BUSINESS CYCLES AND FORECASTING

HOWARD J. SHERMAN
UNIVERSITY OF CALIFORNIA, RIVERSIDE

DAVID X. KOLK
MT. SAN JACINTO COLLEGE

HarperCollins*CollegePublishers*

Executive Editor: John Greenman
Project Coordination, Text and Cover Design: Interactive Composition Corporation
Art Studio: Interactive Composition Corporation
Electronic Production Manager: Eric Jorgensen
Manufacturing Manager: Hilda Koparanian
Electronic Page Makeup: Interactive Composition Corporation
Printer and Binder: RR Donnelley & Sons Company
Cover Printer: New England Book Components, Inc.

For permission to use copyrighted material, grateful acknowledgment is made to the copyright holders on pp. 527–542 ,which are hereby made part of this copyright page.

Business Cycles and Forecasting

Library of Congress Cataloging-in-Publication Data

Sherman, Howard J.
   Business cycles and forecasting / Howard J. Sherman, David
X. Kolk. — 1st ed.
      p. cm.
   Includes bibliographical references and index.
   ISBN 0-06-501139-2
   1. Business cycles. 2. Business forecasting. I. Kolk, David.
II. Title.
HB3711.S4723   1996
338.5'42—dc20   95-5180
                                                 CIP

95 96 97 98 9 8 7 6 5 4 3 2 1

To

Barbara and Wendy

with love

CONTENTS

PREFACE

This book was written to help explain why the U.S. economic system is subject to periods of growth and expansion. The book addresses the question of why the capitalist system has so many people frequently, and involuntarily, unemployed. Why most Americans are concerned on a daily basis about their job security and the effects of a prolonged period of unemployment on their lives and financial security?

We are pleased to acknowledge the help of: Raford Boddy, Gary Dymski, Michael Erickson, James Fain, Jang-Ting Guo, William Hall Jr., Lester Levy, Wayne Murdock, Christopher Niggle, Sheldon Stein, and Martin Wolfson. Some of them agree with our viewpoint and some do not. Some of them liked the manuscript and some did not. But all of them gave us very useful and constructive criticism, for which we are grateful.

Some of the material for this book came from Howard Sherman, *The Business Cycle* (Princeton: Princeton University Press, 1991). All of the material from that book has been suitably rewritten and updated. We also thank Princeton University Press for its permission to use material from that book.

Chapter 8 was drafted independently by Christopher Niggle, whom we thank. The chapter was then extensively edited by the co-authors, so any mistakes are the sole responsibility of the co-authors.

We want to thank two exceptional typists, Joan Noguera and Sandy Schauer, for their fine work typing the various drafts. Wendy Kolk deserves special thanks for extensively editing the final draft. Finally, Howard Sherman thanks the University of California, Riverside, Committee on Research, for funding some of the original empirical research that was used in this book.

— Howard J. Sherman
David X. Kolk

History and Framework
of the Analysis

Part 1 of this book begins with an introduction to aggregate supply, demand, and profits as they relate to the business cycle and presents the framework for analysis that will be used in this book. Then, a brief history of the business cycle in America is given. Finally, a method for measuring the business cycle is introduced.

Part 1 illustrates that a necessary condition for a business cycle to occur is a capitalist economy, where production occurs for private profit. Part 1 will also introduce students to the work of Wesley Mitchell, often called the father of modern business cycle analysis. Mitchell's original work, done in the 1920s and 1930s, is the foundation for much of the work done on business cycles in the last 60 years.

CHAPTER 1

Aggregate Supply, Demand, and Profits

The purpose of this chapter is to introduce the reader to alternative approaches to aggregate supply, aggregate demand, and aggregate profits as they relate to the business cycle. The chapter will provide a framework of analysis for the rest of the book.

An immense gap exists between two types of business cycle theorists. As John Maynard Keynes put it: "What is it that makes the cleavage which divides us? On the one side are those who believe that the existing economic system is, in the long run, a self-adjusting system though with creaks and groans and jerks, outside interference and mistakes. . . . On the other side of the gulf are those who reject the idea that the existing economic system is, in any significant sense, self-adjusting" (quoted in Mirowski 1986, 46). Most classical and neoclassical economists believed that demand automatically adjusts to supply, that the system quickly returns to full employment equilibrium if there is no outside interference, and that all major downturns are due to external shocks to the economy.

On the "other side of the gulf" are those more critical economists including Keynes, Thomas Malthus, Karl Marx, and Wesley Mitchell, who assert that the system does not self-adjust demand to supply, does not necessarily return to equilibrium at full employment, and that recurrent cyclical downturns are primarily due to internal causes. There are, of course, important differences within each of these two groups, but there is a basic division between them. This basic division is clarified in this chapter.

SAY'S LAW

Classical economists argued that, under capitalism, the invisible hand of competition produces a smoothly functioning system which always returns to equilibrium. In line with this view, J. B. Say announced in 1803 the law that "supply calls forth its own demand." In other words, according to *Say's law*, if aggregate supply in the market increases, aggregate demand will also increase until a new equilibrium is reached at full employment. Because the system automatically adjusts to any change or external shock, there can be no involuntary unemployment other than very temporarily. In the classical view, unemployment is caused by either momentary frictions during adjustment, or by external barriers which do not allow the market system to function freely. The classical economists argue that people are just voluntarily unemployed—that is, they prefer not to work at prevailing wages. The classical view does not admit that long-term involuntary unemployment can exist.

Say's law is not just an obsolete theory. It has been refashioned and is currently an important foundation of macroeconomic theory among some U.S. economists (such as the New Classical economists, and supply-side economists). Let us see how this theory, which denies cyclical depressions caused by lack of demand, has evolved.

J. B. Say and other classical economists (particularly James Mill and David Ricardo) argued that the act of production itself creates a level of income sufficient to purchase all that has been produced. The sum of all wages and salaries, rental income, interest income, and profit income will equal the value of all production. The aggregate value of income payments is identical to the value of all things produced for sale, so income is sufficient to demand all that is supplied. Since whatever some people save out of income will be loaned to others anxious to buy beyond their current income, Say believed the total income would be used to buy the total production. Therefore, no matter how large is the potential at full employment output, market forces ensure that all labor resources available for use would be employed.

Say admitted that an excess might be produced in a few product markets, but competition in the market would correct that short-run difficulty. Such temporary maladjustments were sure to be corrected as soon as competition could force capital to switch from one industry to another. In a typical classical statement, Ricardo argued: "Too much of a particular commodity may be produced, which there may be said to be such a glut in the market as not to repay the capital expended on it; but this cannot be the case with all commodities" (reprinted 1891, 286).

The classical economists contended that savings—defined as income not spent for consumption—would always find an outlet as investment. The reason is that people would not forgo the yield offered by investment, which would be lost if one simply "hoarded" one's savings. A high level of savings is healthy and desirable for economic growth, since without high savings there can be no high investment. In sum, the classical economists saw no difficulties inherent in high levels of saving, only benefits.

The kernel of truth in Say's law is the platitude that a dollar's worth of production or supply generates a dollar's worth of income or *potential* demand. Every purchase constitutes a sale, every sale means money income to someone, and that income may be used for more purchases in the next period. Ricardo wrote:

> No man produces but with a view to consume or sell, and he never sells but with an intention to purchase some other commodity which may be useful to him or which may contribute to future production. By purchasing them, he necessarily becomes either the consumer of his own goods, or the purchaser and consumer of the goods of some other person. (Ricardo 1891, 273)

In other words, goods and money have a circular movement in the economy: business produces and sells, it pays income to employees and entrepreneurs, the income is used to purchase consumer goods and producer goods from business, and the process begins again. This is a correct description of circulation when everything works perfectly, but it is not a proof that the system works perfectly.

EVOLUTION OF THE DEBATE ON SAY'S LAW FROM 1800 TO 1930

Say's law was dominant from 1803 when he formulated it until the end of the classical period (about 1870). Say's law remained an important part of the business cycle and monetary theory of the neoclassical economists from the 1870s to the 1930s. However, Say's law became an object of criticism, even ridicule, during the interlude of Keynesian economics from the 1930s to the 1960s. Say's law returned to respectability from the 1970s to the present.

Since Say's law holds that the system automatically reaches full-employment equilibrium, it follows that the only acceptable theories of recession or depression are theories of external shocks which cause temporary deviations from full employment. In fact, the first famous external shock theory was by Stanley Jevons, who lived from 1835 to 1882. Jevons claimed that business cycles are caused by sun spots which cause agricultural declines, which lead to industrial declines.

Several criticisms of Say's law were made by dissenters during the classical period. First, Say's critics argued that there is a limit to profitable investment at any one time. Thus, there may be an excess of savings, some of which will drop out of circulation. The lack of spending causes a decline in demand which results in excess goods with no buyers.

Second, Say's law was criticized on the grounds that the classical economists were confusing private enterprise with earlier systems. Some classical economists even discussed an imaginary Robinson Crusoe island. Under medieval feudalism (or on Crusoe's island), production was just for the use of an isolated group. Under private enterprise, goods are sold in the market for money and production continues only if profit is expected. It is true that every sale brings in income, but that income is not necessarily spent.

Third, a similar criticism of Say's law emphasized that business cycles appear only where there is private enterprise, because this is a monetary economy. Money may be hoarded, so there is less demand and less profit. Production only occurs when a monetary profit is expected; lack of profit leads to unemployment under the private enterprise system. It was contended that business cycles are not found in pre-capitalist societies, which follow Say's law. This view will be explored in the discussion of Wesley Mitchell's historical approach, which is a central element in Chapter 2.

On the theoretical side, the criticisms were answered by an increasingly elegant defense of Say's law by the neoclassical economists (such as Alfred Marshall, Stanley Jevons, and Leon Walras). Neoclassical economists emphasized that equilibrium is always restored, provided that prices, wages, and interest rates are flexible. A lack of demand causes businesses to lower prices, but this results in more demand and less supply, so equilibrium is restored. The arguments for Say's law became still more complex with neoclassical economists in the 20th century (such as A. C. Pigou), but the conclusion remained the same.

THREE ARGUMENTS FOR SAY'S LAW

We discuss here the major classical/neoclassical arguments for Say's law. First, suppose that aggregate supply of commodities is temporarily greater than aggregate demand. It is claimed that flexible prices under competition will quickly cure this imbalance. Under competitive conditions, the excess supply of output will automatically cause prices to drop. At the new lower prices, demand will automatically rise to equal the supply. Since demand will adjust in that manner to any level of supply, including the full employment level of supply—so too, equilibrium may always be reached at the full employment level of supply.

This viewpoint is illustrated in Figure 1.1. This graph illustrates the assumption that the actual price is above the equilibrium level. In that case

FIGURE 1.1

NEOCLASSICAL VIEW OF AGGREGATE SUPPLY, DEMAND, AND PRICES

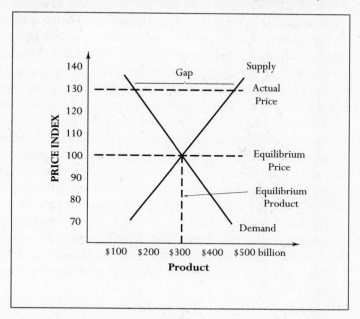

we see that there is a gap between the supply and the demand. The aggregate demand is too small to purchase the aggregate supply at the existing price. But the graph also shows that the actual price may fall toward the equilibrium level. The reason for the falling price is that entrepreneurs are unable to sell all of their goods at the current price, so they lower their prices to attract more customers. As the price declines, the demand increases, while the supply decreases. Finally, an equilibrium of supply and demand is reached at the lower, equilibrium price level. Entrepreneurs can then sell all the goods they are producing at the going price, so there can be no over-production.

Thus, the first neoclassical argument for Say's law argues that if there is insufficient demand, prices will decline until equilibrium is reached at a point where all supply is bought.

The second neoclassical argument for Say's law deals with the possible imbalance of saving and investment. Suppose there is a temporary excess of saving, that is, income not spent for consumption. The supply of savings is above investment demand, so some money is saved, but is not spent. It is claimed that, under competition, flexible interest rates will quickly cure this imbalance. Under competitive conditions, the excess supply of saving will automatically cause interest rates to drop. At the new, lower interest rates, many more investment opportunities will appear profitable. Therefore, investment demand will rise to equal the supply of savings. Again, the argument applies to the full employment level of supply of saving.

The argument is illustrated in Figure 1.2, which shows that the existing interest rate is too high for all savings to be lent to investors. There will be downward pressure on interest rates caused by competition among savers. As the interest rate goes down, we see that investment goes up because borrowing costs less. At the same time, the falling interest rate means that people have less incentive to save, so they will consume more of their income. Eventually, the interest rate falls to an equilibrium where the supply of loans (that is, saving) is equal to the demand for loans (that is, investment). At the equilibrium point, saving is therefore all invested. Thus, all income is spent either on consumption or investment, so there is no hoarding, and all aggregate supply is purchased by aggregate demand.

The third neoclassical argument for Say's law deals with the possible imbalance between demand for labor and supply of labor, which could produce temporary unemployment. Suppose there is a temporary excess of labor supply over the demand for labor, causing temporary unemployment.

FIGURE 1.2
NEOCLASSICAL VIEW OF SAVINGS, INVESTMENT, AND INTEREST RATES

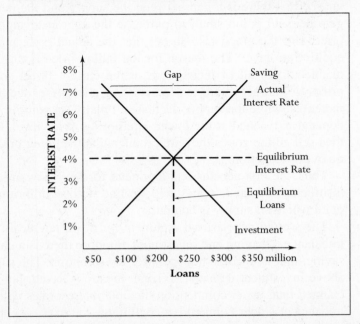

It is claimed that, under competition, flexible wages will quickly cure this imbalance. Under competitive conditions in the labor market, the excess supply of labor (the unemployed) will automatically force employees to accept lower wages. If wages fall, then employees will be able to produce more profit for entrepreneurs. Therefore, at the new lower wages, entrepreneurs will hire more employees until full employment is reached. Full employment is defined to be full employment of those employees seeking jobs at the market wage. Potential employees who are not employed are defined to be voluntarily unemployed or not in the labor force.

Figure 1.3 illustrates the neoclassical view of employment and wages. When wages are too high, more employees will be attracted to the labor market to find jobs. But at that too high wage level, employers will reduce the number of jobs they are willing to offer. Therefore, Figure 1.3 shows a temporary unemployment gap at the existing wage. Wages are pushed down, however, by the competition among workers for the small number of jobs. As the wage level declines, fewer workers go into the job market, but employers offer more jobs. There will therefore be an equilibrium of supply and demand for labor at the full employment level of wages; that is, all employees who want jobs at the equilibrium wage will find jobs offered at

FIGURE 1.3

NEOCLASSICAL VIEW OF LABOR SUPPLY, DEMAND, AND WAGES

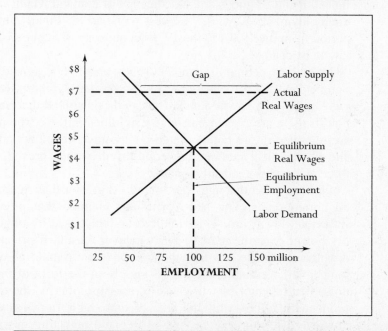

that wage. An interesting point about the classical theories is that because everything was explained by the laws of supply and demand, there is no need for what is now studied as macroeconomics.

CRITIQUE OF SAY'S LAW BY NEO-KEYNESIANS

The advent of the Great Depression, with high unemployment and a fall in the Gross Domesic Product (GDP) from $80 billion in 1929 to $40 billion by 1932, pointed out the failure of economic theory to explain macroeconomic events. Economists were as puzzled as everyone else about how the depression could last seemingly indefinitely. In 1932, the Senate Banking Committee held hearings to probe the causes of the Great Depression that was threatening the political and economic stability of the nation. A parade of eminent businessmen confessed that they had no explanation for the Depression. It was equally clear that the nation's bankers had no idea what the trouble might be. At the Senate hearings, the famous financier and presidential advisor Bernard Baruch spoke for many when he said, "Balance budgets, stop spending money we haven't got. Sacrifice for frugality and revenue. Cut government spending—cut it as rations are cut in a siege. Tax, tax everybody for everything" (Heilbroner 1993).

John Maynard Keynes (1936) attacked Say's law in quite a formal manner, using the style of argument and other tools familiar to neoclassical economists. Since the Great Depression showed everyone that there was indeed a glut of goods and a deficiency of demand which caused 25 percent unemployment, Keynes was very persuasive. Finally, in the Keynesian period from the 1930s to the 1970s, a majority of economists declared Say's law to be dead.

Most U.S. economists in the 1950s and 1960s agreed with what Paul Samuelson called the neoclassical-Keynesian synthesis (these economists were called neo-Keynesians). This synthesis argued that Say's law does not hold if there are certain barriers or rigidities in the economy. If the barriers are removed or are compensated for by government action, then Say's law and neoclassical competitive equilibrium would prevail. They presented three arguments against Say's law.

First, suppose that aggregate supply is greater than aggregate demand for all commodities. The neo-Keynesians claimed that prices are relatively inflexible downward. This rigidity may be caused by oligopoly or monopoly power over the market. For whatever reason, if prices are not flexible downward and do not fall, then supply may remain above demand for a long time. Eventually, the excess supply in the form of increasing piles of unwanted inventories will cause a recession, that is, the quantity of goods produced may fall while the prices remain high. In this case, supply adjusts downward to demand, instead of demand adjusting upward to supply as imagined by Say's law. Broadly speaking, the classical vision always adjusts demand upward to meet supply at the full employment level. The neo-Keynesian vision adjusts supply downward to meet demand.

In terms of Figure 1.1, the neo-Keynesian argument is that the *actual price* remains rigid. There is little or no movement toward the *equilibrium price*. Therefore, at the actual price level, the supply greatly exceeds the demand. The supply is forced down to the demand at the actual price. So the difference between supply and demand on the actual price line is a measure of involuntary unemployment.

Second, suppose that saving is currently in excess of investment. This means that the money put into saving will not circulate as rapidly as before, that is, the *velocity* of money declines. Some neo-Keynesians claimed that there may be a *liquidity trap*, defined as a level below which the rate of interest may not fall. The interest rate stops falling because, below a certain level, lenders expect the interest rate to rise again in the near future. Therefore, potential lenders (those with savings) with a speculative motive may hold cash because they believe there will be higher interest rates in the future. This inflexible interest-rate floor prevents investment demand from rising to meet saving.

In terms of Figure 1.2, the actual interest rate can drop no lower because of this rigidity. Therefore, the actual interest rate does not move toward the equilibrium rate. At the actual interest rate, saving greatly exceeds investment. Eventually, the saving level is forced to move down to the investment level causing less investment and, therefore, less employment. Thus, the initial difference between saving and investment on the actual interest line is one measure of involuntary unemployment.

Third, suppose there is an excess supply of labor over the demand for labor. Neo-Keynesians claimed that wages may be inflexible downward. Wages may be rigid because of trade union strength, or because of minimum wage laws, long term contracts, or for other reasons. In this case, if wages do not fall, the demand for labor will remain below the supply, and involuntary unemployment results.

In terms of Figure 1.3, assuming the actual wage is rigid, it cannot fall to the equilibrium wage. The actual amount of labor is forced down to the labor demanded at the actual wage level. Thus, the difference between the labor supply curve and the labor demand curve at the actual wage level in Figure 1.3 is a good measure of involuntary unemployment.

In any of these cases, according to Samuelson's neo-Keynesian synthesis, government action is required to restore equilibrium at full employment. If wages, prices, and interest rates are rigid, attempts should be made to remove barriers and to restore flexible prices, wages, and interest rates. So long as they are rigid, however, neo-Keynesian theory concludes that government must stimulate the economy by fiscal and monetary means.

POST-KEYNESIAN CRITIQUE OF SAY'S LAW

The Post-Keynesians interpret Keynes in a more radical manner. The problem is not just rigidities, but also cumulative processes that occur if prices and wages do decline, as well as problems of uncertainty in expectations that affect investment.

First, suppose there is excess aggregate supply. If all prices are flexible and do drop, the decline in wages means less demand for the present supply of output. The lower revenue will result in lower aggregate income, which will again lower demand—so the process may be cumulative downward. In other words, one effect of lower prices would be to encourage demand out of a given income. Another immediate effect, however, will be a decline in aggregate income, which will also cause a decline in demand. Moreover, the decline in prices and incomes lower the expectations of consumers and investors for future income, causing a further decline in demand. Thus, flexible prices may become part of the problem. (Post-Keynesians also note that lower prices mean higher interest rates in constant dollars, that is, an increase in the real burden of debt, which increases bankruptcies in business.)

In terms of Figure 1.1, lower prices do mean movement down the curves, which would eventually meet at equilibrium. Lower prices, however, also mean less income. So the aggregate demand curve *shifts* to the left every time prices fall. Thus, demand may actually fall faster than supply, depending on which effect is greater—the direct price effect or the income effect. The direct price effect means that lower prices lead consumers to purchase more goods. The income effect means that lower prices cause less revenue to the firm, leading to lower wage and profit incomes. The post-Keynesians follow Keynes in believing that the negative effect on demand from lower income is very considerable.

Notice that the static graph in Figure 1.1 is not very convenient for showing these shifting relationships, so some post-Keynesians use the dynamic models explained in Part 3 of this book. These dynamic cycle models never end up at equilibrium, but depict a cumulative upward disequilibrium, followed by a cumulative downward disequilibrium. Rather than self-adjustment to optimal, full-employment equilibrium, these models portray an economy of boom and bust, though they may also portray long-run growth.

Second, suppose there is an excess of labor supply over demand, causing unemployment. If wages are flexible and decline precipitously, consumer demand is drastically reduced. Since demand for labor is influenced by the demand for goods, a decline in consumer demand must tend to reduce the demand for workers. Of course, production is also influenced by the declining cost of labor. But if the two factors (consumer demand and labor cost) are falling at the same pace, the two effects cancel each other. Full employment equilibrium is not restored; rather, there may be a downward spiral.

In terms of Figure 1.3, lower actual wages mean that actual demand and supply levels will move along the demand and supply curves. But the post-Keynesians emphasize that lower wages also mean lower demand for products, which means lower demand for labor. So in Figure 1.3, the demand for labor curve may shift to the left as fast, or faster, than the movement along the curve. Lower wages may mean that the equilibrium point shifts downward. The result is less employment—the equilibrium point could be far below full employment—or if the shift is fast enough, the economy does not even reach the lower equilibrium. Again, the static graph in Figure 1.3 needs to be replaced by a dynamic system that allows for cumulative disequilibrium movements.

How does the neoclassical view overlook the fact that cutting wages leads to less aggregate demand? Part of the answer in the post-Keynesian view, is that the neoclassicals concentrate only on individual industries. If wages are cut in one industry, say automobiles, then there may be no noticeable effect on the demand for automobiles. But if wages are cut in all industries, then aggregate demand certainly declines. The mistake of ignoring this aggregate effect has been called the fallacy of composition.

Third, suppose there is an excess of saving over investment. If the expected rate of profit goes below zero, as it has in some depressions, then no positive interest rate can be low enough to induce investment. If insufficient demand causes expected losses, then why would any rational business person wish to borrow at any positive rate of interest? The post-Keynesians have emphasized that the uncertainty of future returns causes investors to react strongly to financial events. If the present rate of profit is rapidly declining, investors may expect a negative future rate. In that case, the equilibrium rate of interest would be negative, so no equilibrium of saving and investment may be possible at the present time.

In terms of Figure 1.2, this argument means that expected lower profit rates lead to expected losses at the actual rate of interest. The investment curve shifts down to the left until the equilibrium rate of interest is below zero. The actual rate cannot go below zero, so there persists an excess of savings over investment. This idle money (or, more precisely, slower circulation) means less demand for investment goods. Eventually, a lower level of income will cause lower saving at every level of interest, so the saving curve also eventually shifts downward. A dynamic downward movement exists that cannot easily be represented in the neoclassical picture of equilibrium supply and demand. Some non-neoclassical economists discuss under-full-employment equilibrium, but others use dynamic models with no long-run equilibrium.

CONTINUED CONTROVERSY ON SAY'S LAW

At present, New Classical theories defend Say's law, while new-Keynesians criticize it. Both are discussed in detail in Chapter 9.

The classical, neoclassical, and New Classical theories are based on the views stemming from Say's law, which sees the system as one that adjusts to full employment equilibrium after every outside shock. The Keynesian, Institutionalist, neo-Marxian, post-Keynesian, and new-Keynesian theories oppose Say's law and argue that the economy does not necessarily adjust to full employment.

Michael Mandel (1993) argues in a *Business Week* column that macro-economics changes every five years, with economists arguing with each other, rather than attempting to explain the things that people are concerned about—inflation, unemployment, and growth. Mandel states, "Ever since the 1970's, when Keynesian ideas came under attack, macroeconomists have been flailing about in all different directions. Monetarists have jostled with supply-siders, who fought with new-Keynesians, who argued with rational expectations theorists."

A good understanding of business cycle theories is gained through knowledge of both. But a good, consistent exposition must, in the end, use one theory or the other as its framework. Therefore, when it is necessary to choose, this book goes with the approach which acknowledges involuntary unemployment and finds that our economy does not automatically adjust to the full employment level of output. Readers who prefer the neoclassical or New Classical framework, which assumes voluntary unemployment in a self-adjusting economy, may read almost any of the textbooks of the 1980s.

THE PROFIT FRAMEWORK OF ANALYSIS

The framework of comparison of points of static equilibrium of supply and demand, used by many modern cycle theorists, always leaves one with the false impression of a self-adjusting equilibrium in the aggregate economy. The same factors can be understood in a different framework, however. A focus on *profit* provides a more realistic starting point. Many investigations of the business cycle begin with an analysis of profits because the expectation of profits is the factor having the clearest effect on investment—an approach that was pioneered by the United States by the works of Wesley Mitchell. Investment is the variable that most directly determines the business cycle, as will be shown in Part 2. Governments, politicians, enterprises, and individual citizens all worry about investment because a decline in investment usually sets off a recession or depression.

Since profits are the key to investment, we must understand what determines profits. The easiest place to start is the truism that profits equal *revenue* minus *costs*. That proposition is an accounting identity with which no one can quarrel. What exactly is *revenue* and what exactly are *costs*?

Let us begin with revenue. Revenue means all that is paid to the enterprise. Obviously, the source of revenue is spending by individuals and by other economic units. And spending reflects demand, so the profit approach is based partly on aggregate demand. Aggregate demand translates into aggregate spending, which becomes revenue.

In the national income accounts (described in Chapter 3), it will be shown that all spending (or demand) is divided by the U.S. Department of Commerce into four flows: (1) consumer spending, (2) investment spending, (3) government spending, and (4) net export spending. Thus, the most useful definition of aggregate revenue is that it equals these four flows. Consumer spending means purchases of such items as food, clothes, and shelter. Investment spending includes purchases of factories and machines. Governments buy things such as hospitals and battleships. Net exports equal exports (bought by foreigners) minus imports (bought by U.S. residents).

An entire chapter will be devoted to each of the four spending flows that together determine aggregate revenue. When we have finished the explanation of the four spending flows, we will have fully explained what factors determine revenue.

What about "costs"? Costs are determined by supply conditions. In particular, there are the costs of the supply of labor (wages and salaries), the using up of plant and equipment (which is reflected in depreciation), and the purchase of raw materials, in addition to interest payments, rent payments, and taxes. There will also be chapters (or large parts of chapters) on these cost components, including labor costs, raw material costs, plant and equipment costs, interest costs, taxes, and depreciation costs. When all of these have been fully explained, the cyclical behavior of costs can be understood.

When the cyclical behavior of aggregate revenue and the cyclical behavior of aggregate costs are fully understood, one can grasp the behavior of profit. When we understand the path of profit, it is then easy to predict the path of investment. This approach provides the framework for the analysis in this book.

HOW THIS BOOK USES THE PROFIT FRAMEWORK

Chapter 2 demonstrates that production for private profit in our present economy is one precondition of the business cycle that has slowly emerged through economic evolution (following the work of Wesley Mitchell). It contrasts the history of the business cycle in our present economic system with economic performance in earlier economic systems. Chapter 3 then introduces the main tools of analysis. It explains how to measure business cycle activity, how the national income accounts are constructed, and finally, how some of the main revenue and cost aggregates move in the business cycle.

Part 2 examines the different components of cost (based on supply) and revenue (based on demand). It begins with aggregate demand by consumers, which is part of the revenue of enterprises. It then examines the demand or spending by investors, which is another flow of revenue to enterprises. Next, it looks at the supply of labor, which is a cost to enterprises. Finally, it examines the supply of raw materials, which is another cost to enterprises. All of these components are described and explained as they change systematically over the business cycle. Each affects profits, so the movement of profits is also examined. The emphasis of Part 2 is on empirical description. Students of the cycle must learn exactly what happens before they can analyze it. Abstract models may be useful, but—unlike many textbooks—the factual description of relationships and institutions is our beginning point.

In Part 3, different theories are presented. It begins with a detailed history of all of the main theories of the cycle, from the classicals to the post-Keynesians and New Keynesians. There follows an analysis of some of the main models which show how the internal dynamics of the economy generate involuntary unemployment. The simplest model is called the multiplier-accelerator theory. Then we explore theories concentrating on lack of revenue or demand. This is followed by theories that emphasize the high cost of supply. Finally, we examine theories where the key factor is profit, which reflects both cost (or supply) and revenue (or demand).

Part 4 is especially interesting because it adds realism to these simple models. A chapter is devoted to the important role of the institutions of money and credit in the business cycle. Another chapter considers the economic role of small, competitive business, versus the role of large corporations with varying degrees of monopoly power—and shows how this institutional situation affects the business cycle. A third chapter explores the international aspects of the business cycle which is now a worldwide phenomenon. Finally, we analyze the usual behavior of the institutions of government over the business cycle, followed by the different views of government policy—asking how government policy may combat involuntary unemployment.

Part 5 presents some of the many ways of attempting to predict the future behavior of the business cycle. Part 5 begins with a brief description of the different types of forecasting methods, both quantitative and qualitative. It then proceeds to detail the various types of modeling techniques. First, indicator forecasting is presented. Indicator forecasting, which looks systematically at what series usually turn ahead of most business, is used as an example of a simple forecasting method. Next, time series models are presented. Time series models identify historic patterns in data and use these identified patterns for forecasting. Finally, we present econometric models that use statistical methods to identify the quantitative relationships between different variables, which are then used to make forecasts. A key question is which type of analysis is most appropriate for each type of problem in forecasting.

Accompanying this book is a data disk which includes most of the data series discussed in the text. The data is presented in Lotus 1-2-3, so students can quickly plot the data and perform simple tests of the data, verifying (or rejecting) the conclusions drawn by the authors. Students are strongly encouraged to become familiar with the data presented and use it as a learning resource.

CONCLUSIONS

Some theories (including the neoclassical theory) contend that demand always adjusts to supply, so all long-run unemployment is voluntary and all recessions are caused by external shocks. Other theories (including those of the Keynesians) contend that demand does not automatically adjust to supply, recessions usually have mainly internal causes, and most unemployment is involuntary. Of course, the two views lead to different policy conclusions, such as whether the government should intervene or not to eliminate unemployment. We believe, however, that the most important point is that the latter view is more realistic and provides a better understanding. No matter what one's political views are, one can suggest better economic policies if the analysis is more realistic. Similarly, if one's aim is to maximize business profits, or to make better forecasts for a business, one can do better with a more realistic analysis.

To avoid thinking of a static equilibrium, the book states the issues in a more dynamic framework. This book focuses on expected profits in relation to expected revenues and expected costs. The next chapter begins the analysis by showing why the profit motivation is one important precondition for recessions caused by lack of effective demand.

KEY TERMS AND CONCEPTS

effective demand

Say's law

neoclassical view of
  Say's law

neo-Keynesian view
  of Say's law

post-Keynesian view
  of Say's law

labor market,
  product market,
  money market

revenue

cost

profit

CHAPTER 2

History of the Business Cycle

Chapter 2 first notes the enormous waste caused by business contractions, then considers the definition of the business cycle. Having defined the business cycle, the chapter examines the historical conditions that must be present to have cycles. Finally, a brief outline of the history of U.S. business cycles is presented.

LOSSES CAUSED BY RECESSIONS AND DEPRESSIONS

During the Great Depression of the 1930s, millions of people lost their jobs. The unemployed did not have enough money to buy the food, clothing, and shelter that they so badly needed. To the degree that this human misery repeats itself—to a much lesser extent—in the contraction phase of every business cycle, a major social problem arises from a seemingly irrational economic situation. It is worth examining the quantitative dimensions of the losses to society, to business, and to workers that occur in every recession or depression.

LOSSES TO SOCIETY

Society suffers many types of losses from the contractions that occur during business cycles. Thousands of factories stand idle and millions of workers are unemployed, so society loses an enormous amount of potential output for current consumption. Society also loses because few new plants and equipment are produced, so there is little growth in productive potential for future expansion. That is the reason every recession or depression lowers the long-run rate of growth. Although the overall long-run U.S. trend has been one of economic growth, the trend rate is lowered by these losses, according to the conclusions presented in this book (Figure 2.1). Society loses inventions that are not discovered because motivation is dampened and less money is being spent for research and development. Society loses because millions of people are unable to work and to create to their full potential. Society loses because millions of people are frustrated and unhappy and the social atmosphere is poisoned.

LOSSES TO BUSINESS

In every contraction, many businesses cannot sell their goods at a profit. Bankruptcies skyrocket and the number of new businesses declines drastically. Thousands of small firms are forced out of business and many owners are left unemployed. Even some large corporations go out of business, leaving their employees jobless.

LOSSES TO INDIVIDUAL EMPLOYEES

The greatest scourge of the business cycle is the unemployment of millions of employees. Every one of these individuals suffers the disruption of useful

FIGURE 2.1
POTENTIAL VERSUS ACTUAL GDP

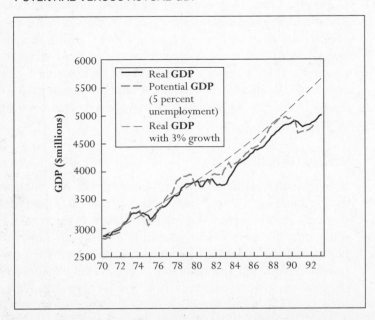

life. Heads of families cannot feed their children. The unemployed feel useless, each believing that he or she is a personal failure. Mental and physical sicknesses increase among the unemployed and their families. Unemployment often leads to alcoholism, divorce, child abuse, crime, and even suicide. A study for the Joint Economic Committee of Congress has documented the grim facts. A sustained one-percent increase in unemployment is associated with the following statistically significant percentage increases: suicide, 4.1 percent; state mental hospital admissions, 3.4 percent; state prison admissions, 4.0 percent; homicide, 5.7 percent; deaths from cirrhosis of the liver, 1.9 percent; deaths from cardiovascular diseases, 1.9 percent (Brenner 1976, v).

Some economists claim that unemployment is voluntary, arguing that employees freely choose to stay employed or choose leisure and unemployment. Voluntary unemployment exists, by definition, when an employee freely chooses not to work at the present going wage in the labor market. Other economists argue that this is nonsense. When fifty thousand employees are given termination slips by, say, General Motors, they are given no choice. According to this view, most unemployment is involuntary, meaning that employees are given no choice about it. Evidence supporting the belief in involuntary unemployment is that within a short time period after millions of employees are fired, advertisements for job openings decline precipitously in every contraction.

DEFINITION OF THE BUSINESS CYCLE

This book describes the business cycle, the recurrent expansion and contraction of the national economy. The root causes and attempted cures of business fluctuations are identified and discussed. Particular attention is paid to the unique characteristics of the private enterprise economy (sometimes called capitalism) that lead to business cycles. The book also examines potential remedies for this curse of the modern private enterprise economic system that causes such pain to average Americans.

We shall find that business cycles occur only in the private enterprise economic system although other types of cycles existed in the old Soviet system, as discussed below. Cyclical unemployment does *not* necessarily mean that capitalism is a bad system and that some other economic system should replace it. Choosing an economic system depends on many criteria, of which unemployment is only one. Which system is most efficient and productive? Which system is most fair and equitable? Which economic system is most likely to cause environmental destruction, racial and gender discrimination, war, and dictatorship? This book does not investigate other economic systems, nor does it discuss these issues. Therefore, although this book discusses the relationships between the private enterprise system and unemployment, it does not reach any overall conclusion on comparisons between economic systems.

Before the evolution of a phenomenon can be traced, it must be carefully defined. Wesley Mitchell, the great pioneer of business cycle research, presented the most useful definition of the business cycle, as follows:

> Business cycles are a type of fluctuation found in the aggregate economic activity of nations that organize their work mainly in business enterprises; a cycle consists of expansions occurring at about the same time in many economic activities, followed by similarly general recessions, contractions, and revivals which merge into the expansion phase of the next cycle; this sequence of changes is recurrent but not periodic; in duration business cycles vary from more than one year to ten or twelve years; they are not divisible into shorter cycles of similar character with amplitudes approximately their own. (Burns and Mitchell 1946, 3)

It is worth examining separately each of the points in Mitchell's definition. First, in Mitchell's view, the business cycle is a phenomenon found under private enterprise and not under other systems. Actually, there were cycles of fast and slow growth in the old Soviet Union, but both the causes and the symptoms were very different than in U.S. cycles (see, e.g., Zimbalist, Sherman, and Brown 1989, 203). For one thing, there was no large scale involuntary unemployment in the Soviet Union. Rather, Soviet employees were often used inefficiently. Bottlenecks occurred and growth slowed, but not because of general unemployment—the Soviets usually had labor shortages.

Second, the business cycle of a private enterprise economy is not limited to a single firm or industry, but is economy-wide and shows most clearly among aggregate measures of economic activity. However, the business cycle affects most economic sectors. Third, all cycles follow the same basic pattern. Cycles are marked by regularities and similar sequences of events. Fourth, cycles differ in many ways, including how long they last, so there is no regular periodicity.

Finally, Mitchell mentioned time periods for a whole business cycle of anywhere from one to twelve years. Some researchers have found short, mild, three to four year cycles as well as longer, sharper ten-year cycles. Mitchell and others do not find that distinction in the evidence. Cycles vary greatly in length, but each repeats roughly the same sequence of events, making them qualitatively similar in their patterns and relationships. There are, of course, some very mild cycles and some very severe cycles; but there is no evidence of two or three mild cycles within severe, longer cycles. Mitchell proved in detail that cycles of shorter duration than the ones he identified show no regular sequence of events, so their alleged patterns would be statistically insignificant.

On the other hand, some authors claim to have found cycles of fifty to sixty years in length. The first person to argue this view was Kondratief, for whom they are named. Their most famous advocate was Joseph Schumpeter (1939). Little evidence was found for the existence of long cycles and discussion of them died away in the prosperous 1950s and 1960s. In the difficult times of the late 1970s, 1980s, and 1990s, there has been a revival of interest in long cycles (see Kotz 1987). This is because dating from the late-1920s, the beginning of the Great Depression, long cycle proponents argue that the next severe world-wide downturn will begin in the 1990s.

Mitchell found no evidence of such long cycles. How could there be much scientific evidence of long cycles when even advocates have discovered, at most, three of them? Later in this chapter it will be shown that, rather than long waves, the private enterprise system has passed through various stages and that the business cycle shows important differences in these stages. For example, there has been a stage with low growth from 1970 to the present, but that historic stage is not part of any identifiable long cycle.

EVOLUTION OF ECONOMIC SYSTEMS

We must distinguish between different types of movements over time. In the very long-run, there has been an evolution from one type of economic system to another, such as from ancient Roman slavery to medieval feudalism in Europe. Economic systems evolve and go through various stages involving considerable changes, but are still recognizably the same systems. For example, the U.S. economic system was characterized by very small economic units in the past, but it is now in a stage characterized by giant corporations.

There are also many long-run (non-cyclical) trends, such as the increasing percentages of women in the labor force. Trends generally occur under one stage of one system, but sometimes cross over several stages. Long-term trends are almost always completely interrupted when there are evolutionary or revolutionary changes from one system to another.

Of course, change may also occur in variables over the business cycle as defined by Mitchell. In addition, many economic series have seasonal variations, such as higher growth rates in construction during warmer months and lower growth rates in colder months. Finally, there are also erratic movements of economic variables not directly connected to any of the above systematic movements. This book concentrates only on the business cycle, but it does introduce long-run trends and stages of private enterprise when necessary as a background.

HISTORICAL PRECONDITIONS OF THE BUSINESS CYCLE

Our modern private enterprise economy has certain institutions and structures, along with business and political practices, that make business cycles possible. Each of these conditions is considered in detail in this section.

PRODUCTION FOR THE MARKET

Most production in a private enterprise economy is solely directed toward the market. England, for example, had fully developed a private enterprise economy by the end of the eighteenth century, and most of its production was designed to be marketed. This feature was rarely true in earlier societies. In hunter-gatherer societies, almost all productive activity was aimed at production of food by gathering or growing fruit and vegetables or hunting animals by the collective unit of all the adults of the tribe. The produce was usually consumed in roughly equal proportions by these same tribal members or their families. Even at a later stage (characterized by agriculture and herding), production was for use, rather than for sale. For example, none of the Indian tribes of the Americas, not even the Aztecs, bought or sold land or produced crops to sell for a profit to others. In fact:

> . . . soil existed only in order to meet the necessities of life, and production, not profit, was the basis of his economy. . . . Unemployment was certainly never a problem in the Indian communities of early America. (Crow 1948, 54)

Since there was little division of labor within the tribe, there was little, if any, trade among its members. In fact, what little commerce was transacted between tribes was mostly limited to small and precious materials for their decorative or magical qualities. Even a relatively more advanced society such as the Inca Empire of South America was based on a self-sufficient economic unit consisting of a few families called the "ayllu," whose only external economic relation was the work-service tax owed to the state and paid in agricultural produce or work on government projects. (See Crow 1948, 26–29.) In fact, all over the world for thousands of years, almost all economic systems—whether tribal or feudal—were based on relatively self-sufficient agricultural units.

In the Roman Empire there was a great deal of trade, but most of it was in luxury goods which did not affect the self-sufficiency of the basic agricultural unit, which was the slave-run plantation. A lack of surplus could bring starvation to large numbers of city dwellers. As one author says:

. . . notwithstanding the phenomenal expansion of trade and industry the vast
masses inside the Empire still continued to win their livelihood from the soil.
Agriculture remained throughout antiquity the most usual most typical
economic activity, and land the most important form of wealth. (Walbank
1956, 11–13)

In Rome, there was unemployment among the urban laborers, most of
whom were former peasants forced off the land by the competition of slavery. This was a long-run phenomenon caused by the complete lack of mass
markets rather than a cyclical breakdown of the market.

Feudal England lacked both extensive trade and towns because the primitive level of technology made the supply of large urban populations impossible. During the feudal period, England traded very little with the rest of
Europe. In the later medieval period there were areas of more highly developed industrial production, such as Flanders and northern Italy, and even
relatively backward areas of England carried on a systematic wool trade
with Flanders. Yet these were exceptions to the general rule of the feudal
economy and may be considered early signs pointing to the beginning of
the end of that economy.

During the feudal period, market institutions, as we know them today,
were not well developed. Surplus production from the slave or feudal estate
might be marketed in return for foreign luxury items for the lord of the
estate, but it was not a matter of life and death for the economic unit. If the
surplus found no market, the manor was still supplied with its necessities
for that year and could continue to produce for the next year's needs.

What could disturb such economically self-sufficient societies? They
were disturbed only by those catastrophes that were more or less "external"
to the economy. These catastrophes included vicissitudes of nature, such as
droughts, plagues, or floods, or the whims of human beings, such as government interference, war, or revolution. These phenomena could and did
depress production and did bring about famines, both at randomly spaced
intervals and seasonally because of the special seasonal sensitivity of agriculture. Such economies could not conceivably face the problem of lack of
effective demand for all commodities, which is a frequent and serious problem in private enterprise market economies. The problem of lack of demand
could not exist because the economic unit directly consumed most of the
products of its own land and could do without trade altogether.

Some modern cycle theories (such as the real business cycle theory)
attribute all economic fluctuations to such external causes as wars, floods,
and so forth. But it has been argued by many economists—and will be
argued in this book—that such external factors were major causes of disruptions only in pre-capitalist societies, such as medieval feudalism. Such factors certainly did disrupt the feudal economy. But there is no cyclical character to these disruptions. They occured at odd intervals and each incident

was quite different in character from the others. One reason they disrupted European feudalism was that the economy was largely agricultural, so floods and droughts had a powerful effect. The modern U.S. economy has a tiny agricultural sector so such factors as floods and droughts do not have much effect on the whole economy.

In the transition period from feudalism to the private enterprise economy, such as occurred in England from the sixteenth through the eighteenth centuries, the majority of the people still depended upon agriculture for their livelihood. More and more products, however, both agricultural and industrial, were delivered to the marketplace. There was increasing long-run unemployment in this period because peasants were removed from agricultural production much more rapidly than employment grew in capitalist industry, but the unemployment was not cyclical.

By the end of the eighteenth century, the private enterprise system of production for the market embraced most of the economic activity of England. Production of commodities for the market was no longer a matter of accident as it had been, but was one of the most essential features of the private enterprise system. Commodities had to be sold in the market or the system would contract. In the nineteenth century, for example, one business entrepreneur might own a factory producing millions of shoes, but the family of the entrepreneur could consume only a few of these. The shoes had to be sold in order to buy other consumer goods for the entrepreneur's family, to pay wages to those working for the business, and to replace and expand the plant and equipment of the business.

In earlier economic systems, the self-sufficient economic unit or the artisan producing a trickle of handmade items for known customers could not possibly be troubled by lack of demand for the products. When almost all that was produced by the economic unit was consumed by it, lack of demand was not going to be a problem. But in the industrialized private enterprise system, the specialized business person produces only for the market and cannot continue production if there is no demand for the products in the market. The advent of a market economy, then, is the first main institutional feature of the private enterprise economy of the late eighteenth century. It was one of three conditions making possible the beginning of large-scale, cyclical unemployment at that time.

REGULAR USE OF MONEY

A second institutional feature that is necessary before there can be a deficiency of aggregate demand is the regular use of money in exchange, which takes the place of the barter system of exchanging goods for goods. What is money? In its simplest form, money has three basic characteristics. First, it is universally accepted as a means of exchange. Second, it is a store of value, so wealth held in money does not deteriorate in value in comparison to other goods. Third, money can be used as a *numeraire*, that is, it is a commodity by which all other goods are measured. For example, if two pair of shoes are equal to one pair of pants in a barter economy, in a money based economy, if shoes cost $0.50, pants would cost $1.00. The major advantage of this is that money simplifies transactions.

Many economists have concentrated on money as the sole necessary condition for the possibility of a lack of effective demand, but that is because they imply the following conditions: first, production for exchange in the market, and second, the regular use of money in exchange. These two conditions might be presented in a single formal statement, but it is analytically useful to separate them.

Among primitive tribal people, where there is very little trade, exchange is often conducted by barter. Although barter is still the only mode of exchange in slightly more advanced societies, certain commodities, such as cows or horses, may be used as "money" in the sense that the value of all other commodities are calculated in terms of them. Only when there is a large volume of trade will a system begin to use a certain amount of precious metals as the known equivalent to certain amounts of all other commodities. At a still later period the metals are stamped into coins, originally with the purpose of figuring amounts more conveniently and facilitating the exchange of goods.

The use of money, however, brings many new complications to the economic scene. In the Roman Empire, for example, vast amounts of money were needed by the government to support wars of expansion, large standing armies, police, and bureaucracy, and to pay for an unfavorable balance of trade (owing to the importing of luxuries from the East). The emperors were eventually forced to the expedient of debasing their coins by clipping or by contaminating them with base metals. As the government debased the coins and as production declined in the later days of the empire, the amount that could be bought with the coins declined rapidly. This was equivalent to a catastrophic inflation.

In spite of the Romans' financial troubles and difficulties in the use of money, they were not confronted with the modern problem of "too many" commodities in the market relative to the money demand for them. Regular use of money was not enough, by itself, to usher in the menace of a lack of aggregate demand so long as most of the Roman economy was still contained in self-sufficient agricultural units. The luxury trade in the empire suffered from the extreme inflation, but only as one more affliction in addition to colonial wars, slave revolts, the extreme inefficiency of employing slave labor, and the Roman citizen's attitude that any participation in the work process was degrading (because work was only for slaves). Moreover, since most of the people still lived on the land, the relatively small amount of trade and commerce that did exist was not absolutely necessary to the continued functioning of most of the economy. This is not to deny that trade was essential to the preservation of the empire as a political unit and for the existence of higher culture in large urban centers, especially Rome. Rome was an importer of grain from Egypt and North Africa, as well as of wine and various fruits from Gaul, to mention only some of the more important imports. When this trade declined in the second century, the Roman cities suffered and also declined, but the agricultural units continued, though in new forms and on an even more self-sufficient basis.

With the breakup of the Roman Empire, trade suffered a considerable decline; in early feudalism the pattern was overwhelmingly that of the isolated, self-sufficient manor. Barter, therefore, grew in importance, and the use of money declined. On each manor, in return for the lord's protection, serfs provided all the necessary articles of consumption and services needed by the lord, his family, and his retinue. In the later medieval period, however, technology began to improve, and industry and commerce slowly began to revive and reach new heights in Western Europe. The widespread trade of the later medieval period eventually led to the replacing of barter by a money economy; at the same time, as noted in the preceding section, production was increasingly designed for sale in the market rather than for use at home. With the increased use of money, exchange in the market required the use of money as an intermediary. If the holder of money, for whatever reason, decided to hold it and abstain from using it for purchase, the demand for market commodities was lower than it otherwise would have been. Some goods available for sale on the market would remain unsold.

Most classical economists denied that the introduction of money into exchange could cause problems. For example, David Ricardo contended that "productions are always bought by productions, or by services; money is only the medium by which the exchange is effected" (Ricardo 1891, 275). It is true that one function of money is to facilitate the exchange of commodities, but it has other uses as well. In the modern economy the seller obtains only money for commodities, which money the seller may or may not use at a later time to buy other commodities. In the meantime, money may be used for the storage of value for future use. It is thus possible for a person to buy or sell without doing the opposite action at the same time. It is not always the case that all buyers will immediately use their money to buy what they want. That is, there is no inherent necessity in a money economy that sellers should find buyers for all commodities brought to market.

The problem is not an aggregate lack of money in the economy. For example, the poor may wish to buy more goods, but may not have enough money. Yet the rich, who have money, may be reducing their spending. The chain of circulation may then be broken at any point at which the flow of money is slowed in its movement. The reduction of the flow of circulation, usually called a decline in the velocity of money, causes a slowdown in the movement of products. Although it is basically true that commodities exchange for commodities even after the introduction of money, the mere necessity of the money bridge makes all the difference in the world. If the bridge is absent, finished commodities may pile up in warehouses while potential consumers are unable to buy them. Only money can make a possible consumer into an actual buyer in the private enterprise system. Thus, the use of money makes possible the lack of aggregate effective or monetary demand for commodities, so it is a precondition of the business cycle.

An excess of supply in this economic system does not mean that everyone is fully satisfied. In every recession or depression, there are millions of poor people who would be happy to have more goods and services. Therefore, the problem is not overproduction of the total commodities of a society in the absolute sense that the supply is greater than what people want or desire; rather, the problem is that there may be too many commodities on the market relative to the monetary or effective demand for them. The term *effective demand* simply means desire combined with money, because desire or need without money has no effect under capitalism.

An additional problem in the sphere of money may arise from the use of tokens or paper money. The government may always cause some degree of inflation by merely starting its printing presses turning out more paper money. The economies of Europe, for example, were brought to their knees by the spectacular collapse of the French and English finance markets in the early 18th century. Excessive printing of paper money by these two governments resulted in a wild speculation in financial securities. The ensuing collapse destroyed numerous fortunes, escalated unemployment, and caused economic distress for nearly a decade.

Still another complication arises from the fact that money may merely be used as a unit of account for indebtedness—that is, in the form of credit. The use of credit intensifies all money problems because not only may a person sell something and not immediately purchase something else, but it is also possible to sell something and not receive the proceeds of the sale for some time. If Brown owes Smith, and Smith owes Johnson, and Johnson owes Martin, then a break anywhere along this chain of credit circulation will be disastrous for all the later parties in the chain. Moreover, the chain in the modern private enterprise economy is usually circular in nature, so that the reverberations reach the starting point and may begin to go around again. This does not, of course, explain why the chain should ever break in the first place.

It has been argued here that no problem of deficient effective demand was possible before money and credit institutions became the usual way of doing business. Does this mean that these institutions are sufficient to explain recessions and depressions? We know that money and credit existed in ancient Rome and in the 16th to 18th centuries in Western Europe, yet the financial disturbances of those times do not seem to have been the same phenomena as the modern type of economic downturn. It is true that after the development of money and credit every catastrophic natural happening or violent political event might be reflected in a sudden distrust of monetary institutions and a panic in the financial markets. For example, when the English fleet was burned by the Dutch in 1667, and also in 1672 when Charles II stopped payments from the Exchequer, there were sudden runs on the London banks. In the 18th century, financial crises resulted from the Jacobite conspiracy in 1708, the bursting of the South Sea Bubble (a stock speculation) in 1720, the fighting with the Young Pretender in 1745, the aftermath of the Seven Years War in 1763, and the disturbances caused by the American revolutionary war.

Wesley Mitchell comments, however, that these panics were unlike the modern business contractions both in cause and effect. First, they were the result of external events, rather than in the endogenous mechanisms that operate (as we shall see) under the private enterprise system. Second, they caused only limited depressions in a few trades, rather than causing the widespread effects of modern recessions. He concludes that the first truly general industrial depression of the modern type appeared as late as 1793 in England (Mitchell 1913, 583–84).

Distress in the financial sector has been a key causal factor in most depressions, but that is not always the case. Usually, the more serious downturns have involved one form of financial catastrophe or another. The contribution of the financial sector to economic problems will be reviewed in later chapters.

PRODUCTION FOR PRIVATE PROFIT

Two necessary conditions have been examined: (1) production for the market and (2) the regular use of money. Both must be present if a business contraction occurs in which demand declines below the full-employment level of supply. Yet, at least one more institutional condition is necessary before it can be said that a downturn may be caused by the fact that total demand is not equal to total supply in an economy. The third condition is the existence of private ownership of production facilities and production for private profit.

In an economy based on private ownership of individual competing units, the sum of decisions to produce may not equal the sum of decisions by other individuals and businesses to spend—that is, to consume and to invest. If the sum of the value of outputs is greater than the sum of the monetary or effective demand, then there is not enough revenue to cover the costs of production and an additional profit for the private entrepreneur. The criterion is decisive because if the private entrepreneur is not making a profit, the entrepreneur will reduce or discontinue production, machinery will stand idle, and many, if not all, of the workers of that enterprise will be unemployed.

The classical economists spent more time discussing the profit motive as the central motivation for production than did any other group. Yet, except in the case of Malthus, the fact that production might prove unprofitable does not often seem to have entered their discussions of business declines. Therefore, they reached the conclusion of the impossibility of a contraction caused by lack of profitability in the private enterprise system. Actually, the possibility always exists that the production of commodities may out-pace the demand for commodities, at least at a price sufficient to cover costs and also yield a profit.

As a tentative conclusion, pre-capitalist societies did not suffer from cyclical downturns due to lack of demand. There were three reasons: (1) they had very little market exchange, (2) the few exchanges were made by barter, and (3) production was not primarily motivated by private profit. These economies, therefore, did not suffer from the modern type of business cycle, but only from external calamities. The modern cycle focuses on demand, whereas feudal disturbances were mainly in supply.

In the 16th and 17th centuries, market exchange became more extensive and there was a gradual spread of the use of money, yet most production was not capitalist and was not focused on private profit. In this transitional period, use of money and credit caused some random disruptions, but no systematic business cycle resulted. The business cycle only emerged in England in the late 18th century when the private enterprise system became predominant. Under the private enterprise (or capitalist) system: (1) most commodities are exchanged in the market; (2) private profit is the primary motivation of production; and, (3) the use of money and credit is the dominant mode of exchange. There is no production unless it is expected that a profit could be made by selling the goods for money in the market. If goods can not be sold at a profit, then workers will be left unemployed.

THE SPREAD OF THE BUSINESS CYCLE

Wesley Mitchell argues that:

> . . . the total number of past business cycles may well be less than a thousand.
> For business cycles are a phenomena peculiar to a certain form of economic

organization which has been dominant even in Western Europe for less than two centuries, and for briefer periods in other regions. (Mitchell and Thorp 1926, 47)

The business cycle of the private enterprise system appears to have made its first appearance in England, at the end of the 18th century. The periods of economic crisis before that time were easily attributable to external or purely political events. It appears that the British business cycle of the nineteenth century was an indigenous product of British economic development. The vast British trading network, however, reached every other country in the world. Therefore, in every other country the cycle must be partly a product of diffusion from England as well as of independent evolution. That does not mean, of course, that England has remained unaffected by the consequent development of other countries or that it is the country that is least influenced by present-day international events.

The business cycle is found in all private enterprise countries, but the forms of the cycle are much influenced by international events and national peculiarities. There is a similar progression of cycle phases in country after country. Yet, no two cycles are exactly the same; they differ in cause, duration, industrial scope, intensity, and importance of various aspects, and also in how rapidly they spread from one country to another. The most highly developed industrial countries, such as the United States, England, France, and Germany, have closely coincident cycles. In the 19th century, however, the less developed and mainly agricultural countries, such as czarist Russia, Brazil, and China, diverged quite considerably from the international pattern (Mitchell and Thorp 1926, 93).

Wesley Mitchell found that the modern business cycle began in England in 1793; in the United States in 1796 (influenced by England); in France in 1847; in Germany in 1857; and in 1888 to 1891 in czarist Russia, Argentina, Brazil, Canada, South Africa, Australia, India, Japan, and China. After 1890, the business cycle assumed a truly international character with regard to major cycles. It also seems significant that there are no records of recurrent cycles in the less developed countries prior to that period, for these countries were mainly agricultural and did not have the private enterprise institutions specified in the three conditions discussed earlier. After 1890, when the European economies came to dominate the rest of the world through colonization, trade, and investment, the cycle became more and more pronounced in the less developed countries. In the 1929 crash, every country in the world felt the impact and went into a depression period (excepting only the Soviet Union). Again in 1938, most countries suffered a relapse together. In Western Europe and Japan, however, recessions in the United States did not cause major downturns in the 1950s and 1960s. In the 1970s, 1980s, and 1990s, however, the international economy became even more integrated, so the European countries and Japan had contractions at about the same time as the U.S. economy. In summary, the business cycle has spread exactly as private enterprise institutions have spread. Moreover, as private enterprise economies became more intertwined, their business cycles became more synchronized.

EVOLUTION OF THE U.S. PRIVATE ENTERPRISE SYSTEM

The business cycle in the United States is not a static thing, but has changed dramatically. These changes in the business cycle reflected changes in the structure of the U.S. private enterprise system. Originally, the United States was a colony and its economy was dominated by England. Even after independence, British domination continued well into the nineteenth century.

U.S. economic development can be divided, somewhat arbitrarily, into four stages. The four stages used here are, roughly, (1) from the Revolutionary War to the Civil War, (2) from the Civil War to the Great Depression, (3) from the Great Depression to about 1970, and (4) from about 1970 to present. The first stage of U.S. private enterprise development was from independence in 1776 to the end of the Civil War against slavery in 1865. It resembled other underdeveloped economies, remaining dependent for investment and trade on England, being mainly agricultural, slowed by underdeveloped small businesses, little government spending, underdeveloped organization of employees, an underdeveloped financial system, and little international power.

It must be emphasized that until the Civil War the U.S. economy was still mainly agricultural. Most people worked on farms, even though there was some commercial capital. Business was very small business, with strong competition in some industries, although regions were isolated from each other. The immature U.S. economy did not, for the most part, generate its own business cycles, but reacted to British business cycles with a time lag.

THE SECOND STAGE

The second stage of U.S. private enterprise was roughly from the end of the Civil War to the Great Depression. The end of slavery opened the South and the West to industrial capital. This period was marked by the rise of giant corporations in industry and finance, the relative decline of agriculture, and the economic independence from England. The U.S. still had little international power until the First World War.

After the Civil War, U.S. private enterprise grew up, with many giant corporations and monopolies or oligopolies in many industries. Mergers came in waves, with a big wave from the 1890s through the 1900s. The impact of corporate growth on business cycles will be examined later.

The U.S. banking and credit system was underdeveloped throughout the nineteenth century, with many financial crises and collapses resulting from its chaotic nature. After the 1907 financial panic, legislation was finally instituted leading to some control of the banking system by the Federal Reserve system. In the 1920s there was much financial innovation and speculative expansion of credit which helped set the stage for the collapse of 1929.

THE THIRD STAGE

The third stage of U.S. private enterprise lasted from the Great Depression until about 1970. This stage witnessed the rise of government power in the United States, both domestically and as the leading international power of the 1950s and 1960s.

The most catastrophic economic event of the twentieth century was the Great Depression. (For a detailed discussion of the causes of the Great Depression, see Devine, 1983.) Although the Great Depression lasted throughout the 1930s in the common view, Geoffrey Moore (1983) analyzes more scientifically the decline from 1929 to 1933 as one unit in terms of its duration, depth or amplitude, and scope. Moore noted that this decline lasted 43 months (Moore 1983, 21). He found that real Gross Domestic Product (GDP) fell 33 percent, industrial production fell 53 percent, non-farm employment fell 32 percent, while unemployment increased by 22 percent (reaching the unprecedented official rate of 25 percent). The scope of the decline was greater than any other in the twentieth century, with 100 percent of all industries declining.

Chandler (1970) tells the tale of the decline more graphically. He describes a complete collapse of the nation's banking system, a real estate market crash, a horrendous decline in national output, and a severe price deflation. The number of unemployed workers swelled from 1.5 million to 12.8 million. Wholesale prices fell over 30 percent in the same period. Investment dropped an amazing 88 percent. Although all industries declined, some key industries were devastated. Iron, lumber, and auto production fell 59 percent, 58 percent, and 65 percent, respectively. Hardship was endemic.

There was a sluggish recovery between 1933 and 1937, even though the economy never recovered to the level achieved in 1929 during this period, and unemployment remained high. A second slump began in 1937. A full recovery was not to be experienced until World War II and the resulting demand for military hardware finally restored the economy.

Trade unions were fairly weak during most of U.S. history, but grew rapidly in the 1930s and 1940s. Unions rose because of labor militancy during the Great Depression, the friendly environment of the New Deal government in the 1930s, and the full employment of World War II in the 1940s.

During the 1930s, many financial controls and regulations were put into effect. The new regulations helped control finances during the war and the prosperous 1950s and 1960s.

Except for war periods, there was very little government spending in the United States until the 1930s. As late as 1929, the U.S. government spent only one percent of GNP. Even in the 1930s, government spending rose to only 3 or 4 percent. In the Second World War, federal spending rose to 40 percent of GNP. Since the Second World War, federal spending has remained very high, with a peak in the Korean War.

Finally, since the end of British domination, the action of international influences on the U.S. economy remained relatively minor until after the Second World War. In the 1950s, the United States was the dominant world power in every respect, including production, trade, and investment. The U.S. impact on other countries was enormous, but others had seemingly little impact on the U.S. economy.

THE FOURTH STAGE

After the enormous expansion of the U.S. economy in World War II and the late 1940s, the 1950s and the 1960s were characterized by moderate growth rates and four minor recessions. These years were also characterized by two very large "limited" wars in Korea and Vietnam, which maintained a high level of military spending in the economy. The military spending led to a high rate of inflation in both wars. At the end of the Vietnam War, however, the inflation continued. It has continued ever since, increasing in expansions, but declining in most contractions.

In addition to continued inflation, the 1970s to the present have been characterized by much lower growth rates, more severe recessions, and higher rates of unemployment. The severe recession or depression of 1982 reduced inflation, but at the cost of 12 million unemployed. The recession of 1990–1991 was followed by continued stagnation for some years. Many other details of the present period, including long-run trends and cycles, will be discussed throughout this book, but a few highlights are described here.

A fourth stage began in about 1970, in which the U.S. growth rate has declined, cyclical contractions have worsened, and the U.S. international economic status has declined drastically in the face of stiff foreign competition. Our trade balance has gone from surplus to deficit, and the government deficit has become enormous.

Government spending rose further during the Vietnam war and with the military spending of the Reagan and Bush years. Since state and local spending has also risen very rapidly, total government spending is now a large percentage of GDP. Revenue did not rise as rapidly, so government deficits are now very large. The government debt tripled in the Reagan-Bush years. Thus, after the model is outlined for the private sphere, the strong government impact on the business cycle will be discussed in detail.

Since the mid–1950s, union strength has waned because of hostile governments, the rise of the service sector, and the decline of the industrial sector. As a result, there has been a major, long-run fall in the percentage of unionized employees, reflected in a decline of union political and economic strength. Whereas one-third of U.S. employees were unionized in 1955, only about one-sixth are now unionized. Weak and declining union power is now a fact of life, though explanations for it differ widely. How the decline of unions has affected income distribution over the business cycle will be discussed in detail when the importance of income distribution is considered.

By the 1970s, the U.S. economy was strongly affected by international relationships. For example, U.S. imports rose from 5.8 percent of Gross Domestic Product in 1949 to 11.4 percent in 1986. Moreover, the U.S. economy faced fierce foreign competition, even in its home market. By the 1980s, exports had risen, but imports rose even faster, and there was a huge trade deficit. The U.S. economy continues to make large investments abroad, but foreign investment in the United States is now very significant. Thus, the much higher level of international connections will be emphasized as another factor in the changes that have occurred in the U.S. business cycle.

Striking new financial innovations as well as deregulation have led to a vastly overextended and vulnerable banking and credit system in the 1970s and 1980s, with some notable failures. Huge amounts of consumer debt, corporate debt, and government debt are another major fact of life in the modern U.S. economy. This book will consider the impact of these kinds of debt on the business cycle.

These long-run structural changes have had several disturbing effects in the U.S. private enterprise system since about 1970. A number of these long-run trends are presented quantitatively in MacEwan (1989), and also in dramatic detail in Harrison and Bluestone (1988). First, from the 1970s to the present, growth of productivity has slowed considerably, with weak expansions and significant declines in recessions. In the four expansions from 1949 till 1970, product per hour rose by 0.65 percent per quarter; but in the four expansions from 1970 till 1991, product per hour rose by *only* 0.39 percent per quarter. Moreover, in the four contractions from 1949 till 1970, product per hour continued to rise by 0.29 percent per hour; but in the four contractions from 1970 till 1991, product per hour actually *fell* by 0.18

percent per quarter (the data come from CITIBASE, a data base distributed by Citibank of New York).

Second, in the stage from the 1970s to the present, the rate of unemployment has risen to a higher rate than in the previous stage, indicating a long-run trend toward higher unemployment in this period. In the four cycles from 1949 till 1970, the unemployment rate averaged only 4.8, but rose to an average of 7.0 in the four cycles from 1970 through 1991.

Third, in the period from the 1970s to the present, real hourly wages (taking inflation into account) have actually declined for long periods; whereas in the 1950s and 1960s, they rose in all phases of the cycle. Thus, in the four cycles from 1949 through 1970, real wages per hour rose by 0.78 per quarter in expansion and by 0.32 per quarter in contractions. In the four cycles from 1970 through 1991, real wages per hour rose only 0.1 percent per quarter in both expansions and contractions. The average weekly wage actually fell over the 1970–1991 period because of the fall in hours per week, in spite of the very slight increase in hourly wages.

Fourth, inequality of income distribution has increased in the stage beginning in 1970. The poor have had declining real incomes since 1973, while the rich have had rising real incomes (see, e.g., Winnick 1988).

Fifth, inequality in wealth distribution has also increased in the 1973 to 1989 period. The increased inequality of wealth has been largely due to the increase of dividends, rent, and interest income (see Harrison and Bluestone 1988, 130).

LONG-RUN CHANGES AND REGULARITY IN THE BUSINESS CYCLE

The historical stages of the private enterprise economy, as well as the long-run trends within each stage, have greatly affected the business cycle. The misery of the Great Depression of the 1930s was followed by a long period of war prosperity in the 1940s, with very mild recessions in the 1950s and 1960s. The 1970s, 1980s, and 1990s have again witnessed severe contractions. The patterns or sequences of cyclical behavior in the 1970s and 1980s resemble the 1930s more than the 1950s and 1960s, although the severity of depressions in the 1970s and 1980s was nowhere near the Great Depression. Because business cycles are unique and change in each historical period, this book will mainly consider the business cycle behavior of the 1970s, 1980s, and 1990s rather than the earlier behavior.

On the other hand, while recognizing that each business cycle is unique, and that long-run trends have changed the cycle, it is also worth emphasizing that the basic dynamics and pattern of the business cycle have persisted over a long time. Zarnowitz and Moore point out that those variables that normally turn before or after the general cycle peak have remained remarkably consistent in the last 100 years in the United States. ". . . the most notable feature of the record is the absence of major changes in the timing relationships among the group of seven." (Zarnowitz and Moore 1986, 571).

Furthermore, Klein and Moore (1985, 81) find that the sequence of turning points in the main business cycle indicators is much the same in all of the advanced private enterprise countries. Their finding is based on examination of six cycles in each of nine countries in addition to the United States: Canada, United Kingdom, West Germany, France, Italy, Belgium, Netherlands, Sweden, and Japan. Thus, there is considerable evidence that the same type of internal mechanism of the business cycle exists in all private enterprise countries at all historical stages of the system, though in very different and unique forms in each cycle.

CONCLUSIONS

Note that the cycle features and trends are very different in different historical stages. This is not, however, an argument for long cycles. First, these stages are not recurrent. Second, the time duration of each historical stage is entirely different.

The U.S. private enterprise system (sometimes called capitalism) is characterized by economic recession or depression every few years. Thus, there have been 37 business cycles in U.S. history, following the precise definition of the National Bureau of Economic Research. Previous societies did not suffer this type of crisis. The private enterprise system is vulnerable to cyclical crises because it (1) has production for the market, (2) has production for private profit, and (3) uses money and credit.

The U.S. economy has suffered recurrent cyclical contractions, but their nature has changed as the structure of U.S. private enterprise has changed. It is now characterized by (1) predominance of giant corporations; (2) enormous use of credit by households, corporations, and government; (3) declining trade union strength; (4) a vast influence of government; and (5) strong international competition. Trends in the 1970s, 1980s, and 1990s include weak growth of productivity, stagnant real wages, increasing income inequality, and severe recessions.

Some major differences were found in the business cycles of three periods. The 1920s and 1930s included the Great Depression. The cycles of the 1950s and 1960s were very mild. The cycles of the 1970s, 1980s, and 1990s were again more violent. There was relatively little unemployment in the

1950s and 1960s, but large amounts of it in the 1930s and again in the 1970s, 1980s, and 1990s. This book will concentrate on the period from the 1970s to the 1990s, with only brief mention of the earlier periods.

SUGGESTED READINGS

A very interesting book on the history of the business cycle is Mirowski (1985). A useful, somewhat eclectic history of the Great Depression is Bernstein (1987). A useful collection of articles, with some historical aspects, has been edited by Philip Klein (1989).

KEY TERMS AND CONCEPTS

unemployment	historical-institutional preconditions of the cycle	definition of the business cycle
Wesley Mitchell		the Great Depression
losses from cyclical downturns	exchange, money, and private profit	

CHAPTER 3

Measurement of the Business Cycle

The pioneer in the empirical description of the business cycle was Wesley Clair Mitchell. Indeed, he helped develop many of our present national income accounts. With the help of Arthur Burns (Burns and Mitchell 1946), he created a method specifically for measuring the business cycle. The method was used in several cycle studies of the National Bureau of Economic Research (NBER), which he founded.

Mitchell's method, called the NBER method in this book, describes the path of a single variable over the average business cycle. The NBER method, the details of which are presented in this chapter, is an excellent method for getting a clear picture of the business cycle. The NBER method may reveal a simple visual relationship of variables, which is helpful in suggesting a hypothesis for testing, but it should be stressed that it does not provide a statistical test of relationships.

DATES OF THE CYCLE

Mitchell's NBER method begins by establishing the trough and peak dates of each cycle, using all available evidence. Mitchell's work on dating the cycle was adopted by the NBER, whose decision is accepted by the U.S. Department of Commerce which publishes the dates of peaks and troughs. The method, as currently used, has many problems because the task of choosing turning points is difficult. For this reason, it is easy to criticize any particular set of rules. The official monthly dates are given in Table 3.1. Critics stress that the many problems in choosing these dates has produced some strange results. The NBER, for example, does not necessarily accept the textbook definition of a recession as two consecutive quarters of decline

TABLE 3.1
BUSINESS CYCLE EXPANSIONS AND CONTRACTIONS IN THE UNITED STATES, 1854 TO 1981

BUSINESS CYCLE REFERENCE DATES			EXPANSION IN MONTHS	CONTRACTION IN MONTHS
Trough	Peak	Trough	Trough to Peak	Peak to Trough
Dec 1854	June 1857	Dec 1858	30 months	18 months
Dec 1858	Oct 1860	June 1861	22	8
June 1861	Apr 1865	Dec 1867	46*	32
Dec 1867	June 1869	Dec 1870	18	18
Dec 1870	Oct 1873	Mar 1879	34	65
Mar 1879	Mar 1982	May 1885	36	38
May 1885	Mar 1887	Apr 1888	22	13
Apr 1888	July 1890	May 1891	27	10
May 1891	Jan 1893	June 1894	20	17
June 1894	Dec 1895	June 1897	18	18
June 1897	June 1899	Dec 1900	24	18
Dec 1900	Sept 1902	Aug 1904	21	23
Aug 1904	May 1907	June 1908	33	13
June 1908	Jan 1910	Jan 1912	19	24
Jan 1912	Jan 1913	Dec 1914	12	23
Dec 1914	Aug 1918	Mar 1919	44*	7
Mar 1919	Jan 1920	July 1921	10	18
July 1921	May 1923	July 1924	22	14
July 1924	Oct 1926	Nov 1927	27	13
Nov 1927	Aug 1929	Mar 1933	21	43
Mar 1933	May 1937	June 1938	50	13
June 1938	Feb 1945	Oct 1945	80*	8
Oct 1945	Nov 1948	Oct 1949	37	11
Oct 1949	July 1953	May 1954	45*	10
May 1954	Aug 1957	Apr 1958	39	8
Apr 1958	Apr 1960	Feb 1961	24	10
Feb 1961	Dec 1969	Nov 1970	106*	11
Nov 1970	Nov 1973	Mar 1975	36	16
Mar 1975	Jan 1980	July 1980	58	6
July 1980	July 1981	Dec 1982	12	17
Dec 1982	July 1990	Apr 1991	88	9

SOURCE: Bureau of Economic Analysis, U.S. Department of Commerce, available in CITIBASE Economic database, machine-readable magnetic file, 1946–present, Citybank: New York, New York.

NOTE: Asterisked figures are the wartime expansions (Civil War, World War I, World War II, Korean War, and Vietnam War). Data originally from National Bureau of Economic Research, Inc.

in GDP. Instead, the members of the NBER look at everything from employment to housing to consumer confidence. They then decide if a decline is sharp enough and broad enough to be offically called a recession. For a serious, scholarly critique of the NBER dates, see Watson (1994).

In spite of the many problems with the NBER dates, the official dates of the NBER are followed throughout this book because they are the most commonly accepted dates. Using these dates, Table 3.1 shows that there have been 31 recessions or depressions in the United States since 1858. There has been one contraction about every 4 to 5 years. But this calculation includes wartime cycles, which the table shows to be much longer than average peacetime cycles. If the wartime cycles are omitted, the average cycle is only 3 to 4 years long. More precisely, from 1945 to 1991, there have been 9 cycles with average expansions lasting 49 months and contractions lasting only 11 months. Although contractions during this period were much shorter than expansions, such has not always been so. For example, in the 14 peacetime cycles from 1854 to 1919, the average expansion was 24 months (or 8 quarters), while the average contraction was also 24 months (or 8 quarters).

Throughout this book, we shall use quarterly data for the reasons stated below. The quarterly dates since the Second World War are given in Table 3.2. Table 3.2 reveals that cycle troughs, the lowest point of each cycle, were reached in 1949, 1954, 1958, 1961, 1970, 1975, 1980, 1982, and 1991. The most serious of these were in 1975, 1982, and 1991. Notice that the quarter of the year in which the trough occurs varies widely with no pattern.

The exact criteria Mitchell used for dating the peaks and troughs were complex and include a number of indicators; the criteria are clearly explained by Burns and Mitchell (1946, Chapter 4) and by Moore (1983, Chapter 1). As noted above, these dates are used both because no better series is available and because the dates are accepted and used by most scholars in the field. The quarterly dates, as Burns and Mitchell (1946) point out at great length, are the best statistics to use in cycle analysis. Statistics given daily or weekly or even monthly tend to contain too much static. Changing the metaphor, the weekly or monthly data lose the forest and

TABLE 3.2
QUARTERLY CYCLE DATES

Cycle	Initial Trough	Peak	Final Trough
Cycle 1	1949.4	1953.3	1953.2
Cycle 2	1953.2	1957.3	1958.2
Cycle 3	1958.2	1960.2	1961.1
Cycle 4	1961.1	1969.4	1970.4
Cycle 5	1970.4	1973.4	1975.1
Cycle 6	1975.1	1980.1	1980.3
Cycle 7	1980.3	1981.3	1982.4
Cycle 8	1982.4	1990.2	1991.2

SOURCE: Bureau of Economic Analysis, U.S. Department of Commerce, available in CITIBASE Economic database, machine-readable magnetic file, 1946–present, Citybank: New York, New York.

NOTE: 1949.4 means the fourth quarter of 1949.

show only the trees. On the other hand, annual data distort many cyclical turning points because the turning points are often in the middle of the year and they are not sufficiently detailed.

REFERENCE CYCLES VERSUS SPECIFIC CYCLES

The dates given in Table 3.2 determine what the NBER calls a reference cycle. A reference cycle is the average business cycle for all sectors of the U.S. economy. Unless stated otherwise, all empirical analyses of cycles in this book refer to reference cycles.

Each specific economic series, however, has peaks and troughs which differ from the average cycle. Sometimes it is necessary to look at the performance of an economic variable over its own particular cycle dates; this is called a specific cycle. It is used rarely, usually for a variable that differs considerably and systematically from the reference cycle. For example, profit rates almost always *lead* the reference cycle, that is, they turn down before the reference cycle peak and turn up before the reference cycle trough. To measure the specific cycle for profit rates, one must first decide where its particular turning points are. Then the rest of the NBER method uses those dates.

Note that a cycle may be measured from trough to trough or from peak to peak. Because it is more common, all cycles in this book are measured from trough to trough.

DIVISIONS OF THE CYCLE

Mitchell called the rising period of the business cycle, from the initial trough to the peak, the *expansion* period. The declining period of the business cycle, from the peak to the final trough, is called the *contraction* period.

The business cycle as defined by Mitchell has four phases: two in the expansion period and two in the contraction period. Starting from the low point or initial trough of the cycle, there is a rapid upturn, called a *recovery* (or revival). Next, there is a further expansion called a *prosperity*. That is followed by a downturn called the *crisis*. Finally, the crisis turns into a contraction called a *depression*. Mild depressions are sometimes called recessions, but this book will use Mitchell's term of depression to describe the final phase of the cycle.

In a more detailed analysis, Mitchell then divides the reference cycle into nine stages. The number of stages is arbitrary, but has a logic to it. Stage 1 is the initial trough of the cycle, the low point from which it begins. Stage 5 is the cycle peak, where most business activity reaches its highest point. Finally, stage 9 is the final trough, from which a new cycle begins. Stage 1, 5, and 9 are, by definition, just three months (one quarter) long. The expansion period lasts from stage 1 to stage 5. The whole expansion (excluding stages 1 and 5) is then divided into three equal time periods. The three periods of equal length in expansion are called stages 2, 3, and 4. Thus, if the whole expansion is 15 quarters long (excluding stages 1 and 5), each of the three stages will be five quarters long.

Similarly, the contraction period lasts from stage 5 till stage 9. The whole contraction (excluding stages 5 and 9) is then divided into three equal time periods. The three periods of equal length in contraction are called stages 6, 7, and 8. Thus, if the whole contraction is six quarters long (excluding stages 5 and 9), then each of the three stages will be two quarters long. Since expansions in recent cycles are normally longer than contractions, stages 2, 3, and 4 are normally longer than stages 6, 7, and 8.

The four phases may now be more precisely defined in terms of the nine stages. Thus, recovery is stages 1 to 3, prosperity is stages 3 to 5, crisis is stages 5 to 7, and depression is stages 7 to 9. The entire expansion period is stages 1 to 5, while the entire contraction period is stages 5 to 9. In other words, recovery is the first phase of expansion (stages 1 to 3), while prosperity is the second phase of expansion (stages 3 to 5). Similarly, crisis is the first phase of contraction (stages 5 to 7), while depression is the last phase of contraction (stages 7 to 9). Mitchell considers that the task of business cycle theory is to explain how each phase leads to the next.

CYCLE RELATIVES

Table 3.3 shows the data for the real national income. The term "real" always means that a variable is expressed in constant dollars, deflated for price inflation. Real GDP is calculated using the implicit price deflator, that is constructed in roughly the same manner to put current GDP into constant dollars. Table 3.3 presents the figures for one cycle, namely the fourth quarter of 1982 through the second quarter of 1991. The first row, called "original data," simply indicates the dollar amounts averaged for each of the nine stages of that business cycle.

The second row of Table 3.3 shows the cycle relatives, which are also pictured in Figure 3.1. The cycle relatives are the original data for a variable divided by the average of that variable for the whole cycle. The average for the whole cycle is called the **cycle base.** The average national income in this cycle was $3,619 billion, so the original data for each stage was divided by that amount to get the nine cycle relatives. To make the relatives more convenient, each ratio is multiplied by 100 to make them percentages.

TABLE 3.3
PATTERN OF REAL NATIONAL INCOME
(1982–1991 CYCLE IN BILLIONS OF 1982 DOLLARS)

	EXPANSION					CONTRACTION			
	TROUGH				PEAK				TROUGH
Stage	1	2	3	4	5	6	7	8	9
Original Data	$3048	$3308	$3602	$3894	$3932	$3918	$3889	$3855	$3850
Cycle Relatives	83.3	91.4	99.5	107.6	108.7	108.3	107.5	106.5	106.4

SOURCE: CITIBASE database, file GYQ.

NOTE: Cycle base, average over the cycle, equals $3619 billion.

FIGURE 3.1
NATIONAL INCOME—IN CYCLE RELATIVES

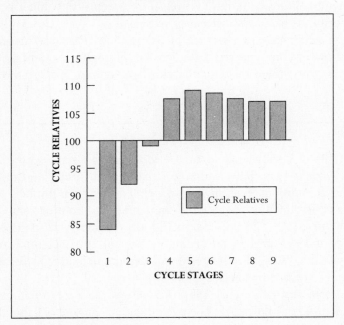

SOURCE: CITIBASE database, file GYQ.

NOTE: This Figure is for one cycle, 1982–1991, in real terms (i.e., constant dollars).

For example, national income in stage 1 was $3,048 billion, which was divided by the cycle base of $3,619 billion. Then it was multiplied by 100 to obtain the **cycle relative** of 83.3. Thus, a cycle relative is just the original data as a percentage of the cycle average (or base) at each stage. This procedure normalizes the data around an average of 100 for the whole cycle. Hence, we can compare the pattern to two entirely different series, such as GDP and interest rates, even though the original units are quite different. We can also compare or average several different cycles of the same variable, even though the cycle base is different in each cycle.

Whereas national income peaks at the cycle peak (stage 5), not all series have individual peaks at the cycle peak. National income is a broad aggregate variable, so it normally reflects the business cycle, moves smoothly upward in the expansion, smoothly downward in the contraction, and neither leads nor lags at turning points.

Some variables, such as profit rates, are called leading indicators, which normally turn down *before* the cycle peak. Others, such as interest rates, are lagging indicators, which normally turn down *after* the cycle peak. The broader and more aggregate a variable is, the more likely it is to behave with regularity and in the same cyclical manner as the average of all business activity. An aggregate which does conform to the cycle, such as GDP, is called a *coincident* indicator.

In Figure 3.1 and in all similar figures based on the NBER method, all stages are shown as if they were the same length. This is not true as a general rule. Usually the expansion (stages 2, 3, and 4) is a different length than the contraction (stages 6, 7, and 8). Most of the cycles in the period since the Second World War have had longer expansions than contractions—but not all of them. For example, the 1981–1982 contraction was longer than the 1980–81 expansion. Moreover, many cycles in past history have had longer contractions than expansions. If one wished to show this in the figures, then every figure showing cycle behavior would require different length stages in expansion and contraction—and some stages would be brief to show clearly. Therefore, all our cycle graphs show an equal expansion and contraction, but students should remember that, in reality, this varies.

RATES OF GROWTH

To study growth or decline, we must examine the change from one period to another. For this purpose, a segment is defined as the period from the middle of one stage to the middle of the next. So there are nine stages, but only eight segments. While national income rises in all four segments of expansion and falls in all four segments of contraction, it does so at different rates of growth or decline.

In Table 3.4 we measure the total change in the cycle relatives for national income from one stage to the next (that is, each segment). The first row of Table 3.4 depicts these amounts of total change in national income in one segment. The second row shows the average number of quarters in each segment (rounded to be whole numbers). Note that in this cycle, 1982–1991, the number of quarters in the expansion varies from 5 to 10 quarters per segment, but in the average contraction there is only about one quarter per segment. Thus, expansions are much longer than contractions in this particular period. This situation—greater length of expansions—does not hold in all periods. In 10 of the last 25 business cycles, the contraction was longer than the expansion.

Finally, in the last row of Table 3.4, we divide the total change in each segment by the number of quarters in that segment to find the rate of growth (or decline) per quarter. These rates of growth are presented in Table 3.4 and Figure 3.2. In the four segments of expansion, national income grew 1.4, 0.8, 0.8, and 0.2 (as a percentage of its average cycle base). This pattern is typical of most private economic activity in expansions under the private enterprise system. In other words, the economy grows most rapidly in the first segment of expansion, less rapidly in the second segment, less rapidly in the third segment, and slowest in the final segment before the peak.

Wesley Mitchell noted that this fact is an important piece of evidence pointing toward the internal generation of business cycle downturns. The economy gets slower and slower and slower until it reaches zero growth and then begins to decline. One could also imagine a pattern that would be dif-

TABLE 3.4

GROWTH RATES OF REAL NATIONAL INCOME 1982–1991 CYCLE, AS PERCENTAGE OF CYCLE BASE

	EXPANSION				CONTRACTION			
Segment	1–2	2–3	3–4	4–5	5–6	6–7	7–8	8–9
Total Change	7.2	8.1	8.1	.0	−0.4	−0.8	−0.9	0.2
Number of Quarters	6	10	6	1	1	1	1	1
Change per Quarter	1.4	0.8	0.8	0.2	−0.4	−0.8	−0.9	0.2

SOURCE: CITIBASE database, file GYQ.

NOTE: The average number of quarters is rounded to the nearest whole number for presentation in this table.

FIGURE 3.2

NATIONAL INCOME—GROWTH RATES PER QUARTER

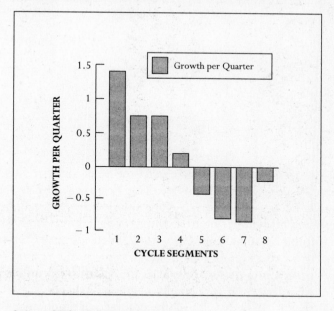

SOURCE: CITIBASE database, file GYQ.

NOTE: This Figure is for one cycle, 1982–1991, in real terms (i.e., constant dollars).

ferent in every cycle and every variable. One could also imagine that growth would be most rapid in the final segment, followed by an external shock, followed by a sharp downturn. On the contrary, Mitchell found that, in reality, during the early expansion of the usual U.S. business cycle, even major external shocks can be survived. The pattern and sequence of events remains the same. Normally, it is only after the peak that an external shock will exacerbate the downturn.

CYCLICAL AMPLITUDE

How can we measure the amplitude (or amount of rise and fall) of a cycle so that we can compare different cycles? In most investigations, there is always a danger in comparing percentages when starting from different bases. Cycle relatives, however, always start from a base equal to 100, so it is easy to compare amplitudes. Table 3.5 measures cycle amplitudes per quarter, that is, the amplitude divided by the number of quarters in an expansion or in a contraction.

TABLE 3.5

CYCLICAL AMPLITUDE OF REAL NATIONAL INCOME

	Expansion Amplitude Per Quarter	Contraction Amplitude Per Quarter
1970–75 cycle	1.2	−1.4
1975–80 cycle	1.5	−1.7
1980–82 cycle	0.8	−0.7
1982–91 cycle	0.8	−0.6
Average	1.0	−1.1

SOURCE: CITIBASE database, file GYQ.

An *expansion amplitude* equals the peak value minus the initial trough value of the cycle in terms of cycle relatives. The expansion amplitudes shown here—in Table 3.5—are divided by the number of quarters to show the growth per quarter of expansion. It was highest (at 1.5 per quarter) in the expansion of 1975–1980, then the growth rate declined in the next two expansions.

A *contraction amplitude* equals the final trough minus the peak in terms of cycle relatives. It is normally negative, indicating a decline from peak to final trough. Table 3.5 shows the contraction amplitudes of national income per quarter for each cycle. The sharpest rates of decline were in the recessions of 1974–1975 and 1980, but the 1981–1982 and 1990–1991 recessions lasted longer, so their total declines were actually greater.

LEADING, LAGGING, AND COINCIDENT INDICATORS

Wesley Mitchell divided all economic time series into coincident, leading, and lagging categories. A coincident series is one that usually reaches its peak at the reference cycle peak and reaches its own trough at the reference cycle trough. So the specific cycle and reference cycle are the same for these series. A leading series is one whose peaks usually come before the reference cycle peaks and whose troughs usually come before the reference cycle troughs. A lagging series is one whose peaks generally come after the reference cycle peaks and whose troughs usually come after the reference cycle troughs.

It was immediately realized that a series that consistently followed one of these patterns would indicate to us where we are in the cycle. So these different groups of series came to be called "indicators." They are important as a basis for understanding theories about the cycle; but they are also important as a means of predicting the cycle. Thus the popular press often tells us that the leading indicators have gone up or down and draw conclusions from that as to what will happen in the future—sometimes their conclusions are right and sometimes they are wrong, for reasons we shall see later. Here we give only a very brief introduction to the indicators because Part 5 contains a whole chapter on appropriate ways to use them for forecasting.

The U.S. Department of Commerce publishes an index of coincident indicators, which is based on a composite of four series that fairly consistently coincide in their behavior with the reference cycle. For example, the gross domestic product and the national income are coincident series. It would be strange if these two aggregates turned up or down at a different time from the reference cycle, which is based on the average behavior of all business activity. Figure 3.3 shows the coincident indicators. It shows that they rise for all four segments of expansion and they fall for all four segments of contraction. Notice also that the coincident indicators rise slower and slower in the expansion, a typical behavior for most broad aggregates.

More interesting, the U.S. Department of Commerce publishes an index of leading indicators, which is based on a composite of 12 series that fairly consistently lead the reference cycle, turning downward before the reference cycle turns downward and turning upward before the reference cycle

FIGURE 3.3
COINCIDENT INDICATORS' INDEX

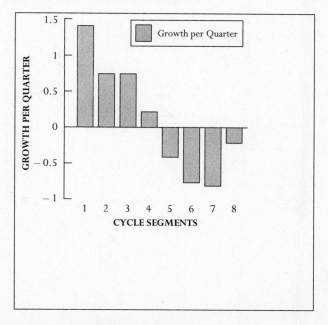

SOURCE: CITIBASE database, file DCOINCQ.

NOTE: This Figure is for the average of four cycles, 1970–1991. Composite index of 4 coincident series.

turns upward. The indicator with the longest lead is usually corporate profit. It is not surprising that profit often turns early because many other series react strongly to whatever profit does. For example, if profit starts rising rapidly, investors rush to increase their investments. If profit falls rapidly for a while, look out for a recession.

Figure 3.4 details an example of the cyclical path of the leading indicators. They rise rapidly in early expansion, but they decline before the reference cycle peak. Then they fall until sometime in the contraction. They begin to rise before the reference cycle trough. Before you rush off to buy or sell stock based on the leading indicators, read Chapter 19 on the strengths and weaknesses of this mode of forecasting.

Finally, the U.S. Department of Commerce publishes an index of lagging indicators, which is a composite of 8 series that fairly consistently turn down some time after the reference cycle peaks and turn up some time after the reference cycle troughs. Who cares about those that lag? While those that lag are hard to use for prediction, they are a big help in understanding the sequence of events in the business cycle. For example, many kinds of

FIGURE 3.4
LEADING INDICATORS' INDEX

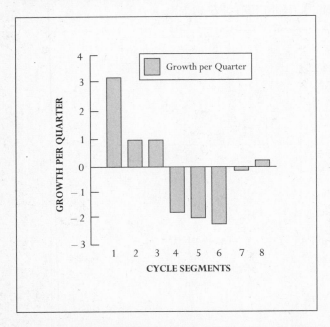

SOURCE: CITIBASE database, file DLEADQ.

NOTE: This Figure is for the average of four cycles, 1970–1991. Composite index of 12 leading series.

interest rates usually lag after the cycle. This means that even when a recession begins, interest rates are still rising, so this is an increased burden on consumers and businesses that are already hurting from the business decline. On the other side, continued low interest rates at the beginning of expansion are a big help to consumers and to businesses.

Figure 3.5 shows that the lagging indicator index rises during most of the expansion, but does not reach its peak till after the reference cycle peak. The lagging indicators then fall for most of the contraction, but they continue to fall after the contraction is over.

CIRCULAR FLOW OF GOODS AND MONEY

National income accounting describes the main flow of money and goods in our economy. We shall define the main aggregates used to describe these flows; then we shall apply the NBER method to take a brief look at how these important aggregates act over the business cycle.

FIGURE 3.5
LAGGING INDICATORS' INDEX

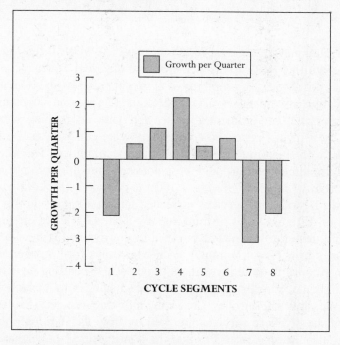

SOURCE: CITIBASE database, file DLAGGQ.

NOTE: This Figure is for the average of four cycles, 1970–1991. It is a composite index of 8 lagging series.

BOX 3.1

THE ARBITERS OF RECESSION

What's a recession? Most economic texts define it as two consecutive quarters of declining output. But don't tell that to the National Bureau of Economic Research, the private group that officially decides when a recession has begun. Says Robert J. Gordon of Northwestern University, one of the seven economists on the NBER panel that makes the call: "I've never heard the committee even discuss that sort of rule." Instead, the panelists take a look at everything from employment to housing to consumer confidence. Then they hash out if the decline is sharp enough and broad enough to be called a recession.

No hurry. There's usually very little argument with the finding. Now mainly known as a sponsor of academic research, the NBER helped pioneer business-cycle dating in the 1920s. The government, a johnny-come-lately, accepts the NBER's judgement because "I don't think we could do a better job," says George R. Green, a top statistician at the Commerce Department.

But don't hold your breath for the next NBER ruling. The panel meets rarely—the last time was in July, 1983—and it usually waits until the evidence is clear. Now a session is unlikely until year-end—and only if the third quarter is a disaster. Says Gordon: "No one will use the big 'R' word until we see a real decline in GNP."

SOURCE: Michael J. Mandel, "The Arbiters of Recession," *Business Week*, August 13, 1990, 32

National income accounting received very little attention and effort before the 1930s. This was because classical and neoclassical economists did not admit any problems of aggregate supply and demand, so no detailed accounts were necessary. The Great Depression so challenged economic theory that government agencies and some economists were receptive when J. M. Keynes proposed certain aggregate concepts as the basis for the new field of economics now called macroeconomics. The U.S. Department of Commerce has translated these concepts into a lot of national accounts.

Gross domestic product (GDP) is defined as the total value of all the finished goods and services produced within a nation during a year. There are four different ways of thinking about the GDP. The circular flow of supply and demand is depicted in these four ways in Figure 3.6. This figure indicates how flow #1, money spending, flows from households to business to buy consumer and investment goods. This spending pays for flow #2, goods sold, the transfer of products from business to households. At the same time, flow #3, services, shows the movement of services from households to business. These services are paid by flow #4, national income, the flow of money income from business to households. Notice that money moves in one direction around the circuit, while goods and services mirror it in their equal and opposite movement. If there is no interruption, the supply and

FIGURE 3.6
THE CIRCULAR FLOW OF SUPPLY AND DEMAND

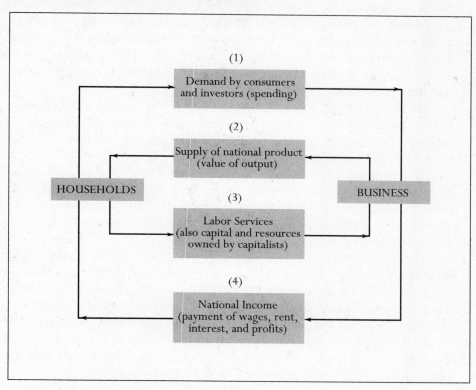

demand will flow smoothly and balance each other in both sets of transactions. All four flows are supposed to be equal and are simply different ways of looking at our aggregate economic activity.

HOW THE NATIONAL INCOME ACCOUNTS ARE DEFINED

GDP is defined as the value of all goods and services produced domestically in the United States for final consumption or investment in a given year. And as noted above, GDP may be calculated in terms of money in two different ways, corresponding to the money flow from households to business or the equal money flow from business to households. In the first, we examine the aggregate money demand for all products, that is, the flow of money spending on consumer goods, investment goods, government purchases, and net exports, each of which is explained below:

$$\$ \text{ GDP} = \$ \text{ spending} = \$ \text{ consumption} + \$ \text{ investment} \qquad (3.1)$$
$$+ \$ \text{ government} + \$ \text{ net exports}$$

Consumption means the total spending of all consumers for goods and services, such as food, clothing, recreation, and transportation. *Investment* is the total spending of all firms and individuals on plant, equipment, and inventories. *Government* means the total spending of all governmental units, federal, state, and local, for all goods and services purchased by them. *Net exports* is defined to mean the total spending of all foreigners on U.S. exports, minus the total spending of all U.S. residents on foreign imports into the United States.

This flow of money spent for products corresponds to the equal opposite flow of products. In the market place the money flow from purchasers is precisely the measure of the value of the GDP sold by business. Thus in Figure 3.6, the two upper loops, labeled (1) and (2), show the movement of money in one direction and the equal movement of goods and services in the other direction. The two are equal by definition because the exchange price has been agreed to by both buyers and sellers. In the next chapter, we will examine what happens when plans for supply and demand do not coincide at present prices.

The second way of calculating GDP in money terms is to add up the money paid out by businesses for all of their costs of production. Most of these costs of production constitute flows of money income to households. These incomes include wages paid for the services of labor, rent for the use of land, interest for the use of borrowed capital, and profit for capital ownership. Thus the two lower loops of Figure 3.6, labeled (3) and (4), depict the movement of goods and services to business in one direction and the equal movement of money as income to households in the other.

Actually businesses have two other major costs that have not yet been discussed. These two costs makes the second way of calculating GDP a little more complicated than suggested by the simple diagram in Figure 3.6. One cost to business is sales taxes (along with other minor taxes, allocated "indirect taxes"). Government spending and taxes are important since governmental units employ over 18 percent of the labor force.

A second cost is depreciation, or the funds set aside to replace the machinery and factory buildings that are eventually worn out in the process of production. These funds are paid out not to any individual but to other businesses when it is time to replace the worn-out instruments of production. So when sales taxes and depreciation are added to the flows of money incomes, we get

$$\$ \text{ GDP} = \$ \text{ labor income} + \$ \text{ rent} + \$ \text{ interest} \qquad (3.2)$$
$$+ \$ \text{ profits} + \$ \text{ depreciation} + \$ \text{ sales taxes}$$

In this way of looking at the GDP, each business pays out labor income to employees. It also pays other businesses to replace the depreciated machinery. The property incomes—rent, interest, and profit—that are received by all owners of property may be grouped together. Then, we may calculate GDP as

$$\$\,\text{GDP} = \$\,\text{labor income} + \$\,\text{property incomes} \qquad (3.3)$$
$$+ \$\,\text{depreciation} + \$\,\text{sales taxes}$$

Thus, we can calculate GDP in terms of all spending to purchase output; or we can calculate GDP in terms of all the money flow through business to employees and property owners (and for replacement of depreciated items to other businesses). By definition, the GDP calculated by either method must be equal to the same money value. Indeed, the U.S. Department of Commerce, which makes these calculations, does always arrive at the same amount by either method, after allowing for statistical mistakes.

National income is defined as the income of the nation in a year's time that is wholly derived from the production of final, usable goods and services. It leaves out depreciation costs and sales taxes. It is the income going to all the economic classes: labor income to employees, rent to landlords, interest to lenders, and profit to entrepreneurs. The national income is simply:

$$\$\,\text{national income} = \$\,\text{labor income} + \$\,\text{rent} + \$\,\text{interest} + \$\,\text{profits} \quad (3.4)$$

In 1991, U.S. national income was $4,544.2 billion, which was composed of $3,390.8 billion of labor income plus $1,153.4 billion of property income. Property income included $47.5 billion of net rental income plus $449.5 billion of net interest income plus $346.3 billion corporate profits plus $368 billion of non-corporate profits (called proprietors' income).

PERSONAL INCOME

The government imposes various taxes on the national income but also adds to the income stream many kinds of transfer payments. A *transfer* payment is a payment that is *not* for current goods or services. The total of payments to all classes in production (that is, the national income) is therefore not the amount of income that households actually have at their disposal. Households' income comes from production plus various transfer payments minus various taxes.

In order to proceed from national income to the income that actually goes to people (that is, personal income), various additions and subtractions must be made. First, corporate profits do not go directly to any individual; corporate profits must be subtracted from national income in the process of determining the personal income actually going to individuals. Second, individuals make various payments of interest on loans to financial institutions and to government; these also must be subtracted to find personal income. Third,

BOX 3.2

THE CONSUMER PRICE INDEX: UNDERLYING CONCEPTS AND CAVEATS

"In 1927, Irving Fisher, in the *Making of Index Numbers*, wrote: Most people have at least a rudimentary idea of a "high cost of living" or of a "low level of prices," but usually have very little idea of how the height of the high cost or lowness of the low level is to be measured. It is to measure such magnitudes that "index numbers" were invented."

The Consumer Price Index (CPI), produced by the Bureau of Labor Statistics, serves as an approximation of an ideal cost-of-living index (CLI). The CPI is "a measure of the average change in the prices paid by urban consumers for a fixed market basket of goods ans services." Measuring price change through the use of a fixed market basket has a long history, dating to the early 1700s. The theory underlying the CLI is much more recent, having been developed by A. A. Konus in 1924.

. . . The measurement of change in the cost-of-living stemming from a change in price is based on an assessment of how a change in the price of goods and services affects consumers' well-being. Consumer well-being can be defined as the level of utility achieved by the consumer through the consumption of goods and services. The underlying assumption is that consumers choose the bundle of goods and services that maximizes their utility for a given expenditure level, or equivalently, minimize expenditures to achieve a given level of utility.

Because a cost-of-living index measures how price changes affect a consumer, one can look at how the minimum expenditure necessary to obtain a certain level of utility responds to price changes. Let the minimum expenditure needed to achieve the level of utility u be denoted by $E(p;u)$, where p denotes the set of prices of goods and services. The cost of living index for a consumer between period t and the base period b can be expressed as a ratio of the minimum expenditures: $I(p^t, p^b, u^b) = E(p^t; u^b) / E(p^b; u^b)$

The level of utility in the base period underpins the comparison between the two expenditure levels.

Consumer Price Index

A Laspeyres fixed-quantity price index that measures the price change of a fixed market basket of goods and services of constant quality bought on average by urban consumers (CPI-U). The CPI-U focuses on urban consumers and the CPI-W focuses on urban wage earners and clerical workers. It is the ratio of a market basket in two periods: the numerator is the value of the market basket at, say, current prices and the denominator is the value of the market basket at base period prices.

Dennis Fixler, *Monthly Labor Review*, December, 1993

individuals pay out of their wage income certain compulsory contributions for social insurance to the government (these are usually payments for Social Security); these also must be subtracted from the national income.

On the positive side, the government makes many transfer payments that shift income to individuals, thus adding to personal income. These transfers include unemployment compensation, farm subsidies, business subsidies, and Social Security benefits. Second, corporations pay dividends out of profits. Third, business makes a few transfer payments, such as retirement benefits. Fourth, a great many wealthy individuals receive interest payments from the government or from corporations. All such payments must be added to national income if we wish to calculate personal income. Totaling all the additions and subtractions from national income, the result is total personal income. The procedure is indicated by the following equation:

$$
\begin{aligned}
\$ \text{ personal income} = {}& \$ \text{ national income} \\
& - \$ \text{ corporate profits} \\
& - \$ \text{ interest paid by individuals} \\
& - \$ \text{ social security taxes} \\
& + \$ \text{ government transfer payments} \\
& + \$ \text{ dividends} \\
& + \$ \text{ business transfer payments} \\
& + \$ \text{ personal interest income} \qquad (3.5)
\end{aligned}
$$

DISPOSABLE PERSONAL INCOME

Finally, there is disposable personal income, which is the amount of money actually at the disposal of individuals and households for spending on consumption or for personal saving. In order to find this quantity, personal income taxes, which are the taxes an individual or a household must pay in proportion to its yearly income, must be deducted. The result is expressed as

$$
\begin{aligned}
\$ \text{ disposable personal income} = {}& \$ \text{ personal income} \\
& - \$ \text{ personal income taxes} \qquad (3.6)
\end{aligned}
$$

Consumers may now spend and save out of disposable personal income. If consumption expenditures are subtracted from disposable personal income, we arrive at personal saving. A simplified listing of the accounts discussed here (with actual figures for 1991) is shown in Table 3.6.

SAVING AND INVESTMENT

Both saving and investment are each by definition equal to national income less consumption. Therefore they must by definition equal each other. Leaving out government and foreign trade, we have:

$$\$ \text{ consumption} + \$ \text{ net investment} = \$ \text{ consumption} + \$ \text{ savings} \qquad (3.7)$$

The equality between saving and investment is only an accounting identity. In terms of planned investment and saving, they may be drastically different. If planned investment is less than saving, then inventories pile up—but accountants call all inventories "investment," even if they are unplanned and unwanted—so saving and investment are equal in the national income accounts by definition.

TABLE 3.6
NATIONAL INCOME ACCOUNTS FOR 1993 (IN BILLIONS OF DOLLARS)

Component of National Income Accounts:	Amount
GROSS DOMESTIC PRODUCT	$6,377.9
+ Net Receipts of factor income from rest of world	+0.2
− Depreciation (or Capital Consumption)	−671.3
− Indirect business taxes (mostly sales taxes)	−565.9
= NATIONAL INCOME	= 5,140.9
− Corporate profits	−467.3
− Interest paid by individuals	−445.6
− Social security taxes and net wage accruals	−605.3
+ Government transfer payments	+890.2
+ Dividends	+158.3
+ Business transfer payments	+21.9
+ Personal interest income	+695.2
= PERSONAL INCOME	= 5,388.3
− Personal income tax	−681.6
= DISPOSABLE PERSONAL INCOME	= 4,706.7
− Consumption expenditures	−4,391.8
− Interest paid by consumers to business	−125.0
= Personal saving	= 189.9

SOURCE: *Survey of Current Business*, March 1994, 7–9.

NOTE: Amounts may be off slightly due to statistical discrepancies and rounding.

CONCLUSION

Measurement of the business cycle is, at best, an imprecise science. The economy is made up of many different sectors, many of which impact different regions of the country differently. People is one part of the country may feel that they are in the midst of the Great Depression, while folks in another part of the country may believe that they are in the midst of an expanding economy. But business cycle theory attempts to gauge overall economic activity, taking into account all aspects of national economic activity. As such, the results are always open to intrepretion and debate. Perhaps the best that can be done is to attempt to agree on a common methodology and use it, until someone develops a better, more consistent methodology that can be used in the future.

SUGGESTED READINGS

The classic, detailed statement of the national income accounts is R. and N. Ruggles, *National Income Accounts and Income Analysis* (New York: McGraw-Hill, 1956). Arthur Burns and Wesley Mitchell (1946) provides the most detailed account of the NBER method and its origins.

KEY TERMS AND CONCEPTS

NBER

reference cycle; specific cycle

cycle relatives; cycle base

stage; segment

change per quarter

leading indicators; lagging indicators

gross domestic product (GDP); national income

Some Components of Revenue and Cost

Part 2 examines the different components of costs and revenues. Aggregate demand by consumers and investment are the primary focus of this portion of the book. Also, the effects of changing the distribution of income are examined.

Part 2 describes the behavior of costs, both labor and raw materials, over the business cycle. Each of these components affects profits, so the behavior of profits over the business cycle is also described.

Part 2 is less concerned with presenting theories of the business cycle than it is in describing how the components of profits change over the business cycle.

CHAPTER 4

Consumption

Profits are dependent on revenue and cost. The aggregate revenue from sale of the gross domestic product (GDP) may be divided into four components: consumption spending, investment spending, government spending, and net exports. Consumption spending is, by far, the largest category of aggregate demand or aggregate revenue. Year after year, consumption absorbs between 60 percent and 65 percent of total GDP (see Figure 4.1). Over 90 percent of personal disposable income is absorbed by consumption. Obviously, the behavior of consumption will have considerable impact upon the behavior of aggregate demand or aggregate revenue. Indeed, in Part 3, an entire chapter will be spent discussing theories that explain all contractions as a result of deficient consumer demand. Chapter 4 explains the cyclical behavior of consumption, leaving its impact on the cycle to be discussed in Part 3.

TYPES OF CONSUMPTION

In the national income accounts, consumption is divided into three categories: (1) consumer non-durable goods, (2) consumer durable goods, and (3) services. In 1990, the money spent on consumption was divided as follows: 13 percent for durable goods (such as refrigerators), 33 percent for non-durable goods (such as food), and 54 percent for services (such as haircutting or financial services). Thus, the demand for services is now the most important category of consumption. Services have slowly grown in relative importance over the last 30 years at the expense of consumption of non-durable goods. The relative roles of these two categories have become almost exactly reversed over that time.

FIGURE 4.1
CONSUMPTION AS A PERCENTAGE OF GDP

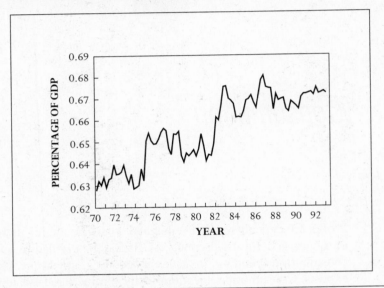

Despite the change in its composition, consumption as an aggregate category has been fairly stable. The ratio of consumption to GDP from 1950 to 1990 has never been below 61 percent and never above 69 percent. Furthermore, no trend is evident. Consumption changes slowly, but it is such a large category that a drop of only 1 percent in a given year amounts to a drop of over $40 billion in aggregate demand (assuming it is not offset elsewhere).

In the four cycles of 1921 to 1938, Wesley Mitchell (1951) found that aggregate consumption rose 15 percent in expansions, but fell by only 10 percent in contractions. In Mitchell's terminology, the expansion amplitude was 15, while the contraction amplitude was 10. When this wide category was disaggregated, Mitchell found that consumer perishables behaved about the same as the aggregate, rising 16 percent and falling 11 percent. Consumer durables, however, reacted more strongly to the cycle—this is because consumers can usually postpone purchases of durable goods. Durable goods had much greater cyclical amplitudes, rising 31 percent while falling 27 percent. Finally, he found consumer services to be much more stable, rising by 14 percent, but falling only 6 percent. He found that services had a rising trend and showed resistance to declines. Obviously, the mix of types of consumption affect cyclical amplitudes. One reason for milder fluctuations in consumption has been the trend to greater weight for services in total consumption.

In the four cycles from 1970 to 1991, aggregate consumption rose 14 percent in expansions, but fell by only 0.2 percent in contractions. Non-durable consumer goods, such as food and other perishables, behaved rather similarly, with an expansion amplitude of 10 percent, while it fell only 1.2 percent in contractions. Consumer durables, such as automobiles, had much greater fluctuations. Durable goods rose 25 percent in expansions and fell 6 percent in contractions, thus conforming rather well to the business cycle. Services, on the other hand, rose in expansions by 14 percent, but continued to rise in contractions by 2 percent, although services rose only a minute 0.2 percent in the most recent contraction. It appears that it was much less risky to invest in consumer services than in consumer durables in the United States in that period.

AGGREGATE CONSUMPTION BEHAVIOR

What has been the cyclical behavior of total consumption, including all three types discussed above? In the four severe recessions of the 1970s, 1980s, and early 1990s, total consumption rose in the expansion but falls in the contraction, though the fall is very slight.

The rates of growth of consumption over the cycle are shown in Figure 4.2. Consumption rises during the whole expansion. It rises most rapidly in the first segment of recovery, then slower and slower until it is rising very slowly indeed in the *prosperity* phase just before the peak. In the crisis at the beginning of the cyclical contraction, consumption falls rapidly, so its decline is quite clear. Unlike consumption during very severe depressions, however, consumption in this period then revives and rises a little during the depression phase of the contraction, so the severity of the contraction in consumer spending was much less than it was between the two wars.

Whatever else one can say about aggregate consumption behavior, it is clearly related to national income. Thus, a formal statement may say:

$$Consumption = f\,(national\ income) \qquad (4.1)$$

where "f" means "function of." If one thing is a function of another, it is influenced, affected, determined, or related to the other.

These relationships are examined econometrically in Part 5. It will be shown that a time lag exists between a change in national income and a change in aggregate consumption. When a person receives income, it takes some time before it is all spent. The aggregate time lag reflects the average of all individual decisions.

FIGURE 4.2
AGGREGATE CONSUMPTION

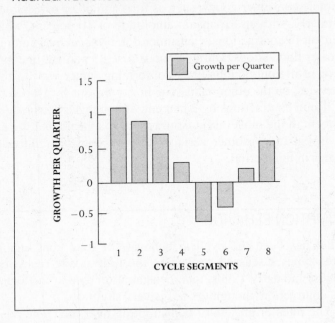

SOURCE: CITIBASE database, file GCQ

NOTE: Quarterly data, in real terms, average of 4 cycles, 1970–1991.

THE PROPENSITY TO CONSUME

Keynes explained consumption in terms of psychological propensities, so almost all economic textbooks today define the ratio of consumption to income as the average propensity to consume, or APC. The ratio of additional consumption to additional income is called the marginal propensity to consume, or MPC. Mathematically, these are expressed as:

$$APC = total\ consumption\ /\ total\ income \tag{4.2}$$

$$MPC = (change\ in\ total\ consumption)\ /\ (change\ in\ total\ income) \tag{4.3}$$

Figure 4.3 pictures the rates of growth of the average propensity to consume in these four cycles. Movements of the APC reflect the differential between the greater fluctuations of national income and the lesser fluctuations of consumption. Thus, throughout the average expansion of this period, the average propensity to consume is declining, reflecting the greater rise of income than of consumption. Throughout the contraction, the average propensity to consume is rising, reflecting the greater decline of

FIGURE 4.3
AVERAGE PROPENSITY TO CONSUME

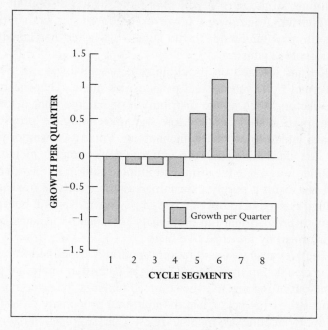

SOURCE: CITIBASE database, files GC/GY.

NOTE: Average propensity to consume out of national income, average of 4 cycles, 1970–1991.

income than consumption. The fact that national income rises and falls more rapidly than consumption may be seen by comparing income behavior in Figure 3.2 with consumption in Figure 4.2. The econometric relation of consumption to income is measured in Chapter 22.

KEYNES VIEW OF CONSUMPTION

Keynes saw a need for a description of the behavior of consumer demand in the aggregate. Previous mainstream economists talked only about individual consumers because Say's law argued that aggregate demand was always sufficient. When Keynes discarded Say's Law, it became important for him to describe aggregate consumer behavior.

Keynes saw aggregate consumer behavior in terms of psychology. He stated the "fundamental psychological law" that "men are disposed, as a rule and on the average, to increase their consumption as their income increases, but not by as much as the increase in their income" (Keynes 1936, 96). He argued that people have a certain habitual consumption expenditure, or standard of living, out of a given level of income. If a person's income rises, he or she will, at first, continue with the same standard of living, so the person will save more. That person will soon adjust his or her consumption upward, however, but more slowly than the rise in income. Therefore, saving tends to rise somewhat faster than consumption in a business cycle expansion.

Keynes focused on psychological propensities. But consumption is not governed by psychological propensities alone. There also are many objective factors, such as the distribution of income, that determine the ratio of consumption to income. Moreover, psychological propensities are by no means innate or eternally unchanging. Present consumer psychological values are determined by the cultural environment, including family background, religion, education, and indoctrination by the advertising media. To call the result a purely psychological propensity is misleading. That terminology is used here only because it is so widespread, but there is always the implicit proviso that the propensity to consume is socially conditioned and constrained by the objective facts.

The Keynesian consumption function is described in beginning economics textbooks, in its simplest form, as a constant marginal propensity to consume out of income. Keynes himself had a far more complex perspective, as indicated by his belief that the marginal propensity to consume (MPC) was likely to decline as income rises. The simplest version of Keynes also assumes that there is some minimum or autonomous consumption level, so that people do not starve even at zero income. Because the theory begins with this minimum consumption, then adds a constant MPC, it reaches the conclusion that the ratio of consumption to income must decline as we get further away from the minimum level. Thus, the usual presentation reaches the conclusion that the average propensity to consume must decline as income rises, but in a rather mechanical way. At any rate, in the view of Keynes himself and in the simplified presentations of his position, APC will fall as income rises in a cyclical expansion, while APC will rise as income falls in a cyclical contraction.

The Keynesian revolution generated a plethora of empirical research on consumption behavior. Cross-sectional studies of different families earning different levels of income in a given year confirmed the view that the APC falls as the income level rises, and the average propensity to save rises. Poor families have a very high APC, and wealthy families have a low APC (for a discussion of the early studies and their relation to later theories, see the excellent surveys by Mayer, 1972, and by Marglin, 1984). Consumption patterns also vary by age group, an important trend in view of the aging of the American population. As the population ages, household formation and expenditures on large durable goods falls. This has some important implications for the economy in the future. Some economic forecasters have identified this trend as a reason for a long-term decline in the future growth rate of GDP, relative to the past performance of the economy. In a study of the expenditure patterns of the elderly, Ruben and Nieswiadomy (1994) stated that the elderly spent less than the nonelderly at the same income level, and the very oldest have the lowest average propensity to consume. Further, the elderly maintain their wealth by reducing consumption, which may result from uncertainty about their health, length of life, and their ability to maintain income levels. These results have interesting implications for the long-term growth of the economy as the population ages for the next few decades. Thereafter, consumption patterns may reverse as the young become a larger portion of the population.

The early studies of monthly or quarterly time-series data for aggregate consumption and income covered relatively short time periods, that is, less than or equal to a whole business cycle. These studies also seemed to confirm that the APC falls as income rises and the APC rises when income falls. The important implication of these early Keynesian studies for business cycle theory was that in every business cycle expansion, consumption rises more slowly than income, with a growing gap between effective consumer demand and output at current prices.

These early results, which are confirmed again by the data presented in this chapter, all seemed to show that Keynes was exactly correct. This view hardened into the dogma that the average propensity to consume always declines as the absolute level of income rises. This simplistic dogma, far less careful and subtle than Keynes's own writing, has been called the Absolute Income Theory. It was affirmed with no limitations as to time or place.

When long-run statistics for the United States became available, some presented averages of 10-year periods as one point, while others used every business cycle as one point. In the long run, defined this way, the APC was found to be very roughly constant. Of course, Keynes was interested mainly in the short run and he never predicted that the APC would fall decade after decade (nor has anyone else suggested such a theory). Moreover, it was later pointed out that many different factors operate together to produce the roughly constant long-run APC in the U.S. economy. An excellent discussion of this whole controversy appears in Green, 1980. Nevertheless, the importance of the long-run constant APC was used as a club to attack Keynes's whole theory, on the assumption that he believed the simplest Absolute Income Theory.

THREE ALTERNATIVES TO KEYNES

Many alternative explanations of aggregate consumption behavior have emerged since Keynes. Three of the well-known alternatives are: the relative income hypothesis of Duesenberry (1949), the life cycle hypothesis of Ando and Modigliani (1963), and the permanent income hypothesis of

Milton Friedman (1957). These are usually explained in detail in any intermediate theory text, so they are mentioned briefly here with respect to their explanation of consumption behavior in the cycle; why does APC fall in expansion, but rise in contractions?

RELATIVE INCOME HYPOTHESIS. This hypothesis explains the rise in APC in contractions by arguing that people spend relative to their previous peak income. As income declines below the peak, people try to maintain their peak consumption. Therefore, they spend a higher proportion of their income to maintain consumption or they dip into savings, so APC rises. In an expansion, when average income goes above the previous peak, people slowly raise their consumption further, so APC falls.

THE LIFE CYCLE HYPOTHESIS. This hypothesis relates mainly to the income and wealth that people usually have at different points in their lives. It argues that people primarily spend in relation to their wealth or the present value of their property. In a contraction, the value of wealth from property falls more slowly than current income. Therefore, consumption falls more slowly than income because it is a function of wealth, so APC rises in contractions. But the value of property rises more slowly than current income in expansions. Since consumption reflects wealth, it also rises more slowly than income, so APC falls in expansions.

THE PERMANENT INCOME HYPOTHESIS. Permanent income is determined by total expected wealth during a lifetime (Friedman 1957). Permanent income determines permanent consumption, the level one expects over a lifetime; the proportion of consumption to income is constant over a lifetime. This true relationship is disguised by short-run changes. During a short-run expansion, the consumer gets transitory income, that income which is known to be a transitory windfall but will not continue. Friedman assumes that APC out of transitory income is lower than APC out of permanent income because people know they must return to their permanent level. Thus, the APC would appear to fall as income rises, while APC would appear to rise as income falls. Of course, the ratio of permanent consumption to permanent income remains constant.

CONTROVERSIES OVER CONSUMPTION HYPOTHESES. A spirited controversy has raged in economics over which of these hypotheses are correct. Well over 200 empirical studies have been done, attempting to prove that one of them fits the facts better than the others. These studies have been summarized and evaluated in three outstanding surveys by Mayer (1972), Marglin (1984), and Green (1980). After lengthy and very detailed discussions, all three surveys reach the same conclusion. The empirical studies do not disprove any of the hypotheses (unless they are given a very rigid form). Neither do the voluminous studies prove any one of them to be the best, correct hypothesis.

This is not unusual in economics. All of the hypotheses explain roughly the same facts. They merely interpret and explain the facts differently. The same conclusion will be found true of the multitude of business cycle theories, though some appear to be far more useful and realistic than others.

Nevertheless, some theories are dominant in economics at any given time, and others are ignored. For various reasons, Keynes was largely ignored in the 1970s and 1980s, while the life cycle and permanent income hypotheses were dominant. They meshed better with the dominant neoclassical microeconomic theory, with the revival of Say's law by the New Classicals, and perhaps were more compatible with the political climate in the Reagan-Bush years.

For the purpose of understanding business cycle theory and policy, it is important to stress that the life cycle and permanent income hypotheses contradicted Keynesian theory on two vital issues: (1) does APC fall in higher income groups? and (2) does APC fall as the economy expands? These appear to be abstruse, academic issues of interest to no one but economists. That is not true, however, because implications of the questions affect policy and influence every budget debate in the U.S. Congress.

Both the life cycle and permanent income hypotheses begin with individual consumer preferences and take these as given psychological facts. In his Presidential address to the American Economic Association, John Kenneth Galbraith (1967) argued that, on the contrary, economists should focus on how preferences are molded and changed by society. By concentrating on individual preferences, these two theories also rule out distinctions between the saving behavior of employees as a group, the saving behavior of entrepreneurs as a group, and the saving behavior of corporations. Their view thus prohibits consideration of what we shall find to be the main hypotheses of post-Keynesians, neo-Marxists, and Institutionalists, all of which concentrate on the differences in behavior among different groups and institutions (see Marglin, 1984, and the literature cited therein).

The concentration on individual preferences by the permanent income and life cycle hypotheses lead to a very clear contradiction with one of Keynes's chief conclusions. Keynes argued that the average propensity to consume declines at higher-income levels. Therefore, Keynes stressed that more inequality, a higher proportion of income to the rich and a lower proportion to the poor, would tend to lower consumer demand. The policy implication is that if it is necessary to increase consumer demand to eliminate unemployment, then there should be greater equality of income.

The life cycle and permanent income theorists argue against Keynes's thesis. These theories are designed, in part, to remove Keynes's thesis from accepted macroeconomic doctrine. For example, Alan Blinder argues thus:

> In the early Post Keynesian days it was commonly assumed, presumably on the basis of Keynes' own intuition, . . . that equalization of the income distribution would increase consumption. With . . . the ascendancy of the . . . [Permanent Income and Life Cycle] models of consumer behavior, this view fell into disrepute in academic circles. (Blinder 1975, 447–48).

Blinder states that the "modern" (permanent income and life cycle) view "does not accord very well with intuition," especially the intuition of "those not schooled in macroeconomics" (Blinder 1975, 448). It is clear that, for Blinder, macroeconomics means only the viewpoint of the neoclassical life cycle and permanent income theories. Macroeconomics does not include the viewpoint of Keynes, the post-Keynesians, Institutionalists, or new-Keynesians.

Whereas Keynes argued that the average propensity to consume falls at higher-income levels, the two neoclassical theories discussed earlier deny this basic finding. They argue that individuals each have a given APC, so the short-run or cross-sectional results can be explained by other, temporary factors. It follows that a change in the distribution of income, in the eyes of these theorists, will not change the average propensity to consume (see Musgrove 1980). The policy implication is that a shift in income distribution from the poor to the rich, or from employees to entrepreneurs, will not lower consumer demand, so it will not have a depressing effect. Similarly, redistribution from the rich to the poor, or from entrepreneurs to employees, will not stimulate the economy.

The second major difference between Keynesian hypotheses about consumption and the life cycle and permanent income hypotheses relates to the behavior of APC over the cycle. Since they take the APC of individuals as given permanently, the fact that APC falls in expansions is seen as "a result of departures from the long-run average rate of growth of income" (Wonnacott 1974, 343–44). Since this is a temporary deviation, it is not perceived as a major problem. For Keynes, on the contrary, limiting the growth of consumer demand would cause serious systemic problems because a lack of effective demand leads to recession or depression.

Finally, almost all economists agree that short-run consumer demand is also affected by several other factors, such as (1) age, (2) income distribution, (3) interest rates, (4) expectations about the future, (5) government taxes, (6) government spending, and (7) international factors. One other alternative to the life cycle and permanent income theories is the post-Keynesians and Institutionalist view of the importance of income distribution.

THE FUNCTIONAL INCOME HYPOTHESIS

Keynes emphasized that increasing inequality may widen the gap between income (or output) and consumer demand, saying: "Since I regard the individual propensity to consume as being (normally) such as to have a wider gap between income and consumption as income increases, it naturally follows that the collective propensity for a community as a whole may depend . . . on the distribution of incomes within it" (Keynes 1939, 129). Keynes was also quite explicit about the effect of an income shift from labor income to property income: "The transfer from wage-earners to other factors is likely to diminish the propensity to consume" (Keynes 1936, 262).

Post-Keynesians have argued that consumer demand is strongly affected by the distribution of income (see Sidney Weintraub, 1958, Michael Kalecki, 1968, Eichner and Kregel, 1975, Darity and Marrero, 1981, Sawyer, 1982, and Marglin, 1984). The poor have high marginal propensities to consume, that is, a high ratio of additional consumption out of additional income. The rich have much lower marginal propensities to consume. Therefore, if the rich get a higher share of income and the poor a lower share than in the previous period, the marginal propensity to consume for the whole country will decline.

Entrepreneurs who receive profits from ownership of property and shares of corporate stocks have, mostly, very high incomes. Even after consuming large amounts of luxury goods, they are able to save and have a low propensity to consume. Recipients of labor income, including wage workers and salaried employees, have much lower average incomes. Recipients of labor income are, on the average, not able to save because they must consume all or almost all their income to meet basic needs.

The functional income hypothesis derives its name from the fact that there are two kinds of income distribution data, individual and functional. Individual income distribution separates people into categories based exclusively on size of income. The term *functional* refers to types of income, mainly the split between labor income and property income, two functionally different groups of income receivers. The functional income hypothesis stresses that there is a lower marginal propensity to consume out of income from profits than out of labor income. This implies that a shift from labor income to property income will cause a lower average propensity to consume for the whole society. A shift from property income to labor income, on the contrary, would raise the overall propensity to consume. For policy purposes, this means that policies (such as those of the Reagan administration in 1981) that shift income from the poor and the wage workers to rich entrepreneurs will restrict consumer demand.

The post-Keynesians (such as Sawyer 1982) contend that entrepreneurs have higher savings ratios and lower consumption ratios than recipients of labor income, for two reasons. First, there is the usual argument that the low income of most people who receive labor income forces them to spend all of it merely to keep at the minimum socially acceptable standard of living. Today, this means a living standard with both husband and wife working at paid jobs. Entrepreneurs, on the other hand, have a high enough income that they may save if they wish to do so.

Second, not only do recipients of property income have savings above the socially necessary minimum, but their institutional situation forces them to invest. For small business persons, it is obvious that they must keep on investing in order to continually expand capital to keep up with competitors so as to avoid being swallowed by competitors. They are under heavy pressure to invest for the survival of the business, even if income is low (see Sawyer 1982, 105; Fichtenbaum 1985, 237). In big business, on the other hand, the decision for further investment is made by the corporation; and only to a lesser extent by individual property income recipients. Corporations pay out only part of profits as dividends to investors. The rest of the profit is retained by the corporation and used as a form of saving destined for investment. As a potentially eternal institution, the corporation has an incentive to invest and expand as rapidly as possible, often contrary to the desire for immediate dividends on the part of many individual shareholders.

The important question is the needs of the corporate institution, not the needs or preferences of individuals, as usually assumed by neoclassical economists. Thus, Sawyer points out that "much of savings is made by firms in pursuit of their objectives (survival, profits, growth, etc.) with little reference to the utility of households who are the nominal owners of the firms" (1985, 170). Marglin (1984, 432) emphasizes the importance of corporate decisions on consumption and saving when we examine reality. Thus, total private saving in the period 1952–1979 was found by Marglin to be 9 percent of disposable income. But of that 9 percent, only 2.5 percent was household saving, while 3.8 percent was corporate saving, and 2.7 percent was pension-fund saving.

Since corporate saving in the form of retained profits is an institutional reality in the modern private enterprise system, it is incorrect to ignore it when considering saving and investment. Yet, most neoclassical studies look only at the personal income (or personal disposable after-tax income) of entrepreneurs and employees when studying consumption and saving tendencies. They exclude corporate and other institutional saving. This neoclassical approach results from their basic methodological view in favor of starting all analyses with individual preference sets. On the contrary, a more realistic and comprehensive theory must include all of the category of national income, which includes not only employee income but also all of retained corporate profits, dividends, interest, and rental income. In that appropriate framework, we shall see that it is quite clear that the APC out of labor income is higher than the APC out of property income. In other words, the ratio of saving out of property income is much higher than the ratio of saving out of labor income (which is, on the average, a net percentage of zero).

CONSUMPTION FROM LABOR INCOME AND FROM PROPERTY INCOME

It is a well-documented fact that in most private enterprise countries, the spending for consumption is quite close in amount to the total wages paid out to workers. One survey of many countries over many years finds the ratio of consumption to total employee compensation to be 1.03 for the United States, 1.04 for Canada, 1.00 for West Germany, 1.00 for the United Kingdom, 1.04 for Switzerland, 0.995 for the Netherlands, 0.98 for Denmark, and 1.04 for Finland. These figures merely reflect the fact that most consumption is from employees' income. In countries with a more equitable income distribution, employees' income is a larger part of total income, so consumption is smaller relative to employees' income. In Sweden, for example, where there is greater equality than in most private enterprise countries, consumption is only 0.85 of employees' income. On the other hand, a high ratio of consumption to employee income means that there is very unequal distribution of income because a small number of property owners have a large part of total consumption. Thus, in countries with a high degree of inequality, we find that the ratio of total consumption to total employee compensation is 1.88 in Mexico, 1.7 in all of Latin America, 1.6 in private enterprise economies in Asia, and 1.5 in Africa.

Moving beyond the simple point that consumption and employee incomes are of roughly the same magnitude, many attempts have been made to estimate employees' propensity to consume as well as entrepreneur's propensity to consume. These studies cover different countries, different time periods, and use different econometric techniques, so the results are also quite different. One study looks at the APC, while the rest look at MPC. Some define employee income as wages only, while others define it as all employee compensation, including salaries, bonuses, and fringe benefits. Some define entrepreneurial income as personal profits only, while others define it as all property income, including interest, rents, and retained corporate profit.

With those warnings, the results of these studies may be considered. For the United States from 1929 to 1952, Klein and Goldberger (1955) find that the MPC from labor income is .62, while the MPC from property income is only .46. For the United States from 1948 to 1950, Milton Friedman (1957) finds that the APC from labor income is .98, while the APC from property income is only .77. For Holland from 1947 to 1954, Lawrence Klein (1962) finds that the MPC from labor income is .85, while the MPC from property income is only .40. For England from 1960 to 1975, Murfin (1980) finds that the MPC out of labor income is .84, while the MPC out of property income is only .23. For the United States from 1949 to 1980, Sherman and Evans (1984) find an MPC of .99 out of labor income, but an MPC of only .13 out of property income. It should be emphasized that those studies with very low estimates of MPC of property income include all property income, including corporate retained earnings, net interest income, and rental income, as well as proprietor's income and dividends. Those studies that find a somewhat higher MPC from property income (but still way below the MPC of labor income) are concerned only with disposable personal income. There are many other studies, all finding a higher propensity to consume from labor income than from property income, see, for example, Burmeister and Taubman (1969), Holbrook and Stafford (1971), Modigliani and Steindel (1977), Steindel (1977), Arestis and Driver (1980), Marglin (1984), and Fichtenbaum (1985). Note that many people have both labor income and property income, so we are examining the consumption from the whole flow of labor income and property income, not just the consumption of particular individuals.

What all these studies have in common is the finding that employee spending from labor income (no matter how defined) shows a higher propensity to consume than entrepreneur spending from property income (no matter how defined). That so many investigators find the same general results for different times and places lends the results some credibility. On the other hand, all of the studies suffer from statistical problems, such as multicolinearity (the variables are not independent, but all move together) and autocorrelation (the results in each period are not independent, but are affected by the previous period), so one should not have much faith in the exact quantitative results.

An interesting and somewhat different approach by Fichtenbaum (1985) finds that consumption is a non-linear function of the ratio of labor to property income, in addition to being a function of total income. His results show the marginal propensity to consume to be a function of the ratio of labor to property income. "Moreover, the results confirm the hypothesis that the MPC out of labor income is greater than the MPC out of property income" (Fichtenbaum 1985, 242). Fichtenbaum has successfully solved some of the earlier statistical estimation problems. His findings support the common sense view that the distribution of income between labor income and property income (or between employees and entrepreneurs) affects consumer demand.

PROPENSITY TO CONSUME AND LABOR SHARE

This section examines the relationship between the propensity to consume and the labor share in the 1970–1991 period.

Labor share is defined to mean the percentage of the national income that goes to labor income. *Property share* is defined as the percentage of all national income going to property income. By definition:

$$\text{Labor share} = \text{labor income} \,/\, \text{national income} \qquad (4.4)$$

$$\text{Property share} = \text{property income} \,/\, \text{national income} \qquad (4.5)$$

Of course, the labor share plus the property share always add up to 100 percent of national income, by definition.

FIGURE 4.4
LABOR SHARE AND AVERAGE PROPENSITY TO CONSUME

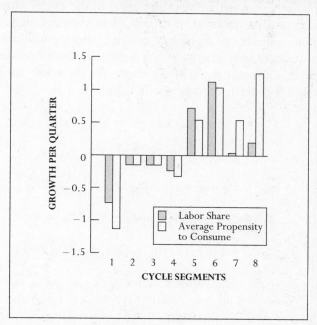

SOURCE: CITIBASE database, files GC/GY and GCOMP/GY. Average propensity to consume means aggregate consumption divided by national income; labor share is all employee compensation divided by national income; average of 4 cycles, 1970–1991.

In Figure 4.4, the rates of growth of the labor share in each cycle segment are revealed for the average of the four cycles, 1970–1991. These growth rates may be compared with the growth rates of the average propensity to consume for the same period. Both fall most rapidly in the recovery phase of expansion, then fall less rapidly in the prosperity phase of expansion. Both rise most rapidly in the crisis phase of contraction, and continue to rise in the rest of contraction.

In the average of the four cycles of the 1970–1991 period, the cycle pattern of both variables in Figure 4.4 shows that the movements of APC and the labor share are quite closely correlated in this period. Both the propensity to consume and the labor share fall in every segment of business expansion. Both the propensity to consume and the labor share rise in every segment of business contraction. Econometric tests for the entire period from 1949 to 1991 show a strong correlation between the average propensity to consume and the labor share. The detailed results, presented in Chapter 22, show this regression relationship with a distributed time lag.

This closely similar behavior gives some support to the hypothesis that the propensity to consume falls in expansion in large part because the labor share falls. The fall throughout the expansion provides support for the view that a low average propensity to consume (caused by a low labor share) limits consumer demand at the peak period of the cycle. Thus, the behavior of the APC and the labor share imply, in this theory, that a lack of demand based on inequality of income distribution limits consumption.

An example may clarify how a decline in the labor share could cause a decline in consumer demand. To dramatize the effect for the reader, a very large shift is described. Suppose (in billions):

$$National\ income = Y = 100 \tag{4.6}$$

$$Labor\ share = W/Y = .80 \tag{4.7}$$

$$Property\ share = \Pi/Y = .20 \tag{4.8}$$

$$APC\ out\ of\ labor\ income = APC_W = 1.0 \tag{4.9}$$

$$APC\ out\ of\ property\ income = APC_\Pi = 0.1 \tag{4.10}$$

Then aggregate consumption (C) equals the APC out of labor income (APC_W) times the amount of labor income (W) *plus* the APC out of property income (APC_Π) times the amount of property income (Π). So, in symbols:

$$C = APC_W(W) + APC_\Pi(\Pi) \tag{4.11}$$

Then, in numbers:

$$C = 1.0(.8 \times 100) + 0.1(.2 \times 100) \tag{4.12}$$

If we do the arithmetic:

$$C = 80 + 2 = 82 \tag{4.13}$$

Now, what happens if the labor share (and the property share) change? Suppose, for simplicity, national income, the APC out of labor income, and the APC out of property income are held constant. Suppose the labor share falls to 50 percent, making the property share 50 percent. Then the new figures are:

$$C = 1.0(.5 \times 100) + 0.1(.5 \times 100) \tag{4.14}$$

If we do the arithmetic, we get:

$$C = 50 + 5 = \$55 \tag{4.15}$$

Thus a lower labor share causes lower consumer demand, all other things being constant. Of course, if national income were rising rapidly enough consumption might rise, but it would rise more slowly than it would have risen if the labor share had not fallen.

CONSUMPTION RELATED TO INCOME DISTRIBUTION

The above exercise gives an arithmetic example of how consumption is related to the distribution of national income between labor income and property income. This could be written as a formal equation relating consumption to these two types of income. Thus:

$$Consumption = f^1 \; (labor \; income) + f^2 \; (property \; income) \qquad (4.16)$$

where f^1 and f^2 are two different functions. Both labor and property income have a positive effect on consumption, but the effect is different. A dollar of labor income will, on the average, result in more consumer spending than a dollar of property income. This is illustrated with some econometric data in Part 5.

Another way to state the same relationship is to say that consumer demand is not only affected by national income, but also by the distribution of national income between labor and property income. The distribution of income may be reflected in the labor share, which is the ratio of labor income to all national income, though it could also be reflected in the property share or in the labor/property ratio of income. Here:

$$Consumption = f^1 \; (national \; income) + f^2 \; (labor \; share) \qquad (4.17)$$

Again, this is spelled out formally in Part 5.

Finally, the same point may be made by relating the average propensity to consume to the labor share. The thesis is that the APC will go up when the labor share goes up, while the APC will go down when the labor share of income goes down. Thus, it may be said that:

$$Average \; propensity \; to \; consume = f \; (labor \; share) \qquad (4.18)$$

Thus, if the labor share of income rises, APC rises. If national income stays the same, then, as shown in the previous section, aggregate consumption will rise as a result of the rising APC. This is another way of saying that aggregate consumption is affected by the distribution of income between labor and property.

CONSUMER CREDIT

In addition to total income and the distribution of income, a vital influence on consumer demand is the amount of consumer credit available and utilized. This factor is investigated in depth in Part 4, Chapter 14.

INFLATION AND INFLATIONARY EXPECTATIONS

If consumers fear that there will be strong price inflation in the near future, they will hurry to spend more money before prices rise any more. This common sense notion has been confirmed by every econometric study using this variable to help predict consumption. The relation of price inflation to the business cycle will be discussed in detail in Part 3, Chapter 15.

THE MULTIPLIER

Keynes emphasized that if government or investors spend additional money adding to national income, this new income is respent by consumers. Respending by consumers magnifies, or multiplies, the impact of any new flows into the economy. The ratio by which consumer respending multiplies the impact of any new addition to the economy is called the multiplier. The multiplier concept is formalized and considered in depth in Part 3 in the chapter on the multiplier-accelerator model.

GOVERNMENT

Governments usually add disposable income by increasing transfer payments or reducing taxes so as to stimulate consumer demand in contractions, while reducing support in expansions. We shall examine the details of this government activity in Part 4, in Chapter 17.

INTERNATIONAL TRADE

As consumer incomes rise in expansions, some consumer demand flows overseas to pay for consumer imports to this country. As consumer incomes decline in contractions, less money flows overseas and imports decline. Of course, payments for exports from this country add to consumer income. These transactions are detailed in Part 4, in Chapter 16.

CONCLUSIONS

The studies discussed in this chapter found that none of the major theories of consumption can be disproved by empirical facts, but neither are they unquestionably supported by the empirical evidence. The facts discovered in previous econometric research, as well as those shown here, are compatible with the functional income theory stated here, though it has not been proven superior to the other theories. The functional income theory says that consumer demand is influenced by the functional distribution of income between employees' labor income and entrepreneurs' property income; though it certainly does not deny the existence of other influences, such as total income.

The empirical evidence compatible with the functional income theory includes:

1. there are higher propensities to consume out of labor income than out of property income;
2. the average propensity to consume declines in expansion and rises in contraction; and,
3. the average propensity to consume is significantly correlated to the labor share of national income.

The evidence of the 1970s, 1980s, and 1990s—that APC and the labor share move together downward for most of the expansion—has been used to support demand-side cycle theories. We shall consider the relevancy of this evidence when discussing those theories.

In addition to the functional distribution of income, consumer demand is obviously influenced by other factors. These include: (1) the level of national income, (2) government taxes and transfer payments, (3) interest rates and availability of credit, and (4) the factors affecting imports and exports.

KEY TERMS AND CONCEPTS

durable, non-durable, services

average propensity to consume, marginal propensity to consume

life cycle hypothesis

permanent income hypothesis

functional income hypothesis

labor income, property income

CHAPTER 5

Investment

Investment, or the accumulation of capital, is the heart of the private enterprise economic system. Moreover, investment is the key variable in the business cycle. Investment fluctuates far more violently than consumption, so it accounts for much of the increase of GDP in an expansion, but it also accounts for much of the decrease of GDP in a contraction. One study concludes: "Investment demand is the centerpiece of the story, both because it is likely to be the most variable and elusive element of aggregate demand, and because of its direct role in the accumulation of capital" (Marglin and Bhaduri 1990). Figure 5.1 illustrates the behavior of aggregate investment, relative to GDP, over time.

Investment means a greater capacity to produce in the long-run and more employment in the short-run. It is important to stress this two-sided effect of investment. More investment means more demand for goods in the area of plants and equipment and inventories. The creation of these capital goods means more employment, which also means more income. On the other side, investment in new plant and equipment means the eventual supply to the market of a new flood of consumer goods.

TYPES OF INVESTMENT

Investment is not a homogeneous category, but a group of several different categories, which perform differently over the cycle. These categories include (1) spending for equipment, (2) spending to construct non-residential structures, such as factories, (3) spending to construct residential structures, and (4) spending to increase inventories. Inventory investment differs enough from the other three (all of which are fixed investments) that it is left for a later section. Table 5.1 indicates the cyclical behavior of

FIGURE 5.1
AGGREGATE INVESTMENT

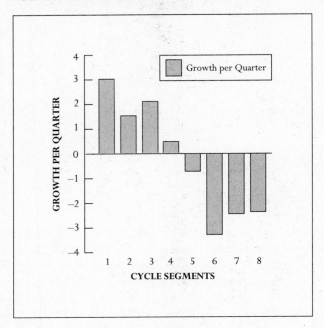

SOURCE: CITIBASE database, file GINQ.

NOTE: This Figure is for the average of 4 cycles, 1970–1991, seasonally adjusted, in real terms, i.e., constant dollars. Investment means gross, private, domestic, non-residential investment.

the first three categories in real terms, giving their expansion and contraction amplitudes.

The table reveals the behavior of these investment components in three very different periods of U.S. capitalism. In the average of the four cycles from 1921 to 1938, Wesley Mitchell's data reflect his finding that equipment had the greatest expansion and contraction amplitudes, because entrepreneurs can react fairly quickly to changes in profit expectations by ordering more or less equipment.

Mitchell's data indicate that factory construction, called nonresidential structures, has a somewhat smaller cyclical amplitude than equipment, though still very large in that period. The lower fluctuation in spending on factories than on equipment is due to the fact that building a factory takes much more planning and preparation, so decision making has a longer time horizon than for purchases of equipment. Once construction for a new factory is started, it is not desirable to stop until it is completed. Therefore, cyclical fluctuations in spending on plant tend to be less than those on equipment.

TABLE 5.1
TYPES OF INVESTMENT

AVERAGE AMPLITUDES, 4 CYCLES, 1921–1938

Type of investment	Expansion	Contraction
Equipment	+46	−39
Non-residential structures	+31	−33
Residential structures	+34	−22

AVERAGE AMPLITUDES, 4 CYCLES, 1949–1970

Type of investment	Expansion	Contraction
Equipment	+30	−12
Nonresidential structures	+18	−0.4
Residential structures	+7	+3

AVERAGE AMPLITUDES, 4 CYCLES, 1970–1991

Type of investment	Expansion	Contraction
Equipment	25	−12
Nonresidential structures	19	−9
Residential structures	18	−17

SOURCES: Data for 1921 to 1938 from Wesley Mitchell, *What Happens During Business Cycles* (New York: National Bureau of Economic Research, 1951). Data for 1949 to 1970 from Bureau of Economic Analysis, U.S. Department of Commerce, *Handbook of Cyclical Indicators: Supplement to the Business Conditions Digest* (Washington, D.C.: GPO, 1984). Data from 1970 to 1991 from Bureau of Economic Analysis, U.S. Department of Commerce, reported in CITIBASE database.

DEFINITIONS: All variables in real terms. "Equipment" means gross private nonresidential fixed investment in producers' durable equipment. "Non-residential structures" means gross private nonresidential fixed investment in structures. "Residential structures" means gross private residential fixed investment.

Because of the severity of the Great Depression, even housing (residential structures) had a very significant decline in the average contraction from 1921 to 1938, though much less than for plants or equipment. In later periods, housing has often been much less correlated with the business cycle than the other categories of investment.

According to Table 5.1 in the mild cycles of 1949 to 1970, the cycle amplitudes of all three categories were much less than in the earlier period. In fact, factory construction has only the slightest decline, while housing actually rose in the average contraction. The table shows that in the four more severe cycles from 1970 to 1991, all three categories of investment again conformed to the business cycle, rising considerably in expansions and falling considerably in contractions, but the fluctuations were smaller than in the 1920s and 1930s.

Residential structures should be in a different category. They are not productive investments, but are more like durable consumption. There is also some indication that construction has a different and longer (15 year) cycle.

Investigation of residential construction cycles was pioneered by Simon Kuznets (1967), with excellent studies also by Long (1939), Guttentag (1961), Gottlieb (1963), and Arcela and Metzler (1973). At any rate, residential construction tends to be much more irregular with respect to the official (NBER—Department of Commerce) business cycle dates than the other categories of investment. Although Table 5.1 shows spending on residential structures conforming to the business cycle, during the more severe recessions and depressions of the 1921–1938 and 1970–1982 periods, during the milder contractions of the 1949–1970 period, residential construction (like consumption) actually rose a little from peak to trough. It also began to decline before the peak. For these reasons, empirical exploration of investment in the next part of this chapter is limited to non-residential investment.

The cyclical behavior of non-residential investment is pictured in Figure 5.2. It shows that non-residential investment is a coincident indicator, rising in reference expansions and falling in reference contractions. It shows, very roughly, that investment rises more slowly in late expansion than in early, and that it falls more slowly in late contraction than in early.

FIGURE 5.2
CYCLICAL BEHAVIOR OF NON-RESIDENTIAL INVESTMENTS

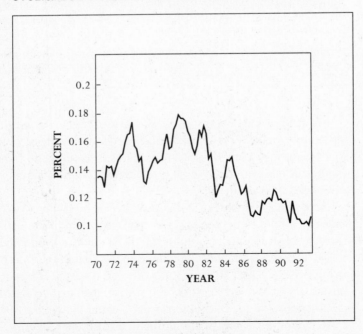

SOURCE: CITIBASE database, files GINQ and GCQ.

CONSUMPTION AND INVESTMENT

Even though consumption spending is much larger than investment spending, investment spending explains more of the business cycle because investment rises and falls far more than consumption.

Table 5.1 shows that real investment has risen faster than real consumption in the average expansion in all the main periods in the last 60 years and before that, as well, to the extent of the available data. Moreover, real investment falls much faster than real consumption in the average contraction in all periods. According to Wesley Mitchell's data shown in the first line of Table 5.2, investment fell drastically in the average contraction of the 1920s and 1930s, a period dominated by the Great Depression. Even in that period, aggregate consumption fell by only less than a third of the percentage decline in investment.

By contrast with the era of the Great Depression, investment fell a relatively small percentage in the mild recessions of the 1950s and 1960s, while consumption actually rose a little, according to Table 5.2. Thus, in the 1950s and 1960s, contraction means contraction in investment, but not in consumption. In the more severe contractions of the 1970s, 1980s, and early 1990s, investment again fell strongly, but Table 5.2 reveals that consumption was stagnant and fell only a tiny amount; so the domestic, private sector decline of this period was again due almost solely to investment.

Figure 5.3 compares real aggregate consumption and real aggregate (non-residential) investment over the business cycle. In the average expansion of the 1970s, 1980s, and 1990s, consumption rose more slowly than investment, though both show the same pattern of a slower and slower growth. In the average contraction, they differ markedly. Investment falls throughout the contraction, while consumption falls only in the first two segments of contraction. In the last half of contraction, investment is still falling, while consumption has begun a slight recovery.

TABLE 5.2
CONSUMPTION AND INVESTMENT

Time period	EXPANSION AMPLITUDE		CONTRACTION AMPLITUDE	
	Consumption	Investment	Consumption	Investment
1921–1938	+21	+55	−16	−49
1949–1970	+17	+24	+1	−10
1970–1991	+14	+23	−0.2	−10

SOURCE: CITIBASE database, file GINQ.

DEFINITIONS: "Consumption" means real aggregate consumption. "Investment" means real gross non-residential private domestic investment.

FIGURE 5.3
CONSUMPTION AND INVESTMENT

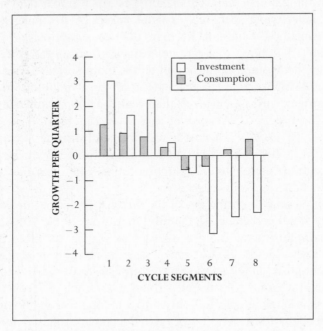

SOURCE: CITIBASE database, files GINQ and GCQ.

NOTE: This Figure is for the average of 4 cycles, 1970–1991, seasonally adjusted, in real terms, i.e., constant dollars. Investment means gross, private, domestic, non-residential investment. Consumption means aggregate consumer spending for all goods and services.

DEMAND (REVENUE) THEORIES OF INVESTMENT: INTRODUCTION TO THE ACCELERATOR

A hypothesis explored by many economists, is that investment is determined by profit and profit expectations. But profit is equal to revenue (influenced by demand) minus cost (influenced by supply). Some theories emphasize the demand aspects of profit, with little attention to costs. Others have emphasized costs, with little attention to the problems of demand or revenue. We begin here with investment theories that focused mainly on demand.

If there is no expectation of future demand for a product, then it would be expected that investment would result in a loss. As a consequence, even if capital is easily available, there will be no investment in this case. The Keynesian view, that lack of demand is the main cause of slower investment, contradicts Say's law. Keynes' view also contradicts the notion that more saving is always good for a private enterprise economy.

If more saving means less consumer demand, it may reduce investment and cause a recession.

In a brilliant and well-known article on the business cycle, Paul Samuelson (1939) argued that the level of investment is a function of the change in consumer demand. This theory is called the "accelerator," and is explained in the first chapter of Part 3. (For the early Keynesian investment models, see Meyer and Kuh 1957.) Later versions of the accelerator theory, discussed below and in Part 3, became far more complex and sophisticated.

Samuelson's idea that consumer demand will influence investment may be stated more formally as follows:

$$Investment = f\,(change\ in\ consumer\ demand) \qquad (5.1)$$

This view, which is the simplest form of the accelerator theory, will be considered further in Part 3, Chapter 11. Note that investment is said to be due to the change in consumer demand, not in the level of demand. If demand stays at any one level, no additional investment in plants and equipment is necessary. Also, when the function is spelled out, there would be a time lag. If demand changes, corporations take time to decide to invest and to actually spend the funds to buy new equipment or to build a new factory.

The first simple models of the relationship of investment to the change in consumer demand were replaced as early as the 1960s by far more complex ones. The simplest accelerator models have been replaced by models (called flexible accelerator models), in which the optimal capital stock, and hence the optimal investment, is viewed as a function of many previous changes in output, rather than merely the most recent changes. Considerable attention has been focused on the most appropriate set of time lags for such a flexible investment function. As in the case of prediction of consumer demand, it is generally agreed that some type of time lag structure distributed over many periods is required. Different views of the most appropriate form of time lag structure range from geometrically declining weights to many more complex forms (for a careful econometric study, see Robert Gordon and John Veitch 1986).

The most common textbook portrayal of the acceleration principle says that investment is determined by the change in national income. That is:

$$Investment = f\,(change\ in\ national\ income) \qquad (5.2)$$

The idea is that there are other spending flows besides consumption, such as investment itself, government spending, and net exports. An increase in any of these spending flows may call forth new investment, but always with a time lag. For example, if government orders more airplanes, then investment in more plant and equipment to make airplanes is required. Since government and net exports are part of GDP and go beyond national income, many economists would use changes in GDP rather than changes in national income to help predict investment.

The more complex forms given to this principle can not be discussed here, but it is worth emphasizing the notion of a whole distribution of time lags, or:

$$Investment = f\,(GDP\ at\ time\ t-1,\ GDP\ at\ time\ t-2,$$
$$\ldots\,GDP\ at\ time\ t-n) \qquad (5.3)$$

In other words, investment is affected by all the changes in GDP (or national income, if that is preferred) from many periods ago $(t-n)$ to the period just before now $(t-1)$. The notion may get pretty complicated and the econometric calculation may be difficult, but the basic idea is very simple. Investors are affected by the recent history of changes in the economy (and of changes in particular industries), rather than just the most recent change.

COST THEORIES OF INVESTMENT

In addition to demand for goods and services, the entrepreneur's profit is affected by the costs of producing that output. Many modern econometric approaches to investment have attempted to combine complex accelerator (demand) theories with theories of the cost of capital. The earlier accelerator theories emphasize output demanded and the level of capital stock, which are assumed to effect profit expectations. Other theories, however, emphasize those variables that affect the marginal cost of funds, including variables showing the interest rate and the rate of corporate cash flow.

The user cost of capital, along with the effect of changes in output demanded, is emphasized by Jorgenson and Hall (1963) and by Grilliches and Wallace (1965). Such theories heavily stress the interest rate and the availability of funds to corporations, variables which were down-played in the early years of the Keynesian revolution, when all eyes were focused on effective demand. Since the 1960s, however, almost all sophisticated investment theories have emphasized the cost side as well as the demand side.

Another approach to investment theory was presented by James Tobin (1969). Tobin called his theory the q-theory of investment, where q is the ratio of the valuation of the existing capital stock to its replacement value. The existing capital stock is held by business. Ownership rights to this capital stock are traded on the stock market, which places a value on the capital stock, determined by the price of each share of that business and the number of shares outstanding. If the value of the capital stock is greater than the cost of beginning a new business with the same capital stock, or $q > 1$, then it would be worthwhile to invest in new business formation. If however, $q < 1$, or the value of the existing capital stock is greater than replacement cost, investors would purchase shares of existing businesses and the rate of capital formation would slow.

It should be stressed that there is no necessary conflict between demand, cost, and profit explanations of investment. The Jorgenson model of investment discusses the importance of changes in output demanded, but also emphasizes cost factors. Jorgenson (1986) synthesizes both revenue and cost factors under the notion that the firm maximizes profits. Since profits equal revenue minus costs, the profit variable encompasses both demand and cost factors. In Jorgenson's model, the revenue side of profits is represented not only by the change in output demanded, but also by the price of output. The cost side of profits is represented in Jorgenson's model by the cost of capital, which includes all related costs, such as the cost of electricity to run machines.

A number of theories have emphasized not only direct costs of capital, but also the availability of money and credit to the firm. Thus, there have been studies of the importance of total profits available for reinvestment, interest rates, cash flow, debt-asset ratio of corporations, and other measures of the liquidity of corporations (see, e.g., Wood 1975, and Evans 1969). These issues are discussed in detail in Part 4 of this book, using the modern literature on money and credit.

Another variety of cost-side theory of investment deals with the costs of raw materials. Many of these theories have become prominent again since the oil shortages of the 1970s. Such issues are discussed in empirical detail in the chapter on cost in this Part and in theoretical models in Chapter 12.

Finally, cost-side theories of profits and investment include those that concentrate on the cost of wages. Industrial businesses buy labor power, in addition to the raw materials, plants and equipment, and borrowed capital, discussed above. Empirical studies of these variables are presented in the next chapter. Theories focusing on the high cost of wages and its presumed negative effect on profits and investment are discussed in Part 3 of this book.

THE PROFIT HYPOTHESIS

One of the most important institutional features of the private enterprise system is the fact that output is produced in order to make a profit. Entrepreneurs invest because they expect to make a profit. That expectation changes according to present and past conditions, including the past rate of profit and any factors that may affect the rate of profit. Factors affecting the rate of profit include: (1) expected demand for goods and services, as evidenced by sales, and (2) present and expected costs, including labor, plants and equipment, raw materials, and the cost of credit, that is, the interest rate.

If planned investment can fall short of planned saving, it is necessary to know what determines decisions to invest. In that perspective, profit is not only important because it influences expectations, but also because actual investment is determined by the availability of funds. Available funds include corporate and individual profits, depreciation allowances, and credit from financial intermediaries of all types. In obtaining credit, past profit performance is one important indicator to creditors of the safety of a loan.

It is apparent and should be emphasized that profit plays a dual role. On the one side, profit performance motivates the investor by affecting expectations of profits. On the other side, profit is one of the sources of available funds for investment. "Today's profits are, on the one hand, a primary source for the accumulation of business capital. Tomorrow's profits, on the other hand, are the lure which attracts business" (Marglin and Bhaduri 1993). Both the favorable expectation and the available funds are necessary for investment.

To say that profit and profit expectations determine investment, however, is only to begin the task. Since almost everything effects profits, economists have spent much time and effort trying to analyze what are the most important elements affecting profits and, consequently, investment. This chapter began with a brief introduction to theories based on demand factors and an introduction to theories based on cost factors. The consumer demand was discussed with empirical detail in the previous chapter. The cost factors are discussed in more empirical detail in the next two chapters, then in complete theories in Part 3.

PROFIT STUDIES

Since demand and cost are both elements in profits, it is not surprising that many economists directly consider profits in relation to investment, rather than the constituents of profits. Robert Eisner conducted an extensive empirical study of both demand (as reflected in sales) and of total profits. He found that investment is "clearly related . . . closely to current and past sales and profits" (Eisner 1978). He lists many other studies that have found a close correlation of investment and profits in time series data.

Some comprehensive studies have found that present and previous total profits do affect investment (see, e.g., Eisner 1978; and Wood 1975). The profit affecting investment may be defined to include corporate profits, noncorporate profits, rental income, and the interest income of financial capitalists; in other words, all property income. In addition to studies of profit, some have found a significant effect of the rate of profit on investment (see, e.g., Sherman and Stanback 1962). Another study finds a statistically significant effect on investment by both total profits and the rate of profits (Sherman and Evans 1984, 173). Using quarterly data from 1949 to 1980, the study found that investment had a statistically significant positive relation to total profit with a two quarter time lag, as well as a statistically significant positive relation to the rate of profit on capital with a three quarter time lag. The econometric estimate is presented in Chapter 22.

What all of these studies reveal may be summarized in more formal terminology. The simplest relation would be to say that investment is determined by the previous change in profits:

$$Investment = f\,(change\ in\ profits) \tag{5.4}$$

So when profits increase, this is followed, with a time lag, by an increase in investment.

It is not realistic, however, to say that only the most recent change influences investors. Investors are influenced by the whole history of changes in profits, though less and less as they recede into the past. Thus, using t for time, we may write:

$$Investment = f\,(profit\ at\ t-1,\ profit\ at\ t-2,$$
$$\ldots profit\ at\ t-n) \tag{5.5}$$

Thus, if profit has been rising for some time, say the last 5 quarters, investors will invest with some confidence.

Investors look not only at the level of profit of a corporation, but also at its rate of profit on investment. Thus, to be realistic, the most general statement might read:

$$Investment = f\,(profit\ at\ t-1,\ profit\ at\ t-2,\ \ldots$$
$$profit\ at\ t-n,\ profit\ rate\ at\ t-1,$$
$$profit\ rate\ at\ t-2,\ \ldots profit\ rate\ at\ t-n) \tag{5.6}$$

This formulation would be difficult to put in an actual model or to calculate from actual data. The basic idea, however, is very simple and is a key to understanding business cycles. It merely states that investors are influenced by the profit performance and the profit rate performance of the economy or of a particular corporation over a number of past periods. If both profits and profit rates have been increasing for a number of quarters, investment is sure to rise.

INVESTMENT AND PROFIT

Corporate profits fluctuate in a strong, pro-cyclical fashion. In the average of the four cycles of 1921 to 1938, Wesley Mitchell (1951, 324) found that corporate profits rose 169 percent in expansions and fell 175 percent in con-

TABLE 5.3
INVESTMENT AND PROFIT: TIMING AND AMPLITUDE

TIMING

Cycle	STAGE AT PEAK		STAGE AT TROUGH	
	Investment	Profit	Investment	Profit
1949–54	5	2	9	7
1954–58	5	3	9	8
1958–61	5	3	9	9
1961–70	5	4	9	9
1970–75	5	5	9	9
1975–80	5	4	9	7
1980–82	5	3	9	9
1982–91	5	4	9	9
Average	5	3.5	9	8.5

AMPLITUDE

Cycle	EXPANSION AMPLITUDE		CONTRACTION AMPLITUDE	
	Investment	Profit	Investment	Profit
1949–54	26	20	−4	−30
1954–58	18	25	−14	−33
1958–61	12	29	−4	−19
1961–70	52	40	−6	−27
1970–75	23	37	−14	−26
1975–80	33	46	−8	−27
1980–82	9	1	−13	−50
1982–91	25	45	−8	−5
Average	25	30	−9	−27

SOURCE: U.S. Department of Commerce data from CITIBASE database, files GINQ and GPIVA.

DEFINITIONS: "Investment" means real, non-residential fixed investment. "Profit" means real corporate profit before taxes. "Expansion Amplitude" is the specific cycle amplitude, that is, from the specific initial trough stage to the specific peak stage of that variable. "Contraction Amplitude" is the specific peak stage to the specific final trough of that variable. The data is for the eight cycles from 1949 to 1991.

tractions. Of course, profitability affects not only investment, but also survival. In the 16 business cycles from 1879 to 1938, Mitchell (1951, 321) found that business failures fell by 62 percent in expansions and rose by 58 percent in contractions.

Table 5.3 compares real investment (all real fixed non-residential investment, including both plant and equipment) with total real corporate profit before taxes for the 8 cycles from 1949 to 1991. Corporate profit is taken before taxes to see its performance before government taxation, but the impact of taxation is discussed in Chapter 17.

Table 5.3 shows that in this period, investment and profit behave fairly similarly but with a time lag. Investment, as always, conforms closely to the cycle, rising throughout the expansion and falling throughout the contraction. Profit, however, leads the cycle, reaching its peak on the average in stage 3, and then declines. Profit may also lead the upturn at the trough of the cycle, though the average lead is very small. This behavior fits most theories, which expect that the affect of profit on investment will have a time lag.

Table 5.3 also shows the cyclical amplitude of investment and profits in each business cycle. What is seen is that when profit expands the most, investment expands the most. When profit declines the most, investment declines the most. So the two appear closely related. It must be emphasized, however, that in the time lag between profit and investment changes, the time lag is long, and the lag is quite variable. So this single relationship is very limited in terms of prediction.

Figure 5.4 illustrates pictorially the relationship between real corporate profit behavior and real non-residential investment behavior in the average of four cycles from 1970 to 1991. Figure 5.4 shows that profit has greater

FIGURE 5.4
PROFIT AND INVESTMENT

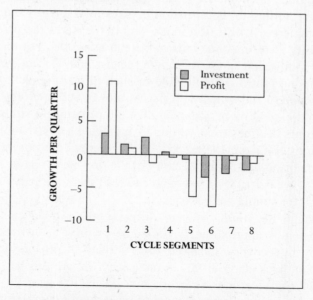

SOURCE: CITIBASE database, files GINQ and GIPVA.

NOTE: This Figure is for the average of 4 cycles, 1970–1991, seasonally adjusted, in real terms, i.e., constant dollars. Investment means gross, private, domestic, non-residential investment. Profit means total corporate profit with inventory valuation adjustments.

fluctuations than investment. Also, profits decline before investment does. Thus, there is a time lag between profit movements and related movements of investment.

TIMING IN DIFFERENT INDUSTRIES

There is a statistically significant correlation between aggregate investment, aggregate profits, and aggregate profit rates (see Sherman and Evans 1984, 173; also see the excellent econometric work by Crotty and Goldstein 1988). But no single aggregate function can explain investment fully and accurately. One reason is that there are vast differences in timing in each industry. All industries do not have rising profits (or profit rates) at the same time, nor do all industries have rising investment in the entire expansion and falling investment in the entire contraction. Most business activity expands and declines with different timing in different industries. In his study of 794 different indicators of economic activity over the business cycle, Mitchell discovered that: "During the four stages of expansion, 74, 77, 78, and 69 percent of all series characteristically rise; during the four stages of contraction, 68, 77, 76, and 63 percent characteristically fall" (Mitchell 1951, 76).

The same phenomenon is shown for sales, profits, profit rates, and investment, according to the diffusion indexes produced by the U.S. Department of Commerce. A diffusion index simply measures the percentage of industries with a rise in some indicator, such as profits. For example, a value of 69 in a diffusion index of profits means that 69 percent of the industries have rising profits. Examination of such diffusion indexes indicate that the percentage of industries with rising sales or rising profits rises in the early and mid-expansion periods, but then the percentage with rising sales or rising profits declines even while the aggregate sales or profits are still rising (see, e.g., Hickman 1959, 535). The economy does not fall apart all at once with no prior sign (as in the story of the one-horse shay). There are advance signs of weakness for those who can read them, though they are not regular enough for simple predictions.

Though the timing is very different, the sequence of events in every expansion is approximately the same in most industries. Total sales rise rapidly in recovery, then rise more slowly in prosperity, so the diffusion index of sales starts to fall in prosperity. In late prosperity, both the profit margin on sales and the profit rate on capital actually begin to decline, which is an early warning signal of recession or depression. Soon thereafter, total profits begin to fall in most industries. Still later, new capital appropriations for expansion by businesses, the first indication of new investment decisions, begin to decline. Finally, at the business cycle peak, total sales and net investment begin an absolute decline. This sequence of events is repeated in the contraction in reverse. (The facts in this paragraph are from Sherman and Stanback, 1962.)

Another reason why aggregate investment functions are unsatisfactory is the fact that the time lags are lengthy and they change in different cycles. On the average, total profits lead investment by one to two quarters, whereas profit rates lead investment by two to three quarters.

Nevertheless, in spite of all of these complications, all the data indicate that profits influence net investment. This point is first put forth in the pioneering work of Michael Kalecki (1968, first published in 1935), which has been followed by most post-Keynesians in its emphasis on the role of profits and profit rates. Profit, in turn, is shaped by such demand factors as the change in output demanded, but it is also shaped by cost factors, such as raw material prices and interest rates on credit, which we will discuss later.

EXPECTATIONS AND UNCERTAINTY

Keynes gave considerable emphasis to the role of expectations in explaining economic performance and in explaining the recurrent crises that affect private enterprise economies. His use of the expression, animal spirits, to describe the formation of expectations is perhaps unfortunate, because the use of this term has occasionally engendered undeserved ridicule. In the use of it, Keynes probably meant that the guesses made about the economic future are not only the consequence of reason, but also of intuition, emotions, peer pressure, and other imprecise forces. Because this is so, expectations about the future returns from investment decisions might be distorted; perhaps grossly so. Various world political and economic events may occasionally generate unjustified pessimism or optimism. Consider, for example, the situation in the late 1920s. There is considerable evidence that until 1929 the public mood was very optimistic; probably unreasonably optimistic (see Galbraith 1972). Investors imagined that all of their investment projects were likely to yield very lucrative returns. Such expectations generated overly optimistic investment assumptions. Likewise, many consumers felt very secure, believing that they would keep their jobs and perhaps experience a robust rise in their standard of living. Thus, their own consumption may have been at artificially high levels, maintained by credit. Then in the autumn of 1929 the stock market crashed, a dramatic event that ushered in a chain of economic calamities. This shocking event burst the optimistic bubble and replaced it with confusion, fear, and gloomy pessimism. Such a sharp change in expectations could and did severely affect the supply of funds, the expectation of profits, and consequently the amount of investment. Keynes and the post-Keynesians have also emphasized the related factor of uncertainty. Paul Davidson makes the distinction between risk and uncertainty (see Davidson 1978, and also Weintraub 1978). When considering risk, some economists wish to impute a certain known probability distribution to future events and, indeed, speak of the "expected value" and measures of dispersion of certain variables in the future. Often, it is thought that a reliable estimate of the probability distribution of future events, such as next year's investment, can be obtained by using accepted techniques in statistical inference on the basis of time-series data. In effect, one employing such techniques would be using the statistical past to predict the probable future. According to Keynes, however, uncertainty cannot be estimated by conventional statistical techniques. Because human beings are so complicated, enigmatic, and emotional, their future behavior is difficult or impossible to predict. Decisions that involve expenditure today (such as investment) in pursuit of uncertain future rewards are made in this uncertain and sensitive environment. The upshot is that investment decisions are quite unstable and very sensitive to even fairly small changes in the environment.

From the discussion of expectations in an uncertain world, the conclusion is drawn that any objective changes in the economy upward or downward will have a much larger effect on investment decisions than would otherwise be predicted. This does not mean the course of events cannot be understood. By hind-sight, it is possible to trace the objective changes that led to the major shift in expectations. Thus it is vital to emphasize that the stock market crash of 1929, and the resulting changes in expectations, did not come out of the clear blue sky, but were the results of changes in real, objectively measurable factors. For example, profit rates turned down some months before the 1929 crash. Thus, after the fact, we can see that future expectations were based on past happenings, but (1) the reactions go far beyond what the statistics would predict, and (2) the reactions are consequently not predictable in detail. At each cyclical turning point, if the actual movements of profits can be explained, then the drastic shifts in expectations can also be explained.

DEPRECIATION AND REPLACEMENT

Gross investment equals net investment plus replacement investment. To this point, the difference has been glossed over. Also, so far it has been assumed that the income allotted to the depreciation allowance is always exactly balanced by the spending on replacement investment. Yet, we have advanced no reason, other than initial simplicity of exposition, for accepting this assumption. This artificial assumption should not prevent us from taking a hard look at actual replacement. Replacement investment is a very large part of gross investment. For example, depreciation (and therefore replacement by assumption) was 63 percent of gross expenditures on construction and producers' durables during the period from 1919 to 1928 (Gordon 1952, 293). In this section, therefore, the differences in the movements of depreciation and replacement investment are considered.

An excess of depreciation allowance over replacement spending means more funds are available for net investment. Of course, this greater amount of funds saved may or may not be invested. If the funds are not invested, there will be no increase in demand at the time. Vice versa, if replacement spending is greater than depreciation allowances, total demand increases.

It must also be recognized that in practice, it is difficult to distinguish between replacement and net investment. Much investment takes the guise of replacement of old capital by new capital. But often the new capital has been improved by innovations. If investment consists of a new innovation, can it be rightly considered a mere replacement?

In each business expansion, a great deal of replacement is hurried into place long before the old capital has fully depreciated. Thus, in expansion, because of optimistic expectations, replacement investment tends to rise rapidly regardless of physical depreciation. On the contrary, in each recession or depression, there is no desire to maintain a high level of output, so many necessary replacements are postponed. Thus, in contraction there is a decline of replacement investment even if depreciation remains constant. Therefore, the very strong cyclical behavior of gross investment is partly due to the cyclical fluctuation of net investment in new plants, equipment, and inventories; but it is also partly due to the cyclical fluctuation of replacement investment. Unfortunately, there are no available aggregate data to separate net investment and replacement except by the false assumption that replacement equals depreciation.

Depreciation, on the other hand, proceeds serenely, changing little in business expansion and contraction (except by changes in the tax law). In an expansion, this source of saving falls behind replacement investment. In a recession or depression, this source of saving may be far greater than the replacement investment in this period. In fact, since depreciation is related to aggregate capital accumulated in many previous years, it declines only very slightly except in very long depressions. For example, in the four cycles from 1921 to 1938, depreciation of all business capital fell an average of only one-half of one percent during the contractions, and even that drop was largely due to the weight of the Great Depression (Mitchell 1951, 142).

In the period from 1949 to 1980, depreciation in constant dollars rose at almost the same pace in recessions as in expansions (see Sherman and Evans 1984, 174). There is simply no cyclical pattern to depreciation, but mostly a smooth increase. If replacement investment was rushed in expansions and postponed in contractions, then actual replacement spending would be greater than depreciation in expansions and much less than depreciation in contractions.

Most new investment is made during expansions, so the average time of purchase of capital will be somewhere around the midpoint of the expansion phase; the average machine will wear out some fixed time after that date. Suppose that expansion lasts five years and the contraction lasts another five years. If the average machine is bought in the third year of expansion and lasts ten years, then the spending for its replacement will not take place until the next expansion period. On these assumptions, the process of replacement intensifies the business cycle because replacement spending exceeds depreciation saving in each expansion, while depreciation saving exceeds replacement spending in each contraction (Einarson 1938).

There are, however, many reasons why replacement needs may be far from a mechanical function of previous investment. In addition to all the technical factors, there is the fact that firms are as strongly influenced by their expectations when making replacements as when making net investments. Even such apparently technical factors as the life span of the machinery become quite flexible when the very standard of scrapping machinery is influenced by business expectations. Accordingly, after a depression begins, firms hold back on replacement; but when a period of prosperity seems to be already under way, they may spend for replacement much sooner than necessary. So physical depreciation has only a minor effect on the duration and intensity of cycles.

The conclusion is that the need for physical replacement, called forth at the end of a lengthy depression, probably has a minor effect on the duration of a contraction, but it is not a very simple relationship. Depreciation allowances have grown at a roughly unchanging rate. Replacement investment, on the contrary, appears to move as an effect of the business cycle, speeding up in expansion and slowing or declining in contraction. Therefore, the cyclical fluctuations of replacement investment intensify cyclical swings. In other words, replacement investment is moved to expand and decline by most of the same factors affecting net investment, but probably somewhat more mildly.

INVENTORY INVESTMENT

The discussion has so far been built on the behavior of investment as if all investment were solely in equipment and factory construction. Aggregate non-residential investment is actually composed of the increase in plant construction, increase in equipment, and the increase in inventories. Inventories include stocks of raw materials, semi-finished goods in process, and finished goods ready for sale.

Changes in inventory investment play a very important role in most business cycles. For example, in the five business cycles from 1919 through

1938, the average change in inventory investment accounted for 23 percent of the average rise in GDP in expansions and 48 percent of the decline in GDP in contractions. In the same period, changes in construction and producer's durable equipment together accounted for an average of only 21 percent of the rise and 37 percent of the decline (see the pioneering study by Abromowitz 1950, 5). This finding was confirmed for the period since the Second World War. From 1945 to the present, changes in inventories again constituted very large percentages of the cyclical changes in gross domestic product (see the excellent studies by Stanback 1963; and Blinder and Holtz-Eakin 1986). In the mild cycles of the 1950s and 1960s, so much of the expansions and contractions were accounted for by the change in inventory investment that the cycle theories of that era tended to focus exclusively on inventories, leaving aside plant and equipment.

If the longer and more severe, or major, depressions and expansions are examined, it appears that much of the change in investment is in plants and equipment. When the shorter, less severe, minor recessions and expansions are examined, however, most of the change is in inventory investment. During the five cycles from 1919 through 1938, considering the whole expansion or the whole contraction as one cycle phase, it was found that for cycle phases lasting eight months to a year, the change in inventory investment was 96 percent of the change in GDP. In that same period, for cycle phases of 1.5 to 2.5 years, the change in inventory investment was 47 percent of the change in GDP. Yet for cycle phases lasting 3.75 to 4.17 years, the change in inventory was only 19 percent of the change in GDP (see Abromowitz 1950, 481–82).

In the period since the Second World War, the same phenomena are observed. Shorter cycle phases show more importance for inventory investment, whereas changes over longer cycle phases show more importance for changes in plant and equipment investment (see Stanback 1963, 6). It seems that the adjustment of inventories to cyclical changes in production is carried out more rapidly than that of plant and equipment, though the latter must make a very large adjustment if the phase lasts long enough.

What is the cyclical behavior of inventories? Most theories predict that, during the expansion phase, inventory investment will increase to meet the demand. Inventory investment does tend to be pro-cyclical, rising in the expansion and falling in the contraction. Why does inventory investment rise in the expansion? The main reason is that in the expansion phase, demand is greater than supply. Sales increase faster than inventories. The greater rise in demand is reflected in the fact that the ratio of inventories to sales declines in the recovery period. The ratio of inventory to sales is counter-cyclical, tending to fall in expansions and rise in contractions. In expansions, the more rapid rise of demand than supply uses up inventories and causes the ratio of inventories on hand to sales to decline. At the same time, the greater demand also motivates a high level of inventory investment in order to return to the desired ratio of inventory to sales.

Of course, inventory investment is not determined by a purely mechanical relationship to the change in sales. The real issue is always the expectation of profits. For one thing, prices are rising in the expansion phase of the cycle; as a result, holding inventories provides the possibility of more profit by selling the goods at an enhanced value. Therefore, some inventories will be acquired on a purely speculative motive. There is also a time lag between the change in sales and the acquiring of inventories. Consequently, inventory investment continues approximately up to the peak of the cycle.

Net inventory investment, the change in business inventories, rises very rapidly in the recovery phase of expansion. Entrepreneurs are very optimistic in this period, so they rapidly increase their inventories of goods on hand, including raw materials, for more production and finished goods for more sales. In the later prosperity phase of expansion, entrepreneurs are more cautious in their purchases of inventories because demand growth is slowing. Therefore, there are sometimes declines as well as increases of inventory investment in the last phase of expansion. In the entire contraction phase, on the other hand, inventory investment declines rapidly because entrepreneurs are very pessimistic about future sales.

These movements of inventory investment are mirrored in the ratio of inventories to sales. In the recovery from recession during the early part of the expansion, sales are booming, so inventories fall behind. Therefore, the ratio of inventories to sales falls in the early expansion. As the expansion progresses, sales growth slows, while inventories continue to grow. The ratio of inventories to sales rises and reaches its desired level (or slightly beyond the desired level). In the contraction, the ratio of inventories to sales rises fairly rapidly and goes way beyond the desired level. The reason is that, even though inventory investment has a very rapid decline, sales fall even faster. The rising ratio of inventories to sales in the recession is a sure symptom of economic illness. In the first part of the contraction, the amount of inventory investment declines rapidly as a result of falling sales, but inventory investment is still positive. There is no planned inventory investment at this point. There is, however, unplanned inventory investment because goods already produced cannot be sold and pile up. Inventories continue to rise many months after each cycle peak (see Stanback 1963, 17). In the last half of the contraction, inventory investment continues to decline and it becomes negative, so there is a big decline in the amount of inventories on hand. Yet, as shown earlier, the amount of sales declines even faster, so the inventory to sales ratio keeps rising.

Whether or not interest rates affect investment in plants and equipment, they seem to have no effect on inventory investment. One careful study says: "We find no strong, systematic influence of real interest rates on inventory investment . . . the conventional literature . . . has consistently failed to uncover an influence of interest rates on inventory investment" (Maccini and Rossana 1981, 21; for more recent econometric study of inventories, see Blinder and Holtz-Eakin 1986).

Many of the same factors cause declines in both categories of investment. To some extent, inventory investment, like other investment, may be affected by the declining profits and profit rates in the last segment of expansion. Less profits mean both less funds with which to purchase inventories and less optimistic expectations for the use of inventories. To some extent also, the decline in the increase of sales will eventually affect inventory investment. There is, however, a very considerable time lag before increased production allows the adjustment of inventories to approach the desired ratio to sales. Furthermore, the beginnings of price decline after the peak will cause a collapse of the speculative motive for holding inventories. Finally, when sales begin an absolute decline, planned inventory investment is pushed downward till it is quite negative.

The length of time necessary to reduce inventories to their desired level is an important factor in determining the duration of the depression. Yet, this does not mean that inventory investment in the recovery increases for some reason different from that for other investment. It is better to consider inventory investment as reacting to most of the same factors as plant and equipment investment. The actual role of inventories is greater the shorter the cycle, while the role of plant and equipment is greater the longer the cycle. Of course, all contractions, and especially the shorter ones, would be much less severe if there were no contractions in inventory investment.

COMPETITION AND MONOPOLY

Firms invest differently depending on whether their industry is highly competitive or not competitive at all. For example, a small number of steel firms had most of the U.S. market for some decades. They became complacent and saw no reason for expensive new innovations, so Japanese steel firms pulled ahead in technology. The effects of different degrees of monopoly power on investment and other economic behavior are discussed in Chapter 15.

CONCLUSIONS

First, the different elements and types of investment have different behavior over the business cycle.

1. Investment in equipment fluctuates more than investment in plants.
2. Investment in plants and equipment together fluctuates more than inventory investment in longer cycles, but less in shorter ones.
3. Replacement is usually above depreciation allowances in expansion, but is below it in contractions.

Second, although their reactions are somewhat different, all kinds of investment react to the same stimuli, namely, profits and profit expectations. Profits in turn are determined by many things, including (1) demand, reflected in sales revenue, (2) labor costs, (3) costs of raw materials, plant and equipment, (4) interest rates, (5) international trade and profit from overseas, and (6) government monetary and fiscal actions. Each of these are discussed in separate chapters in the rest of the book.

KEY TERMS AND CONCEPTS

net and gross
    investment

investment in
    equipment

investment in non-
    residential
    structures

inventory investment

accelerator

multiplier

expectations

interest rates

total profits, rate of
    profit

CHAPTER 6

Functional Income Distribution: Labor Income and Property Income

The distribution of income is of extreme importance in many business cycle theories. Income distribution here does not mean the range of individual incomes, but the functional distribution between economic groups. The main distinction used here is between labor income, which goes to wage and salary employees, versus property income, which goes to entrepreneurs, lenders of finance, and landlords.

In theories stressing lack of effective demand, a key claim is that income distribution shifts from employee's wages to entrepreneur's profit in every business cycle expansion. On the contrary, in theories emphasizing costs of the supply of labor, a key claim is that income distribution shifts from entrepreneur's profits to employee's wages in every business cycle expansion. The chapter begins by exploring the empirical data, the major theories, then how well the theories conform to the facts.

PRESENT U.S. INCOME AND WEALTH DISTRIBUTION

Let us begin by examining personal income distribution in terms of quintiles of U.S. households. A quintile is each 20 percent or one fifth of households (data is from the Census Bureau, analyzed in an excellent article by Amott, 1989). In 1986, according to the usual official measure of income, the lowest quintile had only 4 percent of U.S. income. The second quintile of U.S. population had 10 percent of the income, the middle had 16 percent, and the fourth had 24 percent. The highest quintile of the U.S. population had 46 percent of all income. In other words, the top 20 percent of U.S. households had almost as much income as the bottom 80 percent—a clear measure of severe inequality.

The usual measure, however, understates the inequality because it excludes capital gains which go mostly to the rich. It also includes government transfer payments, which are not part of the private economic system. The Census Bureau has published a new measure, called private-sector income, which includes capital gains, but excludes transfer payments from government. In 1986, the private-sector income was distributed as follows: just 1 percent for the lowest quintile, 8 percent for the second, 15 percent for the middle, 24 percent for the fourth, and 52 percent for the highest quintile. In other words, private-sector income is even more unequally distributed than the usual measure, with the top 20 percent of U.S. households actually holding more income than the bottom 80 percent.

There is also evidence over time that the average American has gotten poorer in the last decade or so. A study published by the National Commission for Employment Policy found that the income growth for prime-age adults slowed sharply in the 1980s, with average income rising by only 33 percent in real terms, compared with 45 percent during the 1970s. Average income gains for those with less than high school diplomas and for African Americans fell from 45 and 39 percent respectively over the 1970s to just 14 percent in the 1980s. In the 1970s only a fifth of prime-age adults suffered real income declines. But in the 1980s, the number of adults suffering real income declines jumped to a third, with half of these people losing more than 25 percent of their income (Rose 1994). For all families (in constant 1985 dollars), the median family income rose by 43 percent in the 13 years from 1960 to 1973. But a peak in median income was reached in 1973. The real median family income fell by 5 percent in the 12 years from 1973 to 1985 (U.S. Bureau of the Census 1986).

At the same time, the rich continued to get richer in the latter period, though not as rapidly as in the former period. For example, families in the 5th percentile from the top (that is, the 95th percentile of income) had their income grow by 48 percent in the 1960–1973 period, but it continued to grow by 7 percent in the 1973–1985 period, whereas the poor had declining real income. (Two excellent publications on income and wealth are by Kloby, 1987, and the comprehensive study by Winnick, 1988.)

If income per year is unequally distributed, then total accumulated U.S. wealth is more so. In 1983, the richest 10 percent of U.S. families owned 72 percent of U.S. wealth. The super-rich, that is, the top 1/2 of one percent of families, had 35 percent of all wealth by themselves (Winnick 1988). The only type of wealth distributed to a large number of families was home ownership.

In fact, if we exclude the value of home ownership, the super-rich had 45 percent of U.S. wealth, while the top ten percent had 83 percent. In terms of the types of wealth, the super-rich owned 36 percent of real estate (excluding private homes), 47 percent of corporate stock, 44 percent of all types of bonds, and 58 percent of all business assets (including corporations, unincorporated business, farms, and professional practices). At the same time, the richest 10 percent of families owned 78 percent of real estate, 89 percent of corporate stock, 90 percent of bonds, and 94 percent of business assets.

What is the share of labor income and what is the share of property income? Since the top 10 percent of families have 94 percent of all business assets and most other property, most business or property income goes to this top 10 percent. The bottom 90 percent of the population by income size, on the contrary, have mostly labor income. Of course, some people receive both labor and property income. On the average, in the period from 1949 through 1982, earnings from labor income (that is, all employee compensation) were 70 percent of all national incomes. The recipients of property income received 30 percent of all national income (calculated from Bureau of Economic Analysis, U.S. Department of Commerce, 1984, BEA series 64).

FRAMEWORK AND DEFINITIONS

This chapter makes use of the official U.S. national income categories, though some of their biases are discussed below. All variables are in real terms, that is, constant dollars. Let labor income (W) be defined to include all employee compensation, namely, wage income, salary income, fringe benefits, bonuses, and commissions. Let property income (Π) be defined to be all the rest of national income, namely, corporate profits, non-corporate profits, rent, and interest. Then, of course, the national income (Y) equals labor income plus property income:

$$Y = W + \Pi \qquad (6.1)$$

The labor share is defined as the ratio of labor income to all national income (W/Y). The property share is defined as the ratio of property income to all national income (Π/Y). It also follows that the labor share (W/Y) plus the property share (Π/Y) equal one.

$$W/Y + \Pi/Y = 1 \qquad (6.2)$$

Thus, if either the labor share or the property share is known, so is the other. This chapter will discuss distribution mostly in terms of labor share (W/Y), but it could just as easily have used property share (Π/Y). National income is used throughout this chapter rather than other measures of output or income because national income includes corporate profit, which is an important part of the analysis.

Another way of measuring income distribution between functional groups is to use the ratio of property income divided by labor income, often called the profit/wage ratio, after its main components. The property/labor ratio (Π/W)—or profit/wage ratio—also equals the property share divided by the labor share (they are equal by definition):

$$\Pi/W = (\Pi/Y) / (W/Y) \tag{6.3}$$

From equations (6.2) and (6.3), if either the labor share or the property share is known, then the profit/wage ratio is also known. Therefore, income distribution by group, called the functional income distribution, may be described here by any of these three ratios. The labor share (W/Y) is used most of the time because it is the most convenient framework for most purposes, but the movements of the profit/wage ratio and the property share are clearly implied. Any statement about the labor share (W/Y) can be restated in terms of the property share (Π/Y) or the property/labor ratio (Π/W).

PROBLEMS WITH MEASURING PROFITS, WAGES, AND PRODUCTIVITY

The biases present in the official definition of many economic variables are discussed in Frumkin (1987). The biases are considerable when it comes to dividing the product or income between labor income and profits property income. In the first place, the Internal Revenue Service always finds more illegal non-reporting of property income than labor income. For example, it is estimated that 58 percent of all rent and interest income is not reported (see Kloby 1987, 3). This does not necessarily mean that employees are more honest than entrepreneurs. The U.S. tax system makes it much easier to hide property income than labor income.

Second, few legal tax loopholes are available for labor income. The law is filled with tax loopholes for property incomes of both individuals and businesses. For this reason among others, corporate taxes are a steadily decreasing percentage of the whole revenue. To note all the legal loopholes would require a long book (see Perlo 1976). The loopholes were reduced by the Tax Reform Act of 1986 (which also drastically reduced progressivity in tax rates), but very large loopholes remain.

On the other hand, labor income, or what is officially called "employee compensation," is greatly overstated. It includes managerial salaries. Many managers' salaries actually contain large amounts of profits in disguise as labor salaries. As salaries, they can then be counted as corporate costs, so they can be tax deductions. Moreover, employee compensation includes fringe benefits, which also disguise much profit income to executives. Most of these executive payments are really profits, so they should not be counted as labor income.

After eliminating just a few of these biases, one careful study found there has been no change in the labor share in 30 years. The labor share was 0.68 in 1948 and 0.69 in 1977, which is quite different from the upward trend reported in the official data (see Bowles and Gintis 1982, 71).

Finally, since more and more self-employed entrepreneurs and small farmers are going bankrupt and becoming employees, the percentage of people earning wages and salaries keeps going up. Another correction should also be made because the labor share goes to a larger and larger percentage of the people. This is a major change over a long period. The portion of wage and salary earners (excluding managers) rose from 20 percent in 1780 to well over 80 percent in 1970. In spite of the biases, the official national income categories are used here because they are readily available, familiar to most economists, and acceptable to most economists.

The bias is strongest in absolute comparisons at a given time. For example, the ratio of property income to national income stated earlier would be much higher than in the official statistics if we corrected for all the biases mentioned earlier. In data on long-run trends, however, there may be less bias because—in a comparison of the growth of two things—there will be a bias in the trend if, and only if, there is an increase in the bias over time. Unfortunately, in this area there is some evidence of the growth of bias. For example, managers are growing in numbers, and their salaries are increasing by leaps and bounds. A large number of managerial salaries are over $1 million a year. For this reason, it is necessary to be extra cautious about presenting trend data.

Finally, data on purely cyclical fluctuations of the labor share will be biased if, and only if, there is a systematic increase in bias at certain points in the cycle. By testing many different definitions, one finds very little change in cyclical results. So the data used most in this book has the least bias.

Another category of data that are very unreliable and biased are the data on productivity, the ratio of product to labor hours. Many writers have pointed out that productivity has a roughly defined meaning for manufacturing output, but is ambiguous for other sectors. For example, one can measure how many widgets a worker produces per hour, but how is the productivity of, say, a lawyer defined? Since the usual definitions give a lower growth rate of productivity in the service sectors than in manufacturing, a shift to services may mean less apparent growth of productivity. Since such a shift is occurring, it may explain some of the apparently lower growth rates in productivity during recent years. On the other hand, this shift from manufacturing to services has been occurring continuously for some time. Therefore, the purely cyclical pattern of productivity should not be much affected, though the absolute levels of productivity growth may be affected by such a shift.

These warnings about biases in the data will not be repeated at later points so as not to bore the reader. But a healthy skepticism about the data in both long-run and cyclical contexts should be kept firmly in mind.

CYCLICAL CHANGES IN INCOME DISTRIBUTION, 1921–1938

Wesley Mitchell (1951) had much less data than are available today, but he did present a few suggestive figures on income distribution for the average of the four cycles between 1921 and 1938 (these figures are mostly dominated by the cycle of the Great Depression). For the average expansion of these four cycles, national income rose by 23 percent of its average cycle base, whereas total employee compensation rose only 19 percent. Therefore, the labor share (W/Y) declined in the average expansion of the 1920s and the 1930s. The decline in the labor share was also reflected more dramatically by the fact that in the average expansion phase of the same four cycles, net profits of all U.S. corporations rose 199 percent!

In the contraction phase of these four cycles, national income fell by 18 percent average whereas total wages fell by only 13.0 percent. Therefore, the labor share (W/Y) rose in the average contraction of the 1920s and the 1930s. Again, the rise in the labor share in the average contraction is emphasized by the fact that net profits of all U.S. corporations fell 175 percent! The fact that the labor share was counter-cyclical in the 1920s and 1930s led many economists, particularly those sympathetic to the labor movement, to endorse the theory that wages always lag behind profits.

LONG-RUN CHANGES FROM 1949 TO 1994

Before examining cyclical patterns in the modern period, it is useful to summarize the relevant changes that occurred in the structure of the U.S. economy from 1949 to 1994. First, monopoly power continued to grow, particularly with the wave of conglomerate mergers beginning in the late 1960s and continuing to the present (this point is discussed in great detail in Chapter 15 on monopoly). Second, trade unions were strong and growing until the mid-1950s, but have suffered a steady decline since then. Third, financial regulations and strong liquidity meant a fairly safe money and credit system in the 1950s and 1960s, but deregulation and new financial innovations led to high debt ratios and increased bankruptcies in the severe cycles of the 1970s, 1980s, and 1990s. Fourth, government military spending remained high after the Second World War, in the 1950s and 1960s. It grew even larger in the 1970s and 1980s, but declined as a percentage of

GDP. Fifth, the U.S. economy totally dominated international trade and investment in the 1950s, but was meeting stiff competition and was suffering trade deficits by the 1970s and since.

These structural changes reduced the demand for U.S. goods and labor so resulted in performance changes: First, a declining growth rate of productivity in expansions and actual declines of productivity in contractions in the 1970s, 1980s, and 1990s. The decline in productivity growth was primarily due to the fact that more severe downturns caused less investment, which meant less embodiment of new technology for future growth. For a different view, see the interesting and important discussion by Weisskopf, Bowles, and Gordon (1983). Second, there have been much higher rates of unemployment in the 1970s, 1980s, and 1990s. Third, there have been much lower rates of capacity utilization in the contractions of the 1970s, 1980s, and 1990s. Fourth, while there was very little inflation in the 1950s and early 1960s, high levels of inflation followed in the 1970s and 1980s. High inflation is one pressure holding down real wages. Fifth, there were rising real weekly wages in the 1950s and 1960s, but declining trends in the 1973 to 1993 period. Inequality has been increasing because lower employee wages have been accompanied by higher executive salaries. Sixth, there were generally more severe contractions in the two decades after 1978 than in the two decades before it. Seventh, effective demand created few problems in the 1950s and 1960s, but this has been the major problem since 1970.

This last fact, the greater deficiency of effective demand in the period since 1970, was documented in detail in articles by Sherman (1986) and Henley (1987b). It was found that consumer demand and business problems of sales were far less important in the mild crises of the earlier period, the 1950s and 1960s, than in the more severe crises of the later period, since 1970. Henley noted that previous research had found demand and sales problems not too important from 1949 to the early 1970s, but he concludes that in the two "cycles from 1975 to 1982 we have found that . . . all the secular decline in the rate of profit is explained by a deterioration in realization conditions, indicative of the general conditions of recession experienced by the U.S. economy at the time" (Henley 1987b, 328).

Henley also separated the share of labor (all employee compensation) income into three parts: the income share of wage (production line) workers, the income share of salaried employees, and the share of supplemental labor costs (fringe benefits). His important contribution shows a secular decline in the wage share, but a secular rise in the salary share as well as in the share of fringe benefits (1987b, 318). His cyclical data indicate that the cyclical pattern of the whole labor share moves with and is dominated by the wage share; but that the salary share and fringe benefit shares move differently, being dominated by their upward trends (1987b, 324).

LABOR SHARE IN THE 1970–1992 PERIOD

The cyclical patterns of labor income and the labor share in the 1970s, 1980s, and 1990s are shown in Figure 6.1. Real labor income is clearly pro-cyclical, rising in expansions, but falling throughout the contractions of this period. On the other hand, the labor share generally moves counter-cyclically, falling in most of business expansion and rising in most of business contraction. Wages and all labor income fluctuate far less than profits and all property income. One way to describe these facts is to say that wages lag behind profits in most of the cycle.

Now let us examine some of the underlying series in greater detail. National income rises throughout expansion although more and more slowly; then it falls throughout contraction. Labor income rises throughout the expansion, but it rises significantly slower than national income. It can rise very slightly in the first segment of contraction; after that, it falls during the whole contraction. Property income rises far more rapidly than labor income during the expansion, but also falls more rapidly than labor income in the whole contraction.

FIGURE 6.1
TOTAL LABOR INCOME AND LABOR SHARE

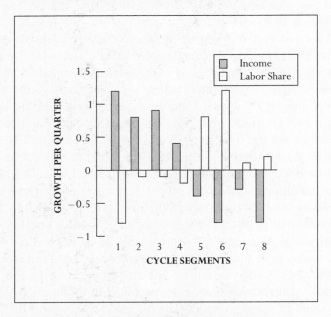

SOURCE: CITIBASE database, files GCOMP and GCOMP/GYQ

NOTE: Average of 4 cycles, 1970–1991, in real terms. Total employee compensation includes all types of labor income, such as wages and salaries. Labor share means total employee compensation divided by national income.

Since labor income rises more slowly than national income in expansion, the labor share as pictured in Figure 6.1 falls in the average expansion. On the other hand, since labor income also falls more slowly than national income, the labor share must rise during the average contraction. During prosperity, the labor share continues to decline, but very slowly. During depression, the labor share continues to rise, but very slowly.

WAGES AND PRODUCTIVITY

The labor share is the ratio of labor income to national income, or W/Y. If real wages, which is the numerator of the labor share, is divided by the number of hours of labor expended in the entire economy (N), the result is: W/N = *real hourly wage.* If real national income or output, which is the denominator of the labor share, is divided by the number of hours of labor expended in the entire economy, the result is: Y/N = *productivity = product per labor hour.* Thus, if both the numerator and denominator of the labor share are divided by the hours of labor (N), the result is: $(W/N)/(Y/N)$ = *labor share.* In words, the labor share equals the average real hourly wage divided by the average product per labor hour. In symbols:

$$W/Y = (W/N)/(Y/N) \tag{6.4}$$

Consider the fact that the income share of employees is equal to the average real hourly wage (or salary) of all employees divided by the average productivity of labor. Obviously, the labor share rises if the hourly wage rises, while it falls if the hourly wage falls, all other things being constant. The labor share falls if productivity rises but it rises if productivity falls, all other things being constant. Throughout the discussion of the labor share, an attempt will be made to explain not only its movements, but also the movements of its two components: (1) real hourly wages, and (2) the product per labor hour.

The term productivity, or labor productivity, used in this chapter just means the total product (real national income) divided by the number of hours of labor; it is an average product/labor ratio. Its changes may reflect not only changes in the amount of labor, but also changes in the quality of labor, changes in capital, changes in technology, or changes in the availability of natural resources—in short, anything that affects output or employment. To avoid confusion, remember that this is very different from the often-used term, marginal productivity of labor, which measures the additional output of additional labor, but with all other factors held constant. The simpler average product/labor ratio, with other factors changing, is more useful for the present analysis.

Notice that, by definition, the labor share is affected positively by higher hourly wages. The labor share is affected negatively by higher productivity,

FIGURE 6.2
REAL HOURLY WAGE AND PRODUCTIVITY

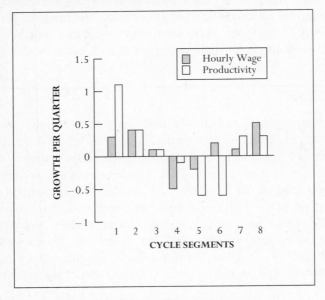

SOURCE: CITIBASE database, files LBOUTU and LBCPUT.

NOTE: Average of 4 cycles, 1970–1991, in real terms. Real hourly wage is total real wages of all non-agricultural workers divided by the number of hours worked. Productivity is the real product per hour worked by all non-agricultural workers.

because the fruits of this higher product of labor automatically go to the capitalist receivers of profits. Figure 6.2 portrays real hourly wages rising more slowly than real productivity per hour in most of the expansion phase. Both series lead the cycle peak in this period, but hourly wages turned down more rapidly than productivity in late prosperity, so the labor share continued to fall in that phase. On the other hand, productivity falls more rapidly than hourly wages in most of the contraction, so the labor share rises in this phase.

According to Figure 6.2, in the 1970–1991 period real hourly wages rose in the average cyclical expansion, but more and more slowly, a normal sort of pattern. It is unusual to find real hourly wages falling before the cycle peak; that occurred in this period because nominal wages were unable to keep up with inflation. Hourly wages continued to fall in the first segment of the crisis phase. The fact that real hourly wages showed a clear and significant rate of decline in two segments of the cycle reflects the severity of these downturns. Real hourly wages did return to slight positive growth in the depression phase of the cycle, so these downturns were nowhere near as severe as in the Great Depression of the 1930s, when real hourly wages declined for several years. Nevertheless, these cyclical declines were severe enough that the long-run trend of real hourly wages reveals zero growth for the whole period.

According to Figure 6.2, productivity rose very rapidly in the recovery phase of the cycle, as is usual in most recorded cycles. In the prosperity phase, productivity continued an anemic rise for one segment followed by a slight decline, reflecting the long-run weakness of productivity growth in this period. In the crisis phase, productivity declined very significantly, again reflecting the greater severity of these cyclical downturns compared with the previous period. In the depression phase, productivity showed a slight recovery. We see once again how the behavior of hourly wages and productivity adds up to the behavior of the labor share. In other words, productivity in expansions usually rises faster than real hourly wages, so the labor share falls. In contractions, productivity falls more than real hourly wages, so the labor share rises.

UNEMPLOYMENT AND CAPACITY UTILIZATION

What determines the cyclical behavior of the labor share (and its components, hourly wages and productivity)? As we shall see, some theories trace behavior of wages and productivity to changes in the level of unemployment, which reflect the supply cost of labor. Other theories trace behavior of wages and productivity to more general changes in demand, reflected in the path of capacity utilization.

LONG-RUN TRENDS.   As a background, let us examine the long-run trends of unemployment and capacity utilization. In the last four decades, there has been a long-run trend toward higher unemployment levels and lower capacity utilization levels. The unemployment rate averaged 4.8 percent in the 4 cycles of 1949 to 1970, but rose to 7.0 percent in the 4 cycles of 1970 to 1991. The capacity utilization rate declined from an average 83 percent in the first 4 cycles of 1949 to 1970 to 79 percent in the last 4 cycles. Looking at the more recent cycles in more detail, the average unemployment rate rose as follows: 4.7 percent (1961–1970 cycle), 5.7 percent (1970–1975 cycle), 7.0 percent (1975–1980 cycle), 8.4 percent (1980–1982 cycle), and 6.8 percent (1982–1991 cycle). At the same time, the capacity utilization rate behaved as follows: 85 percent in the 1961–1970 cycle, 82 percent in the 1970–1975 cycle, 80 percent in the 1975–1980 cycle, 75 percent in the 1980–1982 cycle, and 81 percent in the 1982–1991 cycle.

CYCLICAL BEHAVIOR.   Turning from long-run trends to the business cycle, the cyclical performance of unemployment and capacity utilization are shown in Figure 6.3 for the 1970–1991 period. We see that unemployment fell, as it always does, during the entire expansion. Unemployment rose, as it always does, during the entire contraction. Capacity utilization moves in the opposite direction. Capacity utilization rose in most of the expansion, falling slightly just before the peak, while it fell throughout the entire contraction. Aside from the slight lead at the peak, this is the normal behavior of capacity utilization in all cycles.

Figure 6.3 reveals in detail that in the average expansion of the 1970–1991 period, the unemployment fell during the whole expansion phase—but it fell very slowly. In the contraction phase, the unemployment rate rose with startling speed. Of course, the fact that unemployment fell so slowly in expansions while rising so rapidly in contractions reflects the long-run trend in this period toward rising unemployment.

Finally, Figure 6.3 also portrays capacity utilization as rising in the entire expansion, but at a slower and slower rate, thus revealing the weakening of demand factors. In the entire contraction, capacity utilization declines rapidly, reflecting an absolute decline of demand. The fact that capacity utilization was rising rather slowly in expansion while falling rapidly in contractions, dramatically reflects the long-run trend toward lower use of capacity in this period.

FIGURE 6.3
UNEMPLOYMENT AND CAPACITY UTILIZATION

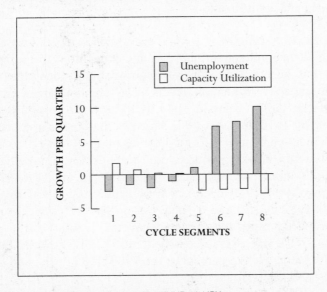

SOURCE:CITIBASE database, files LHUR and IPX.

NOTE: Average of 4 cycles, 1970–1991, in real terms. Unemployment means the percentage of all those in the labor force who are not employed.

DETERMINANTS OF THE LABOR SHARE

Most of the relevant facts have now been described. Next, a general framework is given to explain the facts, then some theories emphasizing particular facts is presented. Last, the consistency of the facts are discussed.

The labor share is directly dependent on the real hourly wage and on productivity. What determines these components of the labor share? The real hourly wage (W/N) is determined by industrial conflict between entrepreneurs and employees within the framework of private enterprise relations of production, under certain economic conditions. It is easy to give a reasonable list of the demand and supply conditions, but which to emphasize is extremely controversial. The conditions under which the wage bargain is struck include: (1) the demand for labor, which is a function of the demand for products; (2) the supply of labor, reflected in the degree of unemployment and in the labor participation rate; (3) the power of labor unions, reflected in percentages of unionization, especially in key firms and industries; (4) the degree of business monopoly power over prices and wages; (5) the power and tactics of the government, including recognition of unions and enforcement of fixed labor contracts for a given period of time; and (6) international events, such as wars or international shifts of economic power. The productivity of labor is affected by industrial conflict in a fight over speedup by the entrepreneurs versus slowdown by the employees. The conditions influencing the outcome of this struggle include (1) demand for labor, reflecting demand for output; (2) the supply of labor, reflected in the rate of unemployment; (3) strength and militancy of unions; (4) power of business monopoly; (5) actions of the government; and (6) international conditions. These influences are similar to the influences on the real hourly wage. In addition, however, labor productivity is also affected by at least three other factors. In the long run, (7) productivity is very much influenced by technological change. In the short run, (8) the productivity of both machinery and labor will differ at different levels of capacity utilization. Finally, (9) productivity will be influenced by the intensity of labor, which is a result of industrial conflict between entrepreneurs and employees (see Bowles and Gintis 1981).

Most economists would agree that all these factors have some effect; the highly controversial issue is: Which ones should be emphasized? We shall examine four hypotheses emphasizing different factors: (1) the wage lag hypothesis, (2) the overhead labor hypothesis, (3) the unemployment hypothesis, and (4) the combined hypothesis.

THE WAGE LAG HYPOTHESIS

One theory may be called the wage lag theory (see, e.g., Sweezy 1942; also Baran and Sweezy, 1966). It contends that in every expansion the labor share falls because wages lag behind national income. On the other hand, the labor share rises in every contraction because wages also lag in the decline. The basic wage lag argument is that, due to the institutions and relations of the private enterprise economy, it is difficult for employees to expand their real wages in expansion to keep up with increasing production, based on rising productivity. It is easier to maintain real wages, or prevent them from falling rapidly, in the face of falling production.

The wage lag theory argues that cyclical changes in income distribution are dominated by the simple institutional fact in the private enterprise economy that the employer owns the product. If, as is always true in expansions, there is increasing productivity, then the employer automatically owns the increased product. To continue to obtain the same share of the increased revenue as they had before the increase in production, employees must struggle and bargain and play catch-up. It is thus not surprising that in an expanding economy the share going to labor normally declines. On the other hand, in a contraction the employer owns a declining product. If employees can hold on to their old wage level, they may receive a rising share of a falling product.

The institutions of our private enterprise system hold back real wage increases in expansion, while making it more difficult to lower wages in contraction. First, wage bargains by organized workers are fixed for a set period. When there are both rapid price and productivity increases, organized workers must always struggle at the end of a two- or three-year contract just to maintain their percentage share. The same two- or three-year contracts prevent any rapid decline in money wages in a contraction. Second, the media often attacks strikes for wage increases, especially if they go beyond the workers' share of price and productivity increases. The media are far more reluctant to attack employees for preventing wage cuts. Third, public opinion also tends to support employees in resisting wage cuts or speed-up, but does not support fights to increase real wages faster than profits or fights to slow productivity. This public opinion is, of course, partly due to the media. Fourth, the government often enters the battle against employees' efforts to raise real wages faster than productivity and strongly opposes efforts to lower productivity. Yet, the government finds it very difficult to attack employees when it is clear that they are merely resisting wage cuts or speed-up.

According to this hypothesis, productivity rises rapidly in expansion and declines rapidly in contraction. Wage lag theorists seem to argue two points to explain productivity behavior. First, technology improves in the expansion because of new research and innovations. In the contraction, on the contrary, there is little research and almost no innovation. This reasoning is at least partially correct, but it does not account for the rapidity of rise in early expansion (when innovations are just beginning to be built), nor does it account for actual declines in productivity in contractions.

Second, some wage lag theorists argue in the short run in a neoclassical vein. In the expansion, factories are used closer to their optimal designed capacity, whereas in contraction operation is far below that level. For example, mass production assembly lines can only work at a certain level. Therefore, labor costs per unit may fall in much of expansion as the optimal minimum cost level is approached, but may rise in contraction as production goes below that level. Again, there is something to this explanation. Yet, many empirical studies have found that costs are constant in a wide range in the short run, so one may be skeptical as to the quantitative importance of a cost explanation of productivity changes.

In summary, the wage lag hypothesis contends that the workings of private enterprise institutions are such that, during expansions, productivity rises faster than hourly wages, so the share of labor declines. In business contractions, private enterprise relationships cause productivity to fall faster than wages, so the share of labor rises.

In a more formal sense, it may be said that the labor share falls during the entire expansion while output and capacity utilization keep rising. In a contraction, the labor share rises while output and capacity utilization keep falling. Thus this theory states, that:

$$Labor\ share = f\ (output) \qquad (6.5)$$

where f means "function of" and where the function is negative. In other words, when output falls, labor share rises; but when output rises, labor share falls. From the data presented in Figure 6.1, it appears that this hypothesis is factually correct to a large extent. Precise econometric testing of this hypothesis is done in Chapter 22.

Since capacity utilization follows the cycle even more closely than output (which has a growth component), we could also say that the labor share is a function of capacity utilization. Then:

$$Labor\ share = f\ (capacity\ utilization) \qquad (6.6)$$

where the function is negative. This means that in expansions, as more and more of productive capacity is utilized, the labor share of national income declines. In the contraction, as less and less of productive capacity is utilized to produce anything, the labor share of income rises.

OVERHEAD LABOR HYPOTHESIS

Overhead labor means employees such as bookkeepers, maintenance people, clerical help, lawyers, accountants, engineers, and security staff—all those people who are needed all the time and are not hired or fired in direct proportion to the amount of production. The overhead labor thesis argues that in the early expansion employers do not need to hire new overhead workers, because the need for these types of workers does not rise directly in proportion to increases in output. Since output and capacity utilization are rising very rapidly, while employment of overhead labor is not expanding as rapidly, measured productivity rises rapidly.

In the last half of expansion, entrepreneurs are forced to begin hiring more overhead labor as well as production line workers to meet the increased labor needs. Yet, the growth rates of output and capacity utilization are declining, so measured productivity growth slows.

The overhead labor theory argues that in the crisis or early contraction phase, entrepreneurs are lowering production. They fire a proportionate number of production line workers. They cannot, however, fire a proportionate number of overhead employees because the need for these types of employees does not decline directly as output falls. Since output is declining, while the total number of workers does not decline as much, the measured (or apparent) product per worker declines. Therefore, less profit is made per worker, counting both production line workers and overhead employees, so the labor share rises in contraction (see Steindl 1952; and Weisskopf 1979). In the depths of the contraction, employers start firing large numbers of all types of employees, so measured productivity becomes constant or even rises again.

The overhead labor hypothesis says that productivity rises as capacity utilization rises, and falls as capacity utilization falls. Therefore, all other things being equal, the labor share declines as capacity utilization rises, that is, the labor share is a negative function of capacity utilization. Since the wage lag hypothesis also maintains that the labor share is a negative function of capacity utilization, the overhead labor thesis tends to support the wage lag view of income distribution behavior. For various interesting variations and critiques of overhead labor, see Oi (1962), Costrell (1981), and Munley (1981). All of the studies give various reasons why higher capacity utilization leads to a lower labor share.

THE UNEMPLOYMENT HYPOTHESIS

The unemployment hypothesis assumes that the labor share rises in the last half of expansion (see Boddy and Crotty 1975; also Gordon, Weisskopf, and Bowles 1987). The reason given is that the decline in the number of unemployed puts labor in a better bargaining position. The argument may be spelled out as follows. As output rises in expansion, employment rises. With a given labor force and a given technology, this means that the unemployment rate must decline. As this occurs, labor militancy rises. Employees are willing to take more chances to back up demands by strikes, which gives them greater bargaining power. At the same time, employers know that there is a smaller number of unemployed available to replace striking employees, so they are less likely to resist employees' demands. Therefore, the greater power and militancy of labor pushes labor income upward.

The bargaining issues are not just wages but also productivity. Employers always wish to increase the intensity of work by speeding up the labor process, while employees wish to reduce the intensity of work and resist speed-up. Employees may also resist new technology if it would replace them with machines. Thus, according to this theory, near the peak of expansion when employee bargaining power is very strong, productivity growth may be stopped. Conversely, in a business contraction, unemployment reduces employees' bargaining power so productivity is assumed to rise. One study by a theorist of this school concludes: "The principal empirical findings are that increases in the general level of unemployment enhance productivity growth" (Rebitzer 1987, 627).

The argument that more unemployment weakens the power of employees, while less unemployment strengthens the power of employees, has also been supported in an article by Schor and Bowles (1987). They contend that more unemployment increases the cost to employees of losing jobs and so makes employees less militant and less willing to strike. They state: ". . . when the cost of job loss is high, it is more difficult for workers to win strikes, and they are therefore less likely to strike" (Schor and Bowles 1987, 584).

According to this theory, when the economy expands toward full employment, the result of higher wages and constant or declining productivity is a rising labor share. Thus, the labor share rises every time business output and employment expand toward full employment. When unemployment has risen sufficiently in a depression, the theory asserts that there will be lower wages and rising productivity, so the labor share will fall.

Someone reading the unemployment hypothesis for the first time might expect the labor share to rise for the entire expansion period and fall for the entire contraction period. This is not true because the labor share always falls in the recovery phase of expansion and always rises in the crisis phase of contraction, according to all studies. The sophisticated formulation of the unemployment hypothesis (see Boddy and Crotty 1975; also Gordon, Weisskopf and Bowles 1987) emphasizes only that the labor share rises in the prosperity phase, the latter part of expansion before the peak. Presumably, for symmetry and internal consistency, the theory would require that the labor share fall again in the latter part of contraction before the trough. The sophisticated unemployment theorists are quite willing to admit that the labor share falls in early expansion and rises in early contraction. They postulate a lag effect. The unemployment theorists postulate a long time lag between changes in unemployment and changes in the labor share, due to a time lag in changes in labor militancy (which require changes in attitude).

If lower unemployment brings more militancy and a higher labor share, why does the labor share fall in the first half of expansion? If higher unemployment brings less militancy and a lower labor share, why does the labor share rise in the first half of contraction? The answer from the unemployment theorists is that there is a subjective time lag after the peak before employee militancy declines, as well as a subjective time lag after the trough before employee militancy rises again. In other words, employees remember the high unemployment levels of recession during the first half of expansion, so they act cautiously. In the first half of contraction, employees still act militantly until unemployment reduces employee resistance. Unemployment theory proponents would also accept some of the arguments of the wage lag theorists, showing objective reasons for a time lag, particularly fixed wage contracts. Thus, the unemployment hypothesis explains the labor share by unemployment with a long time lag. (For a complete cycle theory based on the unemployment hypothesis, see Part 3.)

The unemployment hypothesis says that lower unemployment leads to a higher share, while higher unemployment leads to a lower labor share. So:

$$Labor\ share = f\ (unemployment) \tag{6.7}$$

where the function is negative. In other words, the labor share moves in the opposite direction to the unemployment rate.

According to Figures 6.1 and 6.3, the unemployment rate and the labor share of income usually move the same way. This shows that one cannot accept this hypothesis in any simple way. But, in the first place, those who have supported the hypothesis have clearly stated that there is a long time lag in any such function. Second, when a time lag is considered, falling unemployment in expansion does seem to have some effect toward the end of expansion, when the labor share stops falling very much (and sometimes even rises, as it did in the 1950s and 1960s cycles). So, it appears that unemployment may have some short run effect on the labor share. It is just that for much of the cycle, this effect is overshadowed by other factors (such as output and capacity utilization, which fall in the opposite direction, as noted in the wage lag theory).

The unemployment hypothesis is tested econometrically in Chapter 22, where it is found to have a limited validity in the short-run of a business cycle. Of course, over a long-run period of time, continued unemployment will lower the labor share. In fact, in the 1970s and 1980s, high long-run unemployment rates (rising from cycle to cycle) did accompany a wage share or labor share that fell from cycle to cycle.

THE SYNTHETIC HYPOTHESIS

Whereas the unemployment hypothesis states that the labor share is explained by unemployment, the wage lag hypothesis (and the overhead labor hypothesis) explains it ultimately in terms of changes in capacity utilization (or output) under the conditions of our private enterprise economy. The synthetic hypothesis accepts parts of both theses, so it is a synthesis of them. It assumes that the level of capacity utilization affects the labor share, through the use of overhead labor, through labor strife, and because of private enterprise institutions. Thus, the labor share tends to decline when capacity utilization rises and tends to rise when capacity utilization falls (because wages lag behind profits). But, the synthesis also assumes that the labor share is affected in the opposite direction by unemployment with a time lag. Either one without the other is considered in this viewpoint to be inadequate and incomplete.

The synthesis argues that:

$$Labor\ share = f^1\ (unemployment) + f^2\ (capacity\ utilization) \qquad (6.8)$$

where f^1 is a negative function and f^2 is a different negative function. The point is that these two influences pull in opposite directions. In an expansion, unemployment is falling while capacity utilization is rising. Capacity utilization is the stronger influence, so the labor share of income falls for most of the time in most expansions, but it would fall further if declining unemployment did not exert a positive influence.

In the recovery phase, rising output and rising capacity utilization leads to rapid rises in productivity, but much slower increases in wage rates. The decline in unemployment has no immediate effect. Therefore, the labor share declines.

In the prosperity phase, capacity utilization rises much more slowly, so it has less effect on increases in productivity. Slow wage increases do continue because of the slow increase in demand for labor. Unemployment falls further and begins to cause pressures for higher wages and less productivity growth. The result is that the labor share is relatively stagnant, but often begins to rise a little before the peak.

In the crisis phase of the contraction, capacity utilization falls and pressures develop for a rising labor share through slowly declining wages and rapidly declining productivity. Rising unemployment as yet has no effect.

Toward the end of the depression phase, capacity utilization falls very slowly, with some pressure for further productivity and wage declines. This tends to cause more of an increase in the labor share. But increasing unemployment now exerts its pressure, with a time lag, toward a decline in the labor share. The result is a fairly stagnant labor share, usually rising slightly, but sometimes falling slightly.

BEHAVIOR OF UNEMPLOYMENT AND CAPACITY UTILIZATION

Unemployment results when there is insufficient demand for labor. In one sense, this whole book is about the fundamental causes of unemployment. Its immediate cause, however, is quite clear and simple. The demand for labor is determined by the demand for output. If more output is needed, more employees are hired. If less output is needed, some employees are fired. Thus:

$$Unemployment = f(output) \tag{6.9}$$

Unemployment is a negative function of output, always moving in the opposite direction.

On the other hand, capacity utilization always moves up and down in the same direction as output. When a firm needs more output, if there is some unused capacity, the first thing it does is to put unused machinery into operation. If the demand for a firm's products declines, it reduces the use of its plant and equipment. This may mean less use of machinery in a single plant, or it may mean closing whole plants. In every recession, for example, General Motors closed some plants, lowering its capacity utilization. In recovery, General Motors opens more plants. Thus we may write:

$$Capacity\ utilization = f(output) \tag{6.10}$$

Capacity utilization is a positive function of output, but it does not follow output exactly. Capacity utilization is mainly cyclical, limited to the range from 1 percent to 100 percent of capacity. Output, on the other hand, not only varies cyclically, but can also grow over time. There are sometimes trends in the average capacity utilization over several cycles, but only within its limited range.

Finally, notice that unemployment is a negative function of output, while capacity utilization is a positive function of output. Therefore, capacity utilization and unemployment always move in opposite directions. These movements may be seen clearly in Figure 6.3. If the labor share is influenced by both of them, their influences will contradict and moderate each other.

THEORIES CONFRONTED BY DATA

What do the data at the beginning of this chapter show that is relevant to the theories? To summarize the data, in the average of the four cycles of 1970–1991, (1) the labor share falls in expansions and rises in contractions, but is a leading indicator; (2) productivity rises faster than wage rates in expansions and falls faster than wage rates in contractions; (3) capacity utilization rises in expansions and falls in contractions; while (4) unemployment falls in expansions and rises in contractions. These basic facts appear to support the wage lag and overhead labor hypotheses, but appear to contradict the unemployment hypothesis (because the labor share usually moves in the same direction as unemployment). Before drawing conclusions, however, the econometric evidence should be considered.

The econometric evidence is presented in detail in Chapter 22 of this book, but may be summarized here. If the relation of the labor share to capacity utilization is examined, there appears to be a significant negative relation, as predicted by the wage lag and overhead labor hypotheses. If the relation of the labor share to unemployment is examined separately, the relationship is positive with no time lag (and not significant with time lags), so it appears to contradict the unemployment hypothesis.

But it is incorrect to look at the unemployment and capacity utilization factors separately because they operate simultaneously. If the relationship of the labor share to both capacity utilization and to unemployment are examined, a significant negative correlation of the labor share to capacity utilization with no time lag is found. There is also, however, a significant negative correlation of the labor share to unemployment with a long time lag, as predicted in the unemployment hypothesis and the synthetic hypothesis.

In other words, what appears most likely is that there are two main factors affecting cyclical behavior of the labor share: capacity utilization and unemployment. They push the labor share in opposite directions, so the question is which is strongest at each point and what time lags operate. Capacity utilization is the stronger effect and unemployment operates with a long time lag.

Finally, it is worth noting that capacity utilization is strongly pro-cyclical and has a strong positive relationship to national income. Unemployment is strongly counter-cyclical and has a strong negative relationship to national income. These two facts are well-known and noncontroversial, but help round out knowledge in this area.

EXPLANATION OF CYCLICAL MOVEMENTS OF LABOR SHARE BY CYCLE PHASE

Given the synthetic theoretical approach and the above facts, explanations can be made on the movements of the labor share, real hourly wages, and productivity over the cycle in relation to the influence of unemployment and capacity utilization.

RECOVERY (EARLY EXPANSION)

When output and capacity utilization are rising rapidly in the recovery phase, productivity also rises rapidly, partly because of improving technology, partly because of more optimal use of capacity as more workers are added, and mostly because overhead labor can be more fully utilized. The rise in productivity is greater than the rise in real hourly wages, so profits rise while the labor share declines.

Why do real hourly wages rise more slowly than productivity in spite of the increase in demand for labor? Part of the answer to the slowness of growth of real wages is the fact that unemployment is still high and the memories of the previous recession are still very sharp. A second reason may be that although the employee share in output is falling, they are more aware of the pleasant fact of rising labor income. Third, under private enterprise institutions, wage contracts are fixed at the old levels. It takes time before the next bargaining period is reached. Until there are changes forced through bargaining, all of the increase in productivity automatically goes to the employer because the employer owns the product under the private enterprise system. Fourth, prices are rising, so it is extra difficult to raise real wages. Fifth, the government, the media, and public opinion are all opposed to further wage increases when wages (and prices) are rising.

PROSPERITY (LATE EXPANSION)

In the last half of the average expansion, productivity increases very little, but real wages are also sluggish. As a result, the labor share is stagnant, rising a little in the 1950s and 1960s, but falling a little in the 1970s, 1980s, and 1990s.

Real wages are sluggish toward the end of expansion partly because demand for products, and hence for labor, slows its rate of growth. The increase of consumer demand is limited, as is the increase of investment demand. Yet, unemployment is declining, so workers' bargaining power improves; thus, real wages usually continue to rise in this phase.

Productivity increase is also slowed for several reasons. First, falling unemployment means a better bargaining position for labor, more militancy and more strikes—so speedup is prevented and the rise of productivity is limited. Second, overhead labor is now fully utilized, so there are no more easy gains from this source. Finally, as Wesley Mitchell has noted in all of his books, thousands of new, small and inexperienced firms come crowding into the market at this point. Their entry undoubtedly lowers average productivity.

CRISIS (EARLY CONTRACTION)

In the early stages of the downturn, employment remains fairly high. Employers are hoarding some skilled labor and all overhead labor. Therefore, measured productivity declines very rapidly.

At the same time, fixed labor contracts prevent any rapid decline in hourly wages. Moreover, the government, the media, and public opinion are much more sympathetic to labor's resistance to wage cuts than they were to higher wages.

In summary, as output and capacity utilization decline, wage rates decline very slowly, while productivity rapidly declines. These facts explain the rising share of labor in national income during the crisis phase of contraction.

DEPRESSION (LATE CONTRACTION)

By late contraction, employers fire every possible employee who is not absolutely essential, even some of the overhead labor force. Therefore, measured product per labor hour may finally rise again at the cycle trough.

At the same time, rapidly rising unemployment worsens the bargaining power of employees, lowers their militancy, and reduces the number of strikes. Therefore, real hourly wages usually fall in this phase. As a result of rising or stable productivity and lower real wages, the labor share stops rising and may even decline at the end of the contraction.

SUMMARY

In the fairly severe business cycles of the 1970s, 1980s, and early 1990s, we find: (1) the labor share falls throughout most of expansion and rises throughout most of contraction, (2) wage rates rise more slowly than productivity during expansion, but wage rates also fall more slowly during contraction; (3) capacity utilization is strongly pro-cyclical, while unemployment is strongly counter-cyclical; (4) the labor share is negatively correlated to capacity utilization with no time lag and is negatively correlated to unemployment with a time lag; (5) capacity utilization is positively correlated to real national income; and (6) unemployment is negatively correlated to real national income.

CONCLUSIONS

Since the labor share and unemployment usually move in the same direction, there is little evidence for a crude unemployment hypothesis. But the econometric findings do indicate that unemployment influences the labor share negatively with a time lag, though less strongly than capacity utilization. Therefore, a weak form of the unemployment hypothesis has some validity.

Since (1) the labor share usually moves opposite to capacity utilization, and (2) productivity usually moves with capacity utilization, there is obvious support for the wage lag and overhead labor hypotheses.

The evidence is consistent with the synthetic hypothesis, which says that the labor share is negatively influenced both by capacity utilization, and by unemployment, though the latter influence is weaker and has a long time lag.

Before reaching any final conclusions as to the implications of these findings for business cycle theories, some further discussion is necessary. The next chapter examines non-labor costs to understand their relative importance. Part 3 examines the role of the labor share in both demand-side theories and cost theories.

KEY TERMS AND CONCEPTS

labor income; property income	real output per hour	overhead labor hypothesis
labor share; property share	wage lag hypothesis	synthetic hypothesis
capacity utilization	unemployment hypothesis	
real hourly wage		

CHAPTER 7

Profits and Raw Material Costs

Many theorists, from completely different viewpoints, have argued that a key factor in the business cycle may be that business profits are hurt in the expansion phase by disproportionate rises of the prices of capital goods, that is, plant, equipment, and raw materials. In the contraction phase, on the other hand, profits are helped by disproportionate declines in the price of capital goods. This chapter discusses the empirical findings in this area, while leaving the complete theory to Part 3.

Recall once more that profit equals revenue minus costs. After examining material costs, we will have completed the empirical investigation of (1) revenue from consumer spending, (2) revenue from investor spending, (3) costs of labor services, and (4) costs of material goods. On that basis, we can then turn to a factual examination of profit behavior over the cycle. That is the task of the last half of this chapter.

PREVIOUS EMPIRICAL STUDIES OF PRICE CHANGES

All the books of Wesley Mitchell (e.g., 1913, 1951) have discussed the different rates of change of various prices as a cause of the business cycle. Mitchell points out that in the recovery phase of the cycle, the prices of raw materials remain fairly low at first because there are large stocks of them in reserve left from the recession. By the prosperity phase of expansion, however, reserves are exhausted, so the costs of raw materials rise rapidly. Mitchell notes that these rising costs cut into profit margins (the ratio of profit to total sales) because they rise faster than output prices. According to Mitchell, this negative effect is somewhat balanced by the fact that the wages of production labor and the salaries of overhead labor lag behind output costs, so employees continue to be a source of increasing profit. "For, while the prices of raw materials and wares bought for resale usually rise faster than selling prices; the prices of labor lag far behind, and prices that make up supplementary (overhead) costs are mainly stereotyped for a time by old agreements concerning salaries, leases, and bonds" (Mitchell 1913, 152–53).

In other words, by the middle of expansion, rising raw material prices have become negative factors for business profits, but the lag of wages and overhead costs still increase profits. Mitchell gives several reasons why final output prices do not rise very rapidly in most expansions: (a) public regulation of some prices, (b) long-term contracts for purchases by retailers, and (c) the possibility that the vast new supply of goods in the expansion may outrun the consumer demand.

A considerable number of Mitchell's followers at the National Bureau of Economic Research (NBER) have conducted empirical research in this area (most of these studies are listed in Moore 1983, 175). The NBER study by Thor Hultgren (1965) is a very detailed description of all categories of prices and costs over the cycle. The fascinating NBER study by Ruth Mack (1956) finds that prices of shoes fluctuate less than the price of leather, which fluctuates less than the price of hides. Geoffrey Moore, long associated with the NBER, surveyed the existing empirical studies of costs and profit margins and concluded: "Of course, like the two blades of the proverbial scissors, both prices and costs determine margins, but costs have generally been the widely moving element accounting for the leads in margins" (Moore 1962, 11). It is clear that costs play a major role in the cycle, but it is very controversial as to whether demand or costs play the larger role, and it depends to some extent on which historical period we are discussing.

The best historical study is the NBER report by Frederick Mills (1946), which investigates the cyclical pattern of different categories of prices averaged over many business cycles (from 3 to 20 cycles), all ending in 1938. Mills provides data on the prices of 22 consumer goods, prices, 48 producers' goods (excluding raw materials), and prices of 32 raw materials. During the average expansion he found that the price of consumer goods rose 12 percent (as a percentage of the cycle base), the price of plants and equipment rose 21 percent, and the price of raw materials rose 23 percent. During the average contraction, Mills found that the price of consumer goods fell 18 percent, the price of plants and equipment fell 25 percent, and the price of raw materials fell 26 percent. Thus, the cyclical price fluctuations of consumer goods were least strong, price fluctuations of plant and equipment were in the middle, and prices of raw materials fluctuated the most.

The main explanation for this price behavior by most writers is a combination of accelerated demand with much less fluctuation of supply. In the accelerator theory, a rapid rate of growth of demand for goods and services results in a greater percentage growth of demand for raw materials and other producer's goods. The reason is that demand for raw materials is a derived demand based on the change, rather than the level of output of finished goods. Similarly, when the demand for finished goods and services declines in contraction, the demand for raw materials and other producer goods declines even more rapidly (due to the accelerator).

During the expansion, the supply of raw materials is much harder to expand than the supply of finished goods. Increasing the production of shoes can be done far more quickly than increasing production of cattle hides, since cattle take a number of years to grow. As a result, the quantity of raw materials rises more slowly than the quantity of finished goods, in each expansion, while the price of raw materials rises more rapidly than the price of finished goods. Similarly, in a depression, the flow of manufactured goods may be quickly reduced, but raw materials, such as industrial crops already planted, cannot be cut so fast. Thus, in a depression, the quantity of raw materials usually declines less, while the price of raw materials usually declines more than those of finished goods.

The data of Wesley Mitchell (1951, 312–21) reach the same conclusions. In the average expansion of the four cycles from 1921 to 1938, the price of finished goods rose only 8.6 percent, while the price of raw materials rose 16.0 percent. In the average contraction of the same four cycles, the price of finished goods fell 13.0 percent, but the price of raw materials fell 21.9 percent.

CYCLICAL PRICE MOVEMENTS, 1970–1991

The picture of differential price movements has been very different since the Second World War because of the existence of inflation during much of the period. In most cases, prices continue to rise in the contraction phases as well as the expansion phases. In spite of the inflation, however, striking differences between consumer goods prices and raw materials prices have continued, so it is these differences that are investigated. It turns out that the prices of other capital goods, such as plant and equipment, do not behave very differently from consumer goods prices, so plant and equipment prices are not included in our discussion.

During the period of the 1950s and 1960s, cyclical differences were hidden by long-run changes in the power distribution between advanced countries and the Third World countries. These changes lead to a long-run decline in raw materials prices versus finished goods. The 1970–1991 period, however, resembles the 1920s and 1930s in many ways with respect to price and cost movements. The great inflation is the only difference between the modern period and the cycles of the 1920s and 1930s as to cyclical patterns today. Nevertheless, the differential price movements are the same as in the earlier period.

In the period, 1970–1991, the consumer price index rose an average of 1.7 percent per quarter in the average expansion. In the same period, the price index of all sensitive (that is, flexible and frequently changing) crude and intermediate materials rose by an average of 2.1 percent per quarter in expansions. Thus, in the average expansion phase, the aggregate profits of U.S. businesses were reduced by the greater rise in raw material and intermediate prices. Most of the raw materials were imported from abroad, so it was a net loss to all U.S. firms, rather than a switch from one U.S. firm to another.

In the 1970–1991 period, the consumer price index continued to rise by 2.0 percent per quarter during business contractions as a result of long-run inflation. In the same period, the price index of sensitive crude materials and intermediate goods actually *fell* by 3.1 percent per quarter in the average contraction, in spite of overall inflation. Thus, in the average contraction phase, the aggregate profits of U.S. firms were helped greatly by the decline in raw material and intermediate material prices which were mostly imported from abroad. A graphic portrayal of the differential price movements is presented in Figure 7.1. This graph portrays the ratio of crude and intermediate material prices to consumer goods prices. The ratio rises rapidly in the average expansion, but falls quite considerably in the average contraction. More precisely, the ratio of crude and intermediate material prices to consumer prices rose by 0.46 percent per quarter in the average expansion, while falling by 6.25 percent per quarter in the average contraction. Thus, the cost of crude and intermediate materials was a rising burden on U.S. business in expansions, but was a rapidly declining burden in contractions.

The different movements of this ratio over the cycle can also be investigated through a simple econometric test (as shown in Chapter 22). The ratio of capacity utilization is strongly pro-cyclical and may be assumed to reflect forces of demand in the business cycle. In the 1970s, 1980s, and 1990s, on the other hand, there is a strong and significant positive relation between the ratio of crude and intermediate material prices to consumer prices with the ratio of capacity utilization. This tends to confirm the notion that the cost-price ratio moves up in expansions and down in contractions, so it has a negative effect on profits in expansions and a positive effect on profits in contractions.

To sum up the empirical findings, the cost of raw materials usually rises faster than the consumer price index in expansions. In contractions, the cost of raw materials usually falls faster than the consumer price index (or rises more slowly, if there is inflation). As an indicator of the cyclical

FIGURE 7.1
CRUDE MATERIAL PRICES TO CONSUMER PRICE INDEX, RATIO

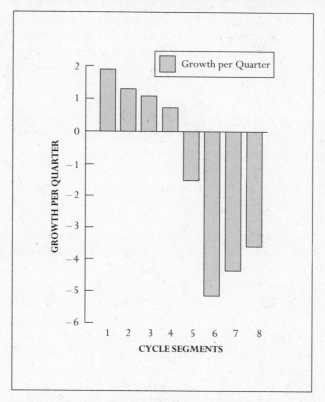

SOURCE: CITIBASE database, files PPSIMC and PUNEW.

NOTE: Average of four cycles, 1970–1991. Ratio of crude and intermediate material prices to consumer price index, quarterly, seasonally adjusted.

expansion and contraction, the clearest index is the index of capacity utilization, which always moves up with the cycle and always moves down with the cycle. Therefore, the ratio of raw material costs to the consumer price index moves in the same direction as the index of capacity utilization. So, we may write:

$$(Raw\ material\ costs)/(consumer\ price\ index) = f\ (capacity\ utilization) \quad (7.1)$$

This relationship is important because it means that raw material costs cut into profits in an average expansion. It also means that falling raw material costs are a help to profits in an average business contraction.

THE COMPONENTS OF PROFITS

Before discussing the behavior of profits, it is useful to review what has been learned so far about the components of profits. Remember that profit equals revenue minus costs. In the aggregate economic data, revenue has four sources. Revenue comes from consumer spending, investment spending, government spending, and net exports. Aggregate costs include labor costs, raw material costs, plant and equipment costs, taxes, rental costs, and interest costs.

In Chapter 4, we considered the cyclical behavior of consumer spending. It was found to be a function of national income, the distribution of income between labor and property incomes, credit, and various other variables. Consumer spending rises and falls as income rises and falls, but more slowly. The behavior of investment spending was considered in Chapter 5. We noted that it is a function of profit expectations, as caused by previous changes in profits and profit rates, as well as by the funds made available by business profits, directly or as a basis for getting credit. It was pointed out that profit is, in turn, a function of the stream of revenue and the stream of costs. It was found that investment rises and falls as income rises and falls, but far more rapidly.

In Chapter 6, real labor costs were found to rise and fall with the cycle. But the share of labor in national income and output was found to be counter-cyclical, that is, the labor share falls as income rises and rises as income falls. So it was anticipated that the labor share is a negative function of output and capacity utilization. The labor share usually falls until the peak of the cycle and usually rises until the trough of the cycle, but sometimes it leads at the peak and trough. The labor share always slows its movement to a crawl before the peak and before the trough of the cycle.

In the beginning of this chapter, the cyclical behavior of raw material costs was examined. Raw materials costs were usually found to rise rapidly in expansion and usually fall in contraction. Specifically, they rise and fall faster than consumer prices. Thus, the ratio of raw material prices to consumer prices rises in expansion as output and capacity utilization rise. But the ratio of raw material costs to consumer prices falls in contractions as output and capacity utilization are falling.

Thus, this part of the book has spelled out some key elements of revenue (consumption and investment spending) and some key elements of costs (labor and raw materials). By investigating these elements of revenue and costs, we have laid the groundwork for understanding profits. Later, in Part 4, some further elements of revenue (government and net exports) and some further elements of costs (taxes and interest) will be discussed, which will help us reach a deeper and more realistic understanding. But one cannot state everything at once without causing confusion, so we now turn to a first approximation to understanding the behavior of profits, keeping in mind

BOX 7.1

AMERICA: WHO REALLY PAYS THE TAXES

If corporations in 1994 paid taxes at the same rate as corporations did through the 1950s, the U.S. Treasury Department would have an extra $250 billion a year. That's two and one-half times as much money as corporations presently pay in taxes. Let's put that $250 billion in more personal terms.

It would be enough money to nearly eliminate the federal deficit.

It would be enough money to provide a 60 percent tax cut for everyone with an income below $200,000.

It would be enough money to pay for health care for everyone who is uninsured — and still have enough left over for a tax cut for individuals.

Business conditions in the 1990s, to be sure, are not the same as they were in the 1950s. And while it might be difficult to generate an equivalent amount of tax revenue, the $250 billion figure provides some insight into just how much taxes corporations once paid, and how little they pay today . . .

During the 1940s, corporate taxes accounted for 33 percent of the federal government's general fund tax collections. The corporate share slipped to 31 percent in the 1950s and to 27 percent in the 1960s. Then it plunged to 21 percent in the 1970s, continuing its free fall in the 1980s to 15 percent, where it remains in the 1990s.

At the same time corporations were contributing an ever smaller share of the cost of running the government, individuals were picking up a growing portion. During the 1940s, individual income taxes accounted for 44 percent of the government's general fund tax collections. This figure rose to 49 percent in the 1950s, to 57 percent in the 1960s, to 66 percent in the 1970s, to 72 percent in the 1980s, and to 73 percent in the 1990s . . .

D. Barlett and J. Steele
Simon and Schuster, New York, 1994, 140

that we will modify and deepen our understanding in Part 4 and will add some econometric description in Chapter 22.

PROFITS AND PROFIT RATES

This part of the chapter explores the behavior of total profits and profit rates over the business cycle, setting the empirical base for a cycle theory centered on profits. Profits are important to cycle theory because of their close relationship to investment, which is the immediate cause of recessions or recoveries.

The main hypothesis of this part of the chapter is that the profit rate, as well as total profits, is strongly pro-cyclical, contrary to some popular misconceptions. One subsidiary hypothesis is that there is no significant long-run trend to the profit rate, contrary to some theories. Another subsidiary hypothesis is that the profit rate leads at the turning points of the business cycle. The lead is not always a long one, but is sometimes very brief. It is also argued that these movements of profits are best explained by both the revenue (demand factors) and the cost (supply factors), contrary to those theories that concentrate on just one or the other.

Each of these empirical issues affect our understanding of the business cycle and the credibility of various cycle theories. For example, the fact that there is no significant long-run trend to profit rates deals a severe blow to the theory that long-run technological changes cause an inevitable decline in the profit rate and that this causes or helps to cause cyclical downturns.

Why are profits important to the business cycle of the private enterprise economy? All theories of the business cycle begin with the fact that the wide fluctuations of investment constitute the proximate cause of business expansions and contractions. But profit expectations determine business investment. In other words, investment is the crucial variable for understanding the business cycle. But profits and profit rates are the keys to understanding investment.

As Keynes emphasized, investment is based on the expectation of profits in the future when the investment produces for the market. But that merely poses the question of what causes our expectations to change. If expectations change on the basis of purely random whims or random impulses from outer space, a helpful theory could not be constructed. Fortunately, there is quite a bit of scientific evidence on the systematic formation of expectations. Klein and Moore (1985) conducted a very extensive review of existing survey data on actual profits and profit expectations; they also considered the actual quantitative measures of past profits. They found that ". . . the survey data of expected profits turn with few exceptions after the turn in both the actual profits survey and the quantitative data" (Klein and Moore 1985, 254). In fact, they found a time lag of three to four months between the actual turns in profits and the turns in profit expectations. Thus, it may be concluded that capitalist expectations by investors of a rise or fall in profits are based on recent increases or decreases in actual profits with a time lag.

It is important to distinguish two different ways in which actual profits affect investment. First, profit expectations are the motivation for investment, but profit expectations are mainly based on past profits. Here, it appears to be not just total profits but, primarily, the rate of profit on investment (or sales) that influences investors, because investors consider profit relative to the amount of their investment (or sales). Long-run decisions are affected by the return on investment, while short-run decisions to invest (such as inventory investment or rapid addition of new equipment) are influenced more by the recent returns on sales.

Second, motivation to invest means little unless the capital funds are available. Funds for investment depend on previous total profits as well as credit. Availability of credit, however, is also based in part on the internal profitability of the firm. So total profit is important as well as profit rates.

In fact, total capital changes very, very slowly in the real world, while profits change very rapidly. Thus, changes in the profit rate mostly reflect changes in total profits, and almost always move in the same direction. Profit rates sometimes turn down before total profits because capital is slowly increasing in an expansion.

DEFINITIONS AND BIASES IN PROFIT DATA

Much profit data comes from the Internal Revenue Service, so it is affected by accounting conventions and by changing tax laws, neither of which are based on any economic theory. Because of the tax laws, entrepreneurs naturally attempt to hide as much profit as possible and also to take advantage of tax loopholes as much as possible. All of this results in under-reporting profits and an underestimated trend in the profit share and the rate of profit (see, e.g., Perlo 1976). Figure 7.2 illustrates how corporate tax payments have remained essentially stagnant for the last 20 years. If corporations paid taxes at the same rate in 1994 as they did in the 1950s, the U.S. Treasury Department would have an additional $250 billion a year, or roughly two

FIGURE 7.2

COMPARISON OF CORPORATE AND PERSONAL INCOME TAX REVENUES, 1970–1992

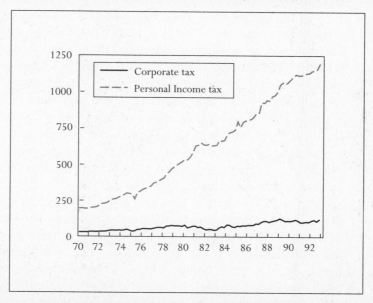

SOURCE: Bureau of Labor Statistics, *Survey of Current Business*, National Income Product Accounts.

and a half times what corporations presently pay in taxes (Barlett and Steele 1994).

For long-run analysis, the denominator of the profit rate should be capital, but that is even more difficult to calculate empirically and is quite problematic as to theoretical meaning. In the short-run, sales can be used as the denominator rather than capital because that is the ratio that probably influences more cyclical decisions. There are also difficult decisions on inclusion and exclusion. For example, should profit be calculated before taxes or after taxes? These decisions on definitions depend on the problem under investigation. Fortunately, the cyclical behavior, as opposed to long-run trends, in profits and profit rates is very similar for a wide variety of definitions (see below, also see Sherman 1968, Chapter 1).

Finally, one could certainly argue that it would be useful to investigate profit rate trends for the non-financial sector or for the whole economy. The investigation here is limited to the manufacturing, mining, and trade sector because (a) it is still an important sector, and (b) quarterly data exist for profit rates in manufacturing, mining, and trade, but there are no quarterly data for the whole non-financial sector or the whole economy. Cyclical analysis must be done with quarterly data, so it is best to be consistent.

LONG RUN PROFIT RATE TRENDS

The official data for the rate of profit on stockholders equity capital in all of U.S. manufacturing, mining, and trade from 1933 to 1982 are shown in Table 7.1. A mistake has been made by some economists when they calculate a supposed long-run trend from the peak of one cycle to the trough of another. For example, an economist may calculate a trend from a peak profit rate period in 1966 to the trough in 1982. Such calculations show a spurious downward trend. To correct that mistake, just one average value is presented for each whole cycle (using quarterly cycle dates from 1949 to 1982).

These statistics reveal no long-run trend in the rate of profit in the past ten cycles (for similar data on the United Kingdom, see King 1975). Of course, one can find a "trend" by taking an appropriate period. From the depths of the Great Depression (1933) to the Korean War, there is a clear upward trend. From the Korean War till the early 1960s, there is a downward trend. These trends, however, prove little except that profit rates tend to rise in wars. Profit rates were obscenely high during the Korean War.

There is also a large literature using other definitions and adjustments to the official data in order to correct for biases in measuring profit rates. Certainly, an extreme enough change in definition can produce a profit-rate trend, but that is beyond the scope of this book. It will be seen below that the cyclical pattern in profit rates is very little affected by changes in defini-

TABLE 7.1
TRENDS IN PROFIT RATES, 1933–1982
(AVERAGE PROFIT RATE FOR EACH CYCLE)

Cycle	Profit Before Taxes to Equity Capital	Profit After Taxes to Equity Capital
1933–1938	3.8%	n.a.
1938–1945	16.2%	n.a.
1945–1949	17.8%	n.a.
1949–1954	24.3%	11.6%
1954–1958	21.0%	10.9%
1958–1961	17.3%	9.3%
1961–1970	19.3%	11.2%
1970–1975	19.4%	11.5%
1975–1980	22.9%	14.2%
1980–1982	18.3%	11.9%

SOURCE: Data for 1933–1949 from U.S. Internal Revenue Service, Statistics of Income, Corporate Income Tax Returns (Washington, D.C.: GPO, 1935–1955). Data for 1949–1982 from Bureau of Census, U.S. Department of Commerce, *Quarterly Financial Report on Manufacturing, Mining, and Trade Corporations* (Washington, D.C.: GPO, 1949–1983).

DEFINITION: Rate of profit to stockholders' equity as a percent in all U.S. Manufacturing, Mining, and Trade.

NOTE: "n.a." means not available.

tion (even when the different definitions do change the absolute level or the long-run trend).

WEISSKOPF'S ANALYSIS OF THE RATE OF PROFIT

Thomas Weisskopf (1979) used a new, innovative framework for analyzing the rate of profit. Within that framework, he conducted an empirical analysis of the components of the profit rate. Let Π be real profit, let Y be real national income, and let K be real capital. By definition, the rate of profit may be written as the profit share of income (Π/Y) times the ratio of output to capital (Y/K):

$$\Pi/K = (\Pi/Y)(Y/K) \tag{7.2}$$

This framework emphasizes that a higher share of profit (and lower share of labor) will raise the rate of profit. This formulation is important to theories emphasizing the cost of labor. It also emphasizes that more product per unit of capital will raise the rate of profit. This latter point is an important consideration for those worried about the long-run effect of technology on the rate of profit.

In looking at business cycles, Weisskopf recognizes that actual output (Y) hardly ever equals the potential output (Z) which might be produced at full utilization of capacity. The ratio between actual output and potential full-capacity output is defined to be the capacity utilization ratio, or Y/Z. By definition, the rate of profit may be written as the profit share (Π/Y) times the capacity utilization ratio (Y/Z) times the ratio of potential full-capacity output to capital (Z/K):

$$\Pi/K = (\Pi/Y)\,(Y/Z)\,(Z/K) \qquad\qquad (7.3)$$

This definition is very useful because it distinguishes three different factors, each of which is important in different theories. The profit share plays a major role in many cost-side theories (especially the unemployment theory). Capacity utilization reflects demand, so it represents revenue, or demand-side theories, according to Weisskopf. The ratio of potential output to capital plays a role in long-run theories, but is also claimed to be important in some cyclical theories. Any macroeconomic change, such as rising aggregate wages, can be traced through its effect on each of these three factors.

When Weisskopf examines the empirical data (mostly for the 1950s and 1960s) within this framework, his most important findings are as follows: first, in recovery or early expansion, the most important influence on the rising profit rate is the rapid rise in revenue or demand, reflected in capacity utilization. Second, in prosperity or late expansion, the most important influence on the profit rate is falling unemployment, which raises the labor share and lowers the profit share. Third, in crisis or early contraction, the most important influence on the profit rate is the falling revenue or demand, reflected in the capacity utilization ratio. Fourth, in depression or late contraction, the most important influence on the profit rate is rising unemployment, which lowers the labor share and raises the profit share. Thus Weisskopf finds demand factors are important in the first two-thirds of expansion and the first two-thirds of contraction, but supply factors are more important in late expansion and late contraction. He strongly implies that the supply factors are the main cause of the downturn and upturn.

Weisskopf's interesting essay has generated an economic upsurge in the production of articles criticizing his work from various points of view (see Munley, 1981; Hahnel and Sherman, 1982a; Hahnel and Sherman, 1982b; Moseley, 1985; and Henley, 1987b). Empirically, some of the critics find that in the 1970s and 1980s, at least, demand factors are far more important than supply factors (such as the unemployment rate). Theoretically, he examines only simultaneous movements, not time lags. But many things in the cycle operate with a time lag, so damages early in expansion (such as falling propensity to consume) may affect profit rates in the later stages of expansion.

CYCLICAL BEHAVIOR OF CORPORATE PROFITS AND PROFIT RATES, 1970–1991

In the four cycles of the 1970–1991 period, both total profits and profit rates conform closely to a pro-cyclical pattern. Figure 7.3 shows the cyclical pattern of the average corporate profit rate on capital, while total corporate profit was shown in Figure 5.3.

In this period, corporate profit rates are pro-cyclical and lead at the peak. Thus corporate profit rates rise in segments 1, 2, and 3, but then fall in segment 4 before the cycle peak. The profit rate then continues to fall during the whole contraction. This behavior is similar to that of total profits, pictured in Figure 5.3. No matter what the definition of profits or profit rates, both profit rates and total profits rise in much of expansion, but lead downward before the peak, and continue to decline for the contraction period.

FIGURE 7.3
PROFIT RATE ON CAPITAL

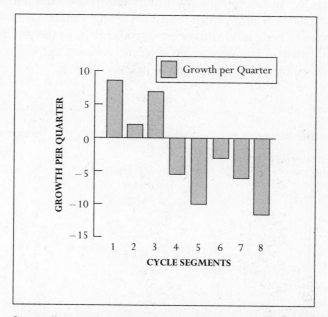

SOURCE: Bureau of Census, U.S. Department of Commerce, *Quarterly Financial Report on Manufacturing, Mining, and Trade Corporations* (Washington, D.C.: U.S. GPO, 1979–1993).

NOTE: Average of four cycles, 1970–1991. Ratio of profits after taxes to stockholders' equity for all manufacturing corporations, quarterly, seasonally adjusted.

CONCLUSIONS ON RAW MATERIAL PRICES

Throughout U.S. history, according to the known data (except for the period of the 1950s and 1960s), raw and intermediate materials prices rose much faster than prices of finished goods in the average business expansion. In the average business contraction, however, raw and intermediate material prices fell much faster (or rose much less) than finished goods prices. This meant that profits of U.S. firms were hurt by this differential price movement in expansions, but were helped by it in contractions. The theoretical implications of this fact for cost theories of the cycle are discussed in Part 3.

CONCLUSIONS ON PROFITS

The conclusion from the data cited above is that profits and profit rates are strongly pro-cyclical. Their normal behavior includes a time lead at the cycle turning points. This behavior is governed by revenue and costs at all times, but revenue appears to be the more strongly moving factor in much of the cycle, though costs are important before the turning points. Briefly, in the recovery period, costs move sluggishly while revenue soars, so profit rates soar. In late prosperity, profits and profit rates fall because revenue growth is very slow while costs are rising somewhat faster. In the crisis, revenue falls rapidly, while costs are sluggish, so the profits and profit rates fall rapidly. In late depression, revenue bottoms out while costs are falling, so profits and profit rates begin to recover.

KEY TERMS AND CONCEPTS

consumer price index

raw material price index

costs; prices

total profit; rate of profit

profit is a leading indicator

rate of profit is a leading indicator

PART 3

Theories of the Cycle

While Part Two described the business cycle, Part Three builds upon the empirical data presented in Part Two and presents various theories of the business cycle. It begins with a detailed history of the main business cycle theories from the classicals to the post-Keynesians and the new-Keynesians.

An analysis is made of some of the main models which illustrate how the economy generates a business cycle. The simplest is the multiplier-accelerator model. Then, various models concentrating on lack of revenue or demand are discussed, followed by analysis of theories that emphasize the high cost of supply. Finally, theories are presented where the key factor is profit.

CHAPTER 8

Business Cycle Theories Before Keynes

This chapter is a summary of all business cycle theories before Keynes, with descriptions of each of the different schools and models. This chapter traces the evolution of business cycle theory up to the 1930s. The next chapter discusses theories of the business cycle in the period from the 1930s to the present. Subsequent chapters present more rigorous and formal versions of selected business cycle theories.

Business cycles are recurrent, non-periodic rises and falls in the overall level of economic activity. Business cycles impose large social costs so they have attracted economists' attention. The factors that cause business cycles ought to be discovered by scientific analysis because they exhibit easily discernible patterns. But because business cycles are non-periodic, or irregular in their timing and duration, the interaction of those causal factors is a complicated process.

TYPES OF BUSINESS CYCLE THEORIES

Economists classify theories and models based upon central distinguishing characteristics. This facilitates communication because complex approaches to economic analysis can be suggested or alluded to by evoking the name of the theory and the model or school of thought which developed it, thus reducing the need to describe these in detail over and over again. Business cycle theories are classified in several ways; they are usually distinguished by their characteristic assumptions and hypotheses regarding the main variables causing the problem. The names given to the theories are descriptive;

for example, *monetarism* for models which emphasize the role of money, and *real business cycle* theory which emphasizes the role of real or non-monetary factors such as technological change. Other names refer to the originator of the theory, such as *Keynesian,* for John Maynard Keynes. Another important distinguishing characteristic of business cycle theories hinges on whether the problem arises within the economy itself or arises outside the economy. It is usually said that a factor determined within the economy, such as the rate of profit, is called an internal or endogenous variable; while a factor determined outside the economy, such as a war or embargo, is called an external or exogenous factor. What is considered internal or external, however, depends on the model. For example, government may be treated as external; but if government behavior is explained within the model, then government is internal or an endogenous factor.

TWO MAIN VIEWS OF BUSINESS CYCLES

Two diametrically opposed approaches to business cycle analysis have co-existed from the earliest attempts to explain economic fluctuations. One tradition was started by the classical economists of the late 18th and early 19th centuries. This tradition is based upon a vision of the economy as essentially stable. In this vision of the economy the normal state is one of fairly rapid economic growth fueled by investment in capital, technological change, the introduction of new products, the discovery of new resources, and population growth. The economy may be deflected from its normal growth path by some external (or exogenous) factor such as war, technological change, or governmental intervention. Otherwise, the economy continues to expand, offering full employment to its labor force and utilizing most of its exploitable resources. If the economy is temporarily deflected from its growth path, strong forces within it automatically and promptly return it to high levels of resource utilization and growth. This vision of the economy originated in the work of the early classical economists, such as Adam Smith and David Ricardo, and has generally dominated economic analysis in the subsequent centuries. As we shall see, it forms the background for much modern theory. We refer to specific theories which adopt this view as within the orthodox or mainstream tradition.

Another competing vision of the private enterprise economy, however, has been the basis of some business cycle theories. This vision appears in the views of dissenting classical economists such as Thomas Malthus, John Maitland, Simonde de Sismonde and Karl Marx, in addition to the pioneering and revolutionary theory of John Maynard Keynes, and the modern work by Institutionalist, Keynesian, and neo-Marxian economists. This approach argues that the private enterprise economy is inherently unstable and is characterized by alternating periods of rapid growth and recession or depression. This tradition contends that factors interrupting growth are inherent in the private enterprise economy. The problems are internal or endogenous to the system itself. These theories have usually been developed and gained their widest acceptance during periods of economic hardship or crisis. Such periods were during the late 19th century and again in the 1930s, when the tendency of private enterprise economies toward instability and depression was revealed by severe and prolonged depressions. This view of the economy is experiencing another rebirth in our own troubled times, forming the basis for much current work in cycle theory, especially among post-Keynesians and new-Keynesians.

FOUR STAGES OF BUSINESS CYCLE THEORY

The evolution of business cycle theory has passed through what may be interpreted as four distinct periods. The first period coincides with the era of *classical political economy,* and appears in the work of the early economists in the late 18th and early 19th centuries. With a few important exceptions, the classical economists largely ignored economic fluctuations, seeing them as inevitable but brief and unimportant pauses in economic growth. As shall be seen, their work provided important insights into the inner logic of private enterprise economies. Although the work of these economists was seriously flawed in several respects, it serves as the starting point for many modern theories of the cycle. The key elements of their theory are known as *Say's law* and the *quantity theory of money*. The dissenters were those economists, including Thomas Malthus and Karl Marx, who criticized Say's law and the quantity theory of money.

A second period began in the 1870s and roughly coincides with the rise of *neoclassical economics,* which developed marginal analysis and general equilibrium theory. The increasing instability of private enterprise economies in the latter third of the 19th century (and again in the 1930s) led to a renewed interest in cycle theory. Most neoclassical theory agreed with the classical economists that the economy is inherently stable. The most interesting dissenter of the second period was the under-consumptionist, John Hobson.

The third period began with the publication of John Maynard Keynes's *General Theory of Employment, Interest and Money* in 1936, which presented a powerful and influential critique of the orthodox classical view that recessions were unimportant, brief interludes in overall growth. Keynes attacked both Say's law and the quantity theory in his theoretical critique of the orthodox doctrine (discussed in detail below). The third period culminated in the Keynesian Revolution of the immediate post-World War II period, during which Keynes's views dominated macroeconomics. Economists using the analytical approaches inspired by Keynes, his followers, and his detractors, combined with modern techniques of empirical analysis, attempted to understand more precisely how the economy works. Some of these economists developed theories which agree with and extend Keynes's views, while others came to conclusions diametrically opposed to his. The principal dissenting economists during this period, roughly from the 1930s through 1970, were the monetarists, led by Milton Friedman.

The fourth, or modern, period began in the 1970s. It is characterized by a conflict of views which can be divided into New Classical, New Keynesian, and dissenting theories. The latter views encompass post-Keynesian, Institutionalist, and Marxian economics.

PERIOD ONE: CLASSICAL POLITICAL ECONOMY

The classical economists who contributed to business cycle theory include Adam Smith, John Baptiste Say, David Ricardo and Thomas Malthus. The classical economists were the first to systematically attempt to explain the sources of economic growth and prosperity. The founder of the school, Adam Smith (1723–1790), used the term, the wealth of nations, to identify what is today called the level of national income. In his book, *The Wealth of Nations*, which was published in 1776, Smith argued that societies become wealthy as the result of increases in the degree of division and specialization of labor. Business expansions are financed by the reinvestment of profit flows in additional capital goods, which increase labor productivity. He also believed that the interaction of self-interest (profit seeking) and competition in a "society of perfect liberty" would automatically lead to the most increase of national, and personal, wealth. The expansion would encourage producers, "as if led by an invisible hand," to extend specialization and thus increase productivity and national wealth. For the classical economists, explaining economic growth required an explanation of the forces which determined the distribution of income across the important social classes involved in production. The classes they discussed were workers, landowners, and capitalists. Capitalists meant property-owning farmers and merchants as well as manufacturers. Classical economists took this approach because it seemed clear to them that although the income streams that flowed to both workers (wages) and capitalists (profits) promoted economic growth, the income streams that went to landlords (rents) and the state (taxes) were not usually productively used. Even more importantly, because rents and taxes reduced the portion of the social surplus that could be invested by capitalists, rents and taxes reduced economic growth. Workers spent their income on necessary consumption, which renewed their labor power. The expenditures of workers created revenue and profits for the firms, allowing firms to expand. Capitalists spent most of their incomes, profits, and interest, on investment in productivity-enhancing capital. But the income streams that went to landlords and the government were spent unproductively. The landlords purchased luxuries for their own personal consumption. The government's expenditures rarely contributed to the accumulation of wealth, being spent mainly on war and the support of bureaucracies, which often interfered in the economy.

Their theory of growth, distribution, and value may be summarized, at the expense of leaving out much rich and insightful detail, in this manner:

1. The key to economic growth is capitalists' investment of their profits in productivity-enhancing fixed capital, in carrying larger inventories, and in hiring more workers.

2. The national income, net of workers' wages, is called the economic surplus. The surplus goes to capitalists who maximize at the expense of that going to landlords and the state. It is good to reduce what goes to landlords and the government because their funds would be used in largely unproductive expenditures.

3. In a competitive economy, workers' wages are regulated by competition and fluctuate around the long-run subsistence cost of renewing the labor forces' ability to work. Subsistence wage meant earning enough money to purchase the necessary subsistence goods, such as food, clothing and shelter. The return to capital, called profits, reflects capital's contribution to output as evaluated by the markets for the goods and services produced by the firms owned and organized by the capitalists. Landlords extract rents at the expense of the capitalists's profits because they have a monopoly on the fixed quantity of land (they own it). Rental value of land is regulated by the prices of agricultural products. The government extracts tax income based upon its political power. Rent and tax revenues should be minimized, if possible, so as to promote growth and wealth.

In the course of their explanation of growth, the classical economists also advanced an explanation for the factors that retarded growth. The factors they emphasized were (1) monopoly, (2) government intervention and regulations, (3) unproductive uses of revenue, and (4) recessions. The classical economists termed recessions as general gluts of commodities which couldn't be sold, or bad trade.

Periods of bad trade were characterized by low levels of sales, production, employment, and profits, and also by declining prices and wage rates. The possibility of a general glut lasting for very long was denied by most classical economists, largely on the basis of Say's law of markets. John Baptiste Say (1767–1832) first formulated the proposition called Say's Law, in his *Treatise of Political Economy,* published in 1803. His book went through five editions, and was probably the most widely read work in economics for twenty years.

Say's law has been interpreted in many ways. On the most general level it is a proposition that the aggregate demand for goods and services newly produced will generally be equal to the market value of the supply of goods and services. Aggregate demand will automatically equal aggregate supply. It is based upon (1) a logical deduction from the premises of profit seeking and the existence of competitive markets for commodities and labor, and (2) the understanding that the value of a commodity is equal to the value of the income streams which its production generates. Since the costs of production all become the incomes of the providers of those factor services, the income generated in the production of a commodity is equal to its market value. Thus, in this theory, aggregate income is always great enough so that aggregate demand will equal the market value of aggregate output or aggregate supply. This is true only if the income is spent. Say's law argues that it will always be spent. Therefore, there will be equilibrium at any output, including the full employment level of output.

The classical refutation of the possibility of persistent wide-spread involuntary unemployment in a private enterprise economy was widely accepted, largely on the basis of that persuasive logic rather than on the basis of empirical proof. In reality, deep and lengthy recessions were already occurring as the doctrine was being formulated. Moreover, Say's law formed an important part of the argument for a philosophy of as little government regulation of the economy as possible. Say's law was also the foundation for the dominant view on the nature and causes of business cycles. Say's law reappears in those modern theories known as the New Classical economics discussed below.

Another important element of classical theory which is relevant to the analysis of business cycles is the quantity theory of money, an early version of which appeared in an essay, "Of the Balance of Trade," by David Hume (1711–1776) in his *Political Discourses*. Hume was both friend and mentor to Adam Smith, who accepted Hume's views on the macroeconomic effects of changes in the quantity of money in circulation.

The classical quantity theory of money can be described in a very simple equation. The quantity or supply of money (M) times the velocity (V) of money must equal the price (P) of all goods and services times the number of transactions (T). Thus:

$$MV = PT \qquad\qquad (8.1)$$

Quantity of money means the amount of money in circulation, including bank accounts that can immediately be turned into money. Velocity of money means the number of times money changes hands in a given time period.

By definition, this is just another statement of the equilibrium of supply and demand. Demand is the amount of money times its speed of turnover. Supply is the amount of goods and services in all transactions times their prices. Thus, MV must always equal PT by definition at equilibrium (which equals GDP).

But the classical economists went further. They assumed that velocity (V) of money was constant (or changed so slowly that we could ignore it). If V is a constant, called k, then

$$Mk = PT \qquad\qquad (8.2)$$

But, the classical economists assumed that total physical transactions (T) was given by the physical amount of labor and capital. If T is given and velocity is constant $(V = k)$, then any change in money supply (M), can only affect prices. In other words, if the supply of money somehow increases, it causes inflation of prices but has no affect on the real amount of transaction.

For our purposes, the essential point of the quantity theory is that money was held to be neutral with respect to the real, physical levels of output and employment. Neutrality means that changes in the quantity of money would not be expected to cause changes in output and employment, or fluctuations in economic activity. The classical economists wanted to discourage inflationist schemes for promoting prosperity (of which there were many during this period). The classical economists wanted to impose fiscal constraints on government spending since they desired the government to be as small as possible. Their monetary theory was intended to provide a logical defense for their policy views, which discouraged the government from printing currency to finance deficits.

The classical theoretical argument about money is straightforward. If an economy is fully utilizing its resources (as can be assumed based upon Say's law), then any increase in the quantity of money will result in an increase in the level of prices and wages. In other words, inflation will result rather than an increase in real output. An increase in the supply of money might result from the discovery of new mines, a trade surplus, or the government printing more money. The classical economists assumed money is spent, as it would most likely be. Hoarding of cash, they claimed, is irrational, since interest income is foregone. Thus they argued that the aggregate demand for goods and services would increase. Firms will attempt to hire more labor to produce more, but since labor is already fully employed, wages will be bid up and firms' costs will rise. Because there are not any more resources to put to work, there will not be any increase in production. The only effect of the increased money would be inflation.

To be fair to the classical economists, most admitted the possibility of a short run change in output occurring in response to changes in the quantity of money. The thrust of their argument however, was that money was neutral, at least in the long run. Say's law and the quantity theory of money are the cornerstones of the classical theory of business cycles. Based upon them, the dominant classical view is that recessions are not inevitable, and are usually short and mild.

DISSENT FROM SAY'S LAW IN PERIOD ONE

Although the classical view dominated formal economic analysis for a century or so, it did not go unchallenged. The dissenters in the classical period included Simonde de Sismonde, Thomas Malthus, James Maitland (Earl of Lauderdale) and Karl Marx. Most of the dissent during the classical period was based upon a critique of Say's law and expressed an *under-consumptionist* theory of unemployment and recession.

Thomas Malthus (1776–1834), for example, argued that aggregate demand could fall below the level of aggregate supply (at least at profitable prices) if aggregate supply increased rapidly enough to furnish a more than adequate amount of necessities for workers and luxuries for the propertied classes. Malthus reasoned that, first, workers' wages tended toward the subsistence level, so they spent all their incomes on necessities. Capitalists spent most of their income on new capital goods, which increased productive potential, rather than on consumption goods. Landlords and other unproductive social classes, such as personal servants, bureaucrats, clergy, and college professors spent income on necessities and luxuries. They also saved, since they had a higher level of income. More troublesome was the fact that they sometimes hoarded their savings in the form of cash. If these latter social classes became satiated with consumer goods, aggregate supply might outstrip aggregate demand.

Other classical economists, including Simonde de Sismonde (1773–1842) and James Maitland (1776–1834), also criticized Say's law from an under-consumptionist perspective quite similar to Malthus's. Under-consumption as a cause of recession appears throughout the history of business cycle theory. The essential points held in common by this group of theories are: (1) the problem is that effective demand for consumer goods increases less rapidly than the potential output of the economy; (2) consumption is largely constrained by the growth in wage income, since most consumers are workers; (3) workers' purchasing power is limited by the ability of the propertied classes to appropriate a large and growing share of money income, and (4) there is a tendency of wages to be held down by competition for scarce jobs. Moreover, (5) the savings of the propertied classes are often channeled into productivity-enhancing investment, which exacerbates the problem by increasing future output, or are hoarded, which reduces current demand. Thus the cause of recession is linked to the manner in which purchasing power (money income) is distributed and spent, and ultimately to the institution of private property.

The most powerful 19th century critique of the orthodox classical view on cycles was Karl Marx's. Marx (1818–1883) denied the validity of both Say's law and the quantity theory of money. He went beyond the simplistic under-consumptionist views of Malthus and his contemporaries to develop a sophisticated and quite plausible alternative theory of the cycle. Most of Marx's views on the causes of recessions and the behavior of the economy during the cycle are in Volume III of his *Capital*. This was written in the period 1853–1865, but not published until 1894. Although his theory of the cycle was not satisfactorily completed, it contained elements which have reappeared in many subsequent theories.

Marx contended that there are two stages in the study of the business cycle. First, its historical preconditions must be understood. Only after understanding its historical setting can its specific causes be explained. Marx discussed the historical preconditions in order to refute Say's law and to show the possibility of depressions due to lack of effective demand. Marx began by criticizing the classical economists for confusing capitalism with earlier economies by describing capitalism as a set of isolated, self-sufficient individual producers, such as Robinson Crusoe on his little island, an example often used by the classical economists. According to classical theory, these individuals choose to barter their goods with each other. Marx points out that in capitalism, unlike Robinson Crusoe's situation, commodities are produced only for exchange in the market. If there is insufficient demand, production is reduced and workers are fired. Second, in capitalism, unlike Robinson Crusoe, goods are not produced for direct consumption by the producers, but in order for capitalists to make profits by selling them. If there is insufficient profit, production is cut back and workers are fired. Third, unlike Crusoe and his man Friday, there is *not* barter of one good for another. The classical economists claimed that money is merely a neutral veil over the exchange of commodities. Rather, there is a monetary economy in which commodities are always sold for money. If someone sells a good and hoards the money, there may be insufficient monetary (or effective) demand, resulting in lower production and employment.

Marx's cycle theory was termed a theory of crises, to call attention to his argument that the onset of depressions were very dangerous episodes for capitalist economies. Marx stressed the role of profits and capitalists' ability and willingness to invest as the key variables. If profits fall for any reason, investment soon falls because profits motivate and finance investment. If investment declines, the economy moves into recession. Marx thought that crises were inevitable, that they would become more frequent and severe as capitalism matured, and that eventually they would destroy capitalism itself. Crises were inevitable because the expansion phase of a cycle sets in motion processes which eventually reduced profits and investment.

Marx envisioned three likely scenarios during expansions, each of which results in recession. Marx's first scenario says that during the expansion phase, the accumulation of capital is often *extensive* rather than intensive, meaning that the new capital goods are similar to the old ones and require additional labor to work them. This increases the demand for labor until eventually full employment is attained. Then the relative scarcity of labor results in wages rising more rapidly than productivity, so that costs of production increase, reducing profits and eventually reducing investment, aggregate demand, and output.

Marx's second scenario states that if the accumulation process in the expansion does not increase the demand for labor enough for wages to rise, another problem appears. The problem is that workers' consumption spending lags behind output in consumption goods industries. Therefore, some commodities can not be sold. Profits fall in those industries, causing a decline in investment and output. Eventually, the expansion halts and recession begins; notice that this scenario is an under-consumptionist explanation. Marx's third possible scenario says capitalists might attempt to maintain profits by investing in labor-saving capital goods. Capitalists introduce machinery which increases the mechanization of production processes, substituting machines for workers. This would have an immediate positive effect on profits since productivity would be increased, lowering costs. Marx argued, however, that the new technologies would rapidly be applied by all firms in each industry in which they were introduced, due to competitive pressures. Then the increased supply of commodities would result in prices falling back to levels at which profits were low. The lower profit rate reduces investment and pushes the economy toward recession.

PERIOD TWO: NEOCLASSICAL ECONOMICS AND BUSINESS CYCLE THEORY

Neoclassical economics refers to an approach to economic analysis which has retained some elements of classical theory, particularly its stress on the efficiency of free markets, and on the power of the competitive interaction of self interest as an incentive system for promoting economic growth. Neoclassical economics rejected other aspects, such as the labor theory of value and the emphasis on linking the distribution of income across the social classes with the rate of economic growth. It originated in the early 1870s with the introduction of marginal analysis and utility theory to explain resource and commodity prices. It also has a theory of general competitive equilibrium, which describes how all the prices and quantities in the entire economy could be interpreted as interdependent and determined together. Neoclassical economics is also associated with the introduction of formal models utilizing mathematics and diagrams. Neoclassical economics emphasizes exploring the nature of equilibrium situations. It is marked by attempts at emulating some of the methods of the natural sciences. Formal hypotheses are defined and, where possible, tested empirically.

Most of the economics done in the period from 1870 through 1930 largely ignored the investigation of macroeconomic growth and fluctuations in favor of what came to be known as microeconomic analysis. Microeconomics examined individual firms and assumed the full employment of resources. Although most economists ignored fluctuations, much interesting work was also done in the field of business cycles, which for the first time became a separate object of analysis, rather than just part of a larger inquiry into the nature of wealth and the sources of economic growth, as in the classical era.

Empirical investigations were made by economists such as William Stanley Jevons (1835–1882), Clement Juglar (1819–1905), and Nikolai Kondratief (1835–1882), who began to systematically collect statistics and look for patterns in the behavior of economic and financial data. National income accounting, with its statistics, such as gross domestic product, investment, consumption and measures of employment and unemployment, did not yet exist.

It is customary and useful to group the neoclassical theories developed during this phase into two types: (1) *pure monetary* theories, (2) *over-investment* theories, including both *monetary* theories of over-investment and *real* theories of over-investment. These theories all use aspects of the neoclassical method of economic analysis, at least in attempting to define formal hypotheses. In addition, many of the economists attempted to demonstrate that their theories accorded with the actual behavior of the economy by citing statistical evidence, thus performing crude statistical tests of their theories.

MONETARY THEORIES

The British economist Ralph Hawtrey (1879–1975) developed a cycle model which is a good example of a pure monetary theory. In Hawtrey's view, the variable that sets off expansions is a decline in interest rates on the loans banks make to merchants. This encourages merchants to borrow and carry larger inventories of the commodities in which they trade. Higher inventory investment, in turn, increases demand for manufactured goods, stimulating output and employment. The recession comes when banks have insufficient reserves to finance additional lending, then interest rates begin to rise, causing a reversal in the process. The increase in bank lending may be due to increased savings flows into the banks or to monetary policy, either of which increases bank reserves and encourages them to reduce interest rates. The reduction in lending comes about because of outflows of reserves due to society's need for more cash, or is caused by tightened monetary policy. The reduction in new credit leads to a recession.

MONETARY OVER-INVESTMENT THEORIES

Another group of theories developed during this period are termed *over-investment* theories, to reflect the importance of investment in determining the behavior of the economy. Good examples of *monetary over-investment* theories are those put forth by Frederick Hayek and Knut Wicksell. Both Hayek and Wicksell distinguished between the actual rates of interest found in markets for loanable funds and the natural rate of interest. The natural rate is the rate which would balance the flow of savings with the demand for loanable funds by businesses. An economy would be in full-employment equilibrium with stable prices if the actual rate of interest equalled the natural rate. If, however, the actual rate fell below the natural rate, aggregate demand would increase as businesses eagerly increased their borrowing to take advantage of the actual rate of interest being below the expected profitability of investment.

Eventually the high level of interest and use of resources would cause prices to rise. High prices would reduce real consumption levels. This reduction in the real level of consumption is termed forced saving, that is, forced by price inflation. Soon actual rates of interest would rise as savers realized that real, inflation-adjusted rates of interest were less than the nominal, market determined rates. When interest rates rose high enough, the process would be reversed and the boom would turn into recession. As Hayek put it, the reduction in interest rates below the natural rate led to over-investment with respect to the economy's ability to produce goods and services at stable prices. The banks' credit expansion led to an artificial boom, and eventual recession, since the increased credit was not financed by an increase in society's preference for capital goods.

The term, over-investment, is used to characterize this type of theory in order to call attention to the strains imposed upon the economy by the increase in investment expenditures. At some point the additional capital goods cannot be profitably used. In other words, there had been too much investment for the economy to profitably absorb.

It is termed a monetary over-investment theory to call attention to the important role played by the expansion of bank credit-money and low interest rates in fueling the expansion. In contrast, Hawtrey's theory is termed a pure monetary theory because the change in interest rate is seen as necessary and sufficient to cause the business cycle.

Joseph Schumpeter presented an example of a *real over-investment* theory in his *Business Cycles* (1939). Schumpeter argued that periods of rapid and sustained growth are caused by the introduction of "epoch making innovations" into the economy. Examples of such innovations would be, the steam railroad system, automobiles and highways, or the electrification of industry. Schumpeter believed that booms come to an end when excess capacity is built in the growth industries because other firms emulate the original entrepreneurs. Eventually, the excess capacity causes profits and profit expectations to decline. Combinations of five factors, according to Schumpeter, can fuel expansions: (1) new products, (2) new production technologies, (3) the opening of new markets, (4) the introduction of new sources of raw materials, and (5) a new organization of economic activity.

Entrepreneurs (or "new men" in Schumpeter's term) introduce these innovations in swarms, or clusters. Industrial innovations cluster because there are often many reinforcing linkages between them. For instance, a new product opens new markets and may generate demand for new sources of raw materials and encourage innovations in production technologies. Although the availability of credit to finance the necessary investment is also critical in his theory, Schumpeter stressed the non-monetary aspects of the innovation process, hence his theory is characterized as a "real" over-investment theory.

DISSENT IN PERIOD TWO: UNDER-CONSUMPTION AND INTERNAL CYCLE THEORIES

Neoclassical economics ruled supreme from the 1870s to the 1930s. There were, however, some significant dissenters. John Maynard Keynes built upon the dissenters, writing to change business cycle theory forever.

JOHN HOBSON. A dissenting British economist, John Hobson (1858–1940), developed a modern version of *under-consumption* theory which he set forth in a series of books including *Imperialism: A Study* (1902), *The Economics of Distribution* (1900), and *The Economics of Unemployment* (1922). Hobson's books were widely read and influenced a great many economists, including both V. I. Lenin and J. M. Keynes. For Hobson, the tendency toward depression was the result of the very unequal distribution of income in favor of those with property income. Property income included interest, profits, and rents. According to Hobson, the propensity to save out of higher income is greater than out of lower incomes. Therefore, the shift toward inequality, which always results from economic development, leads to over-saving, or under-consumption. The lack of consumer demand leads to depression.

WESLEY MITCHELL. There is an amazing degree of agreement from economists over the whole spectrum of opinion that Wesley Mitchell (1890–1948) was the greatest pioneer of business cycle research in the United States. He set up the National Bureau of Economic Research (NBER) and was the inspiration for a myriad of empirical studies and the technique of national income accounting. He described the whole history and evolution of business cycles, showing that the modern type of cycle was not found in prior societies but exists only in private enterprise, industrialized economies which use a monetary system, as described in

Chapter 2. Mitchell also set up a method of measuring the business cycle (see Chapter 3), which came to be known as the NBER method, used throughout this book. His famous definition of the business cycle (given in Chapter 2) clearly defines an endogenous or internal process within the private enterprise system.

CONCLUSIONS

Two contradictory visions of private enterprise economies underlie business cycle theory. One stresses the stability of such private enterprise economies and sees recessions as aberrations. The other view sees private enterprise economies as inherently unstable and recessions as inevitable aspects of such economies.

Four periods in the evolution of cycle theory can be distinguished: (1) classical political economy which believed in Say's law; (2) the rise of neo-classical economics from 1870 until 1930; (3) the Keynesian revolution from the 1930s until the 1970s; and (4) modern business cycle theory. The first two periods were covered in this chapter.

The classical economists believed in Say's law and saw the private enterprise economy as a self-adjusting economy, with competition prevailing as the mechanism leading to equilibrium. There were important dissenting views by Thomas Malthus and Karl Marx, both of whom disagreed with Say's law and discerned a more unstable economy.

The neoclassical economists followed the classical economists in accepting Say's law and the vision of a stable economy achieved by competition. They spelled out these arguments in a rigorous technical fashion, examining separately the labor market, the product market, and the money market, as explained in Chapter 1. They also formulated cycle theories that accepted Say's law, including theories of shocks from monetary institutions and shocks from technological changes. Two important dissenters were John Hobson, who formulated the under-consumptionist theory, and Wesley Mitchell, who described the internal dynamics of an endogenous business cycle in great detail.

KEY TERMS AND CONCEPTS

Say's law of markets	**Karl Marx**	**monetary over-investment theories**
quantity theory of money	**Wesley Mitchell**	
classical and neoclassical economics	**under-consumptionists**	

CHAPTER 9

Business Cycle Theories After Keynes

There had been many dissenters against Say's law in the classical and neo-classical periods, including Malthus, Marx, Hobson, and Mitchell. None of them, however, were able to change the opinions of the (then) mainstream economists.

PERIOD THREE: THE KEYNESIAN REVOLUTION

It was left to John Maynard Keynes to make a clear break within mainstream economics, with the traditional belief in a stable, always expanding economy. Keynes explicitly attacked two central macroeconomic doctrines of traditional economics: Say's law and the quantity theory of money. In doing so, he was very much influenced by the work of Wicksell, Hawtrey, Hobson, Mitchell, Hayek, and his contemporary, Dennis Robertson. Keynes had also read Marx's works but had found him tedious. Although influenced by past theory, Keynes made a revolutionary change in theory. Keynes stressed his radical break with past mainstream theory: "What is it that makes the cleavage which divides us? On the one side are those who believe that the economic system is, in the long run, a self-adjusting system though with creaks and groans and jerks, outside interference and mistakes . . . On the other side of the gulf are those who reject the idea that the existing system is, in any significant sense, self-adjusting" (quoted in Mirowski 1985, 46). Keynes made a successful revolution, partly because he spoke in terms that could communicate with his mainstream colleagues and partly because of the enormous shock of the Great Depression, which convinced economists that some change was necessary.

Keynes' theory stresses the role of money, interest rates, and uncertainty regarding profitability because these factors determine the rate of investment demand. The title of Keynes' best known work is *The General Theory of Employment, Interest and Money* (1936). For Keynes, the problem is not too much investment, but rather too little investment. Thus, his theory falls into its own category, distinguishable from its over-investment predecessors. While it shares with under-consumptionist theories the insight that depressions can be caused by insufficient demand, it differs in arguing that increased investment can offset and even increase low levels of consumption demand. Keynes' views on the business cycle are found in Chapter 22 of the *General Theory*, "Notes on the Trade Cycle," where he explicitly contrasts his views with both the over-investment and under-consumptionist schools. Chapter 18, "The General Theory Restated," presents a succinct version of the theory's essentials.

Keynes' views on the business cycle are extensions of his larger, general theory of the determination of output and employment. Keynes explains how and why economies can plunge into severe depressions and remain there indefinitely. He demonstrates how this can happen in spite of the falling prices, wages and interest rates, which the orthodox tradition argued should return the economy to a full employment equilibrium rapidly (according to Say's law).

The general theory may be summarized as follows: (1) an economy may be in an equilibrium at levels of output below the level which results from full employment of the labor force. The economy might remain in a depression indefinitely. (2) The actual level of output and employment at equilibrium is determined by firms' production plans, which are themselves determined by the expected level of aggregate effective demand for goods and services. (3) Aggregate demand is independent of the current level of output and income. Expenditures in excess of current income may be financed by credit creation. Money may be held, or hoarded, for speculative reasons. Note that this point specifically challenges Say's law. (4) Investment expenditures are unstable. When investment fluctuates, it causes larger, multiplied fluctuations in overall aggregate demand. (5) Investment is determined by two factors. It is affected by the current level of interest rates on bonds, which firms issue to finance investment. But it is also influenced by the expected profit rate on new capital goods, which Keynes termed the "marginal efficiency of capital". (6) Changes in either the level of interest rates or profit expectations result in changes in investment, aggregate demand, output and employment.

Keynes stressed a decline in profit expectations as the most important variable that pushes the economy into crisis and recession. This variable encompasses the whole economic outlook. Keynes argued that profit expectations usually decline for several reasons: (1) The stock of capital increases throughout the expansion, so that the threat of excess capacity increases as expansions mature. (2) Profits in some sectors of the economy inevitably begin to fall, so some firms' expectations of profit are disappointed. Firms interpreted this as perhaps foretelling a general falling off in profits. (3) Current costs of production (especially for new fixed capital) are high and rising. (4) "Doubt (regarding future conditions) spreads rapidly . . ." throughout the business community. As profit expectations fall, so does investment, and the economy rapidly moves into the cumulative avalanche of recession or depression. The crisis is usually exacerbated by a rapid increase in interest rates as pessimism spreads throughout financial markets, resulting in massive selling off of bonds and other securities.

The rapid shift in expectations regarding profits and asset prices thus causes the crisis and the recession itself. Its duration and severity are largely determined by (1) the durability of the capital stock in place and how long before it must be replaced physically, (2) the time necessary to deplete inventories, and (3) what happens to government expenditures, taxes, and monetary policy. Keynes argued that recessions could be avoided by keeping interest rates low and by keeping public expenditures high enough so that aggregate effective demand was consistent with full employment.

In arguing against Say's law, Keynes observed that even if wages were flexible, so that any increase in unemployment rapidly resulted in falling wages, this might exacerbate the recession rather than end it. Falling wages would reduce employees' purchasing power and consumption expenditures. This reduction in demand would increase the objective reasons for business pessimism. Lower demand meant falling prices for commodities, which would further reduce profits and adversely affect business confidence.

Michal Kalecki (1899–1970), a somewhat younger contemporary of Keynes, developed a business cycle theory quite similar to Keynes's in several respects. It also emphasized profits, investment, and profit expectations in causing fluctuations. Kalecki agreed with Keynes that government economic policy could be used to stabilize private enterprise economies. His work will be discussed below in the context of modern cycle theory. Kalecki's theory first appeared in "Business Cycles and Inflation" (1932), and "An Essay on Business Cycle Theory" (1933). Malcolm Sawyer's *The Economics of Michal Kalecki* (1985b) offers a good introduction to the work of this excellent economist.

THE DOMINANCE OF KEYNESIAN ECONOMICS

The early mainstream Keynesian analysis became the new orthodox view in the first decades of the post-World War II era. This version of Keynes' approach is variously referred to as standard textbook Keynesianism, or ISLM Keynesian, or neo-Keynesian, although Joan Robinson called it "bastard" Keynesian because she felt that it distorted Keynes.

Business cycle theory in the 1940s, 1950s, and 1960s was dominated by the standard Keynesian approach. The first generation of Keynesians, such as the Americans, Alvin Hansen, Paul Samuelson, Lawrence Klein, and the Oxford economist, J. R. Hicks (all Noble Laureates), attempted to translate and extend Keynes' rather informal views on the cycle. Their models retained Keynes' emphasis on the instability of the economy, the importance of aggregate demand, and vital role of government spending components in determining output and employment. They also discussed monetary factors as influencing demand. They also assumed, perhaps misrepresenting Keynes a bit, that prices and wages were fixed in the short run. Keynes' own view was that these variables were sticky, or less than perfectly flexible downwards, but not fixed. All of the standard Keynesian theories implied the necessity for government intervention to stabilize the economy.

An early example is Paul Samuelson's *multiplier-accelerator model* (1939). The multiplier-accelerator model is discussed in great detail in the next chapter.

PERIOD FOUR: THE COUNTER-REVOLUTION AGAINST KEYNESIAN ECONOMICS

The policy proposals implicit and explicit in a Keynesian view of the economy are disturbing to many conservative economists. If the economy is dangerously unstable, and if the cause of the instability is inevitable fluctuations in private investment, changes in government spending and taxing might be necessary and sufficient to avoid recessions, depressions, and inflationary booms. Some versions of activist Keynesian theories advocate a counter cyclical monetary policy to smooth interest-rate fluctuations and to stimulate investment. These policies imply a large, powerful, and interventionist state. This view was anathema to conservative free market economists. These philosophical and ideological concerns, coupled with the apparent shortcomings of attempts at Keynesian policy strategies in dealing with inflation and unemployment in the late 1960s and 1970s, led to a counter revolution in academic economics, and especially within the field of business cycle theory. Several new versions of classical economics were developed. In rough chronological order of appearance they were monetarism, rational expectations, and real business cycle theory, all of which might be termed New Classical theories.

These theories incorporate the classical vision of the economy as stable and tending toward full employment. The New Classical economists redefined full employment as a natural rate of unemployment, which is characterized by both high employment and price stability. They retain the classical prejudice against government intervention in the economy. Business cycles are seen as caused by external shocks to the economy, technological change, or well-intentioned but misguided attempts by the government to intervene in the economy. They are based upon the fundamental behavioral premise of neoclassical economics: utility maximizing by rational economic agents within a competitive economic environment. This assumption leads to an argument that markets for goods and resources should reach equilibrium under competitive economies, that is, prices should adjust until supply and demand are equal.

NEW CLASSICAL DEFENSES OF SAY'S LAW

Economic contractions were very weak after the Second World War, so growth and prosperity were dominant in the public perception. Keynesian economics ruled the economic outlook through the 1960s. In the 1970s, however, inflation reared its ugly head and Keynesian economics seemed unable to end it. The opponents of Keynesianism grew stronger. They claimed that government intervention, supported by Keynesian theory, was the problem, causing both inflation and stagnation.

The new view may be called a New Classical school, defined most broadly to include most monetarists, rational expectations theories, and the real business cycle theory (all explained in detail in Part 3). The New Classical school, which was dominant in the 1980s, claims that the economic system reacts to outside shocks by self-adjusting back to a full employment level. It follows that a shock may cause some brief, temporary unemployment, but most of the unemployment is voluntarily, chosen by workers in a system that tends toward full employment. This view was reflected in the non-interference policies of the Reagan and Bush administrations.

The heart of the New Classical view was that the U.S. economy is basically competitive, with monopoly power fairly small in its effect. The New Classical economists argued that all markets in a competitive economy eventually clear. They reach equilibrium. This includes the labor market, except when government interferes. Workers sometimes quit jobs with the mistaken idea that better wages are available elsewhere. But workers could always get work at the going wage in the competitive labor market if they wished to do so. Thus, except for government or union interference, all unemployment is voluntary. For example, the New Classical economist, Robert Lucas, writes that: "To explain why people allocate time to . . . unemployment we need to know why they prefer it to all other activities" (1986, 38).

The New Classical economists attempted to go back to the foundations of economic theory. They argued that the Keynesians merely talked about aggregate concepts, such as consumer demand. They contended that one cannot understand any aggregate, macroeconomic theory without examining its microeconomic foundations. So, in their opinion, aggregate consumer demand must be explained in terms of the theory of individual consumer demand. They thus attempted a counter-revolution against the aggregate economics that had been established by John Maynard Keynes.

MONETARISM

In the first wave of the counter-revolution, *monetarism* was developed over a period from the middle 1950s through the 1970s as a dissent against the Keynesian approach. The dean of the school is Milton Friedman, who taught at the University of Chicago during this period. Monetarism is based upon a restatement of the quantity theory of money. As in classical economics, money is seen as neutral in the long run, but capable of influencing the level of output and employment in the short run. The monetarists begin their attack on Keynesian economies by arguing that fiscal policy cannot change the level of overall aggregate demand. An increase in government expenditures, financed by increased taxes, directly reduces private demand. Moreover, increased expenditures, financed by government borrowing, causes interest rates to rise and leads to the crowding out of private investment expenditures. Since, in their view, government expenditure by itself can not cause fluctuations in the economy, the monetarists focus on changes in monetary policy as the cause of business cycles.

Consider what happens to an economy in a high employment equilibrium when the money supply is increased. For simplicity, suppose a fleet of helicopters unexpectedly dropped money randomly across the territory. The delighted citizenry spends the money on additional goods and services. Prices are bid up and firms eagerly produce more, offering their labor forces higher money wages, if necessary. Workers interpret the higher money wages as equivalent to higher real wages and give up some leisure for the additional wages, anticipating a higher consumption level. Employment and output increase for a while.

Eventually, however, workers realize that they have been fooled. Because prices are rising, higher money wages are worth less in real terms than they had anticipated. When workers realize this, they demand higher money wages. Then the firms are forced to reduce the amount of labor they employ in the interest of profit maximizing. The economy eventually returns to the original real level of output and employment, although at higher prices. This level is, according to monetarism, the only equilibrium consistent with both profit maximizing by firms and utility maximizing by employees and consumers.

The point of the parable is that the monetary authority (the central bank or the treasury) cannot permanently improve the performance of the economy by printing money and delivering it by helicopters or any other way, unless the economy were originally in an equilibrium at less than full employment. The monetarists deny this latter possibility because there can be no equilibrium below full employment. Holding to Say's law, their interpretation of business cycles is that they have generally been caused by incorrect monetary policy. The central bank (the Federal Reserve) first causes inflation by over-expanding the money supply, then it reacts and tightens up on monetary policy, forcing the economy into a recession. If the central bank would stabilize the money supply's growth rate, the economy would tend automatically to grow at a fairly stable rate, with stable prices and high employment levels.

RATIONAL EXPECTATIONS

The adaptive expectations thesis says that economic agents adapt their inflationary expectations to changes in the money supply; so the economy reacts to money supply changes with a time lag. A more radical approach to the explanation of cycles was developed in the 1970s by Robert Barro, Robert Lucas, John Muth, and Thomas Sargent, founders of the *rational expectations school*. This theory also incorporates the monetarist assumption that the economy is basically stable (and holds true to Say's law), but criticizes the adaptive expectations argument. The focus is on the effects of changes in monetary policy on the economy. The rational expectations argument in brief is: (1) if economic agents are rational utility maximizers, they should use all available and useful information in making economic decisions. (2) Rational people should learn from past mistakes, and alter their behavior accordingly. (3) Lucas, Sargent, and their colleagues argue that under these conditions, an increase in the money supply would logically have *no* effect on the economy other than to produce inflation.

Consider the behavior of our citizens confronting a second helicopter drop of money. Once more they gleefully rush to the shops, restaurants, and bars, spending and consuming. Once more prices are bid up and once more firms attempt to hire additional labor services. But would the workers be fooled again? Wouldn't they remember the increase in inflation after the last episode of manna from heaven? Wouldn't they demand higher wages instantly? In fact, if the helicopters began appearing regularly, the workers might even demand higher wages as soon as they heard them overhead, anticipating the inflation which their air drops of money would eventually bring.

Translating this parable into a slightly more realistic model, the rational expectations model argues that only if monetary policy changes are totally unanticipated "surprises," would rational economic actors (employees and lenders) be fooled into offering their services at higher nominal (but not real) rewards. Thus, the only plausible remaining cause of economic fluctuations are surprises in monetary policy. Notice that, in this theory, the private enterprise system itself cannot generate instability and cycles because Say's law is assumed.

REAL BUSINESS CYCLE THEORY

These views became very influential among academic economists, forming part of a new dominant orthodoxy in the 1980s, and are the theoretical starting point for *real business cycle* theory, which presents formal models incorporating these assumptions. Real business cycle theory demonstrates how technological change and other external shocks to the economy can generate behavior in economic models which approximate reality.

The leading figures in the development of this approach are Robert King, Charles Plosser, and Edward Prescott. The best introduction is by Plosser (1989). The theory may be summarized as follows: (1) economic agents maximize through choices, and they are rational in the sense described above. (2) Under competitive conditions, prices will adjust so as to clear markets rapidly. Therefore, as a first approximation assume that markets and the macroeconomy are normally in equilibrium. (3) If the rational expectations hypothesis that monetary and fiscal policy can not alter the real dimensions of the economy is accepted, only technical shocks are likely disturbances which can cause economic fluctuations. Technological shocks equate to changes in the prices of important imported commodities such as petroleum, and shifts in preferences concerning goods and leisure. All of these may affect the supply of resources, goods, and services.

These New Classical theories present critiques of Keynes and Keynesian cycle theory which operate on several levels. First, on the abstract, technical level they argue that the Keynesian approach violates the fundamental neoclassical microeconomic behavioral assumptions of maximizing behavior by rational economic agents. This is known as the Lucas critique of Keynesian micro-foundations based on the work of Robert Lucas (1986). The logically deducible result of beginning with the neoclassical behavioral assumption is that markets should clear and equilibrium would result.

Thus, according to the New Classical theory, business cycle theory should give an account of how economic fluctuations are produced in an economy in which markets are continuously clearing. Or it must abandon the assumption of rational maximizing behavior. On the levels of economic philosophy, political preference, and ideology, these economists are disturbed by the interventionist implications of Keynesian theory. They are disturbed by the larger implications of such intervention for the power of the government in the economy. Their vision of the economy as stable leads them to begin by assuming that government intervention is unnecessary and unwise, and they then attempt to develop economic theory in a direction so as to demonstrate support for their views. Real business cycle theory is explained very clearly by Charles Plosser (1989), while Gregory Mankiw (1989) provides a clear critique of the real business cycle theory.

NEW KEYNESIAN THEORY

Although very influential, the New Classical theories have not gone unchallenged within mainstream economics. One such challenge appears in the form of *new-Keynesianism*. See Gregory Mankiw (1990) for an excellent overview of the New Keynesian approach to macroeconomics; for a more detailed explanation see Mankiw and Romer (1991).

The new-Keynesians, like John Maynard Keynes, make use of the orthodox tools of equilibrium analysis, assumptions about individual psychology, and assumptions about rational expectations and rational maximization. But, while these micro-foundations are similar to the whole tradition of mainstream economics, their analysis and conclusions differ drastically from the New Classical economists.

The new-Keynesians find problems of information stoppages and conflicts over incentives in production that produce somewhat rigid wages, rigid interest rates, and even rigid prices, at levels that prevent full-employment equilibrium. In other words, like Keynes, they find that equilibrium will be reached at a point which is below full employment, so there will be involuntary unemployment. They differ from Keynes and all earlier Keynesians, however, in the types of arguments they use. These arguments about the problems of information flow, as well as the conflicts in the workplace, mark them as being on the frontiers of economic knowledge in the 1990s. The new-Keynesians thus supply rigorous micro-foundations to reach the old Keynesian conclusion that unemployment is caused by structural rigidities in wages and prices (see Mankiw and Romer 1991).

The new-Keynesians make use of the traditional micro-foundations approach, including the usual psychological assumptions, maximization process, and equilibrium analysis. On that basis, they construct models in which markets do not clear for a variety of reasons which are firmly grounded in optomizing behavior by firms and employees. For instance, firms may not choose to lower wages paid to their labor force, even when demand falls, because they fear that at lower wages employees will work less efficiently, thus increasing their costs of production even at the lower money wage rates. This is called the *efficiency wage* theory.

Another problem may be that prices are sticky downward because the cost of changing prices is high. Suppose that it costs a lot of money to advertise each price change, so there is an information cost to changing prices. In this case, it may maximize profits to keep prices stable and suffer declines in sales, laying off production workers and reducing output to cut costs. The new-Keynesians also point to the ubiquity of long-term labor contracts as a reason for sticky wages. They point to monopoly power in most markets for goods and services as a reason for sticky prices. Given these institutional realities of actual economies, price rigidity, wage rigidity, and markets not clearing may in fact represent maximizing behavior by rational economic agents. Thus, the new-Keynesians have used entirely new arguments to reach the Keynesian conclusion that Say's law is incorrect in modern private enterprise, that equilibrium may be reached at a point below full employment, and that involuntary unemployment may, therefore, exist.

DISSENT IN PERIOD FOUR: POST-KEYNESIAN, INSTITUTIONALIST, AND MARXIST THEORIES

An even more fundamental challenge to the orthodox new versions of classical economics appears in the forms of post-Keynesian, Institutionalist, and neo-Marxist business cycle theory. The post-Keynesian economists stress the importance and pervasiveness of instability in financial markets and financial relations in explaining business cycles. The Marxists stress the role of profits in determining investment, the inevitability that profits will decline in expansions, and the importance of investment in determining the level of economic activity. Both groups of theories retain the emphasis on instability and the inevitability of recessions found in the work of Keynes and Marx. Post-Keynesians emphasize the necessity for government intervention in stabilizing the private enterprise economy. The post-Keynesians tend to favor counter-cyclical monetary and fiscal policies, and in some circumstances, wage and price controls, to reduce instability and to prevent inflation and unemployment. The Marxists favor an end to the private enterprise (or capitalist) economy and its replacement by a democratic socialist economy.

The works of Hyman Minsky (1986) and Martin Wolfson (1986) offer the most complete versions of post-Keynesian views on the business cycle. Minsky argues that recessions are inevitable in private enterprise economies, that they are largely due to changes in the financial structure of corporations, and that government intervention can prevent recessions from turning into deep depressions. Wolfson bases his theory on Minsky's argument that financial crises are important recession-enhancing phenomena, but sees a decline in corporate profits as necessary to trigger the onset of recession and financial crisis.

The Minsky-Wolfson post-Keynesian model has these characteristics. First, it emphasizes the importance of endogenous (internal) processes. These endogenous processes in expansionary periods include rising profits and profit expectations, the perceived need for capacity-enhancing investment, and speculation that asset prices will continue to rise and that inflation rates will remain high. These processes lead nonfinancial businesses to increase their borrowing in expansions and encourage banks and other financial institutions to lend. Second, the same processes lead to a reduction in liquidity during expansions. Liquidity means having cash available and not having a mountain of debt. Less liquidity means that firms hold less cash assets.

Third, at some point interest rates begin to rise dramatically, discouraging investment. Higher interest rates have a negative impact because the higher rates of interest increase the cost of new capital, and because the higher rates of interest reduce the present value of all types of existing assets. The sharp rise in interest rates either precipitates a financial crisis or is the result of one. The interest rate increases can be caused by tight monetary policy intended to reduce inflationary pressure by a sharp increase in the demand for funds by firms. Higher interest rates may also happen because pessimism sweeps financial markets. In any case, the higher interest rates mean that real investment by business falls and the economy begins to move into recession. The likelihood of declining investment and recession is enhanced if profits are low or declining when the interest rates rise.

If government expenditures increase dramatically and if the central bank floods the financial system with liquidity, then it is possible that a cumulative avalanche into a deep depression can be avoided. The financial instability models do not give a complete account of the business cycle, primarily because they don't explain the factors which trigger the decline in profitability.

Institutionalist theories largely agree with post-Keynesians in the business cycle area. They emphasize institutional factors rather than abstract psychological assumptions. Wesley Mitchell's work is the best example of Institutionalist views, but the striking work of John Kenneth Galbraith is also Institutionalist.

Writers in the Marxian tradition, such as Broddy and Crotty (1975), Kalecki (1968, first published in 1935), Shaikh (1978), and Weisskopf (1978, 1979), focus on explaining the behavior of profits over the cycle. Their main hypothesis can be summarized as follows: (1) investment is the key to explaining cycles. (2) Investment is determined by expected profits, and expected profits by current profits. (3) Profits are a function of aggregate demand as well as a function of cost factors. The neo-Marxists have also agreed with the post-Keynesians on the importance of financial factors.

CONCLUSIONS

From the 1930s to the 1960s, the theories of John Maynard Keynes dominated business cycle theory. His followers in the 1950s, who may be called neo-Keynesians, developed technical arguments to criticize Say's law in terms of the product market, the labor market, and the money market, mostly emphasizing rigidities that prevent adjustment to full employment equilibrium. Dissenting views developed on the right with Milton Friedman and the monetarists and on the left with the post-Keynesians, who emphasized that the economy often does not self-adjust.

Contemporary work on cycles can be categorized into two groups: (1) the various versions of New Classical economics (monetarism, rational expectations and real business cycle theory), which have attempted to revitalize Say's law, and (2) the dissenting work of new-Keynesians, neo-Marxists, Institutionalists, and post-Keynesian economists, all of who attack Say's law and the notion that the economy self-adjusts to equilibrium.

KEY TERMS AND CONCEPTS

New Classical economics	**monetarists**	**Milton Friedman**
neo-Keynesian, new-Keynesian and post-Keynesian economics		

CHAPTER 10

The Multiplier-Accelerator Model

The multiplier and the accelerator relationships each offer brilliant insights into cyclical behavior and formal cycle theory. Paul Samuelson's synthesis of these two relationships into one theory in 1939 was an outstanding achievement. This chapter examines each of these contributions, as well as their implications and limitations. Their limitations are to some extent the limitations of all cycle models. Their original statement is very simple, clear, and forceful, but omits many of the complex aspects of economic reality. Each limitation has been overcome in more complex and realistic models but the end result is neither clear nor very forceful. Simplicity versus reality is the trade-off in all such models.

THE ACCELERATOR RELATION

The theory of investment called the accelerator relation states that: investment demand is derived from the change in output demanded. The accelerator relation has a long history in economics; it has played a major role in cycle theories by Albert Aftalion, Mentor Bickerdike, T. N. Carver, A. C. Pigou, J. M. Clarke, Roy Harrod, Alvin Hansen, Paul Samuelson, and John Hicks. (For the early history of the accelerator, see Haberler 1960, Chapter 3.)

The basis for this theory is the truism that, in the long run, if technology remains unchanged then increased demand can only be met by more capital investment. In fact, if there is an unchanging technology, the ratio of capital (plant and equipment) required to output produced must be constant. That constant is called the accelerator. The accelerator coefficient may be defined as the ratio of new investment to the change in output.

What is the systematic reasoning that links investment to a change in output? With a given technology, a factory needs a certain amount of capital equipment to produce a given output. Assume there is an increase in demand for a factory owner's products, so the owner wishes to increase the factory's output beyond the present capacity. If the technology stays the same, capital equipment must be increased in proportion to the increase in output demanded. Therefore, the factory owner's demand for new capital (net investment) bears a precise relationship to the desired increase in output.

This reasoning may be extended to the determination of net investment in the whole economy. At a given level of technology, aggregate output can be increased only in proportion to a certain increase in aggregate capital. Therefore, the demand for an increase in capital (net investment) is in some fixed ratio to the decision to increase output. That ratio is, by definition, the accelerator. Thus, in general, we may say that:

$$change\ in\ capital = accelerator \times change\ in\ output \qquad (10.1)$$

Capital is defined as the value of productive facilities. But the expenditure to increase productive facilities is defined as *net investment*. Thus:

$$net\ investment = accelerator \times change\ in\ output \qquad (10.2)$$

Similarly, we could say: the accelerator equals net investment divided by the change in output. It should be remembered that this theory claims that the accelerator ratio is some precise and roughly constant number.

In the United States, yearly output runs at about one-third of the value of all capital. Therefore, it may be assumed that roughly three units of new capital are required to add one unit to national product. The accelerator coefficient would then be roughly equal to 3.

As an example, the output of shoes may be related to the net investment in new shoe machinery. According to the accelerator theory, more demand for shoes will eventually mean more demand for new shoe machinery. But if demand for shoes remains the same, there should be no further investment in shoe machinery. If demand for shoes actually declines, then the accelerator theory would predict negative net investment. Negative net investment (or disinvestment) occurs when old shoe machinery is allowed to wear out but is not replaced.

If the value of the accelerator is known, then exactly how much new investment will result from any increase in desired output can be predicted. Table 10.1 assumes some arbitrary changes in the output of shoes to see what will happen to net investment in shoe machinery at some fixed accelerator. In the table, it is assumed that the accelerator is fixed at three.

TABLE 10.1

ACCELERATOR PRINCIPLE

Time Period	Demand for Shoes	Change in Demand for Shoes	Shoe Machinery	Change in Shoe Machinery
1	$100		$300	
1 to 2		$10		$30
2	$110		$330	
2 to 3		$20		$60
3	$130		$390	
3 to 4		$5		$15
4	$135		$405	
4 to 5		$0		$0
5	$135		$405	
5 to 6		−$5		−$15
6	$130		$390	
6 to 7		−$20		−$60
7	$110		$330	
7 to 8		−$10		−$30
8	$100		$300	
8 to 9		$0		$0
9	$100		$300	
9 to 10		$10		$30
10	$110		$330	

NOTE: The accelerator is assumed to be three, that is, $3 of new capital is required to produce $1 of new output per year. Figures for output of shoe machinery are chosen arbitrarily.

Although the movements of shoe production are arbitrarily chosen, the rest of the table follows by assumption and definition. Thus, from period 1 to period 2, it is assumed that shoe production rises by $10. But because $3 of capital is required to produce $1 of output, capital must rise by $30, that is, net investment is predicted to be $30. In the next interval, a larger rise of $20 in shoe production causes a level of $60 of net investment. On the other hand, from period 3 to 4, a smaller rise of $5 in shoe production causes a decline in net investment to only $15. In the next interval, there is no change in shoe production, so there is no net investment. Finally, in the interval from period 5 to 6, shoe production declines by $5, so net investment in shoe machinery is a negative $15, or $15 of disinvestment. Throughout, we note that the level of net investment (the change in capital) is related to the *change* in output.

The fact that the accelerator theory predicts net investment to be a function of the change in output demanded, has attracted the attention of many cycle theorists. Suppose that demand grows rapidly, which causes a certain high level of investment. If the rate of growth of demand slows, then the level of investment must decline. But, an actual decline in investment will cause a recession or depression. The decline in investment causes a recession because less investment means less employment, which means less demand, and so forth. Thus, a theory may explain business cycle downturns, assuming the accelerator principle is correct, merely by showing why aggregate demand will slow its growth. Using the accelerator, it is not necessary to prove that aggregate demand will decline before investment declines.

LIMITATIONS AND QUALIFICATIONS OF THE ACCELERATOR

The investment process is very complex, so the accelerator has many qualifications and limitations. First the accelerator does not operate instantaneously, but with a time lag. Suppose demand increases from one period to the next. There will be a time lag before new investment ensues, for several reasons. It takes time for the information to be known and recorded. It takes time for concrete plans to be made for new investment. It takes time to borrow new financial capital. It takes time to actually spend money to build a new factory. For all these reasons, most careful theories assume a time lag between the change in demand and the new investment.

In formal terms, suppose that v is called the accelerator coefficient, suppose that I is investment, and Y is the amount of aggregate output demanded. In order to show the time lag, let t be the present time period, let $t-1$ be the previous time period, and so forth. The change in output demanded affecting this period's investment occurred from $t-1$ to $t-2$. Then:

Investment = accelerator × change in output, lagged

or

$$I_t = v\,(Y_{t-1} - Y_{t-2})\tag{10.3}$$

Equation 10.3 shows a time lag of one period from the change in output demanded to the change in investment. In reality, however, the investment response to changes in output demanded exhibits a changing time lag over the cycle, so no fixed time lag is really appropriate.

Second, Samuelson (1939) defined output demanded to mean only consumer demand. Consumer demand is a very important part of aggregate demand, but it is not the only demand to generate new investment. If an entrepreneur owning a machine factory wishes to increase the output of machines, then he or she must invest in new equipment to produce more machines. Therefore, the more general formulation is that the accelerator measures the ratio of new investment to the change in aggregate demand, not just the change in consumer demand.

Third, the accelerator coefficient itself changes over the cycle because of changes in business expectations as to profits. There is no simple technical relationship between demand and investment in the short-run time horizon of the business cycle, but a changing relationship based on changing expectations.

Fourth, the unused capacity at the beginning of expansion would first have to be put into use before an entrepreneur would add to it. For example, if half a factory is idle, no entrepreneur will rush out to build a new factory just because demand rises a little. Therefore, the accelerator will be lower in the recovery phase of the cycle than at the cycle peak.

Fifth, at the peak of profitability, entrepreneurs may desire rapid expansion. The desire is based not on just current demand, but also on speculative expectations. Expansion of investment, however, has a physical limit, which is the total capacity of the economy to produce more plant and equipment. Thus, there is a ceiling to the investment predicted by the accelerator (see the detailed discussion in Hicks 1950).

Sixth, in a severe depression, all businesses may wish to sell their excess capital. One business can sell excess capital to another. In the aggregate, however, the only way to reduce capital is to let it depreciate and not be replaced. So, the limit of reduction of capital is the amount of wear and tear or depreciation suffered in that time period. In other words, the level of depreciation in a given year sets a maximum limit to the amount of disinvestment in that year. Thus, there is a floor to the disinvestment predicted by the accelerator (see the detailed discussion in Hicks 1950).

Seventh, the simplest accelerator investment function deals only with demand and omits the cost variables. In particular, it omits rising labor costs, rising raw material costs, and rising costs of borrowing. If all of these variables are considered seriously, then it is necessary to return to a function based on profits. Only profits reflects both demand and costs. Other variables determining net investment are the degree of monopoly, the amount of government activity, and the amount of net exports, each of which are explored in later chapters.

Some economists have used more and more sophisticated and complex accelerator functions to meet some of these criticisms (see, e.g., Jorgenson 1971). But other studies have questioned the accelerator theory's validity and emphasized the need to consider other variables, such as monetary variables (see, e.g., Gordon and Veitch 1986) or profits (see Eisner 1978). One may conclude that the accelerator is a powerful tool, but requires many qualifications as well as the consideration of other variables if a complete investment function is desired.

THE INVESTMENT MULTIPLIER

Some economists believe that Keynes' most important conceptual contribution to macroeconomics is the consumption function. From this point, the important analytic tool to come out of the Keynesian analysis of consumption is that the multiplier can be derived. The multiplier expresses the relation between the initial increase (or decrease) in one of the components of aggregate demand and the total increase (or decrease) in national income caused by it. The initial spending change may come from any one of the components of aggregate demand, such as investment, or government spending, or net exports. For example, the *investment multiplier* is the ratio of additional income to new investment. The *government multiplier* is the ratio of additional national income to new government spending.

Obviously, it is vital that government policy-makers know how any change in spending, whether in direct government spending or in private investment encouraged by government, will affect national income. The question as to how government spending will affect national income first received considerable attention during the 1930s, when New Deal politicians in the United States debated ways of combating the depression. In England in that period, these questions were debated by a group at Cambridge, including Keynes. The multiplier concept was first rigorously worked out by R. F. Kahn (1931), then a student of Keynes.

In precise terms, the investment multiplier may be defined as the ratio of change in national income to change in investment. The multiplier, however, is more than a definition—a causal relationship running from change in investment spending to change in income is often alleged. Change in investment usually causes a larger change in aggregate income because the money spent on investment is only the direct effect. Often more important is the indirect effect that the new income will be respent by its recipients for additional consumption—this is the main point of the multiplier.

Assume that during a period with some unemployment a firm decides to construct a large new factory. This sudden increase in investment spending will increase the incomes of the contractors who supply the necessary machinery and materials and will provide jobs and wages for previously unemployed workers. Now assume that the initial increase in investment spending is $1000. The recipients of the $1000 of income from investment spending will immediately respend most of it for consumer goods, which will result in new income for business people and employees in the consumer goods industries. These income recipients will, in turn, spend much of their new income on more consumer goods. Exactly how much additional spending occurs in each round will depend on the marginal propensity to consume by the income recipients. But according to this theory, it is already clear that any additional consumer spending must mean that the total income generated will be something more than the original $1000 of investment spending.

The easiest way to see how the multiplier is supposed to work is to study a numerical example. In the example in Table 10.2, only some initial change in investment and a certain marginal propensity to consume need be assumed. One thousand dollars of investment becomes $1000 of income when it is spent. It is assumed that 80 percent, or $800, of that income is respent on consumption, which means another $800 of national income going to other individuals. Individuals will then again spend 80 percent, or $640 of that income, and so it goes. In the first round, 20 percent, or $200, leaks out into saving, and in the second round, 20 percent of the remaining income, or $160, leaks out into saving. The process ends only when the last $1 of the increased income is saved. At that point, the whole $1000 of investment has been saved, but there already have been many rounds of consumption spending in between. In this example, the total of all the rounds of consumption spending (or respending) will eventually approach $4000. Therefore, national income, which includes the initial $1000 plus the $4000 additional spending, will approach a level that is $5000 higher than before.

The new investment may be pictured as a one-time expenditure or it may be conceptualized as a permanent increase in the level of investment. If the $1000 increase in investment is considered as a one-time injection of new spending, then the totals at the bottom of Table 10.2 represent only temporary additions to consumption, saving, and national income. After these one-time increases are realized, however, total spending will eventually return to its original level. But if the $1000

TABLE 10.2
MULTIPLIER RELATION

Time period	Additional Investment	Additional National income	Additional Consumption	Additional Saving
1	$1000	$1000		
2	$0	$800	$800	$200
3	$0	$640	$640	$160
4	$0	$512	$512	$128
5	$0	$409	$409	$103
	.	.	.	.
	.	.	.	.
	.	.	.	.
Total at new equilibrium period	$1000	$5000	$4000	$1000

ASSUMPTIONS: Assume one-time investment of $1000. Assume marginal propensity to consume is .80. Assume the process continues until the additional income approaches $0.

increase is a new stepped-up rate of investment spending that continues throughout all subsequent periods, the totals represent the rise from the old lower levels to the new higher levels of spending flows, which will persist in each future period.

From this description of how the multiplier works, it should be clear that if less is saved out of each increment to income, then each increment to consumption spending will be larger. In other words, if the marginal propensity to consume rises, subsequent increases in consumption and income will be larger.

The multiplier formula is just a shortcut for finding where the process of Table 10.2 ends without repeating the calculation a great many times. The formula can be derived with only one crucial assumption. By definition, the investment multiplier is:

$$multiplier = change\ in\ income\ /\ change\ in\ investment \qquad (10.4)$$

The crucial assumption in the multiplier theory is that there is movement from one equilibrium to another equilibrium position. Therefore, at the end of the process, the theory assumes that the change in saving must equal the change in investment. Substituting saving for investment in equation 10.4, the result is:

$$multiplier = change\ in\ income\ /\ change\ in\ saving \qquad (10.5)$$

Furthermore, by simple mathematical manipulation:

$$multiplier = 1\ /\ (change\ in\ saving\ /\ change\ in\ income) \qquad (10.6)$$

But this ratio, the change in saving to the change in income is simply the marginal propensity to save (MPS). Therefore, the formula to remember is just:

$$multiplier = 1\ /\ MPS \qquad (10.7)$$

Notice that the marginal propensities to save (MPS) and consume (MPC) always add up to exactly 1.0, so MPS equals 1-MPC. Therefore, the multiplier can be expressed as:

$$multiplier = 1\ /\ (1-MPC) \qquad (10.8)$$

The theory says that total increase in income equals increase in investment times the multiplier. In the example in Table 10.2, the increase in investment is $1000. The marginal propensity to consume is 4/5, so the

MPS is 1/5. The multiplier must equal 1 divided by 1/5, which is 5. So it may be calculated that

$$\textit{total increase in income} = \$1000 \times 5 = \$5000 \qquad (10.9)$$

This demonstrates how the multiplier is used to find the end result of investment spending and many rounds of respending for consumption.

Of course, if the multiplier is reduced, then the investment spending has less effect. At one extreme, if the multiplier is just 1, the change in income is just equal to the change in investment. At the other extreme, if the multiplier approaches infinity, any small change in investment will cause an infinite change in income.

The value of the multiplier is controlled by the marginal propensity to consume (MPC). If MPC falls, so does the multiplier because less is respent out of each increase in income. If the MPC is only 1/2, then the multiplier is only 2. If the MPC is zero, everything is saved and there is no respending of the initial income, then the multiplier is 1, that is, the final result for national income just equals the initial investment. But if all income is immediately respent for consumption, which means that the MPC is 1, then the multiplier will be infinity if the process is instantaneous or if the process continues an infinite time.

QUALIFICATIONS AND LIMITATIONS OF THE MULTIPLIER

There are some obvious qualifications that must be kept in mind when the multiplier theory is used. First, it assumes that the economy is in equilibrium, and that saving always equals investment. This is certainly not true in the business cycle, since planned investment is usually greater than planned saving in expansions, while planned investment is usually less than planned saving in contractions.

Second, a time lag must be included because it takes a certain amount of time before income received is respent for consumption and still more time before the second, third, and later rounds of respending may occur. If the time lag happens to be more than one period, then a more complicated multiplier will be needed to get a realistic answer to the change in income for one year. If the time lag is variable, there is no easy answer.

Third, it has been assumed that MPC remains constant until the process is completed. In reality, MPC does change and is affected by many psychological and institutional factors. For example, the accumulated savings of war bonds in World War II greatly increased the propensity to consume in the immediate postwar years. Moreover, saving is not the only leakage from the income stream. Higher or lower taxes will also change MPC out of national income. Furthermore, if purchases of imports (such as

Volkswagens) increase, there will be a leakage from domestic consumer spending. Thus, the domestic MPC may change too often to permit accurate prediction of the multiplier for more than a few months in the future. This international leakage has become very important in the present period and it will be discussed in detail in Part 4.

Fourth, the multiplier formula assumes that investment will remain the same while consumption and national income are expanding rapidly. Obviously, the simple multiplier theory cannot be used if further changes in investment are to be considered. Yet the accelerator assures us that when aggregate income increases, there will be further increases in investment.

For all of these reasons, the conclusion is that the multiplier is a helpful explanatory device, but it cannot be relied on for an exact estimate. Various more realistic multiplier models can obtain better predictions, but they are also more complex and difficult to understand.

THE MULTIPLIER-ACCELERATOR MODEL

The simplest Keynesian model by Paul Samuelson (1939) is called the multiplier-accelerator model. There are just three relationships in this simple demand model.

First, *if there is equilibrium*, then total income or output (Y) will just equal aggregate demand. Leaving aside government demand and net export demand for the moment, the aggregate demand may be defined to be consumption demand (C) plus investment demand (I). Therefore, at each equilibrium point:

Output supplied = consumption + investment

$$Y_t = C_t + I_t \tag{10.10}$$

where t is a time period, such as one quarter. This equation shows what happens at each point where there is equilibrium—but, it assumes that there is disequilibrium between these points as supply adjusts to demand. Remember that Keynes rejected Say's law, which states that demand always adjusts to supply. Thus, this equation provides the contrary assertion; that supply will adjust to demand. If demand is below full employment, output will be below the full-employment level. The equation shows the path taken by demand at each point where supply has adjusted to it. That monetary equilibrium, however, may be below full employment and frequently is in Samuelson's model. In reality in the business cycle, during expansions demand tends to be above supply, while in contractions demand tends to be below supply.

Second, Samuelson adopts his consumption function from Keynes, who describes consumer behavior on the basis of the alleged psychological propensities of consumers. His assumption is that consumption rises and falls with income, but its usual behavior is to rise and fall more slowly than income. The simplest way to portray this Keynesian hypothesis is to assume that aggregate consumption is equal to some minimum level of consumption plus a constant proportion of the aggregate income. Since there is a time lag, it is assumed that consumption is equal to a constant plus the marginal propensity to consume times the aggregate income of the previous time period:

Consumption = constant + (MPC × income, lagged)

$$C_t = a + bY_{t-1} \tag{10.11}$$

where a and b are constants (as are all small letters used in equations in this chapter), and where $t-1$ is the previous time period.

In equation 10.11, the marginal propensity to consume is represented by the constant b. Although the MPC is assumed to be constant (which is an over-simplification), note that there is also assumed to be a minimum level of consumption, a, regardless of income. Therefore, as income rises in an expansion, consumption adds a constant percentage of income, but it is always added to the same constant minimum. Thus, the average propensity to consume (the ratio of all consumption to all income) must fall. Similarly, if income falls in a cyclical downturn, the minimum level becomes a larger part of consumption. Thus, the average propensity to consume rises in a business contraction. Clearly, this picture faithfully follows the psychological laws assumed by Keynes.

Because this consumption function is based on a constant MPC, it is easy to calculate the multiplier in this model. The multiplier equals $1 / (1 - MPC)$. Thus Samuelson's second equation builds the investment multiplier into the system. The multiplier works through this consumption function by controlling the rate of responding of income on consumption.

Third, Samuelson puts the accelerator principle into his model. He assumes that new investment is a function of the change in consumer demand, with a time lag. This relationship is explored later, but for now it may be assumed that new investment is a function of the change in aggregate output demanded (Y), not just consumer demand. Remembering that there is a time lag before the increase in output demanded affects new investment, the relationship is:

Investment = accelerator × (change in output, lagged)

$$I_t = v\,(Y_{t-1} - Y_{t-2}) \tag{10.12}$$

where v is a constant coefficient called the accelerator. As stated earlier, this relationship means that if the growth of output slows down, then investment will actually decline. In this model, the growth of output demanded does slow down because of the consumption function, as we shall see below.

Perhaps the easiest way to see how this model works is to examine a numerical example. Table 10.3 pictures the multiplier-accelerator model over time, showing how we can start from a few simple assumptions and then follow the path of the economy as it moves. The table assumes, arbitrarily, that national income is expanding from $996 billion in the first period to $1,000 billion in the second period. Starting with such an expansion, what happens next? The table assumes a consumption function (such as in equation 10.11) in which consumption is always equal to $96 billion plus 90 percent of the previous period's income. The $96 billion is the constant minimum level of consumption, arbitrarily chosen in this case. Finally, it is assumed that net investment is always just equal to the previous change in output demand. In other words, the form of investment is that of equation 10.12, but it is assumed that the accelerator just happens to equal one.

On these very simple assumptions, when income is at $1,000 billion, consumption in the next period will be $96 billion + 90 percent of $1,000

TABLE 10.3
EXAMPLE OF MULTIPLIER-ACCELERATOR MODEL

Time Period	Consumption	National Income	Net Investment
1		$996	
2		$1000	
3	$996	$1000	$ 4
4	996	996	0
5	992	988	−4
6	985	977	−8
7	975	965	−11
8	964	952	−12
9	953	940	−13
10	942	930	−12
11	933	923	−10
12	927	920	−7
13	928	925	−3
14	928	933	5
15	936	944	8
16	945	956	11
17	957	969	12
18	969	982	13
19	978	991	13
20	987	996	9
21	992	1000	8

ASSUMPTIONS: Income is assumed to be $996 in period 1 and $1000 in period 2. It is also assumed that the constant, *a*, or minimum level of consumption is $96. The marginal propensity to consume, *b*, is .90. The accelerator, *v*, is 1. All figures are in billions. Figures are not exact due to rounding.

billion, that is, $996 billion. On the investment side, when output rises from $996 to $1,000 billion, an accelerator equal to one predicts that the change (+$4 billion) will be equalled by new investment (+$4 billion). Since consumption is $996 billion and investment is $4 billion, the output supplied in the new monetary equilibrium must be $1,000 billion in period 3. These calculations can be repeated each period to obtain all the figures in the table. Notice that national income is constant from period 2 to 3, so net investment is zero in period 4. This causes a decline in national income and begins a recession phase. The recession phase continues for ten periods, then a new expansion begins as net investment again becomes positive.

HOW THE MULTIPLIER-ACCELERATOR MODEL WORKS

The model has been shown in equations and in a numerical example. Now it must be explained verbally in order to answer the four questions always asked of business cycle models. (1) What causes the cumulative process of expansion? (2) What causes the expansion to end and a downturn to begin? (3) What causes the cumulative process of contraction? (4) What causes the downturn to end and recovery to begin?

(1) **THE CUMULATIVE PROCESS OF EXPANSION.**   When expansion begins (as in period 1 of Table 10.3), what causes it to continue? The answer, of course, is the multiplier and the accelerator are acting together. A small increase in investment leads, through the multiplier effect of increased consumer spending, to a larger increase in national income. The increase in national income leads, through the accelerator, to a certain amount of new net investment. The new investment leads to more consumer spending, which leads to more national income, which leads to more investment, and so forth. This model does an excellent job of depicting the cumulative process of expansion.

(2) **CAUSES OF THE DOWNTURN.**   Why does a cumulative expansion ever lead to a downturn? As expansion goes on, the usual behavior of consumption dictates that the increases of consumption become less and less. Since consumption is by far the largest element of national income or output, this means a declining growth of output. The result, via the accelerator, is that sooner or later net investment must decline. This decline of net investment sets off a recession.

(3) **THE CUMULATIVE PROCESS OF DECLINE.**   Why does the decline in net investment cause a downturn to continue for some time? The decline in net investment leads, via the multiplier process of reduced consumer spending, to less national income. The lower national income leads, via the accelerator, to less net investment. The lower investment causes less income, which leads to less consumption, which leads to declining output, which leads to less investment, and so forth.

(4) THE CAUSES OF RECOVERY.   Once there is a cumulative process of downturn, how does the economy ever recover? Consumers reduce their consumption by less than their income is reduced. As consumer demand falls more and more slowly, so does national output, until the accelerator eventually causes net investment to stop falling and have a slight rise. The very slight rise in net investment means more employment and income and through the multiplier process of consumer spending, a greater rise in national income. Thus the recovery begins.

CONCLUSIONS

The multiplier is a useful tool of analysis, provided its limitations and qualifications are remembered, some of which may be removed in more complex models. Similarly, the accelerator is a powerful tool of understanding, so long as its limitations and qualifications are kept in mind. When the multiplier and accelerator are combined, as Samuelson did in 1939, the result is a simple model of the business cycle that offers some very important insights. Even with all the qualifications in more realistic models, these insights remain valid. The model is especially helpful in understanding the cumulative processes of the economy once an expansion or contraction begins. It is somewhat less persuasive in the story that it tells about the causes of the cyclical turns, because it is so abstract. Nevertheless, Samuelson's pioneering effort remains an outstanding contribution to economic knowledge.

Of course, later theories have criticized the weaknesses of the multiplier-accelerator mechanism and have substituted more sophisticated functions to cure each of these weaknesses. Nevertheless, most of the later models have built on and benefited from the knowledge of the multiplier-accelerator model. These models will be examined in the remainder of Part 3.

KEY TERMS AND CONCEPTS

multiplier	accelerator	multiplier-accelerator model

APPENDIX 10 A
FORMALIZING THE MULTIPLIER-ACCELERATOR MODEL

This Appendix presents a formal or mathematical statement of the multiplier-accelerator model. To understand why that may be useful, but also what its limitations are, it is necessary to consider the uses and abuses of mathematics in economics.

THE USES AND ABUSES OF MATHEMATICS

Math is only a tool, but it can be a powerful one (two excellent discussions of the uses and abuses of mathematics in economics are by Mirowski 1986b, and by Ruccio 1988). Before the use of mathematical models of the business cycle became widespread, some theorists wrote underdetermined theories, that is, they used more variables than they gave explanatory relations, so some key variables were left unexplained. On the other hand, some verbal theories gave two or three explanations for the same variable's behavior, so they were overdetermined and internally contradictory. One virtue of a mathematical model is that the reader can tell at a glance whether the number of variables equals the number of independent equations. A mathematical model should normally be consistent and logical, though not necessarily true.

Another virtue of simple mathematical models is that they may offer a clear illustration or reflection of a theory. If the language of mathematics is understood, a model may clarify and illuminate complex relationships.

In spite of the fact that mathematics can be a useful tool, many economists have been worried that it is often misused. Alfred Marshall and J. M. Keynes were both expert mathematicians, but neither used much math in their economics and both had a healthy skepticism about its use (see Turner 1989). Institutionalists, such as Robert Heilbroner (1989) and John K. Galbraith (1989), have expressed dismay over the abuse of mathematics in economics. Wassily Leontief, who won a Nobel prize for his work in mathematical economics, wrote: "Uncritical enthusiasm for mathematical formulation tends often to conceal the ephemeral substantive content of the argument behind the formidable front of algebraic signs. . . . In no other field of empirical inquiry has so massive and sophisticated a statistical machinery been used with such indifferent results" (1985, 272).

What exactly are the alleged abuses of mathematics in economics? First, there is a tendency to write symbols without careful explanation of the concepts and arguments involved. Second, in order to make the model manageable in mathematics, economists often use oversimplified and extremely unrealistic assumptions, but a mathematical model is no better than the assumptions put into it. Third, in order to find problems that can be easily quantified, there is a tendency to choose trivial problems, ones not relevant to the difficult and complex issues facing the world today. Fourth, mathematics must assume given relationships between variables in order to calculate the value of parameters; yet, in reality, not only do the values change, but even the relationships change over time. Nothing is frozen in economics and every relationship is specific to a particular historical period. Finally, for these reasons, as Leontief noted, the vast outpouring of mathematical economics and econometrics has contributed remarkably little to the solution of the most crucial economic problems.

EQUATIONS OF THE MULTIPLIER-ACCELERATOR MODEL

With these limitations in mind, the three equations of the multiplier-accelerator model can be explored. They are:

Output supplied = consumption + investment

$$Y_t = C_t + I_t \tag{10A.1}$$

Consumption = constant + percent of income, lagged

$$C_t = a + bY_{t-1} \tag{10A.2}$$

Investment = accelerator × (change in output, lagged)

$$I_t = v\,(Y_{t-1} - Y_{t-2}) \tag{10A.3}$$

If equations 10A.2 and 10A.3 are substituted into 10A.1, and the terms are collected, the result is:

$$Y_t = a + (b + v)\,Y_{t-1} - vY_{t-2} \tag{10A.4}$$

Equation 10A.4 is called a reduced form equation because it is all in terms of the single variable, Y. This equation is a second order difference equation because it has two time lags or differences. Solving a difference equation means being able to state the time path of the variable (national income) in terms of its initial values, called initial conditions. If there are two time lags, as in a second order equation, then two initial values of national income must be given, from which we can derive the rest of its time path. For this reason, the numerical example in Table 10.3 assumed that two initial values of national income were known.

Begin the solution by ignoring the constant (a) in order to obtain the simplest case of a homogeneous equation. To get a standardized form, let $A = b + v$ and let $B = v$. Then:

$$Y_t - AY_{t-1} + BY_{t-2} = 0 \tag{10A.5}$$

Next, consider a constant, Q, such that:

$$Q^2 - QA + B = 0 \tag{10A.6}$$

This is a simple quadratic equation. From high school algebra, remember that the quadratic formula says:

$$Q = (A + \sqrt{A^2 - 4B})/2 \qquad\qquad (10A.7)$$

When the quantity under the square root sign ($A^2 - 4B$) is negative, the solution will fluctuate in a cyclical manner. In other words, according to the mathematical solution to this equation, there will be cyclical fluctuations in the time path of national income if the parameters are in a certain range, namely, if A^2 is less than $4B$. If, however, A^2 is greater than $4B$, there will be no fluctuations, but constant growth (it is also mathematically possible to have constant decline).

In the range in which there are fluctuations, if $B = 1$, then the fluctuations are of constant magnitude. If B is less than 1, then the cycle is damped, that is, the amplitudes become smaller and smaller till it converges toward some constant value. If B is greater than 1, then the cycle is explosive; that is, the fluctuations become larger and larger. In this particular simple model, the accelerator equals B, so the fluctuations will be regular, damped, or explosive depending on the value of the accelerator. For that reason, in the numerical example in Table 10.3, it was assumed that $v = 1$ in order to obtain regular fluctuations.

Note that only the values of the parameters A and B affect the cyclical fluctuations. If the constant, a, is included in the equation, then it only affects the level around which fluctuations will occur.

DAMPED AND EXPLOSIVE CYCLES

As noted in the previous section, the coefficient B is equal to the accelerator, v, in the above model. Remember that B must equal exactly 1 if cycles are to be constant in amplitude. If B is less than 1, then cycles are damped, that is, the amplitudes get less and less till there are no more cycles. If B is greater than 1, then cycle amplitudes get greater and greater until the economy explodes. Since the business cycle has not disappeared and the economy has not exploded, it appears that the cycle and the economy exist only because this coefficient happens to equal exactly one. Something must be wrong with the assumptions or with the reasoning.

There are several possible solutions. One suggestion is that there is a damped solution to the business cycle equation, but there are exogenous shocks that keep it going. There is a considerable literature on whether the shocks could be purely random, the nature of the shocks, and so forth. But this view approaches the erroneous view that the cycle is due to purely random accidents.

Another solution assumes that the endogenous system is explosive, but that there are so-called floors and ceilings holding it within bounds at every turning point (see Hicks 1950). The ceiling is usually described as the limit of physical production at the full-capacity level, which could increase only very slowly over a long time. The floor is usually described by the fact that aggregate capital can be disinvested only up to the amount of depreciation. In other words, the largest decline that can occur in aggregate capital in one year is the amount of wear and tear of capital.

One problem with this floor-and-ceiling solution is that the private enterprise economy at the peak of the cycle seldom reaches full capacity. Another problem is that disinvestment has seldom, if ever, reached the limit of depreciation. In other words, the economy hardly ever comes near the possible floors and ceilings in the actual, historical business cycle.

Another possibility is that the functions mentioned here have longer time lags than supposed, that is, they are influenced by a number of past periods. The result would be a difference equation with many time lags, that is, a higher order equation. Such an equation allows for a more complex solution, with cycles and growth in a wide range of parameters.

Finally, it has been assumed that all the relations are linear, but that is not true. There are non-linear relations, for example, involving Y^2 and Y^3. Non-linear equations can also generate cycles and growth over a wide range of parameters.

CONCLUSIONS

In summary, the mathematical form of the multiplier-accelerator model is another part of its unrealistic assumptions. Yet a much more complex mathematical form would greatly reduce its usefulness as a tool of understanding. In later chapters, some models that have somewhat more realistic assumptions will be explored, but still keep this simple mathematical form—but the reader should remain skeptical of this simple form.

CHAPTER 11

Demand-Side Theories

Many theorists have contended that the main problems of downturns in private enterprise economies are caused by the lack of consumer demand. The most famous of these theories are the group called under-consumption theories. These theories have been advocated by both mainstream economists and by socialist economists. The two groups approach these theories differently, so the differences must be spelled out. Furthermore, most under-consumption theories have not been business cycle theories at all, but are theories of long-run stagnation. These stagnation theories must also be distinguished from business cycle theories.

LONG-RUN STAGNATION THEORIES

All under-consumptionist long-run stagnation theories include two key components. First, the most important shared belief is that insufficient consumer demand for goods and services is the main cause of depression and unemployment. Second, it is believed that this lack of consumer demand is a problem for the economy at all times, so the usual status of the economy would be stagnation. Certain external or exogenous events, such as wars or new inventions, may pull the economy upward, but it will eventually return to stagnation. Other than the two beliefs that the economic problems are caused by lack of consumer demand and that this results in stagnation, long-run under-consumptionist theories differ in various ways. (Under-consumptionist long-run stagnation theories are discussed in a comprehensive, but very critical, history by Bleany 1976.)

There have been many mainstream under-consumptionist theories, ranging from the earliest with Lord Lauderdale and the Reverend Thomas Malthus in the early 19th century to the later theories of W. T. Foster and W. Catchings in the 1930s (see Haberler 1960, Chapter 5, for a careful but unsympathetic discussion of these theories). In many of these theories, the emphasis was that, on the one hand, industry turns out an increasing flood of commodities. On the other hand, some people save part of their income. As a result, consumer demand does not keep up with the flood of commodities so there is an abundance of unsold goods and production is cut. Less production leads to unemployment, which means still less income and less consumer demand.

Among the classical economists, Malthus was unique in his under-consumption theory. He recommended that society maintain a class of parasites who would consume but not produce. He felt that the landlord class fitted this need because they were magnificent at the art of consumption but did not produce anything. Since the problem was lack of demand and too much saving, according to under-consumptionists, their view ran exactly contrary to the usual classical view that more saving is always good for the economy. While most classical economists recommended more saving for economic growth, some under-consumptionists recommended that everyone be forced to respend all of their income rapidly.

Another form of under-consumption theory was popular with liberal reformers such as John Hobson (1922), a writer whose liberal discussion of imperialism was the basis for much of Lenin's work on that subject. Hobson stressed that the cause of deficient consumer demand is not a general tendency toward too much saving but a lack of demand by the poor. He demonstrated that there was a maldistribution of income, with a few rich people having much income but a large mass of poor people having little income. Most wage workers, he said, are poorly paid, so their income and consumption are very limited. On the other hand, the rich have incomes that are so far above their consumption needs they save most of their income. A lack of consumer demand results because those with large incomes don't need more consumption, while the poor have the need but not the income.

Hobson's solution was a more equal distribution of income. Trade unions often agree with Hobson. At least, unions tend to argue that the way out of any recession or depression is higher wages and more unemployment benefits so that workers will have more money to spend on consumption. Many socialist writers have agreed with Hobson that workers get insufficient pay and therefore cannot purchase all the goods they have produced—but socialists believe the disease can be cured only by ending capitalism (see, e.g., Baran and Sweezy 1966, and J. B. Foster 1986 and 1987).

Theories of under-consumption and stagnation naturally became very popular during the 1930s, after the U.S. economy had suffered ten depressed years. Alvin Hansen, who was a president of the American Economic Association, held an under-consumptionist long-run stagnation theory (Hansen 1964). He argued that stagnation was held off before the Great Depression by certain unique historical factors, including the U.S.

frontier expansion, rapid population growth, and rapid technological innovation in such industries as railroads, automobiles, and electricity (Hansen's theory and similar ones are discussed in R. A. Gordon 1961).

CRITICISMS OF LONG-RUN STAGNATION THEORIES

There have been many criticisms of the under-consumptionist stagnation view from right, left, and center. Haberler comments: "The under-consumption theory is a theory of the crisis and depression rather than a theory of the cycle" (1960, 119). In other words, the long-run under-consumption theory explains why the private enterprise economy declines into stagnation, but it has no explanation as to why the private enterprise economy should ever recover.

If stagnationists simply predict the decline of the private enterprise economy or discuss a "general crisis" as always existing, it does not help them to understand the reality of the private enterprise economy nor does it give them popular credibility. It is easy to observe that in the United States there has been a great deal of prosperity and some periods of rapid expansion. This has occurred even though crises and mass unemployment occur frequently and even though a part of the population does not participate much in the apparent prosperity. To assert that the U.S. economy is in a continuing condition of crisis or decline does not help to understand the private enterprise economy.

Another criticism of the under-consumptionist long-run stagnation theory is the argument that lack of consumer demand is by itself not a sufficient condition for a downturn. Haberler argues, as have many other critics, that even if consumer demand declines, "there is always an equilibrium position possible with full employment" (1960, 125). He is referring to the fact that demand for producers' goods for investment may always fill any gap between total output and consumer demand. Of course, this does not prove that investors will fill the gap, only that it is possible.

The basic criticism of most under-consumptionist theories is that it lacks a theory of investment. Although Keynes shares under-consumptionist worries over lack of demand, his theory is distinguished by its attention on investment. He notes that there will be equilibrium if, and only if, all non-consumed income (that is, saving) is equal to investment plans. It is only if a theory can show that the total demand by both consumers and investors is insufficient to purchase all of the supply on the market at present prices, that a theory can explain a downturn by a demand-oriented theory. In that respect, the multiplier-accelerator theory of Samuelson (1939) is a complete theory, as opposed to incomplete theories that talk only about insufficient consumer demand.

Sweezy (1942) began to solve the problem for under-consumptionists when he followed Samuelson by discussing the accelerator principle. Under-consumptionists had long been saying that capitalism in the private sector, leaving aside military spending, cannot just build more factories to produce more factories and so forth. In other words, private investment does not necessarily grow to fill any gap left by consumption. But why? In fact, it always happens that for some time during every expansion, investment grows faster than consumption. The accelerator principle explains why. It happens because investment is a function of rising growth of consumption. At first, the faster growth of investment is no problem, but is rather the engine of prosperity because the savings are invested to produce output and more employment. Even if consumer demand then becomes stagnant, it is technically possible for the increased flow of goods all to be in the form of investment goods (plant and equipment), which is designed to produce more plant and equipment.

What an under-consumptionist investment function must explain is why this makes no economic sense, primarily because capitalists will not invest if their expectation is for a lack of demand in the near future when the new goods are produced. The accelerator principle does explain why investment must decline when aggregate demand slows down—and it must be emphasized that consumer demand is the largest part of aggregate demand. This defense of under-consumptionism is stated forcefully by John B. Foster, who writes:

> Any continual plowing back of profits into investment would mean that the means of production . . . would expand very much faster than the articles of consumption . . . . This, in fact, is the basic pattern of every accumulation boom. But it is a self-annihilating process. Sooner or later . . . the means of production are built up to such a prodigious extent that a social disproportionality develops between the capacity to produce and the corresponding demand. A crisis of over-accumulation rooted in over-exploitation occurs. (Foster 1987, 61)

Foster's disproportionality thesis could be translated into the action of the accelerator principle which limits investment when the growth of aggregate demand is limited. Of course, there are many criticisms of the accelerator, so what is really required is an adequate investment explanation which may include the accelerator as one part of it. At any rate, the early under-consumptionists were rightly accused of having an incomplete theory as long as they did not explain the path of investment as well as consumption.

The final criticism of the under-consumptionist long-run stagnation theory is the fact that profit expectations are not limited merely by demand, but also by cost considerations. The problem of making profit by the capitalist has two stages. First, the capitalist must have workers create a product with profit embodied in it by keeping costs low enough—including the costs of labor, the costs of raw materials, and the costs of plant and equipment (depreciation). Second, after such a profitable product has been created, it must be sold in order to realize the profit. The under-consumptionists tend to overlook the cost side of the problem.

This issue becomes apparent when some under-consumptionists argue that higher wages will resolve a crisis or prevent a depression. The problem is that higher wages not only create more demand (as both Keynes and Marx emphasized), higher wages also mean higher costs per unit. Therefore, higher wages allow more realization of profit but also allow less production of profit. What each capitalist really wants is lower wages in his or her own plant, but higher wages throughout the rest of the economy.

MARX, KEYNES, AND UNDER-CONSUMPTION

Karl Marx severely criticized the earlier simplistic under-consumption theories. Yet Marx stated his views on the importance of demand very clearly on many occasions. He wrote: "The ultimate cause of all real crises always remains the poverty and restricted consumption of the masses" (1909, vol. 3, 568). Marx argued that capitalist expansions are brought to an end by the limits imposed on consumption by the class structure of capitalism.

John Maynard Keynes refers to the under-consumptionists only in passing as part of the "underground" in the economics profession. Yet he did more to emphasize the importance of the deficiency of effective (monetary) demand than anyone else. He stressed the reasons for a growing gap between consumer demand and national income in an expansion.

Both Marx and Keynes systematically dissected Say's law by showing that lack of effective demand can cause mass unemployment in a private enterprise system. Each demonstrated that dynamic equilibrium is possible in a private enterprise system if, and only if, effective demand grows at a certain rate. Marx and Keynes also showed that entrepreneurs face not one, but two problems: (1) the problem of producing profit and (2) the problem of realizing profit.

The framework of both Marx and Keynes for exploring problems of effective demand is different from that of the early under-consumptionists in that it puts consumer demand and investment on the same footing with respect to aggregate demand. In this framework it is impossible to speak as if lack of consumer demand alone—without specifying investment—is sufficient to explain a downturn.

AN EFFECTIVE DEMAND THEORY OF THE BUSINESS CYCLE

An effective demand theory of the business cycle may be stated within the framework of Keynes's aggregate relationships, on which the U.S. national income accounts are based. Keynes would say that it is a condition of equilibrium that the total output supplied (the real national income) should equal the aggregate consumer spending plus the aggregate investment spending. This chapter considers only the private domestic economy, and it leaves aside government and international trade. In terms of the Keynesian-based national income accounts:

$$National\ income = consumption + investment \qquad (11.1)$$

Second, post-Keynesians would say that income is divided into a stream going to recipients of labor income (wages, salaries, and benefits) and a stream going to recipients of property income (profit, rent, and interest). In terms of the Keynesian-based national income accounts:

$$National\ income = property\ income + labor\ income \qquad (11.2)$$

Note that in the national income accounts, labor income is called employee compensation, while property income is all income that is not employee compensation.

This framework portrays the supply and demand for the two sectors as well as the aggregate property income and aggregate labor income paid out by both sectors. Keynes normally discussed aggregate income, rather than treating labor and property income separately, but he was acutely aware of the importance of the distribution of income. The distinction between labor and property income is crucial in most effective demand models and is incorporated into most post-Keynesian theories (see the survey in Eichner and Kregel 1975).

THE CONSUMPTION FUNCTION

Obviously, an effective demand theory must have a clearly defined consumption function. The basic thrust of such a consumption function is that consumer demand is not only influenced by the total amount of national income but also by the distribution of national income between labor and property owners.

Another way to say the same thing is to assert that the propensity to consume is higher for employees than for employers. In Chapter 4, a large number of empirical studies were cited on this point. All of them found that the propensity to consume (both the APC and the MPC) are far higher out of labor income than out of property income. In other words, an entrepreneur who receives profit income does not need to spend all of it for consumption, but will save some. An unemployed worker, however, is forced to spend all of his or her income for consumption. Furthermore, it was shown that some of corporate income is retained by the corporation and does not go to individuals, so the average propensity to consume out of that income is zero.

Therefore, when the labor share rises so that employees have a larger share of national income, the ratio of consumption to national income will also rise. When the labor share falls so that property owners have a larger share of national income, the ratio of consumption to national income will also fall. In Keynesian terms, both the average and marginal propensities to consume are positively influenced by the labor share. In Part 5 it will be shown that the evidence is consistent with this hypothesis. In other words, an econometric test will be made of the relationship: *Average propensity to consume = f(labor share)*. The best fit is found to have several time lags, but the result is statistically significant, which means that this important hypothesis is not disproved.

A third way to say the same thing, and probably the simplest way to think about it, is to assert that consumer demand includes all of labor income plus some percentage of property income. In other words, wage earners spend all of their income for consumer goods on the average, but entrepreneurs spend only a portion of their income for consumption. Remember that property income includes corporate retained income, none of which is used for consumption. Also remember that there is a time lag between the receipt of income and its expenditure. Thus:

$$Consumption = part\ of\ property\ income,$$
$$lagged + all\ of\ labor\ income,\ lagged \qquad (11.3)$$

It should be noted that this formulation, in which all of wages are consumed, is an over-simplification because the percentage of wages consumed is sometimes somewhat below 100 percent by the usual accounting (see the evidence in Chapter 4). A consumption function of this type was used in 1935 in the pioneering work of Michal Kalecki (see Kalecki 1968, 53; also the discussion in Sawyer 1985b, Chapter 4). Kalecki found the relationship between consumption and the two kinds of income to be statistically significant, as have many other tests since then, as noted in Chapter 4. For technical reasons, however, all tests of this function are suspect (econometricians note that the two kinds of income are not independent of each other, which may bias the test, as discussed in chapter 21).

In fact, all labor income need not be spent for consumption to support the effective demand thesis. It is only necessary that the marginal propensity to consume out of labor income should be significantly higher than the marginal propensity to consume out of property income. This fact was confirmed by almost all the empirical investigations reported in Chapter 4. It was also shown in Chapter 4 that the evidence is compatible with the hypothesis that the average propensity to consume is a positive function of the labor share. In that case, with a given amount of national income, consumer demand will be greater if income is shifted from property income to labor income. Consumer demand will be less, however, if income is shifted from labor income to property income. We must examine the distribution function to find out what does happen to the shares of labor and property income according to this theory.

THE DISTRIBUTION FUNCTION

The cyclical movement of the shares of income of capital and labor was explored in detail in our chapter on the distribution of income (Chapter 6). The important finding from an effective demand point of view is that the profit share generally rises throughout the expansion and falls throughout the contraction. Of course, this means that the labor share generally falls throughout the expansion and rises throughout the contraction.

The effective demand theory relies on the wage lag hypothesis, giving all of the reasons that private enterprise institutions hold back wages from rising as rapidly as profits in a capitalist expansion. These reasons were spelled out in great detail in Chapter 6 and need not be repeated here. The reader is reminded that these reasons include fixed labor contracts, the fact that the corporation owns any extra product produced by high productivity, and the fact that employees do not automatically get higher wages when their productivity rises. It was shown in detail in Chapter 6 that the real amount of wages rises in expansions and falls in contractions, but that real profits rise and fall more rapidly. The conclusion is that the labor share falls during the expansion while it rises during the contraction.

It was found in chapter 6, according to the NBER cycle measures, that the labor share appears to be a negative function of the ratio of capacity utilization. This hypothesis is found to be statistically significant in an econometric test in Chapter 21. The fact that the labor share generally falls when capacity utilization rises is obviously consistent with the fact that capacity utilization is strongly pro-cyclical, while the labor share is strongly counter-cyclical (as we saw in Chapter 6). However, capacity utilization also marches in step with real national income to a large extent (again, the evidence is presented in Chapters 6 and 21). When income and output are rising, more capacity is utilized. So we could also say that the labor share is a negative function of real national income. A rising national income is usually accompanied by a falling labor share, while declining national income is usually accompanied by a rising labor share.

The simplest possible representation of this relationship is to show the labor share as a constant minimum plus some fixed percentage of real national income. As national income rises, labor income rises, but it rises more slowly. As national income falls in a contraction, labor income falls, but it falls more slowly. Therefore:

$$\textit{Labor income} = \textit{constant} + f(\textit{national income}) \qquad (11.4)$$

On this assumption, the labor share is counter-cyclical, because the ratio of labor income to national income falls in expansions and rises in contractions. Since the property share must always move in the opposite direction to the labor share (because they are dividing one pie between them), the property share must be pro-cyclical. A similar empirical distribution function was first found to be statistically significant in 1935 by Kalecki (1968, 40; also see discussion in Sawyer 1985b, Chapter 2).

The counter-cyclical behavior of the labor share is important to an effective demand theory because it affects the amount of consumer demand. A falling labor share in the expansion has a negative effect on consumer demand, while a rising labor share in the contraction will have a positive effect on consumer demand.

THE INVESTMENT FUNCTION

An effective demand business cycle theory may make use of the simplest version of the accelerator, as used by Samuelson (1939). It states that net investment is a function of the previous change in aggregate consumer demand. Specifically:

$$\textit{Investment} = \textit{accelerator} \times \textit{change in consumption} \qquad (11.5)$$

Given this relationship, when consumer demand begins to rise more slowly, net investment will actually decline. Net investment is thus the catalyst for a cyclical downturn (or a cyclical upturn) in this effective demand business cycle model. Unlike the under-consumption models, the effective demand model makes the investment function one of the key foundations of its theory. According to the effective demand model, a decline in the rate of growth of consumer demand leads to an absolute decline in net investment, that leads to a recession or depression.

In Chapter 5, it was found that the empirical truth in this relationship is the fact that investment does indeed fluctuate much more than consumption and many theorists took this to be sufficient evidence of this simple accelerator function. Both the NBER cycle measures presented in Chapter 5 and the econometric tests in Chapter 21 reveal, however, that the matter is actually more complex in reality. Investment is affected by several other kinds of demand, as well as by all of the types of costs. Therefore, we found in Chapter 5 that a more realistic picture made *investment* = *f*(*profits*). Nevertheless, to show the working of the simplest effective demand type of model, *investment* = *f*(*change in consumption*) is used here.

OPERATION OF THE EFFECTIVE DEMAND CYCLE MODEL

The usual questions must be asked as to the causes of expansion, downturns, contractions, and recovery in this theory (using the simple version stated in the five relationships given above, 11.1 to 11.5).

WHAT ARE THE CAUSES OF CUMULATIVE EXPANSION?

As recovery begins, national income is rising, including both property income and labor income. Rising national income causes more consumer spending, leading to more output demanded. As output demanded rises, this process leads, through the accelerator principle, to more new investment. New investment means more employment and income (both wages and profits), which leads to increased spending on consumption and, through the multiplier, to a further rise in national income. Thus, this model makes use of a multiplier-accelerator interaction to cause a cumulative expansion. In this respect, the only difference from Samuelson's model is that the increase in income is separated into property income and labor income.

WHAT ARE THE CAUSES OF THE DOWNTURN?

As expansion continues, rising output is accompanied by a declining labor share. The reasons for the declining labor share include the continued unemployment in the early expansion, the fact that wage bargains are usually fixed for some time period, the fact that employers automatically own any increased product due to higher productivity, and the fact that productivity does rise in expansion. Consistent with this picture of the economy, the distribution function permits total income during the expansion to shift from labor to property income.

The consumption faction in the effective demand model indicates that consumption depends not only on total national income but also on how income is divided between labor and property income. In other words, rising real wages lead to higher levels of consumption. In the average expansion real wages rise more slowly than real profits, causing the marginal propensity to consume to fall. Labor income has a much higher propensity to consume than property income. If the marginal propensity to consume falls, it follows that, if national income were constant, consumption would shrink. In the expansion, national income is growing, so both labor income and property income are growing, even though property income is growing faster. Therefore, the combined result of (1) the shift of income from workers to capitalists and (2) the fact that capitalists spend a lower percentage of income on consumption, is that consumer demand grows, but more and more slowly.

The slower growth of consumer demand is reflected, because of the accelerator principle, in a decline in net investment. The decline of net investment means less income and employment, causing a contraction to begin.

WHAT CAUSES THE CUMULATIVE DOWNTURN?

The decline in net investment causes, through the negative effect of the multiplier process on consumer spending, a greater decline in national income, accompanied by declines in both property income and labor income. The fall in national income causes, through the accelerator principle, a still further decline in net investment. As this process repeats itself, a cumulative decline results.

WHAT CAUSES THE RECOVERY?

As the decline continues, labor income falls more slowly than property income (for all the same reasons that it rises more slowly in expansion, but in reverse). The consequent rise in the labor share raises the marginal propensity to consume. The higher marginal propensity to consume helps stop the decline in aggregate consumption. The slower decline in aggregate consumer demand leads eventually to a small increase in net investment. This sets off the recovery and a cumulative expansion ensues.

CONCLUSIONS

The effective demand cycle theory produces a model that is complete and consistent within itself. Moreover, none of its assumptions are inconsistent with the evidence presented in Chapters 7, 8, and 9. This is an important achievement.

The model also overcomes some of the alleged weaknesses of the long-run stagnation theories of under-consumption. First, unlike the stagnation models, it fully explains the recovery and expansion process as well as the downturn and contraction. Second, unlike some of the earlier stagnation models, it does have a clear and coherent investment function. It can explain a downturn not merely in terms of a lack of consumer demand but in terms of a lack of aggregate demand, combining the behavior of consumption and investment.

There are, however, several remaining weaknesses of the effective demand model. First, this model only discusses the effect on investment of changes in consumer demand but ignores other changes in demand. These include changes in investment, government and international demand. This problem is easy to rectify by basing the investment function on aggregate demand rather than just consumer demand. Aggregate demand usually behaves in the same way as consumer demand because consumption is its biggest component.

Second, the effective demand model leaves out of consideration all of the evidence concerning the cyclical behavior of costs. It says nothing about labor costs, raw material costs, or interest costs. This is a severe limitation. The theory alleges that consumer demand is limited because income shifts from labor to property income. That shift means lower demand, but it also means lower costs per unit. Admitting that lower demand will mean problems in realizing the profits, it nevertheless does not consider the fact that investment demand might also be hurt by rising costs per unit.

Finally, this model is complete in the logical sense that it tells a consistent story. It is very incomplete in the sense that it leaves out some very important aspects of reality. These important variables are brought into theoretical consideration in this book as follows: money and credit are discussed in Chapter 14, the impact of monopoly power is considered in Chapter 15, international relationships are explored in Chapter 16, and government behavior is analyzed in Chapter 17. Each of these variables has a group of economists who contend that macroeconomic analysis should concentrate on that variable. Indeed, no model is complete without consideration of all of these variables. Yet no theory can discuss everything at once, so it is better to approach our complex reality by beginning with a simple abstract model and gradually adding to it in successive approximations. Such abstraction is necessary and legitimate as long as one remembers that the model is not complete until all of the important variables, such as the finance system and the international economy, are fully considered.

KEY TERMS AND CONCEPTS

stagnation theories	**under-consumption theories**	**demand-side theories**

APPENDIX 11 A
FORMALIZING THE EFFECTIVE DEMAND CYCLE MODEL

A simple, basic version of the effective demand model will be presented. The model is restricted to the private domestic economy, so government activity and net exports are omitted. All variables are in real terms.

AN EFFECTIVE DEMAND MODEL

This model consists of five relationships. The first two are identities or definitions, while the last three state behavioral regularities. First, as a condition of equilibrium, it is necessary that the real national income, which is the same as real output, should equal the consumer demand plus the investment demand:

National income = consumption + investment

$$Y_t = C_t + I_t \tag{11A.1}$$

where C is real consumption, Y is real national income, I is real investment, and t is a time period.

Second, following a post-Keynesian approach, the national income must be divided into wages and profits, or more precisely, into labor income and property income.

National income = property income + labor income

$$Y_t = \Pi_t + W_t \tag{11A.2}$$

where Π is property income (mostly profits) and W is labor income (mostly wages).

Third, turning to behavioral assumptions, it is assumed that labor income rises and falls more slowly than national income:

Labor income = constant + percentage of national income

$$W_t = w + gY_t \tag{11A.3}$$

where c ad g are constants—and g is between zero and one.

Fourth, another behavioral assumption is that consumption is determined by spending out of property income and out of labor income, where the former has a much lower marginal propensity to consume than the latter. For simplicity, it is assumed that all labor income is consumed, that is, a marginal propensity to consume of 100 percent.

Consumption = constant + part of profits, lagged + all of wages, lagged

$$C_t = a + b\Pi_{t-1} + W_{t-1} \tag{11A.4}$$

where *a* and *b* are constants, and *b* is between zero and one.

Fifth and last, the behavior of investment is assumed to be determined by the accelerator principle, based on the change in consumer demand.

Investment = accelerator × change in consumer demand

$$I_t = v(C_t - C_{t-1}) \tag{11A.5}$$

where *v* is the accelerator coefficient.

By successive substitutions, this set of five equations and five variables can be reduced to one equation in one variable. That reduced form equation is:

$$
\begin{aligned}
Y_t &= H + AY_{t-1} - BY_{t-2} \\
\text{where:} \quad H &= a + w - bw \\
A &= (b - bg + g)(1 + v) \\
B &= v(b - bg + g)
\end{aligned}
$$

There will be cycles if A^2 is less than $4B$. The cycles will be of constant amplitude if $B = 1$, damped if B is less than one, and explosive if B is greater than one.

It should be emphasized at this point that several criticisms of such a model were made in the chapter. We could add that it is possible to criticize (a) the choice of variables put into and left out of each equation. (b) the form of the equation, including the proper time lags and whether equations should be linear or not linear, as well as (c) whether the parameters are truly constant or whether they change over time. There are also many questions about the limitations of any mathematical model of such a complex process as the economy (see the sophisticated discussion of this problem in Mirowski 1986a).

CHAPTER 12

Supply-Side or Cost Theories of the Business Cycle

Many different theories of business cycles emphasize supply-side problems, the production process, the cost of production, or excess consumption and over-investment. These problems are opposite to those of effective demand, under-consumption, and excess saving emphasized in the previous chapter. The most popular supply-side theory is the view that a rate of taxation which is too high will dry up savings and also make people less willing to work. These theories have come to be called "supply-side theories" in recent decades. They are, however, only one type of supply-side argument and they are not mainly cyclical theories. Similar arguments will be encountered when government policy is discussed in Part 4. Government policy is not discussed here because this chapter is limited to the private economy, not the role of government.

Second, also concerned with the supply side of the economy are most of the theories known as monetary over-investment theories, monetary theories, or monetarism. These theories all relate to money, interest rates, credit, and the financial system and will be discussed in detail only in Part 4.

Third, there is a long-run Marxist stagnation view called the organic composition of capital theory. Since it is not a cycle theory, it is not discussed in this book. An enormous literature has been produced on this theory, for example, Shaikh (1978), Yaffe (1973), Fine and Harris (1976), Bell (1977), and Weisskopf (1978).

Fourth, there is an important set of theories which may be called non-monetary over-investment theories. Most non-monetary over-investment theories argue that the problem with the economy is the high cost of plant, equipment, and raw materials. Some theories are concerned with falling output/capital ratios in the boom (the most interesting in recent years is Devine 1987). These theories are discussed here.

Fifth, economists concerned with size and concentration, beginning with Wesley Mitchell, have noted that the entry of more small, inexperienced firms in a boom may lower capital productivity. That issue is left for the discussion of the cyclical effect of monopoly and competition in Part 4.

Sixth, there is the wage cost theory, which is concerned with the rising cost of labor as full employment is approached. The wage cost theory shall be explored in this chapter.

NON-MONETARY OVER-INVESTMENT THEORY

Many economists have investigated how capital costs rise and fall in the business cycle. These theorists include Spiethoff, Cassel, Tugan-Baranowski, Hayek, and Schumpeter (for a detailed discussion of their theories, see Haberler 1960, Chapter 3). In addition to these theorists, most of whom are conservative, equal concern is given regarding costs of plants, equipment, and raw materials in the radical framework of Karl Marx and Michael Kalecki (see Sherman 1991). All of these theories view the cycle as one of the rise and fall of capital investment. Many such theorists refer to the fact that investment rises and falls more rapidly than consumption. Some refer specifically to the accelerator principle. The radical theorists emphasize that the demand for investment funds outruns the supply of saving, resulting in a shortage of capital. They are concerned that there is too much consumption and not enough saving. This view is exactly opposite those of Keynes or the under-consumptionists, but is very much like that of the classical economists. The decline of the economy is attributed to rising prices of capital goods and/or higher interest rates and/or falling productivity of capital, leading to lower industrial profits.

Recovery in many of these theories depends on technological innovation. The greatest theorist of the cyclical impact of technology is Joseph Schumpeter (1939). Schumpeter discusses in great detail the revolutionary nature of new innovations. He emphasizes the role of entrepreneurs in introducing these innovations. He also shows how once a recovery is begun on the basis of some important new innovation, many other entrepreneurs crowd into the field to expand production and take advantage of the profit opportunities. Such an effect is undoubtedly important. The problem, however, is that Schumpeter offers no independent reason why such innovations should be cyclical in nature. He does a wonderful job of describing the spread of innovations, but that is after recovery has begun. Development of innovations are not, however, the cause of recovery. Entrepreneurs are usually very hesitant to introduce new innovations in a recession or depression because of the lack of a market. Thus, many later economists would accept Schumpeter's emphasis on technology, not only in the long-run, but also in the business cycle, yet not as the cause of the cycle itself. The Schumpeterians go beyond traditional economics to look at what drives technological change. They analyze how growth is affected by support for technical innovation, educational institutions, and rewards to entrepreneurs for developing new products.

The new wave of research from the Schumpeterians focuses on the links between international trade and growth. While traditional theory holds that the payoffs from trade are due to lowered prices, the Schumpeterians argue that free trade encourages the rapid spread of technological change and ideas.

MATERIAL COST THEORIES OF THE BUSINESS CYCLE

All of the economists known as non-monetary over-investment theorists have argued that excessive amounts of investment in a business cycle expansion will mean that the demand for plant, equipment, and raw materials will outrun supply (for a survey, see Haberler 1960, Chapter 3). The excess demand raises the cost of purchasing these goods. Suppose that the price of the product made with this investment is constant or rises very slowly. The over-investment theorists assume that the price of finished goods rises more slowly than their costs. According to this view, the ratio of profit to output per unit must fall, setting off a depression. Other non-monetary over-investment theorists are concerned that approaching capacity limitations may cause chaotic supply conditions, some shortages, and a general lowering of the physical productivity of capital (see the provocative argument by Devine 1987, 275).

The most important over-investment theorist was Frederick Hayek (1939), though theorists as different as Karl Marx have held similar views. Hayek pictures production as being ordered in a series of stages. Each production stage feeds the next one and is part of the cost of the next stage. Production of raw materials may be considered to be the first or earliest stage. The raw materials are then used, at a certain cost per unit, to produce plant and equipment in the second stage. The plant and equipment plus more raw materials, all called producers' goods or capital goods, are used to produce consumer goods at the third stage.

According to Hayek, in every expansion the rising demand for consumer goods generates an even greater percentage increase in demand for plant and equipment and raw materials. The fact that demand for these capital goods (that is, investment in plant equipment and raw materials), is more than proportionate to the increased demand for consumer goods is explained by the accelerator principle, discussed earlier. The large demand for plant and equipment at the second stage generates an even stronger demand (by a further accelerator) for raw materials.

As a result of these pressures, Hayek's theory predicts that in expansions the price of consumer goods will rise least, the price of plant and equipment will rise more, and the price of raw materials will rise most. Hayek argues that the higher costs coming from the earlier stages eventually reduce profit rates in the later stages, thus causing a contraction.

In each contraction, according to Hayek, the accelerator works in reverse, causing a small decline in the output of consumer goods to be reflected in a much larger decline in investment in plant and equipment. Therefore, the price of plants and equipment must fall more than the price of consumer goods. Because of a further accelerator, the demand for raw materials falls even faster than the demand for plant and equipment. In addition, it takes time to reduce the supply of raw materials from agricultural operations, mainly because planning must take place so far in advance. With a more rapid fall in demand and a slower fall in supply, the price of raw materials must fall much faster than the price of finished goods. Hayek argues that the declining costs of material goods help stabilize profit rates at some point in the contraction. Thus, the lower costs help to set the stage for economic recovery.

Hayek's theory is pre-Keynesian, so it is impossible to express it exclusively in Keynesian aggregates. A model of Hayek's cost theory requires some disaggregation into sectors. The national income accounts include the value of finished goods, which is supposed to include raw materials. Thus, a formal model of Hayek's theory would have to disaggregate the economy into a consumer goods producing sector, a capital goods producing sector, and a raw materials producing sector.

A more important problem is that Keynesian national income accounting includes an aggregate profit. Suppose raw material prices rise. All other things remaining constant, the profits of entrepreneurs in the consumer goods sector and in plant and equipment production must decline. But the profits of entrepreneurs in raw material production must rise an equal amount. In that case, it would appear that aggregate profits will remain constant. The point is that aggregate profits for the whole economy may hide the problems of key sectors.

Furthermore, a high proportion of raw materials used in the United States comes from foreign sources. If the price of imported raw materials rises faster than the price of U.S. finished goods, then the profit rates of U.S. businesses relying on imports of raw materials will be hurt. Thus it appears that the disproportionate rise or decline of raw material prices (such as oil prices) could affect U.S. aggregate profits. These issues of international trade are discussed further in Part 4.

A MATERIAL COST MODEL OF THE CYCLE

The main features of the various non-monetary over-investment theories may be used to state a simple model of the business cycle. In so far as possible, the model is stated in the spirit in which the theories were written, but in terms of the usual national income accounting.

Leaving aside foreign and government demand, the condition of equilibrium is that output supplied should equal consumer demand plus investment demand:

$$National\ income\ (Y) = consumption\ (C) + investment\ (I) \tag{12.1}$$

where supply adjusts to demand in each period, but demand may not equal the full employment level of supply.

THE CONSUMPTION FUNCTION

The path of consumption and of investment over the cycle must now be explained. The over-investment theorists assume that there is no lack of consumer demand. Therefore, it may be assumed that consumption is a constant proportion of income:

$$Consumption\ (C) = constant \times national\ income\ (Y) \tag{12.2}$$

Since consumption clearly has no deficiency, investment emerges as the key variable.

THE INVESTMENT FUNCTION

All of the over-investment theorists think of investment as influenced by the profit rate. It may therefore be assumed that the amount of new net investment is a function of the rate of profit:

$$Investment\ (I) = f\ (change\ in\ rate\ of\ profit) \tag{12.3}$$

A rising rate of profit inspires confidence in the future and causes net investment. A falling rate of profit makes entrepreneurs worry and prevents new net investment. It was found in Chapter 5 that this is roughly true, and the econometric test is made in Chapter 22.

DEFINITION OF PROFIT RATE

The profit rate on capital can be thought of as the ratio of profit to output times the ratio of output to capital:

$$Profit\ rate = profit/output \times output/capital \qquad (12.4)$$

This is an identity, true by definition. Spelled out in full, it states: the ratio of profits to capital equals the ratio of profit to output times the ratio of output to capital. It is, however, a very useful definition to explain this theory. The definition separates out the distribution of income between profit recipients and the others who get revenue from producing output (such as labor). The definition makes a separate component of the ratio of output to capital. The output to capital ratio depends on both the physical product of capital (with labor) and the cost of capital goods. The cost of capital goods includes the price of plant, equipment, and raw materials.

THE DISTRIBUTION FUNCTION

The over-investment theories are not directly concerned with the distribution of income between labor and property. At least, that is not the focus of these theories. Therefore, it may be assumed that both the labor share and the profit share remain constant proportions of the total output.

$$Profit\ share = a\ constant \qquad (12.5)$$

This assumption means that the distribution of income plays no important role in this model.

THE COST FUNCTION

Finally the active, crucial part of the model will be examined. The ratio of output to capital reflects both physical quantities and relative prices. The output may be divided into quantity of (finished) output and price of (finished) output. Similarly, the capital may be divided into the quantity of capital goods and the price of capital goods. The physical ratio of the quantity of output to the quantity of capital is governed in the long-run by technology. But, this is a short-run cycle model, so technology may be held more or less constant. The physical ratio could decline if production is pushed beyond the optimum level of capacity utilization, as some over-investment theorists have assumed, but there is no solid evidence for this. Others have speculated that the physical ratio of output to capital may be lowered before the peak of expansion by the entry of large numbers of small inexperienced firms.

The main thrust of Hayek's model, however, is that the ratio of finished output prices to the prices of capital goods (including plant, equipment, and raw materials) must decline as the expansion continues. Empirical data, presented in Part 2, found that this assumption is indeed true. In many previous cycles, consumer goods prices fluctuated less than all capital goods prices. At present, the prices of plant and equipment fluctuate about the same as consumer prices. But, the price of raw materials still fluctuates much more than consumer prices. Therefore, it may be asserted that all capital goods prices fluctuate more than all finished goods prices. It follows that the ratio of output prices to capital goods prices will fall in expansions as output is rising. This fall in an important price/cost ratio is considered of vital importance in these theories. This decline in the ratio of output prices to capital prices may be expressed as a decline in the money value of output to capital. Therefore:

$$Output/capital = negative\ function\ of\ output\ level \qquad (12.6)$$

As costs rise faster than prices in an expansion, the rising cost per unit will lower the profit rate, which causes less investment, leading to a recession or depression. In empirical terms, the closest thing to this assumption was found in Chapter 7, where it was found that raw material costs rise and fall faster than consumer prices. Chapter 22 will show that there is a statistically significant relation between the ratio of raw material prices to consumer prices and the movements of output.

OPERATION OF THE MATERIAL COST THEORY

The usual questions may be asked to see how this theory explains the business cycle.

HOW IS THE DOWNTURN EXPLAINED?

In this model, a rising rate of profit leads to greater investment. The new investment leads to more output. But as the level of output rises, the ratio of output prices to capital goods prices declines. Perhaps, also, as full capacity is approached, the physical output to capital ratio may decline. At any rate, the revenue from output does not rise as rapidly as the cost of capital goods (especially raw materials) for new investment. Therefore, all other things being equal, the rate of profit rises more slowly and eventually declines. The stagnant or declining rate of profit leads to a decline in investment. The decline in investment lowers output and income, so a recession or depression ensues.

HOW IS THE RECOVERY EXPLAINED?

The falling rate of profit causes less investment which leads to less output. As the contraction progresses, however, the cost of capital goods (at least raw material costs) falls faster than the prices of finished output. The physical output to capital ratio may also rise when the economy is no longer above its capacity ceiling and when the most inefficient firms go bankrupt in the depression. Therefore, the revenue from output does not decline as rapidly as the cost of capital goods. Eventually, the rate of profit declines very slowly or starts to rise. The better profit expectations cause a recovery of investment, which leads to greater output and employment.

EVALUATION OF THE OVER-INVESTMENT THEORY

Non-monetary over-investment theories have added to our understanding of the business cycle by the attention paid to price/cost ratios. The ratios of prices to costs, involving a microeconomic perspective, were not often investigated in the dominant period of Keynesian economics, but they are an important part of the story.

On the other hand, theories such as Hayek's do not consider other types of costs, such as labor costs. Above all, they do not consider problems of demand, without which one cannot understand the business cycle. Such theories are a useful part of the whole, but they are incomplete by themselves.

A WAGE COST CYCLE THEORY

Theories that high wages cause recessions are not new. In 1732, it was argued in the House of Commons that: "It is now a universal complaint in the Country that the high Wages given to Workmen is now the Chief Cause of the Decay of our Trade and Manufacturers; our business then, is to take all the Measures that we can think of, to enable our Workmen to work for less wages than they do at present" (quoted in Mirowski 1986b, 15).

Boddy and Crotty (1975) argued a wage cost theory as an explanation of the business cycle (also see the related discussion of long-run and cyclical issues in Glyn and Sutcliffe 1972, and in Gordon, Weisskopf, and Bowles 1987). Boddy and Crotty argued that in every expansion, the increasing output leads to increasing employment which slowly reduces the number of unemployed workers. As full employment approaches, there is a greater demand for labor relative to the supply. This causes the bargaining power of labor to improve. Moreover, as workers eventually come to realize their increased strength, they become more militant.

BOX 12.1

ECONOMISTS FOR AN EXPANDING UNIVERSE

These days, a growing number of economists are asking what propels growth and drawing inspiration from the ideas of Joseph A. Schumpeter (1883 – 1950), the Austrian economist and Harvard University professor. Like Schumpeter, these economists are focusing on technology, innovation and knowledge. And the underlying message of the Schumpeterians is fundamentally optimistic. "The one fact that comes from economic history is the ability of the human mind to break through barriers that weren't imaginable 50 years ago," says Joel Mokyr, economic historian at Northwestern University.

Traditionally, mainstream economics has been unable to explain what determines long-term growth. In the late 1950s, Nobel Laureate Robert M. Solow of Massachusetts Institute of Technology showed that increases in the economy's labor supply and capital stock explained only part of growth. The rest was attributed to technological change, but it was largely unexplainable.

The Schumpeterians go beyond traditional economics to look at what really drives technological change. They are analyzing how growth is affected by the support for technical innovation, educational institutions and rewards to entrepreneurs for coming up with new products. A leading Schumpeterian is Paul Romer of the University of California at Berkeley, perhaps one of the country's most influential young economists. Romer's theoretical work breaks new ground by showing how technological progress can supercharge growth, just as a new jet turbine or a new biotechnology drug spells the difference between a plodding economy and a dynamic one. Romer and other new growth theorists are finding support from such economic historians as Paul David of Stanford University. His empirical studies show the historic interplay between technological change and economic growth.

The most recent wave of research from the Schumpeterians focuses on the links between international trade and growth. In traditional economic theory, the benefits from free trade to a large economy such as the U.S. come mainly because consumers and businesses can pay lower prices for imports. While this is no small potatoes, it doesn't do much to increase growth in the long run.

Yet free trade may have a much bigger payoff than conventional economics allows. Free trade encourages the rapid spread of technology and industrial ideas, according to such trade theorists as Gene M. Grossman of Princeton and Elhanen Helpman of Tel-Aviv University, who have been influenced by the pioneering work of Paul R. Krugman of

Christopher Farrell
Business Week, May 16, 1994, page 64

CONTINUED ON NEXT PAGE...

BOX 12.1 — CONTINUED

MIT. Trade can also invigorate growth by providing access to bigger markets. Conversely, in many cases, barriers to trade slow the rate of technological transmission, leaving a protectionist country lagging far behind.

Take the developing countries of Latin America and the former East bloc nations. They learned the hard way that erecting trade barriers to protect domestic industries isolated them from global technological progress and helped condemn them to years of stagnation. And without fierce competitive pressure from the Japanese auto companies, it's doubtful U.S. carmakers would have felt compelled to engineer productivity gains of 10% a year in the 1980s.

Beyond trade, the theory has far-ranging implications for economic policy. Governments, businesses and universities have a key part to play in affecting the pace of innovation. Some Schumpeterians would like to see stronger government support of commercial technology, especially in the service sector, and others more industry collaboration to develop world-class products. "To achieve long-run success economic policy must support the institutions that generate ideas and technological progress," says Romer.

That militancy is reflected in the fact that the number of strikes rises in expansion and declines in contraction. As a result of their increased strength, employees are able to obtain higher wage rates. They are also able to prevent further speed-up of work, thereby reducing the growth of productivity.

For these reasons, according to this theory, the labor share will rise toward the end of expansion. The rising labor share means a decline in the profit share. All other things being equal (such as demand remaining constant), a decline in the profit share of the product causes a lower rate of profit. Finally, the reduced rate of profit lowers expectations for future profits. This causes a fall in investment, setting off a recession or depression.

In the crisis phase or early contraction, wages remain high due to labor strength and militancy, while productivity is held down. Thus the profit share falls further, the rate of profit is further reduced, and the contraction worsens.

Eventually, however, rising unemployment causes the strength and militancy of labor to disappear. In the last half of the recession or depression phase, the weakened labor movement cannot prevent falling wages and rising productivity. This means that the share of profits begins to rise once more, so the profit rate rises. The rising expectations of profit lead to new investment and an economic recovery begins.

It is important to emphasize that at the beginning of the recovery, unemployment remains very high, so labor remains very weak. Thus the profit share continues to rise in the recovery as productivity grows, but wages are sluggish. Only after the recovery has gone on for a long time does unemployment drop low enough that, with a time lag, labor begins to regain its strength. Thus it is only in the last half of expansion that the share of labor begins to rise once more, setting off the same cycle again.

A MODEL OF THE WAGE COST THEORY

What are the main relationships and assumptions of this theory? As part of its framework, we make the usual assumption that, in equilibrium, real national income equals real consumption plus real investment.

$$Income = consumption\ plus\ investment \tag{12.7}$$

This theory also distinguishes between labor and property income. It may be stressed that these two shares of national income equal the whole thing:

$$Labor\ share + property\ share = 1 \tag{12.8}$$

Thus if the labor share is specified, the property share, which equals one minus the labor share, is known.

THE CONSUMPTION FUNCTION

The path of consumption over the cycle must now be explained. As in the previous model, however, wage cost theorists assume that there is no lack of consumer demand, so it may be simply assumed to be a constant proportion of income. When income rises, it is assumed that consumer demand rises at the same rate. Repeating the same relationship as in the previous model:

$$Consumption = a\ constant \times national\ income \tag{12.9}$$

Since consumption clearly has no deficiency, investment emerges as the key variable.

THE INVESTMENT FUNCTION

Having outlined the less important, but logically necessary, parts of the model, the most vital part of this model may be turned to. As in the previous model, it is assumed that investment is a function of the change in the profit rate.

$$Investment\ (I) = f\ (change\ in\ profit\ rate) \qquad (12.10)$$

A rising rate of profit inspires confidence in the future and causes net investment. As noted before this finding is consistent with the evidence in Chapter 5 and Chapter 21.

DEFINITION OF PROFIT RATE

As in the previous model, the profit rate on capital can be thought of as the property or profit share of output times the ratio of output to capital:

$$Profit\ rate = profit/output \times output/capital \qquad (12.11)$$

This definition is very useful for the wage cost theory because it separates out the distribution of income between labor and profit recipients. It makes a separate component of the ratio of output to capital. Unlike the previous model, the output/capital ratio is not important to the wage cost theorists, but the distribution of income between labor and profit income is the most crucial issue for them. These two relationships are examined in the two following sections.

THE CAPITAL COST FUNCTION

The ratio of output to capital plays no explicit role in this model so it may be assumed to be constant.

$$Output/capital = constant \qquad (12.12)$$

THE DISTRIBUTION FUNCTION

The wage cost hypothesis states that the labor share rises in the last part of expansion and falls in the last part of contraction. The labor share behaves that way, according to this theory, because it is governed by the level of unemployment, with a time lag.

$$Labor\ share = -f\ (unemployment) \qquad (12.13)$$

The labor share is a negative function because greater unemployment weakens labor, which causes a decline in the labor share. Conversely, lower unemployment strengthens labor and produces a higher labor share. The property share is always equal to one minus the labor share, and consequently when the labor share is rising, the property share must fall, and vice versa. This behavior was discussed in Chapter 6, where unemployment was found to have some effect, but less than other variables. Part 5 shows that unemployment must be combined with other variables and be given a time lag to have a significant effect.

THE UNEMPLOYMENT FUNCTION

In this theory, the labor share is a function of unemployment, so we must explain what determines unemployment. The simplest answer is that unemployment and employment are related to the level of output, all other things being equal.

$$Unemployment = -f(national\ income) \tag{12.14}$$

Employment rises when there is a rise in real national income or output. Consequently, unemployment must react negatively to output, that is to say, higher output will lower unemployment. Evidence was found for this relationship in Chapter 6 and the relationship will be found to be statistically significant in Chapter 22.

OPERATION OF THE WAGE COST MODEL

How are these relationships put together? How can the question of why the business cycle exists be answered according to this model?

WHAT CAUSES A DOWNTURN?

When expansion first begins, unemployment is high, so the labor share is low and falling. According to this theory, a lower labor share means more profits for investors, leading to still more investment. The investment creates more jobs, there is more income, more consumption, and less unemployment.

As the expansion progresses, unemployment continues to drop. Employees and unions find that jobs are easier to get and profits are rising. Eventually, the lower unemployment rates give employees more bargaining strength and they become more militant, so the labor share rises. The rising labor share in the last half of expansion means a lower profit share, causing a lower rate of profit. The lower rate of profit reduces expectations. When investors have lower expectations, they invest less, and this leads to a recession or depression.

WHAT CAUSES A RECOVERY?

In the contraction, falling output leads to rising unemployment. As unemployment rises, it slowly undermines the strength of labor and its bargaining power. Employees are not able to keep their real wages from falling. They are forced to work harder, so productivity rises. By the last half of the contraction, because of rising unemployment, the share of labor in the national product begins to fall. A falling share of labor means a rising share of profits and other property returns. The higher rate of profit leads to rising expectations, an increase in investment, and an eventual economic recovery.

EVALUATION OF THE WAGE COST THEORY

The wage cost theory emphasizes some important facts. The rate of unemployment falls in the expansion phase of all business cycles. Wage costs are the largest single element of costs, so higher wages may significantly increase unit costs. Moreover, as a statement of the long-run equilibrium situation, high unemployment is associated with a low wage share.

In the short-run business cycle, however, economic expansion leads to falling unemployment and a falling labor share. Falling unemployment has a weaker effect than countervailing factors. Only at the end of each expansion does it have some noticeable effect, so the labor share is constant or rising just before the peak.

A more telling criticism of the wage cost theory is that the labor share only begins to rise (even in the 1950s and 1960s) *after* the profit rate begins to fall in an expansion. The rise in the labor share may be seen as an effect of the falling profit rate rather than a cause of it, let alone the only cause of it. In other words, wage costs are rising before the profit rate reaches its peak, but they are usually rising less rapidly than profit. Therefore, the *share* of labor is falling until profit reaches its peak. Only when the level of profit begins to fall does the labor share begin to rise. Since a rise in the labor share follows after the profit rate decline, it cannot explain the profit rate decline.

Moreover, what the wage cost theory neglects is the fact that the rate of profit is affected by factors other than the cost of labor. For example, if the cost of labor stays the same, but the cost of raw materials rises, then the profit rate of a firm using those raw materials will decline. There is also the fundamental fact that cost is not the only factor determining profits. Profits are determined by revenue minus costs. So if total cost remains the same, profit may still decline if revenue declines. How much revenue a firm earns depends on demand for its products. If aggregate demand declines then, even if costs stay the same, aggregate profits will decline because some goods remain unsold and/or some capacity remains unused.

The basic criticism of all supply or cost oriented cycle theories is that profit behavior cannot be understood without considering demand as well as cost. A theory based on both demand and cost factors will be presented in the next chapter.

KEY TERMS AND CONCEPTS

| non-monetary over-investment theory | material cost theories | wage cost theories |

APPENDIX 12 A
FORMALIZATION OF MATERIAL COST MODELS

Both the very conservative Frederick Hayek and the radical Karl Marx believed that rising capital costs, particularly rising raw material costs, may lead to a downturn. This appendix uses the analysis developed in this chapter to produce an over-investment model, concentrating on materials costs.

The materials cost model (leaving aside government and foreign trade) is as follows:

Income = consumption + investment

$$Y_t = C_t + I_t \tag{12A.1}$$

Consumption does not play an important role in this theory, so it is assumed that consumption has a constant ratio to income.

$$C_t = b\, Y_{t-1} \tag{12A.2}$$

Investment is a function of the change in the profit rate (Π/K).

$$I_t = r + p(\Pi/K_{t-1} - \Pi/K_{t-2}) \tag{12A.3}$$

The profit rate may be defined as the profit share (Π/Y) times the output-capital ratio (Y/K).

$$\Pi/K = (\Pi/Y)\,(Y/K) \tag{12A.4}$$

But the distribution of income between labor and property owners is not important for this model, so the property share is assumed to be constant.

$$\Pi/Y = k \tag{12A.5}$$

Finally, and most important, it is assumed, mainly because of movements in relative prices, that the ratio of output to capital will decline as the expansion progresses, but rise in business contractions.

$$Y/K_t = a - c\,Y_t \tag{12A.6}$$

These 6 equations and 6 variables may be reduced to one equation in one variable, namely, national income. By successive substitutions, the result is:

$$Y_t = H + AY_{t-1} + BY_{t-2} \tag{12A.7}$$

where
$$H = r$$
$$A = b - pkc$$
$$B = pkc$$

There will be cycles if A^2 is greater than $4B$. The cycles will be of constant amplitude if B equals one, damped if B is less than one, and explosive if B is greater than one.

APPENDIX 12 B
THE WAGE COST CYCLE MODEL

Both Wall Street economists and some Marxists believe that high wage rates may lead to economic downturns. The wage cost model is as follows (leaving aside government and foreign trade):

Income = consumption + investment

$$Y_t = C_t + I_t \tag{12B.1}$$

Income = property income + labor income

$$Y_t = \Pi_t + W_t \tag{12B.2}$$

from which it follows that $\Pi/Y = 1 - W/Y$. Thus, if the labor share is explained, so is the property share.

Consumption does not play an important role in this theory, so it is assumed that consumption has a constant ratio to income.

Consumption is a constant ratio of national income, or:

$$C_t = bY_{t-1} \tag{12B.3}$$

Investment is a function of the change in the profit rate (Π/K). When the profit rate grows more rapidly, investment rises.

Investment = positive function of profit rate, or:

$$I_t = r + p(\Pi/K_{t-1} - \Pi/K_{t-2}) \tag{12B.4}$$

The profit rate may be defined as the profit share (Π/Y) times the output-capital ratio (Y/K).

Profit / capital = profit / output × output / capital

$$\Pi/K = (\Pi/Y)\,(Y/K) \tag{12B.5}$$

But the output-capital ratio plays no important role in this model, so it is assumed to be constant.

Output / capital = constant

$$(Y/K)_t = k \tag{12B.6}$$

The key relationship in this theory is that the labor share is a negative function of unemployment (U) with a time lag.

Wages / income = negative function of unemployment, lagged

$$(W/Y)_t = a - gU_{t-1} \tag{12B.7}$$

Finally, unemployment rises when real income falls and vice versa.

Unemployment = negative function of national income

$$Ut = n - hYt \tag{12B.8}$$

So unemployment is a negative function of output, falling when output rises and vice versa. This means that the wage (or labor) share is a positive function of output.

There are eight variables and eight independent equations in this model, so the model is determined. By a series of substitutions, we obtain the following reduced form equation in terms of national income:

$$Y_t = H + AY_{t-1} + BY_{t-2} \qquad\qquad (12B.9)$$

where
$$H = r$$
$$A = b - pkgh$$
$$B = pkgh$$

This equation will produce cycles in the range where A^2 is less than $4B$. This proves that it is possible to have a logically coherent supply-side wage cost theory of the business cycle; but it says nothing about the realism of the assumptions.

CHAPTER 13

Profit Squeeze (or Nutcracker) Theory of the Cycle

The review of demand-side theories and supply-side theories in the previous two chapters makes clear the opposing points of view. This chapter begins with a general framework in which there is room for both the demand-side factors (which affect revenue) and the supply-side factors (which affect cost); then it turns to a more specific model in which profits are squeezed in the expansion by both limited revenues and rising costs.

A GENERAL FRAMEWORK FOR BUSINESS CYCLE THEORY

Most economists would agree that profits and/or expected profits must play a major role in understanding business cycle behavior. The reader may be reminded of the simple definition that profit equals revenue minus costs. If revenue can be accurately portrayed, a picture of the flow of actual effective demand over the business cycle will be given. If costs can be accurately portrayed, they may give an understanding of supply behavior over the cycle. How to aggregate all of the revenues and all of the costs in the society are difficult and controversial questions.

For aggregate revenue, the road signaled by John Maynard Keynes may be followed:

$$GDP = consumption + investment + government + net\ exports \qquad (13.1)$$

This is a description of the spending or revenue flows, reflecting demand conditions. For aggregate costs, the lead of Wesley Mitchell may be followed:

$$GDP = labor\ costs + depreciation + taxes + rent$$
$$+ interest + raw\ material\ costs + profits \qquad (13.2)$$

This is a description of the flow of income, or costs plus profit, reflecting supply conditions. Notice that profits may be defined on the basis of these two relationships:

From equation 13.2, it can be seen that profit equals GDP minus real costs. But equation 13.1 shows GDP in terms of revenue. By substitution:

$$Profit = (consumption + investment + government$$
$$+ net\ exports) - (labor\ costs + depreciation$$
$$+ taxes + rent + interest + raw\ material\ costs) \qquad (13.3)$$

This equation provides a very general profit framework—revenue minus costs, into which most theories can be fit. Thus a theory may concentrate on consumer spending and ignore most of the other components. A theory might concentrate on interest costs and ignore most of the other components. This formulation stresses that all the components of both revenue and costs must be considered. Most of these components are defined, discussed, and represented empirically in separate chapters in Parts 2 and 4.

THE CONCEPT OF PROFIT SQUEEZE

One specific use of this general framework is to understand the profit squeeze hypothesis. This theory has been called the nutcracker theory because a downturn is caused by the closing of the jaws of the nutcracker on profits from the demand or revenue side, as well as from the cost or supply side. The hypothesis is that profits are limited both by production (through the purchase and use of inputs in the production process) and by the sale of the outputs.

A more precise and scholarly term for the theory might be a profit squeeze theory. The only problem with that name is that it has frequently been used in a careless way by advocates of various supply-side theories, who say that profit is squeezed by rising costs. But it is impossible in the ordinary English use of the words to say that profit is squeezed from one side only. Profit can be squeezed only from both sides. Put an orange on the floor and try pushing it from one side with nothing on the other side. The orange rolls across the floor and is not squeezed. That costs rise 5 percent a year, for example, tells us nothing about the profit rate until we know whether revenue rose more or less than costs. What if revenue rose 10 percent a year?

Elementary economics teaches that profits equal revenue minus costs. Revenues are rising in an expanding economy, so profits are squeezed only if costs rise faster than revenues. When cost theorists tell nothing about demand or its effect on revenue, they cannot tell a logically complete tale about the squeeze on profits. Similarly, if demand-side or revenue theorists tell nothing about supply or its effect on costs, then neither can they tell us a logically complete tale about the squeeze on profits. Thus, the term profit squeeze is used here to mean that profit is squeezed from both sides. To avoid misunderstanding, it should be noted that several possible causes can lead to a profit squeeze: (1) revenue may be constant while costs rise, (2) revenue may rise but costs rise more, (3) revenue may fall, but costs rise or are constant or fall less than revenue. The hypothesis is that profit is squeezed in one of these three senses, and most usually in the second sense, that costs rise faster than revenue in expansions.

SOME PREVIOUS THEORIES AND THE CONCEPT OF PROFIT SQUEEZE

A number of theorists have referred to various aspects of the profit squeeze approach. A number of them will be discussed below.

Karl Marx explicitly addressed the need to consider both costs and demand in a complete theory. He outlined three stages in the process of profit creation. First, the entrepreneur buys capital goods and labor power as cheaply as possible. Second, the entrepreneur uses these inputs in the production process, attempting to get labor to work as hard as possible in order to produce property income known as profit, rent, and interest. Third, the entrepreneur sells the product for as high a price as possible, in order to realize the profit that is embodied in the product through production. Marx writes:

> The creation of . . . surplus value [profit] is the object of the direct process of production. . . . But . . . now comes the second act of the process. The entire mass of commodities . . . must be sold. If this is not done, or only partly accomplished . . . the laborer has been none the less exploited, but his exploitation does not realize as much for the capitalist. (Marx 1909, 3: 286).

If the profit rate declines, either because less profit is embodied in the product in the production process or because less profit is realized through sales, less new investment will result. Less new investment leads to a depression.

According to John Maynard Keynes, new investment is determined by the marginal efficiency of capital (MEC). Roughly, the MEC is the expected rate of profit on investment. Keynes conceptualizes the MEC as the difference between the expected flow of revenue and the expected flow of costs. Keynes emphasized the role of effective demand in determining revenue. He also engaged in an extensive discussion of the role of labor costs, as well as in the role of rising capital goods prices in the expansion (see Keynes 1936, 248).

Keynes asserts that the shape of the business cycle "is mainly due to the way in which the MEC fluctuates" (Keynes 1936, 313). The downturn is due to pessimism over the future of the MEC. "The disillusion comes because doubts suddenly arise concerning the reliability of the perspective yield, perhaps because the current yield shows signs of falling off, as the stock of newly produced durable goods steadily increases. . . . Once doubt begins, it spreads rapidly" (Keynes 1936, 317). Keynes stresses the objective behavior of current profits, though elsewhere he emphasizes subjective uncertainty that affects the animal spirits of investors. (An excellent analysis of Keynes on the business cycle, distinguishing objective and subjective influences on the MEC, appears in Burkett and Wokar 1987.)

Wesley Mitchell had some influence on Keynes. It is not surprising that Mitchell also stressed the centrality of profits. "Since the quest for money profits by business enterprises is the controlling factor among the activities of men who live in a money economy, the whole discussion must center around the prospect for profits" (Mitchell 1913, xi). Mitchell visualized profit as equal to price per unit times output, minus cost per unit times output. Mitchell painstakingly considered the course of each type of price and cost at each stage of the cycle in order to explain profit behavior. (Mitchell's work on cycles is discussed very favorably and in great detail by a number of writers in the collection by Burns 1952, and by Klein 1983.)

Mitchell calls the last half of expansion the prosperity phase, but it is a prosperity nurturing the seeds of its own downfall. He charts the rise of raw material prices, the rise of interest rates, the rise of wages, and the faltering of productivity growth. At the end of expansion, prices do not rise as rapidly as costs, according to Mitchell, for several reasons: (a) public regulation of some prices, (b) long-run contracts for output, and (c) production of a vast new supply of goods, which may outrun consumer demand.

Michal Kalecki (1968) constructs an excellent internal, dynamic model of the business cycle, quite unlike the equilibrium-and-shock approach of many current theorists. "The approach of Kalecki is generally concerned with the evolution of an economic system through time, without imposing any view that the system would reach some equilibrium position or that it would grow at some balanced equilibrium rate of growth" (Sawyer 1985b, 9).

At the heart of Kalecki's model is the influence of profits on investment. Kalecki's investment function includes the change in profits and the change in capital (which will affect the rate of profit). Unlike those who ignore one or the other, Kalecki always stressed the influence of both demand and supply (or revenue and costs) on profits. He considered explicitly how the labor share influences consumer demand and how lack of consumer demand is one of the entrepreneur's problems. Furthermore, he noted the importance of investment demand for profits. Yet, he also emphasizes raw material prices and other costs.

Because he recognized both the demand and supply influences on profits, and because he recognized the interaction of profits and investment, Kalecki's model is far more sophisticated than many later ones. Although his theory was first stated in 1935, it remains one of the best places to begin to understand formal models of the business cycle. Kalecki's tradition has been carried on by many of the post-Keynesians, such as Sawyer (1985) and Eichner (1987).

THE PROFIT SQUEEZE (OR NUTCRACKER) THEORY

Henceforth, the term, profit squeeze, is used to define a theory that views profit as being determined by both revenue and cost. The profit squeeze theory may begin the usual way by stating that in equilibrium, output supplied (that is, gross domestic product, or GDP) must equal output demanded by consumers and investors, leaving aside government and net exports.

$$GDP = consumption + investment \qquad (13.4)$$

It is important to emphasize that any equilibrium is only momentary, at such times as supply catches up to demand. Moreover, the path traced by demand is neither constant nor steadily rising, but is roughly cyclical. Even the notion that supply temporarily catches up to demand is unrealistic. In the expansion, supply is usually below demand because the effective demand can rise rapidly but physical production lags behind. In the contraction, supply is usually above demand, meaning that effective demand can fall rapidly; however, physical production usually declines more slowly.

Nevertheless, it is still the case that by definition (leaving aside depreciation, taxes, rent, and interest):

$$GDP = labor\ income + raw\ materials\ cost + profits \qquad (13.5)$$

Note that since taxes, rent, and interest are excluded from the model, profits are equal to property income.

THE CONSUMPTION FUNCTION

This model uses a consumption function that was developed in the effective demand model. The focus of the consumption function theory is that consumption is not merely a function of national income but is also influenced by the distribution of income; specifically, the share of labor in the national income. If the labor share rises, the average and marginal propensity to consume will rise. The reason is that labor's propensity to consume is higher than that of property owners. Conversely, a falling labor share will lead to a falling propensity to consume. Thus:

$$Consumption = all\ of\ labor\ income + part\ of\ property\ income \qquad (13.6)$$

Equation 13.6 indicates that consumer demand reacts positively to both higher national income and a higher share of labor in the national income. The chapter on consumption (Chapter 4) presented evidence from many empirical studies that the MPC out of labor income is indeed much higher than the MPC out of property income. Part V shows econometric evidence that the hypothesis—aggregate propensity to consume is influenced by the labor share—is statistically significant and cannot be disproved. The model requires only that labor income MPC be higher than property income MPC. Here, for simplicity, it is assumed that the MPC of labor income is equal to one only, as a first approximation.

THE INVESTMENT FUNCTION

The investment function theory uses a broader investment function than that based on demand alone. In order to include not only demand but also the cost side of labor and capital goods, the theory contends that new investment is a function of the change in profit. Remember that profit equals revenue (from demand) minus costs (of supply).

$$Investment = function\ of\ (change\ in\ profit) \qquad (13.7)$$

Thus, investment demand is higher if profit is rising rapidly but will fall when profit is stagnant or declining. In Chapter 5 it was established that the NBER measures imply that there is a positive relationship between investment and profits, as well as profit rates. Investment is probably related both to the level of profit and to the change in profit, though it is not easy to separate out the different influences. Facts are presented in Part V that indicate a statistically significant relationship between investment and profits as well as profit rates, so the hypothesis that profits and profit rates influence investment cannot be disproved.

THE PROFIT FUNCTION

A crucial point of the profit function theory is that profit is related both to demand and to supply variables. Thus, profit is positively related to aggregate demand and is reflected in capacity utilization (as the effective demand theory would argue). The profit rate is, however, also negatively related to labor costs (as argued by the wage cost theorists). Furthermore, profit is negatively related to the cost of raw materials (as argued by the material costs theorists). Higher wages or a higher share of wages in the product will mean higher costs. Ultimately, higher prices of raw materials relative to finished good prices will lead to a higher ratio of costs to revenue. So, it follows that:

$$Profit = (consumption + investment)$$
$$- (labor\ costs + raw\ material\ costs) \qquad (13.8)$$

Notice that this equation is identical with 13.3, except that it has been simplified by leaving out those components that are not essential to the model and that have not yet been discussed in detail.

The fact that labor income has a positive impact on demand (producing higher capacity utilization), while labor income is negative from a cost viewpoint, serves to emphasize the dual nature of labor income. If labor receives higher wages, this means higher costs, yet it also means higher consumer demand. Demand increases revenue, but higher labor costs will increase the cost of production.

It is clear that a change in wages has two separate and opposed effects on aggregate profits: the demand effect versus the cost effect. Which effect is greater cannot be determined by theory alone. Theory can only show that both relationships exist. Which effect will be more powerful will be determined by (1) the actual strength of each variable in each relationship, and (2) the time lags involved in each relationship. Testing the two effects by econometrics would require a model of considerable complexity.

It can be said, however, that in most of each expansion, real wages are rising but profits rise even more. It may be concluded that the demand effect of high wages dominates the cost effect in that period. Similarly, in most of each contraction, real wages decline but profits decline even more. Again, the demand effect appears to dominate in that period. These conclusions are compatible with the empirical findings of Weisskopf (1979). What happens around the turning points is more complex and is discussed below.

THE DISTRIBUTION FUNCTION

The distribution of income in the distribution function model is represented by the labor share of national income (meaning labor divided by national income). The labor share is a negative function of capacity utilization (because wages lag in the expansion of output), but is also a negative function of unemployment. The fact that the labor share goes down when the capacity utilization goes up reflects the wage lag hypothesis. This hypothesis says that wages lag behind property income (that is, profits, rent, and interest). The labor share is also assumed to be a negative function of unemployment, in accordance with the wage cost theory, though with a long time lag.

$$Labor\ share = -f^1\ (capacity\ utilization)$$
$$-f^2\ (unemployment) \qquad (13.9)$$

Thus the distribution function, like the profit function, combines those elements of both demand and supply theories found to be accurate. The capacity utilization effect is dominant, but the unemployment effect exists, though it is weaker and has a long time lag.

Is the hypothesis that the labor share is affected by both capacity utilization and unemployment consistent with the empirical data? In Chapter 6, it was found that the labor share is counter-cyclical, falling in business expansion and rising in the business contraction. Capacity utilization was found to be pro-cyclical, rising in business expansions and falling in business contractions. It therefore appears to be the case that the two do move counter to each other, suggesting a negative function. In Part 5, it will be established that there is a statistically significant negative relationship between the labor share and capacity utilization.

The case for a relationship between the labor share and unemployment is more complex. In the long run, it is obvious that large-scale unemployment leads to lower wages, while full employment leads to higher wages. What exactly is the cyclical relationship? Unemployment is strongly counter-cyclical, falling in expansions and rising in contractions. Thus, the NBER measures in Chapter 6 would lead to the conclusion that any relationship between unemployment and the labor share is positive, since they both usually move the same direction! Furthermore, if the econometric relation between the two by themselves is examined, no significant relation is found.

But there clearly is a relationship. When the relation of the labor share to both capacity utilization and to unemployment is examined, both influences are statistically significant. It is determined that the influence of capacity utilization is stronger and immediate, while the influence of unemployment is weaker and with a time lag. Thus, the econometric evidence does not disprove the hypothesis stated here about the cyclical movement of the labor share.

THE UNEMPLOYMENT FUNCTION

Since the labor share is partly dependent on unemployment, it is essential to know how unemployment is determined. The evidence of the NBER measures presented in Chapter 5 and the econometric evidence of Part 5 both show that unemployment is a negative function of output demanded, or GDP:

$$Unemployment = -f\ (gross\ domestic\ product) \qquad (13.10)$$

As GDP and output rise, unemployment declines. As GDP and output decline, unemployment rises.

THE MATERIAL COST FUNCTION

For pre-World War II cycles, the evidence was presented in Chapter 7 that the cost of capital goods (plant, equipment, and raw materials) rose faster than the price of finished goods in expansions. The price of capital goods also fell faster than the price of finished goods in contractions.

In the period since World War II, there have been two changes: (1) the price of plant and equipment has moved roughly the same as consumer goods, but raw material prices still move differently, and (2) there has been inflation even during recessions. What is still the case, however, is that in the cycles of the 1970s and 1980s, the ratio of raw material prices to consumer goods prices has always risen in expansions and fallen in contractions. Perhaps, the simplest way to describe this is that raw material costs rise and fall with GDP, but fluctuate more:

$$\text{Cost of raw materials} = f\,(\text{gross domestic product}) \qquad (13.11)$$

where the cost of raw materials rises faster than GDP.

Obviously, the rising cost of raw materials hurts profits in the expansion, while the declining cost helps profits in the contraction periods. Empirically, it was found in Chapter 7 that the ratio of raw material costs to the consumer price index is strongly pro-cyclical, normally rising in expansions and falling in contractions. In Part 5, it will be found that the ratio of raw material costs to the consumer price index has a statistically significant relationship to GDP.

CAPACITY UTILIZATION FUNCTION

Capacity utilization always rises and falls with real national output, so its function may be written:

$$\text{Capacity utilization} = f\,(\text{gross domestic product}) \qquad (13.12)$$

It was found in Chapter 6 that capacity utilization is pro-cyclical, rising in expansions and falling in contractions. It moves the same direction as income and output at all times. In Part 5, the econometric evidence shows that there is a statistically significant relationship between capacity utilization and GDP.

OPERATION OF THE PROFIT SQUEEZE MODEL

To see how the model operates requires asking the usual questions as to why there is a cumulative expansion, why it leads to a downturn, why there is a cumulative contraction, and why it leads to a recovery.

WHY DOES RECOVERY LEAD TO A CUMULATIVE EXPANSION?

DEMAND.   Real consumer demand rises most rapidly during recovery. The increase reflects the rise of national income which also rises most rapidly in this phase. As demand for output rises, so does capacity utilization. Real investment demand also rises more rapidly in recovery than at any other time. The reason is the rapid increase in expected profits reflects increases in present profits. New investment, via the multiplier process of consumer responding, leads to even larger increases in national income. Increases in national income, via the accelerator, lead to higher levels of investment.

COST.   Total real labor costs (wages, salaries, and so forth) rise more rapidly in recovery than at any other time. Real labor income, however, does not rise as rapidly as property income, so its share declines. Positive influences on the labor share are the slow increase in per hour wages and the rapid increase in employment, though most of the increases in employment come from the ranks of the unemployed, so there is little pressure on wages. But the wage increase is far outweighed by the large increase in productivity, which is more rapid in recovery than at any other time. The increase in productivity goes automatically to increase business profits, because only with a time lag can employees attempt to renegotiate fixed wage and salary scales.

The rapid increase in production of finished goods means an even more rapid percentage increase in demand for raw materials. As the demand outstrips the supply, the price of raw materials begins to rise. Yet, the price increase is held down somewhat at this period because there are reserves of raw materials and unused capacity from the depression phase.

PROFITS.   In the recovery period, aggregate demand increases very rapidly. At the same time, the unit cost of supply is rising relatively slowly, partly because prices of inputs are rising slowly, but especially because productivity is rising rapidly. As a result, total profits, the profit share of income, the profit rate on sales, and the profit rate on capital are all rising rapidly. The effect of this rise in profitability is (1) rising availability of internal funds for investment and (2) rising profit expectations for the future. Therefore, investment also rises rapidly. Of course, new investment leads, via the multiplier, to more income and more consumption. The greater demand again raises profits, leading to more investment, more employment, more income, and so forth. Thus, there is a cumulative expansion, causing the movement into the phase called prosperity.

WHAT CAUSES THE DOWNTURN OR CRISIS?

CONSUMER DEMAND. Real consumer demand rises slower and slower in prosperity. National income growth also slows down, but not quite as much. So the average propensity to consume continues to decline. The continued decline of the average propensity to consume reflects primarily the continued decline of the labor share. Entrepreneurs may also be saving a higher percentage of their increasing income. At any rate, the growth of consumer demand, which is the largest part of all demand, is very limited near the cycle peak.

COSTS. Real wages per hour are rising very slowly. Productivity is also rising very slowly, but still slightly faster than hourly wages (as explained in Chapter 8). So, the share of labor usually continues to decline, but very slowly (and is usually about constant before the peak). When the labor share stops declining, due to stagnant productivity, the average propensity to consume also stops declining (after a time lag). But profits and profit rates are already declining, so the process leading to contraction is already underway. Why does productivity growth fall from its rapid pace in recovery to a much slower pace in prosperity? As Chapter 8 discussed in detail, overhead workers are now fully utilized, so no further easy gains are possible in this respect. Furthermore, as full capacity is approached, firms may reach or go beyond the optimum use of capacity (though most costs are constant in a wide range). Moreover, many small firms enter the market, some of which are quite inefficient. Demand for raw materials continues to rise to the peak. But supply in many areas is limited to existing mines and farms (with particular amounts of crops planted or animals born), causing supply to increase slowly (often several years). Hence, the price of raw materials rises rapidly at this time.

PROFITS. Aggregate demand is rising more slowly in this phase. An important reason is that consumer demand is limited by a falling propensity to consume. The fall in the propensity to consume is caused mainly by a falling labor share. A time lag causes the propensity to consume to continue to fall even after the labor share stops declining. Declining growth in demand is reflected in declining growth in capacity utilization. Yet at the same time, costs are rising rapidly because of the rising price of raw materials. Therefore, profits are squeezed more and more as the peak is approached. Geoffrey Moore writes: "Whereas at the beginning of an expansion, prices are typically rising faster than costs, at the end costs are typically rising faster than prices . . . putting a squeeze on profits" (1983, 282).

It must be stressed once more that the reader should not confuse total profits with the profit share. The profit share always rises and falls exactly opposite to the movements of the labor share because they divide all income between them (leaving aside rent and interest for simplicity). Profits, however, are determined not only by labor costs (and the profit share of output), but also by other costs and by revenue, which is determined by demand.

This distinction is very important because, in the scenario related here: (1) profits influence investment, but (2) the profit share is only one of the factors determining profits. In the typical expansion, the labor share falls and the profit share rises for most of the expansion. In this period, profits rise because demand rises faster than costs (in spite of a falling propensity to consume).

Eventually, however, usually about one stage before the peak, costs (mainly raw material costs and interest costs) rise slightly faster than demand (held down by a declining propensity to consume). At this point, therefore, real profit begins to decline slowly and a recession becomes inevitable (for reasons discussed below).

Real wages may still inch up slowly (or be constant or even decline a little) so the labor share stops declining and is nearly constant (or rises slightly or continues to fall slightly). The propensity to consume usually continues declining slowly to the peak because it is influenced by the labor share with a time lag. So, demand rises very slowly to the peak while costs rise more rapidly. Thus, profits are declining, though the profit share may be about constant (or with very slight rise or decline) to the peak.

Declining aggregate profits also mean a declining profit rate on capital. The reason is that the amount of capital (by the usual measurements, which are not trustworthy in theory or in calculation) moves extremely slowly relative to the rapid movements of profits. In the above discussion of profits, the term, profit rate, could be substituted for profits since they move almost identically over the cycle.

INVESTMENT.   Why is a contraction inevitable once profits (and profit rates) begin to decline? The reason is that the decline in profits causes a delayed decline in investment. Actually, the profit decline first affects investment decisions (reflected in a reduction of new appropriations for plant and equipment) and then those decisions lead to a reduction of actual new investment. So they cause profits and profit rates to turn down well before the peak, causing actual investment to turn down at the peak. The fall in investment sets off the contraction by causing a fall in employment and income.

WHY DOES A CRISIS TURN INTO A CUMULATIVE DOWNTURN?

DEMAND.   Real consumer demand falls because real income is falling. Yet, the average propensity to consume begins to rise, causing consumption to fall less than income. The main reason that consumption falls less than income is that the labor share of income begins to rise. Real investment demand also falls rapidly in the crisis, reflecting the rapid decline of profit expectations and lack of available profits for reinvestment.

COST.   Real aggregate wages decline in the crisis as a result of falling real wages per hour and rising unemployment (though unemployment usually lags behind output). Yet, the labor share of income begins to rise. The labor share increases because, although real hourly wages are falling, productivity is falling much faster. Productivity falls because employment does not decline as rapidly as output. Although some skilled workers may be retained, the main reason is that most overhead workers, such as bookkeepers or guards, cannot be fired when production fails.

Falling production lowers the demand for raw materials. The supply of raw materials declines very slowly because it means closing mines and planting less crops for the following year. Therefore, prices of raw materials tend to decline in crises, often even when there is general inflation.

PROFITS.   Aggregate demand is falling rapidly because of the decline in consumption demand and the very rapid fall in investment demand. Aggregate cost is falling slower because real wages and raw material prices decline very slowly at first. As a result, aggregate profits and the rate of profit fall rapidly in the crisis. This decline in profits causes production and investment to fall even further (through the accelerator). The decline in production and investment lowers employment, consumer demand, and income once again (through the multiplier process).

WHAT CAUSES THE UPTURN OR RECOVERY?

DEMAND.   Real consumer demand continues to fall, but very slowly (and sometimes rises in mild cycles). The decline in consumption is very slow because income is declining slowly in this phase, but also because the average propensity to consume is rising. The propensity to consume rises mainly because the labor share is rising (though very slowly by the end of the depression).

Real investment continues to decline in the depression so long as profits and profit rates decline, since this means lower profit expectations and less available internal funds. Towards the end of depression profit expectations begin to rise, leading to a recovery in investment at the trough.

COST.   In the depression, aggregate real wages, real hourly wages, and productivity are all falling, while unemployment rises. The share of labor, however, continues to rise slowly in the first part of depression. Near the trough, however, productivity may cease declining and begin to rise. The reason is that business firms now fire every possible worker, even some who are very skilled and also some overhead workers. For this reason, the labor share stops rising and may remain constant before the cycle trough.

In the depression, the price of raw materials continues to fall. Thus, by the end of the depression, total costs are falling rapidly.

PROFITS.   Profits and profit rates continue falling in the early depression phase because demand falls faster than the cost of supply. Yet demand falls slower and slower, while costs are still declining rapidly. Therefore, at some point, often before the trough, but not always, the profit rate and total profits will stop their decline, flatten out, and even rise a little. As soon as profit rates improve even slightly (or possibly if the rate of decline becomes very slight), profit expectations improve. Improved expectations lead to a rise in investment at the trough, marking the beginning of recovery.

CONCLUSIONS

The profit squeeze model succeeds in its main purpose of combining the elements of revenue and cost in one simple model. However, it has many limitations and weaknesses.

The main problem with the theory stated in this chapter is that it still leaves out some very important variables. A complete model would need to incorporate the usual behavior of government, which is obviously vital to the U.S. economy. A complete model would have to incorporate an international sector, which becomes more important to the U.S. economy every day. A complete model would have to incorporate all of the financial factors in the economy which alone can explain why expansions may become booms and why some recessions become deep depressions. Finally, a complete model would have to consider the impact of monopoly power on the economic behavior of the business cycle. With any of these factors left out, a model is extremely incomplete and is, at best, only a first approximation.

Another limitation of the model is its high level of aggregation. The model does not consider different types of consumer demand (such as goods versus services), types of investment, degrees of competition in different sectors, and so forth.

KEY TERMS AND CONCEPTS

| profit squeeze | revenue and cost | capacity utilization |
| nutcracker | demand and supply | |

APPENDIX 13 A
A FORMAL MODEL OF THE PROFIT SQUEEZE (OR NUTCRACKER) THEORY

The first section of this Appendix presents the simplest possible model that integrates both demand (revenue) factors and supply (cost) factors with behavioral equations showing how they squeeze profits at the cycle peak and increase profits at the cycle trough. More realistic and complex equations with the same conclusions are considered in the following section.

If there is equilibrium (ignoring government and net exports), then output (Y) in terms of spending (demand, revenue), equals consumer spending (C) plus investment spending (I):

$$Y_t = C_t + I_t \tag{13A.1}$$

Note that all variables in this Appendix are in constant dollars, and that Y represents the gross domestic product.

If there is equilibrium (ignoring taxes, depreciation, rent, and interest), then output in terms of cost (supply, income) must also equal labor cost (W) plus raw materials cost (M) plus profits (Π):

$$Y_t = W_t + M_t + \Pi_t \tag{13A.2}$$

Since rent and interest are being ignored, property income is the same as profits. Profits or property income (Π) may be derived from equation 13A.2, so:

$$\Pi_t = Y_t - (W_t + M_t) = (C_t + I_t) - (W_t + M_t) \tag{13A.3}$$

This equation merely says that aggregate profit equals aggregate revenue minus aggregate costs (suitably defined to avoid double counting).

Consumer spending is determined by the propensity to consume out of property income and the propensity to consume out of labor income:

$$C_t = a + b\Pi_{t-1} + W_{t-1} \tag{13A.4}$$

Note that it is assumed that the propensity to consume out of labor income equals one, whereas the propensity to consume out of property income is much less than one. This consumption function then says that consumer demand will rise when employees get a higher proportion of national income, but falls when employees get a lower proportion of national income.

Investment spending is a positive function of the change in profits (Π) with a time lag.

$$I_t = v(\Pi_t - \Pi_{t-1}) \tag{13A.5}$$

Although this profit function is oversimplified, it does remind us to consider both the demand and cost aspects of profit-making.

The share of labor, which influences both revenue and cost, is a negative function of both capacity utilization (Y/Z) and unemployment (U), but capacity utilization is a stronger factor than unemployment.

$$(W/Y)_t = w - zY/Z_t - uU_{t-1} \tag{13A.6}$$

Unemployment actually operates only with a long time lag.

Unemployment must now be explained. Unemployment is a negative function of output.

$$U_t = j - kY_t \tag{13A.7}$$

The raw material costs (M) are a positive function of output:

$$M_t = m + nY_t \tag{13A.8}$$

where n is greater than one, since material costs rise faster than total revenue or output. In order to portray total raw material costs as rising faster than total revenue during expansions, it is assumed that the same general price deflator is used to deflate both national output and raw material costs.

Finally, capacity utilization is assumed to be a function of real national income:

$$Y/Z_t = q + rY_t \tag{13A.9}$$

By successive substitutions, it is possible to arrive at one reduced form equation, all in terms of output at times t, $t-1$, and $t-2$. The parameters, however, are much too complex to carry any meaning to anyone reading them, so they are not presented here. For those who like algebra, it is a good exercise to work out the parameters. Although the parameters are a very complex, large group of constants, this is still a second order difference equation, so the solution is well-known. The formal conditions for cycles will be the same as in the previous two chapters.

SOME QUALIFICATIONS OF THE MODEL

First, the functions were stated as simply as possible in this Appendix. A realistic model would allow for much more complex time lags, different for each variable, and distributed across several periods for some variables. Thus, in most of the equations, it should be imagined that there is influence from several previous time periods shown in the equation. This makes the mathematics far more complex because this will be a higher order difference equation, with many time lags.

Second, this model uses only linear relationships. In reality, most relationships are not linear, but are non-linear. If a model is used with far more complex time lags and non-linear relationships, it would be much more realistic, but much less easy to understand. Perhaps what should be emphasized is that the reader may take the general relationships and functions seriously as a picture of the business cycle, but the precise forms of those relationships are not meant to be taken very seriously. The simple model shown above merely illustrated the main lines of the profit squeeze model, but it was not meant for econometric forecasting, for which one must specify more complex functions.

Third, as noted in the chapter, this model leaves out government spending, international relations, taxes, rent, and interest, all of which are discussed in the next part of this book. It is worth looking briefly at some of the particular equations to emphasize these three general points.

If equation 13A.1 is to be realistic, it must include government spending and net exports. If equation 13A.2 is to be realistic, it must include taxes, depreciation, rent, and interest.

Equation 13A.4 on consumption must consider other variables, such as availability of consumer credit. The consumption function must also allow for the influence of several previous periods, so the two types of incomes may be shown over several previous periods. Some of the relationships appear to be non-linear in reality in the consumer equation.

In equation 13A.5 on investment, it is important to consider the influence of profits for several previous periods, the influence, if any, of profit rates on investment independent of total profits, and the possibilities for non-linear forms of relationship. Of course, present and past profits are used in the investment equation as an indicator of future expected profits, so it may be necessary to make this relationship more explicit.

Equation 13A.6 on income distribution should include unemployment at various lagged intervals, not just at one time. Equation 13A.7 on unemployment may involve a non-linear relationship as well as more lagged relationships. Equation 13A.8 on raw material costs undoubtedly should also include more time lags and/or non-linear relations. Equation 13A.9 on capacity utilization is also likely to be non-linear.

Given all of these additional variables and more complex mathematical relationships, the end result would be an extremely complex set of equations. These equations could not easily be put into the form of a single reduced form equation because the general rules about when the system would be cyclical would be hard to calculate and it would be difficult to determine under what conditions the system would be explosive or damped. It would not be of much use, for simple illustration of a theory, but it would be much closer to a realistic econometric model that might possibly be simulated on a computer to find the answers we need.

Adding Realism to the Basic Model

Part 4 builds upon the theories presented in Part 2 and adds realism to these simple models. A chapter is devoted to the important role of the institutions of money and credit in the business cycle. Another chapter considers the economic role of small, competitive businesses and the role of large corporations with varying degrees of monopoly power. The next chapter presents the role of the business cycle in the international economy.

Most importantly, the role of the government in influencing the business cycle is discussed.

CHAPTER 14

Credit and Financial Crises

This chapter explores the vital role of money, credit, and finance in the business cycle, including both its demand aspects and supply aspects. The main hypothesis of this chapter is that the downturn is initiated by the decline in profits, but the credit system plays a crucial role in determining whether a recession becomes a depression. As many other economists have argued, the economic system becomes more vulnerable and financially fragile in an expansion, so a small decline in profit expectations may set off a financial crisis, causing a depression. On the other hand, credit plays a positive role in recovery and early expansion.

MONEY AND CRISIS

During an expansionary period, credit is used to spend on investment beyond immediate income (going into debt) and beyond the objective prospects for profit-making. Since it is beyond the objective conditions, this use of credit is called speculative; it postpones the decline but produces a flood of goods that are beyond the objective limits of the market. Consumers also overestimate their prospects for future income so they use credit to buy more than they can repay out of income. This increasing use of credit for consumption also postpones the decline, but increases vulnerability to personal bankruptcy.

When the contraction occurs, consumers face unemployment or have lower real wages. Consumers are unable to buy and businesses are unable to sell all the goods produced. The excessive debts of firms and of consumers lead to corporate and personal bankruptcies in the contraction, so that loans from banks cannot be repaid. In that case, banks cannot pay all their depositors, there are runs on banks and some banks also go bankrupt. When the collapse comes, everyone wants money and few wants goods.

What is interest and how does it behave? Interest is part of total profit. The owner of industrial capital keeps a certain amount of profit in proportion to his or her equity. But profit also goes in the form of interest to the lenders of financial capital. Because interest is part of total profit, the interest rate is usually below the overall profit rate, except in a crisis.

The level of the interest rate reflects the struggle between the financial and industrial entrepreneurs under given customs, traditions, and laws, with given conditions of supply and demand. The relevant laws (such as usury laws, interest-rate ceilings, and monetary policy) are also determined by that struggle. Before private enterprise, loans were mostly made for luxuries, military expenditure, and other non-productive items. Under private enterprise, consumer credit remains important, but the key to investment is credit lent by financial firms to industrial and merchant firms.

At the beginning of expansion, financial firms are in a weak bargaining position because there is an excess supply of money capital over the market demand for it. As demand starts rising, due to better profit prospects and speculation, the interest rate rises. In the prosperity period, as investment fever takes over, there is much borrowing, higher debts, and higher interest rates (as credit demand passes supply).

After the downturn, demand for credit continues to rise for a while as people and firms need to borrow to pay old debts or routine expenses. So, interest rates rise a little further. Thus, the interest rate tends to be a lagging cycle indicator. The high interest rate and credit rationing, due to the uncertain conditions, do not cause the downturn, but they often transform a mild recession into a severe depression.

In the depression, the decline in profit expectations leads to a rapid decline in business loans, hoarding and accumulation of money capital, and lower interest rates. Thus, when real profit expectations rise, the financial system is again ready to support a new recovery.

It is useful to analyze the equation $MV = PT$ as a truism, where M is the quantity of money, V is velocity of money (the number of times money is respent in a period), P is price, and T is all transactions. Contrary to the classical quantity theory of money, which assumes that velocity is a constant changing ever so slowly in the long run, the velocity of money actually fluctuates cyclically. When consumers and businesses are optimistic as a result of expansion, velocity of spending will climb. When consumers and businesses are pessimistic as a result of contraction, velocity will decline.

EARLY MONETARY AND MONETARY OVER-INVESTMENT THEORIES

Theories making the existence of money the main cause of business cycles have been around a long time. Marx criticized such theories in the mid-nineteenth century. In the 1930s, R. G. Hawtrey argued the extreme view that changes in the flow of money are the sole cause of cyclical changes. (For a detailed discussion of Hawtrey and similar theorists, see Haberler 1960, Chapter 3.) According to Hawtrey, a rising flow of money fuels the expansion. When banks make borrowing more difficult in late expansion, there is less money flow, causing less demand and leading to a downturn. A declining flow of money is reflected in recession or depression. When banks loosen up on credit in late depression, the flow of money increases and a recovery ensues. There would be no problem if there were no limits to the quantity of money, but Hawtrey accuses the government of interference with the banking system in such ways as to limit money.

A related set of theories were the monetary over-investment theories (see Haberler 1960, Chapter 3). These theories held that during much of the expansion the market rate of interest is too low, that is, it is below an equilibrium rate that would just make savings equal to investment. So there is an attempt by entrepreneurs to push investment beyond the available resources. Investment competes with consumption for resources, creating a shortage of capital. This shortage of capital is reflected in lack of available funds to borrow and higher interest rates. The shortage of capital leads to declining investment, which causes a recession or depression. Eventually in the contraction interest rates fall, the demand for new investment funds is less than the real resources available. There is an excess of capital, and a recovery begins.

THE MONETARIST VIEW

The monetarists assume that competitive market private enterprise automatically tends toward full employment, a la Say's law, or in the modern version, towards the natural rate of unemployment. Beginning with Milton Friedman, there is a vast literature for and against monetarist views on every subject (Friedman and the rest of the monetarist literature is all cited in a pro-monetarist book on the business cycle by Courakis 1981). For the monetarists, like the classical economists, money is a medium of exchange between two commodities (goods or services), so demand equals supply as in any barter economy. Since money is not hoarded, it does not cause an endogenous cycle problem. In fact, for the monetarists, the changes in money have no effect on the long-run values of real variables, such as real gross national product. Real GNP is determined solely by resources and technology. The monetarists believe that changes in the money supply determine nominal income and the price level. The money supply affects prices because (1) velocity does not change except very slowly in the long-run, and (2) real production is determined by resources and technology. In the short-run, according to some monetarists such as Milton Friedman, changes in the money supply and government spending may affect real

GNP, but in the long-run these must adjust to the levels given by real factors. On the other hand, rational expectations monetarists claim that even in the short-run, if people have full information, they will adjust immediately, so there is no short-run effect on real GNP.

Since monetarists completely deny the role of a monetary-credit entrepreneurial economy in causing business cycles, why are they called monetarists? Although they deny its role as an endogenous factor, monetarists believe that the change in the money supply is determined exogenously by government policy, namely, Federal Reserve open market operations. When government policy is mistaken, monetarists believe that too much money may cause inflation or too little money may lead to unemployment, inflicting these evils upon an economy that would otherwise be without them. Thus, while money and credit do not cause declines for internal or systemic reasons, exogenous changes in the money supply cause temporary downturns and inflations, so money is the most vital policy factor.

COMMON POINTS IN MARX, KEYNES, AND MITCHELL

This is an area of economics where Marx, Keynes, and Mitchell all agree on two basic points: (1) that the monetary and financial system is a precondition of the cycle and (2) that the credit and financial system intensifies and exaggerates the cycle (on Keynes, see Tobin 1985; on Marx and Keynes, see Crotty 1986, 1987, and Sardoni 1982; on Mitchell, see Woodward 1987). Marx, Keynes, and Mitchell all stress that private enterprise requires the institutions of money and credit, with the use of money as a store of value, not just as a medium of exchange. If Henry Ford produced a million autos, it would be absurd to think of him bartering each one for something else at an auction, as some theorists assume. On the contrary, Ford wants and needs money to act as capital in the next period. Therefore, money is used in this case to sell products, then acts as a method of storing spending power until it is needed, so the logical basis of Say's law is undermined.

Keynes, Marx, and Mitchell all emphasized that private enterprise can be unstable because it is a monetary-credit economy. Mitchell intended to make the monetary economy his main research project, of which the business cycle was only the first part. Mitchell took from Thorstein Veblen the distinction between industry (the useful making of things for people) and the pecuniary economy (the making of monetary profits). Veblen pointed out that in every contraction, entrepreneurs sabotage industry in the sense that they reduce production and employment. They make these reductions to protect their pecuniary profits. Mitchell stressed time and again that entrepreneurs produce if, and only if, they can make a pecuniary profit.

This is the only area where Keynes made an explicit and favorable reference to Marx (see Keynes 1979, 81). What Marx calls a "barter" economy,

Keynes sometimes called a "cooperative economy," which is assumed not to use money because people cooperate together without money (as in most agricultural and pastoral villages). What Marx calls a "monetary" economy, Keynes sometimes calls an "entrepreneur" economy, to stress the monetary profit motive of the entrepreneur as the key to the economy.

Marx pointed out that, when money (M) is first used in feudalism, it is merely the go-between to aid the exchange between one commodity (C) and another, so the economic transaction is represented by C-M-C. But under private enterprise, the enterprise starts with money (M), buys commodities (C) to produce more commodities (C') in order to increase money (M'). It is now the commodity that plays the go-between, so the economic transaction is represented by M-C-M'. Thus, Keynes writes:

> The distinction between a co-operative economy and an entrepreneur economy bears some relation to a pregnant observation made by Karl Marx. . . . He pointed out that the nature of production in the actual world is not, as economists often seem to suppose, a case of C-M-C, i.e., of exchanging commodity (or effort). That may be the standpoint of the private consumer. But it is not the attitude of business, which is the case of M-C-M', i.e., of parting with money for commodity (or effort) in order to obtain more money. (Keynes 1979, 81)

This observation was at the heart of Keynes's attack on Say's law, in which he showed that it is sometimes rational not to use money to immediately buy more commodities.

THE POST-KENESIAN VIEW

The post-Keynesians oppose the monetarists on every major point and stress the following arguments of Keynes (for the best exposition, see Rousseas 1986). Keynes stressed the uncertainty of the investment process. Even roulette, says Keynes, is based on probability, but the economic future cannot be predicted. For example, will there be a war or not? Will there be a new invention as important as the automobile? Technology and wars drastically affect the economy, but there is no calculable probability whatever to these and many other factors impacting the economy. "We simply do not know" (Keynes 1979, 213).

Whereas the neoclassicals imagine a barter economy with certainty (or certain probabilities), the post-Keynesians see a monetary-credit economy with uncertainty. Businesses deal with uncertainty by (1) monopoly and collusion and (2) forward contracts, such as two or three year labor contracts. But these devices are insufficient to overcome the problems of an uncertain credit economy, so the economy is inherently unstable.

The fact of uncertainty makes people want to hold money rather than continuously circulate it. If not for uncertainty, why "should anyone outside of a lunatic asylum wish to use money as a store of wealth?" (Keynes 1979, 216). Rousseas says that money is peculiar as a commodity that may be stored without cost and used in the indefinite future (though there may be uncertainty about repayment and about the value of the dollar). The peculiarity of money permits postponement of decisions in an uncertain world. The peculiarity of money and credit allows borrowing beyond our income. Thus, money can destabilize the economy.

POST-KEYNESIAN THEORIES OF ENDOGENOUS MONEY SUPPLY

According to Keynes, the demand for money is based on a preference for liquidity because of the need for money for current transactions, precautionary holding of reserves, and speculation over the uncertain future. On the other hand, Keynes assumed in the *General Theory* (though not in his earlier *Treatise on Money*, 1930) that the money supply is an exogenous factor, given by the government. Both monetarists and neoclassical Keynesians agree that the government determines the money supply as a factor external to the economy.

The post-Keynesians, however, view the money supply as determined by the economy (see Rousseas 1986, for an excellent discussion of this point). The expansion phase of the business cycle increases output, which produces demand-side pressures for more credit in financial markets, which affect the amount of money and credit. They find that banks usually give credit as needed and only then worry about where to find enough reserves. But if that is the case, where does the banking system get more reserves when they are needed?

The post-Keynesians have advanced two theories to answer this question. One theory states that the Federal Reserve (or central bank) always accommodates their needs because of the political pressure to do so. Remember one function of the Federal Reserve is to maintain orderly markets and to be a lender of last resort in emergencies, so it normally does all that it can do to prevent a large bank from failing, since it wishes to prevent a domino effect. According to this view, the Federal Reserve controls the interest rate, but banks can get any amount they want at that rate (for a detailed and more realistic view of the politics of the Federal Reserve, see Greider 1987).

The second theory states that whenever the Federal Reserve (or other central banks) cannot or does not accommodate business, then the private financial system finds a way to generate enough reserves through liability management and innovative new financial arrangements. It is generally believed by the second group of theorists that the Federal Reserve usually cannot always fully accommodate business. The Federal Reserve has other pressures and constraints on it, such as the need to maintain currency stability. If the Federal Reserve follows only business desires, it may lead to inflation, which the Federal Reserve tries to prevent. Also, the Federal Reserve may make mistakes.

If the Federal Reserve is too restrictive, then the banks will find ways to move funds out of those liabilities which have high reserve requirements (such as demand deposits) to other types of liabilities with lower reserve requirements (such as Certificates of Demand). Since banks use interest rates as a lure to push funds from one area to another, this practice tends to raise overall interest rates.

As reserve ratios tend to fall and their liabilities become more volatile and expensive, the banks become more vulnerable to economic downturns. Yet, if the Federal Reserve fails to accommodate business, a credit crunch occurs. It should also be noted that if innovative liability management does work, then the velocity of money has been increased (because there are more loans per deposit). Many post-Keynesians believe that innovative liability management by the banks is a more important factor than Federal Reserve controls. Dymski, Epstein, and Pollin (1993), however, stress that banks' ability to expand in innovative ways has limits. If the profit rate declines and/or if the Federal Reserve limits liquidity, then banks may be unable to meet all credit needs, thereby helping to precipitate a downturn.

POST-KEYNESIAN THEORIES OF FINANCIAL FRAGILITY

Financial crises result from the convergence of two processes: "(1) business-cycle developments that are endogenous to the normal workings of a private enterprise economy, and (2) the specific institutional structure of the financial system that has evolved historically" (Wolfson 1986, 139–44). Once these two processes create the right conditions, any surprise shock may begin a financial crisis. The surprise events in the U.S. in the postwar period have been bank failures or government actions by the Federal Reserve, for example, or the credit restrictions under President Carter in March, 1980. These surprise events are also caused endogenously, but are unexpected by the financial system.

The long-run theory of financial fragility has been forcefully presented by Hyman Minsky (1986), also see Wojnilower (1988); but for a collection of divergent views, see Semmler (1989). Important contributions by Robert Pollin (1986, 1987) put fragility in terms of empirical trends in corporate and consumer credit. These writers examined the long run tendency toward increasing vulnerability of the financial system in recent decades, as discussed in the next section. In addition, the outstanding book by Wolfson (1986), and the excellent, comprehensive dissertation by Woodward (1987), have demonstrated how the financial system becomes more and more fragile in the expansion phase of each business cycle. Concretely, their work shows that in each expansion (a) the debt/equity ratio of corporations rises, (b) the periods allowed for debt repayment become shorter, and (c) there is less and less liquidity in corporate assets. Since these authors have established this empirical basis for increasing financial fragility in the expansion in great deal, these facts are not repeated here in the empirical analysis, but are considered in the conclusion.

The implications of these facts may be noted briefly at this point. Toward the end of every expansion, real corporate profits decline for endogenous reasons. Since corporations have increased their debt burden, when their own profits start to decline, they have great difficulty paying back their debts. Money suddenly seems in short supply. The inability of corporations and consumers to pay back their debts leads to bank failures, caused initially by the fall in real profits. In the first part of the contraction, this surprise shock of bank failures may lead to a sudden financial crisis, which in turn may cause a deep depression. Although widespread bank failures may always be traced to real factors, only a severe credit crunch or financial collapse can turn a recession (initiated by real factors) into a severe depression.

It is now time to turn to the historical and empirical record to see how well the theories explain the results.

HISTORICAL CHANGES IN THE FINANCE SYSTEM

To understand the present situation, we must go back to the 1930s. The decline in profit rates, corporate failures, and consumers' lack of income beginning in 1929, plus a lack of financial regulation, led to the banking crisis of 1931–1933. The banking collapse made the depression much worse, in fact, made it the Great Depression. The Roosevelt administration felt it necessary to take action to prevent a recurrence. First, and perhaps most important, the Federal Deposit Insurance Corporation was created to guarantee bank accounts up to $2500 (now $100,000), so as to prevent runs on banks. Secondly, many restrictions were put on the expansion of financial institutions, including prohibitions that banks may not act like brokers, brokers may not act like banks, that there shall be no interstate banking, and that Savings and Loans would mainly invest in home mortgages.

By the end of the Second World War, the United States had prosperity, high demand, high profits, and a low debt/equity ratio. This occurred because debt had been liquidated in the depression due to fewer formal restrictions on expenditures in the war period, and because there was little to buy or invest in during the war. The combination of the new regulations described above with these post-war conditions gave the United States a healthy financial system from 1945 to the mid 1960s. The relatively strong U.S. military and economic position after World War II, U.S. ability to impose the Bretton Woods System with the dollar as reserve currency, plus the lack of economic destruction in the United States from the war, all gave it international hegemony. This helped increase U.S. profits, which gave it an even more stable financial system.

By the mid-1960s, prosperity led to less caution and more innovative ways around the restrictions. For example, funds were lured from regular deposits (with high reserve requirements) to Certificates of Deposit (with much lower reserve requirements). The larger Certificates of Deposit meant less protection by the FDIC because they were issued in amounts greater than the insurance limit. Also, there was more U.S. borrowing in the Eurodollar market.

Inflation in the late 1960s hurt the Savings and Loans. They had to borrow at high interest rates because most of their funds were locked into long-run mortgage loans at low rates. Thus, some of the restrictions on permissible types of lending now became very painful. (At least they were painful for those Savings and Loans who followed them, but the regulations were circumvented by many others.)

The 1970s and 1980s witnessed increasing international competition, less U.S. productivity, and lower U.S. profit rates. There was increasing corporate debt, higher debt to equity ratios, and legislative attempts to remove restrictions. This resulted in increased vulnerability and an increasing number of bank failures. The Federal Reserve was used as a lender of last resort to prevent large failures and to keep the system from collapsing in business contractions. One effect of this has been that debts were not wiped out in depressions, so they kept increasing in this period.

The 1980s also saw the systematic looting of the savings and loans industry and the resultant insolvency of the Federal Savings and Loan Insurance Corporation. The deregulation of the savings and loan industry created opportunities for crimes ranging from petty theft to outright looting of different savings and loans, while many honest bankers were forced to adopt high risk lending practices to inflate earnings. The total loss to the taxpayer due to the destruction of the savings and loan industry may ultimately total more than $250 billion, although this figure is still likely to be revised.

Total non-financial borrowing relative to GNP rose from the mid-1960s to the mid-1980s by 60 percent, including increases in household debt, corporate debt, and government debt. "What has occurred since the mid-1960s is that the proportion of the economy's total output (GNP) which is financed by borrowing has departed substantially from a long-term stable path, rising to an unprecedented level" (Pollin 1987, 146). What has caused this large increase in debt?

First, one argument is that the rise in debt was due to inflation which caused falling real interest rates. Second, some economists have argued that the boom psychology has led to corporate speculation. Third, it has been argued that limited profits in the 1970s and 1980s have driven corporations to borrow out of need to keep their growth up to the competition's. These three arguments refer to the demand for credit. A fourth argument states that innovative methods of financing, such as junk bonds for use in mergers, have been used to extend the supply of credit for all corporations (the best discussion of these alternative views is in Pollin 1986).

The increase in corporate debt is an indicator of financial fragility. One result was a doubling in the rate of business failures from 1979 to 1985 (both years of cyclical expansion). Another result was that banks listed as "problems" by the Federal Deposit Insurance Corporation rose from 250 in 1983 to 1,200 in 1986 (see Harrison and Bluestone 1988, 167).

In addition to corporate debt, household debt has risen, partly because the majority of households needed credit merely to prevent their consumption from declining, while the rich have used credit to speculate. The result has been a massive increase in consumer debt (see Pollin 1987). Government has increased its debt through large deficits. Some of the deficits were caused by counter-cyclical activity in depressions with much of this activity automatically required by law. Yet, most of the deficits in the 1980s resulted from the Reagan administration's decisions to drastically lower taxes while greatly increasing military spending.

FINANCIAL INTERNATIONAL TRENDS

International financial trends and their impact on cycles will be discussed in Chapter 15.

TRENDS IN THE INTEREST RATE

Some theories assume that all capital is borrowed and that the interest rate is the most important determinant of investment. In reality, not all capital is borrowed; industrial corporations use large amounts of retained profits for reinvestment. Interest is paid on borrowed capital, but that is only one factor affecting costs.

Nominal interest rates were very low in the 1930s and grew very slowly until the 1960s, with very high rates only in the 1970s and 1980s. Thus, the average prime interest rate charged by banks grew in its average value for the whole cycle as follows in the seven business cycles since 1949: 2.7 percent in the 1949–54 cycle; 3.6 percent in the 1954–58 cycle; 4.4 percent in the 1958–61 cycle; 5.6 percent in the 1961–70 cycle; 7.5 percent in the 1970–75 cycle; 9.4 percent in the 1975–80 cycle; and 16.5 percent in the 1980–82 cycle (see Bureau of Economic Analysis, U.S. Department of Commerce, 1984, series 109). As might be expected, studies from the 1940s and 1950s found little or no empirical evidence of the impact of interest rates on investment (see Meyer and Kuh 1957, 181–89).

In the 1970s and 1980s, when nominal interest rates were very high, one might expect a significant negative effect on investment. In fact, price inflation was faster than the rise of the interest rate (and was a major cause of its rise), causing real interest rates to fall during most of this period. As noted earlier, some theorists have explained much of the rise in borrowing for investment to the fact of a declining real interest rate. Yet, the interest cost is only a small part of the profit picture on which investment borrowing is based, so it is only a small part of the explanation. One empirical study concludes: ". . . the incentive for firms to borrow is bound up with their drive for profits and growth and their need to survive in a competitive environment. The cost of obtaining funds is surely a factor in this equation. But it is not the only factor or even the predominant one" (Pollin 1986, 228).

THE INCREASE IN CYCLICAL INSTABILITY

The mild cycles of the 1950s and 1960s are reflected in mild downturns in the financial variables. The more severe cycles of the 1970s and early 1980s are reflected in and exacerbated by more violent financial downturns. Table 14.1 reveals this change.

All of the financial variables listed in Table 14.1 declined more in the average contraction of the 1970–1982 period than in the 1949–1970 period. The following variables all declined in the earlier period, but declined more

TABLE 14.1
INCREASED SEVERITY OF FINANCIAL DOWNTURNS

	CONTRACTION AMPLITUDE	
	Average of 4 Cycles 1949–70	Average of 3 Cycles 1970–82
Money Supply, M1, real (105)	−0.1	−1.7
Velocity, GNP/M1 (107)	−1.4	−1.5
Private credit, real (110)	−10.8	−35.2
Prime rate (109)	−15.5	−37.7
Short-run interest rate (67)	−15.2	−34.3
Corporate cash flow, Real (35)	−6.4	−13.6
New orders for plant and equip., real (20)	−13.2	−22.1
Money supply, M2, real (106)	2.6	−0.1
Stock prices (19)	3.5	−0.7
Composite financial index (917)	0.5	−3.1

SOURCE: Numbers in parentheses indicate series numbers in Bureau of Economic Analysis, U.S. Department of Commerce, *Handbook of Cyclical Indicators, A Supplement to the Business Conditions Digest* (Washington, D.C.: GPO, 1984).

in the later period: the money supply (M1), the velocity of money, all private non-financial borrowing of credit, the price interest rate charged by banks, the short-term interest rate charged by banks, the corporate cash flow, and new orders for plant and equipment. Three of the financial variables, the money supply (M2), 500 common stock prices, and the composite index of money and financial flows, all actually rose a little in the average contraction of the earlier period, but fell a little in the average contraction of the later period. Thus, Table 14.1 provides quantitative measures of increased financial instability. This evidence of more severe cyclical behavior in financial variables suggests that financial fragility will be an increasingly important source of vulnerability for the advanced private enterprise economy.

CYCLICAL BEHAVIOR OF FINANCIAL VARIABLES, 1970–1991

The previous section shows a change toward greater instability in the financial sector. But some things have remained relatively constant; the cyclical pattern and sequence of financial movements have remained roughly the same in the two periods, even though the movements became more violent. We now examine the cyclical pattern and sequence of turns in financial variables in the average of the four cycles from 1970 to 1991. The expansion amplitude and contraction amplitude data is shown for all the variables under discussion in Table 14.2.

TABLE 14.2
FINANCIAL VARIABLES, 1970–1991

	Expansion Amplitude	Contraction Amplitude
Leading		
Stock prices, New York Exchange (FSNCOM)	32.9	3.7
Real money supply, M2 (FM2D82)	11.4	−0.5
Real money supply, M1 (FM1D82)	4.7	−1.4
Change in business credit outstanding (FCLBMC)	45.7	−63.7
Coincident		
Velocity of money, GDP to M1 (GDPM1)	9.7	−1.7
Velocity of money, personal income to M2 (GMYFM2)	2.1	−1.2
Lagging		
Composite, long-term interest rate (FYGL)	16.9	−8.8
Consumer debt/personal income (CCIPYQ)	8.3	3.4
Short-term prime rate (FYPR)	36.9	−31.3

SOURCE: CITIBASE database, series indicated in parentheses. Average 4 cycles, 1970–1991.

STOCK MARKET PRICES

Stock market prices rose rapidly in the average expansion, but they began to decline in late expansion. After declining for a few stages, they then lose a bit to the end of the cycle. Thus their net change in the average recession was actually slightly positive. Of course, this was period of inflation, with all prices rising. So there is a clear cyclical behavior, though the downturns of this period were still relatively mild compared with the Great Depression. Although stock prices led the cycle peak, they followed after the decline of profits and profit rates, as would be expected.

REAL MONEY SUPPLY

In the period since the Second World War, nominal money supply (M1) as well as credit rose in both expansions and contractions, but rose far more rapidly in expansions (see Benjamin Friedman 1986, 406). But real money supply and real credit supply actually fell at times.

In fact, Table 14.2 shows that the real money supply, both M1 and M2, is pro-cyclical, rising in expansions and falling in contractions. The fact that its cyclical behavior conforms so well to the cycle is compatible with both hypotheses that the money supply is an exogenous cause of the cycle and that it is an endogenous result of the cycle. The monetarists emphasize that the decline in the real money supply leads the cycle peak and they claim that it causes it. The post-Keynesians emphasize that the decline in the real money supply follows after declines in the profit rate and other expectations variables, so it is an endogenous affect of the cycle.

The monetarists believe that the money supply is an exogenous factor and that it is the dominant factor in the cycle, but the evidence is highly controversial (see the comprehensive study by Woodward 1987). The timing sequence is discussed later in this chapter, in order to explain why so many of these financial variables are leaders, and to explain how their timing relates to the real variables.

VELOCITY OF MONEY

The velocity of money also rose and fell pro-cyclically according to B. Friedman (1986, 413). Similarly, Table 14.2 shows that the velocity of money, both for M1 and M2, is pro-cyclical. Velocity is a coincident variable, that is, it rises during the whole expansion and it falls during the whole contraction. The velocity of money rises in expansion because consumers are optimistic as to jobs and wages, while entrepreneurs are optimistic as to profit expectations. During the downturn, entrepreneurs become pessimistic as to profit expectations, while consumers fear lower wages and loss of jobs, so the velocity of spending money declines.

This result disproves the simplest classical quantity theory of money as it applies to cycles—since that theory wrongly assumed a constant velocity.

There is a more sophisticated version requiring only a slowly changing and predictable velocity—but that version of the quantity theory has also been criticized (see Woodward 1987).

BUSINESS CREDIT

In the five business cycles from 1919 to 1938, the total loans of all banks under the Federal Reserve system rose 12.6 percent in the average expansion and fell by 13.2 percent in the average contraction (Mitchell 1951, 330). The recent cyclical performance of business credit in the 1970 to 1991 period is indicated in Table 14.2.

Business borrowing in credit markets is pro-cyclical. We note that the change in business credit rises very rapidly in the expansion, but leads downward before the cycle peak, and then falls in the contraction very rapidly. Thus, the change in credit, like the money supply, rises and falls with the cycle, but with a small lead. It is worth noting, however, that this measure of credit—which is most often used by analysts—deals with the change, not the level of credit. The change in a variable always leads the level of the variable, so it is no surprise that the change in business credit is a leading indicator, whereas the total amount of credit tends to be a lagging indicator. Furthermore, changes in variables usually move more rapidly than the level of a variable, so the very rapid movement of the change in business credit is much greater than the movement in the amount of business credit.

Nevertheless, it shall be seen that the level of business credit moves faster than the real money supply. This is in accord with the post-Keynesian emphasis on the greater importance of credit than of non-credit money, so bank accounts are far more important than paper dollars, while borrowing is even more important.

Credit increases in expansions because firms and consumers become more and more optimistic about the future. The rapid increase of credit in the early and mid-expansion is a major engine of the growth of the economy. Much of this borrowing goes into business investment. Some of it is also borrowed by households to expand consumption. Thus the growth of credit stimulates all sectors of the economy, allowing both consumers and investors to spend far beyond their present incomes. This stimulus is the direct cause of the economic boom and so it pushes the economy beyond the point where it would have otherwise reached.

While business and consumer credit acts as a great boon to economic expansion, it also eventually makes the economy more vulnerable and fragile. Wolfson (1986) has studied the cyclical aspect of this problem in great depth, examining a number of the most important financial ratios that indicate business health or weakness. He finds that the ratio of corporate debt to corporate equity (stockholders' ownership of capital) "has consistently increased as the cyclical peaks are approached" (1986, 135). The fact that debt is increasing faster than capital means that the corporation is in a much weaker position if it must face a decline in its revenues. Paying back the debt becomes more difficult, interest takes a larger bit out of profits, and bankruptcy becomes that much more of a danger.

Wolfson also explores the cyclical behavior in other important ratios. First, the debt maturity ratio, which is the ratio of short-term loans to total credit of non-financial corporations, behaves pro-cyclically. A corporation is, of course, more vulnerable when it has a rising burden of short-term debt that it must pay back quickly. The rise of short-term debt in expansion eventually leads to a greater need to refinance debt sooner than otherwise, and leaves the corporation vulnerable to higher interest rates when it must refinance (see Wolfson 1986, 135).

Second, Wolfson finds that the liquidity rate, which is the ratio of liquid assets to short-term debt of non-financial corporations, behaves counter-cyclically. Liquid assets, such as cash, make a corporation more secure, while any kind of debt makes it more vulnerable. When the liquidity rate falls in an expansion, corporations have less liquid assets to pay back their due debts (Wolfson 1986, 136).

Third, the interest coverage ratio, which is the ratio of (1) profits plus (2) depreciation plus (3) net interest to the net interest paid by the corporation, behaves counter-cyclically. This ratio simply measures the sources with which corporations pay back loans to the amount of such loan payments. When the interest coverage ratio falls in expansions, it indicates that less interest can be covered by corporate income (1986, 137), so the corporation becomes more vulnerable and fragile.

All of these indicators show that corporations fall deeper in debt in the expansion relative to their assets and income. At the end of expansion, when revenues begin to decline, the corporation is far more vulnerable than it was at the beginning of expansion. Thus, a decline in profits and revenue has a greater chance of leading to bankruptcy than earlier in the cycle. If corporations cannot pay back all or even a portion of their debts to banks and other financial institutions, the delicacy of this situation may lead to a bank and credit collapse, as it did in the Great Depression.

CONSUMER DEBT TO CONSUMER INCOME

The crucial ratio for consumers is the ratio of their debts to their income. Robert Pollin (1988a, 1988b) found that there has been a long-run trend upward in the ratio of household debt to household income. He found that this ratio rose rapidly from 1950 to 1965, flattened out from 1965 to 1975, and rose rapidly again from 1975 to 1985.

Pollin concluded that there were two major reasons for this trend. First, inflation has lowered real interest rates, making borrowing to buy assets such as homes somewhat more attractive as a speculative investment. Second, and most important, households have been forced by need to do more borrowing. He points out that from 1973 to 1985 real median household income fell by 4.9 percent, while the real median purchase price of individual family housing rose by 7.4 percent. Thus, some debt increase may have resulted from speculative actions by the rich, but most debt increase has been due to what Pollin calls "necessitous" borrowing by the poor.

The ratio of consumer credit to personal income usually fluctuates pro-cyclically. The average cyclical amplitude of this ratio from 1970 through 1991 is portrayed in Table 14.2. This Table shows that in this period the ratio of consumer credit to income is pro-cyclical, rising in expansions and falling in contractions. It lags behind the cycle by one stage, reaching its low point in stage 2 after the cycle trough, but reaching its high point in stage 6 after the cycle peak.

Why does consumer credit behave this way? In the expansion (from stage 2 to stage 5) more consumers have jobs and a steady income. Therefore, they become more optimistic than previously. Most consumers feel that they may use credit to buy necessities that they could otherwise not afford; they believe they will be able to pay the loans back when they are due. In this phase, therefore, the demand for consumer credit rises more rapidly than consumers' personal income.

When the contraction begins, many consumers become unemployed or receive lower incomes. They cannot pay back their debts, so they rush to get new loans to pay back the old debts and a few are still borrowing for current necessities, hoping the situation will still improve. Thus, the ratio of consumer debt to personal income rises still further in the first stage after the peak.

In the contraction (stages 6 to 9) consumers are pessimistic about future income. They cut back on credit for that reason. Financial agencies may also be unwilling to lend to consumers with uncertain prospects (of course, some bad debts must be written off as households go bankrupt). For both supply and demand reasons, the ratio of outstanding consumer debt to personal income falls.

In the first stage of expansion, personal income grows rapidly. But consumers are still worried by the experience of the last recession or depression; so they do not contract new debts. Hence, the ratio of consumer debt to income continues to fall.

What impact does consumer credit have on the business cycle? In the expansion, optimistic consumers increase consumption faster than current income. Consumer credit in this phase stimulates the economy. This positive stimulation continues, at a slower pace, even into the first stage of contraction, lessening the degree of deficient consumer demand.

In the rest of the contraction, however, the retrenchment of consumer credit pushes consumer demand and the economy downward even faster than current income decline would indicate. Consumers with high debt ratios at the peak are vulnerable to the recession, so they cannot pay back banks or loan companies. For individual consumers this means loss of refrigerators, cars, and homes. These bad debts may also help lead to bankruptcy for some banks, moving them toward financial collapse. This negative effect continues even into the first phase of expansion, but it does little or no harm then because it is more than offset by the rapid rise of income.

CYCLICAL BEHAVIOR OF INTEREST RATES. Wesley Mitchell (1951, 312–32) found that commercial paper rates in New York City in 14 cycles (1858 to 1914) rose an average of 31.4 percent in expansions and fell by 33.9 percent in contractions. He also found that these commercial paper rates lag the cycle, not reaching a peak till stage 6, and not reaching a trough thereafter until stage 2 of the next cycle. Mitchell (1951, 312–32) also found that the weighted average of interest rates in eight northeast U.S. cities in four cycles (from 1919 to 1933) rose by 5.0 percent in expansions and fell by 10.1 percent in contractions. He also found that these interest rates peaked in stage 6 and reached a trough in stage 2 of the next cycle, thus being a lagging indicator of cycles.

In the period from the Second World War to the present, the consensus of all studies is that short-run interest rates continue to be pro-cyclical, they have a high conformity to the cycle, but tend to lag at peaks and troughs (see B. Friedman 1986, 408; Blanchard and Watson 1986, 123–82; and Zarnowitz and Moore 1986, 560–61). Long-run interest rates are also usually pro-cyclical, but with much less amplitude and lower conformity. These views are confirmed in Table 14.2.

This Table shows that the short-run prime interest rate, that is, the interest rate to the most credit-worthy borrowers, is pro-cyclical, rising in the expansion and falling in the contraction. But Table 14.2 also shows that the composite index of all long-term interest rates is equally pro-cyclical. Why are interest rates pro-cyclical? In expansion, (1) there is rising demand for business loans, consumer loans, and mortgage credit; (2) there is increasing expectation of inflation; and, consequently, (3) government attempts to restrict credit by higher interest rates (see Moore 1983, 140). In the contraction, there is decreasing demand for loans, less expectation of inflation, and the Federal Reserve may attempt to lower rates.

Most interest rates lag behind the cycle turns. Thus, Table 14.2 discloses that both short-run and long-run interest rates lag behind the cycle. In the 1970 to 1991 period, both types of interest rate peak quite a bit after the cycle peak; moreover, they do not reach a trough till early in the next expansion. The late turn for interest rates at the cycle peak occurs because firms and consumers desperately need credit at the beginning of the contraction, but credit is already severely restricted.

In early expansion when jobs and profits are rising rapidly, the rate of interest is very low and rising slowly, or still declining, so its cost is easily borne and inconsequential. In the last half of expansion, limited profits and rising interest rates make the cost of interest a more significant negative factor, though far from the main cause of the profit squeeze. In the first half of contraction (the crisis phase), the still rising interest rates are a heavy burden on firms with falling profits and on consumers with falling wages or unemployed. Thus, the cost of interest exacerbates the crisis. Finally, in the last half of the business cycle contraction (the depression phase), interest rates fall rapidly and are one of the factors preparing the conditions for recovery.

THE TIMING OF REAL AND FINANCIAL FACTORS

Each variable is subject to different leads and lags in different cycles, which are themselves of different length. Yet the sequence in which these variables follow one another remains about the same in all cycles. Table 14.3 presents the median number of months by which a variable leads (−) or lags (+) the cycle peak in the average of the long historical period covered by the seven cycles from 1949 through 1982 for which we have detailed monthly data.

Some variables almost always lead the cycle. The longest lead is in real corporate profits; however, profit rates have about the same lead. Part 2 of this book discussed the factors leading to the decline of profits and profit rates. Once profit expectations grow dimmer, the next thing to turn down are the financial variables: there are declines in the real money supply, in the growth rate of consumer credit, and in the growth rate of business credit. The total new private borrowing declines, though it continues to be positive, so loans outstanding still grow. The falling profit expectations mean less desire for new business incorporations, which also decline. Finally, the lowered profit expectations, as well as the lower growth of credit and fewer new businesses, are reflected in reduced orders for plant and equipment.

The specific turning points in some variables are usually coincident with the reference cycle turning points. These variables include most indicators of output, including gross national product, sales of retail stores, the value of goods output, and nonresidential fixed investment, all in constant dollars. The coincident variables also include indicators of employment, including the number of employees on nonagricultural payrolls and the number of employee hours in nonagricultural businesses. One coincident financial indicator is the velocity of money, reflecting the fact that people and busi-

TABLE 14.3
TIMING OF REAL AND FINANCIAL VARIABLES (AVERAGE 7 CYCLES, 1949–1982)

Series	Leading Variables	Median # of Months of Lead (−) or Lag (+)
80	Real corporate profit after tax	−14
106	Real money supply, M1	−11
13	Number of new business incorporation	−10
113	Net change in consumer credit	−10
112	Net change in business loans	−9
20	Orders for new plant and equipment	−8

Series	Coincident Variables	Median # of Months of Lead (−) or Lag (+)
50	Real gross national product	0
54	Real sales of retail stores	0
49	Real value of goods output	0
86	Real nonresidential fixed investment	0
41	Employees on nonagricultural payrolls	0
48	Employee hours in nonagricultural business	0
107	Velocity of money, M1	0

Series	Lagging Variables	Median # of Months of Lead (−) or Lag (+)
109	Prime rate charged by banks	+4
67	Bank rates on short-term loans	+4
56	Real consumer credit	+4
101	Real commercial and industrial loans	+4
95	Ratio, consumer credit/personal income	+4
70	Real manufacturing and trade inventories	+6
77	Ratio, inventories/sales	+8

SOURCE: U.S. Department of Commerce, *Handbook of Cyclical Indicators* (Washington, D.C.: GPO, 1984), 172–73.

NOTE: The series numbers refer to the source.

nesses spend money faster and faster in expansions, but slower and slower in contractions.

A number of the typically lagging variables are financial indicators. Interest rates lag by about one stage (or 4 months), including both the prime rate and the rates on all short-term bank loans to business. This lag occurs because there is an emergency need for loans in the crisis phase. Roughly the same time lag characterizes the quantity-of-credit variables, since these also reflect the urgent need for loans. Those credit variables peaking at the stage after the peak include business credit outstanding, consumer credit outstanding, and the ratio of consumer credit to personal income. Credit props up the economy until one stage into the crisis, but at higher and higher interest rates, and then credit declines rapidly, worsening the contraction.

Finally, there is a long lag before the peak in the real amount of manufacturing and trade inventories, which continue to pile up unplanned and unwanted well into the contraction. This reflection of the worsening situation is also shown in the even longer lag in the ratio of inventories to sales. While sales begin to decline at the cycle peak, inventories continue to rise (as an indicator of unsold goods). Only after a half a year into the contraction, on the average, do unwanted inventories start declining. Even then, unwanted inventories decline more slowly than sales for a little while more. When the ratio of inventories to sales begins to decline at last, it sets the stage for recovery.

MONETARY POLICY

This chapter has discussed the behavior of money and credit over the business cycle. The most important use of that knowledge is to set monetary policy, which is put into an Appendix only to emphasize that policy can be analyzed separately from behavior.

Monetary policy can affect demand by increasing or decreasing the available credit. The Federal Reserve System uses three major tools: (1) reserve requirement changes, (2) controlling the discount rate, and (3) open market operations.

Bank reserves must be held against some liabilities of banks, with the legal minimum set by the *reserve requirement*, which is expressed as a certain percentage of each type of liability. Raising or lowering this reserve requirement will substantially affect the amount of new bank lending and money-credit creation. The greater credit results from new reserves being provided to the banking system. For example, when the reserve requirement on demand deposit liabilities is raised, this reduces the amount of new bank loans. Thus raising the reserve requirement reduces credit. On the other hand, lowering the reserve requirement increases credit.

Banks are also allowed to borrow reserves from the Federal Reserve system through the discount window. The interest rate charged on such loans by banks is called the discount rate. By raising or lowering the discount rate, the Federal Reserve can discourage or encourage the borrowing of bank reserves.

Neither of these two policy options has been used much by the Federal Reserve system in the past. Reserve requirement changes are thought to be too drastic, so they have seldom been used as a counter-cyclical policy. Reserve requirements have gradually been lowered over the long-run, partly in response to pressure applied by commercial banks. The Federal Reserve does change the discount rate periodically, but this usually merely reflects changes in market interest rates. Often the discount rate is below competing market rates because, ideally, banks are supposed to borrow only emergency loans from the discount window, and it is felt that this rate should not be a penalty rate. The discount rate has never been used aggressively as a counter-cyclical policy.

Open market operations are the main vehicle for implementing counter-cyclical monetary policy. These operations are used daily by the Federal Reserve system with the explicit intent of accomplishing policy objectives. Open market operations are overseen by the Federal Reserve Bank of New York. It is here that traders buy and sell U.S. Treasury securities. When the Federal Reserve buys U.S. bonds from banks in return for money, the money reserves of banks are increased. But when the Federal Reserve sells bonds to banks, the money reserves of banks are decreased. An increase in bank reserves allows more bank loans to be made. This means that bank liabilities, including demand deposits (a component of the money supply) grow. These operations, therefore, influence levels of credit, money, as well as interest rates in the economy. The primary tool of implementing Federal Reserve policy is open market operations. This tool has been used almost exclusively in the past and probably will continue to be the dominant tool in the future.

STRICT MONETARISM

Strict monetarism advocates the adoption of a monetary rule (see Friedman 1968). The rule means that the money supply should be forced to grow at some designated rate, say 4 to 5 percent, regardless of economic circumstance. A monetary expansion should not be used to counteract a recession and a monetary decrease should not be used to counteract inflation. So the Federal Reserve should do no counter-cyclical activity. Interest rates should be determined entirely by the market, so the Federal Reserve should not try to influence interest rates.

Why should there be no counter-cyclical monetary policy? Strict monetarists argue that the Federal Reserve tools are too crude for fine tuning. So short-run policies will usually make things worse. Only a constant increase to equal real growth is useful.

The money supply, according to this school of thought, will be controlled by either carefully controlling the level of bank reserves or the monetary base (bank reserves plus currency in the hands of the non-bank public) through open market operations. Through empirical research, the *money multiplier*, which establishes the connection between bank reserves and the money supply, will be determined. Once determined, open market operations will be conducted at a pace sufficient to allow reserves to grow at the correct rate to produce exactly the desired growth in the money supply.

For example, the Federal Reserve might decide to control total bank reserves in their open market operations. Staff economists might conclude, in their research, that if reserves grow at a 3.5 percent annual rate, then the M1 money supply would grow at 4 percent. Presumably, the trading desk at the Federal Reserve Bank of New York would be instructed to purchase Treasury securities gradually at a rate that would allow bank reserves to expand 3.5 percent annually. This they would do faithfully and passively, regardless of market conditions.

If, after a period of time, they discovered that they had guessed incorrectly about the multiplier, so that the money supply growth rate was too fast or too slow, they would presumably adjust the reserve growth rate to compensate. For example, if the Federal Reserve were controlling reserves and the growth rate of reserves was 3.5 percent, but the money supply was growing at 5 percent instead of the desired 4 percent, then the allowed growth rate of reserves might be dropped down a bit until the money supply target would be approximately reached.

Regardless of the practical operating plans of strict monetarism, the policy has one fundamental feature that separates it from any discretionary monetarism. In the conduct of open market operations, there is to be no response whatsoever to prevailing economic conditions. According to this theory, it is *not* the job of the Federal Reserve (or any other central bank) to pursue stabilization or counter-cyclical policies. This strict monetarist policy is the purest form of a laissez-faire policy. The private market economy is to work without intervention.

Strict monetarists justify their policy as the most *workable* monetary policy. In their opinion, the Federal Reserve system can't hope to control interest rates and the measures of monetary aggregates simultaneously. Furthermore, monetarists argue, variations in the money supply growth rate will undoubtedly produce variations in the level of spending, but the lags and amplitudes between money supply changes and spending changes are quite variable, so an expansionary discretionary monetary stimulus might over-stimulate or under-stimulate, producing more confusion and harm than assistance. It is far simpler to have one easy target, using one simple procedure in pursuit of a very elementary objective. The idea is to make it easy for the private sector of the economy to solve its own problems. It is assumed that Say's law operates, so the private economy automatically reaches full employment. Moreover, strict monetarists contend that discretionary government policy unavoidably ends up being inflationary policy. Inflation, monetarists insist, would absolutely be a thing of the past in the presence of a constant monetary rule.

DISCRETIONARY MONETARISM

Advocates of a discretionary monetary policy (such as Paul Volcker, when he headed the Federal Reserve) also identify the money supply as the most important financial variable influencing the level of nominal spending in the economy. The money supply is the primary, if not the exclusive, variable that the Federal Reserve system should attempt to control. These monetary theorists also have considerable faith in the private enterprise system, but they regard it as less stable than their pure monetarist colleagues, so it is occasionally in need of a counter-cyclical stabilization policy.

The policy of the Volcker era at the Federal Reserve was certainly a type of discretionary monetarism. Volcker's policy gave primary emphasis to the control of monetary aggregates, with most attention given to M1. Secondary attention, however, was given to the behavior of interest rates. Strict monetarists would not allow this. An ideal discretionary monetarist policy would always state its objective in meeting monetary targets. The monetary targets, however, rather than being held constant, would be raised and lowered as economic conditions dictated.

The neoclassical-Keynesian critics of monetarism have a number of complaints against both forms of monetarism and especially the monetarist "rule." Generally, the rule is regarded as too inflexible. The critics believe that one of the many roles of the government is to implement counter-cyclical stabilization policies and that the government can do this successfully if appropriate policies are implemented. Rather than regarding the economy as a smoothly-running machine needing an occasional few drops of monetary oil, the critics of monetarism see the private sector as prone to all sorts of disturbances, calamities, and economic mishaps. The monetary rule simply ties the hands of one of the most potentially potent public agencies, rendering it ineffective during times of economic crises. If the finance markets are inherently unstable, with volatile demands for credit, episodic bursts of harmful speculation, and lapses in rational decision making, then monetarist policies are ill-advised. The closer the Federal Reserve moves toward emphasis on narrow monetary growth rate targets, the greater the interest rate volatility is going to be. Without the intervention of the Federal Reserve, any sudden jump in credit demand is likely to drive interest rates up.

Economists who have been influenced by the argument that the money stock is endogenous, such as the post-Keynesians, are also highly critical of monetarism. In the long run, monetarist policies will simply be ineffective, they argue. If a monetary rule is adopted, for example, and either private or government credit demand continues to grow, the resulting high interest rates will introduce a fertile environment for the development of new financial instruments. These new instruments initially are money substitutes and eventually begin to serve money functions, at least at some levels of commerce. With the development of new types of credit, the list of instruments that the Federal Reserve actually controls (such as M1) become increasingly irrelevant to the level of spending. This phenomenon might appear as a rise in velocity of money. In other words, the ratio of spending to the officially defined money supply will shoot up. Velocity increases because the money supply, which the Federal Reserve is controlling with its rule, becomes less important to the level of spending in the economy, while credit becomes more important.

CONTROLLING WIDE AGGREGATES AND CREDIT

Some Keynesian-oriented monetary economists, who are critical of monetarism's focus on narrow monetary aggregates, advise the Federal Reserve to monitor and target much wider liquidity aggregates, such as M3 or some measure of credit. It is felt by these theorists that these inclusive aggregates of credit are much more closely correlated to levels of spending than a narrowly defined money supply (see, e.g., Earley, Parsons, and Thompson 1976).

Such ideas are certainly consistent with the argument that the money stock is endogenously determined by the economy. If near-money substitutes that begin to function as money are developed by banks, then wider financial credit aggregates are more likely to include those instruments (such as money market funds) that begin to serve as money. Hence, an aggregate credit policy is less likely to be surprised by inflation than a policy that concentrates only on money. Advocates of these policies point out that the velocities of wide credit aggregates have tended to be nearly constant for two decades, whereas the velocity of money has fluctuated sharply. This provides strong evidence, in their opinion, that the long-run relationship between wide credit aggregates and spending is far more exact.

Creditists, as they might be called, stress that both the level of spending and the extension of new credit are both *flows*, over a given time period (whereas the monetary aggregates are stocks at a single time). Any variation in credit flows will *directly* cause a variation in spending, whereas expenditures can grow without changes in the money stock. Moreover, changes in the money stock need not necessarily lead to changes in spending, since money changes may be dwarfed by credit changes.

IMPACT OF MONETARY POLICY

The monetarist view is that government fiscal and monetary shocks to the economy are the main destabilizing factors in the U.S. economy. On the contrary, Part 2 of this book showed how the private enterprise economy internally generates the business cycle. Of course, the same evidence of a continuing internally generated business cycle also disproves the hypothesis that the government is able to stabilize the economy by fine-tuning it with fiscal and monetary policy.

The evidence of this book indicates that fiscal and monetary or credit behavior are endogenous to the economic system. Fiscal and monetary behavior are internal in the sense that they are determined by the conjuncture of the business cycle phase and long-term business interests. Government behavior has a significant, but usually limited impact, except in war-driven cycles and a few exceptional instances. In peacetime contractions, the government usually stimulates the economy (a) by running a deficit and (b) by loosening up on credit to encourage borrowing. Thus, government behavior is one of the factors helping the private economy to recover. In peacetime expansions, the declared foe is usually inflation, so fiscal policy is less and less stimulating. In the usual expansion, monetary policy is at first accommodating to business, but usually becomes more and more restrictive towards the peak. The monetary restrictions are usually after the rate of profit has begun to decline, so the private economy is merely pushed along the path it has already taken. Thus, the government usually allows a downturn, but then encourages the recovery. It is an actor, but not the prime actor. Moreover, government acts are mostly predictable, as shown in the previous chapter.

LIMITATIONS OF MONETARY POLICY

Many liberals believe that monetary policy could be effective under the right policies. Even Hyman Minsky, who emphasizes the vulnerability of the private enterprise economy and the incorrect policies of the Federal Reserve, says: "Once endogenous economic processes take the economy to the brink of crisis, Federal Reserve intervention can abort the development of a full-fledged crisis and debt deflation" (quoted in Rousseas 1986, 114). But there are many reasons to be skeptical about the efficacy of any monetary policy. Suppose there is a liberal U.S. administration and a liberal Keynesian head of the Federal Reserve committed to full employment as well as stable prices. Suppose that there is careful coordination of monetary and fiscal policy. Suppose there are no practical problems for the Federal Reserve to control monetary and credit aggregates, though this is probably contrary to reality and to the theory of an endogenous money and credit supply. Even with these simplifying assumptions, there are clear limitations to monetary policy (some of the political and practical issues are detailed in Epstein 1981).

First, take the case of inflation. It is true that sufficiently strong measures will cure inflation. For example, in the winter of 1980, both the Carter administration and the Federal Reserve system agreed to strong measures to reduce credit. These measures succeeded in reducing inflation from about 18 percent to 8 percent in a few months. The trouble is that such measures must be so harsh to have any effect on inflation that they depress the economy. In 1980 the result was a recession and a very considerable rise in unemployment. The same policies appear to have increased unemployment in England under the Thatcher administration and in the United States under the Reagan and Bush administrations.

Second, take the case of severe unemployment. Many Keynesians would support low interest rates and easy credit. Yet Keynesians themselves admit that the interest rate required for a full-employment equilibrium may be so low as to be unattainable. That interest rate might be below the minimum level for speculation, so speculative investors will hold back because they expect it to return to a higher level. The full-employment equilibrium interest rate might even be negative if profit expectations are negative. If losses are expected, a business will borrow only if a bank pays it to borrow! For these reasons, the post-Keynesians see monetary policy at best as an adjunct to (or copartner with) fiscal policy in a deep depression. Low interest rates cannot alleviate unemployment at all if expected profit rates are below zero.

Finally, suppose there is *both* inflation and unemployment. In this case, what should a liberal Keynesian monetary policy be? Should it ease credit and lower interest rates sufficiently to stimulate the economy and reduce involuntary unemployment to zero? If it works, this will cause inflation. Should it reduce credit and raise interest rates in order to reduce inflation to zero? If it is drastic enough to be effective, it will cause severe unemployment.

MONETARY POLICY, WAGES AND INFLATION

In every expansion phase, as soon as real wages start to rise, many economists begin to worry that higher wages will cause inflation. They also worry that higher wages will weaken the U.S. competitive position so as to worsen the trade deficit. For example, Laurence Summers (Professor of Economics at Harvard) worried in 1988 that: "Workers who accepted real wage reductions in 17 of the last 20 quarters will start demanding and receiving wage increases in excess of past price increases, setting off a wage-price spiral" (Summers 1988, 1). Summers paid no attention to the evidence that shows the weakening of unions and the increase of monopoly power over prices. He also paid no attention to the whole analysis of effective demand by Keynes. Rather, he returned to the pre-Keynesian position that favors lowering wages, "reducing consumption and increasing national saving" to cure all evils. He gave that old position a modern twist by arguing that "reduced consumption can make room for increased demand for American products, which will come as the trade deficit declines" (Summers 1988, 1). So lower wages would somehow increase consumption and reduce the trade deficit. What actually happened was that wages remained stagnant and a recession began in 1990.

Similarly, in a synthesis of opinions of many traditional economists, John Berry concluded in 1988: "The compensation of American workers . . . is increasing at the fastest pace in three years, raising concerns of an acceleration in inflation in coming months" (1988, 1). Notice that economists do not seem concerned with wage cuts, only with wage increases. Berry reports that economists are also concerned over falling unemployment because this allows wage increases, and wages represent "about two-thirds of all business costs." In this context, Berry notes that "Federal Reserve Chairman Alan Greenspan warned Congress . . . that if an expected slowdown in the economy does not occur, . . . the Fed will be forced to continue to increase interest rates in order to prevent a new surge in inflation" (1988, 11). Even after 3 years of stagnation, low wages, and high unemployment from 1991 to 1993, Martin Feldstein told the convention of the American Economic Association in 1993 that unemployment was "dangerously low" at 6 percent, while the liberal, Alan Blinder, said it would not be dangerous until it reached 5.5 percent.

Thus, whenever endogenous forces expand the economy and increase employment and wages, the desire of business and most economists to hold down wages is reflected in tighter Federal Reserve policies. But these policies help cause a lack of effective demand, leading to a recession or depression.

CONCLUSIONS: THE CYCLICAL ROLE OF FINANCE

Before analyzing the role of finance in the business cycle, the reader may recall that Part 2 of this book showed how the use of money is a precondition of the cycle. In looking at the specific causes of the business cycle, however, it was noted above that credit (broadly defined) is a far larger amount than money (narrowly defined) and that credit fluctuates far more rapidly than money in the cycle.

It is also worth remembering that the long-term trend had been toward increased financial fragility all the way from 1949 to 1991 (when we had a serious crisis in Savings and Loans as well as in the banking industry). This trend may be one explanation of the deeper contractions of the latter period.

With this background, we may ask a series of questions to focus on the controversial issues concerning finance and credit in the business cycle.

1. WHAT IS THE ROLE OF CREDIT IN THE CUMULATIVE EXPANSION?

With a brief time lag, credit responds to the rising profit expectations and rising personal income expectations. The enormous rise of credit in the expansion—both consumer credit and business credit—increases the growth of the economy at a far greater rate than the multiplier-accelerator mechanism would do if it were based on only real factors. In addition to the income derived from new investment (which is respent on consumption in the multiplier process), income is also increased by credit that is multiplied far beyond current savings by the banking system. In addition to the investment that would be predicted by the accelerator based solely on the change in real income, the existence of credit easily available at relatively low interest rates increases investment beyond the amount of the prediction based on real factors alone.

2. WHAT IS THE ROLE OF CREDIT IN THE DOWNTURN?

Monetarist theories, stating that exogenous shocks causing a decline of money and credit are the main or even sole cause of downturns, are incorrect. Part 2 of this book demonstrated in great detail that the real factors would lead to a downturn even if money and credit caused no problems. Moreover, credit is largely endogenously determined and the amount of credit outstanding continues to expand, though more slowly, through late expansion and into the crisis period. Credit growth slows only *after* mostly real factors have caused a decline in profit expectations; credit declines drastically only one stage *after* a recession begins.

On the other hand, those theories that explain the beginning of the downturn solely by the action of real factors are also incorrect or at least incomplete. The data presented in this chapter show that interest rates rise, with a time lag, throughout the expansion. Granted that interest rates rise because of demand for credit based on real factors (and false optimism spurred initially by real factors), it is still the case that rising interest rates do reduce the profit rate. Yet interest is only a small part of total cost to business, so it is only a small part of the negative factors leading to a downturn. The conclusion is that downturns would occur even if the cost and availability of credit were constant, but the reality is that the rising cost of credit does play a modest role (determined mostly endogenously) in causing the average downturn.

3. WHAT ROLE DOES CREDIT PLAY IN THE CUMULATIVE PROCESS OF CONTRACTION?

If real factors decline and profit expectations dim, a recession will result. But if there were no such thing as credit, it appears that all recessions would be mild. The financial system can turn potentially mild recessions into raging depressions. In the average contraction, after a brief time lag, the amount of consumer and business credit falls—while jobs and output are contracting. In this case, some consumers cannot repay loans to businesses or to banks, while some businesses also cannot repay banks—so some banks go bankrupt.

If the credit collapse is severe enough it leads to a depression, since it greatly magnifies the decline caused by the multiplier-accelerator process. How bad the affect on the economy of the initial decline will be depends on the degree of financial fragility of economic units. This chapter described the endogenous process whereby financial fragility increases throughout the expansion. Businesses become more fragile as they are pressured to borrow more relative to capital, to resort to shorter term loans, use up their liquid assets, and pay higher interest rates. This means that when profits start declining the average business is up against the wall with very little in reserves—tending to cause more businesses to go bankrupt.

The rising ratio of consumer loans to personal income throughout the expansion means that consumer finances also become fragile. Consumers become more and more vulnerable to the loss of jobs or lower incomes, making it impossible to maintain loan payments.

Banks also tend to become more financially fragile throughout the expansion. To make optimal short-term profits, banks reflect their own optimistic expectations by higher and higher ratios of loans to reserves—and by making more loans to less credit-worthy individuals or businesses. Thus, when consumers and businesses are unable to repay loans in a recession, banks are themselves more vulnerable to bankruptcy than in other cycle phases. In brief, the existence of increasing financial fragility in the expansion does not in itself cause a downturn, but it can decide the depth of the decline— and a high enough degree of financial fragility has the potential for causing another Great Depression.

4. WHAT IS THE ROLE OF CREDIT IN CAUSING AN UPTURN?

During a recession or depression interest rates fall (with a time lag). Declining interest rates reduce costs and are one small part of the factors helping profit rates to recover. Financial fragility also declines in the contraction—partly through bankruptcy of the weakest firms. As interest rates remain low in early recovery, they are a small part of the factors helping the recovery to gather steam.

KEY TERMS AND CONCEPTS

cyclical behavior of:
    stock market prices
    interest rates
    real money supply
    velocity of money

consumer debt/
    consumer income

discount rate

endogenous theories
    of money

exogenous theories of
    money

financial fragility

financial crises

money, credit

monetarism

open market
    operations

post-Keynesian
    monetary theory

APPENDIX 14 A
HOW DOES CREDIT MODIFY THE PROFIT SQUEEZE MODEL?

If one wished to formalize the profit squeeze (or nutcracker) model with the addition of financial variables, what modifications would be necessary?

The consumption function must include consumer credit as a positive influence on consumption. Suppose a consumption function that depends only on labor income (W) and property income (Π). When we add consumer credit (D), it becomes:

$$C_t = f(W, \Pi, D, t)$$

$$(14A.1)$$

Of course, the time lags may be complex and the relationship might be non-linear, so the innocuous looking t (time period) in the function indicates that this is not a simple one.

The changes in consumer credit must then be explained. Consumer credit will change when there are changes in consumer needs and expectations, as a function of employment and income. In the simplest case, we may show consumer credit as a function of the unemployment rate and national income:

$$D_t = f(U, Y, t) \tag{14A.2}$$

The investment function must include not only the effect of internal funds, represented by profits, but also the effect of credit available to business. Both the demand and supply of credit to business is strongly influenced by the expected rate of profit, so all those factors influencing profit expectations may also be assumed to affect business credit in a different function. In the simplest case, we might write that investment (I) is some function of profits (Π), the profit rate (Π/K), and business credit (BC):

$$I_t = f(\Pi, \Pi/K, BC, t) \tag{14A.3}$$

while at the same time business credit is itself some function of the level of profits and profit expectations, depending on the profit rate with various time lags and possibly non-linear relationships:

$$BC_t + f(\Pi, \Pi/K, t) \tag{14A.4}$$

One could, of course, explicitly include many other factors, such as output or national income, in this equation, but it should be remembered that all such factors are already implied by profits and profit rates.

Finally, the rate of profit—which influences investment—will be affected by interest costs, among other costs. Therefore, interest costs should be incorporated into the equation determining profit rates. Thus, the definition of aggregate profits would be expanded to include interests costs (IC) as well as labor costs (W) and raw material costs (M):

$$\Pi = (C + I) - (W + M + IC) \tag{14A.5}$$

Obviously, this definition still leaves out other elements of revenue and of cost, dealt with in later chapters.

Another equation would explain interest rates. The simplest function might be as a lagging function of output, though obviously many other factors would have to enter a realistic model.

$$IC_t = f(Y, t) \tag{14A.6}$$

These are some of the functions to be included in a full model.

CHAPTER 15

Monopoly Power, Inflation, and Business Cycles

This chapter is mainly concerned with the effect of monopoly power on the cyclical behavior of prices and profits. As a background, it begins by considering the long-run and cyclical behavior of average prices as well as the trends in monopoly power.

PRICE BEHAVIOR

The Keynesian framework stresses that there may be price inflation if aggregate supply is less than aggregate demand. Demand is conceptualized as consumption spending, investment spending, government spending, and net exports; while supply is thought of as real national output (GDP). The monetary framework ($MV = PT$) agrees that there will be inflation if aggregate supply is less than aggregate demand. Aggregate supply (PT) is conceptualized as prices times output; while aggregate demand (MV) is conceptualized as the supply of money times the velocity of money. Although the two frameworks (both true by definition) emphasize different aspects of demand, both stress inflation as a demand-pull phenomenon, that is, excessive demand causes inflation.

INFLATION IN WARTIME

The easiest type of inflation to explain is wartime inflation. The most spectacular inflations in U.S. history have occurred during, or immediately after, wars. There was enormous inflation in the American Revolutionary War, the War of 1812, the Civil War, and the First World War. In the Second World

War inflationary pressure was held back by strict price controls, but then inflation occurred when controls were lifted after the war. The Korean and Vietnam Wars also resulted in inflation. Similarly, in other countries the most infamous inflations have occurred during wars or their aftermaths, such as Germany experienced after the First World War, Russia during and after the Revolution and Civil War of 1917–1921, and China during its Revolution and Civil War ending in 1948.

Prices rise in wartime because there is vast government spending which competes for products and for workers with consumer spending and investment spending. Employees producing military supplies cannot eat bullets and tanks so they spend their money for consumer goods. Consumer goods are in short supply because labor has been taken away from consumer goods to produce military goods. Private corporations producing non-military supplies add to inflation by competing with military·demand for the limited amounts of plants, equipment, and raw materials that are available. Yet, governments cannot tax away enough of the military-generated wages and profits because they wish to maintain popular support and willingness to work.

LONG-RUN COST-PUSH INFLATION

During the late 1960s, the spending for the Vietnam War caused the usual demand-pull inflation. In other words, the demand from government for enormous amounts of war supplies caused prices to rise for those supplies. In addition, war production meant a high level of employment, giving employees a large amount of purchasing power. The high profits of the war also led corporations to increase their investments, thus creating a third source of demand pulling up prices.

In the early 1970s, when the Vietnam War finally came to an end, historical experience as well as theory would have led to the expectation that inflation would end. It did not end, however, and a high level of inflation continued throughout the 1970s. One major cause of this long-run inflationary trend was the rising price of raw materials, especially oil. From the cries about an oil shortage, one might have thought that the flow of oil suddenly stopped for natural or technological reasons. That was not the case. The shortages and rapidly rising prices were due to changing political-economic relationships in the world.

The Middle Eastern countries achieved some degree of independence from colonialism. Therefore, they began to exercise greater control over their own resources, including oil. They also banded together with other countries into a cartel called the Organization of Petroleum Exporting Countries, or OPEC. In a time of rising world demand for oil, they were able to restrict the supply of oil to a degree and to charge much higher prices.

Before that period, U.S. and European firms controlled oil production. When these firms were pushed out of production by the rising nationalist tide, they continued to control much of refining and distribution. Thus, in addition to the rising price of oil at the production level, Western firms added price increases of their own in refining and distribution.

After many years, the high price of oil eventually led to more supplies being developed as well as to the use of some substitutes. Eventually, downward pressures forced oil prices to decline somewhat, though not back to the pre-OPEC levels. Thus, much of the inflation of the 1970s could be called cost-push, rather than demand-pull.

Notice that part of the cost-push was really rising profit margins, so this part of the price rise might more precisely be called profit-push inflation. Obviously, the degree to which a company can increase prices above the competitive price in any situation depends on the degree of monopoly power. There is no good evidence to show that highly concentrated industries had greater price rises than others in the long-run of the 1970s and 1980s (except for the oil industry and a few others). But it will be shown below that the new cyclical pattern of inflation even in recessions is partly due to increasing monopoly power. Thus, the inflation of the 1970s during recessions appears to be some combination of long-run cost-push and cyclical monopoly profit-push.

Some observers have also attributed the long-run rising prices to the power of unions. It will be shown below, however, that union strength declined in this period and could not have been responsible for the long-run inflation, nor could it have been responsible for the dramatic change in cyclical price behavior over the business cycle.

CYCLICAL INFLATION AND DEFLATION BEFORE WORLD WAR TWO

In most of U.S. history, prices have tended to rise in every business cycle expansion and to fall in every business cycle contraction. The index of U.S. wholesale prices reveals that prices moved in the same direction as real production in 23 of the 26 cyclical expansions and contractions between 1890 and 1938 (see Mills 1946; for similar results, see Zarnowitz and Moore 1986, 526). On the average for the 11 non-war cycles between 1891 and 1938, wholesale prices rose 8.7 percent in expansions and fell 8.9 percent in contractions (see Mitchell 1951, 312–21).

Why did prices usually rise in expansions and decline in contractions in this period? Most simply put, there was inflation in expansions because aggregate demand rose faster than aggregate supply, while there was deflation in contractions because demand fell faster than supply. In Keynesian terms, consumer demand and investor demand rose more rapidly than output of those commodities in the expansion period and vice versa in contractions. In monetary terms, the supply of money and the velocity of money rose faster in expansions than the quantity of output, while the situation was the opposite in contractions.

CYCLICAL PRICE BEHAVIOR SINCE WORLD WAR TWO

As in earlier expansions, the expansions since World War Two have been accompied by rising prices. Unlike previous cyclical contractions, however, the last eight contractions (1949 to 1991) all have shown increasing prices rather than decreasing prices. Although there have been years of no inflation, the inflationary tendency has persisted during the Korean War, the Vietnam War, and the period since then.

Table 15.1 illustrates several important facts. First, inflation in the 1950s and 1960s is very weak overall, but is quite strong in the 1970s and 1980s. Second, as noted earlier, inflation continues even in contractions. The Keynesian and monetarist views both see inflation as the result of excess demand, so the phenomenon of rising prices in contractions seemed to contradict their theories. They have pointed out, however, that although prices have risen, the rate of inflation usually declines in contractions. (For the United States, this is found by Moore 1983, 233). Thus, they argue that as unemployment rises in contractions, the inflation rate declines.

Third, in most of the contractions from 1949 to 1991, the inflation rate does decline, as predicted by orthodox demand-pull theory. Yet, in three of the contractions (1970, 1975, and 1980) the inflation rate actually rose higher in the contraction than in the preceding expansion. In other words, in the 1950s and 1960s, unemployment and inflation mostly moved opposite to each other. In the 1970s and 1980s, however, inflation perversely rose as unemployment rose and fell somewhat as unemployment fell. That inflation rose faster in a period of falling demand obviously contradicts any kind of demand-pull inflation theory. To explain this new phenomenon, other theories must be considered, such as the many types of cost-push and profit-push theories.

TABLE 15.1
INFLATION IN EXPANSION AND CONTRACTION
(CHANGE IN PRICE PER QUARTER AS PERCENTAGE OF ITS CYCLE BASE)

Cycle	Expansion	Contraction
1949–1954	0.8	0.4
1954–1958	0.8	0.2
1958–1961	0.4	0.1
1961–1970	0.7	1.3
1970–1975	1.1	3.3
1975–1980	1.8	3.0
1980–1982	2.3	1.3
1982–1991	0.8	0.8

SOURCE: Implicit Price Deflator for all non-farm business, series LBGDPU in CITIBASE data base.

DECLINING UNION STRENGTH

One popular cost-push explanation of inflation is that labor unions have too much power. The explanation assumes that unions raise wages, leading to higher prices. But union strength has been declining. Union membership has shrunk from a high of 35 percent of the work force in 1945 to 22 percent in 1980 and to only 16 percent in 1994. The collapse of unions in the private sector is even more dramatic, with only 11 percent of private workers now unionized. Total union membership included 36 percent of all nonagricultural workers in 1956, a figure declining to only 17 percent in 1991. In the private, nonagricultural sector, union membership dropped from 38 percent in 1956 to only 13 percent in 1991. Only in the public sector has union strength grown, from 12 percent in 1956 to 41 percent in 1991. Obviously, the increase in unions in the public sector (which is much smaller than the private sector) has not nearly offset the decrease in the private sector.

Whatever the causes of the decline, the increasing weakness of labor unions has been evident for the past three decades. Therefore, the explanation for increasing inflation, especially in recessions and depressions, cannot be found in labor union strength. This is no longer a persuasive theory. In fact, there is good evidence that wage shares in industries have declined when union strength has declined. Henley (1987a) finds a correlation of the wage share with union strength or weakness. Thus, declining union strength was more likely a factor in reducing inflation in this period. The explanation of the inflation trends must be found elsewhere.

THE INCREASE OF MONOPOLY POWER

As late as 1860, small farms and small businesses produced most of U.S. output. After the Civil War had wiped out the slave owners, Northern industrialists had few rivals for power to rule. The Northern industrialists ran the government through the Republican party and used government power to penetrate into the South and the West. For example, huge parcels of land—equal in total acreage to more than many European countries—were given to the railroads. At the same time, technological improvements made a much larger scale of production more profitable, so there was strong motivation to expand. Furthermore, improvements in transportation and communication made expansion of nationwide firms quite feasible.

In 1929, the 200 largest manufacturing corporations held 46 percent of all manufacturing assets. Except for a slight decline during the Second World War (when medium-sized corporations did very well), this index of overall concentration has been rising steadily. The share of the 200 largest manufacturing corporations rose from 47 percent in 1949 to 60 percent in 1973. By 1977 the 100 largest manufacturing corporations produced 33 percent of all manufacturing net output by themselves (see Auerbach 1988, 150). *Fortune*'s 500 largest industrial corporations had 65 percent of sales, 70 percent of employment, and 84 percent of all assets in mining and manufacturing in 1984 (Munkirs and Koedler 1987, 808).

Much of the increase in concentration was due to internal growth of the largest corporations, but some was due to mergers. Since 1950, 1 out of every 5 of the 1000 largest manufacturing corporations has been swallowed by an even larger giant. The nature of these mergers has changed over time. In the 1890s and the 1900s there was a wave of horizontal mergers, that is, mergers between competitors in the same industry. In the 1920s and the 1930s there was a wave of vertical mergers, or mergers between a manufacturer and its suppliers or its retail dealers. In the late 1960s, 1970s, and 1980s, there was an enormous wave of conglomerate mergers or mergers of unrelated firms. These conglomerate mergers have not been limited to manufacturing, but have occurred in every sector of the U.S. economy.

By 1963 (before most of the conglomerate mergers) just four firms had over half the sales in 40 percent of U.S. manufacturing industries (see Blair 1972, 14). In another 32 percent of U.S. industries, just four firms sold between 25 and 50 percent of all sales. Only 28 percent of the industries had less than 25 percent of the sales controlled by four firms. These data on concentration are very impressive, but they still greatly underestimate the concentration of economic power (the latest available data on conglomerates are analyzed in an excellent article by Dugger 1985).

The degree of monopoly power in the United States is a highly controversial issue. Many economists claim that there is actually little monopoly power or that it has little effect on performance. Therefore, these economists base their policy proposals on the assumption of almost pure competition in the United States, believing that prices and wages are usually flexible and can restore full-employment equilibrium. Many other economists, however, believe that monopoly power is the dominant reality in the U.S. economy; for example, see the two powerful book-length studies by Alfred Eichner (1976) and by Joseph Bowring (1986).

These differences cannot be resolved here because although they appear to be differences over facts, they involve fundamentally different approaches, assumptions, and definitions. The definition of monopoly power used here states that monopoly power exists if the structure of the economy shows assets and sales concentrated among a relatively few giant corporations in each industry and in the aggregate economy. If a few corporations own most of the productive capacity and assets of an industry, then it is likely that these firms can influence the price and profit behavior of the industry. The data reported in this section shows concentrated ownership. The data reported in the rest of this chapter tends to confirm the fact that a structure of concentrated ownership tends to produce very different results than a competitive structure (also see the detailed findings of Bowring 1986).

Monopoly power is not only reflected in the concentration of assets, sales, and profits within individual industries, but is also measured by the degree of concentration of all assets, sales, and profits in the entire economy. It is important to distinguish industrial concentration and monopoly power from aggregate concentration (and monopoly power). The data presented above show that the tendency toward increased concentration of assets and sales has proceeded very steadily in the aggregate U.S. economy and shows no signs of a change in that trend.

It is true that the trend toward more concentration is less clear in individual industries. An analysis of the structure of the U.S. economy reveals a high level of concentration in individual industries, but the trend or direction is not so clear for three reasons. First, one problem is that the census industries are too broadly defined, meaning that they include products that are not substitutes and do not compete. This reduces the reported degree of concentration. On the other hand, the reported concentration is increased by not including international competition, which clearly should be included. Adjusting for these two contrary biases (and some other less important biases), W. G. Shepherd found that in most industries concentration is higher than reported (Shepherd 1970, 274–80). A *concentration ratio* in this case may be defined as the percentage of total industry sales controlled by four firms. In 1966, the official unadjusted concentration ratios were lower than Shepherd's adjusted ratios in all major industry groups except one. The changes were substantial; for example, the adjusted ratios rose from 16 to 46 in lumber, and from 32 to 64 in petroleum and coal products.

Second, another reason why concentration ratios in individual industries are not accurate reflections of monopoly power is that each of the 100 largest conglomerates controls some of the biggest firms in several industries, so their power goes far beyond the recorded concentration ratios. Using the census definition that best fits economic theory, there are about a thousand individual manufacturing industries. The concentration ratio was defined earlier as the percentage of sales controlled by the four largest firms in each of these industries. Yet, in a majority of the manufacturing industries, at least one of the four largest firms in that industry is controlled by a large conglomerate (see Blair 1972, 53–54). A *large conglomerate* is defined as one of the 100 largest firms in all of manufacturing.

Third, there are many interlocking directorates among the largest conglomerates, so one person sits on several boards to oversee their collusion or cooperation. In 1965, the 250 largest corporations had a total of 4,007 directorships, but these were held by just 3,165 directors (see Blair 1972, 76). Among the directors, 562 held two or more directorships, and five held six each. It should be noted that interlocking directorates among direct competitors are outlawed by the Clayton Act. There are also various groupings of corporations; for example, large blocks of stock in one group are held by the Rockefellers, whereas large blocks of stock in another are held by the Du Ponts.

Furthermore, banks are interlocked with many industrial corporations to form other important groups that work in a unified manner. Within the banking system itself, there is concentration of assets. In 1968, there were 13,775 commercial banks. Of these, a mere 14 banks (not 14 percent, but just 14) held 25 percent of all deposits. The 100 largest banks held 46 percent of all deposits.

Finally, it is necessary to examine all U.S. corporations, including all sectors of business. Table 15.2 shows the statistics for 1985, the most recent available data. The table reveals that 1.7 million small corporations (54 percent of all corporations) have only $57 billion in assets (less than 1 percent of assets). The highest asset size level (over a quarter of a billion dollars) includes just 4 thousand corporations, but this relatively small group of corporations have $9.9 *trillion* in assets (or 77 percent of all assets).

All of these data lead to two conclusions. First, economic concentration (both industrial and aggregate) among U.S. corporations is very high. Second, aggregate economic concentration among U.S. corporations, as defined by the percentage held by the 100 largest corporations, increased considerably in the 1970s, 1980s, and 1990s. With these facts in mind, one can understand some of the evolution of price behavior of U.S. corporations.

MONOPOLY POWER AND ADMINISTERED PRICES

In the Great Depression of the 1930s—and in the smaller depression of 1938—Gardiner Means (1975) found what he called "administered" prices in the monopoly sector. In the more concentrated industries, Means discov-

TABLE 15.2
DISTRIBUTION OF U.S. CORPORATE ASSETS

Asset Size	Number of Corp.	Amount of Assets	Percent of Corp.	Percent of Assets
Less than 100,000	1,692	$ 57	54%	1%
$100,000-$1 million	1,152	371	37	3
$1 million-$25 million	267	974	9	8
$25 million-$250 million	21	1,517	0.6	12
$250 million or more	4	9,852	0.1	77

SOURCE: U.S. Internal Revenue Service, *U.S. Statistics of Income: Corporation Tax Returns* (Washington, D.C.: U.S. GPO, 1986).

NOTE: Table includes all U.S. corporations in 1985 with at least $1 in assets. Number of corporations is given in thousands. Amount of assets is given in billions of dollars.

ered, prices were not set in a competitive market but were carefully administered or set in the best interests of the monopolies. He found that the competitive prices changed frequently, but that the administered or monopoly prices changed very seldomly.

More specifically, prices in the competitive sector registered large declines in depressions, but administered prices in the monopoly sector declined very little. Means defines the competitive sector as the 20 percent least-concentrated industries, whereas the monopoly sector is defined as the 20 percent that is most concentrated. From 1929 to 1932, prices in the more competitive sector fell 60 percent, but prices in the monopoly sector fell only 10 percent (Means 1975, 8–9). A few prices in the monopoly sector rose a little even in the face of the Great Depression.

Table 15.3 shows that even in the Great Depression the industries with greatest monopoly power lowered their prices very little. These industries kept prices from dropping farther only by reducing their production by very large percentages. The more competitive sectors had no choice but to let their prices be forced down by lack of demand. Production in the competitive sector declined less, because the lower prices brought relatively more demand. The monopoly sector thus held up its prices (and profit per unit) at the expense of great decreases in production and large-scale unemployment. The competitive sector lowered production less, fired fewer workers, but suffered much greater declines in prices and profits per unit. From this data, some observers find that a highly monopolized economy is more apt to produce high rates of unemployment in every business downturn.

Data for more recent business cycles show similar patterns. The competitive sector is defined as all those industries in which concentration of sales by eight firms is under 50 percent. The monopoly sector is defined as all

TABLE 15.3
PRICE AND PRODUCTION IN DEPRESSION, 1929–1932

Industry	Decline in Price	Decline in Production
Motor Vehicles	12%	74%
Agricultural Implements	14%	84%
Iron and Steel	16%	76%
Cement	16%	55%
Automobile Tires	25%	42%
Leather Products	33%	18%
Petroleum Products	36%	17%
Textile Products	39%	28%
Final Food Products	39%	10%
Agricultural Products	54%	1%

SOURCE: National Resources Committee (under the direction of Gardiner Means), *The Structure of the American Economy* (Washington, D.C.: U.S. GPO, 1939), 386.

NOTE: Declines are given as a percentage of their 1929 base.

those industries in which concentration of sales by eight firms is over 50 percent. (This definition, like any definition with a particular dividing point, is purely arbitrary. A more accurate—but far more complex—analysis would look instead at the whole spectrum from the least concentrated to the most concentrated for every statement about corporate performance.) The hundreds of individual industries may be aggregated—by averaging all their concentration ratios, weighted by the value of shipments of each industry—into the major industry groups.

The *expansion amplitude* of a price index is defined as its rise from initial trough to cycle peak, given as a percentage of its average level over the cycle. The average expansion amplitudes for all the prices in the monopoly sector and for all the prices in the competitive sector are given in Table 15.4, for the period 1949 to 1973. The results for the two cyclical expansions of 1949–1953 and 1954–1957 are unusual in that prices in the monopoly sector rose faster than prices in the more competitive sector. In the three

TABLE 15.4
PRICES IN MONOPOLY AND COMPETITIVE SECTORS

EXPANSION AMPLITUDES

Dates of Expansion	Prices in Monopoly Sector	Prices in Competitive Sector
October 1949–July 1953	13.6%	11.1%
May 1954–August 1957	11.0%	4.6%
April 1959–April 1960	2.1%	3.0%
February 1961–December 1969	8.3%	16.3%
November 1970–November 1973	10.2%	23.4%

CONTRACTION AMPLITUDES

Dates of Expansion	Prices in Monopoly Sector	Prices in Competitive Sector
November 1948–October 1949	−1.9%	−7.8%
July 1953–May 1954	+1.9%	−1.5%
August 1957–April 1958	+0.5%	−0.3%
April 1960–February 1961	+0.9%	−1.2%
December 1969–November 1970	+5.9%	−3.0%
November 1973–March 1975	+32.8%	+11.7%

SOURCES: Robert Lanzillotti, Hearings before the Joint Economic Committee of the U.S. Congress, *Employment, Growth and Price Levels* (Washington, D.C.: GPO, 1959), 2238. John Blair, "Market Power and Inflation," *Journal of Economic Issues* 8 (June 1974), 453–78. Kathleen Pulling, "Market Structure and the Cyclical Behavior of Prices and Profits, 1949 to 1975" (Ph.D. dissertation, University of California, Riverside, 1978).

NOTE: Expansion amplitude means rise from trough to peak as a percentage of cycle average, while contraction amplitude means decline from peak to trough as a percentage of cycle average.

later expansions, 1958–1960, 1961–1969, and 1970–1973, the prices in the more competitive sector rose faster than prices in the monopoly sector. This is the same pattern as in the expansion of 1933–1937. It will usually be the case that, in expansions, prices in the more competitive sector rise somewhat faster than prices in the monopoly sector. The theoretical reasons for this behavior are discussed in the next section.

Of most interest, however, are the relative price behaviors in contractions. As noted earlier, average prices for all sectors have behaved differently in recent contractions than in most previous recessions or depressions. Prices have risen instead of fallen, so depression and unemployment no longer guarantee an end to inflation. For this reason, significant inflation has been continuous since 1967, though at different rates. The inflation began in the normal way with the spending during the Vietnam War, but its persistence through periods of falling demand indicates a new kind of animal. How much of this new phenomenon is associated with the competitive sector, and how much with the monopoly sector?

Various investigators have studied competitive prices and monopoly price behavior in the contractions since 1948. Their findings are presented in Table 15.4. The *contraction amplitude* of a price index is defined as its change from the cycle peak to the cycle trough, given as a percentage of its average level over the whole business cycle. The table reveals that the pattern of the 1948 recession was the same as the pattern found by Gardiner Means for the 1929 and 1937 depressions. In all three cases, monopoly prices declined a little, whereas competitive prices declined an enormous amount. In the 1954, 1958, and 1961 recessions the first indications of the new behavior (output stagnation plus price inflation) were found. Competitive prices decline as usual, although by a small amount, but monopoly prices actually *rise* in the recessions, although again by a small amount. The new situation is very clear in the 1970 recession, in which competitive prices decline by a significant amount, whereas monopoly prices rise by a considerable amount. A finer division indicates even stronger price declines in the more competitive industries. While prices in all industries under a 50 percent concentration ratio fell 3 percent, prices in industries under a 25 percent concentration ratio fell by 6.1 percent.

Price data on the 1973–1975 depression indicate that monopoly prices *rose* in the depression by an astounding percentage. This very large price increase throughout the now-dominant monopoly sector caused even competitive prices to show a small *rise* in the depression for the first time on record (because competitive firms have to buy some commodities from the monopoly sector). This undoubtedly caused great disruption in the competitive sector, decreased production, increased bankruptcies, and increased unemployment. Similar differences between competitive and monopoly price behavior have been found in Japan (see Kobayashi 1971).

EXPLANATION OF PRICE BEHAVIOR

In almost all recessions before the 1950s, prices fell. That behavior was predictable and easily explained by traditional economic theory. Traditional microeconomic theory led us to expect that falling demand will cause *both* output and prices to decline.

Similarly, in the aggregate, traditional macroeconomic theory in the 1950s predicted that an excess supply would lead to falling production, unemployment, and falling prices (or stable prices if there are institutional rigidities or monopoly power). On the other hand, traditional macroeconomic theory in the 1950s predicted price inflation only when there was an excess demand above the supply at full employment.

Traditional theory did not predict price inflation in the face of falling demand and unemployment, but this is what occurred in the monopoly sector in the recessions or depressions of 1954, 1958, 1961, 1970, 1975, 1980, 1982, and 1991. Of course, traditional theory would admit that firms with monopoly power can always set prices higher if they wish to restrict their supply enough to do so. But *why*, in the face of falling demand, should monopolies find it profitable to reduce their production so drastically as actually to increase prices?

Only a few economists have provided some answers to this question (see Kalecki 1968; Blair 1974; and Eichner 1973). In most of the monopoly sector, a single large firm in each industry sets prices; others simply follow this price leader. This cost-plus pricing by the large corporations has been confirmed by many empirical investigations (see Eichner 1973; Robinson 1979).

The giant corporations do *not* maximize their short-run profit by setting prices as high as possible at any given moment. Rather, they set prices with a profit margin such as to ensure their maximum long-run growth—and maximum long-run profits. This profit margin must, therefore, be enough to meet fully their expected needs for growth and expansion. Each corporation sets a *target* profit level based on its previous record and the record of the leaders in its industry.

In a business expansion, to achieve their best long-run growth of profits, the giant corporations usually set their prices *below* what the market would pay so as to (1) discourage entry by rivals, (2) gain acceptance of new products in a wider market, (3) stop unions from claiming they have the ability to pay much higher wages, (4) discourage government antitrust actions or attempts to put price controls on their products, and (5) stabilize dividend payments (and stock prices) by preventing them from rising too high so that they won't fall as much in the next recession. This holding down of prices thus gives the monopoly or oligopoly firms more power to maintain or even raise prices in the following contraction—because the giant firm has acquired a larger market, fewer rivals, less government control, and so forth.

What happens if a giant corporation finds its sales revenue falling in a recession or depression? The firm will try to obtain enough revenue to reach its target profit by means of a higher price markup on the remaining sales. This process has been ably illustrated in an arithmetic example in an excellent article by Howard Wachtel and Peter Adelsheim (1976):

> For example, say a firm operating in a concentrated industry has direct costs (raw material and labor) of $200 per unit of output and sets its profit markup above direct costs at 20 percent, therefore selling the product for $240 per unit and making a profit of $40 per unit. Let us say the firm has a target level of profits of $40,000; to realize this profit level it will have to sell 1,000 units at $240 per unit. Now we have unemployment and a recession which causes the volume of sales to fall, say, to 960 units. But if the firm still has a target profit level of $40,000, which it wants to attain, it will have to raise its prices to slightly over $242 per unit from the previous level of $240 per unit. It does this by raising its percentage markup over costs to 21 percent compared to the previous 20 percent. Having increased their profit per unit, the firm now achieves its target profit level, but the resultant manifestation in the economy is the simultaneous occurrence of inflation and unemployment. (Wachtel and Adelsheim 1976, 5).

This illustration assumes little or no further decrease in demand when the price is marked up. But Wachtel and Adelsheim point out that their conclusion, that firms with monopoly power will raise prices in a recession with these policies, holds true even if the price increases cause some further decline in demand. Of course, even the tightest monopoly in reality will lose a few customers from any price rise, but most of them have a strong enough market control, as well as a strong enough image from advertising, to ensure that they will not lose many customers. Just how high a price they can set is a function of their degree of monopoly.

More specifically, their degree of monopoly power over price has three main constraints. First, if the industry raises its prices (led by the price leader), how many customers are willing or able to switch to a substitute product? Second, if the price and profit margins are raised, how many new firms will be able to enter the industry, or how high are the barriers to such new entrants? Third, what is the realistic likelihood of any government intervention if the price-gouging becomes too obvious to be overlooked?

It follows from this cost-plus behavior that such oligopoly firms do not change their prices as frequently as competitive firms. Even if there is rapid inflation of prices and costs, these firms usually keep one price for quite a while then raise it to the new level dictated by their usual profit margin above costs. Thus, there is considerable evidence that in periods of business expansion and rapid inflation it is the prices of the more competitive firms that rise more rapidly and change from day to day.

In a recession, however, the small, competitive firms are forced to drop their prices rapidly as demand falls (because not one of them can restrict the industry supply) *regardless* of the effect on their profit rates. Not so the large, oligopoly firms. In the recession, if costs per unit remain the same (as they do in physical terms over a wide range of output), then the oligopolies may keep their prices the same so as to maintain a profit rate as near constant as possible. Of course, that entails extra reduction of production and the unemployment of many more workers than in a similar competitive industry, but that is not their worry.

Indeed, in recent recessions or depressions, when total sales were declining, the firms with monopoly power actually raised prices as far as they believed necessary to maintain their profit margins and total profit. In order to make these price increases in the face of declining demand, they very drastically reduced their production, thereby worsening unemployment.

MONOPOLY AND PROFIT RATES

If our economy operated under pure and perfect competition, then capital would flow immediately from areas of low profit rates to areas of high profit rates. It follows that the rate of profit would be equal in all industries. The rate of profit, however, is not *equal* in all industries. It is consistently higher in industries with greater monopoly power.

In this case, define a *concentration ratio* as the percentage of industry sales controlled by the eight largest firms. The ratio for each industry group is a weighted average of the ratios in each of its component industries. The *monopoly sector* is defined as all those industry groups over 50 percent concentration in all the census years from 1949 to 1973, whereas the *more competitive sector* is all those groups under 50 percent concentration in all the census years from 1949 to 1973. The *rate of profit* used here is the percentage of profit to sales in each industry group. The average rate of profit on sales for the monopoly sector (over 50 percent concentration) was 11.2 percent for the average of the years from 1949 to 1973. The average rate of profit on sales for the more competitive sector (under 50 percent concentration) was only 6.2 percent for the average of the years from 1949 to 1973; the difference between the two sectors was statistically significant (see Pulling 1978).

Why does the monopoly sector have higher profit rates than the competitive sector? In the first place, monopoly power means the ability to restrict supply and keep prices higher than in the competitive sector (within the three constraints discussed in the preceding section). The higher prices mean lower real wages for all worker-consumers. The profits of small, competitive business and farmers are also hurt by monopoly prices to the extent that they must purchase producer goods from the monopoly sector. Some large firms in the monopoly sector also have extra market power as large buyers of commodities from small competitive business, forcing down the prices charged by these small suppliers.

Large firms in the monopoly sector may also have extra power in the labor market, so they may add to profits by buying labor at a rate lower than the average wage. This factor may, of course, be somewhat offset by trade union action. In U.S. manufacturing, the wage share is lower in industries with high concentration, but is higher in industries with high unionization (see Henley 1987a); where both factors operate, they partially offset each other. In the modern world, wages are not automatically determined by supply and demand in the market. They are determined by the bargaining strength of capital and labor (under given conditions of supply and demand), with monopoly capital usually in the stronger position. Workers are thus squeezed from both sides by monopoly. On the one hand, monopolies can charge workers higher prices as consumers; on the other hand, the monopolies can pay lower money wages by exerting their power in the labor market. (In reality, however, wage rates are usually higher in more concentrated industries because it is easier for unions to organize larger units, and because monopolies usually find it easier to hand on higher wages to consumers as higher prices rather than to fight with unions.)

Additional monopoly profits come from lucrative government military contracts which are financed from the workers' tax money, thus again increasing total profits. Extra-high returns from foreign investments abroad also add to monopoly profits; that is, profits are extracted from workers in foreign countries. In summary, monopolies or oligopolies make profit far above the average rate in several ways: (1) selling at higher prices to consumers, thereby lowering the real wage; (2) selling at higher prices to small business and farmers; (3) buying at lower prices from small business and farmers; (4) buying labor at lower wages from workers (but this is often offset by union organization, as noted above); (5) selling to the government at higher prices; and (6) buying labor power and materials at lower prices in foreign countries. Through these relatively high prices and low costs (always relative to a competitive firm in the same situation), the monopoly or oligopoly firms extract more profits from the worker-consumer-taxpayer here and abroad; they also transfer some profits from small business and farmers to themselves.

Table 15.5 shows the long-run profit rate on the capital investment of all stockholders averaged for the years 1956 through 1975. Each group of corporations is shown by the size of total assets, from the smallest (below a

TABLE 15.5

LONG-RUN PROFIT RATE ON INVESTMENT
FOR ALL U.S. MANUFACTURING CORPORATIONS, 1956–1975

Size (by Assets)	Profit Rate (Profit Before Taxes Divided by Stockholders' Capital)
$0–$1 million	3.7%
$1 million–$5 million	5.3%
$5 million–$10 million	6.7%
$10 million–$50 million	7.4%
$50 million–$100 million	8.1%
$100 million–$250 million	8.5%
$250 million–$1 billion	8.8%
$1 billion and over	11.7%

SOURCE: U.S. Federal Trade Commission, Quarterly Report of U.S. Manufacturing Corporations (Washington, D.C.: GPO, 1956–1975).

million) to the largest (over a billion). The relationship in Table 15.5 is very clear. The profit rate on investment rises monotonically as the size of the corporation increases.

The higher profit rate with size is explained by all the reasons given earlier for the higher profit rate resulting from monopoly power. To a large extent, large size means monopoly power—though there are industries where there are so many giant firms that the concentration ratio by four or eight appears low, and there are industries small enough for a medium-sized firm to have monopoly power. Moreover, examining behavior by size alone eliminates some of the distortion of the concentration ratios caused by one conglomerate's controlling subsidiaries in a number of different industries. The large size also directly affects profitability through economies of scale in production, in distribution, and in nationwide advertising. The large manufacturing corporation may also own its own natural resources. Moreover, the large corporation may have much cheaper access to finance either by its credit rating or by a direct tie-in with a financial institution.

MONOPOLY PROFIT RATES OVER THE CYCLE

We have seen that the large monopoly corporations have higher profit rates in the long run than small competitive firms. We have also seen that, in expansions, the large monopoly firms raise their prices more slowly in order to increase their share of the market. In contractions, the large monopoly firms keep their prices from falling or actually raise them, whereas competi-

TABLE 15.6
AMPLITUDES OF MONOPOLY AND COMPETITIVE PROFIT RATES

Cycle	MONOPOLY SECTOR		COMPETITIVE SECTOR	
	Expansion Amplitude	Contraction Amplitude	Expansion Amplitude	Contraction Amplitude
1949–1954	32.1	−30.8	45.8	−56.9
1954–1958	21.6	−41.3	32.1	−47.8
1958–1961	33.5	−28.6	36.6	−47.1
1961–1970	25.0	−35.1	49.0	−32.3
Average	28.0	−34.0	40.9	−46.0

SOURCE: Federal Trade Commission data complied by Kathleen Pulling, "Market Structure and Cyclical Behavior of Prices and Profits, 1949–1975" (Ph.D. dissertation, University of California, Riverside, 1978).

tive firms have to reduce prices or raise them much less than the monopolies. Given this difference in price conduct, what is the difference in performance of profit rates in the two sectors over the cycle? Table 15.6 shows the cyclical amplitudes of the monopoly and competitive profit rates.

In Table 15.6, the monopoly sector includes all major industry groups with concentration ratios greater than 50 percent in all of the Census of Manufacturers years: 1954, 1958, 1967, and 1972. The competitive sector includes those groups of less than 50 percent in all the same years. An expansion amplitude measures the peak value minus the initial trough value as a percentage of the cycle average. The contraction amplitude is the final trough minus the peak as a percentage.

Table 15.6 shows quite clearly that profit rates in the more competitive sector normally rise and fall more violently than profit rates in the monopoly sector, which is the same pattern as their price behavior. Profit rates in the more competitive sector of manufacturing rose faster than in the monopoly sector in four out of four expansions from 1949 to 1970. And profit rates in the more competitive sector fell further in three out of four contractions.

If we examine the cyclical amplitude of profit rates by size of corporation, the pattern is very similar. Table 15.7 shows the profit rate on sales by size of assets of corporations for the four cycles of 1949 to 1970 and the profit rate on capital by size of corporate assets for the three cycles of 1970 to 1982. The two different definitions of the profit rate are used to show that the change in definition does not change the results.

Table 15.7 reveals that the profit rates of the larger corporations rise less in expansions and fall less in contractions than the profit rates of the smaller corporations. When these findings are combined with the similar findings of Table 15.6 on monopoly and competitive sectors, the conclusion is that the profit rates of large corporations with monopoly power are far more stable than those of small competitive corporations.

TABLE 15.7
AMPLITUDE OF PROFIT RATES BY SIZE

AVERAGE OF FOUR CYCLES, 1949–1970

Asset Size	Expansion Amplitude	Contraction Amplitude
Less than $250,000	+83%	−83%
$250,000–$1 million	+39%	−55%
$1 million–$5 million	+37%	−52%
$5 million–$100 million	+28%	−27%
$100 million and over	+22%	−27%

AVERAGE OF THREE CYCLES, 1970-1982

Asset Size	Expansion Amplitude	Contraction Amplitude
Less than $5 million	+49%	−58%
$5 million–$25 million	+38%	−39%
$25 million–$100 million	+34%	−41%
$100 million–$1 billion	+25%	−37%
$1 billion and over	+24%	−33%

SOURCE: U.S. Census Bureau, *Quarterly Financial Reports of Manufacturing Corporations* (Washington, D.C.: GPO, 1949–1988).

NOTE: Profit rate for 1949–70 is percentage of profit (before tax) to sales for all U.S. manufacturing corporations. Profit rate for 1970–82 is percentage of profit (before tax) to stockholders' equity for all U.S. manufacturing corporations. All amplitudes are for specific cycles.

Why do the large monopoly corporations have more stable profit rates in both boom and bust? First, they attempt to set their prices to maintain a stable profit rate. Second, their monopoly power allows them to set their prices at those levels. They maintain those prices in contractions by restricting their production (and employment). In expansion, they raise prices only slowly while rapidly increasing their production (and employment) to obtain or keep a high share of the expanding market. Third, the costs per unit of the largest corporations remain fairly constant over a wide range of output below full capacity. The unit costs of small corporations rise rapidly when they drop below optimum capacity. Fourth, the interest burden of small corporations, as compared to large corporations, is greater both because they pay higher interest rates and because they borrow a higher percentage of their capital. Fifth, and very important, the small corporations have all their eggs in one basket (with no reserves), whereas the large conglomerates are very diversified, with some investments in industries that may happen to grow despite a contraction (and an ability to shift reserve capital from one area to another).

In summation, it appears that increased monopolization of the economy increases the stability of prices and profits in the sector of high monopoly power but reduces the stability of output and employment in that sector.

Also, the stability of monopoly prices further destabilizes prices in the competitive sector. The instability of the competitive sector probably is the prime factor setting off each new crisis of over-production and contraction. But the drastic decline of output and employment in the monopoly sector (used to keep prices high) greatly deepens the crisis.

CONCENTRATION BY MULTINATIONAL (OR GLOBAL) FIRMS

The present high degree of economic concentration of assets in the whole private enterprise world, by a few enormous multinational or global corporations, constitutes a new structural stage of the international private enterprise economy. The term *multinational* suggests management from many countries, whereas the truth is that each firm is governed mostly by the nationals of one developed private enterprise country. The term *global corporation* may be less misleading. The one viewpoint uniting all these corporations is the notion that the whole globe is their oyster, that vast profits may be made by control of markets in several countries.

In pursuit of profit, U.S.-based global corporations have been rapidly expanding abroad. In 1957, investment in plant and equipment by U.S. firms abroad was already 9 percent of total U.S. domestic investment in plant and equipment. By 1970, that investment abroad rose to 25 percent of domestic investment. In terms of total assets of U.S. industries, by 1974 about 40 percent of all consumer goods industries, about 75 percent of the electrical industry, about 33 percent of the chemical industry, about 33 percent of the pharmaceutical industry, and over half of the $100 billion petroleum industry were located outside the United States (Barnet and Muller 1974, 17).

It is worth stressing, however, that the former U.S. dominance of the global corporations has ended and its share has dramatically declined. Whereas U.S.-based firms held two-thirds of all direct foreign investment in 1961–1970, the share of U.S.-based firms fell to less than half in 1976–1980 (Auerbach 1988, 243). At the same time, the share of German and Japanese-based firms rose dramatically. So one of the most important international facts today is the competition faced by U.S. firms.

It is also important to note that many transactions within and between private enterprise countries are conducted solely between subsidiaries of the same parent corporation. A large-scale sample found that over 50 percent of total foreign trade transactions by the private enterprise countries are of this non-market intracorporate variety between subsidiaries of the same company (Muller 1975, 194). This means that taxes can be shifted to those countries where the rates are lowest. It also means that taxation policies may not operate—or may operate mainly to the benefit of the global giants. Several studies show that the global corporations based in the United States absorb a disproportionate part of all U.S. government spending and tax reductions designed to stimulate the economy (Muller 1975, 188).

The global manufacturing corporations are served by global banks with tentacles almost everywhere (Auerbach 1988, 195–201). At their urging, additional credit has been created as a new currency, the huge pool of Eurodollars (and the special drawing rights which also act as currency). Since there are no reserve deposit requirements on the Eurodollars, they are particularly unstable and contribute a strong impetus to inflationary pressures by further credit creation. This international credit expansion plus rapid monetary flows between corporate subsidiaries across borders make it less possible than ever for any single private enterprise nation to control its money supply by any conceivable monetary policies.

It should also be noted that union bargaining power has been further weakened by the power of the global corporations to shift production rapidly from areas of high wages to low wage areas. For example, if the United States has high wages, they shift production to Mexico, and if even Mexican wages are considered too high, they shift to Hong Kong.

The multinational or global firms are the present instrument whereby enormous profits are extracted from the Third World countries and sent back to the advanced private enterprise countries. For example, U.S. firms' profits from abroad were only 7 percent of total U.S. corporate profits in 1960 but rose to 30 percent by 1974 (Muller 1975, 183). The top 298 U.S.-based global corporations earn 40 percent of their entire net profit overseas, and their rate of profit from abroad is much higher than their domestic profit rate. It is also true that: (1) the rate of profit in U.S. investments abroad is several times higher in the less developed than in the advanced private enterprise countries, and (2) the less developed countries generously make a good-sized contribution to U.S. capital accumulation (the same facts could be shown for European and Japanese investments in the Third World).

Finally, the international concentration of investment decision-making in a relatively small number of corporations plus the very intimate ties of international trade and investment among all the private enterprise countries bind these economies closely together. Therefore, as will be explained in detail in the next chapter, a contraction begun in one country or in just a few global corporations spreads at lightning speed to the others.

CONCLUSIONS

The phenomenon of inflation appears in recessions now because of the vast increase in concentrated monopoly power (both in the U.S. economy and world-wide). In several recessions of the 1950s and 1960s, though competitive prices dropped in each contraction, monopoly prices rose. In the depressions of the 1970s, 1980s, and 1990s, general inflation increased competitive prices a little whereas monopoly prices soared. As a result of the oligopoly control over prices as well as some other factors associated with absolute size, the profit rates in firms with monopoly power are relatively stable, declining relatively little in recession or depression. The small competitive firms, however, bear the full burden of the profit decline in depression (although employees shoulder an even larger burden through reduced real wages). Hence, increasing monopoly power has caused greater declines of production and employment while raising prices through that very restriction of supply.

The existence of monopoly power, therefore, increases cyclical unemployment to a higher level than it would be if there were no monopoly power. Parts 2 and 3 of this book have shown there would continue to be cyclical unemployment even if there were pure competitive private enterprise (with no rigidities or monopoly power), but the existence of monopoly power apparently exacerbates recessions and depressions.

KEY TERMS AND CONCEPTS

monopoly power

degree of concentration

mergers

demand-pull inflation

cost-push inflation

profit-push inflation

long-run profit rate of highly concentrated industries

cyclical profit rate behavior of highly concentrated industries

large size versus concentration

long-run and cyclical profit rate behavior of small, competitive firms

---

APPENDIX 15 A
BIBLIOGRAPHIC ESSAY ON MONOPOLY POWER

The best single study of monopoly power, prices, and profits is by Joseph Bowring (1986). An important pioneering study of monopoly power is by Baran and Sweezy (1966). A thorough follow-up on the pros and cons of the Baran and Sweezy thesis is by John Foster (1986). For a view of monopoly power completely opposed to Baran and Sweezy's views and opposed to the views of the authors, see Willi Semmler (1982). A beautifully and clearly written popular book, from a liberal view, on monopoly and inflation is by John Case (1981). There is a comprehensive and incisive presentation of the post-Keynesian view in Alfred Eichner (1976). A very interesting and useful discussion of monopoly and inflation is by Malcolm Sawyer (1982) who also compiled an excellent survey of theories of monopoly capitalism (1988). A brilliant book on the evolution of monopoly power in the United States is by John Munkirs (1985). A powerful collection of Institutionalist articles on monopoly power is in Wallace Peterson (1988b). The merger movement is analyzed clearly in Du Boff and Herman (1989). A very useful survey and contribution to the debate on monopoly power is in Amitava Dutt (1987). The best discussion of conglomerates is by William Dugger (1985). For neoclassical views of mergers and antitrust policy, see Steven Salop (1987), Laurence White (1987), and Richard Schmalensee (1987). For neoclassical views of takeovers, see Hal Varian (1988), Shleifer and Vishny (1988), Michael Jensen (1988), Jarrell, Brickley and Netter (1988), and F. M. Scherer (1988).

APPENDIX 15 B
A PROFIT SQUEEZE (NUTCRACKER) MODEL WITH MONOPOLY POWER

How should the profit squeeze (or nutcracker) model be modified to reflect the reality of monopoly power? Monopoly power affects price behavior, profit behavior, wage behavior, and investment behavior. The behavior of each of these variables is different in large corporations in concentrated industries than in small firms in more competitive industries. Moreover, by affecting income distribution (as shown by Kalecki 1968, Chapter 1), monopoly power affects consumption and thereby changes the value of the multiplier. By affecting investment behavior, monopoly power changes the value of the accelerator.

In brief, the behavioral function of every variable is different in the monopoly sector (meaning more concentrated industries) than in the competitive sector (meaning more competitive industries). Therefore, the simplest modification is to disaggregate the model into two sectors, each having all the behavioral functions, but also showing how the two sectors will affect each other and will aggregate together in the whole economy. The monopoly sector may be defined as all industries above a certain concentration ratio, while the competitive sector may be defined as all industries below a certain concentration ratio.

As complex as such a model would be, it may be criticized for simplicity. First, concentration ratios are not a very good indicator and certainly not the only indicator of monopoly power. Other indicators, such as barriers to entry, would be needed to create an index of monopoly power for each industry. Second, there are not two clearly distinct sectors, but a range from the largest firms in the most concentrated industries to the smallest firms in the most competitive industries. Instead of a two-sector model, an n-sector model would be needed to show the full spectrum of behavior from competitive to monopoly behavior. Such a model is far too complex to be stated here in formal terms.

CHAPTER 16

The International Economy and Business Cycles

This chapter removes the unreal assumption that the U.S. economy is isolated and self-sufficient. The closed economy assumption was useful until now to clarify the domestic aspects of the business cycle. Its unreal nature, however, is emphasized by Dernberg, who says: "Since there is no such thing as a closed economy . . . it follows that much of macroeconomics [using that assumption] is not only incomplete, but it is also incorrect" (1989, 1). This chapter examines how the U.S. business cycle behaves in the real world of international trade, investment, and finance (an outstanding collection of articles on these issues is MacEwan and Tabb 1989). The chapter begins with the dramatic history of the rise and fall of U.S. economic power. In that historical context, the chapter turns to theories of international transmission of cycles, followed by an empirical analysis of what actually happens. It will be seen in this chapter that the close international integration of the private enterprise economies has increased instability.

U.S. DEVELOPMENT IN THE INTERNATIONAL FRAMEWORK

When a country is in its early stages of industrial development, independence from foreign influences is difficult. Likewise, when a country is small and unable to be self-sufficient, it is usually dependent on foreign supply and demand. In the beginning of the nineteenth century, the United States was both immature industrially and limited in its main centers of commerce and industry to the small area along its Atlantic coast. Therefore, during that period the United States was very susceptible to foreign influences in its economy, especially to the trade and investment of the United Kingdom. The basic direction of influence was surely from the rapidly developing industry of the United Kingdom outward to the less developed industry and commerce of the United States. Depressions developed in England often led to depressions in the United States because of the decline of U.S. exports to England. In the few instances where the American decline began first, the reduction of British investment opportunities may have spread the depression to England.

Investment in the United States brought big profits, but had great risks attached to it, and was subject to violent swings according to the decisions of foreign investors. All the features of the U.S. economy were typical of a less developed country, including the following characteristics of that period (the first half of the 19th century). Two-thirds or more of all U.S. produce was agricultural. Most enterprises in the North and West, whether farm or handicraft, were one-person proprietorships. In the South, there were large slave plantations. There is no indication of internal generation of a business cycle under slavery, but Southern U.S. slavery was affected by business cycles in the rest of the world. Much work was done at home. In cities, shop windows were often merely that part of the home that fronted on the street. There were few urban wage workers because there were few shops of more than one person (with perhaps an apprentice). Markets were limited to the local area. Most families in Northern agriculture were almost completely self-sufficient. There were large unclaimed and unexplored areas in the West. There was much barter, little use of money, and an undeveloped and inefficient banking system. By far the most important section of capital was engaged in commerce—and largely foreign commerce at that. Since it lacked the necessary conditions, the U.S. economy of the early period (at least until 1837) did not have internally generated cycles. (Material in this section is mainly from Lee 1955 and Mirowski 1986b).

In the period of 1837 to 1860, foreign influences were somewhat less important than in 1776 to 1836, so peacetime business cycles were partly the result of internal generation. If not dominant, however, foreign influences certainly played an often decisive part in U.S. development. For example, the British financial panic of 1847 led directly to the moderate U.S. depression of 1848.

The period from the Civil War to the end of the nineteenth century was the period in which the United States reached industrial maturity. By the end of that period the corporate form of business was predominant; only a sixth of all output was agricultural; agriculture itself was more commercial and market-directed; the factory system with thousands of workers replaced the small handicraft shops and the home production of almost all articles. The United States had a system of heavy industry which was as complex and interrelated as any in the world; organized management faced a growing union movement; money had replaced barter in every aspect of the economy; markets were national or international in scope; the frontier had ended; and commerce provided only a small part of the national income. Since it now had the conditions of advanced private enterprise systems, the U.S. economy generated its own cycles but still interacted closely with Western European cycles.

In the United States in the twentieth century, foreign relations have dominated the domestic economy only in the major wars: the First World War, the Second World War, the Korean War, and the Vietnam War. Otherwise, domestic internal mechanisms have dominated the U.S. business cycle, though military spending and international trade and investment have obviously played an increasingly significant role. Major declines in the U.S. economy, such as the Great Depression of the 1930s or the severe recessions of 1975 and 1982, have hurt the rest of the world. The mild recessions that the U.S. economy undergoes every three or four years do not have a major effect on most of the world, although they obviously hurt some specific trading partners. It should be noted that even mild recessions do increase human misery for millions of U.S. employees by involuntary idleness, drastic declines in income, as well as pessimism and alienation, which lead to higher rates of divorce, crime, and suicide.

RISE OF THE U.S. EMPIRE

Until the Civil War, U.S. private enterprise was far behind European private enterprise. It had the advantage, however, of having no feudal or semifeudal encumbrances. After the Civil War, the United States had also abolished slavery which opened the whole country to the private enterprise economy. Moreover, the U.S. economy was relatively short of labor, so it was forced to use the most advanced technology. As a result, U.S. industrialization proceeded very rapidly after 1870, and it eventually overtook and passed British and other European industry. Finally, the two world wars devastated much of Europe and Japan but stimulated the U.S. economy. By 1945 the United States emerged completely dominant in the private enterprise world, though this situation lasted only a brief time in an historical perspective. From 1945 until the mid-1960s, the U.S. economy was far more powerful than Europe's or Japan's, while U.S. military power played policeman trying to maintain imperialist control of the Third World (for an insightful discussion of theories of underdevelopment and imperialism, see Griffin and Gurley 1985).

Between 1945 and 1950, the U.S. gross domestic product (GDP) was equal to that of the whole rest of the world combined. French GDP was only 10 percent of the U.S. product in 1950; West Germany's was only 8 percent; Italy's was only 5 percent; Japan's was only 4 percent; the United Kingdom's was only 13 percent—and all five equalled only 39 percent of the U.S. GDP. In 1950, the United States produced 82 percent of all the world's passenger vehicles and 55 percent of the world's steel production, and consumed 50 percent of the world's energy production (see Szymanski 1975, 65–70).

In the 1950s and early 1960s, U.S. firms also extended their control over much of European industry. By 1965, U.S. firms or their subsidiaries owned 80 percent of computer production, 24 percent of the motor industry, 15 percent of the synthetic rubber industry, and 10 percent of the production of petrochemicals within the entire European Common Market. Furthermore, it is well to remember how concentrated this ownership was. About 40 percent of all U.S. direct investment in Britain, France, and Germany was owned by Ford, General Motors, and Standard Oil of New Jersey. (For most of the data in this section, see Mandel 1970.)

From the Second World War to the early 1960s, U.S. firms maintained a relative superiority over Western European firms because of (1) greater size of capital assets, (2) greater total U.S. savings, and (3) greater technological advances. The size advantage of U.S. corporations was indicated by the fact that, of the hundred largest global corporations, 65 were based in the United States, 11 in the United Kingdom, 18 in other Common Market nations, and 5 in Japan. Because they had greater size and financial power, U.S. firms were able to do more technological research in this period. Furthermore, the continued enormous U.S. military spending subsidized much technological research for U.S. firms. U.S spending on research per capita was three to four times European research spending. Finally, the United States drained away many of the best brains in Europe (after they were trained in Europe). Between 1949 and 1967, about 100,000 of the best doctors, scientists, and technicians left Western Europe for the United States.

DECLINE OF THE U.S. EMPIRE, FROM THE 1960S TO THE PRESENT

In spite of all these initial advantages, the superiority of the U.S. economy in world production faded away and is now replaced by competition by European and Japanese firms, frequently superior in size, research, and industrial innovation. The private enterprise economies of Japan and Western Europe began in 1945 with a skilled labor force but devastated factories. As their industry was rebuilt from scratch, they used the latest technology and began the long march to catch up with the U.S. economy. Whereas the data show that the United States ruled supreme in the early 1950s, it was being challenged by the growing power and competition of Japan and Western Europe in every market by the early 1970s—and they have surpassed the U.S. economy in many areas in the 1990s.

In the 1970s, the United States was still the largest economy, but it no longer was far larger than the combination of all the rest. Thus, by 1972 the French gross domestic product had risen to 17 percent of U.S. GDP, West Germany's rose to 22 percent, Italy's rose to 10 percent, Japan's rose incredibly to 24 percent, and the United Kingdom's to 14 percent—all five of these together now had a GDP equal to 86 percent of U.S. GDP. In specific areas of basic production, the U.S. share of the world total fell between 1950 and 1972 from 82 to 29 percent of passenger vehicles, from 55 to 20 percent of steel production, and from 50 to 33 percent of world energy production.

Since the 1970s, 1980s, and 1990s, the competitive position of Japan and Western Europe has been further strengthened by the fact that their productivity per labor-hour rose much faster than U.S. productivity. On the other hand, Japanese and West European wage levels also rose faster than U.S. wage levels, which hurt their competitive position a little.

The decline of the U.S. empire had several obvious results. First, U.S. corporations can no longer easily sell excess production abroad, so it is no longer possible to increase exports to avoid recession. Second, U.S. corporations have lost some degree of control in some of the Third World, so prices of some raw materials, especially oil, greatly increased in the 1970s (though oil prices have now declined). A third result of the relative U.S. decline is that foreigners have now vastly increased their investments in the U.S. economy. Foreign investments rose to $481 billion, or almost half a trillion dollars, by 1980 (data from U.S. Department of Commerce discussed in Tamalty 1981, 1). These investments were held 50 percent by West Europeans, 7 percent by Canadians, 7 percent by Japanese, and 21 percent by others, including Middle Easterners. Since profits from these investments fluctuate with the U.S. economy, they also help transmit U.S. depressions abroad.

Of course, U.S. investments are still vast, but foreign investment in the U.S. economy has grown faster since 1970. U.S. private investment abroad was $12 billion assets in 1950, but rose to $214 billion assets by 1980. In 1950, U.S. firms repatriated $1.5 billion profits to the United States, but this rose to $43 billion profits by 1980 (see Harrison and Bluestone 1988, 27). Thus, if the rest of the world suffers recession, less profits flow back to the United States. Since these profits are now relatively very important to the U.S. economy, recession abroad may cause a major depressing effect on the U.S. economy.

Fourth, in the 1950s and 1960s, the United States was the largest net creditor and supplier of capital to the rest of the world. Now, the United States is the largest net debtor in the world. In 1981 the net amount of U.S. international investment was plus $141 billion, but by 1987 it was minus $403 billion (see MacEwan 1989, 17). This is a momentous transformation.

Fifth, when the United States was the dominant economic power in the 1950s and 1960s, it was able to maintain a fixed exchange ratio for its currency to gold. Other currencies kept their reserves in dollars and used the dollar as their base. When the U.S. economy relatively weakened in the 1970s, it was forced to go to a flexible exchange ratio. Since the value of the U.S. dollar could then change rapidly, this action greatly increased international financial instability.

Sixth, another reflection of reduced U.S. economic strength versus West European and Japanese competitors is the deficit in the U.S. trade balance. In the 1950s and 1960s the United States exported vastly more than it imported, so all other countries complained of a shortage of dollars, while the United States had a flow of dollars into it. The surplus of dollars from exports was used up by (1) huge U.S. investments abroad plus (2) enormous U.S. military spending and military aid abroad.

The competition of Europe and Japan then reduced the share of the U.S. economy in world exports. The U.S. share of world exports fell from 21 percent in 1957 to 14 percent in 1983 (see Harrison and Bluestone 1988, 27). In the same period, U.S. imports of oil and other products rose in value. Therefore, a trade deficit developed that has persisted and grown. This deficit rose from $25 billion in 1980 to $160 billion in 1987 (for an insightful analysis, see MacEwan 1989). The effect of this deficit is that instead of demand flowing into the United States to pay for net exports, there is actually demand flowing out of the United States to pay for net imports.

It is worth tracing this change in export and import patterns in some detail, as background for the cyclical analysis to follow. According to the official data (Council of Economic Advisors, *Economic Report of the President*, 1988) from 1960 through 1969, U.S. imports averaged 3.1 percent of GDP, while exports were 3.7 percent of GDP, so the United States had a comfortable trade surplus, that is, net exports were +0.6 percent of GDP (having been +0.7 percent in the 1950s). There was a drastic change in the 1970s. From 1970 through 1979, imports rose to 5.9 percent of GDP, while exports rose only to 5.4 percent, so there was a trade deficit, that is, net exports averaged –0.5 percent of GDP. The situation worsened in the 1980s. From 1980 through 1987, U.S. imports grew to an average 8.5 percent of GDP, while exports rose to only 6.3 percent of GNP, so net exports reflected a large deficit at –2.2 percent of GDP. Thus, trade became much more important, while the balance of trade changed from a surplus to a large deficit.

TRADE AND SPREAD OF BUSINESS CYCLE

The channels for international transmission of business cycles are: (1) international trade, (2) international investment, and (3) the international financial system.

One channel of transmission of cycles is international trade. Suppose there is a growth in U.S. exports so that exports become greater than imports (a *favorable* balance of trade). This means a net increase in demand for U.S. products; it will raise income and output if the economy has been below full employment. Of course, if there already was full employment, the increased demand could lead only to higher prices. On the contrary, suppose the United States increases its imports until it has fewer exports than imports (an unfavorable balance of trade). In this case, the U.S. loses buying power to foreign countries, causing less demand and more unemployment.

Suppose the U.S. economy is in a depression and the rest of the world is not. Then since U.S. citizens have less income, the United States will import less from other countries. In that case, the other countries have a decrease in the demand for their commodities, causing depressive effects on their industries. Since the rest of the world then has less income, part of their adjustment will be made by getting fewer imports from the United States. Thus, the process is cumulative.

Just the opposite cumulative process occurs if one country begins to recover from a depression. If U.S. income begins to rise, U.S. citizens have more money to spend, and foreign goods look more attractive. Therefore, the United States imports more of both consumer and investment goods, leading finally to increased income and increased imports in other countries. Of course, in either expansion or depression, we should keep in mind that the cumulative process whereby changes in imports and exports have a multiple effect as they pass from country to country, requires a finite amount of time for each new round of trading. Moreover, not all the increased income that a country gets from increased exports will be respent for imports; some of it will leak into internal spending and will not rebound to increase the exports of another country.

A government may impose trade barriers that lessen trade between countries in order to protect its own industry in a contraction. Such trade barriers may intensify an international contraction. The most famous U.S. action was the very high Smoot-Hawley tariff, which further reduced international trade during the Great Depression. Of course, other countries may retaliate by raising their tariffs against U.S. goods. If the retaliation is of the same magnitude, then U.S. tariffs will reduce U.S. imports, but foreign tariffs will equally reduce U.S. exports. The result is lower world trade but no change in the U.S. balance of trade.

INVESTMENT AND SPREAD OF CYCLES

The second major means of transmitting the business cycle is via international investment. If Japan loans or invests in the United States, then usually part of the money is spent in Japan on equipment and part is spent in the United States on installation and operation of equipment, as well as wages of labor. This transaction will have several effects. It will immediately result in some increase in demand in Japan and some in the United States. To the extent that the money is respent, there will again result cumulative and multiple effects, which may increase a boom or aid a revival from depression. We may note that there will be secondary effects not only on imports and exports of goods and capital, but also to some extent on internal consumption and investment.

Some observers have stressed that investment abroad means less excess of savings at home; thus, "the stability of capital-exporting countries with high rates of saving has . . . been dependent on the recurrent appearance of new opportunities for investment abroad" (League of Nations 1945, 3; see also Severn 1974 and Miller and Whitman 1973). But this very important source of investment opportunities is also very fluctuating and cyclical in nature. The fact that investment abroad has even greater fluctuations than domestic investment is due to the greater sensitivity of investment abroad to changes in the business outlook in other countries. The greater sensitivity is due, in turn, to the greater uncertainty because of distances, different laws, customs, and political trends. Among the most often mentioned problems of international investment are (1) difficulties of management owing to long lines of communication and transportation, (2) inadequate legal protection, (3) ignorance of language and customs, and (4) risk of transfer restrictions on profits or outright confiscation. These factors account for the uncertainty and sensitivity which leads to wide cyclical fluctuation of foreign investments.

The approach of classical economics stressed the ability of foreign investments to raise the average rate of profit of the home country. J. S. Mill mentions investment abroad as

> . . . the last of the counter-forces which check the downward tendency of profits . . . . This is, the perpetual overflow of capital into colonies or foreign countries, to seek higher profits than can be obtained at home . . . . In the first place, it carries off a part of the increase of capital from which the reduction of profit proceeds. Secondly, the capital so carried off is not lost, but is chiefly employed . . . in founding colonies which become large exporters of cheap agricultural produce . . . (Mill 1920, Book 4, 736)

In his view, the rate of profit of the capital-exporting country would be raised by having less competition at home, higher profits from abroad, and a supply of cheap raw materials for its industries. In this context it is possible, if a depression started in a capital-importing country, that the lesser returns on investment would have depressing effects abroad.

The income from investments abroad also has an effect on demand because it is equivalent to an invisible export. The receiver of investment income receives money or credit from the debtor. If that money or credit so obtained is immediately reinvested in the debtor country, then the effect will be expansionary (though most profits are usually repatriated to the home country). In a depression period creditors are more likely than ever to withdraw those funds from the debtor country back to their own country.

Every investment must eventually produce a supply of goods on the market. Thus, though the original effect of an international investment will be to increase demand for the factors of production, it is often claimed that its later effect will be to compete with the industry of the home country. This depends on the type of goods produced and where they are marketed. If the goods are of the same type as already produced by either the capital-exporter or importer and are sold in the same market as the previously established industries, then, of course, the effect may very well be depressing at a future time. On the other hand, if the goods are raw materials needed by the capital-exporter, then their production and sale may even cause the rate of profit in the capital-exporter country to rise.

There does seem to be a considerable degree of agreement on the main points of the trade and investment transmission mechanisms, which might be summed up as follows: If a depression begins in a country that imports a large amount of goods relative to world supply, then the rest of the world feels a sudden decline in the demand for many kinds of goods. This seems initially to be the main instrument of spreading the depression. Then, however, in the exporting countries the lower demand for their goods lowers their income, their consumption, and the investment opportunities in their countries. When the effects reach back to the initiating countries, not only may there be some drop in demand for their finished goods exports, but usually the demand for their capital export drastically declines in view of the drying up of investment opportunities abroad.

INVESTMENT AND TRADE IN THE GREAT DEPRESSION

In the Great Depression, the flow of U.S. investment abroad declined from over $1.3 *billion* in 1929 to $1.6 *million* dollars in 1932 (League of Nations 1934, 220–30). Countries may still desire most strongly to find or conquer new markets for goods and capital export during a depression, as Britain did in the nineteenth century, but this easy road to recovery has seldom been open in the twentieth century. As one exception, it is possible that massive U.S. aid to Europe during the Marshall Plan period moderated early postwar U.S. recessions.

As might be expected, the U.S. depression of the thirties had the worst effect on (1) those in debt to the United States who had been paying back principal, interest, and dividends by exports to the United States; (2) exporters of producers' goods (especially raw materials), because these had constituted 85 percent of U.S. imports in the previous period; and (3) those who exported consumers' goods to the United States (mostly food), which constituted the other 15 percent of U.S. imports. For this reason, Argentina and Australia, large exporters of raw materials, were immediately among the hardest hit and were the first to go off the gold standard. On the other hand, the immediate detrimental effects of the Great Depression did force a positive long-run adjustment in some countries. For example, several Latin American countries, such as Brazil, defaulted on their debts and shifted to import-substituting industrialization which led to a growth spurt in the period from 1945 to 1960. The growth in Latin America eventually led to more U.S. exports to that area.

When there is a period of expansion in the United States it also appears that some of the increased income is used for increases both in the import of finished products for consumption, which are mostly luxuries, and in the import of producers' goods for new investment, most of which are raw materials. Though U.S. imports were a small portion of U.S. income in 1929, a decrease of U.S. income meant a larger than proportional decrease of imports. This is because a larger than proportional part of the increase in income is devoted to investment in raw materials (because of the acceleration principle) and to consumption of luxuries (because demand for these items reacts most strongly to changes in income). Therefore, in the boom of the twenties, imports increased faster than national income; while in the depression of the thirties, imports decreased even faster than the rapidly falling national income.

In the 16 non-war business cycles from 1867 to 1938, imports rose by 26 percent in the average expansion and fell by 19 percent in the average contraction (see Mitchell 1951, 312–32). By contrast, there was much less cyclical movement in U.S. exports because these were related to the cyclical movements of national income in other countries which were only partly synchronized with U.S. national income. Thus, in the same 16 business cycles, U.S. exports rose 15 percent in the average expansion and fell only 1 percent in the average contraction.

Since imports rose more than exports in expansions, it followed (by definition) that net exports fell in expansions. Since imports fell more than exports in contractions, net exports tended to rise in contractions. Thus, net exports were counter-cyclical. Since net exports were falling long before the peak, they exacerbated the downturn in profits by a reduction in demand. On the other hand, the usual rise in net exports in the depression helped set the stage for recovery.

Underdeveloped countries are hardest hit by these wide fluctuations in trade. International investment and international trade in primary products—that is, in raw materials, both agricultural and mineral—show the greatest fluctuations. Therefore, it was observed in the Great Depression "that any country whose economy is intimately dependent on foreign investment or whose trade is greatly dependent on primary commodities will be seriously affected by swings of business arising outside its own borders" (League of Nations 1945, 92). Of course, this is still true.

The physical output of agriculture was stable or showing a slow rise during the entire 1920s and the 1930s. Manufactured products, on the other hand, rose up to 1929, then dropped off rapidly. World manufacturing output in 1933 was only about 40 percent of that of 1929. It then rose slowly until manufacturing reached the 1929 level in 1938, only to fall off again. Mining activity and the output of minerals show even greater fluctuation in world statistics. In the period from 1918 to 1939, mineral production rose about as fast as manufacturing in expansions, but minerals fell faster than manufacturing in depressions (League of Nations 1945, 80). In price terms also, the fluctuations of raw materials are much greater than those of finished products.

During the expansion of the twenties, raw material prices rose faster than finished goods prices, then dropped much faster to the depression trough of 1933, and rose more slowly until 1938. In the 1938 recession, raw material prices again dropped faster. The *prices* of iron and steel in the world market had very small fluctuations in this period, but the *prices* of both nonferrous metals and farm products had very large cyclical variations. Since raw materials are relatively expensive in the boom, the Third World raw materials producing countries tend to have a favorable balance of trade and good terms of trade in expansions. In the Great Depression, however, the Third World suffered both unfavorable balance of trade and poor terms of trade. Moreover, although their exports were cut back in the depression, most of their imports were necessities which could not be cut back so easily.

The drop in demand for exported commodities can have one of two effects, either lowering the price or lowering the amount, or both. The physical output and amount taken of most agricultural products for consumers is relatively stable because on the demand side they are necessities of life and on the supply side they are largely governed by nature and produced under extremely competitive conditions. Therefore, almost the total drop in such food products as crops and livestock is a drop in prices, so that there is a proportionate drop in the people's income in these countries even though they still do the same amount of production.

The situation with minerals and industrial crops, which are used as raw materials for which the demand fluctuates very greatly, is quite different. In the case of raw materials, especially minerals, there is a great drop in output and employment as well as in price and income. In the brief recession of 1937 to 1938, for example, not only did the amount of tin exported from Bolivia (its main export) drop precipitously, but the price of tin fell by 45 percent.

CYCLICAL PATTERN OF IMPORTS AND EXPORTS SINCE THE SECOND WORLD WAR

When the demand of other countries for imports rises, then the United States can export more. Thus, one quantitative study in the 1950s concluded: "During expansions in world imports, U.S. export quantities, prices, and values rose; during contractions in world imports, they fell (or rose at a slower rate)" (Mintz 1959, 305). It is still true today that a rise in world income results in more imports from the United States.

So U.S. exports rise in the expansion phase of other countries. "U.S. exports to Canada, the United Kingdom, West Germany, and Japan, for example, grew six times as fast when those countries were in an expansion phase of their growth cycle than when they were in a contraction phase" (Klein and Moore 1985, 306; also see Klein 1976). In a later section, however, it will be shown that the cycles of the leading private enterprise countries tend to move together. Therefore, U.S. exports tend to expand in U.S. expansions because these foreign economies are expanding. U.S. exports tend to fall in U.S. contractions because these foreign economies are contracting. Thus, Dornbusch and Fischer (1986, 462) find that U.S. exports are roughly pro-cyclical from 1950 to 1980.

What about U.S. imports? When U.S. income is expanding in a cyclical expansion, our imports rise because we demand more of foreign goods. Thus, for Canada, the United Kingdom, West Germany, and Japan, "exports out of those countries to the United States (our imports from them) grew more than three times as fast as during upswings in the U.S. growth cycle as during its downswings" (Klein and Moore 1985, 306). So U.S. imports tend to be pro-cyclical because they are a function of U.S. income; Dornbusch and Fischer find that imports conform to the cycle better than exports (1986, 462).

The reason is that U.S. imports are closely tied to the U.S. cycle because they are a function of U.S. income. U.S. exports, however, are only indirectly related to the U.S. cycle. U.S. exports fluctuate pro-cyclically only to the degree that other countries' cycles are synchronous with the U.S. cycle in timing and in amplitude. Foreign cycles are not in perfect timing synchronization with U.S. cycles. Moreover, the United States is subject to greater economic instability, reflected in higher cyclical amplitude of cycles in production and income than other private enterprise countries. Since the rest of the world is not perfectly synchronous with the U.S. economy and since the U.S. economy usually has greater fluctuations, it follows that U.S. exports usually have a smaller cyclical amplitude than U.S. imports.

Thus, net exports tend to be counter-cyclical (this analysis is also supported by Dornbusch and Fischer 1986, 462). This means that the flow of money demand out of the U.S. economy rises faster than the flow of money demand into the U.S. economy in the average expansion. Net export demand, as a result, declines in the expansion and appears to be a depressing factor. On the other hand, net exports tend to rise in the contraction, so they appear to be a stimulating factor at that time.

According to Table 16.1, in the last four cycles, U.S. imports and U.S. exports rose at roughly the same speed during expansion periods. There is little difference between the expansion amplitudes of imports and exports, so there is only a small decline in net exports. This is rather different from earlier historical experience when imports usually rose much faster than exports, so net exports fell strongly in expansions.

We shall find that the new behavior of exports is due to the closer coordination of cycles in the whole private enterprise world, conforming more closely to the U.S. cycle. Remember that U.S. exports are based on the economic health of the rest of the world. This means that U.S. exports conform to the U.S. to the degree, and only to the degree, that world cycles conform to U.S. cycles.

During business contractions, according to Table 16.1, imports fell rapidly, while there was little change in the level of exports. Actually, exports continued to rise for a little while beyond the peak, then declined a little for the rest of the contraction. The fact that U.S. imports declined rapidly while exports lagged behind and declined only slowly, meant that net U.S. exports rose by 7 percent in the average U.S. contraction of this period.

Although exports don't conform as well to the cycle, both imports and exports do tend to be pro-cyclical. Net exports, however, tend to be counter-cyclical because imports move further up and down than do exports. In this

TABLE 16.1
U.S. EXPORTS AND U.S. IMPORTS

	Expansion Amplitude	Contraction Amplitude
Imports	30.4	−7.8
Exports	30.2	−0.4
Net Exports	−0.2	7.4

SOURCE: CITIBASE database, files GEXQ and GIMQ.

NOTE: Average of four cycles, 1970–1991, in constant inflation-adjusted dollars.

period, Table 16.1 shows a slight decline in our net exports during expansions, but a large increase in our net exports in contractions.

INTERNATIONAL FINANCE AND TRANSMISSION OF CYCLES

The third major transmission belt for international instability and cycles is the financial system (see the classic study by Morgenstern 1959). After the Second World War, the U.S. dominance in production and trade carried over into financial dominance (see the excellent studies by Magdoff 1969, 1979). One reflection of this dominance was the negotiations of the Bretton Woods agreement in the way desired by the United States, making the U.S. dollar the international currency. U.S. banks also spread their branches and influence around the world. In the 1970s and 1980s, however, since the decline of U.S. production and trade relative to other countries, the U.S. has also lost some of its financial dominance. This loss of dominance is reflected in many ways, including stiff competition in finance from banks of other countries.

The evidence on the present high degree of international integration of finance is clear, but there is a considerable controversy on its effects. One major characteristic of financial integration is mobility of capital across international frontiers. Most economists in this area have argued that international capital mobility has increased (see the excellent article by Epstein and Gintis 1988, but see the qualifications by Zevin 1988). There has also been a large literature arguing that those explanations of saving and investment which assume a closed economy are obsolete. Rather, it is argued that all macroeconomics must be considered anew in an international model (see, e.g., Dornbusch 1980; also see Dernberg 1989). In practical terms, that means an increase in the power of business to shift to other countries, as well as a decrease in the power of governments to control their own economies. One example, the early Mitterand government attempted to expand the French economy by increasing buying power, but most of the added spending went into imports, not domestic sales.

Increases in financial integration are also reflected in the growth of the market in Euro-currency, greater use of computer-facilitated information flow, opening up of stock markets to foreign nationals, the increase in international banking cited above, and various reductions in government controls on capital flows. It is certainly true that the age of electronic miracles has made information flow around the world almost instantaneous. But this has not resulted in a new international equilibrium mechanism wherein all private firms and all countries adjust smoothly and flexibly to all changes in a financially integrated world. On the contrary, careful studies by MacEwan (1986) and Gordon (1988) find a world in which the world financial system is highly integrated, but integration exacerbates economic problems because the instability of one country is rapidly transmitted to all other countries. For example, in the stock market collapse of October 1987, the news traveled immediately so that U.S., Japanese, and European markets all fell in unison (though at very different rates). In this example, close financial integration did not result in equilibrium, but in the spread of instability. As Dernberg states: ". . . the combination of flexible exchange rates and a high degree of international capital mobility have created a climate in which macroeconomic shock transmission from one country to another is enormous" (1989, 7).

The tendency toward spreading instability has been very clear since the old U.S.-dominated financial order disappeared in the mid to late 1960s, to be replaced by anxious competition and considerable chaos. Gordon points out: "Because of movement toward flexible exchange rates after the collapse of the Bretton Woods system in 1971, there was an increasing synchronization of business cycles among the advanced countries after 1971, leading to increasingly volatile fluctuations of economic activity. When one economy sneezed, others echoed" (1988, 11).

In addition to stock market shocks and violent exchange rate fluctuations, another mechanism for spread of business cycle instability is through the banking system. MacEwan comments:

> There is substantial disagreement over the causes of the Great Depression of the 1930s, but there is little dispute over the fact that the failure of the capitalist world's financial system made a major contribution to the depth and duration of the economic crisis. When Austria's Kreditanstalt failed in 1931, international financial markets spread the impact through a run on German banks, a depreciation of sterling, extensive liquidation of dollars for gold, and eventually the widespread bank closings in the U.S. (MacEwan 1986, 178)

The phenomenon of bank failures leading to other bank failures is not new, but the spread of bank branches all over the world and the almost instantaneous flow of information may make the international repercussions even greater today than previously.

One other mechanism of transmission of instability is especially important at the present time; this is the enormous mound of debt in the Third World owed to U.S. and European banks. The crisis in the Third World debt, and its effects, is analyzed in detail by MacEwan (1986); George (1988); and Pollin (1989). Repayment of these debts is improbable because they are so large relative to export earnings—especially in Brazil, Mexico, and Argentina, where in 1984 the ratios of debt to merchandise exports were, respectively, 45 percent, 69 percent, and 141 percent (MacEwan 1986, 180). If these debts are not repaid, they must be written off as bad debts by the banks, which makes their own position visibly weaker. An excellent book on these issues, with policy suggestions, is Pool and Stamos (1989).

SYNCHRONIZATION OF BUSINESS CYCLES

So far, this chapter has found increased integration of trade, investment, and finance in the private enterprise world. These increasingly integrated economies transmit instability very quickly from one to another. As a result, we would expect increased synchronization of production cycles. Moreover, if the production cycle in the leading capitalist countries is closely synchronized, the transmission mechanisms described above may have more violent effects as results of instability reverberate from one country to another. To what degree has increased synchronization occurred?

There have been several excellent studies of the degree of synchronization of the business cycle in various capitalist countries (see Morgenstern 1959; Mintz 1959, 1967; Hickman and Schleicher 1978; MacEwan 1984; and Klein and Moore 1985). Klein and Moore comment that "to varying degrees these researchers discovered evidence of synchronized economic movements among developed countries" (1985, 286). It is worth noting that in the 19th century, (1) as countries became industrialized they joined the international business cycle, and (2) countries that became colonies of the industrialized countries also became part of the international business cycle. Part 1 of this book discussed in detail Wesley Mitchell's extensive studies of how synchronization of cycles increased among countries as private enterprise spread, with almost world-wide synchronization in the Great Depression of 1929.

Klein and Moore (1985) constructed an international composite coincident index, composed of the coincident indexes for seven countries (the United States, Canada, United Kingdom, West Germany, France, Italy, and Japan). They found much the same indicators (both coincident and leading) were consistent in performance in the seven countries. They found that their index showed clear business cycles, with troughs in 1958, 1961, 1963, 1967, 1971, and 1975—though some of these, such as 1963 and 1967, were only declines in the rate of growth and not absolute declines.

Klein and Moore found very little deviation from the international business cycle dates by the individual countries. In fact, they checked to see how many months each of nine foreign private enterprise countries was in phase with the international cycle. They found that: Japan was in phase 86 percent of the time; Canada, 88 percent; France, 83 percent; United

Kingdom, 78 percent; United States, 77 percent; Netherlands, 77 percent; Belgium, 68 percent; Italy, 66 percent; Sweden, 48 percent; and the average was in phase 75 percent of the time.

By far the best study of how much the synchronization of the cycle has increased in the 1970s and 1980s over the 1950s and 1960s is by Arthur MacEwan (1984). He examines monthly data—using three month moving averages—for the United States, Japan, West Germany, France, Italy, United Kingdom, and Canada, based on both the index of industrial production and the coincident composite index for each country. He begins by examining the simple question as to how often various pairs of countries' composite indexes move in the same direction. In the 1950s and 1960s, he finds *no* statistically significant synchronization of cycles between the U.S. economy and any of the others—except for Canada, which does usually fluctuate with the U.S. economy. From 1970 through June 1981, however, he finds statistically significant synchronization of downturns with every country except Italy (MacEwan 1984, 67). This is an impressive confirmation of the hypothesis that synchronization has increased in this period. Also for the 1970s and early 1980s, he finds a statistically significant synchronization of U.S. upturns with Japan, West Germany, and Canada, some non-significant synchronization for France and the United Kingdom, but again little synchronization with Italy.

MacEwan also finds increased synchronization among the United States, Japan, and Europe when he uses upturns and downturns of indexes of industrial production, regression analysis based on composite indexes, and regression analysis based on indexes of industrial production. Within Europe, however, synchronization was high in the 1950s and 1960s, but did not increase in the 1970s. His findings indicate that increasing synchronization and rising economic integration are related. "The high degree of integration within Europe was associated with a relatively high degree of synchronization early on, and the growing synchronization of the United States and Japan within the group more recently has been associated with their growing integration into the world economy" (MacEwan 1984, 75). He cautions that trade integration is a large part of the story, but is not the only important aspect of integration. He puts a heavy emphasis on expansion of international credit and movements of liquid financial capital, as well as growing financial integration.

The simplest way to compare the degree of synchronization among the advanced capitalist countries is to examine their cyclical amplitudes and cyclical patterns over the reference cycle dates for U.S. business cycles. According to all the data, the United States had fairly mild downturns during the 1950s and 1960s. In that period, however, Japan and most of Europe had no downturns at all. Therefore, there was no synchronization of turning

TABLE 16.2

AMPLITUDES OF INDUSTRIAL PRODUCTION BY COUNTRY

(AVERAGE OF FOUR CYCLES, 1970–1991)

Country	Expansion Amplitude	Contraction Amplitude
United States	21.1	−7.8
Canada	18.3	−7.1
Japan	25.6	−6.0
OECD	13.9	−3.7
Germany	14.6	−4.0
United Kingdom	8.9	−3.5
Italy	17.8	−6.9
France	12.8	−3.1

SOURCE: CITIBASE database, files IPFR, IPIT, IPUK, IPWG, IPCAN, IPJP, IPOECD, and IP.

NOTE: OECD means Organization for Economic Development and Cooperation. It covers all of the countries of the European Community Common Market.

points nor of amplitudes of decline. The only evidence of synchronization in the 1950s and 1960s was that the rate of growth of Japan and of Europe was much slower during U.S. contractions than during U.S. expansions.

The situation became strikingly different in the 1970s, 1980s, and 1990s. All of the European countries and Japan suffered actual downturns at about the same time as the U.S. economy did. Sometimes one lagged, sometimes the other. So synchronization is not perfect, but it is at a high level.

One kind of evidence for synchronization may be seen in Table 16.2. This table shows the amplitudes of expansion and contraction for each country. The important point is that the dates used for turning points for every country are purely U.S. dates. So if there were no synchronization, cyclical amplitudes of other countries would be random for U.S. dates. Instead, Table 16.2 shows that during the period 1970 to 1991, each of the countries had significant expansions when the U.S. economy expanded. Moreover, each of the countries suffered significant business contractions during U.S. contractions.

The causes of this behavior are not mysterious. After the Second World War, Japan and Western Europe had very little production capacity and needed everything. Therefore, to the extent that financing was available (and much came from the United States), production grew rapidly in the 1950s and 1960s. Thus, even during U.S. recessions, when their exports to the United States declined, these countries continued to grow, though at a slower pace. In the later period, the 1970s, 1980s, and 1990s, demand no longer grew so rapidly, so they were more vulnerable to economic recessions spreading from the United States. Furthermore, ties to the U.S. economy continued to grow stronger, both in trade and in reciprocal investment.

CONCLUSIONS

This chapter noted the rise and decline of U.S. domination over the world economy. Relevant international trends in the later period include: (1) foreign competitors with higher sales and productivity growth than the U.S. economy, (2) change to flexible exchange rates, (3) change of U.S. economy from net creditor to net debtor, (4) an end to the U.S. trade surplus and an enormous rise in the U.S. trade deficit, and (5) a huge Third World debt to U.S. banks, with many defaults happening or expected. These long-run international trends have increased the vulnerability of the U.S. economy.

This chapter analyzed and described empirically three major channels of transmission of instability and cycles. First, the simplest mechanism is the fluctuations of imports and exports. A relative decline in other countries' imports (because their income is contracting) results in less demand for U.S. exports. Second, foreigners may increase or decrease their direct investment in the United States, depending on their own investment resources or needs. Similarly, U.S. firms may make more or less profits abroad and may invest more or less abroad. Third, there are several mechanisms for transmission of instability in the financial sector: (1) one stock market collapse leads to another, (2) one bank failure leads to another, (3) violent exchange rate fluctuations may adversely affect trade, (4) bad debts of some countries may lead to bank failures in another country. It is important to remember that these mechanisms do not operate only between independent firms in different countries but also within and through the large conglomerate global firms that now dominate the global economy (as detailed in the previous chapter).

Private enterprise economies are more highly integrated than in previous periods, so these transmission mechanisms operate rapidly to spread instability. As a result, boom and bust periods of the private enterprise countries are more closely tied together than ever before. In the 1950s and 1960s, the U.S. economy was subjected to only minor cycles—and it was the dominant economic power. Almost all other private enterprise economies showed continued growth with no absolute declines, but with lower growth rates in U.S. recessions. In the 1970s, 1980s and 1990s, however, the U.S. economy suffered severe downturns. These U.S. downturns were echoed by synchronized declines in the West European and Japanese economies (as well as in most Third World economies). These downturns had reverberations that worsened the U.S. contractions. Thus, all of the transmission mechanisms for international instability cited above were working furiously with dramatic effect in the latter period.

When all of these economies decline together, the negative effects reverberate and cause cumulative international decline. They also tend, however, to recover together in a cumulative international expansion. As shown in the survey of long-run trends and in the section on financial transmission mechanisms, there is both more financial fragility and quicker transmission in this period, so downturns may be made more severe and recoveries more difficult. At any rate, the close international economic relationships are factors for increased instability at this time.

International trends and the synchronized instability make effective government responses to private enterprise contractions by any single government very difficult (as will be discussed in the next chapter).

KEY TERMS AND CONCEPTS

rise of U.S. economic power, 1950–1970

relative decline of U.S. economic power, 1970–1990

three mechanisms of cyclical spread

how exports and imports spread cycles

net exports

U.S. investment abroad

foreign investment in U.S.

international financial shocks

synchronization of cycles

APPENDIX 16 A
FORMAL MODEL OF INTERNATIONAL CYCLES

Obviously, if international trade is going to be in our model, we must include net exports (*NE*) as one of the elements of aggregate demand:

$$Y_t = C_t + I_t + NE_t \qquad (16A.1)$$

Net exports is defined as exports (*EX*) minus imports (*IM*), so we may write:

$$NE_t = EX_t - IM_t \qquad (16A.2)$$

The next question, naturally, is what determines U.S. exports and imports?

Imports are easy because they clearly rise and fall with U.S. income. Thus we may write:

$$IM_t = f(Y_t) \qquad (16A.3)$$

As U.S. national income rises, imports rise as some proportion is spent on imports. As U.S. national income falls, some amount less than before is spent for imports.

Now comes the difficult question. What determines U.S. exports to other countries? The main answer is that the cyclical behavior of U.S. exports to the rest of the world is determined mainly by the income of all the other countries of the world. Thus we may write:

$$EX_t = f\,(Y \text{ rest of world at } t) \tag{16A.4}$$

Finally, what determines the income of the rest of the world? In a complete model, this must be determined and not taken as given. The answer is clear but difficult to implement. The income of the rest of the world depends on the entire cycle model of the rest of the world. It would require all of the same equations as in the U.S. case, but with world wide data. Of course, one could demand still more realism and have a separate model for each region, such as Europe, Japan, and so forth—but that would probably be too complex to yield much of importance.

The mechanisms of international investment and international finance are still more complex but could be added along the same lines. The U.S. model would yield a certain amount of capital interested in investing abroad, but the actual investment abroad would depend on the rest of the world economy. Similarly, the model of the rest of the world would yield a certain amount of capital interested in investing in the United States, provided our profit outlook is optimistic enough. The strength of U.S. finance would be one factor determining how much it could offer in loans abroad, while the state of other economies would determine how much was actually loaned. Vice versa, the rest of the world will generate a certain amount of loanable capital, but how much would flow to the United States would depend on the perceived health of the U.S. economy. These very specific and complex functions are far beyond the scope of this book.

CHAPTER 17

Government Fiscal Behavior and Policy

This chapter discusses how government spending and tax policy has actually behaved over the cycle. Various policy positions are then considered.

THE ENDOGENEITY OF GOVERNMENT BEHAVIOR

The endogeneity of government monetary behavior was discussed in Chapter 14. Here, we focus exclusively on the question of the endogeneity of fiscal behavior. Fiscal behavior is the behavior of government spending and taxation. Endogenous behavior of government means that government behavior may be explained as a reaction to a given economic situation. The political aspect raises the question as to what determines government behavior; the economic question is whether there is a roughly constant pattern of behavior every cycle.

Most economists view government economic behavior as external to the economic system. Others, such as Institutionalist and post-Keynesians, have viewed government behavior as part of an integrated political-economic system. The latter economists have emphasized two ways in which economic interests influence government fiscal behavior. First, economic power translates into political power through ability to give money to candidates, ownership of the media by the wealthy, lobbying by business interests, more political participation and voting by the wealthy, and lack of participation and voting by most lower-income employees and the unemployed. It is an institutional fact that half of Americans don't vote and the participation rate for the poor often drops below 15 percent (see Piven and Cloward 1988; Burnham 1982).

Second, even if candidates are elected opposed to the power of wealth, the structure of the private enterprise economy forces most representatives to support business interests. For example, billions of dollars were used to bail out the savings and loan institutions in the 1989–1994 period. The extensive debate on the process and degree of endogenous control of government behavior is discussed thoroughly in Carnoy (1984); Sherman (1987); Miller (1986); Veblen (1975); and Dugger (1989).

In addition, we will see that government fiscal policy is determined in part automatically by previous laws. For example, the tax system automatically reacts to higher or lower income levels. Since the result is supposed to stabilize the economy, economists call such policies automatic stabilizers. Such automatic fiscal policy is distinguished from discretionary fiscal policy, which results from current decisions.

This book is not the place to explore the determinants of government behavior in detail, but a working assumption will be that it is endogenously determined. Government fiscal behavior reflects (1) in part the long-run interests of business, (2) in part the opposing interests of employees, and (3) in part a given phase of the business cycle, as well as (4) single-issue interest groups, such as pro-choice or anti-abortion groups. What will be explored in detail in this chapter is the fairly regular pattern of government fiscal activity over the business cycle, reflecting these economic interests.

THE IMPACT OF FISCAL BEHAVIOR

Few, if any, economists until the 1930s blamed the peacetime business cycle on government fiscal policy. In fact, it was impossible that fiscal policy should cause the business cycle, at least until the 1930s, for two reasons. First, total government spending was a tiny proportion of GDP. Second, most government spending was state and local, which was controlled by 48 different governments, and which was usually balanced even in the 1930s (see Miller 1986). In 1929, on the eve of the Great Depression, federal spending was only one percent of GDP. Federal spending rose a little in the 1930s, grew enormously in the Second World War, and has remained very significant ever since.

So-called "automatic fiscal policy" was largely enacted in the 1930s. There was instituted, or greatly increased: (1) unemployment compensation, (2) farm and business subsidies, and (3) various welfare spending. These spending flows automatically increase in contractions and automatically decrease in expansions. On the other side, corporate and personal income taxes became important. These tax flows automatically increase as a percentage of GDP in expansions and automatically decrease as a percentage of GDP in contractions. As a result, the government deficit, which is spending minus taxes, tends to increase in contractions but decrease in expansions, as shown below. Discretionary fiscal policy, which is a new decision to spend or to tax, has since the 1930s tended to reinforce this pattern.

An important hypothesis is that there would be a business cycle in the private enterprise economy even with no government fiscal activity. One piece of evidence is the fact that the cycle did exist before the 1930s although government fiscal activity was negligible. Since the Second World War, fiscal activity was stimulative in every peacetime contraction. In expansions, government policy was either depressing or less and less stimulative. Nevertheless, the hypothesis considered here is that government was not the determining factor in cycle turns in peacetime. Note that this hypothesis, which is post-Keynesian, is quite contrary to the monetarist view that the cycle is primarily the result of external fiscal-monetary shocks overwhelming the private sector.

A completely different hypothesis is the political business cycle theory. It argues that politicians manipulate fiscal policy before elections to stimulate the economy and to please voters. Then politicians depress the economy after the election to reduce inflation. Although there are a few obvious examples of such attempts, the evidence shown below indicates that the business cycle and the fiscal reaction to it remains mostly determined by the behavior of the private sector.

LONG-RUN TRENDS IN FISCAL BEHAVIOR

How has the government actually behaved over the long run? Aside from the jumps in spending during the First and Second World Wars, total government spending (federal, state, and local) has risen fairly continuously in the twentieth century. Total government spending was 7.7 percent of GDP in 1902, rising to 8.1 percent in 1913 on the eve of World War I. It continued to rise to 21 percent of GDP in 1940 (see Ransom 1980, 2). After the Second World War, total government spending rose from 26 percent of GDP in the 1949–1954 cycle to 37 percent in the 1980–1982 cycle. It generally rose during conservative as well as liberal administrations. Ironically, the biggest jump in federal spending as a percentage of GDP came in the conservative Reagan administration during the 1980s.

In the 1980s and 1990s, the level of government spending was 35 to 40 percent, which implies a whole new stage of private enterprise in symbiosis with government. Fiscal policy can and does change the distribution of income, the allocation of resources, the inflation rate, and the course of the business cycle. When most people think of the growth of government spending, they think of federal spending. In wartime that is correct, but otherwise it is much less true. Federal spending was only 1 percent of GDP in 1929 before the Great Depression. During the Second World War, federal government spending, which was almost all military, rose to the incredible

TABLE 17.1
GOVERNMENT SPENDING AS PERCENTAGE OF GDP

Cycle Years	Federal Purchases of Good and Services	Federal Spending	State and Local Spending	Total Spending
1949–1954	12.1	18.0	7.5	25.5
1954–1958	11.4	18.0	8.6	26.6
1958–1961	11.1	19.1	9.8	28.9
1961–1970	10.6	19.4	11.4	30.8
1970–1975	8.4	20.5	13.7	34.2
1975–1980	7.5	21.8	13.7	35.5
1980–1982	8.2	23.8	13.1	36.9
1982–1991	8.2	23.0	13.3	36.3

SOURCE: CITIBASE database, files GGFEX, GDP, GGSEX, GGFEQ.

height of 42 percent of GDP in 1944 but fell after the war. Table 17.1 shows that federal spending rose from 1949 to 1991 only from 18 percent to 23 percent of GDP.

Total government spending rose enormously in the 1949 to 1991 period, from 26 to 37 percent of GDP, but not much of that increase was due to the federal government. Most of the rise in spending was done by state and local governments, whose spending almost doubled in this period as a percentage of GDP. In this period, federal government purchases of goods and services actually *declined* from 12.1 to 8.2 percent of GDP. Total federal spending did rise, but not because of more purchases of goods and services. Federal expenditures have grown because of the growth of transfer payments, especially social security and interest payments. Transfer payments simply transfer income from those being taxed to the recipients of government payments. Most federal interest payments arise from debt due to military spending and are paid to the wealthy. Federal interest payments equaled 20 percent of the personal income tax in 1980, but had risen to 38 percent in 1986, which constituted a major redistribution of income from taxpayers to wealthy bond-holders (Harrison and Bluestone 1988, 152).

TAXATION

The federal personal income tax is called "progressive" because it charges higher tax rates in higher income brackets. The corporate income tax and the property tax are also somewhat progressive. By the end of the Second World War, official tax rates on the wealthiest taxpayers rose to 90 percent, but the actual effective rates were always much lower because of legal loopholes. The Social Security payroll tax is "regressive," that is, lower income brackets pay a higher percentage of their income. State and local sales taxes are also regressive because the wealthy pay lower percentages of their income (see Pechman 1985, 6–7).

Reformers in U.S. history have always argued the tax system should redistribute income to reduce the extreme inequality. But a study of 1985 data shows that if one added up all the effects of progressive and regressive taxes, "it is clear that the tax system has very little effect on the distribution of income" (Pechman 1985, 5). Pechman's study is careful, detailed, and uses various alternative assumptions about the impact of taxes on different groups.

In the period of his study—between 1966 and 1985—Pechman finds a decline in the importance and progressivity of corporate taxes, property taxes, and personal income taxes—all of which are progressive taxes. At the same time, the regressive Social Security payroll tax became more important. As a result, "the effect of these changes was to reduce the progressivity of the tax system" (Pechman 1985, 8). What is even more interesting, in the light of the important effect of income distribution on consumption, is the fact that in 1966 the taxes paid out of property income were higher than those paid out of labor income. But by 1985 the tax burden on labor income was substantially higher than on property income (Pechman 1985, 9).

GROWTH OF THE DEFICIT

The increase in the 1980s in interest payments was partly due to higher interest rates but partly also due to the increase in the national debt. A deficit measures an increase in the debt, while a surplus measures the decrease of the debt in a year. In the 1950s and 1960s, there were five years with surpluses; but in the 1970s and 1980s, there was a deficit every year. The average deficit grew relative to GDP. Thus, the deficit was 0.4 percent of GDP in the 1950s; the deficit was 0.8 percent of GDP in the 1960s; the deficit averaged 2 percent of GDP in all of the 1970s; but the deficit averaged 3.8 percent of GDP from 1980 through 1992.

MILITARY SPENDING

Much of the deficit was due to the increase in military spending. Total military spending was well over a trillion dollars during the Reagan administration. The U.S. Department of Defense is the largest planned economy in the world and it spends more than the net income of all U.S. corporations. But military spending goes far beyond Department of Defense spending. The most careful study of military spending to date (Cypher 1972) includes half of all "international affairs" spending, veterans' benefits, atomic energy, and space appropriations because these were mostly military related. Military-related spending also included 75 percent of the interest on the public debt since at least that much of the debt was used to pay for wars. Other military spending on which it is impossible to get exact data are major parts of the budget for research and development, the CIA, and other intelligence agencies. Cypher's study found military spending to be about 13 percent of GDP for the whole period he studies. For its total effect, we would have to know the multiplier for military spending.

Some large corporations benefit strongly from the high level of military spending. This benefit is based on the fact that the rate of profit is very high in military production and that most of these profits go to a few very large firms. Just one hundred corporations have received 85 percent of all military contracts in the last two decades.

There is a controversy over the cyclical impact of military spending. Tom Riddell (1988) argues that military spending is used to boost profit rates whenever they decline, while others emphasize that military spending is pushed by the military-industrial complex at all times (see Melman 1988). These issues can be clarified by looking at the actual cyclical pattern of government spending.

CYCLICAL SPENDING PATTERNS IN WAR AND PEACE

There is a vast difference in the pattern of federal government spending during war-dominated cycles and peacetime cycles. The Korean War dominated the 1949–1954 cycle, while the Vietnam War dominated the cycle of 1961–1970. In the average of these two war-dominated cycles, the index of military equipment production rose 1.1 percent per quarter for the entire lengthy expansions, but fell 5.8 percent per quarter in contractions (series 557, Bureau of Economic Analysis, 1984). Since military spending was the largest part of federal purchases of goods and services, the huge rise and decline in military production caused a similar rise and fall in federal purchases. Thus, in the average of the two war-dominated cycles, real federal purchases of goods and services rose 3.1 percent per quarter in expansions and fell by 5.0 percent per quarter in contractions (series 253, Bureau of Economic Analysis, 1984). It appears, therefore, that in these two cycles, the rise of military spending helped fuel the expansion while the postwar decline of military spending was one important cause of the contraction.

We must consider, however, not only the two war cycles, but also the six peacetime cycles in the period from 1949 to 1991. In this period in the peacetime cycles, the behavior of military spending has a less important cyclical role. Moreover, military spending changes from pro-cyclical in war-related cycles to counter-cyclical in peacetime cycles! In the average peacetime expansion, military production rose only 0.3 percent per quarter, while government purchases of all goods and services rose only 0.1 percent per quarter. During the average peacetime business contraction, military production rose to 0.5 percent per quarter, while all federal purchases of goods and services rose 0.7 percent per quarter. It thus appears that military spending and other federal purchases during peacetime were used to prop up the sick economy during recessions but were cut back in expansions. In the 1990s, there seems to be a broad consensus, except among military producers, that there should be no military spending done whose purpose is simply to bolster the economy, which can be done in other ways.

CYCLICAL PATTERS OF FEDERAL EXPENDITURES

Goods and services are only part of federal spending. Let us now turn to total federal expenditures which include goods and services but also include all kinds of transfer payments. Transfer payments are payments, such as farm subsidies, that are not payments for current production; they transfer income from taxpayers to some other group. We shall examine data for each of the war cycles and each of the peace cycles. Table 17.2 shows spending rates of growth per quarter of all federal expenditures in expansion and contraction for each cycle.

TABLE 17.2
FEDERAL GOVERNMENT EXPENDITURE
(RATE OF GROWTH PER QUARTER, CONSTANT DOLLARS)

TWO WAR CYCLES

Cycle	Rate	EXPANSION Politics	Rate	CONTRACTION Politics
1949–54	4.0	Truman, Korea	−4.1	Eisenhower
1961–70	1.1	Johnson, Vietnam	0.9	Nixon
Average	2.6	N.A.	−1.6	N.A.

SIX PEACETIME CYCLES

Cycle	Rate	EXPANSION Politics	Rate	CONTRACTION Politics
1954–58	0.3	Eisenhower	3.2	Eisenhower
1958–61	0.1	Eisenhower	1.9	Kennedy
1970–75	0.4	Nixon	2.9	Ford
1975–80	0.9	Carter	3.0	Carter
1980–82	0.8	Reagan	2.1	Reagan
1982–91	0.7	Bush	0.7	Bush
Average	0.5	N.A.	2.6	N.A.

SOURCE: CITIBASE database, file GGFEX.

NOTE: N.A. means not applicable.

Not surprisingly, given the enormous increase in military spending, federal government expenditures rose at 2.6 percent per quarter in the average wartime expansion, but only at 0.5 percent per quarter in the average peacetime expansion. In the two contractions following wars, expenditures *fell* by an average 1.6 percent per quarter. By contrast, in the six peacetime contractions, government expenditures *rose* by an average 2.6 percent per quarter. The impact in contractions, therefore, was pro-cyclical in the average war cycle, but counter-cyclical in the average peacetime cycle.

What is fascinating is that there is no evidence that it matters which party, Republicans or Democrats, is in power. There is no evidence whatsoever that Republicans spend less than Democrats in business contractions. In every one of the five peacetime cycles, regardless of who was in power, the pattern is the same: a slow rise of federal government spending in expansions followed by a rapid rise in federal spending in contractions. This pattern is shown graphically for the last four cycles, 1970 to 1991, in Figure 17.1.

Why does federal spending rise slowly in expansions then rapidly in contractions? The slow rise in expansions reflects the long-run increases in military spending and in constructive spending on goods, services, business subsidies, welfare, and interest on the debt. The far more rapid rise of spending in contractions is mostly not discretionary policy but is automatic under present laws.

FIGURE 17.1
FEDERAL GOVERNMENT SPENDING

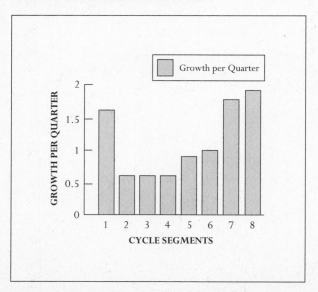

SOURCE: CITIBASE, series GGFEX.

These are the so-called *automatic stabilizers* that tend to increase income in recession or depression while tending to decrease it in expansions. Some of the expenditures that automatically increase in every recession or depression are farm subsidies, unemployment compensation, and business subsidies. One result is that personal income falls more slowly than GDP, thus supporting more consumer spending than would be done by the private sector by itself. In expansion, these same automatic stabilizers tend to fall, thus reducing the growth of income.

FEDERAL RECEIPTS AND DEFICITS

In addition to spending, government fiscal impact is determined by receipts (mostly taxes). Table 17.3 presents federal receipts, as well as resulting deficits, in terms of their cyclical amplitude as a rate of growth per quarter for each cycle.

Receipts behave about the same in wartime and peacetime. They rise in every expansion and decline in every contraction. Again, this is an automatic fiscal behavior, not discretionary. Government tax receipts mainly reflect the rise and fall of corporate and individual income. Since the federal

TABLE 17.3
FEDERAL RECEIPTS AND DEFICITS
(RATE OF GROWTH PER QUARTER, CONSTANT DOLLARS)

TWO WAR CYCLES

Cycle	EXPANSION			CONTRACTION		
	Receipts	Deficit	Politics	Receipts	Deficit	Politics
1949–54	0.6	3.4	Truman, Korea	−4.2	0.0	Eisenhower
1961–70	1.3	−0.2	Johnson, Vietnam	−2.5	3.7	Nixon
Average	1.0	1.6	N.A.	−3.4	1.9	N.A.

FIVE PEACETIME CYCLES

Cycle	EXPANSION			CONTRACTION		
	Receipts	Deficit	Politics	Receipts	Deficit	Politics
1954–58	1.3	−1.0	Eisenhower	−3.2	6.3	Eisenhower
1958–61	2.4	−2.3	Eisenhower	−0.8	2.7	Kennedy
1970–75	1.4	−1.0	Nixon	−1.0	3.9	Ford
1975–80	1.2	−0.3	Carter	−0.9	4.2	Carter
1980–82	1.7	−0.9	Reagan	−2.0	4.0	Reagan
1982–91	0.9	−0.6	Bush	−0.9	3.1	Bush
Average	1.6	−1.1	N.A.	−1.6	4.2	N.A.

SOURCE: CITIBASE database, files GGFR, GGFNET.

NOTE: N.A. means not applicable.

taxes are income taxes, this rise and fall is automatic. Moreover, to the extent that higher income brackets pay a higher percentage of income to taxes, it follows that the automatic change of taxes is higher than the percentage change of income.

This automatic functional relationship is strong enough that it outweighs most discretionary policy changes due to war and peace or changes in political administration. Figure 17.2 reveals for the last four cycles (1970–1991) the dramatic pro-cyclical behavior of federal revenues.

Contrary to mythology, the federal deficit also behaves somewhat the same in all peacetime cycles, regardless of which party is in power. Thus, the deficit rose (or the surplus declined) in every contraction of peacetime. The deficit rose in recessions under Eisenhower, Kennedy, Ford, Carter, and Reagan. The deficit fell (or the surplus rose) in every expansion of peacetime. So the deficit fell under Eisenhower, Nixon, Carter, and Reagan. In spite of the Vietnam War, the same cyclical pattern held for the deficit in the 1961–1970 cycle (under Johnson and Nixon). Only the very rapid rise and fall of military spending in the Korean War cycle, 1949–1954, under Truman and Eisenhower, reversed the normal pattern.

FIGURE 17.2
FEDERAL GOVERNMENT TAXATION

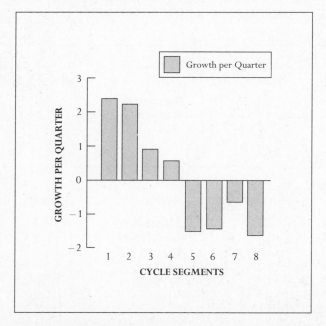

SOURCE: CITIBASE, series GGFR.

Figure 17.3 pictures for the last four cycles, 1970 to 1991, the clearly counter-cyclical pattern of the federal deficit in peacetime. Therefore, we may assume as a stylized fact of the cycle that the federal deficit is counter-cyclical; that is, it falls in expansion and rises in contraction. The implications of this important fact are discussed in a later section after we have examined state and local fiscal behavior and total government fiscal behavior.

STATE AND LOCAL FISCAL BEHAVIOR OVER THE CYCLE

Table 17.4 shows the behavior of state and local spending, receipts, and deficits, cycle by cycle. The table is not split into war and peace cycles because there is no noticeable change in cyclical behavior between those two categories at the state and local level, since it does not involve military spending.

State and local revenues (mostly sales and property taxes) grew rapidly in both expansions and contractions in the 1950s and 1960s. Revenues grew

FIGURE 17.3
FEDERAL GOVERNMENT DEFICIT

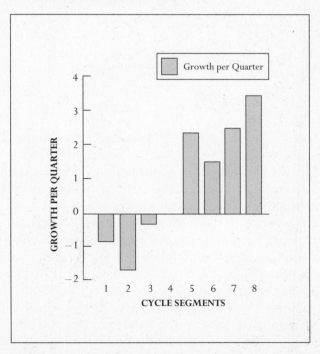

SOURCE: CITIBASE, series GGFNET.

TABLE 17.4
STATE AND LOCAL SPENDING, RECEIPTS, DEFICITS
(RATE OF GROWTH PER QUARTER, CONSTANT DOLLARS)

EXPANSIONS

CYCLE	Expenditures	Revenues	Deficits
1949–54	1.2	1.1	0.1
1954–58	1.5	1.5	0.0
1958–61	1.0	1.7	−0.7
1961–70	1.6	1.7	−0.1
1970–75	1.0	1.4	−0.4
1975–80	0.4	0.8	−0.4
1980–82	−0.7	−0.2	−0.5
1982–91	1.1	0.9	0.2
Average	0.9	1.1	−0.3

CONTRACTIONS

CYCLE	Expenditures	Revenues	Deficits
1949–54	2.4	0.9	1.5
1954–58	2.7	1.9	0.6
1958–61	2.4	1.9	0.5
1961–70	2.8	1.8	1.0
1970–75	1.0	−0.1	1.4
1975–80	−0.2	−0.1	−0.1
1980–82	0.2	0.0	0.2
1982–91	1.0	0.4	0.6
Average	1.6	0.9	0.7

SOURCE: CITIBASE database, files GGSR, GGSNET, GGSEX.

far more slowly in the 1970s, 1980s, and 1990s as the economy expanded more slowly.

State and local spending grew during expansions at about the same rate as taxes in the first two cycles, 1949 to 1958. So state budgets were balanced. After that, spending actually grew less than taxes in expansions, so deficits declined in expansions. On the other hand, in every contraction (except one), spending rose more rapidly than revenues. Hence, in every contraction (except one), the deficit rose. Thus, the state and local deficit became counter-cyclical, much as the federal deficit.

The only exception was the situation in the 1980 contraction when revenue fell, but there was a fiscal crisis, that is, actual large deficits for the first time. In reaction, state and local governments felt constrained to lower spending even more, worsening the decline of income. In general, however, state and local deficits rose in contractions and fell in expansions.

CYCLICAL BEHAVIOR OF TOTAL GOVERNMENT FISCAL ACTIVITY

Total government activity includes federal, state, and local activity. For the four business cycles from 1970 through 1991, Table 17.5 reveals the cyclical behavior of total government spending, receipts, and deficits. Table 17.5 provides a comparison of the separate behavior of federal activity, state and local activity, and total government activity.

In the average cycle, total real government expenditures rise moderately in recovery, then rise more slowly in prosperity, pick up speed again in the crisis, and rise most rapidly in the depression phase. They are counter-cyclical in that they rise faster in contractions than in expansions.

By contrast, the tax receipts (or revenue) from total government activity rise most rapidly in recovery then less so in prosperity. The receipts actually decline in crisis and depression. Thus, tax receipts are very pro-cyclical. Receipts follow the pattern of real national income, but rise and fall somewhat faster. The more rapid rise and fall of taxes are due mostly to the fact that income taxes are a higher percentage in higher income brackets. As incomes expand, not only are more taxes collected, but the average tax rate must rise.

TABLE 17.5
CYCLICAL PATTERN OF FISCAL ACTIVITY (AVERAGE, 3 CYCLES, 1970–1991, RATE OF GROWTH PER QUARTER, CONSTANT DOLLARS. INCLUDES ALL FEDERAL, STATE AND LOCAL, AND TOTAL GOVERNMENT ACTIVITY.)

EXPENDITURES

	Expansion	Contraction
Federal	0.8	1.8
State and Local	0.3	0.5
Total Government	0.6	1.1

RECEIPTS

	Expansion	Contraction
Federal	1.4	−1.2
State and Local	0.6	−0.1
Total Government	1.2	−0.7

DEFICITS (EXPENDITURES – RECEIPTS)

	Expansion	Contraction
Federal	−0.6	3.0
State and Local	−0.4	0.5
Total Government	−0.5	1.8

SOURCE: CITIBASE database, files GGFEX, GGFR, GGSR, GGSEX, GGFNET, GGSNET.

As a result of the spending and taxing pattern, deficits from total government activity fall at a considerable pace in recovery. Deficits decline in recovery because tax receipts rise much faster than spending. In prosperity, when receipts rise only a little faster than spending, total government deficits fall only very slightly.

During the first part of contraction, in the crisis, total government deficits rise rapidly. Deficits rise rapidly in the crisis (early contraction) because spending is rising while taxes are falling in real terms. In the depression phase, total government deficits rise most rapidly. Deficits rise very rapidly in depression because spending rises rapidly, while receipts are still falling. Thus, total government deficits fall in expansions and rise in contractions, being a significant counter-cyclical factor. As noted earlier, this pattern is changed very little (if at all) by the declared fiscal ideology of the party in power.

SUMMARY OF FISCAL BEHAVIOR

In the wartime cycles, it is obvious that government has a massive impact. In the Second World War, the Korean War, and the Vietnam War during the expansions, government military spending was the single largest and most rapidly rising factor. After each war there was a recession caused in part by the decline of military spending.

In the average peacetime cycle, however, the government role is quite different. In the recovery phase, while the private economy is booming (with rapidly rising output and profits), the government deficit declines rapidly. This action is mostly automatic under present law.

In the prosperity phase, however, when the private economy is slowing its rate of growth, the further decline of deficit spending removes more support for expansion, helping set the stage for a business contraction. One cannot say that government fiscal actions cause the downturn, since some deficit spending continues, but the decline in the deficit does further reduce the rate of growth of demand. The deficit decline in prosperity is inherent in the automatic stabilizers under the present legal and economic structure. Therefore, government fiscal policy does play a role in the internal dynamics of the cycle—and it is a factor in the events leading to the downturn by reducing its stimulation. Yet the downturn is caused by the private economy because the private sector declines even though the government is still stimulative, albeit with a weaker and weaker force.

In the average contraction, including both the crisis and depression phases, the government deficit increases relatively rapidly. Thus, contemporary U. S. fiscal behavior, derived from the automatic stabilizers under present laws and from economic activity, is counter-cyclical in the contraction. It therefore appears to operate as one internal cause of the recovery—though there is a controversy on this point, discussed in the next section.

IMPACT OF FISCAL BEHAVIOR

In the Keynesian view, government behavior provides a major support to the cyclical tendency of the private economy to recover at the bottom of depression. Thus, in the Keynesian view, the evidence of the contemporary historical period confirms that (1) government activity is determined by the level of the economy (given the legal structure), and (2) government has a significant but limited impact in peacetime.

From this view, it is also worth emphasizing that earlier in U.S. history, long before fiscal policy was quantitatively significant enough to affect the economy with enough impact to cause upturns or downturns, there was a business cycle in the private sector. Government spending and taxation in peacetime was not that significant until the 1930s—and there were many business cycles before then.

In contemporary peacetime cycles of the 1990s, total government deficits, the aggregate result of federal, state, and local fiscal decisions, fall in business expansions and rise in business contractions. If Keynes is correct, a high deficit stimulates the economy. Therefore, this behavior means that government tends to stimulate the economy in contractions but tends to reduce stimulation in expansions. Liberal Keynesians will applaud this counter-cyclical behavior of the deficit. In the Keynesian view, a rising deficit in contractions will tend, all other things being equal, to decrease unemployment and encourage recovery. The falling deficit in expansions will tend to prevent overheating and inflation.

On the other hand, monetarists will point out that the rising deficit in contractions may lead to higher interest rates. This view is the "crowding out" argument of the monetarists and others, which says that government demand for loans drives up interest rates for all borrowers. Monetarists have also decried the fact that deficit spending has continued in recent cycles during expansions even though it is at a declining rate of growth. The existence of deficit spending over the whole cycle means to monetarists that the government is continually pumping money into the economy. In their view, this action may be the major cause of a long-run inflationary trend in the economy. We shall return to this dispute below.

GOVERNMENT POLICY: WHAT IS TO BE DONE?

Next, we discuss various approaches to the control of the business cycle through fiscal policies. To follow the evolution of the debate, we begin with the neo-Keynesian policies of the 1950s and 1960s, then discuss all of the criticisms of these policies, which brings out the alternative views of other economists.

KEYNESIAN COUNTER-CYCLICAL POLICIES

There is no one set of policies that every economist would agree to call "Keynesian" because there are several different schools of Keynesians, ranging from the neoclassical-Keynesian synthesis of the 1950s and 1960s to the contemporary new-Keynesians to the very different post-Keynesians. What is clear is that a great deal changed in counter-cyclical policies as a result of the impact of John Maynard Keynes.

One pre-Keynesian argument contended that unemployment could be cured by reducing wages, because lower wages will encourage investment. According to Keynes, this is incorrect because (1) lower wages mean less consumer demand, and because (2) consumer demand is an important determinant of investment.

Another pre-Keynesian argument—by the under-consumptionists—contended that higher wages would reduce unemployment by raising consumer demand. According to Keynes, this is incorrect because (1) costs are an important determinant of investment (via expected profits), and (2) wages are the largest component of costs.

What Keynes did insist upon was the importance of aggregate effective demand, in which he included not only consumption, but also investment, government demand, and net export demand.

In the 1950s and 1960s there was an overwhelming consensus among most U.S. economists and most U.S. politicians on a demand-oriented fiscal policy, usually considered to be liberal and Keynesian. In its textbook description, it relied on two simple government fiscal policies to fine-tune the economy, prevent inflation, and prevent cyclical contractions (they also advocated certain monetary policies). In the first case, if there is unemployment but no inflation, (1) increase government spending and (2) reduce government taxes. Then just allow the resulting deficit spending to stimulate demand. In the second case, if there is inflation but no unemployment, (1) reduce government spending and (2) increase taxes. Then let the resulting surplus of government taxes over spending soak up excess demand.

In the modern U.S. context, these policies are said to be liberal because they would increase government activity in order to prevent the evils of unemployment and inflation. Policies are called conservative in the modern U.S. context if they would reduce government anti-cyclical activity, relying on the private enterprise system to automatically correct any problems.

These liberal policies were often called Keynesian, but Paul Samuelson renamed them the policies of the neoclassical-Keynesian synthesis because they are Keynesian in the sense of requiring government activity to prevent unemployment and inflation, but they are neoclassical in the sense that once full employment is restored, it is assumed that the private enterprise economy performs in an optimal way. The analysis of the 1950s was also neoclassical in the sense that adjustment to full employment was assumed to be prevented only by wage rigidities, price rigidities, or imperfections in the competitive process.

Whether this view was called a neoclassical-Keynesian, neo-Keynesian, or something else, it held strongly that fiscal policy could fine-tune the economy to eliminate the business cycle. There were many statements by noted economists in the 1960s that the business cycle had disappeared. Franco Modigliani stated that the dominant view was that "a private enterprise economy using an intangible money *needs* to be stabilized, *can* be stabilized, and *should* be stabilized by appropriate monetary and fiscal policy" (1977, 27). Paul Samuelson said that in "the writings of Solow, Tobin, and myself, attention was focused on a managed economy which through skillful use of fiscal and monetary policy channeled the Keynesian forces of effective demand into behaving like a neoclassical model" (quoted by Lekachman 1960, 30).

There are three kinds of limitations on this liberal, neoclassical-Keynesian synthesis of fiscal policy: (1) administrative inadequacies, (2) political constraints based on economic interests, and (3) inherently conflicting economic goals.

ADMINISTRATIVE CONSTRAINTS UPON FISCAL POLICY

In reality, administration of these neo-Keynesian policies is difficult because it requires precise and prompt government planning within an unplanned private enterprise economy. First, there is the information-gathering problem. There is always delay before available data can reveal changes in unemployment and inflation. Second, there is a much longer delay for interpretation of the data. Some government economists must determine that rising unemployment or inflation exist before something can be done about it.

Third, there is a further delay in order to decide what to do about it. Economists must estimate how much of an increase or cut in spending or an increase or cut in taxes, or both, is required to meet the goals. This is not only time-consuming, but very, very difficult. No two economists agree on the amounts, and government estimates are always totally inaccurate (a conclusion for which past evidence is overwhelming). If there is to be spending for the purchase of equipment or construction, engineers must also make plans.

A fourth administrative delay must occur while Congress goes through the lengthy process of deliberation (that is, conflict among vested interests in more or less polite debates) and legislation. A fifth administrative delay must occur before the plans can be put into effect. A plan to build a new battleship does not put money into immediate circulation, but adds it slowly over many years. An immediate tax cut still requires time for the estimated amount to be spent by consumers or investors.

Because of these five delays (information, interpretation, planning, legislation, and execution), as well as the gross mistakes in planning, the results seldom have any resemblance to the plans. In fact, it has frequently happened that new spending, designed to end a recession, actually helps overstimulate an expansion. Similarly, tax cuts to stimulate the economy may occur in time to increase inflation.

POLITICAL CONSTRAINTS UPON FISCAL POLICY

The political constraints on fiscal policy are much worse problems for the process than the administrative constraints. The interests of the business groups are dominant in the budget process. These interests frequently conflict with the reasonable national goals assumed by neo-Keynesian economists. For example, full employment—defined as a situation with no one unemployed—would provide labor with a much greater power to raise wages, so it is *never* an actual goal of U.S. fiscal policy. Neo-Keynesians have gotten Congress to adopt some pious statements about full employment, but with no enforcement procedure. In practice, the U.S. government has usually adopted the conservative view that some unemployment is "natural," such as 6 or 7 percent. Of course, if unemployment is "natural," it is good.

Increases or decreases in government spending hurt some groups and help others. Increases or decreases in taxes hurt some groups and help others. There is no interest-group-neutral fiscal policy. There is also no U.S. agency called "government waste" which can be reduced for painless cuts. The question is always this: spending or cuts *for whom*? The ability to ignore this issue is the greatest weakness of neo-Keynesian fiscal policy. For example, the question of spending for health care is always heavily lobbied by interest groups representing the doctors, the insurance companies, and the hospitals, with their own profit in mind.

Not only is the distribution of income directly affected, but so also is the allocation of resources. Fiscal policies determine the use of private resources (such as Cadillacs) versus public resources (such as mass transit). They decide on spending for hospitals or schools versus bombs or battleships. Again, none of this is interest-group-neutral, but on the contrary strongly affects distribution of income. Suppose by some miracle that a large majority agrees on a certain total amount of government spending to combat unemployment. The prime political question, however, is spending on what, for it is here that vested interests come into play. For example, even small vital expenditures on free medical care have sometimes been defeated after lobbying by the American Medical Association. Powerful vested interests oppose almost every item in the civilian budget as soon as economic expansion proceeds beyond the necessary minimum. What kinds of interests must be defeated to have the necessary spending to fill the enormous deficiency in demand in an economic contraction? Constructive projects like the Tennessee Valley Authority could develop dams, irrigation, and cheap power, but these have been fought tooth and nail by the private power interests because they might lower profit rates. There could be large-scale public housing, but lobbying by private contractors has long kept such programs to a minimum.

There might be other constructive spending. For example, there is great need for spending on hospitals and schools. The rich, however, see these projects as subsidies to the poor for things that the rich can buy for themselves out of their own pockets (such as education and health care). Proposals to increase unemployment compensation or lower taxes paid by the poor encounter even greater resistance because they would transfer income from the rich to the poor. Likewise, billions could usefully be spent in aid and loans to the less developed world, where poverty and human suffering are so widespread—but that is opposed by many U.S. interests with strong lobbies.

Businesses do not like government competition with private enterprise or policies that significantly alter the relative distribution of income in favor of the poor or middle class. They therefore tend to oppose all government non-military spending—except business subsidies or highway spending, which is strongly pushed by the automobile producers.

From all the facts just given, it must be concluded that peaceful constructive spending on a large scale is opposed by many special interests. On the other hand, military spending does not violate any vested interests. Military spending is considered an ideal anti-depression policy by military-related business for three reasons. First, such expenditures have the same short-run effect on employment and profits as would expenditures on more socially useful projects. Second, military spending means big and stable profits for big business, whereas any type of constructive spending may shift income from rich taxpayers to poor recipients. Third, the long-run effect of military spending is even more favorable to business because no new productive equipment is created to compete with existing facilities. On the other hand, most studies conclude that military spending provides fewer jobs per dollar than nonmilitary spending.

It is an historical fact that only the military spending of the Second World War brought the United States out of the Great Depression. It is an historical fact that the strong expansions and mild contractions of the 1950s and the 1960s were powerfully supported by the high level of Cold War spending in the Korean War and in the Vietnam War. In the 1990s, there has finally come to be some consensus for reduction of the military, but there is no consensus on what other public projects are a good idea—except some kind of health care.

The 1981 Reagan budget was perhaps the most classic example of business interests at work. It made huge increases in military spending. At the same time (with continued high unemployment), it made the largest cuts in spending in public service job programs, while the job-producing Young Adult Conservation Corps was eliminated. Other spending cuts tending to reduce employment were in the following: education programs, aid to disadvantaged children, specific health programs, medicaid payments to states, medicare for the elderly, public housing (with increases in rents), food stamps, mothers' and infants' nutrition, school lunches, day care, aid to families with dependent children, the Economic Development Administration, urban development action grants, the Consumer Product Safety Commission, mass transit aid, funds for water cleanup projects, funds for more parks, funds for arts and humanities, funds for legal services for the poor, funds for the postal service, funds for public broadcasting, and funds for community action programs. These cuts were followed by more cuts in the Bush administration and by still more cuts in the Clinton administration.

All the cuts in spending were types that tend to hurt the poor and the middle class. Most of the Reagan and Bush tax cuts, as well as the increase in military spending, increased the after-tax profits of business. A cautious summary of the Reagan tax bill said: "Although the bill contains massive tax cuts for business and a host of tax breaks for special interests, there are only a handful of changes to help the average worker" (United Press International 1981, 1). This section has shown that there are political constraints on any constructive government spending. (See Box 17.1.)

ECONOMIC CONSTRAINTS UPON FISCAL POLICY

To make reasonable fiscal policies, one must understand the economic constraints set on policy by the structure of the private enterprise economy. The four major constraints within the system allegedly are: (1) redistribution to

BOX 17.1

HOW WOULD YOU CUT THE GOVERNMENT DEFICIT?

An interesting "game" that can always be played is "Where should the reductions in government spending be made?" In the table below is the Federal budget for the past three years. In order to balance the budget, spending cuts of approximately $250 billion dollars need to be made. See if you and a few of your friends can balance the budget. Then consider the problems that legislators have, with the various special interest groups and others lobbying to insure that budget cuts don't hurt them. Finally, remember that you need to get reelected next time.

SOURCE OR TYPE	1991	1992	1993
RECEIPTS			
All sources	1,054,265	1,091,692	1,153,147
Individual income taxes, net	467,827	476,465	509,680
Withheld	404,152	408,352	430,427
Presidential election campaign fund	32	30	28
Nonwithheld	142,693	149,342	154,772
Refunds	79,050	81,259	75,546
Corporate income taxes, gross receipts	113,599	117,951	131,548
Refunds	15,513	17,680	14,027
Social security taxes and contributions, net	396,011	413,689	428,300
Employment taxes and contributions	370,526	385,491	396,939
Self employment taxes and contributions	25,427	24,421	20,604
Unemployment insurance	20,922	23,410	26,556
Other net receipts	4,563	4,788	4,805
Excise taxes	42,430	45,570	48,057
Customs deposits	15,921	17,359	18,802
Estate and gift taxes	11,138	11,143	12,577
Miscellaneous receipts	22,852	27,195	18,211
OUTLAYS			
All types	1,323,757	1,381,895	1,408,122
National defense	272,514	298,188	290,590
International affairs	16,167	16,100	17,175

CONTINUED ON NEXT PAGE . . .

BOX 17.1 — CONTINUED

SOURCE OR TYPE	1991	1992	1993
General science, space and technology	15,946	16,234	17,055
Energy	2,511	4,519	4,445
Natural resources and environment	18,708	19,870	20,088
Agriculture	14,864	14,968	20,257
Commerce and housing credit	75,639	9,752	−23,532
Transportation	31,531	33,747	35,238
Community and regional development	7,432	7,924	10,395
Education, training, employment and social services	41,479	43,586	48,827
Health	71,183	89,571	99,249
Social security and medicare	373,495	406,570	435,137
Income security	171,618	199,395	207,933
Veterans benefits and services	31,344	33,973	35,715
Administration of justice	12,295	14,481	14,983
General government	11,358	12,874	13,039
Net interest	195,012	199,422	198,807
Undistributed offsetting receipts	−39,356	−39,280	−37,386

SOURCE: Economic Report of the President

the poor may reduce entrepreneurial incentives to invest; (2) government competition may reduce investment in private enterprise; (3) conflict may occur between policies to reduce the internal deficit and policies to reduce the trade deficit; and (4) there may be conflict between anti-unemployment and anti-inflation policies. In addition, there is the alleged conflict between government borrowing and private investment borrowing. It should be noted that all of these problems are seen as barriers to any government activism by conservative economists. To the extent that these barriers are real and not just rhetoric to stop social action, they point to conflicts within the system and lead to arguments on the need to change the system.

CROWDING-OUT?

The neo-Keynesian policy leads to deficit spending in depressions. Indeed, deficit spending is an automatic, built-in effect under present U.S. laws. Conservatives argue that government borrowing raises interest rates; therefore, it reduces or crowds out private borrowing for investment. Thus, government spending, according to conservative fiscal theory, reduces private spending by an equal amount and has no other effect. It appears reasonable to argue that government borrowing may raise interest rates. But how much? Is it significant? Is it overshadowed by other effects?

Other effects of fiscal spending include the multiplier effect of increase in income by consumer spending. Moreover, in most of U.S. history, interest rates were relatively low, so they had little quantitative effect on investment. Chapter 14 also referred to the fact that most empirical studies have found no statistically significant negative effect of interest rates on investment.

The historical record of the business cycle shows why one would not expect to find good evidence that deficit spending raises interest rates or that higher interest rates lower investment. In the historical experience of the United States, during the average expansion, the government deficit declines (mainly because of rising revenues), yet interest rates also rise (mainly because of rising private demand). Moreover, in spite of rising interest rates, private investment rises rapidly in expansions (mainly because of improved profit expectations). On the other hand, in the average contraction the government deficit rises, yet interest rates fall, while private investment also falls.

There is no convincing evidence that government spending crowds out private spending. It does seem clear that deficit spending has a net stimulative effect because the multiplied demand effect is far greater than the effect of higher interest costs.

Although deficit spending has stimulated the economy in every war period, it has had its most dramatic effects in two periods. First, in the Second World War under President Roosevelt, the government bought 40 percent of GDP. Given that enormous new demand for goods and services, the vast unemployment of the Great Depression disappeared. By 1943, the official unemployment rate fell to 1 percent. The expansion lasted till the end of the war.

Second, in the years from 1980 to 1988, under President Reagan, military spending was vastly increased, while taxes were considerably reduced. The result was an historically unprecedented deficit. This deficit helped the recovery from depression and continued to feed an unusually long expansion. Thus, President Reagan provided the best evidence available in support of Keynes' theories for a peacetime period.

REDISTRIBUTION OF INCOME

Keynes said that private enterprise is at fault because of (1) "failure to provide for full employment" and (2) "its arbitrary and inequitable distribution of wealth and income" (quoted in Rousseas 1986, 372). Keynes argued that fiscal policy should redistribute income to the poor (see Hotson 1976,

13–14) and that this would help alleviate the lack of effective demand. If, however, a drastic reduction of income equality by fiscal means were to be legislated by a liberal government, then entrepreneurs might refuse to invest. This sort of refusal to invest was called "sabotage" by Thorstein Veblen. Generally, a decline in investment has not resulted from minor reforms, which increases taxes or welfare spending. But a really drastic redistribution policy might lower business confidence and make entrepreneurs hoard or flee the country with their capital. Such capital flight did occur in Chile under the socialist government of Salvadore Allende and also in the first year of the socialist government of Francois Mitterand in France.

Another more immediate problem of redistribution is the fact that the enormous national debt of the United States means enormous interest payments from the average taxpayer to the wealthy holders of Treasury bonds. The huge deficits of the Reagan administration, at high interest rates, thus greatly increased the inequality of income. Continuous high deficits cause an interest burden on the middle class and shift of income to the wealthy.

GOVERNMENT COMPETITION WITH PRIVATE ENTERPRISE

If the U.S. government sponsored a successful energy corporation, the lower prices would compete with present private energy corporations. These private energy corporations might then go on strike by not investing or by fleeing overseas. As conservatives frequently and correctly point out, *any* peaceful constructive direct investment by government does compete with private capital. Therefore, enough government investment might cause an investment strike or capital flight. Of course, one remedy would be still more government investment.

The same constraint, the worry over possible income distribution, may apply to competition with elite professionals. If free national health care were instituted, doctors might get reasonable payments instead of outrageous monopoly revenues. Doctors might also flee, but where would they go? Every other industrialized country (except South Africa) already has free national health care.

GOVERNMENT DEFICIT VERSUS TRADE DEFICIT

When the U.S. economy is stimulated, income grows. Higher incomes lead to an increase in imports. If exports do not change (and that does not depend on the U.S. economy), then this causes net exports to decline. A decline in net exports causes the trade deficit to increase. Thus, if the economy improves so that the government deficit declines, the trade deficit may increase. Yet a higher trade deficit means lower demand for U.S. products.

A related problem is the fact that a stronger U.S. economy leads to a higher exchange rate for the U.S. dollar. But a higher exchange rate reduces U.S. exports. Again, internal policy may conflict with trade policy.

INFLATION AND UNEMPLOYMENT

Perhaps the most difficult problem for U.S. fiscal policy is how to find policies that reduce both unemployment and inflation, two goals that are in conflict with each other. In the 1970s and 1980s, the U.S. economy actually was faced with both unemployment and inflation. In the early 1970s, Paul Samuelson said that economists knew how to prevent either unemployment or inflation, but he sadly admitted that there was no policy to solve both: "Experts do not yet know . . . an income policy that will permit us to have simultaneously . . . full employment and price stability" (Samuelson 1973, 823). Typical neo-Keynesian policies for full employment stimulate the economy with a high level of demand, but the usual Keynesian policy to reduce inflation is to reduce demand. It is impossible to do both at once.

It is true that unemployment and inflation sometimes moved together in the 1970s, so under some circumstances it would appear at first glance that the two could be cured together by the same policy. Closer examination, however, reveals that they sometimes increased together, but almost never decreased together. So a single policy can make both worse, but may not be able to make both better. A drastic enough rise in demand to cause full employment would also probably lead to more inflation. A drastic enough fall in demand to cause zero inflation or stable prices would also cause much more unemployment.

ALTERNATIVE POLICIES: MONETARY, DIRECT CONTROLS, PLANNING

Monetary policy must always be coordinated with fiscal policy. It was discussed in detail in Appendix 14B.

It is also possible to use direct controls on prices and wages in conjunction with fiscal policy. Such controls were used extensively during the First and Second World Wars. They were also used in peacetime during the Nixon administration, an example that is discussed in some detail in Appendix 17B.

Finally, it is possible to have national planning with an emphasis on control of investment. To be effective, such planning must be based on democratic, public ownership and/or control of a significant part of the economy.

This is very controversial and is outside of the bounds of this book (see Sherman 1987 for a complete discussion).

CONCLUSIONS

It was found that government automatically, under the present legal and economic structure, tends to decrease the deficit during every expansion and tends to increase the deficit during every contraction.

New Classical economists urge *no* government counter-cyclical intervention. New-Keynesians and post-Keynesians urge government use of fiscal, monetary, and/or direct control policies. Radical and neo-Marxian economists urge a change to democratic planning and economic democracy or democratic socialism. The authors have indicated the different positions, but there is no consensus among economists on these controversial issues.

SUGGESTED READINGS

There is a vast literature on policy from various points of view. For the most conservative see George Gilder (1981). The supply-side view is given by Arthur Laffer (1982). For the monetarist view, see Milton Friedman (1968); but also see Franco Modigliani (1977). Middle of the road views are expressed by Charles Kindleberger (1978), and by James Tobin (1981). Post-Keynesian views of government policy are given by John Hotson (1976) and by Hyman Minsky (1986). An Institutionalist view is stated by Wallace Peterson (1988a). Neo-Marxian view of fiscal policy is given by John Miller (1986). Some radical policy programs are presented in Bowles, Gordon, and Weisskopf (1990); Dugger (1989); and Dymski, Epstein, and Pollin (1991). A variety of views on Keynes and policy are stated in a collection by Harold Wattel (1985).

KEY TERMS AND CONCEPTS

fiscal policy	reserve ratio	automatic fiscal behavior
automatic fiscal policy and discretionary fiscal policy	direct wage and price controls	war-cycles and peace-cycles
monetary policy	deficit	federal government
Federal Reserve system	debt	state and local government
open market operations	pro-cyclical	
	counter-cyclical	

APPENDIX 17 A
GOVERNMENT IN A FORMAL CYCLE MODEL

In a business cycle model, government spending is an element of demand which increases profits by allowing their realization through more sales. Government taxes reduce demand which reduces profits. Government fiscal policy (spending and taxes) will affect the consumption function as well as the investment function, with the relative impact depending on the type of spending and the type of taxes.

To begin with, government may be inserted into both the aggregate revenue relationship and the aggregate cost relationship. Thus,

$$Revenue = Consumption + Investment \\ + Net\ Exports + Goverment \quad (17A.1)$$

and

$$Cost = Labor\ Income + Raw\ Material\ Costs \\ + Interest\ Costs + Depreciation + Taxes \quad (17A.2)$$

We know that revenue minus cost equals profits and that profit is a key variable in determining investment.

$$Profit = Revenue - Cost \quad (17A.3)$$

and

$$Investment = F\ (Profit,\ Profit\ Rate,\ Taxes) \quad (17A.4)$$

Government spending and government taxes also obviously affect consumption, so a complete consumption function would have to include these two government variables.

$$Consumption = F\ (Income,\ Labor\ Share,\ Credit, \\ Government\ Spending,\ Taxes) \quad (17A.5)$$

and, of course, the labor share of national income is affected both by government spending and by taxes.

$$Labor\ Share = F\ (Unemployment,\ Capacity\ Utilization, \\ Government\ Spending,\ Taxes) \quad (17A.6)$$

In light of its fairly regular cyclical behavior, the easiest way to depict government fiscal activity is as a function of capacity utilization. The deficit is a negative function of capacity utilization (or business health). It rises as capacity utilization falls, but declines as capacity utilization rises.

$$Government\ Deficit = F\ (capacity\ utilization) \qquad (17A.7)$$

That gives enough indication of what a formal model might look like, but a few more verbal notes may be added. If the government spending and revenue are separated, then two functions are needed. One could say that government revenue is a positive function of capacity utilization, rising as capacity utilization rises, and vice versa. The growth rate of government spending may be seen as a negative function of capacity utilization. As capacity utilization (and economic health of business) increases, the growth rate of government spending falls. As capacity utilization (and the economic health of business) declines in a cyclical contraction, the rate of growth of government spending rises. These functions would reflect the endogenous role of government fiscal behavior in the business cycle.

APPENDIX 17 B
INCOME POLICY: DIRECT CONTROLS OF WAGES AND PRICES

We have noted the concerns of some economists that neither fiscal policy nor monetary policy (nor their combination) can end a situation of unemployment plus inflationary pressures. Therefore, when the combination of unemployment and inflation became an obvious evil in the early 1970s, even the conservative Nixon administration decided to try the drastic solution of enlarged military spending plus an income policy. An income policy meant in this case direct wage and price controls. Because direct controls are a possible addition to monetary and fiscal policy, it is very instructive to examine this episode as a case study (relying on the excellent dissertation by Harris 1978).

On August 15, 1971, President Nixon announced a new economic policy designed to save America, reduce inflation and unemployment, and increase corporate profits. Phase 1 ran for 90 days from August to November 1971. In Phase 1, all wages, prices, and rents were frozen. Profits were not frozen. In actuality, all wage increases were prevented, but some prices continued to creep upward.

Phase 2 lasted from November 1971 until January 1973. The freeze was ended, but there were mandatory controls on wages, prices, and rents, though not on profits. Under this system, inflation continued, though at a reduced rate of about 4 percent per year. Unemployment, according to the official definition, fell from its highest level of about 6 percent in the 1970 recession down to about 5 percent. Wages were successfully kept to a very, very slow increase in this period, but profits rose spectacularly. Phase 3—from January to June 1973—was supposed to phase out the wage and price controls and move back to the private, competitive market. It removed all controls over prices in all industries except food, health, and construction, so it substituted voluntary controls. The voluntary controls were no controls at all because they had no enforcement procedure. Therefore, business paid no attention to them so prices increased rapidly, rising at about 8 percent a year. In the end, even the administration admitted failure in holding down prices. On the other hand, a striking feature of Phase 3 was the pressure kept on the unions to abide by voluntary controls and the extent to which the unions did restrain employees from asking for wage raises. As a result, there was a very slight rise in money wages, but the real earning power of employees declined. Again there were no controls on profits, which continued to increase.

After another brief price freeze, Phase 4 began in August 1973 and ended in April 1974. It was again a mandatory system of controls over prices, wages, and rents, but not over profits. It was very effective in holding down wages, but prices continued to rise at about 10 percent per year. In all of 1973, the actual buying power of employees declined by 4 percent, whereas profits rose rapidly. In the first half of 1974, unemployment rose to 6 percent and a recession began, but the rate of inflation rose to 12 percent.

DO CONTROLS CAUSE INEFFICIENCY AND CORRUPTION?   Economists of most ideological views criticized the controls, but for different reasons. The conservatives, such as Milton Friedman, were horrified at the violation of the First Commandment of laissez-faire economics: Thou shalt not interfere with the market process of setting wages and prices (see Friedman 1971, 45). Conservatives have always argued that resources, including capital and labor, cannot be efficiently allocated if prices are not set by competition in the market. If the government arbitrarily sets prices, how can a business-person calculate most efficiently what to produce or what technology to use? If a business-person does follow the arbitrary prices set by the government, then he or she will not produce what consumers desire and will not produce it in the cheapest possible way. It will not be produced as cheaply as possible because those prices do not correctly reflect the true scarcities of resources. Moreover, it will not be the combination of goods that consumers desire because those prices do not correctly reflect true consumer preferences. Thus, wage-price controls doom a private enterprise economy to inefficiency.

It is strongly argued by most economists that direct controls do not mix well with a private enterprise economy. This policy would mean a combination of bureaucratic planning with private greed in a market economy. The controls might improve the situation over a pure market economy for a short time, in periods such as rapid inflation and unemployment. It is often argued, however, that this is not a stable solution over a long time because of increasing inefficiency as supply and demand conditions change.

DO CONTROLS INCREASE INEQUALITY?   One reason that the combination of controls and private enterprise is said to be unstable is that it means political control of relative incomes. Given the political strength of business interests, political determination of relative incomes will usually tend to increase the inequality of income. For example, it was claimed that during President Nixon's controls, wages were restricted while profits soared. In fact, in his speech announcing the wage-price controls, President Nixon stated: "All Americans will benefit from more profits. Profits fuel the expansion . . . mean more investment . . . and . . . mean . . . more tax revenues. That's why higher profits in the American economy would be good for every person in America" (Nixon 1971). Vice President Agnew argued the same theory in favor of the controls, saying: "Rising corporate profits are needed more than ever by the poor" (Agnew 1971). President Nixon and Vice President Agnew were successful in limiting wages and raising profits.

The mechanism for setting wages was a Pay Board, to which President Nixon appointed an equal number of business representatives, "public" representatives, and union representatives. Eventually, the union representatives from the American Federation of Labor-Congress of Industrial Organizations (AFL-CIO) resigned. They pointed out that the so-called "public" representatives appointed by President Nixon were always more aggressively opposed to wage increases than the business representatives, so labor lost every vote by a 2 to 1 margin. This specific result reflected the particular administration in power, but it has been claimed that the general tendency would be the same in any private enterprise country.

APPENDIX 17C
ECONOMIC POLICY SINCE 1980

Consider the economic situation when Ronald Reagan was elected President in 1980. The nation was suffering through stagflation, or a period of high unemployment coupled with high inflation. Many people believed that Reagan's election was a mandate for new economic policies that would reduce the government's impact on the economy.

The cornerstone of Reagan's economic plan was developed by Arthur Laffer of the University of Southern California. Laffer argued that the relationship between tax rates and government revenues could be depicted as in Figure 17.1a. There is a point, shown as *t*, where government revenues are maximized by a particular average tax rate. If the average tax rate is greater than t, people will choose not to earn additional income, choosing instead to take additional potential earnings in the form of leisure or other non-monetary renumeration. If the average tax rate is less than t, the government is not maximizing its potential tax revenues.

In agreement with Laffer, Reagan argued that the tax structure was hindering economic growth and the large government infrastructure was riddled

FIGURE 17.1A
THE LAFFER CURVE

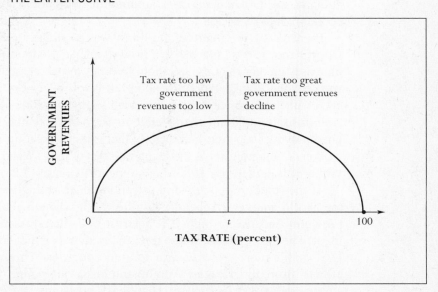

with waste and inefficiencies. His presidential campaign was based upon reducing the tax burden, curbing government spending, and reducing regulation of the private sector. Reagan argued that these proposals would unleash the private sector for a return to the prosperity of the 1950s and 1960s.

The Laffer curve was not universally accepted, and it would take the Administration until 1981 to persuade Congress to pass a tax reduction package. In the meantime, the Administration used monetary policy to begin the attack on inflation.

EARLY MONETARY POLICY

The Federal Reserve, under Chairman Paul Volcker, had been criticized for allowing real interest rates to go negative during the Carter Administration. There was some argument that the relative impotence of monetary policy in the late 1970s had helped, or at least had not slowed, the growth of inflation. Under Reagan, however, the Fed was not constrained and could mount a full-scale attack on inflationary pressures in the economy.

The Fed responded to the lessening of political constraints upon it by beginning to increase interest rates in early 1980. Over the next 18 months, interest rates on 3-month treasury bills increased from less than 8 percent to over 16 percent. The immediate response by the economy was the 1981–82 recession. Interest rate hikes caused an immediate reduction in demand for the housing and automobile industries, leading the overall economy into recession.

The goal of the interest rate hikes was to break the wage-price spiral. During the 1960s and 1970s, it was alleged that unions gained wage increases greater than the inflation. In order to reduce the wage demands by workers, the Reagan Administration felt it was necessary to create high levels of unemployment for an extended period of time. While the Reagan Administration did not characterize its actions as creating a reserve army of unemployed, its action had exactly that effect—creating a large number of workers competing for a shrinking number of jobs. Wage growth came to a virtual halt in the early 1980s (see Appendix Figure 17.2a).

At the same time, the Administration began strengthening the dollar on the world market (Appendix Figure 17.3a) which already had upward pressures because of high U.S. interest rates that attracted foreign investment. The strong dollar made foreign goods less expensive in the U.S. and U.S. goods more expensive in foreign countries. This had two desirable effects from the Reagan Administration's viewpoint. The effect of the strong dollar was to reduce inflationary pressures in the U.S. by making foreign goods less expensive. Also, the less expensive foreign goods

FIGURE 17.2A
UNEMPLOYMENT RATE

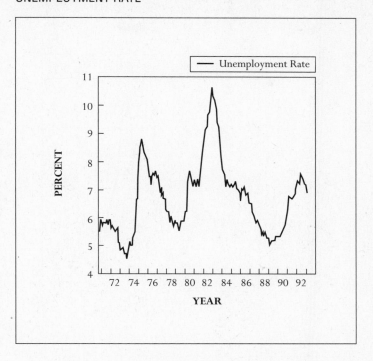

increased competitive pressures on U.S. firms, holding both wage and price increases down.

The strong dollar had a negative effect on the U.S. economy. U.S. manufacturing firms found it increasingly difficult to compete on the world markets. As a result, there was an increasing trend to relocate manufacturing companies from the U.S. to overseas sites, further reducing domestic employment.

The results of the Fed's actions in the early 1980s, in addition to the increasing value of the dollar, essentially broke the inflationary spiral of the late 1970s. The Fed received much of the credit for its aggressive anti-inflationary policies, although its actions required strong political support from the Reagan Administration (because of its depressing economic effects).

However, beginning in the mid-1980s, interest rates began a long, gradual downward decline, lasting until 1993. The decline in interest rates was the result of both a weak world economy and decreasing inflationary pressures in the overall economy (Appendix Figure 17.4a). Most importantly though, the decline of world oil prices that had partially been responsible

FIGURE 17.3A
TRADE WEIGHTED VALUE OF THE DOLLAR

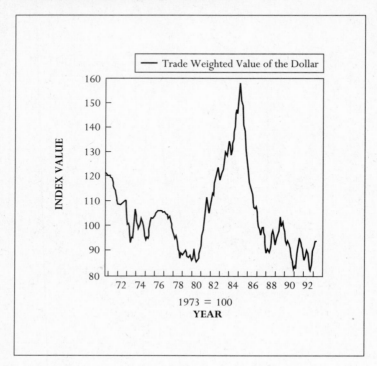

1973 = 100
YEAR

for the inflationary pressures in the economy were now offset by a collapse in world oil prices that began exerting strong downward price pressure.

FISCAL POLICY

As a presidential candidate, Reagan rallied against the Federal deficit. Reagan argued that the increasing federal deficit was crowding out private investment and only a reduction in the Federal deficit would allow interest rates to fall enough to encourage private investment.

In taking this position, Reagan was implicitly rejecting Keynesian economic theories in favor of a return to the supply-side theorists. Reagan and his economic advisors argued that Keynesian economics had an inflationary bias and resulted in income redistribution at the expense of long-term economic growth.

However, reducing the government deficit is more difficult than having everyone agree that it should be done. While the common, and mistaken, belief is that the poor benefit more from the various government entitlement

FIGURE 17.4A
90-DAY T-BILL RATE

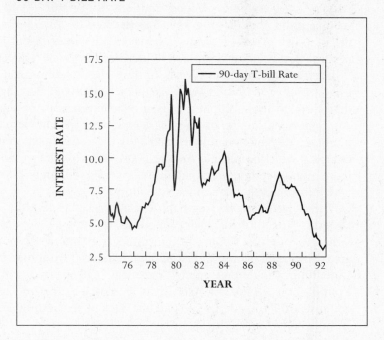

programs, it is the upper and middle classes that receive the vast majority of government benefits. Any attempt to reduce their benefits, or the benefits of various agricultural programs, or other programs designed to benefit retirees, immediately results in a political reaction.

Reagan had two stated goals in his fiscal policy. First, increase defense expenditures to offset the perceived growing Soviet military advantage and, secondly, reduce the overall deficit. In order to gain the necessary political support to accomplish these two goals that would result in the reduction of other Federal programs, Reagan invoked the promise of the Laffer curve. By reducing taxes to high income households, private investment would soar and the economy would grow. The fast growing private sector would generate additional government tax revenues. The Administration could then fund increased defense expenditures while maintaining, or expanding, social programs. At the same time, the government deficit would fall, reducing the long-term interest rate, further encouraging private investment.

Reagan was successful in selling the necessity of a tax cut in 1981. The results, however, were not exactly what had been promised to the American people. The government deficit soared, increasing to over $200 billion annually. Since 1982, the high government deficit has been used as the reason for attempting to reduce entitlement programs and other forms of income redistribution programs. Yet, because of congressional deadlock and the inability of either political party to pass meaningful budget reduction proposals, the deficit continued to increase for the next decade.

In effect, the remaining years of the Reagan Administration (1982–1988) saw strong economic growth, partially because of the huge budget deficit that, through the multiplier, caused a strong increase in aggregate demand. As important, much of the increase in aggregate demand was due to increased demand for military goods by the government that did not directly compete with the private sector. Thus, some of the inflationary effects of increased government expenditures were contained by the decision of where to stimulate the national economy.

There were strong regional effects based upon the composition of Federal expenditures. The economies of regions with a strong defense industry, such as Southern California, the industrial northeast, and the areas around St. Louis and Atlanta all benefited from increased government expenditures in defense related industries. Other regions of the country, for example, the Oklahoma and Texas economies, suffered as a result of the collapse of the price of oil and the lack of offsetting Federal economic stimulus programs.

In addition to the stimulating effect of the Federal budget, the Administration encouraged wage restraint on the part of corporations, including union busting (begun by the Administration itself in response to the decision of air traffic controllers to strike and the Administration's unwillingness to become involved in some major job actions such as the Greyhound strike).

SUMMARY OF THE REAGAN YEARS

By 1986, the economy had reached low levels of inflation, characterized by high levels of unemployment and small wage growth. The distribution of income was reversing, with the poor becoming poorer and the wealthy becoming wealthier. Any attempt on the part of wage earnings to strike or increase earnings was countered by corporations with plant closures or the hiring of replacement workers at low wages.

Also, technological changes in the marketplace, primarily the rapid advancement in computer technology, has reduced the ability of low-skilled workers to exert any significant pressure on corporations for wage increases. The large number of unemployed guaranteed someone would be willing to work at the same wage, or even lower, in many cases. Unions have been increasingly willing to attempt to bargain for job security rather than increased wages and benefits, or even to buy job security for a portion of the workers through reductions in wages and benefits.

Thus, the Reagan years can be summarized as a period of growth in GDP but a decline in the wealth of many Americans. Large corporations, through buy-outs and takeovers, continued to expand their importance in the economy. Economists at the University of Chicago began developing a defense of large corporations, arguing that economic efficiency led to a few large producers in many markets rather than the exercise of monopoly power.

The Reagan years were characterized by a large increase in economic growth. However, the benefits of this growth were concentrated among fewer people than at any time since the period 1890–1910. Thus, if controlling inflation is the only measure of the success of an administration, the Reagan Administration should be commended for a good job of managing the economy between 1980 and 1988.

THE BUSH ADMINISTRATION

Many problems that the Reagan Administration had managed to postpone came to light during the Bush Administration. This, including the negative effects on the economy of the collapse of the savings and loan industry, calls for effective means of controlling the growth of inequality and the negative effects of the disintegration of the Soviet Union.

Inflation remained low during the Bush Administration, primarily due to the weak world economy which caused commodity prices to stay weak. Economic growth was somewhat lackluster as defense expenditures declined, reversing the regional stimuli of the Reagan Administration.

Also, a fear of many economists was realized in 1990, when the economy entered the first economic slowdown since 1981. Many households and businesses had responded to slow income growth in the mid-1980s by adding to debt. As long as the economy was growing, households were able to make payments on their debt. However, as soon as the economy stopped growing, many households began defaulting on their debt, putting increasing pressure on corporate profits which were also being strained by the slowdown in the economy.

Thus, what had begun as a slowdown in the economy slowly turned into a fairly significant recession. Many of the regional economies, such as that in Southern California, had regional recessions that were the worst since the Great Depression.

The effects of the economic slowdown were exacerbated by the continuing slow world economy and by the recession in Japan. Germany, preoccupied with the reunification of East and West Germany into a single nation, was concerned with inflationary pressures in its economy and refused to attempt to stimulate the European economy.

The Fed responded to the slowdown in economic activity by attempting to stimulate the economy through cuts in the discount rate, driving interest rates down to under 4 percent.

However, even though the cost of money was low, capacity utilization remained low and aggregate demand was low. Firms would not invest in the face of over capacity in the economy. Instead, firms were interested in reducing labor costs. Consumer confidence remained low and layoffs continued to increase.

Even though the NBER declared the recession over in early 1991, many consumers were unwilling to believe that the recession was over. President Bush's continued claims that the recession was over were not received with any belief by people on Main Street.

The Bush Administration was also constrained in its ability to attempt to use fiscal policy to stimulate the economy as a result of the large budget deficits left from the Reagan Administration. Hence, without an increase in aggregate demand, monetary policy by itself was unable to stimulate the economy, while fiscal policy was unavailable to the Administration. Essentially, the Administration was in the position of waiting for consumer demand to increase to pull the economy out of the recession with enough strength that firms would begin to invest, thereby completing the upturn.

There was one other interesting, but unfortunate, aspect of the recovery during the Bush years. The recovery was accomplished without any corresponding increase in employment. Partially as a result of the end of the cold war and a worldwide trend towards free trade, firms were interested in cutting labor costs. The recession had shown firms that the results of a decade of investment in office equipment (fax machines, personal computers, etc.) had increased productivity enough that many of the jobs eliminated during the recession were simply not replaced, even with the economy growing. Also, the emergence of a large temporary work force that allowed firms to hire employees on a part-time basis without paying benefits, gave firms the flexibility to delay hiring full-time employees.

THE CLINTON ADMINISTRATION

The Clinton Administration entered office with several major goals. These included balancing the Federal budget, restoring economic growth, including employment growth, and keeping inflationary pressures low. The Administration seized upon development and commercialization of high technology, particularly the information superhighway, as a cornerstone of long-term economic growth.

Even though the Clinton administration has been in office now for two years, it is difficult to judge the success of its economic policy. In many ways, it appears that the Administration was fortunate in that the economy was recovering as Clinton took office, giving Clinton a political boost while lowering the deficit. However, partisan bickering over the type of economic policies that the Administration could embrace, including a return to government fiscal stimulus versus a Republican continuance of the Reagan doctrine of government inactivity, has stopped or slowed the development of some of the Administration's economic policies.

Many of the difficulties faced by the Administration have centered around two issues—health care reform and deficit reduction. In the area of health care reform, the Administration was stopped by the Republicans and it appears that the issue has faded from the political agenda. In the area of deficit reduction, the Administration has been successful in cutting the Federal deficit from $282.7 billion in 1992 to $241 billion in 1993 to an estimated $165 to 190 billion in 1994. Both friends and foes of the Administration point out that much of the reduction has been due to the high growth rate of the economy, which grew over 3.2 percent, in real terms, in 1993 and 1994.

However, as pointed out in Chapter 17, many lawmakers believe that defense expenditures have been cut too deeply while the poor believe that various social programs have been too deeply slashed.

REPUBLICAN SPENDING CUTS AND UNEMPLOYMENT

The Republican majority in Congress in 1995, led by House Speaker Newt Gringrich and Senate Majority Leader Robert Dole, have proposed spending cuts of approximately $150 billion annually during each of the next seven years, in an attempt to balance the Federal budget. If government revenues remained constant, the proposed spending cuts would mean a balanced budget by the year 2002.

However, critics could argue that massive spending cuts would mean a reduction in aggregate demand. A reduction of $150 billion in Federal government demand, with a multiplier of two, would mean a $300 billion annual reduction in aggregate demand over each of the next seven years, with a corresponding loss of government tax revenues. In addition, the resulting lower aggregate demand would lead to lower levels of employment, followed by increased demand and spending on government social services. The end result of the Republican budget proposals could be no more than reduced employment, reduced levels of government services, government services, and the same deficit.

One may ask whether a better response to the government deficit would be increasing employment, so that tax revenues increase and demands for social services decrease.

Forecasting

Part Five presents some of the forecasting methods used to predict the behavior of the business cycle. The various forecasting models, both quantitative and qualitative, are presented. Then, additional detail is added to the various modeling techniques.

Indicator forecasting is presented. Indicator forecasting looks systematically at what economic series turn ahead of, and with, the business cycle.

Next, time series models are presented. Time series models are based upon identifying the past behavior of a variable and using the past behavior to forecast the behavior of the series in the future.

Next, econometric models are discussed. Econometric models identify the relationships between variables and use this identified relationship to forecast.

Finally, a series of examples of the different types of forecasting models are presented.

CHAPTER 18

How to Prepare a Forecast

The value of accurate and timely information on the future direction of the economy is enormous. Should the business person begin expanding production to meet a future increase in demand? Is now the best time to refinance debt, before interest rates begin to rise? Should policymakers adopt an economic stimulus package or is the economy rebounding from a recession without need for additional government intervention? Forecasting is the practice of predicting the future. Forecasts are the predictions.

People have always attempted to forecast the future. The Oracle of Delphi provided answers for the Greek kings and Roman emperors. Aztecs sacrificed captives to various gods to divine the outcome of battles. Most ancient civilizations have had some method, shielded in mysticism, for predicting the future. In more modern times, large computer models of the economy have replaced soothseers as the source of knowledge of the future, sometimes successfully. Throughout history, knowledge of the future has been a way to power, wealth and wise policy judgments for society.

Only in the last forty or fifty years has forecasting developed into a systematic study of the possibilities that lie in the future. A major difference in today's forecasts from those done hundreds of years ago is the degree of statistical analysis included in the forecasting methodology. In the last three decades the computer has facilitated analysis of large amounts of data. A smaller difference lies in the scope of the forecast. Early forecasts tended to be long-term, describing how society would change as new social orders and technologies were adopted. Today, forecasts deal with every aspect of business and society, from next quarters' sales of the smallest firm to long-term changes in the structure of the economy and society. Now, almost every large business or government agency performs some type of formalized forecasting.

The foundations of modern forecasting were laid by William Stanley Jevons in 1865. In *The Coal Question*, Jevons argued that manufacturing had replaced agriculture as the dominant sector in English society. Jevons' work included studies of economic fluctuations and extrapolations of the ultimate limiting factor of coal production on economic development.

Studies of the business cycle had been on-going since the mid-1850s. Although stylized forecasting methods continued to be developed for the next sixty years, it was not until the 1930s that economic forecasting became widely accepted in the United States. Acceptance of forecasting methods was based not so much on the improved skills of forecasters, but upon necessity. In the 1920s forecasting services had begun preparing forecasts that were used primarily for stock market speculation. The Great Depression created yet another impetus for methods that would identify business cycle fluctuations. The transition from an agrarian society to an industrialized society meant that business fluctuations created crisis, not only in business but in the lives of workers due to changes in employment levels.

The advent of Keynesian economics provided a further impetus for development of accurate forecasting methods. Government adoption of Keynesian economic policies meant government had to stimulate demand when it was deficient and restrain it when it was excessive (Blackaby 1979). To perform this type of market intervention requires some idea of where the economy is headed.

Today, forecasting has evolved into a major industry. From stock market forecasters to economic forecasters to psychics, thousands of people are involved in predicting some aspect of the future. The reasons for the forecast are always the same—identify what is likely to happen in the future so as to be able to take the greatest advantage of it.

USE AND MISUSE OF FORECASTS

In spite of the enormous sums of money paid to them, economists have a poor record forecasting changes in the business cycle.

Incorrect forecasts can occur for numerous reasons. Among these reasons is a tendency of forecasters to be momentum followers. A momentum follower assumes that whatever happened over the past several months will continue over the next few months. Forecasters are concerned about the validity of their forecasts when they differ significantly from other forecasters' results. It is not uncommon for forecasters to look to other forecasters for verification of their results. This concern tends to drive forecasts towards each other, preventing forecasters from identifying significant shifts in the business cycle. If everyone else using the same data forecasts the economy will continue growing, why should you forecast that the economy is going to change directions and begin contracting?

Another source of error in forecasts is in the data itself. The U.S. has a long tradition of accurately gathering timely information on the performance of the economy. In the last decade, however, gathering this data has been slowed, or in some cases discontinued, as a result of the budget deficits and efforts to curb government spending. As such, while good faith efforts are still made to collect and publish economic data, sometimes the data is subject to large revisions that impact forecasts made using the original data.

When evaluating a forecast, one needs to consider the methodology used, the data requirements, and the variable being forecast. Careful attention should be given to the needs of the ultimate user of the forecast and to sound principles of model building. At the same time, it is necessary to be realistic about modeling limitations and constraints.

One of the primary considerations of forecasting is accuracy. A forecast has no value if we cannot be sure that it has a reasonable chance of being correct. A standard of reasonableness needs to be identified at the outset of the forecasting process that is consistent with real world constraints. Accuracy can be improved by choosing an appropriate forecasting technique at the beginning of the forecast process.

Another consideration is cost. While forecasts are intended to save money in the long run, much of the savings could be lost if the development, operation, and maintenance of the forecasting models are high. This often implies keeping data requirements simple.

Because of the complexities involved in developing a forecast, many forecasters use simple models and compare their results with results from other models.

People sometimes misuse forecasts, primarily because of a lack of knowledge of what a forecast is really saying. A forecast is always a range around some value. For example, suppose you read that the government forecasts GDP to grow by 2.2 percent next year. This does not mean that if the economy grows at 2.3 or 1.8 percent the forecast is wrong. Instead, the 2.2 percent forecast value represents the midrange of the forecast. It suggests growth will be in a range about 2.2 percent.

For some applications, the general magnitude of the change in the forecast variable is sufficient to provide meaningful results. For other applications, a small variation from the point forecast can have a large impact on government decisions and businesses. For example, suppose demand for a product is forecasted to grow at a 6 percent annual rate for the next twelve years. This means that in about twelve years demand would double. But if demand only grew at 4 percent annually for the first three years, any business plans made using this forecast would have resulted in over 7 percent excess capacity. Table 18.1 shows how even a small variation in actual to forecasted values causes a large effect over a long time period.

TABLE 18.1
EXAMPLE OF A FORECAST ERROR COMPOUNDED OVER TIME

Year	Forecasted Sales	Actual Sales	Excess Capacity
1	100.0		
2	106.0	104.0	2.0
3	112.4	108.2	2.2
4	119.1	112.5	6.6
5	126.2	117.0	9.2
6	133.8	121.7	12.1
7	141.8	126.6	15.2

Let us take an example of how a forecast can be used incorrectly, especially when construction of production facilities takes many years. In the electric utility industry, demand had grown by six percent annually during the 1950s and 1960s. Forecasters assumed that demand would continue to grow at the same rate into the 1970s and began construction of generating stations to meet this demand. When demand slowed to 2 percent in the early 1970s, the question was not if the forecasts were wrong for some reason, but when would demand return to its forecasted levels of growth. By the early 1980s, the electric utility industry had over 35 percent excess generation capability, with some utilities having 50 to 60 percent excess generation capability.

This example does not imply that forecasting is not a useful tool or a worthwhile exercise. Instead it shows that forecasting is essential in the decision making process, but a tool that needs to be used carefully, examining alternative forecasts and using common sense. With this guideline in mind, both the forecaster and the decision maker can avoid the pitfalls and misuse of forecasts.

To protect themselves against the impacts of actual results not meeting forecasted results, many businesses use several different forecasting techniques and different assumption sets. A popular application of this type of analysis is called scenario forecasting, where different assumption sets representing ranges of assumptions are used. For example, forecasts employing optimistic, pessimistic, and neutral views of the economy identify what risks (and rewards) the businessperson might face if the future economy was stronger, or weaker, than previously thought.

Scenario forecasting allows the full value of forecasting to be realized. Good use of forecasts is not so much based on the belief that the forecasted value of a variable will actually be realized but on the need to identify likely alternative risks to a business, Federal, state or local agency, or the overall economy. Scenario forecasting identifies what should be guarded against before financial damage occurs.

TYPES OF FORECASTING MODELS

Forecasting methods used can be as simple as a consensus of experts in the field, based strictly upon good judgment, intuition, and awareness of the state of the economy (the Delphi method). More complex forecasts may be the result of complicated statistical models using hundreds of equations that determine the relationship between many variables.

TIME SERIES MODELS

Suppose you had been asked to provide a forecast of the economy for the next year, including estimates of personal income and consumption. You would begin by examining the behavior of the economy for the past several years to determine if there is any trend or seasonal patterns that might affect your forecast. This historical data is called a *time series*. A time series is a set of observations measured at successive periods of time. Most macroeconomic time series use either quarterly or monthly data.

A specific observation in a time series is identified by the series name and date. For example, $GDP_{1992.4}$ refers to the fourth quarter gross domestic product (GDP) for 1992. In a general model, t identifies the current time period, while prior periods are referred to by subtracting the number of periods, n. That is, X_t is the time series X at time t, while X_{t-3} refers to the observation 3 periods ago.

Different groups within the government prepare and release economic time series data. The Bureau of Economic Analysis (BEA), of the Department of Commerce, publishes the *Survey of Current Business*. The *Survey of Current Business* is one of the primary sources of data for economists and includes quarterly data on national income and product accounts, as well as current business statistics on a monthly basis. Data on financial institutions and monetary policy is collected by the Federal Reserve and published in the *Federal Reserve Bulletin*. Other sources of time series data includes the Bureau of the Census, Department of Agriculture, Department of Energy, and various other Federal agencies. A good summary of the various data sources is *Business Statistics*, published by the Department of Commerce annually. The BEA also publishes a *User's Guide to BEA Information, Publications, Computer Tapes, Diskettes and Other Information Services* in the *Survey of Current Business* that provides large amounts of free information. Several computerized information services also make databases, such as "Citibase," electronically published by Citibank, available for subscription that includes economic time series data.

In contrast to time series data is *cross-section* data. Cross-section data captures the relationship between variables at a single point in time. For example, suppose you were attempting to determine what variables influence

FIGURE 18.1
RELATIONSHIP BETWEEN DIFFERENT FORECASTING MODELS

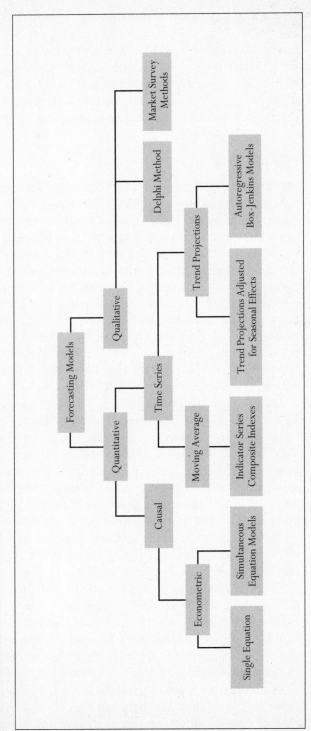

the price of homes. You would want to gather data on home prices and other statistics such as square feet, number of rooms and lot sizes. In addition, you would consider locational characteristics of each home, such as distance from shopping centers, employment centers, recreational areas, etc. You would then estimate home prices based upon these different characteristics. This type of analysis would allow you to determine why the same home sells for different amounts at different locations and which characteristics of a home add the most value. Box 18.1 presents a summary of some of the different forecasting methods. The less complex methods are introduced in the remainder of Part 5.

QUALITATIVE VERSUS QUANTITATIVE MODELS

Forecasting methods are either qualitative or quantitative. Figure 18.1 shows the relationship between many of the modeling methods described in this chapter. Qualitative models use the judgment of experts in the field in situations where no historic data is available or political or other events that cannot be forecast have a large impact on the variable.

QUALITATIVE FORECASTING MODELS

Qualitative methods tend to provide reasonably good forecasts in the short term because of the familiarity of experts with ongoing changes in their field. The qualitative methods work best when the forecasting scope is limited. The primary problem with qualitative methods is identifying experts in the appropriate fields and then getting them to agree on a common forecast.

Examples of qualitative methods include the Delphi method and market research methods. The Delphi method involves asking various experts what they anticipate in the future, without attempting to attach high degrees of precision to the forecast results. The California Energy Commission uses the Delphi method for forecasting crude oil prices. This method is used because of the influence Mideastern political actions have on oil prices, often overshadowing typical supply and demand considerations.

Market research methods involve surveys and questionnaires of people's subjective reactions to new products. Researchers interview people after they try a product in an attempt to identify the product's characteristics that make it desirable, or how it could be improved. A major difficulty with market research models is identifying an appropriate sample group that is representative of the tastes of the nation or region where the good is marketed.

QUANTITATIVE FORECASTING MODELS

Quantitative models are based upon an analysis of historical data, attempting to find relationships or trends that can be used for forecasting. Quantitative

BOX 18.1

SUMMARY OF SOME DIFFERENT FORECASTING METHODS

BRIEF DESCRIPTION OF METHODS

JUDGEMENT METHODS	COUNTING METHODS	TIME SERIES METHODS	ASSOCIATION OR CAUSAL METHODS
NAIVE EXTRAPOLATION: the application of a simple assumption about the economic outcome of the next time period, or a simple, if subjective, extension of the results of current events.	**MARKET TESTING:** representative buyers responses to new offerings, tested and extrapolated to estimate the products' future prospects.	**MOVING AVERAGES:** recent values of the forecast variables averaged to predict future outcomes.	**CORRELATION METHODS:** predictions of values based on historic patterns of covariation between variables.
SALES-FORCE COMPOSITE: a compilation of estimates by salespeople (or dealers) of expected sales in the territories, adjusted for presumed biases and expected changes.	**CONSUMER MARKET SURVEY:** attitudinal and purchase intentions data gathered from representative buyers.	**EXPONENTIAL SMOOTHING:** an estimate for the coming period based on a constantly weighted combination of the forecast estimate for the previous periods and the most recent outcome.	**REGRESSION MODELS:** estimates produced from a predictive equation derived by minimizing the residual variance of one or more predictor (independent) variable.
JURY OF EXECUTIVE OPINION: the consensus of a group of "experts," often from a variety of functional areas within a company.	**INDUSTRIAL MARKET SURVEY:** data similar to consumer surveys but fewer, more knowledgeable subjects sampled, resulting in more informed evaluations.	**ADAPTIVE FILTERING:** a derivation of a weighted combination of actual and estimated outcomes, systematically altered to reflect data pattern changes.	**LEADING INDICATORS:** forecasts generated from one or more preceding variable that is systematically related to the variable to be predicted.
SCENARIO METHODS: smoothly unfolding narratives that describe an assumed future expresses through a sequence of time frames or snapshots.		**TIME SERIES EXTRAPOLATION:** a prediction of outcomes derived from the future extension of a leastsquares function fitted to a data series that uses time as an independent variable.	

BOX 18.1 — CONTINUED

BRIEF DESCRIPTION OF METHODS

JUDGEMENT METHODS	COUNTING METHODS	TIME SERIES METHODS	ASSOCIATION OR CAUSAL METHODS
DELPHI TECHNIQUE: a successive series of estimates independently developed by a group of "experts" each member of which, at each step in the process, uses a summary of the group's previous results to reformulate new estimates.		**TIME SERIES DECOMPOSITION:** a prediction of expected outcomes from trend, seasonal, cyclical and random components, which are isolated from a data series.	**ECONOMETRIC MODELS:** outcomes forecast from an integrated system of simultaneous equations that represent relationships among elements of the national economy derived from combining history and economic theory.
HISTORICAL ANALOGY: predictions based on elements of past events that are analogous to the present situation.		**BOX–JENKINS:** a complex, computer-based iterative procedure that produces an autoregressive, integrated moving average model, adjusts for seasonal and trend factors, estimates appropriate weighting parameters, tests the model, and repeats the cycle as appropriate.	**INPUT–OUTPUT MODELS:** a matrix model showing how demand changes in one industry can directly affect aggregate national or regional economic activity.

SOURCE: David Georgoff and Robert Murdock, "Manager's Guide to Forecasting," *Harvard Business Review*, January–February 1986, 110.

models are separated into two basic types, time series and causal models. Time series models attempt to identify patterns or trends in the data. These identified patterns are then used to predict the future, under the assumption that past trends will continue.

Causal models attempt to estimate the mathematical relationship between a dependent variable and one or more independent variables. An independent variable is one whose behavior is determined outside the model, while the behavior of the dependent variable depends upon, or is a function of, the independent variable. For example, consumption expenditures are dependent upon total income (among other things). Consumption expenditures would be the dependent variable and total income would be the independent variable.

Causal models begin with a theory about the behavior and types of variables that affect the dependent variable. A forecasting model that is consistent with the theory is then built. Causal models assume that the relationship between the independent and dependent variables remains unchanged, but allows for changing the importance of the various independent variables.

Causal models may be preferred over time series models because they are based upon some underlying theoretical foundation. This structure allows for investigation of changes in the independent variables. For example, how will lowered personal tax rates affect consumption and GDP? Or on a smaller scale, the effect of changes in price on sales of an individual product can be studied.

The choice of which type of model to use is difficult. Time series models are relatively inexpensive to construct, but assume that past trends will continue into the future. This makes them unacceptable for identifying the effects of other variables on the independent variable, such as determining the effect of a tax cut on GDP. Causal models are more acceptable for this type of study but are difficult and more expensive to construct. Causal models also make the assumption that the identified relationships that have existed between variables will continue into the future.

Choosing the appropriate modeling approach depends primarily on the use of the forecast. For simple, short-term forecasts, a qualitative model may be appropriate. For longer term forecasts under relatively stable conditions, a time series model may be best. Other types of applications, for example identifying the effects of changes in price on demand, require a causal model. It is important to recognize that there is no one best forecasting method. The final choice of a model will be made on the basis of cost, data sources, accuracy requirements, and expected use of the forecast.

ISSUES IN DEVELOPING A FORECAST

Forecasting is not an exact science. Forecasters bring their own biases and beliefs about how the economy works to the modeling forum. Some forecasters attempt to use simple, easily understandable models while others develop complicated models that account for the influence of many different variables. Regardless of what methodology is adopted, or what beliefs or assumptions about the forecast subject are held, the ultimate test of the forecast is in the final result. The forecasters work is measured by how accurately the forecast actually predicts what will happen to the economy as well as how consistent the forecast is with economic theory.

Consistency with theory is important in understanding how a model accounts for the results. Suppose you were asked to develop a forecast of the demand for new homes. Regardless of how accurate the forecast turns out to be, if the model predicts a positive relationship or correlation between home prices and sales (that is, as prices rise, demand rises) the forecast will not be accepted. People's intuition gives rise to questions about the underlying theoretical model. Some acceptable reason for the positive relationship between price and demand must be identified for a result that conflicts with generally accepted theory.

How the assumption set is formulated is another key area of developing forecasts. Many forecasters use the same primary data set, such as "Citibase," a computer data set of various government data sets, and they use the same general types of modeling techniques. Their models have had to show that they replicate the past behavior of the economic time series accurately. Moreover, they must show that their forecasts were developed within the constraints of good economic theory. Based on all these factors, even forecasters who approach a forecast with totally different beliefs about the importance of various factors, such as those between monetarists and Keynesians, will develop similar forecasts if they are constrained by the same assumption set.

Much of the difference in forecasts prepared by different groups is due to differences in future assumed values of key variables. For example, in the late 1970s and early 1980s, forecasters were attempting to develop long-term forecasts of oil prices. These forecasts were used by shale oil developers, solar energy companies, conservation groups, coal and natural gas firms, as well as other sectors of the economy to determine how to respond to the rapid rise in oil prices in the 1970s. These price increases were a major concern to the economy and would help determine how much of the nation's investments would be channeled into alternative energy development over the next decade. Forecasts of oil prices, which ranged from $35–120 per barrel by the early 1990s, were partially due to different beliefs about the long-term political stability of the Organization of Petroleum Exporting Countries (OPEC) and its ability to manipulate supply in the future.

Traditional economic theory suggests that a cartel has a tendency to collapse because of the economic incentive for members to cheat by lowering prices in an attempt to gain market share. Some forecasters believed that OPEC's ability to manipulate supply was limited in the long-term and that eventually prices would be determined by supply and demand considerations. Other forecasters believed that the oil market was different than other industries because of the split between the large oil companies which purchased, refined, and marketed petroleum, and the supplying countries that produced the crude oil. OPEC attempted to use the oil companies as a way of discouraging cheaters by threatening to cut off crude supplies to companies that helped an OPEC country lower prices or exceed its production quota. In effect, OPEC was using the oil companies to enforce its own production and price decisions (Adelman 1976).

Forecasters who accepted the market strength of OPEC eventually produced results showing ever higher prices, justifying enormous investments in nuclear, coal, and conservation technologies to offset the nation's dependence on foreign crude supplies. Forecasters who believed that OPEC would eventually self-destruct, as most cartels historically had, eventually produced forecasts with lower energy prices. As is often the case, the actual events were a compromise. OPEC members did cheat and prices did not rise as much as the worst case scenarios suggested. However, OPEC has been able to maintain some control of production, even though this control varies according to other, political, factors in the Mideast. Still, prices are not as low as they might be in the absence of OPEC. All forecasters, however, had to make some assumption of how OPEC's market influence would affect the oil market in the long-term. The differences between forecasters about this key factor in the oil markets were reflected in the forecasts.

Currently, forecasters are attempting to determine how the nation will rebound from the last recession. In the Pacific coast states of California, Oregon and Washington, which have a large amount of aerospace and defense related industries, federal legislative decisions on how fast to downsize the military will have a large impact on regional economic growth. But, it is not possible to quantitatively forecast what Congress and the Administration will ultimately decide. Instead, forecasters are limited to preparing scenario forecasts bracketing the effects of various ranges of changes in defense expenditures, based upon potential actions in Washington. The forecasters who guess best at what Federal policy makers ultimately decide will have the best forecasts.

PREPARING A FORECAST—THE INITIAL STAGES

The steps in preparing a forecast that are presented in this chapter are, in some cases, optional. Each forecaster works in his or her own way. Some of these recommended steps will be discarded or combined with other steps in the forecast process as the student gains more familiarity with what is required in preparing a forecast.

When beginning the forecast process, there are several basic steps that must be performed. These include:

1. Identification of the problem. What is going to be forecasted and what time period is of concern;

2. Theoretical considerations. What work has been performed on forecasts of the same variable(s) in the past and how relevant is this work to your problem. What does economic theory say about the variables that might influence your forecast;

3. Data concerns. How easy will it be to acquire the necessary data to prepare a forecast;

4. Determining the assumption set. What assumptions will you, as the forecaster, be required to make;

5. Modeling methodology. What type of models are most appropriate for your problem;

6. Preparing the forecast. The actual data analysis necessary to prepare the forecast;

7. Forecast verification. How will you determine if your forecasts are reasonable. How will you check your forecast against the actual behavior of the data.

There are other substages to each of these areas of major concern to the forecaster, but the seven items above address the primary areas that forecasters should identify before beginning the forecast procedure.

1. IDENTIFYING THE PROBLEM.   Suppose you were asked to develop a forecast of some variable. The first question that should come to mind is how long a time frame will the forecast cover. For some industries, such as the electric, natural gas, and water utility industries, forecasts can cover decades, reflecting the difficulties in building new infrastructure. For other industries, such as the computer, telecommunications, and other high technology sectors of the economy, a two year time period may be stretching the limits of acceptability, because of the pace of change.

Forecasts are generally broken into four arbitrary classifications—immediate term, short term, intermediate term, and long term. Immediate term forecasts are one to two month forecasts. Short term forecasts are two months to six months. Intermediate term forecasts are six months to two years and long term forecasts are generally greater than two years.

The forecast duration may have an impact on the type of model that is ultimately chosen. For immediate and short term forecasts, time series models generally perform best, especially if seasonality factors are involved. Long term forecasts of the economy that use input-output models and regression models generally perform best. But these types of models are often not appropriate for some types of questions pertaining to an individual firm. For example, you may be able to show that long term demand for a sector will grow, but you cannot always show how demand for a firm's product within the sector will behave.

Generally, short and intermediate term forecasts do not have any particular modeling technique associated with them. For short-term forecasts with seasonality factors, however, time series models often perform best. The forecasting model needs to be chosen to match the characteristics of the data. In many instances, it may be preferable to prepare forecasts using more than one type of model to provide a check on the final forecast.

Long-term forecasts tend to be dominated by political and technological developments that are difficult to foresee. How many forecasters in the late 1970s who were preparing forecasts for the 1990s would have identified the effects of the personal computer on the computer industry or the video cassette recorder on the entertainment industry? Forecasting the rate of technological change is a factor that can often be ignored in intermediate and short term forecasts but may dominate the forecast in the long term (Mansfield 1968).

2. THEORETICAL CONSIDERATIONS. No forecast is performed without some idea of what variables are important or how the variable will behave over time. A basic recognition of the underlying theoretical model that will be used both limits the potential forecast outcome and determines the model construction. Theoretical consistency also serves to verify the model results by showing conformance with expectations with theory about what does influence the dependent variable.

Performing a literature search to see how other forecasters have prepared forecasts of the same variable is also useful in speeding up and improving the forecast process. While the statistical models in most cases will not be identical, observing how others have approached the forecast process will identify unique problems and identify what sources of data exist.

Economic theory provides a starting point for model construction. Causal models require that a set of independent variables be chosen to explain the dependent variable. A forecaster cannot check every combination of possible independent variables to identify those that influence the independent variable. Economic theory provides a starting point as to which possible variables should influence the forecast. In many cases, variables will be added or dropped from the set of explanatory variables, due to peculiarities of the specific variable being forecast. This does not mean, however, that the underlying economic theory is wrong, just that in this particular case these variables are not statistically significant in explaining the dependent variable. In some circumstances, the effect of a variable may also be overwhelmed by other variables or conditions.

Adding or deleting variables from the independent variable set is often done because of the difference between the regional and national economies. In one area of the country the economy may be weak, even though the national economy is showing strong growth. The weak regional economy may mean that modeling results are different than those that use nationwide statistics. However, this type of discrepancy is easily understood. More subtle differences occur in demand forecasts when variables show non-significant results, or even reversed signs, than those expected. This is usually due to a different variable that is highly correlated with another and masks the expected statistical effects. There are tests to identify and correct this type of correlation, but the very presence of it often makes the modeling process more difficult than is first expected.

When using time series models, there is less concern with the underlying economic theory than with causal models. This is because time series models are attempts to extrapolate the past behavior of a variable into the future, without regard for what is making the variable behave as it does. The major concern with time series models is that the model itself is specified correctly, rather than whether or not the model follows some underlying theoretical construct.

3. DATA CONSIDERATIONS. Gathering data to prepare a forecast is one of the most arduous and important tasks that a forecaster has to face. This is especially difficult if the forecaster is dealing with regional, industry, or individual firm forecasts where the data is not readily available.

It is relatively easy to acquire national economic data and data on major industries. This data is usually available at Federal government depositories which receive copies of most Federal government publications. Much of this data is also available through computerized databases and can be easily accessed.

Data at the state and local level is not as easy to acquire. Some data pertaining to Standard Metropolitan Statistical Areas (SMSAs) is published by the Bureau of Labor Statistics, the Bureau of Economic Analysis, and the Department of Commerce, although the amount of data has been reduced in the last few years as a result of budgetary constraints. Some states have sources of major economic variables, although in many cases the quality of the data has deteriorated in the last few years as many states have also faced budgetary problems.

For regional and local forecasters, the problem of data acquisition is severe, and in many instances, insurmountable. In many cases, census data is the only source of data for a small region and could be as much as eleven years old. In a few instances, local agencies or industry groups attempt to gather some information on a small region basis, usually through small samples. Modelers may use national economic variables, or variables that hopefully capture the same information at the regional level, as proxy variables for local economic conditions. For example, if forecasters are trying to forecast the potential success of a proposed shopping mall, they may be forced to rely on personal income data from a larger area that may or may not be representative of the personal income in the area the mall would actually draw. This could have an influence on the type of store that the mall is able to attract.

For an individual business, data problems may be even more severe. Many firms do not keep time series available for many years and the data may be suspect as different types of accounting practices are followed. In this instance, the forecaster may be faced with the problem of performing a forecast with only a few years of historic data as guide.

When faced with these problems, the forecaster must adapt. Firms or regional governments do not like to be told that because they have kept poor records in the past, a forecast cannot be done for the future. Instead, the forecaster must identify whatever data is available and use that data as a proxy for the nonexistent or limited local data that would be available in a perfect world. It is essential to note that your success in identifying the appropriate available data to use in the forecasting process will determine your overall success as a forecaster.

4. THE ASSUMPTION SET.   Earlier in this chapter we touched on how forecasters tend to use the same models and same data as other forecasters in preparing their forecasts. We are now ready to go even further with this concept. The choice of the assumptions used in the forecast process will ultimately decide the outcome of the forecast process.

With the possible exception of the modeling and data acquisition steps, there is no more important stage in preparing a forecast than identifying the assumption set that will be used in the forecast. This step is so important that in many regulatory forums the assumption set is given to the industry by the regulators to ensure consistency in the forecast preparation. As much time is spent in identifying the baseline assumptions as is spent studying the results of the forecast process.

To show how important the assumption set is in preparation of the forecast, consider a forecast of California's state tax revenue. Projected tax revenues and expenditures determine the fiscal health of the state government and its ability to provide government services to the population.

Tax revenue is dependent upon (among other things) the number of people employed, the average hourly salary, the inflation rate, taxable sales, health of the state's business and the tax rates for sales tax, personal income tax, and the corporate tax.

Some of the major sectors of the California economy are the defense and aerospace industry, construction industry, tourism, and the export sector, primarily exports to Pacific Rim countries. Forecasters can identify the historic relationship between these various sectors and the national economy, interest rates, the level of defense expenditures, and the performance of major trading partner's economies. How do you make your assumptions about what values should be included for the level of defense expenditures and other key variables for the future?

A forecast is prepared by identifying the statistical relationship between two or more variables as it was in the past, or:

$$Y_t = f(X_{1,t}, X_{2,t}, \ldots, X_{n,t}) \tag{18.1}$$

where $f(..)$ is the estimated statistical relationship between the variables. The forecast is then prepared by using this estimated relationship to obtain future values of the independent variables, or:

$$Y_{t+1} = f(X_{1,t+1}, X_{2,t+1}, \ldots, X_{n,t+1}) \tag{18.2}$$

The forecast of Y_{t+1} is dependent upon the forecasted or assumed values for $X_{i,t+1}$. In many cases, other equations in the forecast model will be used to provide the future values for X_i. However, not all future values of X_i can be forecasted. The value of these variables must be assumed.

In the case of the California economy with its heavy dependence upon defense expenditures, the key to the forecast of tax revenue is the question of what would be the future level of national defense expenditures. A secondary issue is what portion of defense expenditures would be spent within California, as opposed to other areas of the nation.

If the problem was approached in 1990 with the belief that defense expenditures would be unchanged from prior years, the forecast of tax receipts would be relatively unchanged from previous forecasts. The state government could then plan upon maintaining the same levels of government expenditures. If, however, a forecaster began the forecasting process with the assumption that defense expenditures would be reduced by 10 percent and California would suffer a greater proportion of reduction in defense expenditures, then a much different picture would emerge.

The reduction in defense expenditures would lead to employment declines among the highly paid defense industry employees. The decline in income would have multiplier effects on the rest of the California economy, particularly home sales and retail sales. State tax revenues would decline due to the reduction in personal income tax and state sales tax revenues. At the same time, demand for government services would increase, primarily because of the need for job retraining, medical assistance, and other types of income assistance programs.

How could one judge what would happen to defense expenditures in this instance? Historical patterns were no longer valid as the cold war ended and the Soviet Union collapsed into different ethnic states. Essentially, the forecaster had to take an educated guess as to what might follow, although few forecasters like to call any aspect of their work a guess.

By examining proposed Federal budgets for the level of defense expenditures, the forecaster is able to identify some proposed level of defense expenditures and the type of programs that could be impacted. Data exists to identify what sort of defense expenditures are made in California versus the rest of the nation, so the forecaster can approximate the level of defense expenditures in the state. Problems in identifying which military bases would be closed would be another consideration that needs to be faced, although this is another area that is not subject to formal forecasting techniques.

The forecaster can estimate some level of effects of the change in the geopolitical situation on state defense expenditures. However, the ultimate change of defense expenditures will lie with Congress and the Administration. If the forecaster makes reasonably good guesses about how the political situation will affect the level and composition of defense expenditures, the forecasts of the impact on the state will be good. But it is still an assumption about a key economic variable that will have a major effect on the final forecast.

In the last few years, forecasters have found themselves under increasing scrutiny over which assumptions are made in the forecast process. This is particularly true for forecasters who work at the regional level in various environmental impact processes, a portion of which is the effect of new development on the local economy. Opponents of different large construction projects, such as dams, transmission lines, and other major projects have found that they can stop or delay construction of these facilities by challenging the assumptions underlying the studies, rather than the study methodologies or results. By forcing studies to be redone using more conservative assumptions, opponents have been able to challenge the sizable economic benefits that proponents have claimed for their projects. This has resulted in stopping some major projects.

In the last few years, scenario forecasting has gained popularity as a means around the problems of developing the assumption set. In scenario forecasting, a series of different assumption sets are developed using the baseline assumption set and then conservative and optimistic assumption sets. For example, if one were making assumptions about GDP growth, a high, medium, and low growth assumption set might be developed. This allows the forecaster to identify how sensitive the forecast is to (expected) deviations between the assumption set and the actual values. More on different ways to attempt to compensate for deviations between future events and assumed values is presented later in the book.

In summation, when preparing a forecast, at least some portion of it will depend upon your assumptions about key variables (or guesses). Care must be taken to develop assumptions in a reasonable and defensible manner or the entire forecast process could be challenged and invalidated.

5. CHOOSING THE MODELING METHODOLOGY. Once a forecaster has identified the problem, gathered the data, and prepared an assumption set, the next step is to determine which of the various modeling methodologies available should be used.

If the model is going to be used for an immediate or short-term forecast, then a time series model should be considered first. Time series models tend to provide good short-term forecasts and they often avoid the difficulties with gathering data and preparing assumption sets.

If the forecaster is preparing an intermediate or long-term forecast, then an input-output model (discussed in Chapter 22) or regression model should be the first choices that come to mind. These types of models are more appropriate for modeling the changes in the economic structure that will occur in the long term. Long-term changes tend to invalidate the underlying assumption in time series models.

In addition to the term of the forecast, a modeler should be concerned with what is being studied. If the effect of changing economic or demographic conditions on a region is the problem, time series models would not be considered. Time series models are not appropriate for determining the effects of other variables on the dependent variable. Thus, even if the forecast was for a short time period, a causal model would be chosen over a time series model, given these circumstances. In the same vein, a time series model might be preferred to causal models even for longer terms if there was reason to believe that there would not be significant changes in the variables that could impact the independent variable.

An example of using time series models for longer-term forecasts could be illustrated by the problem of estimating attendance at a national park. In this example, a moving average model would provide good results in predicting annual results for a longer time period. There would not be any reason to go through the additional expense and difficulty of gathering data and development of the assumption set if a time series model could be used.

Accuracy is another prime consideration in the choice of the modeling methodology. In some circumstances it is acceptable just to identify the future direction of the variable, while in other cases estimating period to period changes is essential. If you were forecasting whether or not a new manufacturing facility was needed in a region, showing that demand would grow is often sufficient to justify construction. If you were trying to determine when to construct the facility, then greater accuracy would be required to ensure that the facility came on line at the appropriate time to minimize associated carrying costs.

Accuracy is always important in forecasting and the above example is not meant to minimize it. It does show that identifying what is important to the people using the forecast may allow for coarser estimates than the forecaster is able to provide.

It is not uncommon for a forecaster to choose two or more different modeling methods in preparing a single forecast. The primary advantage of using more than one modeling method is that each type of model brings different strengths to the forecast process. If different modeling methodologies provide the same forecast, the forecaster can be confident of the overall accuracy of the forecast. If the forecasts differ, then the forecaster can review the forecast process to identify the cause of the discrepancy. When the reason for different forecasts is identified, the forecaster can either explain the discrepancy or take whatever steps are necessary to correct the wrong forecast model. In either situation, having a check on the final forecast result is valuable.

The preceding discussion demonstrates that for most arguments in favor of a particular forecasting methodology there is usually a counter argument in favor of a different modeling approach. Except for the limitations of not being able to use time series models to examine the effects of one variable on another, a forecaster has a variety of choices available. Which model to use will depend upon many different factors, including the desires of the forecaster and the ultimate user of the information generated in the forecast process.

6. PREPARING THE FORECAST.   Now that the forecaster has identified the problem, gathered the appropriate data, chosen an assumption set, and determined which modeling methodology to use, he or she is ready to begin preparing the forecast.

In most cases, the forecaster will have some preconceived notions about what the forecast should show. If the national economy is expanding, someone forecasting government revenues would expect tax revenues to increase. If a regional economy is expanding, the electric demand forecaster will assume that the forecast would show an increase in demand from one year to the next. Some knowledge about what the forecast should say is a useful check of the first results from the forecast models. In spite of some preconceived notion about what the forecast results should be, it is important not to let these beliefs force your forecast to that result. If the models have been correctly specified and the assumption set reasonably accurate, the forecast results should prove to be fairly good.

However, one of a forecaster's biggest concerns is that decisions made as a result of his or her models prove to be wrong because the forecast itself was incorrect. Forecasting is nothing more than an attempt to reduce the uncertainty associated with future events. Entities that can successfully manage uncertainty through accurate forecasting will be more successful than those entities that are at the mercy of unforeseen events.

7. VERIFICATION OF THE FORECAST.   Once the forecast is prepared, it is necessary to compare the results with actual data to see how the modeling methodology replicates the time series. One of the most common methods of accomplishing this is to prepare an ex-post forecast, that is, a forecast after the actual events have occurred. To see if the modeling methodology actually duplicates the data with some reasonable degree of accuracy, the data set used to prepare the forecast is stopped several periods before the data ends. Some of the historic data is used to prepare the forecast and then compared against the behavior of the known data. If the forecast methodology provides reasonably accurate results, then the forecast is redone using all the available data. If the model provides an accurate representation of data during the ex-post period, it is reasonable to assume that it will provide an accurate forecast, in the absence of any major changes in the ex-ante (or before the fact) forecast period.

CONCLUSIONS

This chapter has presented some of the steps in preparing a forecast. These steps should be followed in some general format whenever one is preparing a forecast. The major thing to realize is that everyone prepares their forecast differently. How you do it will depend upon what sort of models you feel comfortable with and the type of manpower, budget, and data constraints you labor under.

KEY TERMS AND CONCEPTS

Delphi method	**long-term forecasts**	**short-term forecasts**
causal models	**qualitative models**	**scenario forecasting**
cross-section data	**quatitative models**	**time series data**

CHAPTER 19

The Indicator Approach

This chapter will introduce one of the forecasting tools used by the Federal government to determine where the economy is on the business cycle, the Composite Indexes of Leading, Coincident, and Lagging Economic Indicators. Other economic forecasting models are discussed in later chapters.

COMPOSITE INDEXES OF LEADING, COINCIDENT, AND LAGGING ECONOMIC INDICATORS

A primary forecasting tool of the Federal government is the Composite Indexes of Leading, Coincident, and Lagging Indicators, or, for short, the Composite Indexes. The Composite Indexes are based upon work first performed by Wesley Mitchell and Arthur Burns in the 1930s. The composite indexes are a type of time series model that predicts by assuming past trends and relationships will continue into the future.

Mitchell and Burns, the best known business cycle economists of the 1930s, were attempting to develop a method to determine when the recession that began in 1937 would end. Before the computer, economists were very limited in their abilities to forecast. Analytic methods were unable to handle large amounts of data. Data was gathered slowly, with initial errors and large revisions between periods, making analysis more difficult.

Mitchell and Burns (1938) developed the concept of leading, coincident, and lagging indicator series. An indicator series is a time series that has a definite relationship with changes in the overall NBER business reference cycle. A leading indicator is one that declines before most business activity declines and rises before most business activity rises. Coincident indicators are those that move in tandem with most business activity. Lagging indicators are those that decline after most business activity has exhibited a decline and rise after most business activity has risen. Mitchell and Burns (among others working at the National

Bureau of Economic Research, or NBER) examined over eighty different time series and classified fifty of them as leading, coincident, or lagging.

Each of the various indicator series is tracked by the BEA and is referenced by the series title and reference number. Thus, the Index of Hourly Compensation (BEA series 345) identifies a particular indicator series. No single indicator series can capture the economy's diverse activity. Instead, it is necessary to track many different series to attempt to identify in which direction the economy is moving.

The leading indicator series tend to represent anticipations and early links in the sequence of business decisions as well as the early stages of production. Each of the leading indicator series measures focuses on some narrow aspect of economic activity. For example, some of the leading indicator series are Average Weekly Hours (BEA series 1), Index of Net Business Formation (BEA series 12), and Manufacturer's New Orders for Durable Goods (BEA series 7). Each of these leading indicator series tend to rise in anticipation of growth in business activity (or in GDP).

The coincident indicators tend to be broader, comprehensive measures of aggregate economic activity. Examples of coincident indicators include such time series as Manufacturing and Trade Sales (BEA series 57), Industrial Production Indexes (BEA series 47), and Personal Income (BEA series 52). Each of these series tends to move in tandem with GDP.

The lagging indicators tend to be measures of production costs or debt that rise in the latter stage of the business cycle. Some examples include Consumer Installment Credit Outstanding (BEA series 66), Unemployment Rate (BEA series 44), and Yield on New High Grade Corporate Bonds (BEA series 114).

It is necessary to recognize that the indicator series are imprecise measures of the direction of the economy. The relationship between each of the indicator series and general business activity varies according to the various forces that are causing the economy to change direction. Indicator series can help identify the direction of the economy, but they are an imprecise and temperamental forecasting method.

In the early 1950s, Geoffrey Moore (1950) updated the 1938 work of Mitchell and Burns and developed a list of indicator series that predict the beginning and end of a business cycle. Since the early 1950s, the various indicator series have been adjusted to reflect technological, legal, and structural changes in the economy. For example, in Moore's original list of leading indicators, freight car loadings were an important indicator of current economic activity, that is, a coincident series. Since the 1950s however, this series has declined in importance due to the emergence of the truck industry as an important mode of transportation, as well as the growth of the service industry that has reduced the importance of manufacturing in the economy. In 1961, Julius Shiskin of the NBER developed Composite Indexes that capture and smooth the data contained in several of the various indicator series. The three Composite Indexes are made by averaging the behavior of the different indicator series that make up each composite series.

The timing and strength of each indicator series relationship with general business activity, reflected in the reference cycle, changes over time. This imprecise relationship makes forecasting changes in the business cycle difficult. Shiskin was able to identify a small number of indicator series that, when their behavior was averaged, provided a more precise indication of the direction of the economy.

Today, the Composite Indexes and indicator series are prepared by the Bureau of Economic Analysis (BEA) and published monthly in the *Survey of Current Business*. Table 19.1 shows the current components of the three Composite Indexes. Figure 19.1 shows the behavior of the three indexes relative to business cycle expansions and contractions from 1970 through 1992.

TABLE 19.1
ECONOMIC INDICATOR SERIES COMPRISING THE COMPOSITE INDEXES

COMPOSITE INDEX OF LEADING INDICATORS

Series #	Series Title
1	Average Weekly Hours
5	Average Weekly Claims for Unemployment Insurance
8	Manufacturer's New Orders–Consumer and Materials Industries
19	Stock Prices
20	Contracts and Orders for Plant and Equipment
29	New Private Housing Units Authorized
32	Vendor Performance
83	Index of Consumer Expectations
92	Changes in Manufacturers' Unfilled Orders
99	Change in Sensitive Materials Prices
106	Real M2 Money Supply

COMPOSITE INDEX OF COINCIDENT INDICATORS

Series #	Series Title
41	Employees on Nonagricultural Payrolls
47	Industrial Production
51	Personal Income Less Transfer Payments
57	Manufacturing and Trade Sales

COMPOSITE INDEX OF LAGGING INDICATORS

Series #	Series Title
62	Change in Index of Labor Costs of Output, Manufacturing
77	Ratio of Manufacturing and Trade Inventories to Sales
91	Average Duration of Unemployment
95	Ratio of Consumer Installment Credit Outstanding Personal Income
101	Commercial and Industrial Loans Outstanding
109	Average Prime Rate Charged by Banks
120	Change in Consumer Price Index for Services, Smoothed

FIGURE 19.1
SURVEY OF CURRENT BUSINESS
CYCLICAL INDICATORS
COMPOSITE INDEXES: LEADING INDEX COMPONENTS

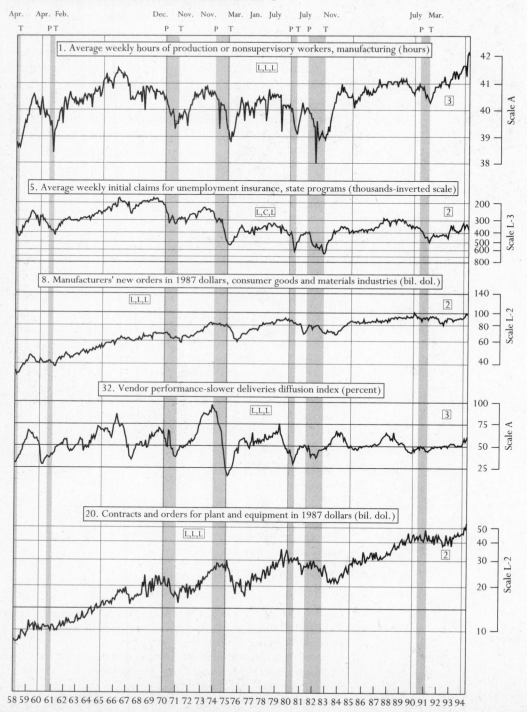

FIGURE 19.1 (CONTINUED)

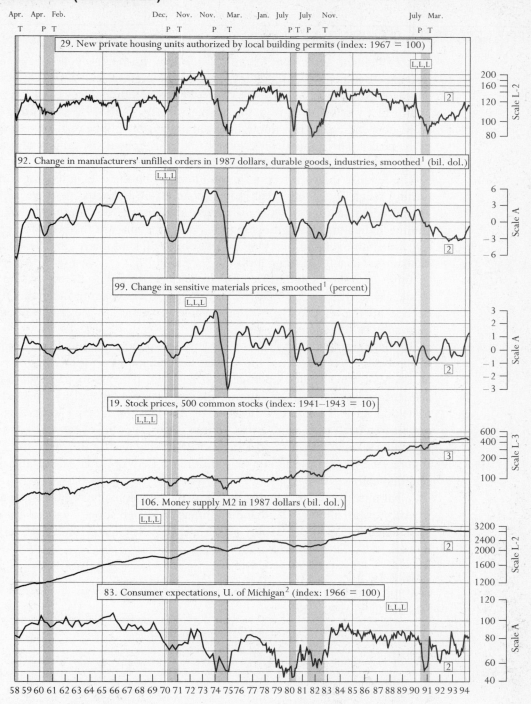

1. This series is smoothed by an autoregressive-moving-average filter developed by Statistics Canada.

2. This is a copyrighted series used by permission; it may not be reproduced without written permission from the University of Michigan, Survey Research Center.

USEFULNESS OF THE COMPOSITE INDEXES

The coincident indicators clearly show the business cycle peaks and troughs. Together with GDP, they indicate the highest and lowest points of general business activity. This is very useful in telling business and government exactly where we are in the business cycle. Table 19.2 shows that the coincident indicators rise throughout the expansion and peak at stage 5 (the cycle peak). The coincident indicators fall throughout the contraction and reach a trough at stage 9 (the cycle trough).

The leading indicators concentrate attention on the events leading to the turning point. By seeing what indicator series are impacted first, we gain a greater understanding of what may cause an upturn or downturn. Also, since leading indicators lead the cycle turns, many people use them for forecasting; we shall examine this tool in detail but will find many limitations and weaknesses as a forecasting tool.

Table 19.2 shows that the leading indicators rise during the expansion up to stage 4, a whole stage before the cycle peak. The leading indicators then decline all the way to stage 8, one whole stage before the trough, before beginning to rise again.

The lagging indicators are also very useful in understanding the workings of the business cycle. They show what lags behind at a turning point, such as interest rates. Their importance is that they help us to understand the sequence of events, so the lagging indicators are as useful as the leading indicators in that respect. Table 19.2 shows that the lagging indicators do not reach a peak until stage 7 (two whole stages after the cycle peak) and do not reach a trough until stage 2 (a whole two stages after the cycle trough). Figure 19.2 illustrates the dramatic difference between the leading and lagging indicators.

What must be stressed is that the same overall sequence of events appears in every cycle, although lead and lag times differ. This fact is crucial for the understanding and forecasting of business cycles using indicator series.

TABLE 19.2
LEADING, LAGGING, AND COINCIDENT INDICATORS AVERAGE OF
FOUR CYCLES 1970–1992

INDICATORS	CHANGES PER QUARTER							
	SEGMENT				PEAK			
	1–2	2–3	3–4	4–5	5–6	6–7	7–8	8–9
12 Leading	2.1	1.0	1.0	−0.9	−2.1	−2.3	−0.1	0.3
4 Coincident	3.7	1.1	1.1	0.5	−2.0	−2.2	−1.7	−1.9
6 Lagging	−1.5	0.6	1.2	2.3	0.5	0.8	−3.1	−2.0

FIGURE 19.2
SURVEY OF CURRENT BUSINESS
CYCLICAL INDICATORS
COMPOSITE INDEXES

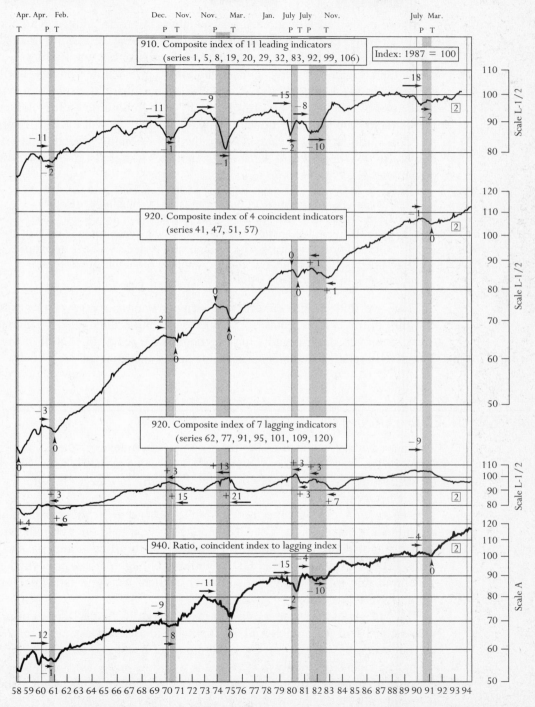

NOTE: The numbers and arrows indicate length of leads (+) and lags (−) in months from business cycle turning dates.

Moreover, all countries with capitalist business systems exhibit the same behavior (Moore 1983).

Moore examined indicators in six countries (Canada, United Kingdom, West Germany, France, Italy, and Japan) using U.S. cycle turning points as bench marks. He found that "the sequence of turns among the leading, coincident and lagging groups in each country corresponds roughly to the sequence in the United States" (1983, 77). The most extensive survey of indicators by Klein and Moore (1985) looked at both so-called classical cycles (actual upturns and downturns and so-called growth cycles (upturns and downturns in growth rates). When the U.S. economy suffered classical downturns, Europeans and Japanese sometimes suffered only growth-rate downturns. Klein and Moore found:

> So far we have seen that most of the leading and lagging indicators that display consistent behavior at classical turning points in the United States have a similar record of leading and lagging growth cycle turning points in at least nine additional countries. The . . . indicator systems we have developed suggest that the cyclical interrelationships among economic processes are quite similar in each of them. (1985, 109)

Thus, we find clear regularities in sequential processes over the cycle, not only in the United States but in all the leading private enterprise countries. Moreover, the indicators turn at roughly the same time in all of these countries in relation to the business cycle peaks and troughs.

COMPOSITE INDEX OF LEADING INDICATORS

The most widely watched of the three composite indexes is the Composite Index of Leading Indicators (CLI). The CLI was constructed with the goal of identifying the future direction of the economy in time to modify fiscal and monetary policy.

Construction of a CLI is not a simple task, due to the performance requirements placed on it. The CLI needs to give a long enough indication of a change in direction of the business cycle to allow policymakers to react. If the CLI does not lead GDP by a long enough period, policymakers will be unable to use the various counter-cyclical instruments available to them to avert a recession.

The CLI should provide a uniform lead period. If the CLI does not provide a consistent warning period, the knowledge that a recession is coming, but not when, is of little use for determining if fiscal and monetary policy should be changed. Finally, a CLI that is wrong as often as it is right does not provide the necessary justification for major changes in economic policy if it predicts a recession is imminent.

The basic idea behind the construction of the CLI is that overall business activity is generally proceeded by a turning point in many of the indicator series. This does not imply causality or that these indicator series cause the change in GDP. Instead, it describes how changes in economic activity work through the economy. For example, if monetary policy was tightened (leading to higher interest rates) it would have an impact on variables such as durable orders, plant and equipment orders, profits, building permits, and installment debt among other variables, before GDP turned downwards. Thus, many of the different leading indicator series will signal any future turn in economic activity.

Which of the indicator series react first and strongest depends upon the reason behind the economic changes. Therefore, it is necessary to design a CLI that gathers many different signals of changes in economic activity from different indicator series. The CLI does this by averaging a broad group of indicator series, each impacted most strongly by different events, yet all leading changes in GDP.

CONSTRUCTION OF THE COMPOSITE INDEXES

To determine which indicator series to include in the three composite indexes, the BEA ranks each indicator series by seven different measures. These measures include:

1. Timing: The time relationship between the indicator series and GDP. For the leading indicator index series, that means the longer, and more consistently, changes in the time series leads changes in GDP;
2. Conformity: How consistent is the relationship between GDP and the indicator series;
3. Smoothness: Is the indicator series subject to large fluctuations between turning points or is it relatively smooth;
4. Currency: The speed with which the indicator series is available for use;
5. Statistical adequacy: An evaluation of the statistical reporting system for the series;
6. Economic significance: The economic justification for including the indicator series in the indicator series. For example, while sunspots may lead changes in GDP, the theoretical justification for including sunspots in an indicator series is weak;
7. Revisions: The extent to which data revisions affect the series. Some time series revisions tend to be small, reflecting the statistical reporting system for the time series. Other series (such as trade statistics) tend to have large revisions that could change any forecasts made using this series.

Each of these seven selection criteria are assigned a weight, shown in Table 19.3, with timing being the most important. These weights are arbitrarily assigned by the BEA and reflect the importance of the different characteristics of a good indicator. The BEA then evaluates each of the different indicator series to determine which belong in the different composite indexes.

Once the indicator series that make up the composite indexes are identified, the index itself is calculated. Because most of the indicator series that make up the indexes are in different units, it is necessary to normalize these indicator series, or put them into the same units. That is, it is not possible to compare money supply (BEA series 106) which is in dollars, to average weekly changes for unemployment insurance (BEA series 5) which is in individual's filing claims.

The first step in constructing composite indexes is to convert all the series into their percentage changes. The percentage change in each indicator series is then divided by the long-run average percentage change of each series. This step standardizes the changes and prevents indicator series that have large percentage changes from dominating the composite indexes. The standardized changes are then summed to calculate the change in the indexes.

WHY THE COMPOSITE LEADING INDICATOR LEADS

The CLI is constructed by averaging the performance of different indicator series relative to GDP. But a theoretical basis for including each indicator series must exist, even if the indicator series exhibits a strong statistical relationship with GDP. Each of the series currently included in the CLI captures some part of changes in aggregate economic activity by examining changes in either consumption or business activity.

Some of the indicator series such as Average Weekly Hours (BEA series 1) and Average Weekly Initial Claims for Unemployment Insurance (BEA series

TABLE 19.3
WEIGHTING VALUES ASSIGNED TO INDICATOR SERIES

Criterion	Weight
Timing	0.267
Conformity	0.167
Smoothness	0.133
Currency	0.100
Statistical Adequacy	0.067
Economic Significance	0.167
Revisions	0.100

SOURCE: U.S. Department of Commerce, *Handbook of Cyclical Indicators*

5) capture the demand by business for more workers necessary to expand output. If business is laying workers off or reducing hours prior to reducing the labor force then one would expect business conditions to decline.

The Index of Consumer Expectations (BEA series 83) measures how consumers view the future. The more pessimistic consumers are, the less likely they are to spend or go further into debt. The more optimistic consumers are, the more likely they are to spend, leading manufacturers to expand output.

The Money Supply, M2 (BEA series 106) has a strong, inverse relationship with interest rates. As the money supply increases, interest rates decline, leading to increased purchases of high priced goods, such as homes and automobiles. Conversely, a decline in the money supply tends to lead to higher interest rates and a decline in large capital purchases.

Manufacturers' New Orders (BEA series 8), Contracts and Orders for Plant and Equipment (BEA series 20), New Private Housing Units Authorized (BEA series 29), Vendor Performance (BEA series 32), Changes in Manufacturers' Unfilled Orders (BEA series 92) and Changes in Sensitive Materials Prices (BEA series 99) all measure the performance of the manufacturing sector. As new orders for manufactured goods are received or firms have trouble meeting production backlogs, production will increase. If firms are reducing their production backlogs or new orders are slowing down, production levels will decline.

The last indicator series, Stock Prices (BEA series 19) is one of the most difficult to interpret. It may be a measure of the anticipation of the direction of the economy. Or it may be that at business cycle peaks, interest rates rise and purchasers switch from stocks to interest earning assets, or at a trough, interest rates are low and people move from interest assets, such as bonds, into stocks. Or it may be a measurement of wealth and consumer expectations. Whatever the reason, stock prices remain the most consistent series of all the indicator series with one of the longest lead times.

USE OF THE COMPOSITE LEADING INDICATOR AS A FORECASTING TOOL

Remember that one of the reasons forecasters have a poor record is that they tend to be momentum followers, or that they assume what has happened the last few months will continue the next few months. But the key question economic forecasters are attempting to answer is when will the economy reach a peak or trough in the business cycle.

The CLI was designed to provide a signal of impending changes in the direction of GDP. However, there is not an agreed upon methodology to interpret changes in the CLI. The reason is that the CLI is not a consistent indicator of the timing of changes in the business cycle. That is, the CLI has

BOX 19.1
SURVEY OF CONSUMERS

The Surveys of Consumers are conducted by the Survey Research Center at the University of Michigan. Begun in 1946, the surveys have long stressed the important influence of consumer spending and saving decisions in determining whether the national economy slips into recession or is propelled toward recovery and growth.

The Surveys of Consumers have proven to be an accurate indicator of the future course of the national economy. The Index of Consumer Expectations, derived from the Surveys of Consumers, is included in the Leading Indicator Composite Index published by the U.S. Department of Commerce, Bureau of Economic Analysis.

The inclusion of data from the Surveys of Consumers is a significant confirmation of its usefulness for understanding and forecasting changes in the national economy. Each series included in the composite Index of Leading Indicators is selected because of its performance on six important characteristics: economic significance, statistical adequacy, consistency of timing at business cycle peaks and troughs, conformity to business expansions and contractions, smoothness, and prompt availability. No other consumer survey meets these rigorous criteria.

The Index of Consumer Expectations includes three questions: how consumers view prospects for their own financial situation, how they view prospects for the general economy over the near term, and their view of prospects for the economy over the long term. The Expectations Index represents only a small part of the survey data that is collected on a regular basis.

Each monthly survey contains approximately 20 core questions, each of which probe a different aspect of consumer attitudes and expectations. The samples for the Surveys of Consumers are designed to be representative of all American households, excluding those in Alaska and Hawaii. Each month, 500 interviews are conducted by telephone from the Ann Arbor office.

The core questions cover three broad areas of consumer sentiment: personal finances, business conditions, and buying conditions. Overall assessments of past and expected changes in personal finances are supplemented by measures of the expected change in nominal family income, as well as expected real income changes. Attitudes towards business conditions in the economy as a whole, over the near and the long-term horizon, are measured in detail. Specific questionnaire items concerning expected changes in inflation, unemployment, and interest rates, as well as confidence in government economic policies, supplement the more general assessments. Finally, several questions probe for the respondent's appraisal of present market conditions for large household durables, vehicles, and houses.

For each area, consumers are not only asked to give their overall opinions but are also asked to describe in their own words their reasons for holding these

CONTINUED ON NEXT PAGE . . .

BOX 19.1 — CONTINUED

views. These follow-up questions reflect the interest of the surveys in not only projecting what consumers will do, but also understanding why consumers make certain spending and saving decisions. Understanding the rationales that consumers give for their actions helps us to anticipate why consumers react differently to the same economic phenomena at different times.

The response of consumers to the sudden news of the plunge in stock prices in October 1987 both highlighted the importance of consumer expectations and suggested that consumer reactions would be different than many analysts expected. Following the crash, the most common assessment was that consumer confidence would play a pivotal role in determining whether a recession would develop. The surprise was that the fear and panic on Wall Street did not spread to Main Street. Consumers displayed a more measured response, assessing the direct damage to their own financial situation as limited and the overall influence of the crash as unlikely to spread and engulf the entire economy.

Not only are purchases of homes, vehicles, and household durables, as well as the occurrence of debt and acquisition of financial assets, important economic decisions for individual families, but in the aggregate, the timing of these decisions influences the course of the entire economy. These large and infrequent spending and saving decisions are often associated with planning and deliberation on the part of consumers, rather than with impulse or habit. Moreover, these decisions are not based solely on consumers' current economic situation but also depend on their expectations about household income employment, prices, and interest rates.

Economic optimism promotes consumer confidence and a willingness to make large expenditures and debt commitments, while economic uncertainty breeds pessimism and a desire to curtail expenditures and rebuild financial reserves. When many people change from an optimistic to a pessimistic view of economic prospects at the same time, it has been repeatedly found that a widespread shift toward postponement of expenditures follows. It is in this manner that the economic optimism and confidence of individual families exert their influence on the course of the aggregate economy.

The importance of consumer optimism and confidence in shaping the course of the economy has been recognized in many countries. Other countries that now regularly monitor consumer sentiment through studies that are patterned after the Surveys of Consumers include Austria, Australia, Belgium, Canada, Denmark, Finland, France, West Germany, Great Britain, Greece, Ireland, Italy, Japan, Luxembourg, Norway, Spain, Sweden, Switzerland, and Taiwan.

The Surveys of Consumers, founded by George Katona, have been directed by Richard Curtin since 1976.

Thanks to the Survey Research Center at the University of Michigan given varying lead times for economic downturns or upturns in the economy. Table 19.4 shows the number of months that the CLI has led the economic downturn or recovery. Additionally, not every upturn or downturn in the CLI should be associated with a change in the direction of the economy. Thus, interpreting the information contained in the CLI is an art to itself.

Table 19.5 shows the behavior of the CLI between 1988 and 1992. The CLI varies from month to month. No easily discernible pattern or trend is apparent in the behavior of the CLI. Any forecast made from the behavior of the CLI on a monthly basis would be revised again and again. For example, using the CLI only, the forecast for January 1989 shows the economy is improving, followed in February and March by a forecast of a slowdown, but a pickup in economic activity forecasted in April, and so forth.

The CLI was not designed to be used in this manner. Even if the economy is expanding, the CLI will exhibit declines as the various components of the CLI grow slower. Instead, the CLI is most useful when it is used to identify trends or changes in the business cycle. To do this however, requires a set of guidelines to interpret the behavior of the CLI.

One of the proposed set of guidelines (Hymans 1973) for using the CLI are:

1. Forecasts are made one month at a time, with the forecast being no change, a peak is coming or a trough is coming;
2. The signal obtained in month t determines the forecast for month $t + 1$;
3. During an economic upturn, two consecutive declines in the CLI lead to a forecast of a peak for the month following the second decline;
4. If after a peak is forecasted, there are two consecutive increases in the CLI then the forecast of a peak is revised to no change;

TABLE 19.4

CHANGES IN THE COMPOSITE LEADING INDICATOR IN MONTHS FROM BUSINESS CYCLE TURNING DATE

UPTURN		DOWNTURN	
July 1953	5	May 1954	6
Aug. 1957	20	April 1958	2
April 1960	10	Feb. 1961	10
Dec. 1969	8	Nov. 1970	1
Nov. 1973	8	March 1975	1
Jan. 1980	15	July 1980	2
July 1981	2	Nov. 1982	10
July 1991	2	March 1991	2
Average:	8.75		4.25

TABLE 19.5

USING THE CLI TO FORECAST THE BUSINESS CYCLE

		Level	Change From Preceeding Period	Forecast
1988	July	142.7		U
	August	144.1	+1.4	U
	September	143.7	−0.4	U
	October	143.9	+0.2	U
	November	144.0	+0.1	U
	December	145.0	+1.0	U
1989	January	146.0	+1.0	U
	February	145.6	−0.4	U
	March	144.7	−0.9	U Peak has been reached
	April	145.8	+1.1	U
	May	144.2	−1.6	U
	June	144.0	−0.2	U
	July	144.1	+0.1	NC
	August	144.8	+0.7	NC Revise forecast to
	September	145.0	+0.2	N continued growth
	October	144.5	−0.5	U
	November	144.7	+0.2	U
	December	145.3	+0.6	U
1990	January	145.4	+0.1	U
	February	144.1	−1.3	U
	March	145.4	+1.3	U
	April	145.2	−0.2	U
	May	146.0	+0.8	U
	June	146.2	+0.2	U
	July	146.2	0.0	D
	August	144.4	−1.8	D
	September	143.2	−1.2	A Peak has been reached
	October	141.5	−1.7	D
	November	139.9	−1.6	D
	December	139.7	−0.2	D
1991	January	138.7	−1.0	D
	February	140.4	+1.7	D
	March	140.4	0.0	D
	April	141.5	+1.1	U
	May	141.9	+0.4	A Trough has been reached
	June	143.0	+1.1	U
	July	143.9	+0.9	U
	August	145.6	+2.6	U
	September	145.5	−0.1	U
	October	145.2	−0.3	U
	November	144.9	−0.3	U
	December	144.7	−0.2	U

TABLE 19.5 (CONTINUED)

1992			
	January	146.3	+2.4	U
	February	147.3	+1.0	U
	March	147.9	+0.6	U
	April	148.3	+0.4	U
	May	149.2	+0.9	U
	June	148.8	−0.4	U
	July	149.0	+0.2	U
	August	148.5	−0.5	U
	September	148.4	−0.1	U
	October	149.2	+0.8	U
	November	150.3	+1.1	U
	December			

(1) A U means that the economy is expanding, or moving upward on the business cycle, a D means that the economy is contracting, and a NC means that the economy did not change, or was stagnant in that month.

5. The rules during an economic downturn are exactly symmetrical, with two consecutive increases in the CLI required for a forecast of a trough. But two consecutive declines after a forecast of a trough changes the forecast to no change.

Because the CLI averages almost a nine month lead in predicting peaks and a five month lead in predicting troughs, the forecast of a peak is implicitly a forecast of a peak within the next nine or so months. A forecast, based on the fact that a trough has occurred, means that the economy will begin improving during the next five months.

Table 19.5 is used to show how these guidelines are used to make forecasts about the future direction of the economy. With the economy growing slowly through the late 1980s, forecasters were looking for indications that the economy was slipping into recession. The CLI did not exhibit two consecutive declines, that would have signaled a business cycle peak, until February and March, 1989. However, the business cycle did not reach a peak, instead stagnating during the third quarter of 1989, exhibiting no real growth.

By August, 1989, the CLI again exhibited two consecutive periods of growth, requiring the forecast to be changed from a peak to no change in the direction of the economy (continued growth). By mid-1990, the CLI had begun to fall, even though the economy was still expanding. The CLI continued to fall for the next six months. Using the guidelines above, the two consecutive declines in the CLI in August and September 1990 signaled a peak in the business cycle within the next nine months. (In this particular case, the CLI only provided a two month warning of a peak.) The CLI continued to decline, which meant that there was no need to revise the forecast, or that the economy would continue to grow after a short sputter.

The CLI did not begin to increase again until early 1991, signaling a business cycle trough within the next four months. In fact, the NBER identified March, 1991, as a cyclical trough in U.S. economic activity. The naming of March, 1991, as the cycle trough provoked much controversy because the economy continued to stagnate for at least two more years.

In this case, the CLI worked as well as could be expected, with the business cycle peaks and troughs coming within the average time frames that would be expected. However, the short warning of the impending recession did not provide policy-makers with the necessary time to take appropriate expansionary action, if they had so desired.

While in this case the CLI did forecast that an economic slowdown was coming, this has not always happened. In 1983, the CLI dropped for several months, signaling a cyclical peak. In fact, the economy slowed from the high levels of real economic growth that it reached after the recession of 1981–82. However, the economy did not slip back into recession. Instead, the economy stabilized at a comfortable long-term growth level.

There are other guidelines used to interpret the CLI than those proposed by Hymans. For example, it has been suggested that a three month decline in the CLI is necessary to forecast a peak during an economic upswing or a three month rise necessary to signal a trough. None of the different criteria however, guarantee that a correct forecast will be realized. As a longer time frame is required for forecasting a change in the business cycle, the shorter the period policymakers have to attempt to mitigate the effects of the change in the business cycle. The fewer observations of the CLI used to predict a peak or trough, the more likely the forecast is to be wrong, harming the credibility of the forecasting method.

A key point to recognize with indicator forecasting is that only the direction of the economy (up or down) is the goal of the forecasting methodology. This method does not attempt to forecast how fast the economy will grow. This point illustrates an important fact in forecasting—determine what the goal of the forecasting process is and design the methodology around it, rather than attempt to forecast more precisely or in greater detail than is necessary, unless the forecast can be improved upon with little or no effort.

WEAKNESS OF THE CLI AS A FORECASTING TOOL

The CLI, in general, does a good job of identifying changes in the business cycle. However, it has several weaknesses that must be guarded against. The major problem is the large variation in changes in the CLI relative to changes in GDP. A small change in the CLI may predict a tiny change in GDP, or the beginning of a major downturn in economic activity. Also, because of the difference in time lags from cycle to cycle, we do not know when downturns in the CLI will show as downturns in general business activity.

Furthermore, to the extent that the CLI is correct in predicting an imminent turn in the business cycle, policymakers might act on this information, making the predictions false. That is, as counter-cyclical economic policies are enacted, the forecasts of the CLI become wrong as the economy reacts.

VERIFICATION OF THE CLI. In addition to the CLI, the composite coincident and lagging indicator series provide valuable information. The composite coincident index summarizes the state of actual business activity. Note that the indicator series that make up the composite coincident index reflect current economic activity, such as personal income, employment, and industrial production. It tends to validate the forecasts of the CLI, as well as giving some precision to the timing of swings in economic activity.

By examining the behavior of the composite coincident index once forecasts of the business cycle have been made, it is possible to verify the predictions of the CLI. A forecasted decline in business activity made using the CLI can be discarded if the composite coincident index does not exhibit any signs of weakness after some appropriate time. The problem is identifying an "appropriate time" to wait before assuming the forecast is a false signal. Typically, if nine months to a year have passed and the coincident indicators have not begun to fall, a false signal is assumed.

THE INDEX OF COINCIDENT INDICATORS

The Index of Coincident Indicators (ICI) is designed to have turning points that coincide with those of the business cycle. The BEA constructs the ICI from four components: Employment on Nonagricultural Payrolls (BEA series 41), Personal Income Less Transfer Payments (BEA series 51), Industrial Production (BEA series 47) and Real Manufacturing and Trade Sales (BEA series 57).

Over the last eight business cycles, all but one of the turning points in the ICI were in the same quarter or an adjacent quarter to the business cycle turning points. Because of the close correlation between the ICI and aggregate economic activity, the ICI is a good measure of changes in business cycles.

The ICI is constructed in basically the same way as the CLI. That is,

1. Monthly symmetrical percent changes are calculated for each of the four component indices;
2. Each series of changes is standardized so that its average absolute value is 1.0. This standardization is accomplished by dividing each series of changes by its average absolute value;
3. The standardized component changes are averaged;
4. The series of average standardized changes is cumulated into a preliminary ICI with a value of 100 for the initial month;

5. The trend of the preliminary ICI is subtracted from the trend of real GDP to derive a trend adjustment factor;

6. The trend adjustment factor is added to the average standardized changes calculated is step 3;

7. The trend adjusted average standardized changes are cumulated into an ICI;

8. The final ICI is calculated by dividing each month by its average value in 1982.

Why would one want to calculate a series that shows where economic activity currently is? Notice that the series that make up the ICI are all monthly series. Most measures of aggregate economic activity are quarterly. Thus, the ICI can provide up to six months of warning of changes in the business cycle.

For a detailed discussion of the mathematics of the calculation of the ICI, see Green and Beckman (1992).

CONCLUSIONS

This chapter introduced some of the basic problems associated with forecasting. Both the strengths and weaknesses of forecasts were briefly discussed. Then the different types of forecasting models, both qualitative and quantitative, were introduced.

There are different types of forecasting models and methodologies. Later chapters will introduce these different methodologies and show how the strengths and weaknesses can be identified and compensated for. It was shown here that the CLI is a very useful tool for understanding the business cycle, but has serious weaknesses as a forecasting tool. Notice that the CLI is an example of a forecasting methodology that is more concerned with identifying changes in the direction of the economy rather than the strength of the economy. This is in comparison to other types of forecasting methods that attempt to determine the level of growth of GDP. The ICI was also introduced, more to illustrate that it is sometimes necessary to forecast the present due to lags in data collection and analysis, rather than as a tool to forecast the future.

KEY TERMS AND CONCEPTS

Composite indexes of
leading, lagging,
and coincident
indicators

indicator series

CHAPTER 20

Time Series Models

In Chapter 18, various types of quantitative models were briefly described. This chapter introduces one of the major quantitative forecasting methodologies, time series models.

Time series models are based upon the identification of a variable's historic behavior and an extrapolation of the behavior into the future. As a forecasting method, time series models provide good forecast results when the economic and political situation remains stable during the forecast period. Best results are obtained when time series models are used for short time periods.

The primary limitation of time series models is the inability to account for the effects of changes in economic conditions that impact the variable under study. For example, a forecast of consumption expenditures using historic patterns could be done. But if a change in tax law should occur, either increasing or decreasing after-tax income, a time series model will not identify the effect on consumption expenditures.

In spite of this limitation, time series models are used widely. They are relatively simple to construct and provide accurate forecasts under many circumstances.

STRENGTHS AND LIMITATIONS OF TIME SERIES MODELS

Time series models are most accurate when the forecast horizon is short. A short time period is one in which historical patterns dominate and there have been no exogenous shocks to the economy. Consider the oil industry in the early 1970s. After years of increasing demand for petroleum, industry forecasters had no reason to anticipate demand would slacken. Yet, beginning with the first Arab Oil Embargo in 1972, oil prices increased over the next three years by 300 to 500 percent.

Because gasoline has a low short-run demand elasticity, higher prices for gasoline did not cause demand to immediately decline. Some industry analysts predicted that Americans would continue to use gasoline in the same quantity that they had before the embargo. However, once the embargo ended, gasoline demand declined as people adjusted to the higher prices by purchasing more fuel-efficient cars, investing in energy saving appliances, and conserving. In fact, gasoline demand declined for the rest of the 1970s. In the short-term, people would not trade in their cars or appliances just to save gasoline or energy. But when they finally did replace their cars and appliances, they choose more energy efficient appliances and automobiles.

Beginning in the late 1970s, oil prices began a long-term decline, from $42.50 per barrel to as low as $9.00 per barrel. Many forecasters believed that Americans would continue in their fuel-efficient ways and that demand would not increase substantially. Again, some forecasters were wrong. Americans responded to lower gasoline and energy costs by increasing demand, although with a lag between the price decline and increased energy use.

In both cases, forecasters who relied upon time series models to forecast gasoline demand were wrong. External shocks to the system upset the historical patterns of the variable. Forecasts of petroleum demand made using time series were wrong, because of the external shock due to the rapid increase in oil prices.

Time series models provide accurate forecasts when any changes in the variable's environment are occurring slowly or consistently. However, they do not provide accurate forecasts for variables that exhibit a large degree of variability or for long-term forecasts. For example, time series models do not forecast the balance of trade well. The large change in monthly trade patterns do not lend themselves to time series forecasts, although the seasonal component of the trade balance can be forecasted with time series models.

An advantage of time series models is that they are relatively simple and inexpensive to construct and to use. In forecasting, it is frequently the case that the simpler the model, the better the forecast. However, one should not choose the least expensive model if resulting inaccurate forecasts cause the wrong decision to be recommended. The primary principle behind accurate forecasting is to choose the modeling methodology that best captures the patterns or relationships exhibited by the variable under study.

THE MULTIPLICATIVE TIME SERIES MODEL

A time series is made up of four separate components that interact with each other. These four components are the: (1) trend, (2) seasonal, (3) cyclical, and (4) irregular component, or:

$$Y_t = T_t \times S_t \times C_t \times I_t \tag{20.1}$$

where:

$\quad Y_t \quad = \quad$ the time series value at time t.

$\quad T_t \quad = \quad$ the trend component of a time series.

$\quad S_t \quad = \quad$ seasonal component of the time series.

$\quad C_t \quad = \quad$ the cyclical component of the time series.

$\quad I_t \quad = \quad$ the irregular component of the time series.

This way of describing a time series is called the *multiplicative time series model*. The trend component is measured in units of the variable being forecasted, dollars, shoes, etc. The seasonal and cyclical components are measured in relative terms, with values above 1.0 indicating the time series is above the normal or average value. Values below 1.0 represent below annual average levels. The irregular component cannot be forecasted and partially explains forecast error, even in a perfectly constructed forecasting model.

To show how the multiplicative model works, consider sales of snow skis. The trend component would be the number of skis sold quarterly, for example, 500,000 pairs. The seasonal component would indicate the effects of each time period on ski sales. During the first and fourth quarters of each year, ski sales are above the average sales for each quarter, causing the seasonal component to be greater than 1.0. During the second and third quarter sales would be below the annual average, causing the seasonal component to be less than 1.0. Assume that the four seasonal indices for the first, second, third, and fourth quarters are 1.25, 0.8, 0.8, and 1.15 respectively. The average of the seasonal components must be equal to one.

The cyclical component could represent the effect of the economy on ski sales. For simplicity, assume that the cyclic effect is 1.0.

To estimate ski sales by quarter, you would then have:

$$\text{sales in quarter 1} = 500{,}000 \times 1.25 \times 1.0 = 625{,}000$$

$$\text{sales in quarter 2} = 500{,}000 \times 0.8 \times 1.0 = 400{,}000$$

$$\text{sales in quarter } 3 \ = \ 500{,}000 \ \times \ 0.8 \ \times \ 1.0 \ = \ 400{,}000$$

$$\text{sales in quarter } 4 \ = \ 500{,}000 \ \times \ 1.15 \ \times \ 1.0 \ = \ 575{,}000$$

Note that the total sales during the year are equal to 2,000,000 skis, or four times the average quarterly sales given by the trend component.

There is no value or measurement of the irregular component. If some portion of the variation in the irregular component could be identified, the effects would be captured in the trend, seasonal or cyclical components. The irregular component is a random, non-measurable impact that will vary from time period to time period.

If a time series contains any variation, then a forecast requires forecasting of at least the trend and seasonal components. Forecasting the cyclical component is very difficult and is often ignored.

TREND COMPONENT.   Time series are measured on some regular time basis, such as weekly, monthly, quarterly, or annually. While there will be some random fluctuation due to the irregular component, the entire time series may show gradual shifts or movement over some long period. The gradual shifts are often due to long-term factors, such as changes in population, demographic characteristics, technological progress, or changes in consumer preferences.

For example, if nominal federal tax receipts are graphed against time, as shown in Figure 20.1, receipts would be higher every year, even though there is a substantial variation between periods. This type of trend is classified as a linear trend, because a line can approximate the overall direction of money supply growth. Some other possible trend patterns include non-linear trends, such as that exhibited by population growth or a hyperbolic function (Figure 20.2).

SEASONAL COMPONENT.   Some time series show a regular pattern of variability according to the time of year. Bathing suit sales and airline traffic both increase during the summer, while demand for heavy clothing and snow shovels is highest during the winter months. The seasonal component of the time series describes this annual variability due to seasonal influences.

Estimating the seasonal effects on time series is important in determining economic policy because the seasonal effects tend to obscure the effects of economic trends. For example, suppose unemployment drops between the third and fourth quarters. Is this drop due to an improvement in economic conditions or just reflective of increased hiring of part-time seasonal workers? To answer this question requires that the seasonal effects on employment be identified. Then it is possible to determine if the

FIGURE 20.1
EXAMPLE OF A TREND COMPONENT

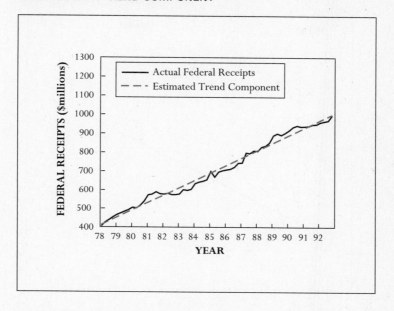

FIGURE 20.2A
EXAMPLE OF DIFFERENT TRENDS—NON-LINEAR DECLINING

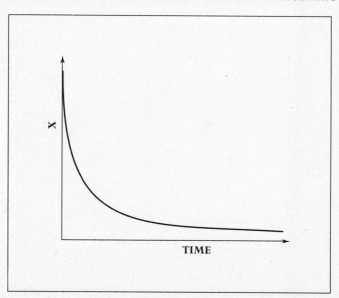

FIGURE 20.2B
EXAMPLE OF DIFFERENT TRENDS—INCREASING TREND

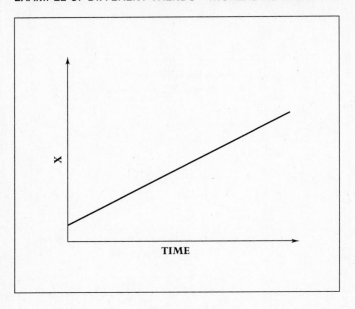

FIGURE 20.2C
EXAMPLE OF DIFFERENT TRENDS—DECLINING TREND

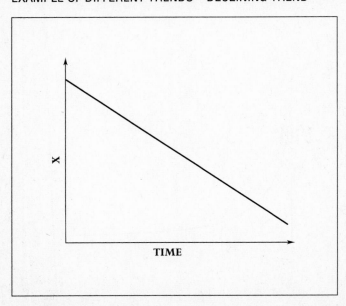

FIGURE 20.2D
EXAMPLE OF DIFFERENT TRENDS—GEOMETRIC GROWTH

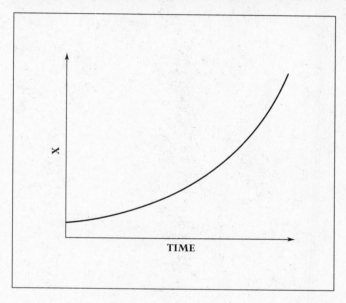

decline in unemployment is as great as would normally be anticipated. Figure 20.3 shows the seasonal component of employment, where employment is higher in the third quarter of each year, droping in the fourth quarter.

CYCLICAL COMPONENT. Many time series exhibit cyclical behavior with a regular number of observations below and above the trend line. Any regular pattern about the trend line is attributable to the cyclical component of the trend line.

Often this cyclical behavior is the normal behavior of a variable around its trend. Federal government receipts are an example of this cyclical behavior of the economy, varying about the long-term trend line. Figure 20.4 shows an example of the cyclical component of a time series.

The changes in behavior of the cyclical component over time does not lend itself to forecasting. Time series models rely on an underlying assumption that the series behaves in a predictable pattern. The cyclical component however, does not necessarily repeat itself, often varying in length and intensity.

IRREGULAR COMPONENT. The irregular component of a time series, sometimes called *white noise,* is the remaining random variability within the time series after the effects of the trend, cyclical and seasonal components.

FIGURE 20.3
EXAMPLE OF A TIME SERIES WITH A SEASONAL COMPONENT

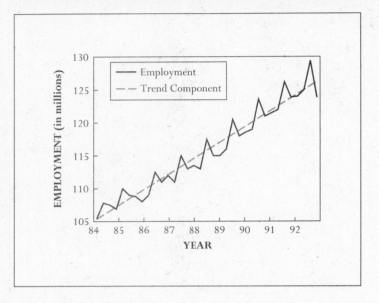

FIGURE 20.4
EXAMPLE OF THE CYCLICAL COMPONENT

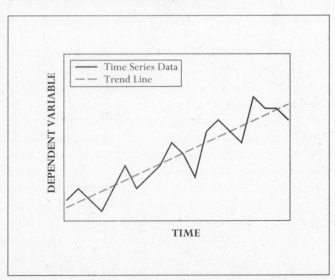

The irregular component is caused by the short-term, unexpected, non-recurring factors that impact the time series. The irregular component cannot be forecast and accounts for most forecast error in a properly specified model.

TIME SERIES FORECASTING MODELS

Time series models vary in complexity, ranging from simple to very complicated. The discussion of the various types of models begins with the simpler types of models. These models are best used in situations where there is very little data available or the time series exhibits a great deal of random variability between periods.

NAIVE MODELS. If a time series shows little change, no trend component and no identified seasonal or other patterns, then the simplest of all forecasting models can be used. The naive model uses the last observed value of the time series as the forecast of all future values, or:

$$Y_{t+1} = Y_t \tag{20.2}$$

Surprisingly, this model can be quite useful, especially if little or no historical data exists on which to base a forecast or if the time series is fairly stable.

MEAN FORECAST MODEL. Another simple model for forecasting a time series is to use the mean of the time series for the forecast for the next period, or:

$$Y_{t+1} = \bar{Y} \tag{20.3}$$

where $\bar{Y}$ is the mean or average value of the time series. $\bar{Y}$ is calculated as:

$$\bar{Y} = (\Sigma Y_t)/n \tag{20.4}$$

where n is the number of observations.

When using the mean forecasting model, the forecast for each period will be the mean value. This model is best used when the variable exhibits a large amount of variability between periods with no identifiable pattern, especially a trend pattern that would cause the mean to drift upward or downward over time.

The naive and mean forecasting models are typically used only under severe circumstances. For example, when other methods provide poor results that are unacceptable for some reason or the variable under examination either exhibits little or no change from period to period or large amounts of random variability. Neither of these models will provide good results if the time series has a long-term trend component. In most cases, more sophisticated models provide better forecasts of the future.

MORE SOPHISTICATED TIME SERIES MODELS

Recall that the multiplicative time series model is written as:

$$Y_t = T_t \times S_t \times C_t \times I_t \qquad (20.5)$$

If a time series contains the four components, a forecast of the time series requires forecasting at least the trend and seasonal. If the cyclical component can be identified it should be included in the forecast, or:

$$Y_{t+1} = T_{t+1} \times S_{t+1} \times C_{t+1} \qquad (20.6)$$

where Y_{t+1} is the forecast value of the time series. The irregular component cannot be forecast and so is excluded from equation 20.5.

After the naive models, the easiest time series forecasting techniques are those that are appropriate for a fairly stable time series, meaning those that exhibit no significant trend, cyclical or seasonal effects. In these situations, the object is to smooth out the irregular component of the time series through an averaging process. The first of these methods is the moving average method.

MOVING AVERAGE MODELS.   This type of model uses the average of the most recent values as the forecast for the next time period. Mathematically, the moving average model is shown as:

$$Y_{t+1} = (Y_t + Y_{t-1} + Y_{t-2} + \ldots + Y_{t-n})/n \qquad (20.7)$$

where: Y_{t+1} = forecast value of Y at time $t + 1$

Y_{t-n} = past n values of Y

Table 20.1 shows how a four period moving average model is used to develop a forecast.

The easiest way of utilizing a moving average model is to use the time series average as the forecast of the period. The moving average forecast-

TABLE 20.1
DEVELOPMENT OF A FOUR PERIOD MOVING AVERAGE MODEL

Observation	Time Series Value	Fitted Value
1	105.8	
2	107.8	
3	107.9	
4	108.1	
5	107.6	107.4
6	110.9	107.9
7	110.2	108.6
8	110.6	109.2
9	110.2	109.8
10	113.5	110.5
11	113.0	111.1
12	113.7	111.8
13	112.9	112.6
14	116.2	113.3
15	115.5	114.0
16	116.0	114.6
17	115.8	115.2
18	118.7	115.9
19	117.5	116.5
20	117.7	117.0
21	118.1	117.4
22	118.3	118.0
23	117.8	117.9
24	117.5	118.0
25	116.8	117.9
26	116.9	117.6
27	116.8	117.3
28	116.8	117.0
29	117.1	116.8
30	117.6	116.9
31	117.7	117.1
32	117.7	117.3
		117.5 = *Forecast Value*

The time series is quarterly U.S. Employment (in millions).

ing method is most useful when the time series exhibits large variability between periods, with no apparent pattern or trend. If the time series exhibits an increasing or decreasing trend, a forecast using a moving average model will underforecast data points in a series with an increasing trend and overforecast data points in a time series with a decreasing trend.

To use moving average models, one must first select the past number of data points to include in the models. Adding more past or lagged values to the moving average model has two unintended results. First, the more lagged variables, the more data points are discarded. Secondly, the forecast values for Y_{t+n} will exhibit less variation as the number of lags increases. Figure 20.5 illustrates the effects of adding more lags to the forecasting model. To choose the appropriate number of past values of the variable to use in the moving average forecasting model, measures of judging the accuracy of the forecast must be developed.

FORECAST ERROR

No forecasting model will generate the exact value of the time series for every observation. The difference between the time series value and the forecast value is known as the forecast error, e_t, or:

$$e_t = Y_t - \hat{Y}_t \tag{20.8}$$

FIGURE 20.5
EFFECTS OF ADDING MORE LAGGED VARIABLES TO THE MOVING AVERAGE MODEL

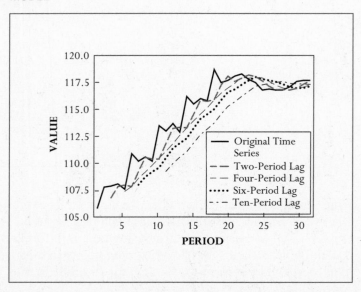

where $\hat{Y}_t$ is the forecasted or "fitted" value of Y_t.

One measure of the forecast accuracy is to sum the e_t. However, if the e_t are random, some will be positive and some negative, resulting in a sum near zero, regardless of the size of the individual errors. This result can be avoided by squaring each of the individual e_t and then calculating the average value. The average of the sum of the squared errors is called the *mean square error* (MSE) and is a common measure of the accuracy of a forecasting model. Mathematically, the MSE is:

$$\text{MSE} = (\Sigma(Y_t - \hat{Y}_t)^2) / n \tag{20.9}$$

The MSE can be used to calculate the number of past observations to use in developing a moving average model. An approach to use in choosing the number of observations to include in the moving average model is to use a trial and error method that minimizes the MSE. Beginning with a small number of past values, calculate the MSE then add more past values. Choose the number of lags that minimizes the MSE as the number of lags to include in the moving average model.

Another measure of forecast error is the mean of the absolute values of the error term, or the *mean absolute deviation* (MAD), or:

$$\text{MAD} = (\Sigma(\text{absolute value}(e_t))) / n \tag{20.10}$$

The major difference between the MSE and MAD is that the MSE is influenced much more by large forecast errors than small errors. That is, if there are several large e_t, then the MSE will be quite big compared to a different lag structure that has smaller errors across all observations.

Table 20.2 presents an example of calculating the goodness-of-fit using the different measures of forecast error. Which measure of forecast accuracy to use is not a simple matter, although most measures of accuracy are based upon methods that attempt to minimize the MSE. As is the case with choosing a forecasting method, there is no single right answer when attempting to choose the right measure of accuracy.

WEIGHTED MOVING AVERAGE MODELS

One variation of moving average models is the *weighted moving average*. In moving average models, each observation receives the same weight or importance in forecasting the time series. Usually, weighted moving average models place more importance on recent values of the time series with the weights declining for older data values. This is not always the case.

TABLE 20.2
CALCULATION OF MEAN SQUARED ERROR AND MEAN ABSOLUTE DEVIATION

Observation	Time Series Value	Forecast Value	Forecast Error	Error Squared	Absolute Value of Error
1	170				
2	210				
3	190				
4	230				
5	180	200.0	−20.0	400.0	20.0
6	160	202.5	−42.5	1806.3	42.5
7	200	190.0	10.0	100.0	10.0
8	180	192.5	−12.5	156.3	12.5
9	220	180.0	40.0	1600.0	40.0
10	200	190.0	10.0	100.0	10.0
11	150	200.0	−50.0	2500.0	50.0
12	220	187.5	32.5	1056.3	32.5
13	130	197.5	−67.5	4556.3	67.5
14	160	175.0	−15.0	225.0	15.0
15	155	165.0	−10.0	100.0	10.0
16	165	166.3	−1.3	1.6	1.3
17	165	152.5	12.5	156.3	12.5
18	140	161.3	−21.3	451.6	21.3
19	170	156.3	13.8	189.1	13.8
20	180	160.0	20.0	400.0	20.0
			$\Sigma = -101.25$	$\Sigma = 13798.44$	$\Sigma = 378.75$

Number of observations = 16

Mean square error = $(\Sigma(Y_t - \hat{Y}_t)^2) / n = (13798.44 / 16) = 862.40$

Mean absolute error = $(\Sigma(\text{absolute value}(Y_t - \hat{Y}_t))) / n = 378.75/16 = 23.67$

Some weighted moving average models place more emphasis on observations two or three periods ago with nearer term observations having less weight. This is because some variables react with some lag. For example, some farm commodities are more responsive to production several periods earlier as a result of farmer's knowledge of output levels.

For a n period weighted moving average model, the forecast for period t would be:

$$Y_t = (w_1 Y_{t-1} + w_2 Y_{t-2} + \ldots + w_n Y_{t-n}) \tag{20.11}$$

where the w_i are the weights attached to the past 3 observations. If the sum of the w_i are less than one, the forecast will show a declining trend over time, while weights greater than one will cause the forecast to show an increasing trend. If the time series does not exhibit a trend, then the sum of the w_t will will equal one.

Table 20.3 shows how a forecast using the weighted moving average model is developed. There is no exact way to calculate the best w_i. A trial and error method, attempting to minimize the MSE or MAD, is the only way to determine the correct w_i.

TABLE 20.3

EXAMPLE OF A 3 PERIOD WEIGHTED MOVING AVERAGE MODEL

Observation	Time Series Value	Weighted Average	Forecast Error	Error Squared	Absolute Value of Error
1	112.9				
2	116.2				
3	115.5				
4	116.0	115.0	1.0	0.95	1.0
5	115.8	115.9	−0.1	0.02	0.1
6	118.7	115.8	2.9	8.56	2.9
7	117.5	117.3	0.2	0.04	0.2
8	117.7	117.4	0.3	0.11	0.3
9	117.1	117.9	−0.8	0.64	0.8
10	118.3	117.4	1.0	0.90	1.0
11	117.8	117.9	0.0	0.00	0.0
12	117.5	117.8	−0.3	0.06	0.3
13	116.8	117.8	−1.0	0.95	1.0
14	116.9	117.2	−0.3	0.11	0.3
15	116.8	117.0	−0.2	0.05	0.2
16	116.8	116.8	0.0	0.00	0.0
17	117.1	116.8	0.3	0.08	0.3
18	117.6	117.0	0.6	0.42	0.6
19	117.7	117.3	0.4	0.18	0.4
20	117.7	117.5	0.2	0.03	0.2
		117.7			
			3.15	12.14	8.70

The weights are $w_1 = .5$, $w_2 = w_3 = .25$

Number of observations = 17

Mean square error = ($\sum$(error squared)) / n = 12.14 / 17 = .714

Mean absolute error = ($\sum$(absolute value (error))) / n = 8.7/17 = .511

FORECASTING A TIME SERIES USING TREND PROJECTION

Moving average models are appropriate for time series that do not exhibit any significant trend component. However, for time series that exhibit some overall upward trend, moving average models will tend to under forecast the actual value of Y_t, while over forecasting the value of Y_t for downward trending time series. The pattern of the error terms is useful in determining if the moving average model is appropriate for the particular time series being studied. If the error terms are predominantly all positive or negative, then the time series exhibits some long term trend. If error terms tend to be positive, the time series has an upward trend. If the error terms are all negative, the time series has a downward trend.

A time series has a linear trend if a line can be used to approximate the long-term behavior of the time series. The trend component does not need to capture all of the variations in the time series. Instead, the trend component need only reflect the gradual shifting of the time series over time.

For a time series exhibiting a linear trend, the value of the time series can be written as:

$$Y_t = B_0 + B_1 t \tag{20.12}$$

where:
$$
\begin{aligned}
Y_t &= \text{the forecast of the time series at } t \\
B_0 &= \text{intercept of the trend line} \\
B_1 &= \text{slope of the trend line}
\end{aligned}
$$

The formulas for calculating the slope and intercept are:

$$B_1 = (\Sigma t\, Y_t - (\Sigma t\, \Sigma Y_t)/n)/((\Sigma t^2 - (\Sigma t)^2/n) \tag{20.13}$$

$$B_0 = Y - B_1 t \tag{20.14}$$

$$\overline{Y}, \overline{t} = \text{average values of } Y \text{ and } t$$

The formulas in 20.13 and 14 minimize the MSE for the actual and fitted values of Y_t, where the fitted values are the results of substituting $t = 1, 2, \ldots, t$, into equation 20.12 and calculating the fitted value of Y_t.

Using these relationships for the data shown in Table 20.4, we can make the following calculations:

$$\overline{t} = 210/20 = 105 \tag{20.15}$$

$$\bar{Y} = 2339.4/20 = 116.97 \tag{20.16}$$

$$B_1 = (24636.4 - ((210 \times 2339.4)/20))/((2870 - 210^2/20)) = .116 \tag{20.17}$$

$$B_0 = (2339.3/20) - (.026 \times (210.20)) = 155.75 \tag{20.18}$$

Thus, the trend component of the time series is:

$$Y_t = 115.75 + .116(t) \tag{20.19}$$

TABLE 20.4
EXAMPLE OF CALCULATING THE TREND COMPONENT OF A TIME SERIES

Observation (t)	Employment (in millions)	Observation * Employment	t squared
1	112.9	112.9	1
2	116.2	232.4	4
3	115.5	346.5	9
4	116.0	464.0	16
5	115.8	579.0	25
6	118.7	712.2	36
7	117.5	822.5	49
8	117.7	941.6	64
9	118.1	1062.9	81
10	118.3	1183.0	100
11	117.8	1295.8	121
12	117.5	1410.0	144
13	116.8	1518.4	169
14	116.9	1636.6	196
15	116.8	1752.0	225
16	116.8	1868.8	256
17	117.1	1990.7	289
18	117.6	2116.8	324
19	117.7	2236.3	361
20	117.7	2354.0	400
Totals 210	2339.4	24636.4	2870

$\bar{t} = (210/20) = 10.5$

$\bar{Y} = (2339.4/20) = 116.97$

$B_1 = ((24636.4 - (210 \times 2339.4/20) / (2870 - (210^2 / 20)) = 0.116$

$B_0 = (2339.4 / 20) - (.026 \times (210 / 20)) = 115.75$

Trend Component = 115.75 + .166(t)

The slope value, B_1, shows the average change in Y on a period to period basis. Thus, to use the trend component for forecasting, substitute the value of t into the model. For example, substituting $t = 21$ into the formula gives the following forecasted value of Y_{21}.

$$Y_{21} = 115.75 + .116 \times 21 = 118.186 \qquad (20.20)$$

Figure 20.6 shows the actual and forecast values for this example.

FORECASTING SEASONAL COMPONENTS

Earlier in this section we discussed the problems that seasonal components of a time series introduce in determining the behavior of a time series. This section introduces a forecasting model for a time series that has both a trend and seasonal component. The approach first removes the seasonal effects from the time series, leaving only a trend component.

FIGURE 20.6
EXAMPLE OF FITTING A TREND LINE TO DATA

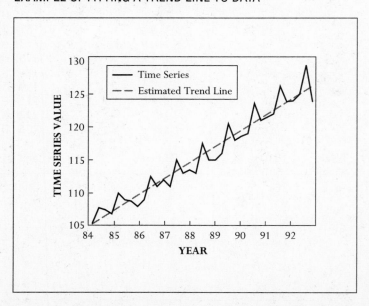

FIGURE 20.7

SMOOTHING EFFECT OF A FOUR–QUARTER MOVING AVERAGE MODEL AND A CENTERED MOVING AVERAGE MODEL.

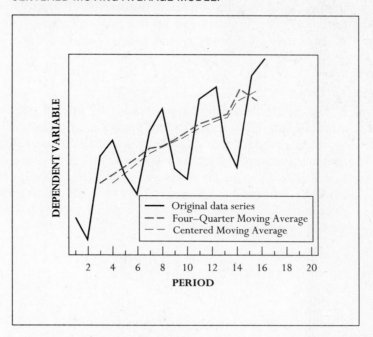

Using the trend forecasting method discussed above, the trend component is forecast. Then, the effects of the seasonal components are incorporated back into the trend forecast to yield the final forecast.

The multiplicative time series model is used to represent a time series that has a trend, seasonal and irregular component. Quarterly data will be used to illustrate this methodology, although monthly data could just as easily be used.

CALCULATING THE SEASONAL INDEXES. Figure 20.7 shows that employment data tends to be above the trend line in the third quarter and drop in the second quarter of each year. To isolate the seasonal and irregular components, S_t and I_t, a moving average model is constructed that uses one year of data in each calculation.

The seasonal adjustment begins by calculating a four quarter moving average time series, YA_t, where:

$$YA_t = (Y_{t-4} + Y_{t-3} + Y_{t-2} + Y_{t-1})/4 \qquad (20.21)$$

The process of calculating the YA_t loses four data points from the original series, two at the beginning and two at the end of the series.

YA_t is calculated to provide an average value of Y_t for each four periods. That is, YA_t provides an average of the middle quarter of the moving average group. However, using monthly or quarterly data, it is difficult to identify the middle quarter. YA_t does not correspond directly to the original quarters of Y_t. This problem can be fixed by calculating the *centered moving average,* YAC_t, by averaging successive points in YA_t, or:

$$YAC_t = (YA_t + YA_{t-1})/2 \qquad (20.22)$$

The centered moving average tends to smooth out fluctuations in the original time series, as shown in Figure 20.7. Because the moving averages were calculated for four quarters of data they do not include the seasonal or irregular components of the time series. Table 20.5 illustrates the procedure to calculate the centered moving average. The next step in this process is to calculate the seasonal component, S_t, for each observation. This is accomplished by dividing the values of Y_t within a year by the corresponding centered moving average, or:

$$S_t = Y_t / YAC_t \qquad (20.23)$$

TABLE 20.5

DEVELOPMENT OF A CENTERED MOVING AVERAGE MODEL

Observation	Value	Four Quarter Moving Average	Centered Moving Average
1	96		
2	82		
3	120	107.0	109.50
4	130	112.0	114.75
5	116	117.5	119.50
6	104	121.5	123.25
7	136	125.0	125.50
8	144	126.0	127.00
9	120	128.0	129.75
10	112	131.5	133.00
11	150	134.5	135.25
12	156	136.0	136.75
13	126	137.5	138.75
14	118	140.0	141.50
15	160	143.0	
16	168		

TABLE 20.6
DEVELOPMENT OF THE SEASONAL INDEXES

Observation	Value	Centered Moving Average	Seasonal Irregular Component
1	96		
2	82		
3	120	109.5	1.096
4	130	114.75	1.133
5	116	119.50	0.971
6	104	123.25	0.844
7	136	125.50	1.084
8	144	127.00	1.134
9	120	129.75	0.925
10	112	133.00	0.842
11	150	135.25	1.109
12	156	136.75	1.141
13	126	142.00	0.887
14	118	145.25	0.812
15	160		
16	168		

The seasonal component is then used to calculate the seasonal index, SI_t, by averaging all of the S_t for each of the quarters. Table 20.6 illustrates the entire series of steps necessary to calculate the four seasonal indexes corresponding to each quarter, while Table 20.7 shows how the final seasonal indexes are calculated.

The seasonal indexes provide some useful information about a time series. A seasonal index greater than one means that the series tends to be above the average annual value in that period. An index less than one means that the periods' observation tends to be below the average annual in that quarter. Employment data, for example, shows the greatest seasonal index in the third quarter as students enter the job market for the summer and drops in the fourth quarter as they return to school.

TABLE 20.7
DEVELOPMENT OF THE SEASONAL INDEXES

Quarter	Seasonal—Irregular Component			Seasonal Index
3	1.096	1.084	1.109	1.096
4	1.133	1.134	1.141	1.136
1	0.971	0.925	0.887	0.928
2	0.844	0.842	0.812	0.833

It should be noted that monthly data can also be seasonally adjusted using the same procedure described above, except a twelve period moving average is calculated, rather than a four period moving average. Additionally, there are twelve seasonal indexes.

The multiplicative time series model requires that the average of the seasonal indexes equal one. If the average is not one, each of the indexes must be adjusted by normalizing them, or multiplying each SI_t by the sum of the SI_t divided by four (or twelve in the case of monthly data).

DESEASONALIZING THE TIME SERIES.   By dividing each observation in the time series by the appropriate seasonal index, the effects of each season are removed. Most data presented in the various economic and business publications, such as the *Survey of Current Business*, has been adjusted for seasonal effect.

FORECASTING THE DESEASONALIZED TIME SERIES.   Once the effects of the seasonal component of the time series have been eliminated, the time series can be forecasted as a simple trend line, using the method described earlier. The multiplicative time series models can then be used to create the forecast, Y_{t+1}, by multiplying the trend forecast for each time period by the appropriate seasonal index.

EXPONENTIAL SMOOTHING

Decomposition of time series into the various components is seldom done today in forecasting because of the widespread use of exponential smoothing techniques. Exponential smoothing uses a weighted average of past time series values to forecast the time series. The exponential smoothing model is based on the equation:

$$F_{t+1} = \alpha Y_t + (1 - \alpha)F_t \qquad (20.24)$$

where:
$$
\begin{aligned}
F_{t+1} &= \text{forecast of the time series for time } t + 1\\
Y_t &= \text{actual value of the time series at time } t\\
F_t &= \text{forecast of the time series for time } t\\
\alpha &= \text{smoothing constant } (0 < \alpha < 1)
\end{aligned}
$$

To illustrate how the exponential smoothing model uses all previous values of the time series in calculating F_{t+1}, set F_t equal to Y_t at time $t = 1$. Then, using equation 20.24:

$$F_{t+1} = \alpha Y_t + (1 - \alpha)F_t, \text{ but since } Y_t = F_t \qquad (20.25)$$

$$F_{t+1} = \alpha Y_t + (1 - \alpha)Y_t \tag{20.26}$$

$$F_{t+1} = \alpha Y_t + 1Y_t - \alpha Y_t \tag{20.27}$$

$$F_{t+1} = Y_t \tag{20.28}$$

$$F_2 = Y_t \tag{20.29}$$

That is, the exponential smoothing forecast for period 2 is equal to the value of the time series in period 1.

Then, since $F_{t+1} = F_2 = Y_t$, F_3 would be equal to:

$$F_3 = \alpha Y_2 + (1 - \alpha)Y_1 \tag{20.30}$$

and:

$$F_4 = \alpha Y_3 + (1 - \alpha)(\alpha Y_2 + (1 - \alpha)Y_t) \tag{20.31}$$

$$F_4 = \alpha Y_3 + (1 - \alpha) Y_2 + (1 - \alpha)^2 Y_1 \tag{20.32}$$

and so F_5 would then be a weighted value of Y_t through Y_{t+4}, etc. Notice that the sum of the coefficients α always equal 1. That is, the exponential

TABLE 20.8
EXAMPLE OF EXPONENTIAL SMOOTHING MODEL

Period	Sales (000s)	$\alpha = .8$	Forecast Error
1	34	34.0	0.0
2	42	34.0	8.0
3	38	40.4	-2.4
4	46	38.5	7.5
5	36	44.5	-8.5
6	32	37.7	-5.7
7	40	33.1	6.9
8	36	38.6	-2.6
9	44	36.5	7.5
10	40	42.5	-2.5
11	30	40.5	-10.5
12	44	32.1	11.9
13	38	41.6	-3.6
14	39	38.7	0.3
15	44	38.9	5.1
Forecast		43.0	

smoothing model is a weighted moving average of all the past values of the Y_t.

The primary advantage of the exponential smoothing model is that it requires very little historical data to perform a forecast. Only two pieces of information are required. These are the actual and forecasted values for the time series at time t. But the smoothing constant, α, must be identified in advance. The more observations in the time series, the better the choice of the smoothing constant will be.

To illustrate how the exponential smoothing model works, consider the data shown in Table 20.8. The exponential smoothing forecast for period 2 is set equal to the actual value of Y_t in period 1, as shown in equation 21.29. Continuing with the forecast gives the results shown in Table 20.8. The forecast error for the fitted observations are shown in column 3.

Each different value of α will provide a different fitted value for the known observation points with some, unknown, α providing the minimum mean squared error. That is, α is chosen by a trial and error method to minimize the mean square error. This value of α is then used to forecast the time series. Most software packages that are used for exponential smoothing includes an algorithm to determine the best value of α by minimizing the MSE.

The criteria for selecting a good value of α can be seen by rewriting equation 20.25 as:

$$F_{t+1} = \alpha Y_t + (1 - \alpha)F_t \qquad (20.33)$$

$$F_{t+1} = \alpha Y_t + F_t - \alpha F_t \qquad (20.34)$$

$$F_{t+1} = F_t + \alpha(Y_t - F_t) \qquad (20.35)$$

Equation 20.35 shows that the forecast value is equal to some adjustment in the forecast error for the prior period. A value of α close to 1 means that the forecast adjusts quickly to forecast errors, while values of α close to 0 means that the forecast does not overreact to errors. The choice of α then, depends upon the random variation in the time series.

Figure 20.8 shows how the time series forecast value changes as different values of α are used, depending on how quickly the forecast adjusts to errors between the fitted and actual time series value. Also, note how using the exponential smoothing model tends to smooth out the variations in the data over time.

EXAMPLE OF THE FORECAST PROCESS

To illustrate how a forecast is prepared, let us take a simple example and examine some of the steps in the forecasting process. Again remember that

FIGURE 20.8
EXAMPLE OF AN EXPONENTIAL SMOOTHING MODEL

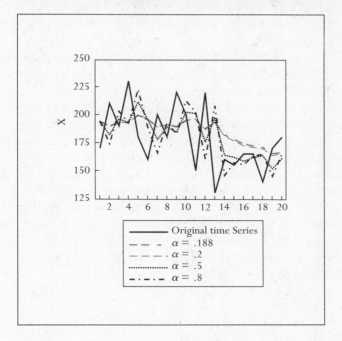

TABLE 20.9
MONTHLY SALES DATA (IN 000s)

	Year 1	Year 2	Year 3	Six Month Forecast
January	484	526	564	598.10
February	470	473	510	534.43
March	464	494	530	562.38
April	356	386	410	437.76
May	368	386	420	443.34
June	280	298	320	339.78
July	290	314	332	
August	304	321	348	
September	220	244	252	
October	260	260	296	
November	304	334	346	
December	412	460	470	

each forecaster has their own manner of attacking a problem. Over time, each student who works in the forecasting field will develop his or her own preferred method of preparing a forecast. The process represented here is an example of one of the potential ways of attacking a problem, but is not the only method.

The data in Table 20.9 represents store sales (in real terms) for the past thirty-six months. Suppose you had been asked to prepare a forecast of the product sales for the next twelve months. How would you proceed?

In this instance the task is to prepare a forecast of combined sales from a store, rather than for an individual product. Attempting to use price as an explanatory variable is difficult because of the various effects of price on individual items, rather than on aggregated data. Also, the forecaster is preparing a short-term forecast. In view of these two considerations, a time series model may be the best model to use.

A first step in the forecasting process would be to graph the sales data against time, shown in Figure 20.9. The graph shows if there is any apparent trend and possible seasonal influences on the data. The next step would then be to determine if a moving average, trend model or a trend series with seasonal data is appropriate.

FIGURE 20.9
PLOT OF MONTHLY SALES AND FITTED TREND LINE

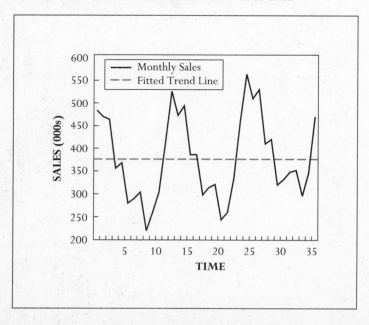

TABLE 20.10
ESTIMATED TREND LINE FOR SALES DATA

REGRESSION OUTPUT:	
Constant	375.7111
Standard error of Y	95.70160
t^2 Statistic	3.925860
R^2	0.000006
No. of Observations	36
Degrees of Freedom	34

X Coefficient(s)	−0.02342	
Std Err of Coef.	1.535407	
t^2 Statistic	−0.01525	

The data appears to indicate that a linear trend model is an appropriate place to begin, as opposed to a moving average model. This is because the data exhibits a cyclical pattern (possibly due to seasonality in the data) around the trend line. A moving average model tends to lag the actual data as it changes direction. Thus, in this case, a moving average model would tend to underforecast in November, December, and January, while overforecasting in April, May, and June.

Table 20.10 shows the equation of the estimated trend line. While the y axis intercept is statistically significant (meaning that it is not equal to zero), the slope parameter is not statistically significant. The implication is that there is no relationship between time and the dependent variable. In effect, the mean value of the dependent variable has become the forecast. Obviously, this model could be improved upon.

The data suggests that there is a significant seasonal effect. As a result of the failure of the simple trend model, it is necessary to adjust the trend model for seasonal effects. The steps, and the data, are shown in Table 20.11. Setting $t = 25, 26, \ldots$, etc., the forecast for the next six months are shown.

The forecast for the next few months appears to be good, but is it a reasonable forecast? A common way of verifying the forecast, given that the forecast demonstrates a good fit with historic data, is to check the magnitude of the period to period changes. Between month 1, 13, and 25, sales increased by an average of $40,000. The forecast shows a change of $31,000 between month 25 and 37. Month 4, 16, and 28 showed an average change of $32,000, while the forecast predicts a change of $27,000. Other months show the same rough equivalence of the forecasted change in sales from the same month one year ago as the average change from the same month. That is, the forecasted sales by month are consistent with what would be expected in the absence of other factors, such as output limitations, bad weather, or other things that could impact the historic relationship of growth.

TABLE 20.11
DEVELOPMENT OF THE FORECAST

Time Period	Sales (000s)	12 Month Moving Average	Centered Moving Average	Seasonal Average	Seasonal Indexes	Deseasonalized Trend	Seasonally Adjusted Forecast
1	484						
2	470						
3	464						
4	356						
5	368						
6	280	351.00	352.75	0.822			
7	290	354.50	354.75	0.857			
8	304	355.00	356.25	0.618			
9	220	357.50	358.75	0.725			
10	260	360.00	360.75	0.843			
11	304	361.50	362.25	1.137			
12	412	363.00	364.00	1.445			
13	526	365.00	365.75	1.301	1.443	364.52	526.00
14	476	366.50	367.50	1.344	1.299	366.39	476.00
15	494	368.50	368.50	1.047	1.344	367.68	494.00
16	386	368.50	369.75	1.044	1.041	370.88	386.00
17	386	371.00	373.00	0.799	1.049	367.99	386.00
18	298	375.00	376.58	0.834	0.800	372.48	298.00
19	314	378.17	379.58	0.848	0.829	378.77	314.00
20	322	381.00	382.50	0.638	0.852	377.93	322.00
21	244	384.00	385.00	0.675	0.628	388.54	244.00
22	260	386.00	387.42	0.862	0.701	370.90	260.00
23	334	388.83	389.75	1.180	0.853	391.56	334.00
24	460	390.67	391.42	1.441	1.160	396.55	460.00
25	564	392.17	393.25	1.297		390.86	564.00
26	510	394.33	394.67	1.343		392.56	510.00
27	530	395.00	396.50	1.034		394.47	530.00
28	410	398.00	398.50	1.054		393.94	410.00
29	420	399.00	399.42	0.801		400.40	420.00
30	320	399.83	376.33	0.882		399.98	320.00
31	332	352.83	331.58	1.050		400.48	332.00
32	348	310.33	288.25	0.874		408.45	348.00
33	252	266.17	249.08	1.188		401.27	252.00
34	296	232.00	214.50	1.613		422.25	296.00
35	346	197.00				405.63	346.00
36	470					405.17	470.00
37 Forecast						407.38	598.10
38 Forecast						409.59	534.43
39 Forecast						411.80	562.38
40 Forecast						414.01	437.76
41 Forecast						416.22	443.34
42 Forecast						418.43	339.78

Another consideration the forecaster needs to consider is when to update the forecast. In a perfect situation, the forecast would be updated whenever additional data became available. In real life, especially in planning situations, the forecast will be updated when the results begin to diverge too greatly from the actual data, reducing the confidence in the forecast to the point no one believes the forecast any longer.

CONCLUSIONS

Time series models are the easiest type of forecasting models, usually providing fairly good short-term results. However, time series models require that the forecasting environment be fairly stable. That is, time series models may not provide good forecasts in a period of rapid change or upheaval. The next chapter presents a different type of forecasting method that may provide better results in some situations.

KEY TERMS AND CONCEPTS

autoregressive models

cyclical component

deseasonalized time
  series

expotential smoothing
  models

irregular component

mean squared error

moving average
  models

multiplicative time
  series models

naive forecasting
  models

smoothing constant

trend component

weighted moving
  averages

CHAPTER 21

Econometric Models

Chapter 20 introduced students to time series modeling, a quantitative modeling technique. Time series models identify historic patterns in the data and use these patterns to develop a forecast of the future, under the assumption that these patterns will continue. Time series models do not attempt to determine how the forecast variable is affected by other variables.

This chapter introduces another quantitative modeling technique, econometric models. Econometric models are causal models that statistically identify the relationships between variables, or how changes in one (or more) variables cause changes in another variable. Econometric models then use this identified relationship to predict the future.

Econometric, or regression, models estimate the statistical relationship between two or more variables. The regression models presented here are linear, although the relationship between the variables might not be. That is, a dependent variable might be linearly related to the square of an independent variable.

The forecast variable is called the dependent, or endogenous, variable. The endogenous variables' value is determined within, or by, the model. The value of the dependent variable is determined by a set of independent, or exogenous, variables. The value of the exogenous variables are determined outside the model, either from the results of another model, known values, or assumed values. In a Keynesian model of the economy, for example, the level of government spending for the next few time periods is given, based upon the Federal budget, while GDP is dependent upon the level of government expenditures, investment, and consumption.

There are two types of data used in regression analysis. Economic forecasting models predominantly use time series data, where the value of the variables change over time. In addition to time series data, there is cross-section data, which is a set of observations at a single point in time.

WHAT IS AN ECONOMETRIC MODEL

Throughout this book, the functional relationship between two or more variables has been discussed. An econometric model is a way of determining the strength and statistical significance of a hypothesized relationship. Econometric models are used extensively in economics as a means of proving, or disproving, the existence of a casual relationship between two or more variables.

Suppose that we are attempting to determine the relationship between two variables. To describe this relationship we need a set of observations on each variable and a mathematical form of the relationship that connects them. Econometric models, such as linear regression, are a means of estimating the functional relationship or equation between two or more variables.

To use regression analysis we must assume the form of the relationship between the variables. In the simplest form, an independent variable, Y, is assumed to be linear related to X, or $Y = \beta X$. In this form, Y is always BX. A one-unit change in X causes a β units change in Y. Regression analysis is concerned with ways to estimate β that provide the best estimate of how Y would change as X changes.

THE CLASSICAL REGRESSION MODEL

The classical regression model estimates the relationship between a single independent variable and dependent variable, or:

$$Y_t = \beta_0 + \beta_1 \times X_t + e_t \tag{21.1}$$

where β_i stands for the true, but unknown, value of the slope and intercept terms.

In this model, β_0 is the intercept term, β_1 is the slope, and e_t is the error term. Because β_0 and β_1 are not known, they must be estimated. The values of β_0 and β_1 are estimated by B_0 and B_1, or:

$$Y_t = B_0 + B_1 \times X_t + e_t \tag{21.2}$$

β_0 and β_1 are estimated as:

$$B_1 = (n\Sigma(X_tY_t) - (\Sigma X_t)(\Sigma Y_t)) / (n \Sigma X_t^2 - (\Sigma X_t)^2) \tag{21.3}$$

$$B_0 = \overline{Y} - (B_1 \times \overline{X}) \tag{21.4}$$

where $\overline{Y}$ and $\overline{X}$ are the mean values of the dependent and independent variables and n is the number of observations.

The error term is calculated as:

$$e_t = (Y_t - \hat{Y}_t) \tag{21.5a}$$

or,

$$e_t = Y_t - (B_0 + B_1 X_t) \tag{21.5b}$$

where $\hat{Y}_t$ is the fitted value of Y_t, and B_0 and B_1 are the estimated parameter values. The fitted value of Y_t is the value of Y_t calculated by substituting the estimated numeric values of B_0 and B_1 into equation (21.5b).

Equations (21.3) and (21.4), used to estimate β_0 and β_1, were derived by minimizing the sum of the square of the error terms, e_t. This method of estimating the regression equation parameters is therefore called the ordinary least-squares method, or OLS for short, based upon the criteria used to estimate the parameters. Figure 21.1 illustrates the relationship between the calculated regression line and the data.

Notice that B_0 and B_1 are calculated the same way in which the trend component of a time series was calculated in the previous chapter. That is, a time series trend line is estimated by determining the relationship between

FIGURE 21.1
THE ESTIMATED REGRESSION LINE MINIMIZES THE SUM OF THE E_t^2

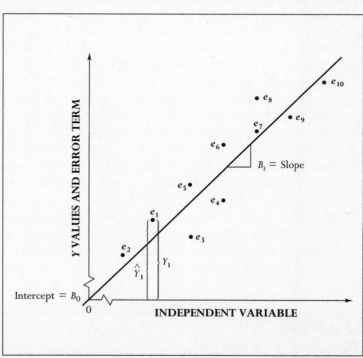

time periods and the dependent variable, or time (t) is the independent variable and Y_t is the dependent variable.

B_0 and B_1 are called *best linear unbiased estimators*, or BLU estimators. On average, the estimated values of B_0 and B_1 are equal to β_1 and β_0 (or unbiased) and no other linear estimator has a smaller variance than estimates of β_0 and β_1 derived using this method.

Estimating the regression parameters, B_0 and B_1, is a mechanical process. Any two variables can be regressed against each other and some relationship identified. However, the skill, and art, of regression analysis is in determining which variables to use in an equation that give the best results.

EXAMPLE OF ESTIMATING THE CLASSICAL REGRESSION MODEL

Now that we have seen how to calculate the coefficients of a regression model, let us use a simple example to illustrate the regression model.

Consider the simple Keynesian consumption function. The portion of money spent each year varies because of changes in the economic environment facing individuals. If it is assumed that income is the sole determinant of consumption then the relationship between income and consumption can be estimated. However, other factors such as an individual's wealth, perceptions about the future of the economy, among other things, all impact consumption expenditures. This simple model ignores these other factors. If the effect on consumption of these factors is small then the model will give good results and the fitted values of the equation will be close to the actual values of consumption, resulting in small error terms, e_t. If however, the independent variable does not explain consumption well, then the fitted values of consumption will not be close to the actual values and the difference between the fitted and actual values will be large. In the example, shown in Table 21.1, the relationship between disposable personal income (X_t) and consumption (Y_t) is estimated. Now that the regression coefficients have been calculated, the effect of personal income on consumption can be more readily seen. The intercept term, B_0, estimates what consumption would be if income were equal to zero, while the slope coefficient, B_1, estimates the portion of income that is consumed. As income changes, consumption will change by the estimated B_1 amount times the change in income. But does personal income do a good job explaining consumption? To answer this, various ways to evaluate the regression equation must be introduced.

MEASURES OF GOODNESS OF FIT

Estimating a regression equation is just the beginning of the regression modeling process. The next step is determining how well the estimated equation

TABLE 21.1
EXAMPLE OF CALCULATING A REGRESSION EQUATION

Date	Personal Consumption (Y_t)	Disposible Income (X_t)	$X_t \cdot Y_t$	Fitted Value of Y	Error Term e_t	Error Term Squared	$(X_t - \overline{X})^2$	$(Y_t)^2$	$(X_t)^2$
1965.3	1503.1	1672.7	2514235.	1476.9	26.2	685.3	955899.100	2259309.6	2797925.3
1965.4	1540.6	1703.0	2623641.	1505.6	35.0	1223.9	897568.514	2373448.4	2900209.0
1966.1	1559.6	1713.0	2671594.	1515.1	44.5	1981.6	878720.495	2432352.2	2934369.0
1966.2	1566.1	1720.2	2694005.	1521.9	44.2	1953.3	865273.762	2452669.2	2959088.0
1966.3	1582.0	1741.2	2754578.	1541.8	40.2	1616.9	826646.323	2502724.0	3031777.4
1966.4	1587.6	1762.9	2798780.	1562.3	25.3	638.1	787657.893	2520473.8	3107816.4
1967.1	1600.2	1788.6	2862117.	1586.7	13.5	182.9	742700.835	2560640.0	3199090.0
1967.2	1620.8	1802.6	2921654.	1599.9	20.9	435.4	718766.41	2626992.6	3249366.8
1967.3	1629.4	1819.5	2964693.	1615.9	13.5	181.2	690396.348	2654944.4	3310580.3
1967.4	1639.0	1834.9	3007401.	1630.5	8.5	71.9	665041.760	2686321.0	3366858.0
1968.1	1672.9	1859.6	3110924.	1653.9	19.0	360.6	625366.104	2798594.4	3458112.2
1968.2	1696.8	1889.4	3205933.	1682.1	14.7	215.2	579122.409	2879130.2	3569832.4
1968.3	1725.2	1889.9	3260455.	1682.6	42.6	1814.3	578361.658	2976315.0	3571722.0
1968.4	1735.0	1908.2	3310727.	1699.9	35.1	1229.6	550862.214	3010225.0	3641227.2
1969.1	1754.7	1908.5	3348844.	1700.2	54.5	2968.2	550416.983	3078972.1	3642372.3
1969.2	1765.0	1927.9	3402743.	1718.6	46.4	2153.9	522007.587	3115225.0	3716798.4
1969.3	1775.0	1967.8	3492845.	1756.4	18.6	346.9	465944.024	3150625.0	3872236.8
1969.4	1790.1	1985.6	3554422.	1773.2	16.9	284.6	441960.271	3204458.0	3942607.4
1970.1	1800.5	1990.6	3584075.	1778.0	22.5	507.8	435337.261	3241800.3	3962488.4
1970.2	1807.5	2020.1	3651330.	1805.9	1.6	2.6	397279.257	3267056.3	4080804.0
1970.3	1824.7	2045.3	3732058.	1829.8	−5.1	25.7	366147.130	3329530.1	4183252.1
1970.4	1821.2	2045.2	3724718.	1829.7	−8.5	71.7	366268.160	3316769.4	4182843.0
1971.1	1849.9	2073.9	3836507.	1856.8	−6.9	48.3	332353.317	3422130.0	4301061.2
1971.2	1863.5	2098.0	3909623.	1879.7	−16.2	261.5	305146.782	3472632.3	4401604.0
1971.3	1876.9	2106.6	3953877.	1887.8	−10.9	119.1	295719.447	3522753.6	4437763.6
1971.4	1904.6	2121.1	4039847.	1901.5	3.1	9.3	280159.470	3627501.2	4499065.2
1972.1	1929.3	2129.7	4108830.	1909.7	19.6	384.6	271129.454	3722198.5	4535622.1
1972.2	1963.3	2149.1	4219328.	1928.1	35.2	1241.8	251302.618	3854546.9	4618630.8
1972.3	1989.1	2193.9	4363886.	1970.5	18.6	346.5	208393.095	3956518.8	4813197.2
1972.4	2032.1	2272.0	4616931.	2044.4	−12.3	152.4	143187.260	4129430.4	5161984.0
1973.1	2063.9	2300.7	4748414.	2071.6	−7.7	59.6	122290.737	4259683.2	5293220.5
1973.2	2062.0	2315.2	4773942.	2085.4	−23.4	545.4	112359.660	4251844.0	5360151.0
1973.3	2073.7	2337.9	4848103.	2106.8	−33.1	1098.9	97656.8287	4300231.7	5465776.4
1973.4	2067.4	2382.7	4925993.	2149.3	−81.9	6703.4	71663.7857	4274142.8	5677259.3
1974.1	2050.8	2334.7	4788002.	2103.8	−53.0	2811.1	99667.0746	4205780.6	5450824.1
1974.2	2059.0	2304.5	4744965.	2075.2	−16.2	263.1	119647.450	4239481.0	5310720.3
1974.3	2065.5	2315.0	4781632.	2085.2	−19.7	386.7	112493.781	4266290.3	5359225.0
1974.4	2039.9	2313.7	4719716.	2083.9	−44.0	1938.9	113367.513	4161192.0	5353207.7
1975.1	2051.8	2282.5	4683233.	2054.4	−2.6	6.7	135351.091	4209883.2	5209806.3
1975.2	2086.9	2390.3	4988317.	2156.5	−69.6	4840.2	67652.4916	4355151.6	5713534.1
1975.3	2114.4	2359.4	4988715.	2127.2	−12.8	164.1	84681.5388	4470687.4	5566768.4
1975.4	2137.0	2389.4	5106147.	2155.6	−18.6	346.7	68121.4833	4566769.0	5709232.4
1976.1	2179.3	2424.5	5283712.	2188.9	−9.6	91.4	51031.2283	4749348.5	5878200.3
1976.2	2194.7	2434.9	5343875.	2198.7	−4.0	16.1	46440.6490	4816708.1	5928738.0
1976.3	2213.0	2444.7	5410121.	2208.0	5.0	25.1	42312.8709	4897369.0	5976558.1
1976.4	2242.0	2459.5	5514199.	2222.0	20.0	399.9	36443.1635	5026564.0	6049140.3
1977.1	2271.3	2463.0	5594211.	2225.3	46.0	2114.5	35119.1070	5158803.7	6066369.0
1977.2	2280.8	2490.3	5679876.	2251.2	29.6	878.0	25632.3064	5202048.6	6201594.1
1977.3	2302.6	2541.0	5850906.	2299.2	3.4	11.7	11968.5625	5301966.8	6456681.0
1977.4	2331.6	2556.2	5960035.	2313.6	18.0	324.9	8873.81444	5436358.6	6534158.4
1978.1	2347.1	2587.3	6072651.	2343.0	4.1	16.6	3981.72685	5508878.4	6694121.3
1978.2	2394.0	2631.9	6300768.	2385.3	8.7	76.4	342.284260	5731236.0	6926897.6

CONTINUED ON NEXT PAGE . . .

TABLE 21.1 (CONTINUED)
EXAMPLE OF CALCULATING A REGRESSION EQUATION

Date	Personal Consumption (Y_t)	Disposable Income (X_t)	$X_t \cdot Y_t$	Fitted Value of Y	Error Term e_t	Error Term Squared	$(X_t - \overline{X})^2$	$(Y_t)^2$	$(X_t)^2$
1978.3	2404.5	2653.2	6379619.	2405.4	−0.9	0.9	7.83481567	5781620.3	7039470.2
1978.4	2421.6	2680.9	6492067.	2431.7	−10.1	101.3	930.193519	5864146.6	7187224.8
1979.1	2437.9	2699.2	6580379.	2449.0	−11.1	123.0	2381.34963	5943356.4	7285680.6
1979.2	2435.4	2697.6	6569735.	2447.5	−12.1	145.9	2227.75259	5931173.2	7277045.8
1979.3	2454.7	2715.3	6665246.	2464.2	−9.5	91.0	4211.88981	6025552.1	7372854.1
1979.4	2465.4	2728.1	6725857.	2476.4	−11.0	120.1	6037.14611	6078197.2	7442529.6
1980.1	2464.6	2742.9	6760151.	2490.4	−25.8	664.3	8556.07870	6074253.2	7523500.4
1980.2	2414.2	2692.0	6499026.	2442.2	−28.0	782.5	1730.48296	5828361.6	7246864.0
1980.3	2440.3	2722.5	6643716.	2471.1	−30.8	946.0	5198.27648	5955064.1	7412006.3
1980.4	2469.2	2777.0	6856968.	2522.7	−53.5	2858.7	16027.3255	6096948.6	7711729.0
1981.1	2475.5	2783.7	6891049.	2529.0	−53.5	2863.5	17768.6431	6128100.3	7748985.7
1981.2	2476.1	2776.7	6875386.	2522.4	−46.3	2142.1	15951.4561	6131071.2	7710062.9
1981.3	2487.4	2814.1	6999792.	2557.8	−70.4	4956.1	26797.3868	6187158.8	7919158.8
1981.4	2468.6	2808.8	6933803.	2552.8	−84.2	7086.4	25090.2666	6093986.0	7889357.4
1982.1	2484.0	2795.0	6942780.	2539.7	−55.7	3103.9	20908.8922	6170256.0	7812025.0
1982.2	2488.9	2824.8	7030644.	2567.9	−79.0	6246.1	30415.0370	6194623.2	7979495.0
1982.3	2502.5	2829.0	7079572.	2571.9	−69.4	4817.7	31897.6292	6262506.3	8003241.0
1982.4	2539.3	2832.6	7192821.	2575.3	−36.0	1297.3	33196.5025	6448044.5	8023622.8
1983.1	2556.5	2843.6	7269663.	2585.7	−29.2	854.7	37325.8822	6535692.3	8086061.0
1983.2	2604.0	2867.0	7465668.	2607.9	−3.9	15.2	46915.1588	6780816.0	8219689.0
1983.3	2639.0	2903.0	7661017.	2642.0	−3.0	8.9	63806.2922	6964321.0	8427409.0
1983.4	2678.2	2960.6	7929078.	2696.5	−18.3	336.0	96223.4655	7172755.2	8765152.4
1984.1	2703.8	3033.2	8201166.	2765.3	−61.5	3780.0	146535.131	7310534.4	9200302.2
1984.2	2741.1	3065.9	8403938.	2796.2	−55.1	3041.3	172639.480	7513629.2	9399742.8
1984.3	2754.6	3102.7	8546697.	2831.1	−76.5	5851.7	204574.452	7587821.2	9626747.3
1984.4	2784.8	3118.5	8684398.	2846.1	−61.3	3752.6	219116.743	7755111.0	9725042.3
1985.1	2824.9	3123.6	8823857.	2850.9	−26.0	675.4	223917.363	7980060.0	9756877.0
1985.2	2849.7	3189.6	9089403.	2913.4	−63.7	4056.2	290735.641	8120790.1	10173548.2
1985.3	2893.7	3156.5	9133964.	2882.0	11.7	135.9	256136.272	8373499.7	9963492.3
1985.4	2895.3	3178.7	9203290.	2903.1	−7.8	60.3	279099.911	8382762.1	10104133.7
1986.1	2922.4	3227.6	9432338.	2949.4	−27.0	727.6	333158.771	8540421.8	10417401.8
1986.2	2947.9	3281.4	9673239.	3000.3	−52.4	2748.0	398159.831	8690114.4	10767586.0
1986.3	2993.7	3272.6	9797182.	2992.0	1.7	2.9	387131.687	8962239.7	10709910.8
1986.4	3012.5	3266.2	9839427.	2985.9	26.6	706.1	379208.499	9075156.3	10668062.4
1987.1	3011.5	3295.2	9923494.	3013.4	−1.9	3.6	415765.845	9069132.3	10858343.0
1987.2	3046.8	3241.7	9876811.	2962.7	84.1	7068.4	349634.595	9282990.2	10508618.9
1987.3	3075.8	3285.7	10106156	3004.4	71.4	5099.0	403604.913	9460545.6	10795824.5
1987.4	3074.7	3335.8	10256584	3051.8	22.9	522.7	469771.890	9453780.1	11127561.6
1988.1	3128.2	3380.1	10573628	3093.8	34.4	1184.2	532460.738	9785635.2	11425076.0
1988.2	3147.8	3386.3	10659395	3099.7	48.1	2317.6	541547.447	9908644.8	11467027.7
1988.3	3170.6	3407.5	10803819	3119.7	50.9	2587.3	573199.007	10052704.4	11611056.3
1988.4	3202.9	3443.1	11027904	3153.4	49.5	2445.6	628371.822	10258568.4	11854937.6
1989.1	3203.6	3472.9	11125782	3181.7	21.9	481.1	676504.726	10263053.0	12061034.4
1989.2	3212.2	3450.1	11082411	3160.1	52.1	2716.9	639518.609	10318228.8	11903190.0
1989.3	3235.3	3455.7	11180226	3165.4	69.9	4889.0	648506.598	10467166.1	11941862.5
1989.4	3242.0	3480.9	11285077	3189.2	52.8	2783.4	689728.712	10510564.0	12116664.8
1990.1	3259.5	3516.8	11463009	3223.2	36.3	1314.9	750647.355	10624340.3	12367882.2
1990.2	3260.1	3523.9	11488266	3230.0	30.1	908.3	763000.632	10628252.0	12417871.2
1990.3	3273.9	3513.7	11503502	3220.3	53.6	2872.6	745285.291	10718421.2	12346087.7
1990.4	3248.0	3511.6	11405676	3218.3	29.7	881.2	741663.845	10549504.0	12331334.6
1991.1	3223.5	3488.7	11245824	3196.6	26.9	722.1	702745.337	10390952.3	12171027.7

CONTINUED ON NEXT PAGE . . .

TABLE 21.1 (CONTINUED)
EXAMPLE OF CALCULATING A REGRESSION EQUATION

Date	Personal Consumption (Y_t)	Disposible Income (X_t)	$X_t \cdot Y_t$	Fitted Value of Y	Error Term e_t	Error Term Squared	$(X_t - \overline{X})^2$	$(Y_t)^2$	$(X_t)^2$
1991.2	3239.3	3505.2	11354394	3212.3	27.0	731.5	730681.457	10493064.5	12286427.0
1991.3	3251.2	3511.5	11416588	3218.2	33.0	1087.7	741491.615	10570301.4	12330632.3
1991.4	3249.0	3530.8	11471569	3236.5	12.5	156.3	775102.529	10556001.0	12466548.6
1992.1	3289.3	3565.7	11728657	3269.5	19.8	390.2	837772.395	10819494.5	12714216.5
1992.2	3288.5	3576.0	11759676	3279.3	9.2	84.6	856733.645	10814232.3	12787776.0
Column Sum:	259500.3	286243.3	7.2E+08	259500.3	0	150981.8	35459992.8	655472425.	794119500.2
Mean:	2402.8	2650.4	6679255.2	2402.8	0.0	1398.0	328333.3	6069189.1	7352958.3

$$B_1 = ((n \times \Sigma X_t Y_t) - (\Sigma X \Sigma Y)) / ((n \times \Sigma X_t) - \Sigma X_t^2)$$

$$= 0.946975$$

$$B_0 = \overline{Y} - B_1 \overline{X} = -107.083$$

fits the actual data points, or how well the estimated equation explains variations in the dependent variable. Measures of goodness of fit are necessary to determine whether or not the independent variable adequately explains changes in the dependent variable. Additionally, because estimating a regression equation is a fairly mechanical process, measures of goodness of fit help identify which variables are the best in the forecast process.

COEFFICIENT OF DETERMINATION

The most widely used measure of goodness of fit is the *coefficient of determination*, or R^2. R^2 is a statistic that ranges between 0 and 1. A R^2 of 1 means that all the variation of the dependent variable is explained by the independent variable, while a R^2 near zero means almost none of the variation is explained.

The R^2 statistic measures the portion of the variation in the dependent variable from its mean value that is explained by the independent variable. Figure 21.2 illustrates how the variation in the dependent variable is separated into the explained and unexplained variation. The total variation of the dependent variable is defined as:

$$Total\ variation = \Sigma(Y_t - \overline{Y})^2 \tag{21.6}$$

The total variation in the dependent variable can be written as the sum of the deviations from its mean value, or:

$$Total\ Variation = unexplained\ variation + explained\ variation \tag{21.7}$$

FIGURE 21.2

THE TOTAL VARIATION IN THE DEPENDENT VARIABLE,
$(Y_t - \overline{Y})^2$, IS EQUAL TO THE EXPLAINED VARIATION, $(\hat{Y}_t - \overline{Y})^2$,
PLUS THE UNEXPLAINED VARIATION, $(Y_t - \overline{Y})^2$.

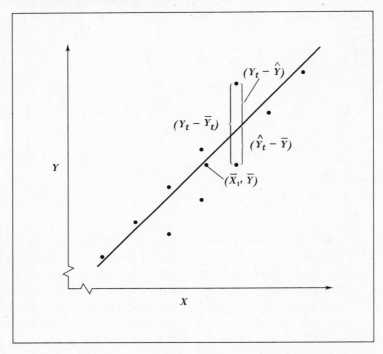

The explained variation is the difference between the fitted regression values, $\hat{Y}_t$, and the mean value of $\overline{Y}$, while the unexplained variation is the difference between the actual value of the dependent variable, Y_t, and the fitted value, $\hat{Y}_t$, or:

$$\Sigma(Y_t - \overline{Y})^2 = \Sigma(Y_t - \hat{Y}_t)^2 + \Sigma(\hat{Y} - \overline{Y})^2 \tag{21.8}$$

R^2 is the proportion of explained variation to total variation and is then defined as:

$$R^2 = Explained\ Variation\ /\ Total\ Variation \tag{21.9}$$

or,

$$R^2 = \Sigma(\hat{Y}_t - \overline{Y})^2 / \Sigma(Y_t - \overline{Y})^2 \tag{21.10}$$

If the explained variation is close to the total variation, the R^2 will be close to one. A R^2 of 1.00 means that all the Y_t lie on the regression line, while if the explained variation is small, relative to the total variation in Y_t, the R^2 will be close to zero.

A regression equation with a high R^2 is a good sign that the equation has a good statistical relation between the independent and independent variable, or that a large portion of the total variation of the dependent variable is explained by the independent variable. However, a high R^2 is not, by itself, the measure of a good regression. In the multivariate regression model, adding more variables to the regression equation will almost always increase the R^2, even though none of the independent variables added have any significant relationship with the dependent variable.

What is a good value of R^2 for a regression equation? This is strictly a matter of judgment, based upon the variability of the dependent variable. In some cases, a R^2 of 0.90 is good, in other cases, a R^2 of as low as 0.25 is good. A high R^2 is often a sign of a good equation, but a low R^2 is not necessarily a sign of a bad equation. In general, the more variation between periods in the dependent variable, the lower the R^2 can be, while still having an equation that helps explain changes in the dependent variable.

TESTS OF SIGNIFICANCE

The R^2 statistic is a measure of the ability of the regression equation to explain variation in the dependent variable. It does not measure the statistical validity of the independent variable. To determine if the estimated coefficients of the regression equation are statistically different from zero, statistical tests of significance are used, based upon the normal distribution.

THE NORMAL DISTRIBUTION

A random variable is any variable that takes on alternate values according to chance. Random variables are described by the process that generates their values. This process is called a *probability distribution* and lists all possible outcomes of the random variable and the probability that these outcomes will occur. One of the most useful probability distributions is the normal distribution, shown in Figure 21.3.

The shape of the normal distribution is determined by two parameters, the mean and standard deviation. The population mean, μ (mu) determines where the distribution is centered and the standard deviation σ (sigma) determines how spread out the curve is. The greater the standard deviation, relative to the mean, the flatter is the distribution. Figure 21.4 shows how

---

FIGURE 21.3
THE NORMAL DISTRIBUTION

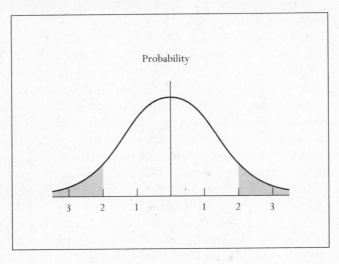

different values of σ change the shape of the normal distribution. μ and σ are calculated as:

$$\mu = (\Sigma X_t) / n \qquad\qquad (21.11)$$

$$\sigma = (\Sigma(X_t - \mu)^2) / n \qquad\qquad (21.12)$$

where *n* is the total number of observations in the population.

The area under the normal distribution is equal to one because the normal distribution represents the probability that a random variable will fall within the upper bound (infinity) and the lower bound (minus infinity). Because the value of a random variable will fall within these two extremes, the probability will equal one.

To calculate the probability that a random variable lies within some range, the standard normal distribution, Z, with mean zero and standard deviation 1 is used. For example, if $0 < Z < 1.50$, then Z lies within 1.50 standard deviations to the right of 0, the mean. Values for the standard normal distribution are in Mathematical Appendix Table I at the end of this book. Looking at the Z value of 1.50 shows 43.32 percent of the values lie between 0 and 1.50. Because the standard normal distribution is symmetric, the same percent of values lie between $-1.50 < Z < 0$. Table 21.2 presents

FIGURE 21.4

HOW THE NORMAL DISTRIBUTION IS AFFECTED BY DIFFERENT VARIANCES

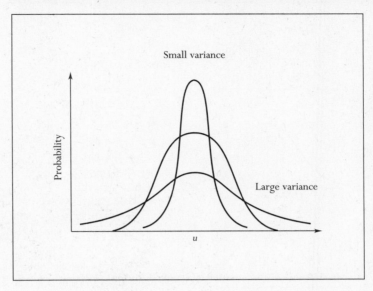

some examples of calculating the proportion of data that lies within different values of Z.

The difficulty in using the standard normal distribution in economics is that the population parameters are seldom known. Instead, samples that approximate the population distribution are used. A close approximation of a normal population is the *t* distribution.

THE STUDENT *T* DISTRIBUTION

If the distribution of the underlying population parameters, β_0 and β_1, is not known, then the Student *t* (*t*) distribution must be used to determine the probability that a random variable falls within some range. The *t* distribution is a symmetric distribution with a mean equal to zero. The *t* distribution has the same general shape as the normal distribution, although there is more weight in the tails. As the number of observations increases, the *t* distribution approaches the normal distribution. Figure 21.5 compares the normal distribution with the *t* distribution.

The most common *t* test checks the hypothesis that the regression parameters, β_0 and β_1, are significantly different from zero, given that B_0 and B_1

TABLE 21.2
EXAMPLES OF CALCULATING Z VALUES

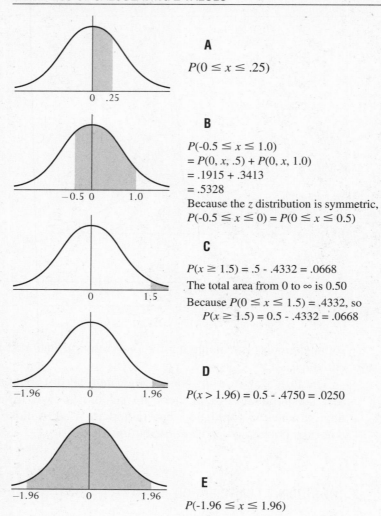

A

$P(0 \leq x \leq .25)$

B

$P(-0.5 \leq x \leq 1.0)$
$= P(0, x, .5) + P(0, x, 1.0)$
$= .1915 + .3413$
$= .5328$
Because the z distribution is symmetric,
$P(-0.5 \leq x \leq 0) = P(0 \leq x \leq 0.5)$

C

$P(x \geq 1.5) = .5 - .4332 = .0668$
The total area from 0 to ∞ is 0.50
Because $P(0 \leq x \leq 1.5) = .4332$, so
$\quad P(x \geq 1.5) = 0.5 - .4332 = .0668$

D

$P(x > 1.96) = 0.5 - .4750 = .0250$

E

$P(-1.96 \leq x \leq 1.96)$

The total area under the z distribution is 1.0.
From part (D) above, we saw: $P(x \geq 1.96) = .0250$.
Because the z distribution is symmetric: $P(x \leq -1.96) = .0250$
So the total area under the two tails is 0.05.
Thus, the probability $P(-1.96 \leq x \leq 1.96) = 1.00 - .05 = .95$

FIGURE 21.5
A COMPARISON OF THE NORMAL DISTRIBUTION AND THE STUDENT
T DISTRIBUTION

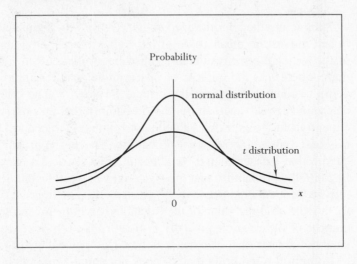

were estimated as shown above. In the example of the effect of personal income on consumption, it is expected that consumption will be positively related to personal income. A test of the hypothesis $\beta_1 = 0$ is performed with the goal of either rejecting this hypothesis, or accepting the alternative hypothesis, β_1 does not equal 0. Hypothesis tests are set up in the hope of rejecting the *null hypothesis*, or a statement that assumes a certain effect is not present. For example, to test the validity of the consumption model, the following test could be performed:

Null Hypothesis: $\beta_1 = 0$

Alternative hypothesis: $\beta_1 = 0$

To test a hypothesis requires that the rules for acceptance and rejection be identified before the data are examined.

To test the null hypothesis, it is necessary to standardize the estimated regression coefficient by subtracting the estimated regression coefficient, B_1, by subtracting the hypothesized true value, β_1, and dividing by the estimate of its standard error, s, or:

$$t_{n-2} = (B_1 - \beta_1) / s_B = (B_1 - \beta_1) / (s / \sqrt{\Sigma(X_t - \overline{X})^2}) \qquad (21.13)$$

where *s* is calculated as:

$$s = \sqrt{(\Sigma e_t^2 / (n - 2)) / (\Sigma(X_t - \overline{X})^2)} \tag{21.14}$$

Subtracting the hypothesized value, β_1, from the estimated regression coefficient moves the mean value of $(B_1 - \beta_1)$ to zero. Dividing by the estimate of the standard error results in a *t* distribution that has $n - 2$ degrees of freedom; where *n* is the number of observations in the sample. The calculated *t* value is compared against the critical *t* value, t_c. The critical value of *t* is determined in advance and is the probability that an observation will lie far enough from the expected value that it is unlikely to occur. The most common t_c is based upon a 2.5 percent probability, or that the probability that a calculated value greater than t_c will occur only about 2.5 percent of the time. Because the probability that the observed value can be either positive or negative, or be at either extreme in the *t* distribution, there is a 5.0 percent possibility that the absolute value of the calculated *t* will be greater than t_c. For a large number of observations, usually *n* greater than 30, the t_c is 1.96, or a calculated *t* of greater than 1.96 has less than a 2.5 percent chance of occurring.

If the null hypothesis that β_1 does not equal zero is being tested, then β_1 equals zero and the *t* test becomes:

$$t_{n-2} = B_1 / (s_b) \tag{21.15}$$

where s_b is:

$$s_b = \sqrt{(\Sigma e_t^2) / ((n - k) / \Sigma(X_t - \overline{X})^2} \tag{21.16}$$

and *k* is the number of regression coefficients, excluding the constant term.

If t_{n-2} is greater than the t_c for the desired level of confidence then we can reject the null hypothesis, β_1 equals zero. In general, if the calculated value of t_{n-2} is greater than 2.0 then the null hypothesis can be rejected, or that the estimated regression parameter is significant.

T TESTS OF THE REGRESSION COEFFICIENTS

The statistical test for rejecting the null hypothesis that a relationship between the independent and dependent variable exists is based upon the *t* distribution. If the null hypothesis, β_1 equals zero is not rejected, then it cannot be said that there is a relationship between the independent and dependent variable. To use the *t* test, the estimated regression coefficient B_1 is standardized by dividing by the estimate of the standard error:

$$t_{n-2} = B_1 / (\sqrt{(\Sigma e_i^2 / (n-2))} / \Sigma (X_i - \overline{X})^2) = B_1 / s_{B1} \qquad (21.17)$$

The term $n - 2$ is the number of degrees of freedom in the model. n is the number of observations and there are two parameters, causing the loss of two degrees of freedom. In a more general case, there are $n - k$ degrees of freedom, where k is the number of regression parameters estimated.

According to the null hypothesis, β_1 equals zero so the appropriate test statistic is B_1 / s_{B1}. If the ratio of the estimated parameter to its standard error is greater that or equal to t_c in absolute value, the null hypothesis, that t_c is the critical value of t for the required level of confidence of the test, is rejected. For a large sample size (n greater than 30) and 5 percent level of significance, $t_c = 1.96$.

Most econometric software calculates the t statistic for the various parameters automatically, allowing the user to quickly determine if the estimated regression parameter is significantly different than zero.

Up to now, the t tests have been done on the slope coefficient, B_1, of the regression equation. This verifies that there is a significant relationship between the independent and dependent variable. However, in many cases researchers are interested in determining if the regression line goes through the origin. For example, in our attempt to construct a single equation model of consumption, the slope was 0.947 and the t statistic was 149.42, allowing the null hypothesis that B_1 equaled zero to be rejected. However, what would happen if income dropped to very low levels? Does the estimated regression line pass through the origin? To test this hypothesis, the t statistic is calculated as:

$$T_{n-2} = B_0 / \sqrt{(((\Sigma e_t)^2 / n - 2) \times (\Sigma X_t^2 / n \Sigma (X_t - \overline{X})^2))} \qquad (21.18)$$

Table 21.3 shows how the t test is used to verify the significance of parameters of a regression equation, using the data and regression results presented in Table 21.1.

THE F DISTRIBUTION

A high R^2 means that there is a good fit of the regression line with the dependent variable (assuming the e_t are not correlated), while a low R^2 generally implies a poor fit. However, a low R^2 can occur for several reasons. For example, the chosen independent variable may not be a good explanatory variable. Or, there may be large variation in the underlying data.

If one is using the classical regression model, a high R^2 and a significant t statistic for B_1 tends to validate the model. A second test of significance is the F test.

TABLE 21.3
EXAMPLE OF A T TEST ON THE REGRESSION COEFFICIENTS

Beginning with the regression equation calculated in Table 21.1:
Consumption $= -107.08 + (.947 \times (Disposable\ Income))$

We calculate:

$$Sum\ of\ the\ error\ terms\ squared = \Sigma e_L{}^2 = 150981.80$$
$$Sum\ of\ the\ (X_t - \overline{X})^2 = \Sigma(X_t - X)^2 = 35459992.85$$

$s_{B1}{}^2 = ((\Sigma e_t)^2 / (n - 2)) / (\Sigma(X_t - \overline{X})^2) = 0.000040$

$s_{B1} = \sqrt{s_{B1}{}^2} = 0.006$

From equation (21.15):

$t_{n-2} = B_1 / S_{B1} = .947 / .065 = 149.420$

Since t is greater than t_c from Mathematical Appendix table, we can reject the null hypothesis that disposable income and consumption are not related.

To test the null hypothesis that the intercept term is zero, or $B_0 = 0$, we must first calculate the standard deviation.

$S_{B_0}{}^2 = ((\Sigma e_t)^2 / (n - 2)) \times (\Sigma X_t / (n \times (\Sigma(X_t - \overline{X})^2))) = 295.3535$

$S_{B_0} = \sqrt{S^2{}_{B_0}} = 17.18585$

From equation (21.16):

$t_{n-2} = B_0 / S_{B_0} = -6.231$

The critical value of t from Mathematical Appendix Table II for $t = 1.96$. Because $t > t_c$, we can reject the null hypothesis that the intercept term is equal to 0.

The F test is:

$$F_{1,n-2} = explained\ variance\ /\ unexplained\ variance$$
$$= (B_1{}^2\ \Sigma(X_t - \overline{X})^2)\ /\ s^2 \qquad (21.19)$$

If there is a strong statistical relationship between the independent and dependent variable then there should be a large ratio of explained to unexplained variance. This ratio follows the F distribution with 1 and $n-2$ degrees of freedom in the numerator and denominator, respectively.

The F distribution is not symmetric like the normal distribution. Instead, it begins at zero and asymptotically approaches the x axis (see Figure 21.6).

The only way that $F_{1,n-2}$ can be zero is if the explained variance is zero, while the ratio can get very large.

The F test can be used to reject the null hypothesis of no relationship between the independent and dependent variable. If the critical value of the F distribution from Mathematical Appendix Table II at the 5 percent significance with 1 and $n-2$ degrees of freedom is greater than the calculated value we cannot reject the null hypothesis, while if the calculated value of $F_{1,n-2}$ is greater than the critical value the null hypothesis can be rejected in favor of the alternative hypothesis, that there is a statistical relationship between the independent and dependent variable.

Table 21.4 shows how the F test is used to test the null hypothesis that there is no relationship between income and consumption.

SUMMARY OF STATISTICAL TESTS OF THE REGRESSION EQUATION

Three different tests of the regression equation—the R^2, the t and the F test have now been introduced. These three tests together allow a forecaster to determine if a regression equation identifies a strong statistical relationship between the independent and dependent variable.

FIGURE 21.6
THE F DISTRIBUTION

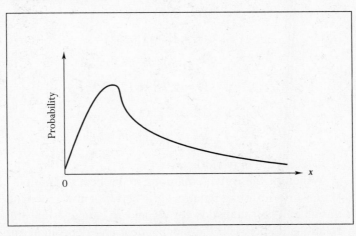

TABLE 21.4
USING THE F TEST TO VERIFY A STATISTICALLY VALID RELATIONSHIP BETWEEN THE INDEPENDENT AND DEPENDENT VARIABLE

Total sum of squares = error sum of squares + regression sum of squares

or:

$$\Sigma(Y_t - \overline{Y}) = \Sigma(Y_t - \hat{Y}_t) + \Sigma\,(\hat{Y}_t + \overline{Y})$$

From Table 21.1 we can calculate:

Total sum of squares =	31950151.0
Error sum of squares =	150981.8
Regression sum of squares =	31799169.2

R_2 is defined as:

$R_2 = 1 -$ *(explained variation in Y / total variation in Y)*

   = *(regression sum of squares / total sum of squares)* = 0.995

The *F* statistic is defined as:

F = *(explained variation in Y) / (unexplained variation in Y)*

   = *(regression sum of squares) / ((error sum of squares) / N − 2)* = 22325.3

Since $F > F_c$, we reject the null hypothesis that the dependent and independent variables are not related.

Consider two different regression equations:

$$Y_t = 2.56 + 12.50\,X_t \tag{21.20}$$
$$(2.34)\,(5.54)$$
$$R^2 = .80 \quad F = 345.29$$
$$Y_t = 2.56 + 12.50\,X_t \tag{21.21}$$
$$(.23)\,(3.45)$$
$$R^2 = .80 \quad F = 2.56$$

(*t* statistics are in parenthesis).

Which of these two equations is the best? Equation 21.20 has a high *F*, suggesting a strong relationship between the independent and dependent variable. The *t* statistics for B_0 and B_1 suggest that there is a good linear relationship between the independent and dependent variable and the R^2 of .80 says 80 percent of the total variation in the dependent variable is explained by the independent variable.

Equation 21.21 also has a high R^2, but the small F statistic suggests that the relationship between the independent and dependent variable is weak. The low t on B_0 suggests that the intercept term might be zero, or that the regression line might go through the origin.

In spite of the apparent differences, it is difficult to determine which equation is best. The significance tests of equation 21.20 suggests a stronger relationship between the independent and dependent variable than equation 21.21. However, this is where the skill in modeling comes into play. It is possible that forcing the regression line through the origin improves the fit. However, setting the intercept term to zero, or forcing the regression line through the origin, is something that should be done with care. Also, a regression of the form:

$$Y_t = B_1 X_t \tag{21.22}$$

requires that some measures of goodness of fit be interpreted differently.

THE ERROR TERM AND THE CLASSICAL MODEL

The regression model makes several important assumptions about the error term. These are:

(1) The error term is normally distributed;

(2) The error term has a mean value of 0;

(3) The variance of the error term is a constant;

(4) Consecutive error terms are not related to each other.

The first assumption, requiring the error term to be normally distributed, is important in the statistical tests we discussed above. The F and t tests are based upon an assumption of a normal distribution of the error terms.

The assumption that the error terms have an expected value of zero is a simplifying assumption. If the expected value is not zero, the model is equivalent to a new model with the same slope, but a different intercept term.

The first three assumptions together mean that the error term has a zero mean value and that the size of the error term does not depend upon the value of the independent value, X_t.

The last two assumptions are often violated and need to be checked for and corrected to ensure that the estimates of B_0 and B_1 remain unbiased and that the estimated variances are correct. Assumption (3) means that the size of the error is not related to the dependent variable. If the error term has a constant variance, as assumed, it is called homoscedastic. If the variance is changing, it is called heteroscedastic. If Assumption (3) is violated, a fix to

FIGURE 21.7
EXAMPLES OF HETEROSCEDASTIC ERROR TERMS

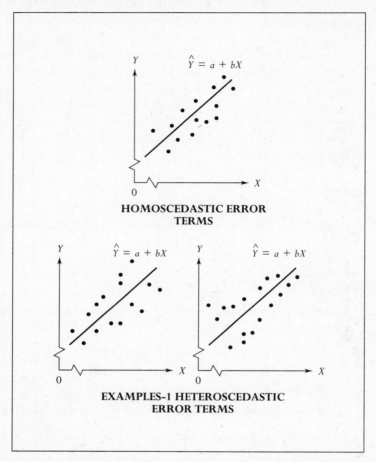

HOMOSCEDASTIC ERROR TERMS

EXAMPLES-1 HETEROSCEDASTIC ERROR TERMS

the model needs to be made, so that the model remains statistically valid. Figure 21.7 shows examples of homoscedastic and heteroscedastic error terms.

Assumption (4) means that a positive error term is not generally followed by another positive error term, and negative error terms are not generally followed by other negative values. In econometric models using time series data this assumption is often violated. If the error terms are correlated with each other, the error terms said to be *serial correlated*, or *autocorrelated*. Figure 21.8 presents examples of autocorrelation in the error term.

FIGURE 21.8
EXAMPLES OF AUTOCORRELATION

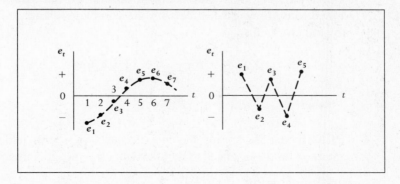

IDENTIFYING AND CORRECTING HETEROSCEDASTICITY

If heteroscedasticity is present in a model, the least-squares procedure used to estimate the parameters of the regression model will place more importance on the observations that have large variances than those that have small variances. This is because the sum of squared residuals associated with the large variance error terms is greater than the sum of squared residuals of the small error terms. Fortunately, identifying and correcting heteroscedasticity is a fairly simple procedure. There are many different tests for heteroscedasticity, but only one is discussed here (for a discussion of other tests, see Johnston 1984, or Intrilligator 1978).

A common test for heteroscedasticity is the Goldfeld-Quandt test. This is an easy test to construct and use if enough data points are available. This test is carried out by first arranging the data according to the magnitude of the independent variable. The data is then broken into five groups of approximately equal size. The middle fifth of the data is then ignored for the purposes of this test.

Regression equations for the lowest two-fifths and upper two-fifths of the data are then calculated. The sum of the square of the error terms is then calculated for each of the two regression equations. The ratio of the two sums (with the largest values in the numerator of the ratio) is distributed as an F statistic with $(n - (n/5) - 4))/2$ degrees of freedom in both the numerator and denominator. The null hypothesis of heteroscedastic error terms can be rejected if the calculated value of F is greater than the critical value of F for a desired significance level.

The major concern with the Goldfeld-Quandt test is that if autocorrelation is present in the model it will not always be valid.

If heteroscedasticity is present in the model, the data need to be transformed to eliminate the effects on the parameter estimates. The most common transformation is:

$$Y_t / X_t = B_0^* + B_1 \times (1 / X_t) + e_t \qquad (21.23)$$

where: $B_0^* = B_0(1 / X_t)$

This model transforms the non-constant error term into a constant. The regression results just need to be used with care, recognizing the transformation.

AUTOCORRELATION

Another major area where the underlying assumptions of the classical model break down is the assumption that succeeding error terms are not related. This is known as first-order autocorrelation, or as it is sometimes called, serial correlation. It is quite possible that error terms are correlated with the error terms two or three or more periods back. This is known as second- or third-order autocorrelation, but the tests for this are quite difficult and will not be discussed here.

Autocorrelation is primarily a problem when using time series data. If cross sectional data exhibits autocorrelation then the data can simply be reordered to eliminate the effects. However, most macroeconomic data and models are time series, making autocorrelation a serious problem that needs to be addressed.

If autocorrelation is present in a model, the parameter estimates will not be affected. However, the estimates of the standard error will be biased downward. This leads to the conclusion that the parameter estimates are more precise than they truly are. T tests of the parameters will reject the null hypothesis that B_i equals zero more than it should, often leading to incorrect model specification.

The most common test for autocorrelation is the Durbin-Watson (DW) statistic. The DW statistic is defined as:

$$DW = \Sigma(e_t - e_{t-1})^2 / \Sigma e_i^2 \qquad (21.24)$$

The DW statistic lies between 0 and 4, with a value near 2 indicating no autocorrelation. The reason that the DW statistic lies between 0 and 4 is that the DW statistic is approximately equal to:

$$DW = 2(1 - \rho) \qquad (21.25)$$

where ρ is the first-order autocorrelation between the error terms. The correlation must be in the range $0 < \rho < 1$ (in absolute value) by definition.

Most tables include test statistics that vary with the number of independent variables and observations. Two limits, d_1 and d_u, are given. If you are testing the possibility of positive serial correlation a calculated value for DW smaller than d_1 allows you to reject the null hypothesis that positive serial correlation is present. If DW is greater than d_u, the null hypothesis is not rejected. For values of DW between d_1 and d_u the test is inconclusive.

If you are testing for negative autocorrelation, the null hypothesis is rejected if the calculated DW statistic is greater than $4 - d_1$ and the null hypothesis is accepted if DW is less that $4 - d_u$. Within the range $4 - d_u$ and $4 - d_1$ the test is inconclusive.

Table 21.5 shows how the DW statistic is used to test a regression equation for the existence of autocorrelation.

If serial correlation is present, the DW statistic gives us an approximate value for t, the correlation between the error terms. To correct for serial correlation, a transformed regression equation is calculated:

$$Y_t - Y_{t-1} = B_0 \times (1 - \rho) + B_1 \times (X_t \times (1 - \rho)) \tag{21.26}$$

There are alternative means for identifying the best estimate of t. Most methods involve testing for the minimum sum of squared residuals, beginning with the approximate value determined by the DW statistic.

Table 21.6 shows the effects of correcting a regression for autocorrelation. Notice how the parameter values do not change much, although the t statistics are much lower.

TABLE 21.5
CALCULATING THE DURBIN—WATSON STATISTIC

The DW statistic is defined as:

$$DW = \Sigma(e_t - e_{t-n}) / \Sigma e_t^2$$

Using the regression results from Table 21.1, we find:

$$DW = 59424.3 / 1562965 = 0.395380$$

From Mathematical Appendix Table IV, $DW_{L/u} = 1.65$ and $DW = 1.69$

Since the calculated value of DW is less than DW, we conclude serial correlation is present in this model specification.

TABLE 21.6
EFFECTS OF AUTOCORRELATION ON THE REGRESSION
PARAMETER ESTIMATES

Using the data in Table 21.1, we estimated the following equation:

$$Y = -108.083 + .947 \times (X)$$

Table 21.5 suggests the presence of autocorrelation in the data. Correcting for autocorrelation, we calculate the following equation:

$$Y = 16536.063 + .257 \times (X)$$

where $R^2 = .999$

In addition, the t statistics are:

$$B_0 = .234$$

$$B_1 = 4.218$$

That is, correcting for autocorrelation suggests that the intercept term, B, is not significantly different than 0 and the parameter results are less certain than indicated in the original model specification.

THE MULTIVARIATE MODEL

In many situations, the behavior of a dependent variable cannot be adequately explained by just one independent variable. Two, or more, independent variables can be used to explain the behavior of an independent variable in the multivariate regression model of the form:

$$Y_t = \beta_0 + \beta_1 X_{it} + \ldots + \beta_n X_{nt} + e_t \tag{21.27}$$

where the X_i are the various explanatory variables and the B_i the estimated effect of the corresponding independent variable on the dependent variable. The multivariate regression model and the measures of goodness of fit can, in general, be interpreted the same way as in the classical model, expect more problems can be expected due to the possibility of a high degree of correlation (or multicollinearity) between the explanatory variables.

    INTERPRETING THE MULTIVARIATE MODEL. Estimating the coefficients, β_i, in the multivariate model will not be discussed here. This is because the parameter estimates depend upon the number of explanatory variables. Thus, as the number of independent variables change, the formula for the different β_i change. For a detailed method of calculating the β_i, see

Johnston (1984) or Pindyck and Rubinfeld (1981). In the same manner, the variance estimates for β_i also are dependent upon the total number of explanatory variables.

While the fact that the parameter mean and variances are dependent upon the number of independent variables, most software packages will automatically compute these values. Thus, as is the case in the classical model, computing the values is less important than knowing how to interpret the results.

The coefficients, B_i, estimate the change in the dependent variable, Y, due to a change in X_i, assuming that all other explanatory variables remain constant. (In calculus terms, the B_i correspond to the partial derivatives of Y with respect to the various X_i.)

All the measures of goodness of fit, the t test, R^2, Durbin-Watson, and F test have the same interpretation in the multivariate model as in the classical model. That is a high R^2, t values greater than 2.0 for all B_i, and a high F are necessary for a good model fit. However, adding variables to a multivariate model will result in the R^2 increasing, even if the variables being added to the model have little, or no statistical relationship with the dependent variable (see Johnston 1984, or Intriligator 1978). To fix this problem, we use the *corrected R^2*, which adjusts the R^2 for the number of observation and independent variables. The corrected R^2 is defined as:

$$R^2 = 1 - (1 - R^2)(N - 1 \,/\, N - k) \tag{21.28}$$

where N is the number of observations and k is the number of variables. Notice that if there is only one variable, the corrected and original R^2 are equal to each other, while if there is more than one independent variable, the corrected R^2 is greater than the original R^2. Also, the corrected R^2 can be negative as the number of variables added to the model increases, or it does a poor job of explaining the dependent variable.

MULTICOLLINEARITY. The major difference between the classical regression model and the multivariate model is the need to check for multicollinearity in the multivariate model. Multicollinearity is a high degree of correlation between two (or more) independent variables. Correlation exists between variables when they tend to move together in a predictable pattern. However, in the multivariate model the B_i explain how the independent variable behaves if there is some change in one of the independent variables, with all else being held constant. If some of the independent variables are correlated, then it is impossible for one of them to change and the other to stay constant (or else they would not be correlated).

It is possible to calculate the parameters if the correlation is not perfect (or close to 1) in the multivariate model. If two or more variables have a perfect correlation (or one independent variable is a multiple of another) then it is not possible to estimate the B_i. However, even if the B_i can be estimated, interpretation of the parameters becomes difficult. In general, if two independent variables have a higher degree of correlation between themselves than with the dependent variable, multicollinearity will be a problem that needs to be addressed. For a more in-depth discussion of multicollinearity and the various ways to test and correct for multicollinearity, the student is best served by reading one of the fine econometric texts available to them, such as Pindyck and Rubenfeld (1981) or Intriligator (1978).

EXTENSIONS OF THE BASIC MODEL

The classical regression model provide some guidance to a modeler in some straight forward situations where an easily identified relationship exists between the dependent and independent variables. However, in many instances, the relationship between variables is more difficult to determine and other modeling techniques need to be employed.

LAGGED VARIABLES

In many macroeconomic applications, a long time period may pass between a change in one variable and its effect on a dependent variable. That is, it is unlikely that all economic decisions occur without some time lag between the action and response. For example, consumption may be determined by income last quarter, or defense expenditures may change as a result of government policy decisions made several quarters ago. In some cases, this lag is the result of inertia in the economic system. People do not immediately respond to changes in income. Aerospace firms cannot immediately hire employees or begin investing in new plant just because government increases or decreases proposed defense expenditures. Farmers cannot change their crop mix as a result of changes in current prices. In many instances, economic decisions are made on the basis of prior information.

The effects of a change in an independent variable may be felt over a number of time periods. This time adjustment is modeled by the use of various forms of distributed lag models.

In its general form, the distributed lag model can be written as:

$$Y_t = B_0 + B_1 X_t + B_2 X_{t-1} + B_3 X_{t-2} \ldots + B_n X_{t-n} \tag{21.29}$$

The distributed lag model refers to the ability of the model to account for the effects of an independent variable over a number of time periods. A series of lagged independent variables, X_{t-n}, accounts for the time adjustment process.

If the number of lags is small, then the equation can be estimated using ordinary least-squares regression. However, autocorrelation is likely to be present in the model because the X_i and X_{i-1} are likely to be highly correlated. If the time period covered by the lag structure is long or if the modeler is unsure of how the lagged variable affects the dependent variable, then the estimation process becomes more difficult. However, there are several shortcuts, based upon prior identification of the lag structure, to minimize the problems in dealing with distributed lag models.

GEOMETRIC LAG. One of the most common lagged variable structures is the geometric lag. The geometric lag structure assumes that the weights of lagged explanatory variables are all positive and decline geometrically over time. Figure 21.9 illustrates the geometric lag structure.

One of the attractions of the geometric lag structure is that it implies that the effects of the independent variable are greatest in the near term, declining over time, but never reaching zero. That is, changes in the dependent variable, possibly years ago, still have some effect on the independent variable. Yet after some time period, the effects become small and can be safely ignored.

The geometric lag is defined as:

$$Y_t = B_0 + B_1(X_t + wX_t + w^2X_{t-1} + w^3X_{t-2} + \ldots.) + e_t \qquad (21.30a)$$

FIGURE 21.9

EXAMPLE OF A GEOMETRIC LAG STRUCTURE

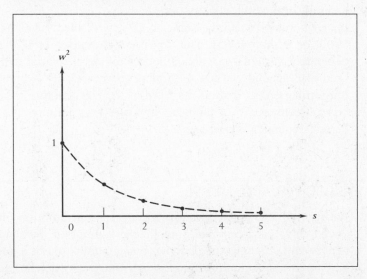

or

$$= B_0 + B_1 \, w^n X_{t-n} + e_t \qquad (21.30b)$$

where w is the weight associated with the declining importance of past variables.

In this form, the geometric lag looks difficult to estimate. However, it can be shown (for example, see Johnston 1984) that the geometric lag of equation (21.30a) can be rewritten as:

$$Y_t = B_0(1 - w) + wY_{t-1} + B_1X_t + u_t \qquad (21.31)$$

That is, the geometric lag model allows the dependent variable to be written as a function of itself, lagged one period. This ability to use the dependent variable as a function of its last value both simplifies the data collection effort and reduces the search time necessary to determine the appropriate weight. This structure also (almost) guarantees a good fit of the regression equation because Y_t and Y_{t-1} often track each other closely.

Many models use lagged dependent variables for the reasons stated above, ease of data collection, and computational ease. Ordinary least squares regression can be used to estimate the parameters, β_i, under certain circumstances. In general, however, autocorrelation is a serious problem. The Durbin-Watson statistics that is used to test for autocorrelation in a regression equation does not always detect autocorrelation in a regression with lagged dependent variables, even though it usually is used, for lack of anything better.

There are many different lag structures besides the geometric lag. A more general form of the lag structure is the polynomial distributed lag, although this is somewhat cumbersome to deal with (see Johnston 1984, Griliches 1967, or Almon 1965). The key point to recognize is that often a lagged dependent variable provides a good explanatory variable that should not be ignored, especially when the independent variable's effects are felt over a long time period. Even if the form of the lag structure is known, the loss of observations due to a long lag structure may require that the modeler use lagged dependent variables.

EXAMPLE OF A LAGGED VARIABLE MODEL

Earlier in this chapter, a simple Keynesian consumption function was introduced. It's worth emphasizing that consumption does not react instantaneously to changes in income but operates with a lag. The simplest Keynesian consumption function is usually shown as a linear function with no time lag, or:

$$C = a + bY \tag{21.32}$$

where:
C = real aggregate consumption (21.)

Y = real aggregate disposable income

b = a constant representing the marginal propensity to consume

a = a constant

Consumption lags behind income since people do not spend their money immediately. To more accurately model consumption, a lag function must be used, or:

$$C_t = a + b_1 Y_{t-1} + b_2 Y_{t-2} + \ldots + b_n Y_{t-n} \tag{21.33}$$

In this type of specification, the effects of changes in disposable income would be felt most in the earlier periods, then declining to close to nothing over time. Without an examination of the data it is not possible to tell if b_1 or b_2 is larger, or how long it takes people to adjust consumption to changes in income.

Table 21.1 presented the results of the regression equation shown in equation 21.30, without correcting for autocorrelation. In this example, disposable personal income is used to explain real consumption expenditures from 1965.3 through 1992.2. The regression results appear to show that consumption will change by $0.95 for each $1.00 change in current period disposable income.

Notice, however, the residual, or error pattern, of the regression, shown in Figure 21.10. It shows a nice, smooth pattern. While the R^2, t statistics, and F statistics of the regression are all good, the low Durbin-Watson (DW) statistic and the smooth residual pattern are signs of serial correlation in the regression.

To correct for serial correlation, a new regression using the Cochran-Orcutt procedure was estimated. A comparison of the two regressions is shown in Table 21.6. The DW statistic improves and the R^2 and F statistics are high, but the t statistic on current period consumption declines. The residual plot, shown in Figure 21.11, now has a more random pattern than the regression shown in Figure 21.10.

The next step is to add lagged values for disposable income. Again, a Cochran-Orcutt correction is performed on the data to correct for serial correlation. The results, shown in Table 21.7, are much better in that the coefficients have the correct signs, with a high R^2 and high F statistic, although the low t statistic on lagged personal income is somewhat unexpected.

FIGURE 21.10
RESIDUAL PLOT OF THE FITTED VALUE OF CONSUMPTION

Residual Plot	obs	RESIDUAL e_t	ACTUAL CONSUMPTION	FITTED CONSUMPTION
	65.3	−254.106	1503.10	1757.21
	65.4	−222.075	1540.60	1762.67
	66.1	−206.603	1559.60	1766.20
	66.2	−202.528	1566.10	1768.63
	66.3	−191.612	1582.00	1773.61
	66.4	−190.863	1587.60	1778.46
	67.1	−182.232	1600.20	1782.43
	67.2	−165.116	1620.80	1785.92
	67.3	−161.146	1629.40	1790.55
	67.4	−155.912	1639.00	1794.91
	68.1	−129.024	1672.90	1801.92
	68.2	−112.224	1696.80	1809.02
	68.3	−86.9998	1725.20	1812.20
	68.4	−82.3154	1735.00	1817.32
	69.1	−64.9969	1754.70	1819.70
	69.2	−60.8592	1765.10	1825.96
	69.3	−60.0438	1775.00	1835.04
	69.4	−50.8534	1790.10	1840.95
	70.1	−44.8634	1800.50	1845.36
	70.2	−46.1543	1807.50	1853.65
	70.3	−36.0104	1824.70	1860.71
	70.4	−43.4795	1821.20	1864.68
	71.1	−23.7759	1849.90	1873.68
	71.2	−18.5551	1863.50	1882.06
	71.3	−10.2266	1876.90	1887.13
	71.4	12.2695	1904.60	1892.33
	72.1	31.7657	1929.30	1897.53
	72.2	60.1208	1963.30	1903.18
	72.3	74.3664	1989.10	1914.73
	72.4	100.123	2032.10	1931.98
	73.1	121.162	2063.90	1942.74
	73.2	108.987	2062.00	1953.01
	73.3	109.794	2073.70	1963.91
	73.4	86.2068	2067.40	1981.19
	74.1	65.8143	2050.80	1984.99
	74.2	67.7519	2059.00	1991.25
	74.3	59.9193	2065.50	2005.58
	74.4	24.9258	2039.90	2014.97
	75.1	33.8712	2051.80	2017.93
	75.2	39.9087	2086.90	2046.99
	75.3	63.9248	2114.40	2050.48
	75.4	71.5307	2137.00	2065.47
	76.1	99.5863	2179.30	2079.71
	76.2	106.783	2194.70	2087.92
	76.3	113.176	2213.00	2099.82
	76.4	129.078	2242.00	2112.92
	77.1	147.574	2271.30	2123.73
	77.2	139.566	2280.80	2141.23
	77.3	139.713	2302.60	2162.89
	77.4	154.556	2331.60	2177.04
	78.1	152.328	2347.10	2194.77
	78.2	172.679	2394.00	2221.32
	78.3	164.745	2404.50	2239.75
	78.4	161.206	2421.60	2260.39
	79.1	157.837	2437.90	2280.06
	79.2	138.226	2435.40	2297.17
	79.3	133.050	2454.70	2321.65
	79.4	121.303	2465.40	2344.10
	80.1	91.7940	2464.60	2372.81
	80.2	38.1304	2414.20	2376.07
	80.3	35.5651	2440.30	2404.73
	80.4	27.0678	2469.20	2442.13
	81.1	7.52485	2475.50	2467.98
	81.2	−5.59038	2476.10	2481.69
	81.3	−24.2348	2487.40	2511.63
	81.4	−56.5735	2468.60	2525.17
	82.1	−48.8030	2484.00	2532.80
	82.2	−64.5862	2488.90	2553.49
	82.3	−68.7146	2502.50	2571.21
	82.4	−45.6298	2539.30	2584.93
	83.1	−42.1451	2556.50	2598.65
	83.2	−17.3569	2604.00	2621.36
	83.3	−8.94960	2639.00	2647.95
	83.4	−3.57476	2678.20	2681.77
	84.1	−17.4887	2703.80	2721.29
	84.2	−2.37126	2741.10	2743.47
	84.3	−13.9204	2754.60	2768.52
	84.4	−0.52281	2784.80	2785.32
	85.1	24.6711	2824.90	2800.23
	85.2	10.6627	2849.70	2839.04
	85.3	54.5715	2893.30	2838.73
	85.4	31.1255	2895.30	2864.17
	86.1	28.4133	2922.40	2893.99
	86.2	29.6580	2947.90	2918.24
	86.3	66.5938	2993.70	2927.11
	86.4	77.1470	3012.50	2935.35
	87.1	44.1301	3011.50	2967.37
	87.2	87.3241	3046.80	2959.48
	87.3	81.7493	3075.80	2994.05
	87.4	42.0612	3074.70	3032.64
	88.1	66.0579	3128.20	3062.14
	88.2	63.2549	3147.80	3084.55

CONTINUED ON NEXT PAGE . . .

FIGURE 21.10 (CONTINUED)

Residual Plot	obs	RESIDUAL e_t	ACTUAL CONSUMPTION	FITTED CONSUMPTION
	88.3	56.2430	3170.60	3114.36
	88.4	54.1444	3202.90	3148.76
	89.1	20.9753	3203.60	3182.62
	89.2	17.0947	3212.20	3195.11
	89.3	23.8335	3235.30	3211.47
	89.4	0.14812	3242.00	3241.85
	90.1	−25.5704	3259.50	3285.07
	90.2	−48.6082	3260.10	3308.71
	90.3	−56.5941	3273.90	3330.49
	90.4	−110.189	3248.00	3358.19
	91.1	−138.173	3223.50	3361.67
	91.2	−146.055	3239.30	3385.36
	91.3	−150.869	3251.20	3402.07
	91.4	−178.339	3249.00	3427.34
	92.1	−171.555	3289.30	3460.86
	92.2	−194.802	3288.50	3483.30

FIGURE 21.11
RESIDUAL PLOT OF THE FITTED VALUE OF CONSUMPTION CORRECTED FOR AUTOCORRELATION

Residual Plot	obs	RESIDUAL e_t	ACTUAL CONSUMPTION	FITTED CONSUMPTION
	65.4	18.6593	1540.60	1521.94
	66.1	1.14377	1559.60	1558.46
	66.2	−10.8176	1566.10	1576.92
	66.3	−2.27491	1582.00	1584.27
	66.4	−12.4097	1587.60	1600.01
	67.1	−5.06517	1600.20	1605.27
	67.2	3.20042	1620.80	1617.60
	67.3	−9.04303	1629.40	1638.44
	67.4	−7.89106	1639.00	1646.89
	68.1	15.5405	1672.90	1657.36
	68.2	5.77266	1696.80	1691.03
	68.3	11.8402	1725.20	1713.36
	68.4	−7.21756	1735.00	1742.22
	69.1	3.71659	1754.70	1750.98
	69.2	−6.79822	1765.10	1771.90
	69.3	−8.22779	1775.00	1783.23
	69.4	−1.84876	1790.10	1791.95
	70.1	−5.90928	1800.50	1806.41
	70.2	−10.6079	1807.50	1818.11
	70.3	0.06290	1824.70	1824.64
	70.4	−19.4219	1821.20	1840.62
	71.1	10.9588	1849.90	1838.94
	71.2	−3.70910	1863.50	1867.21
	71.3	−2.64999	1876.90	1879.55
	71.4	11.7004	1904.60	1892.90
	72.1	8.91729	1929.30	1920.38
	72.2	18.2528	1963.30	1945.05
	72.3	8.23059	1989.10	1980.87
	72.4	23.6004	2032.10	2008.50
	73.1	15.0026	2063.90	2048.90
	73.2	−18.2910	2062.60	2080.29
	73.3	−4.95593	2073.70	2078.66
	73.4	−25.1520	2067.40	2092.55
	74.1	−30.7825	2050.80	2081.58
	74.2	−7.00664	2059.00	2066.01
	74.3	−11.5110	2065.50	2077.01
	74.4	−41.8520	2039.90	2081.75
	75.1	−2.31689	2051.80	2054.12
	75.2	11.7392	2086.90	2075.16
	75.3	13.3948	2114.40	2101.01
	75.4	4.64376	2137.00	2132.36
	76.1	24.7538	2179.30	2154.55
	76.2	0.30314	2194.70	2194.40
	76.3	1.99761	2213.00	2211.00
	76.4	12.3944	2242.00	2229.61
	77.1	13.7099	2271.30	2257.59
	77.2	−8.24771	2280.80	2289.05
	77.3	2.61362	2300.00	2299.99
	77.4	12.5841	2333.80	2319.02
	78.1	−1.97842	2347.18	2349.08
	78.2	26.3790	2300.00	2367.67
	78.3	−6.83635	2400.00	2411.34
	78.4	−0.98281	2423.60	2422.58
	79.1	−1.35784	2437.90	2439.20
	79.2	−19.1746	2435.40	2454.57
	79.3	−0.05129	2454.70	2454.75
	79.4	−7.84467	2465.40	2473.24
	80.1	−21.5364	2464.60	2486.14
	80.2	−62.2277	2414.20	2476.43
	80.3	4.85528	2440.30	2435.44

CONTINUED ON NEXT PAGE . . .

FIGURE 21.11 (CONTINUED)

Residual Plot	obs	RESIDUAL e_t	ACTUAL CONSUMPTION	FITTED CONSUMPTION
	80.4	4.70022	2469.20	2464.50
	81.1	−13.6813	2475.50	2489.18
	81.2	−15.1153	2476.10	2491.22
	81.3	−10.1917	2487.46	2497.59
	81.4	−34.4824	2468.80	2503.08
	82.1	1.60990	2484.90	2482.39
	82.2	−13.4011	2490.90	2502.30
	82.3	−3.67609	2502.50	2506.18
	82.4	21.0050	2539.30	2518.30
	83.1	1.67261	2556.50	2554.83
	83.2	28.8938	2604.00	2575.11
	83.3	15.3519	2639.00	2623.65
	83.4	17.2081	2678.20	2660.99
	84.1	1.82414	2703.80	2701.98
	84.2	19.7520	2741.10	2721.35
	84.3	−4.81513	2754.60	2759.42
	84.4	14.8407	2784.80	2769.96
	85.1	25.6148	2824.90	2799.29
	85.2	2.15202	2849.70	2847.55
	85.3	34.8813	2893.30	2858.42
	85.4	−15.4624	2895.30	2910.76
	86.1	8.03445	2922.40	2914.37
	86.2	8.53886	2947.90	2939.36
	86.3	34.4248	2993.70	2959.28
	86.4	8.00080	3012.50	3004.50
	87.1	−20.0741	3011.50	3031.57
	87.2	30.2399	3046.80	3016.56
	87.3	9.23707	3075.80	3066.56
	87.4	−22.1420	3074.70	3096.84
	88.1	35.5479	3128.20	3092.65
	88.2	4.52037	3147.80	3143.28
	88.3	5.19756	3170.60	3165.40
	88.4	13.1776	3202.90	3189.72
	89.1	−18.0660	3203.60	3221.67
	89.2	−2.69531	3212.20	3214.90
	89.3	10.4673	3235.30	3224.83
	89.4	−10.7484	3242.00	3252.75
	90.1	−4.52154	3259.50	3264.02
	90.2	−14.4769	3260.10	3274.58
	90.3	−0.68699	3273.90	3274.59
	90.4	−42.4260	3248.00	3290.43
	91.1	−32.7612	3223.50	3256.26
	91.2	0.17867	3239.30	3239.12
	91.3	−1.19454	3251.20	3252.39
	91.4	−18.2705	3249.00	3267.27
	92.1	21.2191	3289.30	3268.08
	92.2	−15.7272	3288.50	3304.23

The next step is to perform a distributed lag regression where consumption is regressed on itself, lagged one period, but is also regressed on changes in income. The regression model, shown in Table 21.8 is the best of the different models presented, with a high R^2, good t statistics, all the coefficients have the correct sign, and the F statistic is high.

A word of caution, however. The DW statistic is not always valid when using lagged dependent variables, but there is no other easy test to use for testing for autocorrelation. Therefore, autocorrelation may be making the regression results look better than they truly are, but there is nothing to test the results against.

The regressions presented above suggest that other variables, in addition to income, determine consumption expenditures. For example, wealth, belief about the future direction of the economy, distribution of income, and so forth, all affect consumption decisions. The regressions above demonstrate that income, although an important determinate of consumption, is not the only factor determining current consumption expenditures. If one is

TABLE 21.7
EXAMPLE OF LINEAR REGRESSION

Least squares
Sample range: 1966.1 − 1992.2
Number of observations: 106

Variable	Coefficient	Standard Error	*t* Statistic	2-Tail Significance
Consumption	3493.782	2514.401	1.390	0.1677
Disposible income	0.150	0.089	1.679	0.0961
Disposible income (−1)	0.008	0.891	0.095	0.9241

R-squared:	0.999
Adjusted *R*-squared:	0.999
Standard error of regression:	17.1419
Log likelihood:	−449.5707
Durbin-Watson statistic:	1.667
Mean of dependent variable:	2419.399
Standard deviation of dependent variable:	537.7871
Sum of squared residuals:	29972.23
F Statistic:	34414.48
Probability (*F* statistic):	0.0000

TABLE 21.8
EXAMPLE OF LINEAR REGRESSION

Least squares
Sample range: 1966.1 − 1992.2
Number of observations: 107

Variable	Coefficient	Standard Error	*t* Statistic	2-Tail Significance
Consumption	24.052	8.0859	2.975	0.0036
Consumptions (−1)	0.994	0.0040	248.479	0.0000
Change in disposible income	0.1516	0.0871	1.7403	0.0848

R-squared:	0.999
Adjusted *R*-squared:	0.999
Standard error of regression:	17.087
Log likelihood:	−454.010
Durbin-Watson statistic:	1.661
Mean of dependent variable:	2411.186
Standard deviation of dependent variable:	541.9448
Sum of squared residuals:	30367.67
F Statistic:	53257.91
Probability (*F* statistic):	0.0000

interested only in forecasting consumption, then the final regression provides fairly good results.

An important note—the regressions presented here are only intended to illustrate the process of estimating a regression equation. They are not intended to present the state-of-the-art of statistical studies of the determinents of consumption.

SIMULTANEOUS EQUATION MODELS

Although single-equation models are often used to forecast economic activity, economic relationships may be so complex that a multiple equation model may be required. This is particularly true when forecasting macroeconomic variables such as gross domestic product (GDP). To illustrate how simultaneous equation models are used in forecasting, consider a very simple three equation model of the national economy that can be used to forecast GDP.

$$C_t = a_1 + b_1 GNP_t + e_{1t} \qquad (21.34A)$$

$$I_t = a_2 + b_2 P_{t-1} + e_{2t} \qquad (21.34B)$$

$$GNP_t = C_t + I_t + G_t \qquad (21.34C)$$

where:
$$C_t = \text{consumption expenditures in year } t$$
$$I_t = \text{investment at time } t$$
$$P_t = \text{profits at time } t$$
$$G_t = \text{government expenditures}$$
$$e_{it} = \text{stochastic disturbance (random error term)}$$

Equation 21.34A states that consumption expenditures in year t (C) are a linear function of GDP in the same year. Equation 21.34B estimates investment in year t as linear function of profits in the previous year. Equation 21.34C defines GDP in any year as the sum of consumption expenditures, investment, and government expenditures in the same year.

Variables C, I, and GNP, (the left-hand variables or variables to the left of the equals signs in Equations 21.34A-C) are called endogenous variables. These are the variables that the model seeks to explain or predict from the solution of the model.

Exogenous variables are those determined outside the model. In the above model, P_{t-1} and G are the exogenous variables. Their values must be supplied from outside the model in order to be able to estimate the model. When (as in the above model) some of the endogenous variables also appear on the right of the equals signs, this means that they both affect and are in turn affected by the other variables in the model or they are simultaneously determined.

The above very simple macromodel contains three endogenous and two exogenous variables, and two structural and one definitional equations. Most large models of the U.S. economy contain hundreds of variables and equations. They require estimates of tens, if not hundreds, of exogenous variables and provide forecasts of an even greater number of endogenous variables, ranging from GDP to consumption, investment, and exports and imports by sector, as well as for numerous other real and financial variables.

Equations 21.34A and 21.34B are called structural (behavioral) equations because they seek to explain the relationship between the particular endogenous variable and the other variables in the system. Equation 21.34C is a definitional equation or an identity and is always true.

Note that equation 21.34C has no parameters or coefficients to be estimated. Given the value of the exogenous variables, the system can be solved to estimate the values of the endogenous variables. A change in the value of an exogenous variable will affect directly the endogenous variable in the equation in which it appears and indirectly the other endogenous variables in the system.

For example, an increase in P_{t-1} leads to a rise in I, directly (equation 21.34B). The induced increase in I_t then leads to an increase in GDP, and through it in C_t as well.

Since the endogenous variables of the system are both determined by and in turn determine the value of the other endogenous variables in the model (i.e., they also appear on the right-hand side in equations 21.34A and 21.34B), ordinary least squares methods cannot be used to estimate the parameters of the structural equations (the a and the b in equations 21.34A and 21.34B). More advanced econometric techniques are required to obtain unbiased estimates of the coefficients of the model. The student is referred to more advanced econometric books available to learn how to use two stage least squares, necessary to estimate these types of models (for example, Johnston 1984).

EXAMPLE OF CONSTRUCTING A REGRESSION MODEL

Suppose the forecaster were asked to forecast retail employment in a region for the next five years. Retail employment includes such classifications as store clerks, salespersons, etc. The data is graphed in Figure 21.12. What type of model would be chosen? To begin with, five years is too long a period to assume that other economic factors will remain constant. This

FIGURE 21.12
FORECASTING EXAMPLE OF RETAIL EMPLOYMENT

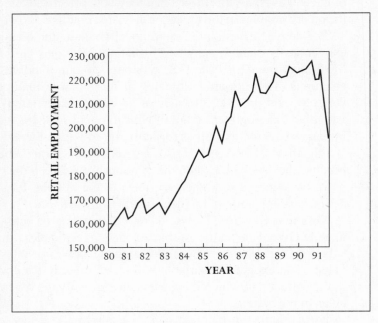

violates the basic assumption of time series models, that the historic pat-terns of the variable will repeat. A regression model would appear to be best suited for this problem.

What basic assumptions should the forecaster consider as he begins constructing the basic model? To begin with, retail employment might be closely tied to changes in personal income. Personal income generally moves in tandem with the national economy, but is commonly tied to some measure of population levels, such as number of households or pop-ulation. You would also assume that personal income growth or some other variable reflecting economic well-being should be used in the fore-cast model. Similarly, the data suggests some level of seasonality, perhaps reflecting that retail sales peak in the fourth quarter of each year, during the holiday season.

It is not unreasonable to assume that as an area grows in population some relatively constant number of new retail establishments open, adding to the regions' retail base. As the personal income of the population changes in tandem with the state or national economy, retail employment should change in roughly the same pattern. Whether or not the economy leads or lags retail employment will need to be determined.

Because the behavior of a regional variable is being examined rather than a national variable, data considerations will be important. What measure of national economic activity can be used to approximate regional economic well-being, understanding that any measure of regional personal income will take a long time to collect and be published. The relationship of the regional economy to the national economy will also need to be considered. Some areas of the nation have economies that lag or lead the nation, depending upon the structure of the local primary industries. For example, if the regional economy is heavily dependent upon natural resources, such as in the Rocky Mountain states, the economy will tend to lag the national economy. If however, the economy is dependent upon high technology industries, such as in the Northeast, it will tend to lead the national economy.

There are two variables that can be examined first; GDP (in real terms) and population. Both should have some relationship to the level of personal income growth in the regional economy. The data is shown in Table

TABLE 21.9
DATA USED IN ESTIMATING THE RETAIL EMPLOYMENT REGRESSION

Date	GDP	Population	Retail Employment
1980.1	4510.2	216164	156300
1980.2	4394.6	217647	158900
1980.3	4395.6	219136	162400
1980.4	4483.9	220610	166800
1981.1	4545.2	221662	161867
1981.2	4526.2	222727	163367
1981.3	4549.9	223797	167767
1981.4	4477.6	224855	169667
1982.1	4422.3	225996	163800
1982.2	4439.9	227151	164700
1982.3	4420.3	228311	165866
1982.4	4426.4	229459	168200
1983.1	4454.5	230158	163433
1983.2	4575.8	230866	166800
1983.3	4643.9	231576	170733
1983.4	4723.7	232279	174166
1984.1	4814.8	233280	176770
1984.2	4878.9	234293	180500

CONTINUED ON NEXT PAGE . . .

TABLE 21.9 (CONTINUED)
DATA USED IN ESTIMATING THE RETAIL EMPLOYMENT REGRESSION

Date	GDP	Population	Retail Employment
1984.3	4905.3	235311	184000
1984.4	4938.1	236318	188400
1985.1	4970.5	237388	184730
1985.2	5009.4	238471	186270
1985.3	5073.2	239559	190670
1985.4	5102.1	240635	197370
1986.1	5169.2	241173	190600
1986.2	5165.9	241717	200593
1986.3	5195.2	242264	204780
1986.4	5212.3	242805	212765
1987.1	5251.0	243959	204933
1987.2	5316.1	245127	207667
1987.3	5367.9	246300	213033
1987.4	5445.8	247460	221767
1988.1	5480.9	248664	211500
1988.2	5539.2	249884	210267
1988.3	5574.2	251108	212767
1988.4	5627.4	252320	215533
1989.1	5672.0	254334	221033
1989.2	5697.2	256374	218267
1989.3	5697.2	258422	219333
1989.4	5718.0	260449	223400
1990.1	5767.0	262247	219900
1990.2	5789.2	264068	221033
1990.3	5776.7	265896	221933
1990.4	5730.4	267705	224300
1991.1	5695.8	268330	218067
1991.2	5716.8	268962	217500
1991.3	5736.8	269597	217833
1991.4	5745.0	270225	221433
1992.1	5794.9	270597	195300
1992.2	5835.5	270973	193933

21.9. The regression equation using these two variables is (t statistics in parenthesis):

$$Retail\ Employment = -35,579 + 48.99 \times GDP - 0.00024 \times Population$$

$$(-1.99)\ (6.47)\ (-0.01) \qquad\qquad (21.35)$$

$$R^2 = 0.95\ DW\ statistic = 1.078\ F\ statistic = 412.05$$

The equation is not very good in explaining the level of retail employment. Examining the regression reveals several things. First, a test for autocorrelation should be made and, secondly, the seasonal effects on retail employment need to be measured.

BINARY VARIABLES. One method for identifying the effects of seasonal variations on a variable is to use binary variables. Binary variables (which are sometimes called dummy variables) are variables that can take on two or more distinct values if a desired effect is present.

Binary variables are very useful in regression analysis. They can be used to change the slope of a regression equation or the intercept term, depending on what effects the forecaster is attempting to incorporate.

Consider estimating the consumption function, using data from 1940 to 1990. It is reasonable to believe that during war years consumption is lower than during other years because of shortages, people voluntarily reducing consumption in support of the war effort, etc.

A regression equation can be set up as:

$$C_t = B_0 + B_1 \times Y_t + B_2 \times D_1 \tag{21.36}$$

where:
$$
\begin{aligned}
C_t &= \text{consumption expenditures at time } t \\
Y_t &= \text{personal income at time } t \\
D_1 &= \text{a binary variable, equal to one during war} \\
&\quad \text{years and 0 otherwise}
\end{aligned}
$$

During war years, the regression equation would be:

$$C_t = (B_0 + B_2) + B_1 \times Y_t \tag{21.37}$$

While during peacetime, the equation would be:

$$C_t = B_0 + B_1 \times Y_t \tag{21.38}$$

That is, if B_2 is statistically significant, the consumption function changes during war years in comparison to peacetime.

This regression equation can be further modified by using the dummy variable interactively with Y_t, as:

$$C_t = B_0 + B_1 \times Y_t + B_2 \times D_t + B_3 \times (Y_t \times D_t) \tag{21.39}$$

During the war years, the regression equation then becomes:

$$C_t = (B_0 + B_2) + (B_1 + B_3) \times Y_t \tag{21.40}$$

While during the non-war years, the regression equation is then:

$$C_t = B_0 + B_1 \times Y_t \qquad\qquad (21.41)$$

In this case, assuming that the parameter estimates on the binary variables are both significant, both the slope and intercept parameter estimates are changed, reflecting the change in consumption expenditures due to the different wars.

When using binary variables, there must be at least one fewer binary variable than the number of effects being measured. In the above example, the effects of two conditions, war or peace, were examined, so we could use one binary variable. If the effects of three conditions were being studied, two binary variables would be necessary, etc. This is because of the method by which the regression parameters are estimated. Essentially, if two binary variables in the above equation were used, the sum in any year would be one (either it would be war or peace, one of the binary variables would have a value of one and the other zero). In this case, it is not possible to separate the effects of the two binary variables and the regression results. If a result could even be found, it would be meaningless.

Binary variables have many different uses in forecasting. One of the most useful is allowing forecasters to measure seasonality effects. If quarterly data is being used, there can be three binary variables, each measuring the impact of seasonal effects from the quarter that is not associated with a binary variable.

For example, suppose we were looking at quarterly consumption data for the past ten years. A regression equation of the form:

$$C_t = B_0 + B_1 \times D_1 + B_2 \times B_2 + B_3 \times D_3 + B_4 \times Y_t \qquad (21.42)$$

can be estimated, where D_1 is 1 in the first quarter and 0 otherwise, D_2 is 1 in the second quarter and 0 otherwise, D_3 is 1 in the third quarter and 0 otherwise. This form of the regression assumes that there is no slope change between quarters, or that the marginal propensity to consume is the same in all quarters.

In the prior section, we began an example of estimating a regression equation of retail employment. The example can now be completed, using binary variables to account for the effects of seasonal changes in retail trade employment.

Recall that retail employment was estimated, using GDP and population as the two independent variables. In deciding what binary variables to add to the equation, it is believed retail employment increases during the fourth quarter, due to extra help being hired to help during the holidays, then retail employment declines in the first quarter of the following year. There is no reason to believe retail employment in the second or third quarter changes due to seasonal effects.

A binary variable, D_1, is defined that is set equal to 1 in the first quarter and 0 other times. It would be expected that the parameter estimate will be negative, reflecting a decline in retail trade employment in the first quarter.

Using the new regression form, a regression equation (*t* statistics in parenthesis) is estimated as:

$$Retail\ employment = -62,899.5 - 3,184.4 \times D1 + 33.13 \times GDP$$

$$(-3.00) \qquad (-3.27) \qquad (3.18)$$

$$+.05 \times Population \qquad\qquad (21.43)$$

$$(1.59)$$

$$R^2 = 0.975 \quad DW = 1.80 \quad F\ statistic = 478.2 \quad AR(1) = -0.59$$

The *t* statistic for population is a little low, but we decide to keep it in the equation as it improves the regression fit. It is also believed that there is some level of retail employment that is dependent upon the population level. Correcting for autocorrelation has led to a good DW and R^2 and the *F* statistic is high. Based upon all these different measures of goodness-of-fit it is concluded that the regression equation does a reasonably good job of explaining retail employment. This equation can now be used for forecasting once future values of population and GDP are ready.

Population growth is relatively stable in the region, averaging about 700 people per quarter. There is no reason to assume that it will change significantly in the future. Therefore, we just project population growth into the future, using the average quarterly growth rate. Assumed GDP growth was taken from an independent forecasting firm.

Using these assumed values, the forecasted value of retail employment is derived. But what if the assumed future values of the two dependent variables is wrong? That is, suppose GDP growth or population growth is greater or weaker than anticipated. What difference does it make in the forecast of retail employment?

In the first quarter, differences between the assumed values of the dependent variables and the actual values have little effect on the forecast. In fact, even if both GDP and population grew twice as much as anticipated, the forecast would only change by about 150 people per quarter, well within the normal forecasting error. Within a few years, however, the effects of the differences in assumed versus actual growth could be very large. In this type of a situation, we would expect to update the forecast at some regular basis, attempting to reduce the long-term error associated with differences in forecasted versus actual values of the dependent variable.

In this particular example, the model does not exhibit any strong effects of variations in the assumption set. This is not always the case. Depending on what variable is being examined, even a small difference in the assumed versus actual value of the dependent variable can make a large difference in the forecast, depending on the size of the estimated coefficient(s) in relationship to the intercept coefficient and the variation in the independent variable.

The more sensitive the forecast is to changes in the independent variables, the closer the variables have to be monitored. While this may seem an obvious undertaking, it is often not done until the forecast results have gotten so bad that they are no longer useful. Here again, the ability to consistently monitor the relationship between the forecast and actual behavior of a variable is dependent upon many items, such as the importance of the variable and time and budgetary constraints. There are very few organizations that have the ability to constantly monitor every forecasted variable to see how it relates to actual values and determine why the forecast was wrong.

SUMMARY

This chapter has presented a basic introduction to regression analysis, primarily relying on a single independent variable as an explanatory variable. In the vast majority of cases however, multivariate models are used. Multivariate models, aside from their computational difficulty (which has been significantly reduced by econometric computer software packages) have the same measures of goodness of fit and interpretations as the classical regression model. The primary difference between the two models is the need for check for multicollinearity in the multivariate model, a procedure that can be difficult to perform and for which it is difficult to correct the model results.

KEY TERMS AND CONCEPTS

autocorrelation	*F* distribution	normal distribution
binary variables	geometric lag	null hypothesis
classical regression model	heteroscedasticity	*t* distribution
coefficient of determination (R^2)	lagged variables	tests of significance
	least-squares	
Durbin-Watson statistic	measures of goodness of fit	
error term	multicollinearity	

CHAPTER 22

Examples of Forecasting and Models

The preceding chapters have introduced the basics of time series and econometric models. These two types of models are the primary modeling methods available to forecasters. This chapter will illustrate how these modeling techniques are commonly used in forecasting and it will present another modeling technique, Input-Output (I-O) models. Additionally, a method is presented to simulate the behavior of a variable into the future.

Time series and econometric models, as usually used in macroeconomic forecasting, rely on time series data. I-O models use cross-section data to describe the economy at a single point in time. I-O models are often used in conjunction with regression or time series models. Each of these different modeling methods has various strengths and weaknesses, ranging from computational difficulty to data acquisition problems. Each of these modeling techniques has an appropriate niche in forecasting, increasing the number of tools available to the forecaster.

WHICH MODELING TECHNIQUE IS BEST?

As discussed earlier, there is no single best forecasting technique for all situations. Each forecasting problem needs to be evaluated on the basis of several different criteria to determine which modeling methodology will provide the best results in a given situation.

Over the years, different economists have attempted to determine what is the best modeling method (Mahmoud 1984). Recently, McNees and Tootell (1991) attempted to determine the leading indicators of economic activity for the New England region. As with the national economy, there is no single indicator series that captures the behavior of a regional economy. In creating this index of leading indicators for the region, they encountered several problems, the most basic of which was determining what variable best represents regional economic activity. That is, at the national level, GDP is the measure of economic activity, so at the regional level gross state product or gross regional product would be the corresponding measure. However, measures of gross state product suffer from a problem of timeliness, with estimates of gross state product taking some five years to develop.

McNees and Tootell decided upon employment as the measure of regional economic activity for several reasons, including data availability and timeliness—the data was available and it was collected and published with a short lag. Employment trends were expected to be dominated by the national business cycle, yet there would be differences in regional versus national employment trends due to the industry mix in the New England area. That is, the New England economy has a much smaller percentage of gross output in the agricultural, mining, and non-durable goods sectors but a much larger percentage of output in the durable goods sector than the national economy. Factors that impact the agricultural or mining sectors nationwide would be expected to have a smaller effect on the New England economy. Factors that impacted the durable goods sector would be expected to have a greater effect on the New England economy than on the nation.

McNees and Tootell regressed different economic series on employment in New England, with different lag structures depending on such factors as data availability. They then ranked the various measures according to the indicators ability to predict employment. Of the 26 regional indicators examined, 6 predicted employment better than employment itself—that is, in comparison to estimating a time series model with a lagged structure for employment, other variables more accurately predicted employment. The ranking of the different variables used in the analysis is shown in Table 22.1.

It is important to recognize that both regional and national economic activity influence New England employment. A national downturn will decrease demand for goods in the region, especially in the New England region that has a much higher portion of durable good manufacturing than the nation as a whole. Similarly, anything that affects region-specific industries will impact employment within the area. An example of this is the decline in oil prices in the early 1980s that sent the Texas and Oklahoma economies into a recession which stimulated the rest of the nation through lower energy prices.

McNees and Tootell illustrate a key point in the different types of forecasting models. The various leading economic indicator series are examples of binary forecasting that focus on whether the economy is still expanding or contracting. Indicator forecasting is also fairly simple, although this is the strength of the method. There is no attempt to determine the future strength of the economy. Most forecasting models attempt to estimate a continuous relationship between the dependent and independent variable.

TABLE 22.1
REGIONAL INDICATORS OF EMPLOYMENT GROWTH IN NEW ENGLAND

Indicator	Number of Lags	R^2
Value of Residential Construction	1 to 21	.44
Average Weekly Initial Claims for Unemployment Insurance	0 to 15	.43
Value of Total Construction Contracts	1 to 16	.43
Index of Help-Wanted Advertising	1 to 17	.38
Total Retail Sales Index	2 to 16	.37
Total Existing Home Sales	1 to 19	.35
Total Payroll Employment	1 to 15	.35
Index of Housing Authorized by Local Building Permits	1 to 23	.33
Housing Permits Authorized, Single Family	1 to 21	.33
Index of Consumer Expectations	0 to 24	.32
Index of Consumer Sentiment	0 to 14	.29
Ratio of Civilian Unemployment in New England to the U.S.	0 to 23	.26
Value of Non-Residential Construction	1 to 20	.25
Civilian Unemployment Rate	0 to 14	.25
New Business Incorporation	2 to 16	.19
Commercial Electricity Sales	3 to 22	.14
Civilian Employment	0 to 10	.14
Retail Sales Index	2 to 13	.13
Industrial Electricity Sales	3 to 22	.13
Civilian Labor Force	0 to 4	.12
Consumer Price Index (Boston)	1 to 24	.11
Average Hours of Production Workers	1 to 14	.08
Precipitation, Deviation From Average	0 to 0	.03
Temperature, Deviation From Average	0 to 0	.00
Residential Electricity Sales	3 to 3	$-.01$
Average Hourly Earnings	1 to 1	$-.01$

After examining many different indicator series, McNees and Tootell concluded that the problem with indicator series is not that good indicator series are difficult to find, but that with so many different series from which to choose, identifying the best few series is difficult. The question is, can some other modeling method provide better results.

McNees and Tootell constructed multivariate forecasting models of the New England economy. Multivariate analysis, as opposed to the univariate analysis of the indicator approach, may identify variables that become more important as they account for partial effects of changes in employment that single variables do not capture. The regression analysis began by including into a single model the variables with the best relationship to employment growth identified in the indicator analysis. Then variables were added to the regression equation one at a time. This method of adding variables separately tends to make the final result dependent upon the first set of variables in the model. As a result, it is necessary to vary the order in which variables are added. The final results in this case were not dependent upon order of inclusion.

The final model, shown in Table 22.2, uses lagged employment, initial claims for unemployment insurance, help-wanted advertising, and value of construction as the independent variables. Claims for unemployment insurance and help-wanted advertising are both good indicators because of the timeliness of the data—unemployment claims are available weekly and firms advertise for jobs before filling it. Construction should signal future employment in the construction industry.

The estimated regional indicators do not include any of the components of the national index of leading economic indicators. This is unusual, given the importance of the national economy on regional economic activity. McNees and Tootell then examined how different national economic variables could be used to form a leading indicator series for the New England economy.

TABLE 22.2
SOME OF THE MULTIVARIATE MODELS OF NEW ENGLAND EMPLOYMENT

AUTOREGRESSIVE:

$$\text{Payroll employment} = \text{constant} + \text{payroll employment} (-1)$$

REGIONAL MODEL:

Payroll employment = constant + payroll employment (-1 to 3) + average e weekly initial claims for unemployment insurance (-1 to 3) + value of non-residential construction (-1 to 3) + index of help-wanted advertising (-1)

NATIONAL:

Payroll employment = constant + payroll employment (-1 to 3) + difference in yields of federal funds minus the yield on treasury bills (-1 to 3) + National Index of Help-Wanted Advertising (-1 to 2) + national new orders for plant and equipment (-1 to 3) + trade component for national payroll employment

The numbers in parenthesis are the lags of each variable used in the equation.
The regional model, so called because it is restricted to only regional data, provides the best result of regional employment.

The final result of their studies is that a model using New England variables tends to perform best in predicting employment. The best overall approach is to combine the results from several different types of models—the regional indicators, the national indicators, and the recent history of employment changes. In summary, each type of model provides insight into the various forces impacting employment. Their results illustrate that there is no one best economic forecasting model or approach that can be used in all situations.

INPUT-OUTPUT MODELS

Another major modeling method used by forecasters is I-O models. I-O models are linear, intersectional models of output determination. The I-O model's main strength is that it provides policy makers with a detailed view of the interdependence of business, government, and consumers in the economy. (For example, see Isard 1960, Miernyk 1965, Richardson 1972, and Rose and Kolk 1984.)

I-O analysis can trace its origins back to 1758, when Francois Quesnay published *Tableau Economique,* stressing the interdependence of economic activities. Quesnay showed how a single establishment, a farm, created successive rounds of wealth resulting from an increase in final demand. In effect, the *Tableau Economique* was a forerunner of modern multiplier analysis.

Other economists, primarily Leon Walras, Gustav Cassel, and Vilfredo Pareto, advanced the concept of general equilibrium over the next 150 years. But in 1936 Wassily Leontief, who was later awarded a Nobel prize in economics for his work, published a general theory of production based upon economic interdependence and published the first I-O table of the United States (Leontief 1951). Leontief's work was classified by the Federal government during the war years for fear it could be used by foreign saboteurs to identify where to strike at the U.S. economy.

Today, I-O analysis is one of the most widely used models in economic analysis. One of its major uses, especially in developing countries, is to identify sectors of the economy that must be expanded to prevent production bottlenecks or to increase the multiplier effects of an increase in final demand.

An I-O table provides an explicit set of economic accounts for a given geographic area. This accounting system is based upon a fundamental identity: total production of any sector or industry equals the amount of its products used by other industrial sectors to produce their output and the amount demanded for final consumption by consumers, business and government. Total production within a region is known as gross output.

A schematic portrayal of the major components of an I-O table is shown in Figure 22.1. Quadrant I of the table corresponds to final use of goods and services or the net output of the economy. Quadrant II contains interindustry

FIGURE 22.1
STRUCTURE OF AN INPUT-OUTPUT TABLE

USE TABLE: COMMODITIES USED BY INDUSTRIES AND FINAL USES

	INDUSTRIES										FINAL USES (GDP)							TOTAL COMMODITY OUTPUT
	Agriculture	Mining	Construction	Manufacturing	Transportation	Trade	Finance	Services	Other*	Total use (intermediate)	Personal consumption expenditures	Gross private fixed investment	Change in business inventories	Exports of goods and services	Imports of goods and services	Government purchases	GDP	
COMMODITIES Agricultural products																		
Minerals																		
Construction																		
Manufactured products																		
Transportation																		
Trade																		
Finance																		
Services																		
Other																		
Noncomparable imports																		
Total intermediate inputs																		
VALUE ADDED Compensation of employees																		
Indirect business tax and nontax liability																		
Other value added**																		
Total																		
TOTAL INDUSTRY OUTPUT																		

Legend:
☐ Total Commodity Output
▨ Primary Product of the Industry
■ Total Industry Output

Source: Survey of Current Business, April 1994, 77.

transactions reflecting the technological needs, or goods produced for industrial purposes rather than to meet consumer needs. Quadrant III corresponds to returns to primary factors, or the value-added in production (wages, salaries, profits, taxes, etc.). Quadrant IV represents value added associated with final demand activities, such as domestic help, government payrolls, interest on debt, etc.

At any time, the I-O table provides an excellent and compact look at the economy. It portrays the diversity of an economy, the leading purchasing and consumer sectors, and the role of imports and exports. To a businessperson, it shows how sales to various customers compare with those of competitors.

To illustrate the workings of an I-O model, a small hypothetical I-O model is present in Table 22.3. The table contains only three aggregated sectors in order to keep the example simple. I-O models range in size from just a few sectors at the regional level up to the U.S. I-O table that shows the interrelationship between 537 industries, or over 288,000 transactions between industries.

Each sector is listed in the I-O table twice, once as a seller and once as a purchaser. Sales to other sectors are shown by row entries, while purchases from other sectors are represented by a column entry. The final demand column represents all sales for final use from the various sectors. Each column, then, is the national production function of that sector.

By dividing the entries in each column by the corresponding Gross Output (or column sums), a table of direct requirements is calculated. The direct requirements table, shown in Table 22.4, shows the proportion of total outlays spent in each of the productive sectors. Table 22.4 shows that for each dollar spent by mining, $0.50 was an internal transaction within the sector, $0.25 was spent on manufactured goods, and $0.125 was spent on services.

Note that the sum of the columns does not add to $1.00. The difference is the percentage of value added, or, essentially, wages, salaries, and profits within the industry. Also, final demand, value added, and gross output are not considered in the construction of the direct requirements table, as we are interested in identifying the effects on each industry of changes in total outlay, or final demand.

A key assumption in I-O is that the direct requirements table remains constant for short time periods. This allows the forecaster to examine the effects of any changes in final demand on all sectors of the economy.

To illustrate this point, assume that final demand for services increases by $100. Service sector gross output initially rises by $100 to meet the increase in final demand. But when gross output increases, purchases from other sectors must also increase. The service sector will have to increase purchases from other sectors in the economy by the amounts shown in Table 22.5. Remember that the column entries correspond to the industry production function. Thus, an increase in demand for output from sector i requires that sector i increase purchases from all sectors.

TABLE 22.3
AN EXAMPLE OF AN INPUT-OUTPUT MODEL

SELLERS	PURCHASERS				
	Mining	Manufacturing	Services	Final Demand	Gross Output
Mining	100	25	50	25	200
Manufacturing	50	150	25	175	400
Services	25	100	100	275	500
Value added	25	125	325		
Gross output	200	400	500		

TABLE 22.4
DIRECT REQUIREMENTS PER DOLLAR OF GROSS OUTLAY

SELLERS	PURCHASERS		
	Mining	Manufacturing	Services
Mining	.500	.063	.100
Manufacturing	.250	.375	.050
Services	.125	.250	.200

TABLE 22.5
INCREASE IN PURCHASES FROM OTHER SECTORS DUE TO A $100 INCREASE IN DEMAND FOR SERVICES

Mining	$100 × .10 = $10.00
Manufacturing	$100 × .05 = $ 5.00
Services	$100 × .20 = $20.00

To meet this increased demand for intermediate goods, or goods used to produce other goods, all sectors of the economy must purchase more inputs, shown in Table 22.6.

However, this is not the end of the process, as successive rounds of additional inputs are needed to produce the $7.30 of services, $5.35 of manufacturing goods, etc. The total effect of a change in final demand is then equal to the direct increases in final demand and the cumulative effects of all second, third, and higher order purchases made to satisfy the initial increase in final demand.

Going through the above calculations is useful to understand the effects of changes in final demand but is not necessary to determine the overall effects. The final total change in gross output of each sector can be read directly from Table 22.7, the total requirements table.

TABLE 22.6
INCREASE IN DEMAND FOR INTERMEDIATE GOODS

	Mining: $10	Manufacturing: $5	Services: $20	Total
Mining	$10 × .5 = 5	$5 × .06 = .30	$20 × .1 = 2.	7.30
Manufacturing	10 × .25=2.5	5 × .375 =1.85	20 × .05 = 1	5.35
Services	10 × .125=1.25	5 × .25 =1.25	20 × .20 = 4.0	6.50

TABLE 22.7
TOTAL REQUIREMENTS TABLE

	Mining	Manufacturing	Services
Mining	2.249	.346	.303
Manufacturing	.951	1.787	.231
Services	.649	.613	1.361

The total requirements table shows the total increase in output in each sector due to a $1.00 change in final demand for that sector's output.

I-O analysis requires the use of matrix manipulation to derive most of the results due to changes in final demand. As such, we will not present the mathematics underlying I-O analysis here, but a brief summary is included in the Appendix to this chapter. For a more detailed account of the underlying mathematics, see Miernyk (1965) or Richardson (1972).

Once the total requirements table is calculated, it can be used to calculate the regional gross output, by sector, by multiplying the total requirements matrix by a final demand column. The final demand column is the demand by sector for goods and services used for final consumption. Underlying the mathematics of I-O analysis is that the total requirements table shows how much of a sector's output is required to produce $1.00 of final output. Note that the total requirements table has numbers greater than one on the diagonal. This means that to produce a $1.00 of output in a sector, such as mining, $1.00 is used to meet final demand and almost $1.25 of intermediate goods from within the mining sector is used. In addition 34.6 cents of manufacturing goods and 30.3 cents of services is required.

USE OF INPUT-OUTPUT MODELS IN FORECASTING

I-O models are one of the most widely used models in both national and regional forecasting. It is possible to use I-O analysis to show how changes in demand for the output of one (or more) sector will impact total output and employment in the region covered by the I-O model.

As useful as I-O models are at the national level, it is within the field of regional economics that I-O has become an indispensable tool. Data limitations at the regional level often preclude forecasters from gathering the necessary data for accurate forecasting. Regional I-O models can be constructed using various types of scaling methods to regionalize the U.S. national I-O table, using just employment data or any other available data. The various methods available for regionalizing the national I-O table range from very sophisticated approaches to essentially just scaling the national table, based upon the percentage of regional employment to national employment. For examples of various methods of regionalizing I-O tables, see Morrison and Smith (1974) or Stevens (1983). Regardless of the sophistication of the regionalizing methodology in a region where data is not available, having an I-O table, however crudely constructed, can form the basis of a forecast in the absence of any other information.

Another major use of I-O models is in impact analysis. Impact analysis identifies the output, employment, and income effects on a region due to the addition or removal or a major project or business in a region. For example, suppose you were asked to determine the effects of closing a military base in a region that had little economic data available, other than employment data. An I-O model created for that region could be created using the employment data. Then, the final demand of the military base could be estimated by determining the amount of goods and services purchased locally, along with estimates of the military salaries and civilian wages paid. Wage and salary income could then be distributed among the various sectors in the same proportion as either national consumer spending patterns or state spending patterns, if available.

Usually the data for this type of study is compiled by identifying the economic sector and location of expenditures of the base by going through statistics of the base's budget. This is a time consuming and difficult exercise, but is usually performed by opponents or proponents of base closures.

Once the final demand column of the base has been determined, then the base's final demand can be inserted into the I-O table. This allows the modeler to estimate the regional gross output and employment effects of the base and estimate the proportion of the local economy dependent upon the base.

The employment effects are usually calculated by multiplying the change in final demand by the average employment per million dollars of gross output. This can be expanded by using local employment statistics to calculate the effects on each occupation from within a sector, again using the average employment by occupation for some standard level of output.

This same type of analysis can be followed for any type of business or large construction project (such as a major dam or highway) in a region. In general, the larger and more diversified an economy, the smaller the overall effect of a base closing or other project will be. However, for a region that is dependent upon just a few economic sectors for the majority of regional gross output, the more devastating the effects of a factory or base closure.

IMPACT ANALYSIS

As an example of the use of I-O in estimating the economic impacts of a major industrial plant closure on a regional economy, consider the case of the closing of the Kaiser Steel Corporation's Fontana plant in December 1983. Kaiser was started by Henry J. Kaiser, one of the most progressive industrial leaders in America. He had made his fortune during the New Deal era and had always attempted to work with labor, rather than against it. In fact, many of the business community considered him a socialist, especially other steel leaders. He was one of the first employers to provide medical care (through Kaiser Hospital) and various forms of employee recognition and rewards. Pay levels at Kaiser were high compared to the rest of the industry because Kaiser would routinely accept the contract terms between other companies and the United Steelworkers of America and then add salary or benefits to it.

The closing of Kaiser sent shockwaves through the Riverside and San Bernardino County economies, two developing regions some 35 miles from downtown Los Angeles. As late as 1981, Kaiser employed 10,815 people and was the largest non-government employer in the two county area. Only the region's military bases (which were ultimately closed or scaled back only eight years later) employed more people.

Kaiser had been opened during World War II to supply fabricated steel to the West Coast shipyards. However, fear of Japanese attack caused the plant to be built 55 miles inland. As a result of the distance from a deepwater port, Kaiser was forced to contend with high transportation costs. During the boom years of the late 1940s through the late 1960s (ignoring the two recessions in 1952 and 1959), Kaiser prospered because of its position as the only fully integrated steel manufacturing facility on the West Coast and a series of government contracts to supply steel for the Korean War and the Vietnam war.

Beginning in the early 1960s, foreign steel imports (primarily Japanese) began cutting into Kaiser's market share. While this was not initially a serious problem, by the early 1970s, Kaiser realized that the plant, with its original equipment, could not compete with the modern foreign steel facilities.

Between 1975 and 1978, Kaiser invested some $250,000,000 in upgrading the plant facilities. However, by then it was too late, and between 1976 and 1980 the combined company lost over $229,000,000. In 1981, the company essential gave up to the foreign companies and announced that it would close by the end of 1983. (For a good biography of Henry Kaiser, see Foster 1985. Also, Toruno 1985 provides a good overview of the Kaiser facility).

When examining the effect of an industry on a region, three types of effects are usually considered:

1. Direct effects: The output, income, and employment effects on the region due to production, or output, of the industry.
2. Indirect Effects: The output, income, and employment effects on the region due to secondary impacts to support the output of the industry under study.
3. Induced effects: The output, income, and employment effects on the region due to changes in wages and salaries caused by the direct and indirect effects.

An example of what is meant by regional multipliers would be useful here. (Note that a region can include anything from a small city to the entire nation. In this sense, the region is defined as the area under study). Suppose a producer of radios is located in a region and several companies which sell components to the radio producer are also located there. Now let the demand for radios increase. The direct impact on the region will be the purchases the radio producer makes in the region to support higher production levels. These impacts include hiring more people, buying more electronic components locally, etc. The indirect effects will be those associated with the increased demand for inputs from the companies supplying the radio producer. That is, an increase in demand for radios is indirectly an increased demand for radio components. The induced effects will be the demand for goods and services associated with greater income in the region which, directly or indirectly, receive wages due to increased demand for radios. Note that this cycle also works in the opposite direction—a decline in the demand for radios causes the radio producer to reduce employment and purchases from other firms.

The strength of the regional multipliers depends upon the degree of integration of the local economy. If all the firms necessary to produce radios are within the region, the change in demand will affect the region more strongly than if only a few, if any, firms are within the region. Hence, the makeup of imports and exports within a region is important.

From the above, we can derive the two types of multipliers, type I and type II. Type I multipliers are the ratio of direct and indirect effects to direct effects. Type II multipliers are the ratio of direct, indirect, and induced effects to direct effects. Thus, a type II multiplier of 1.5 means that for any $1.00 change in output in the region causes total output to increase by $1.50.

Whenever one is using an I-O table for analysis of a particular industry, it is convenient to measure change in a standard unit figure, for example, $1,000,000. Because the I-O model assumes linearity, the results can then be scaled to reflect the size of the project under examination.

When estimating the effects of a reduction in output or the total closure of the Kaiser plant, there are two main areas to examine. First, the effects of income, employment, and output due to the reduction in Kaiser's output must be examined and, secondly, the effects of the loss in wages and salaries due to the closure of Kaiser. While these two effects are distinct, the total effects of the closure will be the total reduction in gross output.

An I-O table for the two county area was created (Lofting 1980). This table was used to calculate the type I and type II output multipliers for the region. The type I multiplier was 1.68 and the type II multiplier was 3.98. That is, a $1,000,000 in Kaiser output leads to a $1,680,000 change in direct and indirect effects, and an additional $2,300,000 in income effects. Notice that the type II multiplier is larger than the type I multiplier. This is always the case, as the type II multiplier takes into account more effects (the effect of income on the region) than the type I multiplier.

The type I and II multipliers can be derived directly from the total requirements matrix (of the type shown in Table 22.7). The type I multipliers are the column sum of the total requirements matrix. The type II multipliers are the column sum when the matrix is "closed," or when the income and value added sectors are included in the matrix.

Using the multipliers, we are able to calculate the effects Kaiser had on the two county area, the major results are summarized in Table 22.8.

Using this information, the effects of the closure of Kaiser had the following effects on the two county area:

Employment:	−24,249 (person year equivalents)
Income:	−$618,618,000
Output:	−$1,407,360,000

In relationship to the two county area, these effects were the equivalent of reducing regional employment by some 14.4 percent, income by 12 percent, and regional output by 15.4 percent.

However, the effects were tempered by federal, state, and union transfer payments, such as food stamps, trade adjustment assistance, unemployment insurance, and union benefits. These benefits, at least in the short run, reduced the effects of the closure by up to one-third. Thus, the total impact of the closure, taking into account these transfer payments, was:

Employment:	−16,224 (person year equivalents)
Income:	−$408,287,000
Output:	−$924,000,000

This type of impact analysis cannot be done using time series or econometric modeling techniques. In both methodologies, an underlying assumption is that the structure of the economy does not change significantly between the period covered by the historic data and the period covered by the forecast. Removing or adding a major sector to the regional economy violates this assumption.

TABLE 22.8
SECTOR EFFECTS OF KAISER STEEL ON THE TWO COUNTY REGION

	OUTPUT		INCOME	EMPLOYMENT	
Type I		Type II	Type II	Type I	Type II
1 Steel Production $1,311,850		Steel Production $1,312,280	Steel Production $397,000	Steel Production 11.40	Trade 18.07
2 Utilities $56,130		Trade $332,634	Trade $2,232,000	Trade 1.5	Steel Production 11.54
3 Business Services $52,574		Real Estate $212,247	Real Estate $154,000	Transportation 1.00	Health Services 6.16
4 Transportation $51,232		Health Services $150,264	Health Services $111,930	Business Services 0.36	Banking 2.61
5 Industrial Chemicals $32,639		Utilities $35,672	Construction $77,490	Fabricated Metal Products .36	Transportation 1.50
6 Scrap $18,039		Banking $76,280	Utilities $34,440	Construction .33	Personal Services 1.41
7 Construction $16,660		Transportation $54,435	Banking $29,652	Banking .26	Amusement .98
8 Fabricated Metal $12,714		Communications $45,600	Car Repair $22,386	Utilities .25	Food & Kindred .85
9 Copper and Aluminum Products $11,412		Industrial Chemicals $41,479	Personal Services $22,386	Industrial Chemicals .25	Construction .78
10 Misc. Machinery $10,315		Construction $38,476	Amusement $12,054	Misc. Machinery .22	Business Services .68
Total Change in Region					
$1,679,820		$3,980,000	$861,490	19.56	49.04

Impact analysis is just one of the uses of I-O in modeling. The other primary use is in conjunction with time series or econometric models of final demand. For a complete discussion of this use, see Almon (1975).

FORECASTING COMMODITY PRICES

In Part II, the affects of price pressures on profits were discussed. The example presented here discusses how forecasting techniques are used to forecast commodity prices.

Price movements in the commodity market often foreshadow changes in inflationary pressures in the economy. Figure 22.2 shows how commodity prices vary with the cyclical movement of the economy. However, while the overall movement of commodity prices is important to the macroeconomist, commodity speculators are concerned with forecasting the price movements of a single commodity or commodity group.

WHAT IS THE COMMODITY MARKET

The commodity market is actually a series of different markets, such as the Chicago Board of Trade (CBOT) where grains (among other things) are

FIGURE 22.2
COMMODITY PRICES

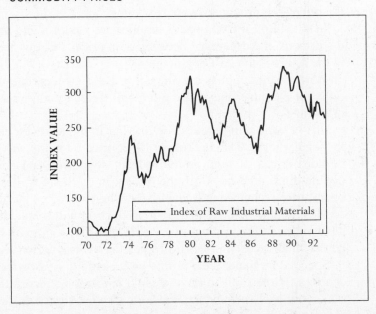

sold, the Commodity Exchange in New York (COMEX), and several regional commodity exchanges, where other raw materials are bought and sold. The commodity market can even include financial instruments such as treasury bill futures.

There are two basic types of entities in the commodities market. There are those entities, such as Ralston-Purina, General Mills, and General Motors, that actually use the raw resources in their production process. The other group active in commodity markets is the speculators who are not necessarily interested in actually taking delivery of the commodity, but instead are interested in making money from changes in the price of a commodity. It is the speculators who create a liquid market, enabling large orders to be filled without disrupting the market. When speculators buy or sell commodity futures, they are exposing themselves to risk because they believe they will make a profit. Speculators are drawn to the commodity market because of the chance to make large profits in a relatively short time period.

Speculators set a price for the future delivery of commodities, allowing farmers and miners (among other raw materials producers) to determine which crops to plant or which metal mining capacity should be expanded.

To illustrate how a market for a single commodity works, consider the case of corn. Every few months a future market for corn is established. The market is for delivery of a set amount of corn at some predetermined time, based upon crop harvest dates. Prices are established through the bid and sell prices, where the bid price is the bid by speculators and the sell price is the price corn producers want for their product.

In the simplest case, where supplies are plentiful and there are no market disruptions, the difference between corn prices this quarter and two quarters in the future is the cost of storage.

However, if supplies are subject to large swings, due to weather disruptions for example, the future price will differ by more or less than the cost of storage.

In 1993, the rain-related crop disaster in the Midwest caused grain prices to begin rising. The February, 1993 price of corn was the highest in a decade. Prices of high-protein wheat, soybeans, and sorghum all posted double-digit increases from the prior year. U.S. stockpiles of corn and soybeans were at their lowest levels since the 1970s.

Most people believe that grain production will rebound in 1994. Farmers have an incentive to plant every acre that they can, with corn prices up 30 percent and soybean prices up 16 percent over the prior year.

Speculators make their profits on their ability to correctly forecast price changes. If they fail to have a good forecasting record, they will join the ranks of the ex-speculators, watching or working for those who are better at forecasting price movements.

FORECASTING COMMODITY PRICES

There are two schools of thought on forecasting price changes in the commodity market, although most price analysts use both approaches to forecasting. These two methods are the fundamentalist approach and the technical approach. The fundamentalist approach is used to forecast price movements over some long period of time. In this context, a long period of time could mean until the next harvest or until the supply of a particular metal can be appreciably affected by new production. The technical approach is a short-term forecasting approach that is only concerned with the likely price movement over the next few days.

THE FUNDAMENTALISTIC APPROACH TO COMMODITY PRICE FORECASTING. The fundamentalist approach relies on calculating supply and demand functions for a particular commodity and then using these calculated functions to determine the future direction of the market. For example, suppose that the fundamentalist determines that the demand for corn can be characterized as:

$$Qc = C(P_{corn}, P_{grains}, \text{personal income, population, trade weighted value of the U.S. dollar)} \tag{22.1}$$

where:

P_{corn}	=	price of corn
P_{grain}	=	index of grain prices
Population	=	population of the U.S.
Personal income	=	U.S. per capita personal income
Trade weighed value of the U.S. dollar	=	index of the average value of the U.S. dollar relative to trading partners

Quantity demanded of corn is an inverse function of price, so the expected coefficient of price should have a negative sign. There is a strong cross-price elasticity of demand between all grains and corn. Demand for corn is positively related to personal income growth and population. The trade weighted value of the U.S. dollar captures the change in foreign demand for U.S. corn in a stable market.

This demand function is an obvious simplification of the demand curve for corn, but it will suffice for our purposes.

Supply is often more easily estimated than demand. The U.S. Department of Agriculture surveys regions in the U.S. for crop yields and for planting information, and, for most grains, accurate historical data on production exists. Using this data, fundamentalists estimate the supply curve of various commodities.

The estimated supply and demand equations are then used to forecast where commodity prices will be in the future. By itself, this analysis is somewhat boring if the market is in equilibrium and nothing is disrupting the world markets. However, the analysis quickly becomes more interesting as the effects of world politics and trade patterns are considered.

Again, consider the 1994 grain outlook. U.S. corn farmers have about 80 million acres to plant. With a normal yield per acre, and higher prices encouraging farmers to plant every acre, the projected output is 8.8 billion bushels, up 39 percent from 1993. This would be enough to meet expected demand and rebuild a comfortable inventory. Combined with record soybean harvest in the rest of the world, grain prices would be expected to remain steady, holding inflation down.

In the past however, low crop yields were the result of droughts rather than flooding. The flooding has drowned the soil microbes and washed away soil nutrients. Because the market is so tight, commodity prices will move widely as speculators attempt to guess the effects of any change in weather patterns or yields.

As crop estimates change, grain prices will change. An expected 8.4 billion bushel corn crop would result in corn prices increasing to the $3.20–3.25 level, while a 7.5 billion bushel crop would push prices into the $4.00 per bushel rate, from the current $3.00 per bushel level.

Note also that meat prices would also be impacted by price increases in grain prices. Since feed prices would increase, the price of cattle and pigs would increase, driving up the nation's overall inflation rate.

THE TECHNICAL APPROACH TO COMMODITY PRICE FORECASTING. The technical approach to commodity price forecasting relies on identifying patterns in trading and prices. In general, technicians use price charts to attempt to forecast short-term price movements of a commodity. There are several patterns that commodity speculators look for, using a chart of historical commodity prices such as that shown in Figure 22.3. These patterns include price trends, support and resistance levels, and rectangles.

The technical approach depends upon identifying extreme highs and lows of a commodity's price movements. An extreme high is the highest price before prices dipped. An extreme low is the lowest price before price climbed.

PRICE TRENDS. Technical analysts often draw a straight line through the extreme lows in an attempt to identify an upward trend or the extreme highs in an attempt to identify the downward trend.

Technical analysts watch the trendline closely. If there is an upward trend in prices and prices drop below the trendline it is an indication that the ongoing trend is losing force. However, this does not mean that the price movement is changing direction, just that a period of market consolidation may be taking place. Figure 22.4 shows how a price trend is identified.

FIGURE 22.3

EXAMPLES OF A CHART OF HISTORICAL COMMIDITY PRICES USED BY COMMODITY TECHNICIANS

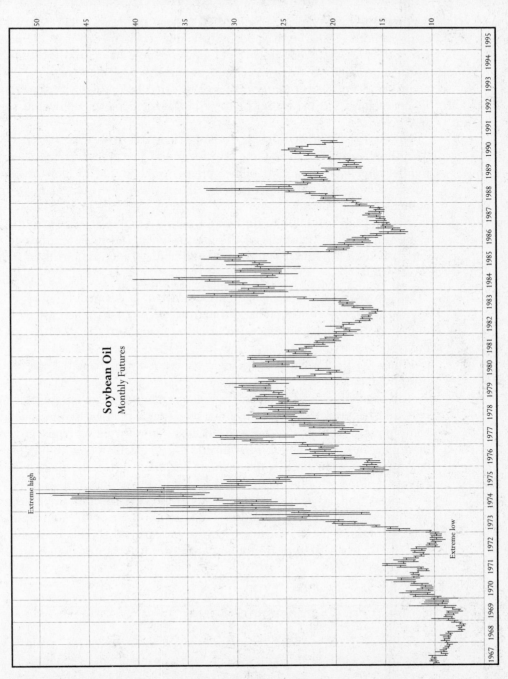

SUPPORT AND RESISTANCE LEVELS.   A price support level is the price at which any market decline is expected to stop, while a price resistance level is the price at which any increase is likely to stop. The fact is, commodity prices tend to stop near the point where they have stopped before. This market behavior is due to the behavior of the people in the market. At every price level, some people have sold positions (or gone short) and some people have purchased positions (or gone long). Suppose the market initially rallies, and price increases. The speculators who are long see the value of their holdings increase, while the shorts realize losses.

Now let the market rally fizzle and prices return to their earlier level. The shorts want to cover their positions, and the longs, having seen the market already can support higher prices, want to add to their positions. Also, people who were not involved in the market do not want to miss another upside market move. Each of these different groups causes the market to keep from falling through its earlier price resistance level. In the same sense, if the market had initially dropped and now returned to the earlier level, the same psychology would hold, except the positions would be reversed.

RECTANGLES.   A rectangle price pattern is formed by trading for several weeks or even months in a narrow price range. When prices break out of the rectangle, an extended price movement in the direction of the breakout usually occurs.

Figure 22.5 shows how a rectangle pattern is formed and the effects of a price breakout.

The psychology of the rectangle is the same as that underlying the support and resistance levels of the market. The market has consolidated at some point. Once a price breakout occurs, shorts need to begin covering their positions, longs add to their position, and speculators with no position begin taking a position in the market, all which drive the market in the direction of the price breakout.

This section has presented the basics of the two different methods used by some speculators to forecast commodity prices. Of course, every speculator uses these two tools, and permutations, secret methods, and other tools in an attempt to divine the future direction of the commodity market.

MODEL OF FUNCTIONAL INCOME HYPOTHESIS

Part II presented some of the theories of consumption. This section will illustrate a method of attempting to use consumption expenditures as a means of verifying, or disproving, one of the theories of aggregate consumption, the functional income hypothesis.

FIGURE 22.4
EXAMPLES OF TRENDLINES

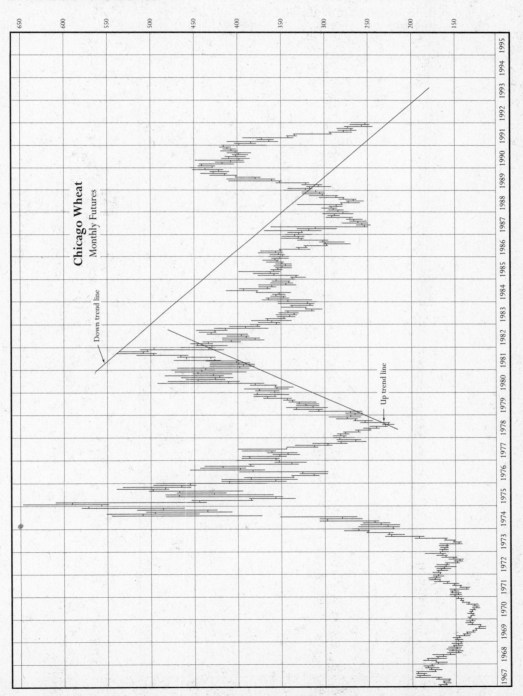

Chicago Wheat
Monthly Futures

Down trend line

Up trend line

FIGURE 22.5
EXAMPLE OF A RECTANGLE TRADING PATTERN, WHERE PRICES ARE TESTING THE SUPPORT AND
RESISTANCE LEVELS BEFORE AN UPWARD PRICE BREAK-OUT OCCURS

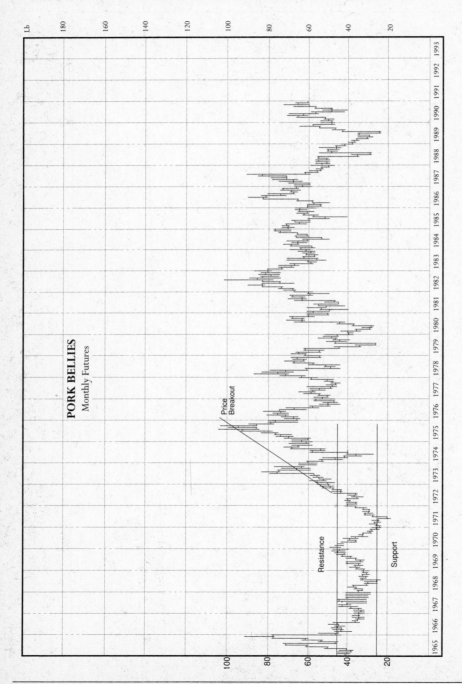

PORK BELLIES
Monthly Futures

A simple way to represent the functional income hypothesis:

$$C_t = W_{t-1} + a + bR_{t-1} \tag{22.2}$$

where W is wages and all other types of labor income, while R is profits and all other types of property income. Notice that it is assumed for simplicity that the coefficient of W is one, though that is not necessary. For the functional income hypothesis to be true, it is only necessary that the coefficient of W be greater than that of R. To estimate this equation properly, we should also include time lags distributed over several previous periods. But this equation cannot be estimated without a bias because W and R are not really independent of each other, since their total includes all income.

Another form of equation for the functional income hypothesis could be the statement that consumption is a function of both income (Y) and the labor share (W/Y):

$$C_t = a + bY_{t-1} + c(W/Y)_{t-1} \tag{22.3}$$

where b is the MPC of consumer spending for all income and c is the positive effect of a greater labor share. Once again, if we were to estimate this equation, we would have to include time lags for several periods. This equation also would provide a biased estimate because Y and W/Y are not independent of each other.

Finally, a third way to portray the functional income hypothesis is to show that the average propensity to consume is a function of the labor share. An econometric test (using the ARMA method to correct autocorrelation) was run from the first quarter of 1949 to the first quarter of 1992. The test correlated the average propensity to consume (C/Y), consumption/national income) to the labor share $(W/Y$, labor income/national income). National income is used as the denominator for both ratios to show the full effect of property income, including the full effect of corporate saving. The result was:

$$C/Y_t = 5.54 + .70W/Y_t + .37W/Y_{t-1} + .20W/Y_{t-2}$$

$$(2.01)\ (6.74)\ (3.13)\ (1.71) \tag{22.4}$$

For this equation, $R^2 = .96$, that is, the correlation coefficient squared is .96, a high correlation. Also, the Durbin-Watson coefficient is 1.99, which indicates that there is no significant autocorrelation in this case. The t-statistics indicate that there is a strong statistical significance to the relation between the propensity to consume and the labor share with no time lag, with a weaker significance for the influence from earlier periods. The evidence is consistent with the functional income hypothesis. Of course, the evidence is also consistent with other hypotheses because other possible variables were not included in the regression.

ESTIMATING INVESTMENT

In Chapter 21, lagged variables were presented. The next sections show how lagged variables are used in econometric models of important economic variables, beginning with investment.

The simplest demand-oriented equation for investment says that:

$$I_t = v\,(C_{t-1} - C_{t-2}) \tag{22.5}$$

where I is real investment, C is real consumption, and v is the accelerator coefficient, relating investment to the change in consumer output demanded. A slightly more sophisticated equation substitutes total demand (Y) for consumption:

$$I_t = v\,(Y_{t-1} - Y_{t-2}) \tag{22.6}$$

A still more sophisticated demand-oriented equation will consider investment to be the result of the change in output at several previous periods:

$$I_t = f\,(Y_{t-1}, Y_{t-2}, Y_{t-3} \ldots Y_{t-n}) \tag{22.7}$$

Many such distributed lag functions have been estimated econometrically (see, e.g., Jorgenson 1971).

The profit hypothesis may be stated as the relation of investment to profits and profit rates in many previous periods:

$$I_t = f\,(\Pi_{t-1}, \Pi_{t-2} \ldots \Pi_{t-n};\ \Pi/K_{t-1}, \Pi/K_{t-2} \ldots \Pi/K_{t-N}) \tag{22.8}$$

where Π is total profit and Π/K is the rate of profit on capital.

The relationships of investment, profits, and profit rates were tested econometrically using the official government sources (as reported in CITIBASE database) the period from the first quarter of 1949 to the first quarter of 1992.

First, real nonresidential investment (CITIBASE file GNQ) was regressed on real total corporate profit before taxes (CITIBASE file GPIVA) with the result (using the ARMA method) that:

$$I_t = 404.6 + .23\Pi_t + .12\Pi_{t-1} + .14\Pi_{t-2} \tag{22.9}$$
$$(4.96) \qquad (5.49) \quad (2.90) \qquad (3.41)$$

$$R^2 = .98 \qquad DW = 2.00$$

where R is the correlation coefficient and DW is the Durbin-Watson test. There is a high correlation (and no significant auto-correlation) when investment is regressed on profits with a distributed time lag. According to the t-statistics (in parentheses) there is a strong relationship with no time lag, but some significant relationship with time lags of one and two quarters.

Second, real nonresidential investment (CITIBANK file GINQ) was regressed on the ratio of profit before taxes to stockholders' equity capital (*R/K*). The data is from Federal Trade Commission data, 1949–1993, US. Printing Office, Washington D.C. The result (using the ARMA method) was:

$$I_t = 708.8 + 1.19\Pi/K_t + 1.01\Pi/K_{t-1} + .67\Pi/K_{t-2} + .67\Pi/K_{t-3} \quad (22.10)$$
$$\quad (5.54) \quad (5.86) \quad (5.16) \quad (3.50) \quad (3.45)$$

$$R2^5 .99 \qquad DW = 1.98$$

Investment appears to be correlated with the profit rate (with no significant autocorrelation). There is a significant relationship of investment with the profit rate for several previous periods, with a declining strength as we go back in time (according to the *t*-statistics).

Finally, investment can be correlated to both profits and profit rates in a multiple regression, but one should remember that the results are biased by the fact that profits and profit rates are not independent of each other. With that qualification in mind, real nonresidential investment (I, series #86) was regressed on real corporate profits before taxes (Π, series #286) and on the ratio of profits before taxes to stockholders' equity capital (*R/K*) with the result (using the ARMA method) that:

$$I_t = 365.5 + .26\Pi_t + .57\Pi/K_{t-1} + .68\Pi/K_{t-2} \qquad (22.11)$$
$$\quad (6.01) \quad (6.13) \quad (2.91) \quad (3.60)$$

$$R^2 = .99 \qquad DW = 2.00$$

Investment has a statistically significant correlation with both total profits and profit rates. The relation of investment with profit rates is strongest with a two-quarter time lag.

ESTIMATING LABOR SHARE

A brief formalization of the hypotheses presented in chapter 6 would be as follows: The wage lag and and overhead labor hypotheses emphasize that the labor share (*W/Y*) is a function (f^1) of capacity utilization. Capacity utilization is the ratio of actual output (*Y*) to Z, where Z is the possible output at optimum utilization.

$$W/Y_t = f^1(Y/Z)_t \qquad (22.12)$$

The unemployment hypothesis emphasizes that the labor share is a function (f^2) of unemployment (U) with a time lag (g).

$$W/Y_t = f^2(U_{t-g}) \qquad (22.13)$$

The synthetic hypothesis, however, contends that the labor share is influenced by both capacity utilization and by unemployment, pulling in different directions. So this view would say that it is more reasonable to combine the two factors into one equation. That equation states that the labor share is a function of both capacity utilization (with no measurable time lag) and of unemployment (with a long time lag).

$$W/Y_t = f^1(Y/Z)_t + f^2(U_{t-g}) \qquad (22.14)$$

Using data from the sources indicated in Figures 6.1 and 6.3, econometric tests were made from the first quarter of 1949 to the first quarter of 1991. (Autocorrelation was corrected in all regressions by the ARMA method, based on the correction suggested by Cochrane and Orcutt 1949.) The results of a simple regression of the labor share (W/Y) on the capacity utilization ratio (Z/Y)—with all rates expressed as percentages—were:

$$W/Y_t = 81.0 - 0.10(Y/Z)_t \qquad (22.15)$$
$$(46.6) \qquad (-5.6)$$

$$R^2 = 0.97 \qquad\qquad DW = 1.99$$

where the figures in parentheses are t-statistics, showing a high level of statistical significance of the regression coefficients. R^2 is the correlation coefficient squared, and DW is the Durbin-Watson coefficient, showing almost no autocorrelation in this case. It does appear that the labor share is highly and negatively correlated with capacity utilization, but this result could be misleading until we add the unemployment factor in a multiple regression.

A multiple regression attempts to explain the labor share with both capacity utilization and with the unemployment rate:

$$W/Y_t = 82.7 - .11(Y/Z)_t - .28U_{t-3} \qquad (22.16)$$
$$(43.1) \quad (-6.54) \quad (-3.38)$$

$$R^2 = 0.97 \qquad\qquad DW = 1.99$$

The t-statistics indicate that the regression coefficients are statistically significant. There is a high correlation and no significant autocorrelation. Thus, it appears that the labor share is negatively correlated with capacity utilization, but also is negatively correlated with unemployment with a time lag. Of course, this does not prove cause and effect. Moreover, the high correlation in the main merely reflects the fact that most economic variables conform to the business cycle, so they move together pro-cyclically (or move inversely if one of them is counter-cyclical). We must also remember the biases in the data that make it suspect—as well as the various statistical problems in such time data (such as the fact that capacity utilization and unemployment are not really independent of each other). At any rate, the evidence is at least compatible with the hypotheses suggested here.

Much less controversial is the hypothesis that unemployment is closely related to real national income (Sources in Figure 6.3):

$$U_t = 62.5 - 0.01Y_t \qquad (22.17)$$
$$(8.7) \quad (-11.5)$$

$$R^2 = 0.97 \qquad DW = 1.99$$

Unemployment has a significant negative correlation with real national income.

Similarly, it is obvious that capacity utilization is closely related to real national income:

$$Y/Z_t = -179.1 + 0.05Y_t \qquad (22.18)$$
$$(-5.7) \quad (12.2)$$

$$R^2 = 0.93 \qquad DW = 2.00$$

Capacity utilization has a significant positive correlation with real national income.

DETERMINING RAW MATERIAL PRICE BEHAVIOR

The ratio of raw and intermediate materials prices (P_m), to all consumer goods prices (P_c), may be shown as P_m / P_c. This ratio is pro-cyclical in most periods. It may therefore be explained as a function of the ratio of capacity utilization, which perfectly reflects the business cycle. Capacity utilization (Y / Z) is the ratio of actual output (Y) to potential output at full capacity (Z). In equation form:

$$(P_m/P_c)_t = f(Y/Z)_t \qquad (22.19)$$

where the ratio of raw intermediate material prices to finished goods prices is a positive function of the ratio of capacity utilization.

The data used here are from CITIBASE database (files IPX, PPSIMC, and PUNEW). All data are seasonally adjusted quarterly and expressed as percentages. The ratio of sensitive raw and intermediate materials prices

(P_m), to the consumer price index (P_c), was regressed against the ratio of capacity utilization (Y/Z).

The results for the period from 1970 through 1992 are:

$$(P_m/P_c)_t = 37.1 + 0.78Y/Z_t \qquad (22.20)$$
$$ (1.4) \quad (3.0)$$

$$R^2 = 0.92 \qquad\qquad DW = 1.99$$

In this period, there is a high correlation between the two ratios. There is no significant autocorrelation. Moreover, the coefficient for capacity utilization is statistically significant.

The econometric conclusion is that there was a statistically significant correlation between the ratio of raw and intermediate material prices to consumer prices and the ratio of capacity utilization in the 1970s, and 1980s and 1990s (when both ratios were pro-cyclical).

MONTE CARLO SIMULATION MODELS

When a forecaster is using an econometric model for forecasting purposes the choice of assumptions often essentially determines the results of the forecast process. For example, if one were forecasting electricity use, which is closely tied to GDP growth, assuming that GDP will grow by 3.00 percent annually for the next five years usually will guarantee that the model output will show an increasing level of electricity growth. Because we are making forecasts about the future, assumptions are necessary. But how do expected variations in the assumption set impact the forecast results?

Simulation models attempt to identify the range of possible forecast outputs as the assumption set varies about the point estimates.

There are many different types of simulation models, ranging from mathematical models of the universe to the behavior of fish populations in a pond. We are concerned only with econometric simulation models that begin with an estimated relationship between two (or more) variables as shown in Chapter 22. Some simulation models are used to perform forecasts without evaluating the effects of different assumption sets. For example, every time you use an econometric model to prepare a forecast you are performing a simulation of the future.

There are different ways to use simulation models. A common application is a forecast, which simulates the behavior of an equation, such as an econometric equation, into the future, beyond the time frame that was used to estimate the model parameters.

More sophisticated simulation models attempt to identify how normal variations in the assumption set affect the forecast results. That is, if the assumed growth of GDP is 3.00 percent annually, it is unlikely that each quarter's growth rate will be exactly 3.00 percent. One would anticipate that GDP growth will vary around the assumed growth rate, between (for example) 2.8 and 3.2 percent. One way to approach the uncertainty of GDP growth is to perform a series of forecasts based upon a high, low, and medium growth rate. This is fine, as long as you have only one variable that you are concerned with. If, however, you have two or more, then the number of possible results begins to grow. For example, suppose you were making assumptions about GDP growth and defense expenditures. Then you would need to have 9 cases, associated with high GDP growth and high, medium, and low defense expenditures, medium GDP growth with high, medium, and low defense expenditures, etc. With three variables there would be 27 possible outcomes. As the number of variables and the number of possible ranges are increased, the number of potential forecast outcomes quickly grows to unmanageable levels. Also, it is possible that in the first quarter of the forecast, horizon high GDP growth is accompanied by low defense expenditures, while in the next quarter there is low GDP growth but high defense expenditures.

A Monte Carlo simulation model (or stochastic model, reflecting the probabilistic nature of the model) begins with an assumed value of every variable and a probability distribution around the assumed value. For each time period, a random choice of each variable is made and a forecast value prepared. But the forecast is done many times, each time choosing from the assumed variable set. For example, it is not uncommon to perform the simulation 50 to 100 times (or more), using a different combination of assumptions each time. The various simulations help identify the potential range of outcomes, which have now taken into account variations in the assumption set. Monte Carlo simulation models are just one of many simulation methods. An advantage of Monte Carlo simulations over other methods is that it allows for determining the probability that the forecast or simulation results will fall within various ranges.

A disadvantage of a Monte Carlo simulation is the large amount of mathematical calculations involved and the sheer amount of data generated. While this problem has been mitigated by modern computers, it is not something that should be overlooked when deciding to perform a simulation using several exogenous variables.

This example presents a Monte Carlo simulation that is used only for forecasting purposes. We will begin with an econometric model, the parameters having already been estimated using the standard least-squares methodology, using a data set that extends from some time in the past to today. The question is then how to perform a forecast and determine the potential range of outcomes.

In a Monte Carlo simulation, the distribution of the exogenous variables is determined. The distributions have a mean value equal to the assumed growth value in the future and variance based upon historical data. Once the distribution has been identified, random draws are taken from the distribution of the assumed (or exogenous) variables. These random values of the exogenous variables are then used as input to the forecasting model.

AN EXAMPLE OF A MONTE CARLO SIMULATION–LOAD FORECASTING

Forecasting electricity demand is done by most state regulatory commissions and almost every electric utility in the nation. Peak demand forecasts form the basis of electricity rates and the need for new generation plants to meet this demand. Electric utilities have become one of the most sophisticated modeling industries in the world because of the number of different factors that influence electricity demand as well as the long time period necessary to construct new generation facilities. For example, it is not uncommon for a new generation plant to take twelve years to construct and the cost to exceed several billion dollars. Electric utilities are loath to invest the money in plants that might sit idle for several years if the demand forecasts are too high, while failure to have the necessary generation capacity means that the utility would have to purchase high priced electricity from other utilities.

In the Southwest, electricity demand is influenced by population and income growth, the growth of the regional economy, and temperature. Demand for electricity is greatest during the hot summer months when consumers and businesses turn on their air conditioners. For an individual utility, demand can vary as much as 25 percent per day in the summer, depending upon temperature. There is no means available to a utility forecaster in 1993 to predict the effects of temperature on the electric system ten years from now, even though that is exactly what he or she must do if now generation capacity is to be available by then.

To forecast electricity demand, a simple regression model was estimated:

$$\text{Demand} = 0.012 \times \text{Max}T^2 + 0.105 \times DDCD - 0.065 \times DDHD + .0004 \times \text{ElecSales} - 17.267 \times \text{ElecPrice} - 21.423 \times DQ3 \qquad (22.21)$$

Demand	=	maximum annual demand (in megawatts)
$\text{Max}T^2$	=	maximum temperature, squared
$DDCD$	=	a measure of heat build-up for the summer months

where: $DDHD$ = a measure of cold for the winter months

ElecSales = sales of electricity for the entire quarter

ElecPrice = the price of electricity

$DQ3$ = a dummy variable equal to 1 for the summer, 0 otherwise

This equation shows that quarterly demand is dependent upon the maximum temperature (squared), a measure of air conditioning load on any particular day and heat build-up. If it suddenly got hot one day, many people might not turn on their air conditioners, and office buildings have cooled during the nighttime. If, however, there was a heat wave lasting several days, people would turn on their air conditioners as soon as temperature started to increase and building air conditioners would need to work harder to handle the higher building ambient temperature. $DDCD$ and $DQ3$ are two binary variables that attempt to isolate the effects of temperature in the summer months. The price of electricity has a negative effect on demand. As electric bills get higher during the summer months, people are less likely to turn on the air conditioner until the temperature gets very high. Finally, total sales for any quarter (estimated in a different model) reflect economic conditions and the vacancy rate for commercial and industrial buildings in the region.

Note that the use of binary variables in the equation essentially breaks the model into two different equations. During the winter months, the two summer dummy variables ($DDCD$ and $DQ3$) drop out, while in the summer months, the winter dummy variables ($DDHD$) is zero. That is, trying to estimate the effects of temperature without the use of binary variables would tend to underestimate the effects by using temperature in the winter, when demand is low, rather than restrict the effects of temperature to the summer months when demand is high.

If this model was going to be used for estimating demand several years into the future, the forecaster would have several concerns. First, how hot will it get in each quarter. Next, how hot would the quarter be. Finally, how good is the forecast of total sales.

The forecast of total sales uses employment in the different customer classes as an explanatory variable, which is forecast using estimates of GDP growth (among other variables).

To prepare the forecasts of demand, 100 random draws from the distributions of temperature, GDP and $DDCD$ (and other important variables) were made for each quarter to estimate the range of demand forecasts. The results of the various simulations are shown in Figure 22.6.

Notice that the range of forecasts tend to be centered around the forecast of demand estimated using the point estimate of each of the different variables. Yet, the plot of the various forecasts shows that it would be possible to have a demand that ranges from 473 *MW* to 543 *MW*, or a deviation of some 70 *MW* by 1991. This is valuable information to forecasters. Even if the forecasting model is correct, the effects of (primarily) temperature variations would mean that the forecast could over or underestimate the actual demand by significant amounts. To the extent that forecasters were now purchasing new generation capacity, they could determine the extent to which they were willing to buy capacity to meet the highest value of

FIGURE 22.6

EXAMPLE OF MONTE CARLO SIMULATION

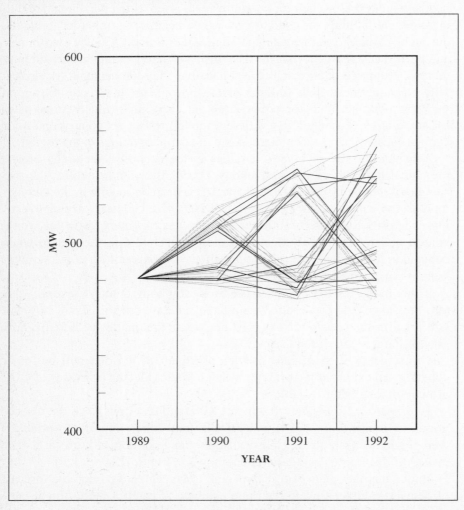

demand, the lowest value, or any level in between the two extremes, recognizing the potential financial implications of their choice.

THE CALIFORNIA STATE FORECASTING AND REVENUE MODEL

A major use of forecasting is estimating economic activity and tax revenues by different government agencies, either at the federal, state, or local level. These types of forecasting models use all the techniques discussed above, including simultaneous equation models and I-O models.

An example of an elaborate forecasting model is that used by the California Commission on State Finance (the CSF model). This model is used to forecast California economic activity and the general fund revenues, or tax moneys available to fund general government expenditures. (For a complete discussion of the CSF model, see the California Commission on State Finance 1987).

Figure 22.7 shows the conceptional model structure. The model structure and equation specifications are estimated in advance, using time series and econometric modeling techniques. Assumptions on basic economic policy are used to drive the model. The assumption set is used to estimate national economic conditions which then feed into the state economic forecast. The state economic forecast, in conjunction with the tax revenue forecast block, then becomes the input for the forecast of the tax base and liabilities which then becomes the input for the various tax receipts.

This type of state forecasting model is not unique. While California may be linked more closely to the national economy than other regions, most areas produce primarily for national rather than regional markets. California's economy is closely tied to the aerospace and electronics industries that are dependent upon defense spending and business spending on capital equipment. Thus, it is necessary to model both the national economy and the statewide linkages in order to estimate the performance of the regional economy.

In order to account for the various factors that impact the California economy, the forecasting model is conceptionally broken into two blocks, an export block (manufacturing, mining, and agriculture) where employment and income are primarily influenced by non-California demand, and a state block (services, trade, and construction) that is determined by statewide demand.

Figure 22.8 illustrates how the model is tied together. Note that this forecasting model used all the various techniques that we have discussed, including an I-O model of the national economy that drives California industrial output by sector, simultaneous equation models, and time series models.

The domestic block is solved simultaneously because of the contemporaneous nature of the variables in this part of the model. For example, retail

FIGURE 22.7
DESCRIPTION OF REVENUE ESTIMATING PROCEDURES

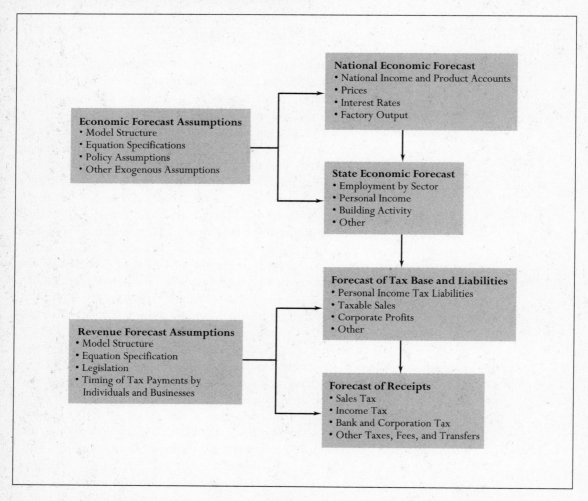

employment is determined by retail spending which is determined by income which is partially determined by retail employment. This feedback or simultaneous determination of demand requires that the domestic block be solved using a simultaneous equation system. Figure 22.9 illustrates how the domestic block is tied together.

THE EXPORT SECTOR

It is not unusual for a regional model to consider exports as output sent to the national economy, rather than just foreign exports. In California, the

FIGURE 22.8

HOW THE NATIONAL ECONOMY AFFECTS CALIFORNIA EMPLOYMENT, SPENDING, AND INCOME

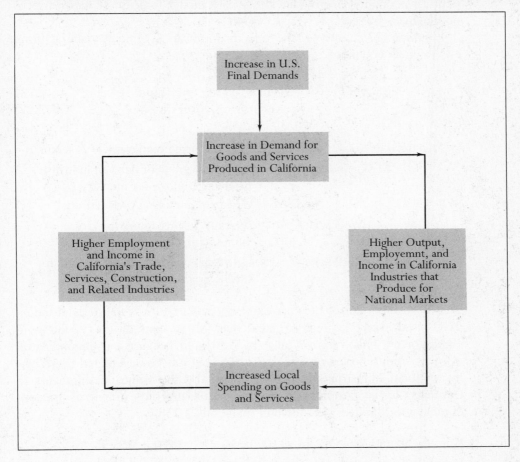

export sector includes mining, agriculture, and manufacturing, industries whose output is primarily tied to levels of national economic activity. By far the most important sector is manufacturing which forms the core of the California economy. This sector includes the electronics, aerospace, and defense sectors, some of the most important economic sectors in the California economy. However, the manufacturing sector only employs about 20 percent of the work force. Yet changes in this sector strongly affects the state's economy because a large share of employment in the services, trade, and finance sectors is closely related to the production, distribution, financing, and sales of manufactured products. Also, employment in the relatively high-paying manufacturing sector generates strong income effects in the California economy as the income is spent locally on goods and services.

Employment in the export sector is assumed to be based primarily on national economic activity. The key linkage between the California and national economy is provided by an I-O model forecast of national economic levels by sector.

Equation 22.22 shows the specification of a typical manufacturing employment equation:

$$EM_i = a\, b_1 \times \text{MAvg}(\text{IndProd}_i) - b_2 \times \text{Prod} \\ - b_3 \times \text{WeeklyHrs} - b_4 \times \text{RelWages} \qquad (22.22)$$

where:

EM_i	=	manufacturing employment is sector i
MAvg(IndProd)	=	moving average of derived industrial production index for industry i
Prod	=	U.S. manufacturing productivity
WeeklyHrs	=	Average weekly hours for U.S. manufacturing
RelWages	=	California average wages divided by U.S. average wages

The most important of the four explanatory variables is the derived industrial output variable, that explains over 80 percent of the variation in employment. This variable must be estimated because current industrial activity is not reported on a regional basis but must be estimated by weighing national industrial production indices by the value of shipments in California for each industry. For example, the derived estimate of the nondurable goods industry is shown in Equation 22.23:

$$\text{Nondurable Industry Output} = 10936.5/1.49 \times \text{IP20} + 355.5/0.892 \\ \times \text{IP22} + 2565.4/0.873 \times \text{IP23} \\ + 1978.4/1.093 \times \text{IP26} + 5473.2/1.202 \\ \times \text{IP27} + 4058.5/1.038 \times \text{IP28} \\ + 4155.5/0.842 \times \text{IP29} + 2398.4/1.120 \\ \times \text{IP30} + 216.7/0.816 \times \text{IP31} \qquad (22.23)$$

In this equation, the 10,936.5 represents the value of shipments in California (in millions) for industry 20 (food and kindred products). The 1.49 equals U.S. industrial production index for industry, 20 and IP20 represents the national forecast value of the index.

The second and third variables in equation 22.23, U.S. output per manhour and average weekly hours, identify the effects of variations in output per employee over the business cycle. For example, in the early stages of the business cycle, firms meet increased production not by hiring additional workers but by increasing overtime. This increases output but holds down the growth in employment that might otherwise be expected in view of rising output.

The final variable in equation 22.23, relative wages, explains the effects of differential wages costs in California versus the rest of the nation. Relative wages are only one of many factors that cause relative growth rates of specific industries to differ between California and the rest of the nation. Other factors could include the natural resource base, energy costs, taxation, etc. With the exception of taxation, which has fallen in California with regard to the rest of the nation since 1978, the effects of the other variables can be regarded as constants and ineffective as explanatory variables.

THE DOMESTIC SECTOR

Employment in the domestic sector is primarily related to market demand within California, as opposed to the export sector which depends upon demand from sources outside the state. Employment in the trade industries is related to local spending patterns (as measured by taxable sales), construction employment is related to building activity in California, utilities and business spending is dependent upon California income, and manufacturing activity and other services are primarily related to California personal income. Yet, even within the domestic sector, national economic activity influences California. For example, housing activity is primarily related to interest rates which are determined primarily by national financial conditions.

The first example of employment equations, Equation 22.24, in the domestic sector is for nonbusiness services.

$$\text{ESVNB/PopCa} = a + b_1 \times \text{CADIperm/CaPop} + b_2 \\ \times \text{CADITrans/PopCa} + b_3 \times \text{CS/C} \qquad (22.24)$$

$$\text{ESVNB} = \text{California nonbusiness services employment}$$

where: $\text{PopCA} = \text{California population}$

$$\text{CADIPerm} = \text{Permanent California disposable income expresses as a four quarter moving average of real disposable income}$$

$$\text{CADITrans} = \text{Permanent California disposable}$$

$$\text{CS} = \text{U.S. real personal consumption expenditures on services}$$

$$\text{C} = \text{U.S. total real personal consumption expenditures}$$

FIGURE 22.9
"EXPORT" SECTOR (MANUFACTURING, MINING, AGRICULTURE)

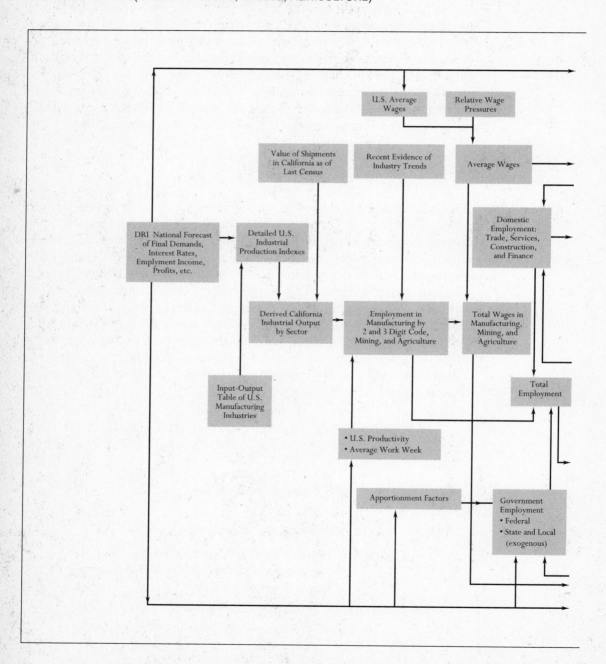

FIGURE 22.9
DOMESTIC SECTOR (TRADE, SERVICES, REAL ESTATE, FINANCE, CONSTRUCTION, REGULATED INDUSTRIES)

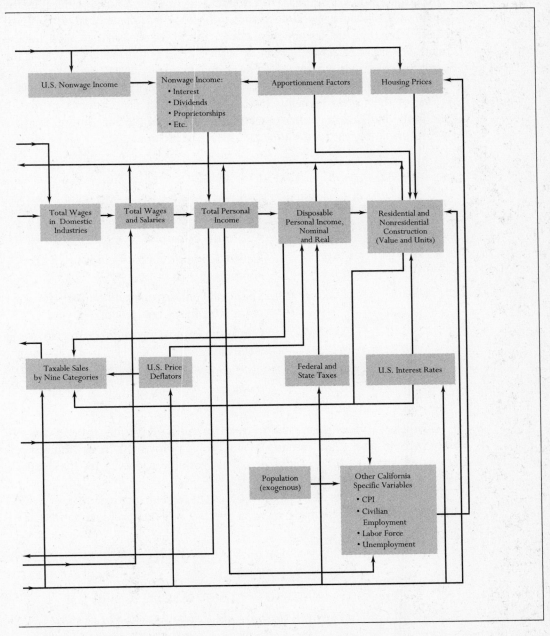

This equation assumes that nonbusiness services employment is determined by (1) consumer spending on services and (2) hiring practices of employers in response to changing business conditions.

Also, note how Friedman's Permanent Income Hypothesis underlies the equation. Consumer spending is first influenced by households' perceptions of their ongoing or permanent income. Initial increases in income have a relatively small effect on services; larger increases will occur only after the additional earnings are perceived as permanent.

The next equation, 22.25, shows the equation for business services. This is one of the fastest growing sectors of the California economy, primarily due to the increasing complexity and importance of the accounting, marketing, information services, and legal aspects of business.

$$EVSB = a + b_1 \times (CAE357 + CAE366 + CAE367) + b_2 \times (CADIPerm) \tag{22.25}$$

where:

$EVSB$	=	California business services employment
$CAE357$	=	California employment in industry 357, computers
$CAE366$	=	California employment in industry 366, communications equipment
$CAE367$	=	California employment in industry 367, electronics
$CADIPerm$	=	California permanent real disposable income

Business services are related to two variables, (1) permanent real disposable income and, (2) a moving average of employment in the three most important manufacturing industries. This variable accounts for the cyclical effects on the manufacturing sector.

Another important sector is the trade employment sector, Equation 22.26. This is an example of using a moving average in a regression equation.

$$CAETrade = a + b_1 \times MAvg(CATSR) \tag{22.26}$$

where:

$CAETrade$	=	California trade employment
$MAvg(CATSR)$	=	three-quarter moving average of real California taxable sales for the retail trade category

The above set of equations 22.25 through 22.26 are examples of some of the employment equations in the domestic block of the model. There are many more employment equations that help explain California employment by sector. The next step in the model is then to estimate the unemployment rate, which is simply an identity, shown in Equation 22.27.

$$CAUR = (1 - (CAHHEMP / CALF)) \times 100 \qquad (22.27)$$

where:
$$
\begin{aligned}
CAUR &= \text{California employment rate} \\
CAHHEmp &= \text{Civilian employment} \\
CALF &= \text{Civilian labor force}
\end{aligned}
$$

The civilian employment estimate is derived by Equation 22.28:

$$CAHHEmp = CAE + Resid$$

$$Resid = a + b_1 \times UR + b_2 \times Time \qquad (22.28)$$

where:
$$
\begin{aligned}
CAHHEMP &= \text{California civilian employment} \\
CAE &= \text{California wage and salary employment} \\
Resid &= \text{Difference between wage and salary} \\
&\quad\ \text{employment and civilian employment} \\
UR &= \text{U.S. unemployment rate} \\
Time &= \text{Time trend}
\end{aligned}
$$

Once employment estimates are prepared, the next stage is to estimate California income from both wage and salary and non-wage and salary sources. The forecasting equations are shown in Equation 22.29.

$$\text{Total Income} = CAEmp_i + CANWI_i \qquad (22.29a)$$

$$CAW_i = a + b_i \times CAEmp_i \times AvgWage \qquad (22.29b)$$

$$CANWI_i = a\, b_1 \times MAvg(CAPI/PI) \times NWI_i \qquad (22.29c)$$

where:
$$
\begin{aligned}
CAW_i &= \text{California wage and salaries in industry } i \\
CAEmp_i &= \text{California employment in sector } i \\
AvgWage &= \text{U.S. average wages per employee} \\
CANWI_i &= \text{California non-wage income in category } i \\
MAvg &= \text{Lagged moving average}
\end{aligned}
$$

$$\text{CAPI} = \text{California disposable income}$$
$$\text{PI} = \text{U.S. disposable income}$$
$$\text{NWI}_i = \text{U.S. nonwage income in category } i$$

Note that these equations use as inputs the outputs of the various employment forecasts derived earlier in the model.

The discussion above shows how a large scale model of an economy, either regional as is this example or national, can be constructed. However, the model by itself is only of limited interest. More important is how the model is used to simulate the behavior of the economy under study. Also, because the CSF model output, employment, and income by sector is used to forecast state sales tax receipts and other sources of state revenues which form the basis of the state budget, accuracy and an ability to estimate the effects of changes in national economic variables is important.

To verify the model results, a dynamic simulation of the period 1980–85 was performed. In a dynamic simulation all of the explanatory variables in the simultaneous block of the model are based on the model's estimates. Thus, the error in any variable is affected by errors in all other equations in the model. The final result, in this case total income, should then represent the errors of all prior equations. The forecast and actual changes in personal income are shown in Figure 22.10. Notice how the model underestimated the impact on income of the 1981–82 recession, but performed fairly well over the six year simulation period.

Once the modeler is fairly comfortable that the model fairly accurately forecasts, it is then possible to begin varying the assumption set and performing different simulations of the future of the economy under various scenarios. Only then can the sensitivity of the model to changes in economic conditions be identified.

CONCLUSIONS

This chapter has presented different examples of how various forecasting methods are used. Most forecasting problems are best approached using a specific forecasting methodology, although forecasters often try several different methodologies to verify the forecast results.

Hopefully, as the student gains experience in preparing forecasts, he or she will recognize when a different type of model is best used and apply the methodology that best fits a particular situation.

FIGURE 22.10
RESULTS OF THE DYNAMIC SIMULATION OF THE CALIFORNIA FORECASTING MODEL

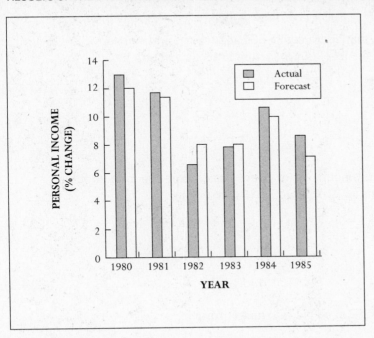

KEY TERMS AND CONCEPTS

impact analysis

input-output models

multipliers

Monte Carlo simulation models

APPENDIX 22 A
MATHEMATICS OF INPUT-OUTPUT ANALYSIS

The mathematics of I-O analysis are based upon the basic balance equation:

$$X_i = x_{i1} + x_{i2} + \ldots + x_{ij} + Y_i \qquad (22A.1)$$

$$X_i = \text{gross output of sector } i$$

where: $\quad x_{ij} = \text{sales of sector } i \text{ to sector } j$

$$Y_i = \text{final demand for sector } i\text{'s output}$$

Assuming that intermediate demand for output from sector i to sector j is a function of the level of production in sector j, then:

$$x_{ij} = a_{ij} \times X_j \tag{22A.2}$$

where:

$$a_{ij} = x_{ij} / X_j \tag{22A.3}$$

where a_{ij} is the amount sector j buys from sector i per unit of output.

By substituting 22A.3 into 22A.1, we obtain:

$$X_1 = a_{i1}X_1 + a_{12}X_2 + \ldots + a_{in}X_n + Y_1 \tag{22A.4}$$

or

$$X_i = \sum_{j=1}^{n} a_{ij}X_j + Y_i \tag{22A.5}$$

Equation 22A.5 can be put into matrix form as:

$$AX + Y = X \tag{22A.6}$$

$$A = n \times n \text{ matrix of the } a^{ij}$$

where: $\quad X = n \times 1 \text{ vector of the gross output}$

$$Y = n \times 1 \text{ vector of final demand}$$

All the equations given in 22A.4 through 22A.6 are equivalent and can be solved for gross output in the following manner:

$$AX + Y = X \tag{22A.7}$$

$$X - AX = Y \tag{22A.8}$$

$$(I-A)X = Y \tag{22A.9}$$

$$X = (I-A)^{-1}Y \tag{22A.10}$$

The matrix of X's, known as the F, or flow, matrix, represents total purchases of sector j from sector i in dollar amounts. By reading down the column of the basic I-O table, each entry is the dollar amount purchased by the jth industry from the ith industry. At the national level these data are compiled by direct survey by the U.S. Department of Commerce. Most regional tables however, are constructed from the U.S. table using non-survey methods.

The A matrix, or technological matrix, can be calculated from the flow matrix by their respective column sums. The A matrix standardizes the purchases of the jth industry from the ith industry on a unit basis.

The matrix $(I-A)^{-1}$ is referred to as the Leontief Inverse and contains coefficients defined as total direct and indirect requirements per unit of output. By assuming that the technology remains constant, final demand can be varied to see the effects on the entire economy of a change in final demand.

The assumptions underlying I-O analysis are: (1) in order to produce a unit of output, an industry buys a fixed set of inputs and (2) that over a relatively short time period the input mix remains relatively constant. Work by Anne Carter (1970) suggests that the technology matrix changes slowly enough so as not to cause statistical errors in the model for up to three years. But beyond that, technological change in some industries begins to warp the model.

I-O MULTIPLIERS

There are three types of effects that economists are interested in measuring: direct, indirect, and induced. Direct effects pertain to employment and output required for general operation of an industry. Indirect effects include the employment and output changes produced in supporting industries required to provide materials and services for the directly effected industry. Induced effects include labor and output required to meet the increased demand for goods and services generated by the increased spending by wage earnings due to direct and indirect effects.

From the $(I-A)^{-1}$ matrix we can derive two types of income multipliers. Type I income multipliers are defined as the ratio of direct and indirect effects to direct effects.

Type I multipliers are estimated as:

$$\text{Type I multipliers} = H'(I-A)^{-1}(\text{diag}(H))^{-1} \qquad (22A.11)$$

where:

H is a vector of employment compensation and Diag(H) is the diagonalization of the H vector.

In order to capture induced effects, it is necessary to add a row and column, or close the model. The added row is a combination of employee compensation and proprietary income from the value-added sector of the model. The added column is the personal consumption column from final demand.

Type I income multipliers are calculated as:

$$\text{Type II multipliers} = (H')^{-1}(\text{diag}(H))^{-1} \qquad (22A.12)$$

We can derive type II multipliers are the ratio of direct, indirect, and induced effects to direct effects. The degree to which type II multipliers are larger than type I multipliers reflects the amount of income received from a given industry and then respent within the region. For very labor intensive industries, the type II multiplier can be three or four times as large as the type I multiplier.

MATHEMATICAL APPENDIX

TABLE I
THE NORMAL DISTRIBUTION

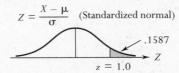

$$Z = \frac{X - \mu}{\sigma} \quad \text{(Standardized normal)}$$

z	.00	.01	.02	.03	.04	.05	.06	.07	.08	.09
0.0	.5000	.4960	.4920	.4880	.4840	.4801	.4761	.4721	.4681	.4641
0.1	.4602	.4562	.4522	.4483	.4443	.4404	.4364	.4325	.4286	.4247
0.2	.4207	.4168	.4129	.4090	.4052	.4013	.3974	.3936	.3897	.3859
0.3	.3821	.3783	.3745	.3707	.3669	.3632	.3594	.3557	.3520	.3483
0.4	.3446	.3409	.3372	.3336	.3300	.3264	.3228	.3192	.3156	.3121
0.5	.3085	.3050	.3015	.2981	.2946	.2912	.2877	.2843	.2810	.2776
0.6	.2743	.2709	.2676	.2643	.2611	.2578	.2546	.2514	.2483	.2451
0.7	.2420	.2389	.2358	.2327	.2296	.2266	.2236	.2206	.2177	.2148
0.8	.2119	.2090	.2061	.2033	.2005	.1977	.1949	.1922	.1894	.1867
0.9	.1841	.1814	.1788	.1762	.1736	.1711	.1685	.1660	.1635	.1611
1.0	.1587	.1562	.1539	.1515	.1492	.1469	.1446	.1423	.1401	.1379
1.1	.1357	.1335	.1314	.1292	.1271	.1251	.1230	.1210	.1190	.1170
1.2	.1151	.1131	.1112	.1093	.1075	.1056	.1038	.1020	.1003	.0985
1.3	.0968	.0951	.0934	.0918	.0901	.0885	.0869	.0853	.0838	.0823
1.4	.0808	.0793	.0778	.0764	.0749	.0735	.0721	.0708	.0694	.0681
1.5	.0668	.0655	.0643	.0630	.0618	.0606	.0594	.0582	.0571	.0559
1.6	.0548	.0537	.0526	.0516	.0505	.0495	.0485	.0475	.0465	.0455
1.7	.0446	.0436	.0427	.0418	.0409	.0401	.0392	.0384	.0375	.0367
1.8	.0359	.0351	.0344	.0336	.0329	.0322	.0314	.0307	.0301	.0294
1.9	.0287	.0281	.0274	.0268	.0262	.0256	.0250	.0244	.0239	.0233
2.0	.0228	.0222	.0217	.0212	.0207	.0202	.0197	.0192	.0188	.0183
2.1	.0179	.0174	.0170	.0166	.0162	.0158	.0154	.0150	.0146	.0143
2.2	.0139	.0136	.0132	.0129	.0125	.0122	.0119	.0116	.0113	.0110
2.3	.0107	.0104	.0102	.0099	.0096	.0094	.0091	.0089	.0087	.0084
2.4	.0082	.0080	.0078	.0075	.0073	.0071	.0069	.0068	.0066	.0064
2.5	.0062	.0060	.0059	.0057	.0055	.0054	.0052	.0051	.0049	.0048
2.6	.0047	.0045	.0044	.0043	.0041	.0040	.0039	.0038	.0037	.0036
2.7	.0035	.0034	.0033	.0032	.0031	.0030	.0029	.0028	.0027	.0026
2.8	.0026	.0025	.0024	.0023	.0023	.0022	.0021	.0021	.0020	.0019
2.9	.0019	.0018	.0018	.0017	.0016	.0016	.0015	.0015	.0014	.0014
3.0	.0013	.0013	.0013	.0012	.0012	.0011	.0011	.0011	.0010	.0010

SOURCE: Based on *Biometrika Tables for Statisticians,* Vol. 1, 3rd ed. (1966), with the permission of the *Biometrika* trustees.

NOTE: The table plots the cumulative probability $Z > z$.

TABLE II
THE *t* DISTRIBUTION

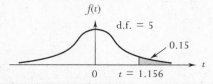

Degrees of Freedom	PROBABILITY OF A VALUE AT LEAST AS LARGE AS THE TABLE ENTRY					
	0.15	0.1	0.05	0.025	0.01	0.005
1	1.963	3.078	6.314	12.706	31.821	63.657
2	1.386	1.886	2.920	4.303	6.965	9.925
3	1.250	1.638	2.353	3.182	4.541	5.841
4	1.190	1.533	2.132	2.776	3.747	4.604
5	1.156	1.476	2.015	2.571	3.365	4.032
6	1.134	1.440	1.943	2.447	3.143	3.707
7	1.119	1.415	1.895	2.365	2.998	3.499
8	1.108	1.397	1.860	2.306	2.896	3.355
9	1.100	1.383	1.833	2.262	2.821	3.250
10	1.093	1.372	1.812	2.228	2.764	3.169
11	1.088	1.363	1.796	2.201	2.718	3.106
12	1.083	1.356	1.782	2.179	2.681	3.055
13	1.079	1.350	1.771	2.160	2.650	3.012
14	1.076	1.345	1.761	2.145	2.624	2.977
15	1.074	1.341	1.753	2.131	2.602	2.947
16	1.071	1.337	1.746	2.120	2.583	2.921
17	1.069	1.333	1.740	2.110	2.567	2.898
18	1.067	1.330	1.734	2.101	2.552	2.878
19	1.066	1.328	1.729	2.093	2.539	2.861
20	1.064	1.325	1.725	2.086	2.528	2.845
21	1.063	1.323	1.721	2.080	2.518	2.831
22	1.061	1.321	1.717	2.074	2.508	2.819
23	1.060	1.319	1.714	2.069	2.500	2.807
24	1.059	1.318	1.711	2.064	2.492	2.797
25	1.058	1.316	1.708	2.060	2.485	2.787
26	1.058	1.315	1.706	2.056	2.479	2.779
27	1.057	1.314	1.703	2.052	2.473	2.771
28	1.056	1.313	1.701	2.048	2.467	2.763
29	1.055	1.311	1.699	2.045	2.462	2.756
30	1.055	1.310	1.697	2.042	2.457	2.750
(Normal) ∞	1.036	1.282	1.645	1.960	2.326	2.576

SOURCE: Reprinted from Table IV in Sir Ronald A. Fisher, *Statistical Methods fro Research Workers*, 14th ed. (copyright © 1972 by Hafner Press, a Division of Macmillan Publishing Co., Inc.) with the permission of the publisher and the late Sir Ronald Fisher's Literary Executor.

TABLE III

THE *F* DISTRIBUTION: 5% (ROMAN TYPE) AND 1% (BOLDFACE TYPE) POINTS FOR THE DISTRIBUTION OF *F*

n_2	n_1 DEGREES OF FREEDOM FOR NUMERATOR											
	1	2	3	4	5	6	7	8	9	10	11	12
1	161	200	216	225	230	234	237	239	241	242	243	244
	4,052	**4,999**	**5,403**	**5,625**	**5,764**	**5,859**	**5,928**	**5,981**	**6,022**	**6,056**	**6,082**	**6,106**
2	18.51	19.00	19.16	19.25	19.30	19.33	19.36	19.37	19.38	19.39	19.40	19.41
	98.49	**99.00**	**99.17**	**99.25**	**99.30**	**99.33**	**99.34**	**99.36**	**99.38**	**99.40**	**99.41**	**99.42**
3	10.13	9.55	9.28	9.12	9.01	8.94	8.88	8.84	8.81	8.78	8.76	8.74
	34.12	**30.82**	**29.46**	**28.71**	**28.24**	**27.91**	**27.67**	**27.49**	**27.34**	**27.23**	**27.13**	**27.05**
4	7.71	6.94	6.59	6.39	6.26	6.16	6.09	6.04	6.00	5.96	5.93	5.91
	21.20	**18.00**	**16.69**	**15.98**	**15.52**	**15.21**	**14.98**	**14.80**	**14.66**	**14.54**	**14.45**	**14.37**
5	6.61	5.79	5.41	5.19	5.05	4.95	4.88	4.82	4.78	4.74	4.70	4.68
	16.26	**13.27**	**12.06**	**11.39**	**10.97**	**10.67**	**10.45**	**10.27**	**10.15**	**10.05**	**9.96**	**9.89**
6	5.99	5.14	4.76	4.53	4.39	4.28	4.21	4.15	4.10	4.06	4.03	4.00
	13.74	**10.92**	**9.78**	**9.15**	**8.75**	**8.47**	**8.26**	**8.10**	**7.98**	**7.87**	**7.79**	**7.72**
7	5.59	4.74	4.35	4.12	3.97	3.87	3.79	3.73	3.68	3.63	3.60	3.57
	12.25	**9.55**	**8.45**	**7.85**	**7.46**	**7.19**	**7.00**	**6.84**	**6.71**	**6.62**	**6.54**	**6.47**
8	5.32	4.46	4.07	3.84	3.69	3.58	3.50	3.44	3.39	3.34	3.31	3.28
	11.26	**8.65**	**7.59**	**7.01**	**6.63**	**6.37**	**6.19**	**6.03**	**5.91**	**5.82**	**5.74**	**5.67**
9	5.12	4.26	3.86	3.63	3.48	3.37	3.29	3.23	3.18	3.13	3.10	3.07
	10.56	**8.02**	**6.99**	**6.42**	**6.06**	**5.80**	**5.62**	**5.47**	**5.35**	**5.26**	**5.18**	**5.11**
10	4.96	4.10	3.71	3.48	3.33	3.22	3.14	3.07	3.02	2.97	2.94	2.91
	10.04	**7.56**	**6.55**	**5.99**	**5.64**	**5.39**	**5.21**	**5.06**	**4.95**	**4.85**	**4.78**	**4.71**
11	4.84	3.98	3.59	3.36	3.20	3.09	3.01	2.95	2.90	2.86	2.82	2.79
	9.65	**7.20**	**6.22**	**5.67**	**5.32**	**5.07**	**4.88**	**4.74**	**4.63**	**4.54**	**4.46**	**4.40**
12	4.75	3.88	3.49	3.26	3.11	3.00	2.92	2.85	2.80	2.76	2.72	2.69
	9.33	**6.93**	**5.95**	**5.41**	**5.06**	**4.82**	**4.65**	**4.50**	**4.39**	**4.30**	**4.22**	**4.16**
13	4.67	3.80	3.41	3.18	3.02	2.92	2.84	2.77	2.72	2.67	2.63	2.60
	9.07	**6.70**	**5.74**	**5.20**	**4.86**	**4.62**	**4.44**	**4.30**	**4.19**	**4.10**	**4.02**	**3.96**
14	4.60	3.74	3.34	3.11	2.96	2.85	2.77	2.70	2.65	2.60	2.56	2.53
	8.86	**6.51**	**5.56**	**5.03**	**4.69**	**4.46**	**4.28**	**4.14**	**4.03**	**3.94**	**3.86**	**3.80**
15	4.54	3.68	3.29	3.06	2.90	2.79	2.70	2.64	2.59	2.55	2.51	2.48
	8.68	**6.36**	**5.42**	**4.89**	**4.56**	**4.32**	**4.14**	**4.00**	**3.89**	**3.80**	**3.73**	**3.67**
16	4.49	3.63	3.24	3.01	2.85	2.74	2.66	2.59	2.54	2.49	2.45	2.42
	8.53	**6.23**	**5.29**	**4.77**	**4.44**	**4.20**	**4.03**	**3.89**	**3.78**	**3.69**	**3.61**	**3.55**

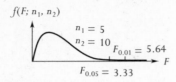

14	16	20	24	30	40	50	75	100	200	500	∞	n_2
245	246	248	249	250	251	252	253	253	254	254	254	1
6,142	**6,169**	**6,208**	**6,234**	**6,258**	**6,286**	**6,302**	**6,323**	**6,334**	**6,352**	**6,361**	**6,366**	
19.42	19.43	19.44	19.45	19.46	19.47	19.47	19.48	19.49	19.49	19.50	19.50	2
99.43	**99.44**	**99.45**	**99.46**	**99.47**	**99.48**	**99.48**	**99.49**	**99.49**	**99.49**	**99.50**	**99.50**	
8.71	8.69	8.66	8.64	8.62	8.60	8.58	8.57	8.56	8.54	8.54	8.53	3
26.92	**26.83**	**26.69**	**26.60**	**26.50**	**26.41**	**26.35**	**26.27**	**26.23**	**26.18**	**26.14**	**26.12**	
5.87	5.84	5.80	5.77	5.74	5.71	5.70	5.68	5.66	5.65	5.64	5.63	4
14.24	**14.15**	**14.02**	**13.93**	**13.83**	**13.74**	**13.69**	**13.61**	**13.57**	**13.52**	**13.48**	**13.46**	
4.64	4.60	4.56	4.53	4.50	4.46	4.44	4.42	4.40	4.38	4.37	4.36	5
9.77	**9.68**	**9.55**	**9.47**	**9.38**	**9.29**	**9.24**	**9.17**	**9.13**	**9.07**	**9.04**	**9.02**	
3.96	3.92	3.87	3.84	3.81	3.77	3.75	3.72	3.71	3.69	3.68	3.67	6
7.60	**7.52**	**7.39**	**7.31**	**7.23**	**7.14**	**7.09**	**7.02**	**6.99**	**6.94**	**6.90**	**6.88**	
3.52	3.49	3.44	3.41	3.38	3.34	3.32	3.29	3.28	3.25	3.24	3.23	7
6.35	**6.27**	**6.15**	**6.07**	**5.98**	**5.90**	**5.85**	**5.78**	**5.75**	**5.70**	**5.67**	**5.65**	
3.23	3.20	3.15	3.12	3.08	3.05	3.03	3.00	2.98	2.96	2.94	2.93	8
5.56	**5.48**	**5.36**	**5.28**	**5.20**	**5.11**	**5.06**	**5.00**	**4.96**	**4.91**	**4.88**	**4.86**	
3.02	2.98	2.93	2.90	2.86	2.82	2.80	2.77	2.76	2.73	2.72	2.71	9
5.00	**4.92**	**4.80**	**4.73**	**4.64**	**4.56**	**4.51**	**4.45**	**4.41**	**4.36**	**4.33**	**4.31**	
2.86	2.82	2.77	2.74	2.70	2.67	2.64	2.61	2.59	2.56	2.55	2.54	10
4.60	**4.52**	**4.41**	**4.33**	**4.25**	**4.17**	**4.12**	**4.05**	**4.01**	**3.96**	**3.93**	**3.91**	
2.74	2.70	2.65	2.61	2.57	2.53	2.50	2.47	2.45	2.42	2.41	2.40	11
4.29	**4.21**	**4.10**	**4.02**	**3.94**	**3.86**	**3.80**	**3.74**	**3.70**	**3.66**	**3.62**	**3.60**	
2.64	2.60	2.54	2.50	2.46	2.42	2.40	2.36	2.35	2.32	2.31	2.30	12
4.05	**3.98**	**3.86**	**3.78**	**3.70**	**3.61**	**3.56**	**3.49**	**3.46**	**3.41**	**3.38**	**3.36**	
2.55	2.51	2.46	2.42	2.38	2.34	2.32	2.28	2.26	2.24	2.22	2.21	13
3.85	**3.78**	**3.67**	**3.59**	**3.51**	**3.42**	**3.37**	**3.30**	**3.27**	**3.21**	**3.18**	**3.16**	
2.48	2.44	2.39	2.35	2.31	2.27	2.24	2.21	2.19	2.16	2.14	2.13	14
3.70	**3.62**	**3.51**	**3.43**	**3.34**	**3.26**	**3.21**	**3.14**	**3.11**	**3.06**	**3.02**	**3.00**	
2.43	2.39	2.33	2.29	2.25	2.21	2.18	2.15	2.12	2.10	2.08	2.07	15
3.56	**3.48**	**3.36**	**3.29**	**3.20**	**3.12**	**3.07**	**3.00**	**2.97**	**2.92**	**2.89**	**2.87**	
2.37	2.33	2.28	2.24	2.20	2.16	2.13	2.09	2.07	2.04	2.02	2.01	16
3.45	**3.37**	**3.25**	**3.18**	**3.10**	**3.01**	**2.96**	**2.89**	**2.86**	**2.80**	**2.77**	**2.75**	

TABLE III (CONTINUED)

n_2	n_1 DEGREES OF FREEDOM FOR NUMERATOR											
	1	2	3	4	5	6	7	8	9	10	11	12
17	4.45	3.59	3.20	2.96	2.81	2.70	2.62	2.55	2.50	2.45	2.41	2.38
	8.40	**6.11**	**5.18**	**4.67**	**4.34**	**4.10**	**3.93**	**3.79**	**3.68**	**3.59**	**3.52**	**3.45**
18	4.41	3.55	3.16	2.93	2.77	2.66	2.58	2.51	2.46	2.41	2.37	2.34
	8.28	**6.01**	**5.09**	**4.58**	**4.25**	**4.01**	**3.85**	**3.71**	**3.60**	**3.51**	**3.44**	**3.37**
19	4.38	3.52	3.13	2.90	2.74	2.63	2.55	2.48	2.43	2.38	2.34	2.31
	8.18	**5.93**	**5.01**	**4.50**	**4.17**	**3.94**	**3.77**	**3.63**	**3.52**	**3.43**	**3.36**	**3.30**
20	4.35	3.49	3.10	2.87	2.71	2.60	2.52	2.45	2.40	2.35	2.31	2.28
	8.10	**5.85**	**4.94**	**4.43**	**4.10**	**3.87**	**3.71**	**3.56**	**3.45**	**3.37**	**3.30**	**3.23**
21	4.32	3.47	3.07	2.84	2.68	2.57	2.49	2.42	2.37	2.32	2.28	2.25
	8.02	**5.78**	**4.87**	**4.37**	**4.04**	**3.81**	**3.65**	**3.51**	**3.40**	**3.31**	**3.24**	**3.17**
22	4.30	3.44	3.05	2.82	2.66	2.55	2.47	2.40	2.35	2.30	2.26	2.23
	7.94	**5.72**	**4.82**	**4.31**	**3.99**	**3.76**	**3.59**	**3.45**	**3.35**	**3.26**	**3.18**	**3.12**
23	4.28	3.42	3.03	2.80	2.64	2.53	2.45	2.38	2.32	2.28	2.24	2.20
	7.88	**5.66**	**4.76**	**4.26**	**3.94**	**3.71**	**3.54**	**3.41**	**3.30**	**3.21**	**3.14**	**3.07**
24	4.26	3.40	3.01	2.78	2.62	2.51	2.43	2.36	2.30	2.26	2.22	2.18
	7.82	**5.61**	**4.72**	**4.22**	**3.90**	**3.67**	**3.50**	**3.36**	**3.25**	**3.17**	**3.09**	**3.03**
25	4.24	3.38	2.99	2.76	2.60	2.49	2.41	2.34	2.28	2.24	2.20	2.16
	7.77	**5.57**	**4.68**	**4.18**	**3.86**	**3,63**	**3.46**	**3.32**	**3.21**	**3.13**	**3.05**	**2.99**
26	4.22	3.37	2.98	2.74	2.59	2.47	2.39	2.32	2.27	2.22	2.18	2.15
	7.72	**5.53**	**4.64**	**4.14**	**3.82**	**3.59**	**3.42**	**3.29**	**3.17**	**3.09**	**3.02**	**2.96**
27	4.21	3.35	2.96	2.73	2.57	2.46	2.37	2.30	2.25	2.20	2.16	2.13
	7.68	**5.49**	**4.60**	**4.11**	**3.79**	**3.56**	**3.39**	**3.26**	**3.14**	**3.06**	**2.98**	**2.93**
28	4.20	3.34	2.95	2.71	2.56	2.44	2.36	2.29	2.24	2.19	2.15	2.12
	7.64	**5.45**	**4.57**	**4.07**	**3.76**	**3.53**	**3.36**	**3.23**	**3.11**	**3.03**	**2.95**	**2.90**
29	4.18	3.33	2.93	2.70	2.54	2.43	2.35	2.28	2.22	2.18	2.14	2.10
	7.60	**5.42**	**4.54**	**4.04**	**3.73**	**3.50**	**3.33**	**3.20**	**3.08**	**3.00**	**2.92**	**2.87**
30	4.17	3.32	2.92	2.69	2.53	2.42	2.34	2.27	2.21	2.16	2.12	2.09
	7.56	**5.39**	**4.51**	**4.02**	**3.70**	**3.47**	**3.30**	**3.17**	**3.06**	**2.98**	**2.90**	**2.84**
32	4.15	3.30	2.90	2.67	2.51	2.40	2.32	2.25	2.19	2.14	2.10	2.07
	7.50	**5.34**	**4.46**	**3.97**	**3.66**	**3.42**	**3.25**	**3.12**	**3.01**	**2.94**	**2.86**	**2.80**
34	4.13	3.28	2.88	2.65	2.49	2.38	2.30	2.23	2.17	2.12	2.08	2.05
	7.44	**5.29**	**4.42**	**3.93**	**3.61**	**3.38**	**3.21**	**3.08**	**2.97**	**2.89**	**2.82**	**2.76**
36	4.11	3.26	2.86	2.63	2.48	2.36	2.28	2.21	2.15	2.10	2.06	2.03
	7.39	**5.25**	**4.38**	**3.89**	**3.58**	**3.35**	**3.18**	**3.04**	**2.94**	**2.86**	**2.78**	**2.72**
38	4.10	3.25	2.85	2.62	2.46	2.35	2.26	2.19	2.14	2.09	2.05	2.02
	7.35	**5.21**	**4.34**	**3.86**	**3.54**	**3.32**	**3.15**	**3.02**	**2.91**	**2.82**	**2.75**	**2.69**

14	16	20	24	30	40	50	75	100	200	500	∞	n_2
2.33	2.29	2.23	2.19	2.15	2.11	2.08	2.04	2.02	1.99	1.97	1.96	17
3.35	**3.27**	**3.16**	**3.08**	**3.00**	**2.92**	**2.86**	**2.79**	**2.76**	**2.70**	**2.67**	**2.65**	
2.29	2.25	2.19	2.15	2.11	2.07	2.04	2.00	1.98	1.95	1.93	1.92	18
3.27	**3.19**	**3.07**	**3.00**	**2.91**	**2.83**	**2.78**	**2.71**	**2.68**	**2.62**	**2.59**	**2.57**	
2.26	2.21	2.15	2.11	2.07	2.02	2.00	1.96	1.94	1.91	1.90	1.88	19
3.19	**3.12**	**3.00**	**2.92**	**2.84**	**2.76**	**2.70**	**2.63**	**2.60**	**2.54**	**2.51**	**2.49**	
2.23	2.18	2.12	2.08	2.04	1.99	1.96	1.92	1.90	1.87	1.85	1.84	20
3.13	**3.05**	**2.94**	**2.86**	**2.77**	**2.69**	**2.63**	**2.56**	**2.53**	**2.47**	**2.44**	**2.42**	
2.20	2.15	2.09	2.05	2.00	1.96	1.93	1.89	1.87	1.84	1.82	1.81	21
3.07	**2.99**	**2.88**	**2.80**	**2.72**	**2.63**	**2.58**	**2.51**	**2.47**	**2.42**	**2.38**	**2.36**	
2.18	2.13	2.07	2.03	1.98	1.93	1.91	1.87	1.84	1.81	1.80	1.78	22
3.02	**2.94**	**2.83**	**2.75**	**2.67**	**2.58**	**2.53**	**2.46**	**2.42**	**2.37**	**2.33**	**2.31**	
2.14	2.10	2.04	2.00	1.96	1.91	1.88	1.84	1.82	1.79	1.77	1.76	23
2.97	**2.89**	**2.78**	**2.70**	**2.62**	**2.53**	**2.48**	**2.41**	**2.37**	**2.32**	**2.28**	**2.26**	
2.13	2.09	2.02	1.98	1.94	1.89	1.86	1.82	1.80	1.76	1.74	1.73	24
2.93	**2.85**	**2.74**	**2.66**	**2.58**	**2.49**	**2.44**	**2.36**	**2.33**	**2.27**	**2.23**	**2.21**	
2.11	2.06	2.00	1.96	1.92	1.87	1.84	1.80	1.77	1.74	1.72	1.71	25
2.89	**2.81**	**2.70**	**2.62**	**2.54**	**2.45**	**2.40**	**2.32**	**2.29**	**2.23**	**2.19**	**2.17**	
2.10	2.05	1.99	1.95	1.90	1.85	1.82	1.78	1.76	1.72	1.70	1.69	
2.86	**2.77**	**2.66**	**2.58**	**2.50**	**2.41**	**2.36**	**2.28**	**2.25**	**2.19**	**2.15**	**2.13**	
2.08	2.03	1.97	1.93	1.88	1.84	1.80	1.76	1.74	1.71	1.68	1.67	27
2.83	**2.74**	**2.63**	**2.55**	**2.47**	**2.38**	**2.33**	**2.25**	**2.21**	**2.16**	**2.12**	**2.10**	
2.06	2.02	1.96	1.91	1.87	1.81	1.78	1.75	1.72	1.69	1.67	1.65	28
2.80	**2.71**	**2.60**	**2.52**	**2.44**	**2.35**	**2.30**	**2.22**	**2.18**	**2.13**	**2.09**	**2.06**	
2.05	2.00	1.94	1.90	1.85	1.80	1.77	1.73	1.71	1.68	1.65	1.64	29
2.77	**2.68**	**2.57**	**2.49**	**2.41**	**2.32**	**2.27**	**2.19**	**2.15**	**2.10**	**2.06**	**2.03**	
2.04	1.99	1.93	1.89	1.84	1.79	1.76	1.72	1.69	1.66	1.64	1.62	30
2.74	**2.66**	**2.55**	**2.47**	**2.38**	**2.29**	**2.24**	**2.16**	**2.13**	**2.07**	**2.03**	**2.01**	
2.02	1.97	1.91	1.86	1.82	1.76	1.74	1.69	1.67	1.64	1.61	1.59	32
2.70	**2.62**	**2.51**	**2.42**	**2.34**	**2.25**	**2.20**	**2.12**	**2.08**	**2.02**	**1.98**	**1.96**	
2.00	1.95	1.89	1.84	1.80	1.74	1.71	1.67	1.64	1.61	1.59	1.57	34
2.66	**2.58**	**2.47**	**2.38**	**2.30**	**2.21**	**2.15**	**2.08**	**2.04**	**1.98**	**1.94**	**1.91**	
1.98	1.93	1.87	1.82	1.78	1.72	1.69	1.65	1.62	1.59	1.56	1.55	36
2.62	**2.54**	**2.43**	**2.35**	**2.26**	**2.17**	**2.12**	**2.04**	**2.00**	**1.94**	**1.90**	**1.87**	
1.96	1.92	1.85	1.80	1.76	1.71	1.67	1.63	1.60	1.57	1.54	1.53	38
2.59	**2.51**	**2.40**	**2.32**	**2.22**	**2.14**	**2.08**	**2.00**	**1.97**	**1.90**	**1.86**	**1.84**	

TABLE IV
THE DURBIN-WATSON TEST STATISTIC d

SIGNIFICANCE POINTS OF d_L AND d_U: 5%

n	$k = 2$		$k = 3$		$k = 4$		$k = 5$		$k = 6$	
	d_L	d_U	d_L	d_U	d_L	d_U	d_L	d_U	d_L	d_U
15	1.08	1.36	0.95	1.54	0.82	1.75	0.69	1.97	0.56	2.21
16	1.10	1.37	0.98	1.54	0.86	1.73	0.74	1.93	0.62	2.15
17	1.13	1.38	1.02	1.54	0.90	1.71	0.78	1.90	0.67	2.10
18	1.16	1.39	1.05	1.53	0.93	1.69	0.82	1.87	0.71	2.06
19	1.18	1.40	1.08	1.53	0.97	1.68	0.86	1.85	0.75	2.02
20	1.20	1.41	1.10	1.54	1.00	1.68	0.90	1.83	0.79	1.99
21	1.22	1.42	1.13	1.54	1.03	1.67	0.93	1.81	0.83	1.96
22	1.24	1.43	1.15	1.54	1.05	1.66	0.96	1.80	0.86	1.94
23	1.26	1.44	1.17	1.54	1.08	1.66	0.99	1.79	0.90	1.92
24	1.27	1.45	1.19	1.55	1.10	1.66	1.01	1.78	0.93	1.90
25	1.29	1.45	1.21	1.55	1.12	1.66	1.04	1.77	0.95	1.89
26	1.30	1.46	1.22	1.55	1.14	1.65	1.06	1.76	0.98	1.88
27	1.32	1.47	1.24	1.56	1.16	1.65	1.08	1.76	1.01	1.86
28	1.33	1.48	1.26	1.56	1.18	1.65	1.10	1.75	1.03	1.85
29	1.34	1.48	1.27	1.56	1.20	1.65	1.12	1.74	1.05	1.84
30	1.35	1.49	1.28	1.57	1.21	1.65	1.14	1.74	1.07	1.83
31	1.36	1.50	1.30	1.57	1.23	1.65	1.16	1.74	1.09	1.83
32	1.37	1.50	1.31	1.57	1.24	1.65	1.18	1.73	1.11	1.82
33	1.38	1.51	1.32	1.58	1.26	1.65	1.19	1.73	1.13	1.81
34	1.39	1.51	1.33	1.58	1.27	1.65	1.21	1.73	1.15	1.81
35	1.40	1.52	1.34	1.58	1.28	1.65	1.22	1.73	1.16	1.80
36	1.41	1.52	1.35	1.59	1.29	1.65	1.24	1.73	1.18	1.80
37	1.42	1.53	1.36	1.59	1.31	1.66	1.25	1.72	1.19	1.80
38	1.43	1.54	1.37	1.59	1.32	1.66	1.26	1.72	1.21	1.79
39	1.43	1.54	1.38	1.60	1.33	1.66	1.27	1.72	1.22	1.79
40	1.44	1.54	1.39	1.60	1.34	1.66	1.29	1.72	1.23	1.79
45	1.48	1.57	1.43	1.62	1.38	1.67	1.34	1.72	1.29	1.78
50	1.50	1.59	1.46	1.63	1.42	1.67	1.38	1.72	1.34	1.77
55	1.53	1.60	1.49	1.64	1.45	1.68	1.41	1.72	1.38	1.77
60	1.55	1.62	1.51	1.65	1.48	1.69	1.44	1.73	1.41	1.77
65	1.57	1.63	1.54	1.66	1.50	1.70	1.47	1.73	1.44	1.77
70	1.58	1.64	1.55	1.67	1.52	1.70	1.49	1.74	1.46	1.77
75	1.60	1.65	1.57	1.68	1.54	1.71	1.51	1.74	1.49	1.77
80	1.61	1.66	1.59	1.69	1.56	1.72	1.53	1.74	1.51	1.77
85	1.62	1.67	1.60	1.70	1.57	1.72	1.55	1.75	1.52	1.77
90	1.63	1.68	1.61	1.70	1.59	1.73	1.57	1.75	1.54	1.78
95	1.64	1.69	1.62	1.71	1.60	1.73	1.58	1.75	1.56	1.78
100	1.65	1.69	1.63	1.72	1.61	1.74	1.59	1.76	1.57	1.78

NOTE: n = number of observations; k = number of explanatory variables, including the constant term.

SIGNIFICANCE POINTS OF d_L AND d_U: 1%

n	k = 2		k = 3		k = 4		k = 5		k = 6	
	d_L	d_U	d_L	d_U	d_L	d_U	d_L	d_U	d_L	d_U
15	0.81	1.07	0.70	1.25	0.59	1.46	0.49	1.70	0.39	1.96
16	0.84	1.09	0.74	1.25	0.63	1.44	0.53	1.66	0.44	1.90
17	0.87	1.10	0.77	1.25	0.67	1.43	0.57	1.63	0.48	1.85
18	0.90	1.12	0.80	1.26	0.71	1.42	0.61	1.60	0.52	1.80
19	0.93	1.13	0.83	1.26	0.74	1.41	0.65	1.58	0.56	1.77
20	0.95	1.15	0.86	1.27	0.77	1.41	0.68	1.57	0.60	1.74
21	0.97	1.16	0.89	1.27	0.80	1.41	0.72	1.55	0.63	1.71
22	1.00	1.17	0.91	1.28	0.83	1.40	0.75	1.54	0.66	1.69
23	1.02	1.19	0.94	1.29	0.86	1.40	0.77	1.53	0.70	1.67
24	1.04	1.20	0.96	1.30	0.88	1.41	0.80	1.53	0.72	1.66
25	1.05	1.21	0.98	1.30	0.90	1.41	0.83	1.52	0.75	1.65
26	1.07	1.22	1.00	1.31	0.93	1.41	0.85	1.52	0.78	1.64
27	1.09	1.23	1.02	1.32	0.95	1.41	0.88	1.51	0.81	1.63
28	1.10	1.24	1.04	1.32	0.97	1.41	0.90	1.51	0.83	1.62
29	1.12	1.25	1.05	1.33	0.99	1.42	0.92	1.51	0.85	1.61
30	1.13	1.26	1.07	1.34	1.01	1.42	0.94	1.51	0.88	1.61
31	1.15	1.27	1.08	1.34	1.02	1.42	0.96	1.51	0.90	1.60
32	1.16	1.28	1.10	1.35	1.04	1.43	0.98	1.51	0.92	1.60
33	1.17	1.29	1.11	1.36	1.05	1.43	1.00	1.51	0.94	1.59
34	1.18	1.30	1.13	1.36	1.07	1.43	1.01	1.51	0.95	1.59
35	1.19	1.31	1.14	1.37	1.08	1.44	1.03	1.51	0.97	1.59
36	1.21	1.32	1.15	1.38	1.10	1.44	1.04	1.51	0.99	1.59
37	1.22	1.32	1.16	1.38	1.11	1.45	1.06	1.51	1.00	1.59
38	1.23	1.33	1.18	1.39	1.12	1.45	1.07	1.52	1.02	1.58
39	1.24	1.34	1.19	1.39	1.14	1.45	1.09	1.52	1.03	1.58
40	1.25	1.34	1.20	1.40	1.15	1.46	1.10	1.52	1.05	1.58
45	1.29	1.38	1.24	1.42	1.20	1.48	1.16	1.53	1.11	1.58
50	1.32	1.40	1.28	1.45	1.24	1.49	1.20	1.54	1.16	1.59
55	1.36	1.43	1.32	1.47	1.28	1.51	1.25	1.55	1.21	1.59
60	1.38	1.45	1.35	1.48	1.32	1.52	1.28	1.56	1.25	1.60
65	1.41	1.47	1.38	1.50	1.35	1.53	1.31	1.57	1.28	1.61
70	1.43	1.49	1.40	1.52	1.37	1.55	1.34	1.58	1.31	1.61
75	1.45	1.50	1.42	1.53	1.39	1.56	1.37	1.59	1.34	1.62
80	1.47	1.52	1.44	1.54	1.42	1.57	1.39	1.60	1.36	1.62
85	1.48	1.53	1.46	1.55	1.43	1.58	1.41	1.60	1.39	1.63
90	1.50	1.54	1.47	1.56	1.45	1.59	1.43	1.61	1.41	1.64
95	1.51	1.55	1.49	1.57	1.47	1.60	1.45	1.62	1.42	1.64
100	1.52	1.56	1.50	1.58	1.48	1.60	1.46	1.63	1.44	1.65

REFERENCES

Abromowitz, Moses. *Inventories and Business Cycles.* New York: National Bureau of Economic Research, 1950.

Agnew, Spiro. Speech at National Governors' Conference September 4, 1971.

Almon, C., et al. *Inter-Industry Forecasts of the American Economy.* Lexington: Lexington Books, 1985.

Almon, S. "The Distributed Lag Between Capital Appropriations and Expenditures." *Econometrica* 33(1965): 178–196.

Amott, Teresa. "Re-slicing the Pie." *Dollars and Sense,* 146 May 1989, 10–11.

Ando, A., and Franco Modigliani. "The Life Cycle Hypothesis of Saving." *American Economic Review* 53 (March 1963): 55–84.

Arcela, Francisco and Allan Metzler. "The Markets for Housing and Housing Services." *The Journal of Money, Credit, and Banking* 5 (February 1973): 78–99.

Arestis, P., and C. Driver. "Consumption out of Different Types of Income in the U.K." *Bulletin of Economic Research* 32(December 1980): 23–36.

Auerbach, Paul. *Competition, The Economics of Industrial Change.* New York: Basil Blackwell, 1988.

Baran, Paul, and Paul Sweezy. *Monopoly Capital.* New York: Monthly Review Press, 1966.

Barnet, Richard, and Ronald Muller. *Global Reach.* New York: Simon and Schuster, 1974.

Bartlett, D., and I. Steele. *America—Who Really Pays the Taxes.* New York: Simon and Schuster, 1994.

Bell, Peter. "Marxist Theory, Class Struggle, and the Crisis of Capitalism." In Jesse Schwartz, ed., *The Subtle Anatomy of Capitalism*, pp. 170–194. Santa Monica: Goodyear Publishers, 1977.

Bernstein, Michael. *The Great Depression.* New York: Cambridge University Press, 1987.

Berry, John. "Labor Costs Raise Fears of Inflation." *Washington Post* July 27, 1988.

Blackaby, F. "Economic Forecasting." In R. Whitson, ed., *Use and Misuse of Forecasting*, pp. 42–68. London: McMillian Press, 1979.

Blair, John. "Market Power and Inflation." *Journal of Economic Issues* 8 (June 1974): 453–478.

Blair, John. *Economic Concentration.* New York: Harcourt, Brace, Jovanovich, 1972.

Blanchard, Oliver, and Mark Watson. "Are Business Cycles All Alike?" In Robert Gordon, ed., *The American Business Cycle*, pp. 123-182. Chicago: University of Chicago Press, 1986.

Bleany, Michael. *Underconsumption Theories*. New York: International Publishers, 1976.

Blinder, Alan, and Douglas Holtz-Eakin. "Inventory Fluctuations in the United States Since 1929." In Robert Gordon, ed., *The American Business Cycle*, pp. 183–236. Chicago: University of Chicago Press, 1986.

Blinder, Alan. "Distribution Effects of the Aggregate Consumption Function." *Journal of Political Economy* 83 (July 1975): 446–461.

Boddy, Raford, and James Crotty. "Class Conflict and Macro-Policy." *Review of Radical Political Economics* 7 (Spring 1975): 1–17.

Bowles, Samuel, and Herbert Gintis. "The Crisis of Liberal Democratic Capitalism." *Politics and Society* 11 (1982): 69–79.

Bowles, Samuel, David Gordon, and Thomas Weisskopf. *After the Wasteland*. Armonk: M. E. Sharpe, 1990.

Bowles, Samuel, and Herbert Gintis. "Structure and Practice in the Labor Theory of Value." *Review of Radical Political Economics* 12 (Winter 1981): 1–27.

Bowring, Joseph. *Competition in A Dual Economy*. Princeton: Princeton University Press, 1986.

Brenner, Harvey. *Estimating the Social Costs of National Economic Policy: Implications for Mental Health and Criminal Aggression*. Prepared for the Joint Economic Committee, U.S. Congress, Washington, D.C.: GPO, 1976.

Bureau of Economic Analysis, U.S. Department of Commerce. *Handbook of Cyclical Indicators, A Supplement to the Business Conditions Digest*. Washington, D.C.: GPO, 1984.

Burkett, Paul, and Mark Mohar. "Keynes on Investment and the Business Cycle." *Review of Radical Political Economics* 19 (Winter 1987): 39–54.

Burmeister, E., and P. Taubman. "Labor and Non-Labor Income Saving Propensities." *Canadian Journal of Economics* 2 (October 1969): 1–15.

Burnham, Walter Dean. *The Current Crisis in American Politics*. New York: Oxford University Press, 1982.

Burns, Arthur, ed. *Wesley Clair Mitchell: The Economic Scientist*. New York: National Bureau of Economic Research, 1952.

Burns, Arthur, and Wesley Mitchell. *Measuring Business Cycles*. New York: National Bureau of Economic Research, 1946.

California Commission on State Finance, *The Economic and Revenue Models: Documentation*. Sacramento: California Commission on State Finance, 1987.

Carnoy, Martin. *The State and Political Theory*. Princeton: Princeton University Press, 1984.

Carter, A., *Structural Change in the American Economy*. Cambridge, MA, harvard University Press, 1970.

Case, John. *Understanding Inflation*. New York: Penguin Books, 1981.

Chandler, Lester. *America's Greatest Depression, 1929–1941*. New York: Harper and Row, 1970.

Costrell, Robert M. "Overhead Labor and the Cyclical Behavior of Productivity and Real Wages." *Journal of Post Keynesian Economics* 4 (Winter 1982): 277–290.

Courakis, Anthony, ed. *Inflation, Depression, and Economic Policy in the West.* Totowa: Barnes and Noble, 1981.

Crotty, James R. "Marx, Keynes, and Minsky on the Instability of the Capitalist Growth Process." In Suzanne Heldurn and Daird Bramhall, eds., *Marx, Schumpter, and Keynes*, pp. 297–327. Armonk: M. E. Sharpe, 1986.

Crotty, James R., and Jonathan P. Goldstein. "A Marxian-Keynesian Theory of Investment Demand: Empirical Evidence." Paper presented at Conference on International Perspectives on Accumulation and Profitability, New York University, September, 1988.

Crotty, James R. "The Role of Money and Finance in Marx's Crisis Theory." In Cherry, et. al., eds., *The Imperiled Economy* 1: 71–82. New York: Union for Radical Political Economics, 1987.

Crow, John A. *The Epic of Latin America.* Garden City: Doubleday, 1948.

Cypher, James. "Military Expenditures and the Performance of the Post-War Economy, 1947–1971." Ph.D. Dissertation, University of California, Riverside, 1972.

Darity, William, and Wanda Marrero. "Distribution, Effective Demand, and the Orthodox Macromodel." *Journal of Macroeconomics* 3 (Fall 1981): 455–487.

Davidson, Paul. *Money and the Real World.* New York: Wiley, 1978.

Dernberg, Thomas. *Global Macroeconomics.* New York: Harper and Row, 1989.

Devine, James. "Underconsumption, Over-Investment, and the Origins of the Great Depression." *Review of Radical Political Economics* 15 (April 1983): 1–27.

Devine, James. "Cyclical Over-Investment and Crisis in a Labor-Scarce Economy." *Eastern Economic Journal* 13 (July–September 1987): 271–280.

Dornbusch, Rudiger. *Open Economy Macroeconomies.* New York: Basic Books, 1980.

Dornbusch, Rudiger, and Stanley Fischer. "The Open Economy." In Robert J. Gordon, ed., *The American Business Cycle*. Chicago: University of Chicago Press, 1986.

Du Boff, Richard, and Edward Herman. "The Promotional-Financial Dynamic of Merger Movements." *Journal of Economic Issues* 23 (March 1989): 107–134.

Duesenberry, J. *Income, Saving, and the Theory of Consumer Behavior.* Cambridge: Harvard University Press, 1949.

Dugger, William. "Centralization, Diversification, and Administrative Burden in U.S. Enterprises." *Journal of Economic Issues* 19 (September 1985): 687–70l.

Dugger, William. *Radical Institutionalism.* New York: Greenwood Press, 1989.

Dutt, Amitava Krishna. "Competition, Monopoly Power, and the Uniform Rate of Profit." *Review of Radical Political Economics* 19 (Winter 1987): 55–72.

Dymski, Gary, Gerald Epstein, and Robert Pollin. *Transforming the U.S. Financial System*. Armonk: M. E. Sharpe, 1991.

Earley, James, Robert Parsons, and Fred Thompson. "Money, Credit, and Expenditures." *Bulletin of the Graduate School of Business, New York University* 3 (February 1976).

Eichner, Alfred, and J. A. Kregal. "An Essay on Post-Keynesian Theory: A New Paradigm in Economics." *Journal of Economic Literature* 13 (December 1975): 1293–1314.

Eichner, Alfred. "A Theory of the Determination of the Mark-up Under Oligopoly." *Economic Journal* 83 (December 1973): 1184–1199.

Eichner, Alfred. *The Megacorp and Oligopoly*. Armonk: M. E. Sharpe, 1976.

Eichner, Alfred. *Macrodynamics of Advanced Market Economies*. Armonk: M. E. Sharpe, 1987.

Einarson, Johan. *Reinvestment Cycles*. Oslo: J. Chr. Gundersens Boktrykkeri, 1938.

Eisner, Robert. *Factors in Business Investment*. Cambridge: Ballinger, 1978.

Epstein, Gerald, and Herbert Gintis. *An Asset Balance Model of International Capital Market Equilibrium*. Presented at Conference on Financial Openness (WIDER), Helsinki. Revised paper presented at Conference on International Perspectives on Profitability and Accumulation, C. V. Starr Center for Applied Economics and New York University, September 1988.

Epstein, Gerald. "Domestic Inflation and Monetary Policy." In Tom Ferguson and Joel Rogers, eds., *The Hidden Election*, pp. 141–195. New York: Pantheon, 1981.

Evans, Michael K. *Macroeconomic Activity*. New York: Harper and Row, 1969.

Fichtenbaum, Rudy. "Consumption and the Distribution of Income." *Review of Social Economy* (October 1985): 234–244.

Fine, Ben, and Lawrence Harris. "Controversial Issues in Marxist Economic Theory." In R. Miliband and J. Seville, eds., *The Socialist Register*, pp. 141–178. New York: Monthly Review Press, 1976.

Fisher, I. *The Making of Index Numbers*. New York: Houghton Mifflin, 1927.

Fixler, D. "The Consumer Price Index: Underlying Concepts and Caveats." *Monthly Labor Review* (December 1993):

Foster, John B. *The Theory of Monopoly Capital*. New York: Monthly Review Press, 1986.

Foster, John B. "What Is Stagnation?" In Robert Cherry, et al., eds., *The Imperiled Economy*, Book 1. New York: Union for Radical Political Economics, 1987.

Foster, Mark., "Giant of the West: Henry J. Kaiser and Regional Industrilization, 1930-1950," *Business History Review* 59 (Spring 1985) page 17.

Friedman, Milton. "Price Controls." *Newsweek* August 30, 1971.

Friedman, Milton. *A Theory of the Consumption Function*. Princeton: Princeton University Press, 1957.

Friedman, Benjamin. "Money, Credit, and Interest Rates in the Business Cycle." In Robert Gordon, ed., *The American Business Cycle*, pp. 395–458. Chicago: University of Chicago Press, 1986.

Friedman, Milton. "The Role of Monetary Policy." *American Economic Review* 72 (January 1968): 1–24.

Frumkin, Norman. *Tracking America's Economy*. Armonk: M. E. Sharpe, 1987.

Galbraith, John Kenneth. *The Great Crash*. Boston: Houghton-Mifflin, 1972.

Galbraith, John Kenneth. *The New Industrial State*. Boston: Houghton Mifflin, 1967.

Galbraith, John Kenneth. "A Look Back." *Journal of Economic Issues* 23 (June 1989): 413–416.

George, Susan. *A Fate Worse Than Debt: The World Financial Crisis and the Poor*. New York: Grove Press, 1988.

Gilder, George. *Wealth and Poverty*. New York: Bantam Books, 1981.

Glyn, Andrew, and Bob Sutcliffe. *British Capitalism, Workers, and the Profit Squeeze*. London: Penguin, 1972.

Gordon, David M. "The Global Economy: New Edifice or Crumbling Foundations?" *New Left Review* 168 (March/April 1988): 24–65.

Gordon, David, Thomas Weisskopf, and Samuel Bowles. "Power, Accumulation and Crisis." In Robert Cherry, et al., eds., *The Imperiled Economy*, Book 1, pp. 43–58. New York: Union for Radical Political Economics, 1987.

Gordon, R.A. "Investment Opportunities in the United States." In R. A. Gordon, ed., *Business Cycles in the Post-War World*. New York: Oxford University Press, 1952.

Gordon, R. A. *Business Fluctuations*, 3rd ed. New York: Harper and Row, 1961.

Gordon, Robert, and John Veitch. "Fixed Investment in the American Business Cycle, 1919–1983." In Robert Gordon, ed., *The American Business Cycle*. Chicago: University of Chicago Press, 1986.

Gordon, Robert J., ed. *The American Business Cycle*. Chicago: University of Chicago Press, 1986.

Gottlieb, Manuel. "Long Swings in Urban Building Activity." In *43rd Annual Report of the NBER*. New York: National Bureau of Economic Research, 1963.

Green, George and Beckman, "The Composite Index of Coincident Indicators and Alternate Coincident Indexes." *Survey of Current Business*, June, 1992 Page 42-44.

Green, Francis. "A Critique of the Neo-Fisherian Consumption Function." *Review of Radical Political Economics* 16 (Spring-Summer 1984): 95-114.

Green, Francis. "A Note on the Overestimated Importance of the Constant U.S. Saving Ratio." *Southern Economic Journal* 47 (April 1980): 510-516.

Greider, William. *Secrets of the Temple: How the Federal Reserve Runs the Country*. New York: Simon and Schuster, 1987.

Griffin, Keith, and John Gurley. "Radical Analyses of Imperialism, the Third World, and the Transition to Socialism." *Journal of Economic Literature* 23 (September 1985): 1089–1143.

Griliches, Z. "Distributed Lags: A Survey." *Econometrica* Volume 35, page 16-49, 1967.

Griliches, Z., and N. Wallace. "The Determinants of Investment Revisited." *International Economic Review* 6, No. 3 (September 1965): 311–329.

Guttentag, J. M. "The Short Cycle in Residential Construction." *American Economic Review* 51 (June 1961): 292–308.

Haberler, Gottfried. *Prosperity and Depression,* 4th ed. Cambridge: Harvard University Press, 1960.

Hahnel, Robin, and Howard Sherman. "Income Distribution and the Business Cycle." *Journal of Economic Issues* 16 (March 1982a): 49–73.

Hahnel, Robin, and Howard Sherman. "The Profit Rate over the Business Cycle." *Cambridge Journal of Economics* 6 (June 1982b): 185–194.

Hall, Robert. "The Role of Consumption in Economic Fluctuations." In Robert Gordon, ed., *American Business Cycle*. Chicago: University of Chicago Press, 1986.

Hansen, Alvin. *Business Cycles and National Income*. New York: Norton, 1964.

Harris, Joe. "The Impact of the 1971–1974 Wage and Price Controls on Profit Levels and Distribution of Income." Ph.D. Dissertation, University of California, Riverside, 1978.

Harrison, Bennett, and Barry Bluestone. *The Great U-Turn: Corporate Restructuring and the Polarizing of America*. New York: Basic Books, 1988.

Hayek, Frederick. *Profits, Interest, and Investment*. London: Routledge, 1939.

Heilbroner, R. "Anti-Depression Economics." *Atlanta Monthly* (April 1993): 100.

Heilbroner, Robert. "Rereading 'The Affluent Society'." *Journal of Economic Issues* 23 (June 1989): 367–378.

Henley, Andrew. "Trade Unions, Market Concentration and Income Distribution in United States Manufacturing Industry." *International Journal of Industrial Organization* 5 (March 1987a): 193–210.

Henley, Andrew. "Labour's Shares and Profitability Crisis in the United States." *Cambridge Journal of Economics* 11 (December 1987b): 315–330.

Hickman, Bert, and Stefan Schleicher. "The Interdependence of National Economies." *Weltwirtschaftsliches Archiv* 114 (July 1978): 642–708.

Hickman, Bert. "Diffusion, Acceleration, and Business Cycles." *American Economic Review* 49 (September 1959): 535–565.

Hicks, John R. *A Contribution to the Theory of the Trade Cycle*. Oxford: Oxford University Press, 1950.

Hobson, John A. *Imperialism*. London: Allen and Unwin, 1938.

Hobson, John A. *The Economics of Distribution*. Clifton: Augustus Kelly, 1972.

Hobson, John A. *The Economics of Unemployment*. London: Allen and Unwin, 1922.

Holbrook, Robert, and Frank Stafford. "The Propensity to Consume Separate Types of Income: A Generalized Permanent Income Hypothesis." *Econometrica* 39 (January 1971): 1–21.

Hotson, John. *Stagflation and the Bastard Keynesians*. Waterloo: University of Waterloo Press, 1976.

Hultgren, Thor. *Costs, Prices, and Profits: Their Cyclical Relations*. New York: National Bureau of Economic Research, 1965.

Hymans, S. "On the Use of Leasing Indicators to Predict Cyclical Turning Points." In *Brookings Papers on Economic Activity*. Vol. 2. Washington, D. C., Brookings Institute, 1973.

Intriligator, M. *Econometric Methods, Techniques and Applications*. Englewood Cliffs: Prentice-Hall, 1978.

Isard, W. *Introduction to Regional Science*. Englewood Cliffs: Prentice-Hall, 1976.

Jarrell, Gregg, James Brickley, and Jeffry Netter. "The Market for Corporate Control." *Journal of Economic Perspectives* 2 (Winter 1988): 49–68.

Jensen, Michael. "Takeovers." *Journal of Economic Perspectives* 2 (Winter 1988): 21–48.

Johnston, J. *Econometric Methods*. New York: McGraw-Hill, 1984.

Jorgenson, Dale. "Econometric Studies of Investment Behavior: A Survey." *Journal of Economic Literature* 9 (February 1971): 1111–1147.

Jorgenson, Dale, and M. Hall. "Capital Theory and Investment Behavior." *American Economic Review* 53 (May 1963): 247–259.

Kahn, R.F. "The Relation of Home Investment to Employment." *Economic Journal* (June 1931): 1-20.

Kalecki, Michal. *Theory of Market Dynamics*. New York: Monthly Review Press, 1968.

Keynes, John M. *The General Theory of Employment, Interest and Money*. New York: Harcourt Brace Jovanovich, 1936.

Keynes, John M. "Mr. Keynes on the Distribution of Incomes and 'Propensity to Consume': A Reply." *Review of Economics and Statistics* 27 (August 1939): 128–130.

Keynes, John M. *Collected Writings* 29. London: MacMillan, 1979.

Kindleberger, Charles. *Manias, Panics, and Crashes: A History of Financial Crises*. New York: Basic Books, 1978.

King, M. A. "The United Kingdom Profits Crisis: Myth or Reality." *The Economic Journal* 85 (March 1975): 33–54.

Klein, Philip. "Institutionalism Confronts the 1990s." *Journal of Economic Issues* 23 (June 1989): 545-554.

Klein, Philip, and Geoffrey Moore. *Monitoring Growth Cycles in Market-Oriented Countries*. Cambridge: Ballinger, 1985.

Klein, Philip. "The Neglected Institutionalism of Wesley Clair Mitchell." *Journal of Economic Issues* 17 (December 1983): 867-899.

Klein, Lawrence, and A. S. Goldberger. *An Econometric Model of the United States, 1929–1952*. Amsterdam: North Holland Publishing Company, 1955.

Klein, Lawrence. *An Introduction to Econometrics*. Englewood Cliffs: Prentice-Hall, 1962.

Kloby, Jerry. "The Growing Divide." *Monthly Review* 39 (September 1987): 1–9.

Kobayashi, Yoshihiro. "Movements of Price and Profits in the Periods of Rapid Growth in the Japanese Economy." *Economic Studies Quarterly* 6 (August 1971).

Koetz, G. "Was the Last Decade so Cruel? Yes." *Business Week*, January 17, 1994.

Kolk, D. "Kaiser Steel Company" *Southwest Administrative Review* 1 (1984): 14.

Kotz, David. "Long Waves and Social Structures of Accumulation." *Review of Radical Political Economics* 19 (Winter 1987): 16–38.

Kuznets, Simon. *Secular Movements in Production and Prices*. Reprint New York: A.M. Kelley, 1967.

Laffer, Arthur. *Supply Side Economics*. Pacific Pallisades: Goodyear, 1982.

League of Nations. *Economic Stability in the Post-War World*. Geneva: League of Nations, 1945.

League of Nations. *Statistical Yearbook, 1932–1934*. Geneva: League of Nations, 1934.

Lee, Maurice W. *Economic Fluctuations*. Homewood: Irwin, 1955.

Lekachman, Robert. *Keynes' General Theory*. London: MacMillan, 1960.

Leontief, Wassily. "Theoretical Assumptions and Unobserved Facts." In W. Leontief, ed., *Essays In Economics*, pp. 272–282. New Brunswick: Transaction Books, 1985.

Leontief, W. *The Structure of the U.S. Economy, 1919-1939*. New York: Oxford University Press, 1951.

Lindblom, Charles. *Politics and Markets*. New York: Basic Books, 1977.

Lofting, E. "Southern California Input-Output Table." Computer tape, Berkeley: Engineering-Economics Associates, 1980.

Long, C. D. "Long Cycles in the Building Industry." *Quarterly Journal of Economics* 51 (May 1939): 371– 403.

Lucas, Robert. "Models of Business Cycles." Paper prepared for the Yrjo Jansson Lectures. Helsinki, Finland, (March 1986).

Maccini, Louis, and Robert Rossana. "Investment in Finished Goods Inventories." *American Economic Review* 71 (May 1981).

MacEwan, Arthur. "International Debt and Banking: Rising Instability Within the General Crisis." *Science and Society* 50 (Summer 1986): 177–209.

MacEwan, Arthur. "Interdependence and Instability: Do the Levels of Output in the Advanced Capitalist Countries Increasingly Move Up and Down Together?" *Review of Radical Political Economics* 16(1984): 57–79.

MacEwan, Arthur. "International Trade and Economic Instability." *Monthly Review* 40 (February 1989): 10–21.

MacEwan, Arthur, and William Tabb, eds. *Instability and Change in the World Economy*. New York: Monthly Review Press, 1989.

Mack, Ruth. *Consumption and Business Fluctuations: A Case Study of the Shoe, Leather, Hide Sequence*. New York: National Bureau of Economic Research, 1956.

Magdoff, Harry. *Age of Imperialism*. New York: Monthly Review Press, 1969.

Magdoff, Harry. *Imperialism, From the Colonial Age to the Present*. New York: Monthly Review Press, 1979.

Magnusson, P. "Need An Economic Forecast? Maybe the I Ching Can Help." *Business Week*, September 13, 1993.

Mahmoud, E. "Accuracy in Forecasting: A Survey." *Journal of Forecasting* 3 (1984).

Mandel, Ernest. *Europe vs. America: Contradictions of Imperialism*. New York: Monthly Review Press, 1970.

Mandel, M. "Lost in the Wilderness of Economic Theory." *Business Week*, October 25, 1993.

Mandel, M. "Arbiters of Recession." *Business Week*, August 13, 1990.

Mankiw, Gregory, and David Romer. *New Keynesian Economics*. Cambridge: Massachusetts Institute of Technology Press, 1991.

Mankiw, Gregory. "A Quick Refresher Course in Macroeconomics," *Journal of Economic Literature* 29 (December 1990): 1063–1078.

Mankiw, Gregory. "Understanding Real Business Cycles." *Journal of Economic Perspectives* 3 (Summer 1989): 78–91.

Mansfield, E. "Technological Change and the Rate of Imitation." *Econometrica* 1961: 741-766.

Mansfield, E. *The Economics of Technological Change*. New York: Norton, 1968.

Marglin, Stephen. *Growth, Distribution, and Prices*. Cambridge: Harvard University Press, 1984.

Marglin, Stephen, and Amit Bhaduri. "Profit Squeeze and Keynesian Theory." In Stephen Marglin, ed., *The Golden Age of Capitalism: Lessons for the 1990s*. London: Oxford University Press, 1993.

Marx, Karl. *Theories of Surplus Value*. New York: International Publishers, 1952.

Marx, Karl. *Capital*. Vol. 3. Chicago: Charles Kerr, 1909.

Mayer, Thomas. *Permanent Income, Wealth, and Consumption: A Critique of the Permanent Income Theory, The Life-Cycle Hypothesis, and Related Theories*. Berkeley: University of California Press, 1972.

McNees, S., and Tootell, G. "Whither New England." *New England Economic Review* (July/August 1991).

Means, Gardiner. "Inflation and Unemployment." In John Blair, ed., *The Roots of Inflation*. New York: Burt Franklin, 1975.

Melman, Seymour. "Economic Consequences of the Arms Race: The Second-Rate Economy." *American Economic Review* 78 (May 1988): 55–59.

Meyer, John, and Edwin Kuh. *The Investment Decision*. Cambridge: Harvard University Press, 1957.

Miernyk, W.H. *The Elements of Input-Output Analysis*. New York: Random House, 1965.

Miliband, Ralph. *The State in Capitalist Society*. New York: Basic Books, 1969.

Mill, John Stuart. *Principles of Political Economy*. Reprint. Edited by W. L. Ashley. London: Longmans, Green, 1920.

Miller, Norman, and Marina Whitman. "Alternative Theories and Tests of U.S. Foreign Investment." *Journal of Finance* 28 (December 1973): 1131–1150.

Miller, John. "The Fiscal Crisis of the State Reconsidered." *Review of Radical Political Economics* 18 (Spring and Summer): 236-260.

Mills, Frederick. *Price-Quantity Interactions In Business Cycles*. New York: National Bureau of Economic Research, 1946.

Minsky, Hyman. *Stabilizing an Unstable Economy*. New Haven: Yale University Press, 1986.

Mintz, Ilse. *Trade Balance During Business Cycles*. New York: National Bureau of Economic Research, 1959.

Mintz, Ilse. *Cyclical Fluctuations in the Exports of the United States Since 1879*. New York: National Bureau of Economic Research, 1967.

Mirowski, Philip. *The Birth of the Business Cycle*. New York: Garland Publishing Co., 1985.

Mirowski, Philip. "Mathematical Formalism and Economic Explanation." In Philip Mirowski, ed., *The Reconstruction of Economic Theory*, pp. 179–240. Boston: Kluwer-Nijhoff, 1986a.

Mitchell, Wesley. *Business Cycles*. Berkeley: University of California Press, 1913.

Mitchell, Wesley. *What Happens During Business Cycles*. New York: National Bureau of Economic Research, 1951.

Mitchell, Wesley and Burns, A., "Statistical Indicators of Cyclical Revivals," Bulletin 69. New York: National Bureau of Economics Research, 1938.

Mitchell, Wesley, and W. L. Thorp. *Business Annals*. New York: National Bureau of Economic Research, 1926.

Modigliani, Franco. "The Monetarist Controversy Or, Should We Forsake Stabilization Policies?" *Economic Review of the Federal Reserve Bank of San Francisco* 25 (March 1977): 21-25.

Modigliani, Franco, "The Monetarist Controversy, Or Should We Forsake Stabilization Policies?" *Economic Review* (March):21-35.

Modigliani, Franco, and Charles Steindel. "Is a Tax Debate an Effective Policy Tool for Economic Stabilization." *Brookings Papers on Economic Activity* 1: 175-209.

Moore, Geoffrey. *Business Cycles, Inflation, and Forecasting*, 2nd ed. Cambridge: Ballinger, 1983.

Moore, Geoffrey. "Tested Knowledge of Business Cycles." In *42nd Annual Report of the National Bureau of Economic Research*. New York: National Bureau of Economic Research, 1962.

Morgenstern, Oskar. *International Financial Transactions and Business Cycles*. New York: National Bureau of Economic Research, 1959.

Morrison, W. I., and Smith, P. "Non-Survey Input-Output Techniques at the Small Area Level: An Evaluation." *Journal of Regional Science* 14 (January 1974): 1-13.

Moseley, Fred. "The Rate of Surplus Value in the Post-War U.S. Economy: A Critique of Weisskopf's Estimates." *Cambridge Journal of Economics* 9 (January 1985): 43–51.

Muller, Ronald. "Global Corporations and National Stabilization Policy." *Journal of Economic Issues* 9 (June 1975): 183–184.

Munkirs, John. *The Transformation of American Capitalism*. Armonk: M. E. Sharpe, 1985.

Munkirs, John, and Janet Knoedler. "The Dual Economy: An Empirical Analysis." *Journal of Economic Issues* 21 (June 1987): 803–811.

Munley, Frank. "Wages, Salaries, and the Profit Share." *Cambridge Journal of Economics* 5 (April 1981): 235–242.

Murfin, A. J. "Saving Propensities from Wage and Non-Wage Income." *Warwick Economic Research Papers* 174 (1980): 1–19.

Musgrove, Philip. "Income Distribution and the Aggregate Consumption Function." *Journal of Political Economy* 88 (June 1980): 504–525.

Nixon, Richard. Televised presidential address to the nation, August 15, 1971.

Oi, Walter. "Labor as a Quasifixed Factor." *Journal of Political Economy* 70 (December 1962): 538–555.

Pay, W. A. "Geography of Money." *National Geographic*, December 1927, p. 744.

Pechman, Joseph. *Who Paid the Taxes, 1966–1985*. Washington, D.C.: The Brookings Institution, 1985.

Perlo, Victor. "The New Propaganda of Declining Profit Shares and Inadequate Investment." *Review of Radical Political Economics* 8 (Fall 1976): 53–64.

Peterson, Wallace, ed. *Market Power and the Economy*. Norwell: Kluwer Academic Publishers, 1988b.

Peterson, Wallace. *Income, Employment, and Economic Growth*, 6th ed. New York: W. W. Norton, 1988a.

Pindyck, R., and Rubinfeld, D. *Econometric Methods and Economic Forecasts*. New York: McGraw-Hill, 1981.

Piven, Frances Fox, and Richard Cloward. *Why Americans Don't Vote*. New York: Pantheon Books, 1988.

Plosser, Charles. "Understanding Real Business Cycles." *Journal of Economic Perspectives* 3 (Summer 1989): 51–78.

Pollin, Robert. "Abyss of Third World Debt." *Monthly Review* 40 (June 1989): 54–58.

Pollin, Robert. 1988b. "The Growth of U.S. Household Debt: Demand-side Influences." *Journal of Macroeconomics* 10 (Spring 1988a): 231–248.

Pollin, Robert. "Structural Change and Increasing Fragility in the U.S. Financial System." In Cherry, et al., eds., *The Imperiled Economy* 1:145–158. New York: Union for Radical Political Economics, 1987.

Pollin, Robert. 1988. *Deeper in Debt: The Changing Financial Conditions of U.S. Households*. Report prepared for Joint Economic Committee, U.S. Congress. Washington, D.C.: GPO.

Pollin, Robert. "Alternative Perspectives on the Rise of Corporate Debt Dependency." *Review of Radical Political Economics* 18 (Spring and Summer 1986): 205–235.

Pool, John Charles, and Stephen Stamos. *International Economic Policy Beyond the Trade and Debt Crises*. Lexington: Lexington Books, 1989.

Pozdena, R. "Do Interest Rates Still Affect Housing." *Economic Review of the Federal Reserve Bank of San Francisco* 3 (1990).

Pulling, Kathleen. "Cyclical Behavior of Profit Margins." *Journal of Economic Issues* 12 (June 1978): 1–24.

Ransom, Roger. "In Search of Security: The Growth of Government in the United States, 1902–1970." *University of California Riverside Working Papers* 40 (January 1980).

Rebitzer, James. "Unemployment, Long-term Employment Relations, and Producitivity Growth." *Review of Economics and Statistics* 69 (November 1987): 627–635.

Ricardo, David. *The Principles of Political Economy and Taxation*. London: Gonner, Bell, and Sons, 1891.

Ricardo, D. *The Principles of Political Economy and Taxation*. London: Gonner, Bell, and Sons, [1817] 1891.

Richardson, H. *Input-Output and Regional Economics*. New York: Wiley, 1972.

Riddell, Tom. "U.S. Military Power, the Terms of Trade, and the Profit Rate." *American Economic Review* 78 (May 1988): 60–65.

Robinson, Joan. "Solving the Stagflation Puzzle." *Challenge* (November-December 1979): 40–46.

Rose, A., and D. Kolk, *Forecasting Natural Gas Demand in a Changing World*. Greenwich: JAI Press, 1984.

Rose, Arnold. *The Power Structure*. New York: Oxford University Press, 1967.

Rousseas, Stephen. *Post Keynesian Monetary Economics*. New York: M. E. Sharpe, 1986.

Rubin, R., and Nieswiadomy, M. "Expenditure Patterns of Older and Nonretired Persons." *Monthly Labor Review* 117 (April 1994): 4.

Ruccio, David. "The Merchant of Venice or Marxism in the Mathematical Mode." *Rethinking Marxism* 1 (Winter 1988): 36–68.

Ruggles, Richard. *National Income Accounts and Income Analysis*. New York: McGraw-Hill, 1956.

Salop, Steven. "Symposium on Mergers and Antitrust." *Journal of Economic Perspectives* 1 (Fall 1987): 3–12.

Samuelson, Paul. *Economics*, 9th ed. New York: McGraw-Hill, 1973.

Samuelson, Paul. "Interaction Between the Multiplier Analysis and the Principle of Acceleration." *Review of Economic Statistics* 21 (May 1939): 75–78.

Sardoni, Claudio. *Marx and Keynes on Economic Recession*. New York: New York University Press, 1982.

Sawyer, Malcolm. "Theories of Monopoly Capitalism." *Journal of Economic Surveys* 2 (January 1988): 47-76.

Sawyer, Malcolm. *Macroeconomics in Question: The Keynesian-Monetarist Orthodoxy and the Kaleckian Alternative*. Armonk: M. E. Sharpe, 1982.

Sawyer, Malcolm. *The Economics of Michal Kalecki*. Armonk: M. E. Sharpe, 1985b.

Sawyer, Malcolm. "Toward a Post-Kaleckian Macroeconomics." In Philip Arestis and Thanos Skouras, *Post Keynesian Economic Theory*. New York: M. E. Sharpe, 1985a.

Say, J. B. *Theatise on Political Economy*. Philadelphia: Grigg, [1800] 1834.

Scherer, F. M. "Corporate Takeovers." *Journal of Economic Perspectives* 2 (Winter 1988): 69–82.

Schmalensee, Richard. "Horizontal Merger Policy." *Journal of Economic Perspectives* 1 (Fall 1987): 41–54.

Schor, Juliet, and Samuel Bowles. "Employment Rates and the Incidence of Strikes." *Review of Economics and Statistics* 45 (November 1987): 580–596.

Schumpeter, Joseph A. *Business Cycles: A Theoretical, Historical, and Statistical Analysis of the Capitalist Process*. New York: McGraw-Hill, 1939.

Semmler, Willi. "Competition, Monopoly, and Differential Profit Rates." *Review of Radical Political Economics.* 13 (Winter 1982): 39–52.

Semmler, Willi, ed. *Financial Dynamics and Business Cycles*. Armonk: M. E. Sharpe, 1989.

Severn, Alan. "Investor Evaluation of Foreign and Domestic Risk." *Journal of Finance* 29 (March 1974): 545–550.

Shaikh, Anwar. "An Introduction to the History of Crisis Theories." In Union for Radical Political Economy, ed., *U.S. Capitalism in Crisis*, pp. 219–248. New York: Monthly Review Press, 1978.

Shepherd, William. *Market Power and Economic Welfare*. New York: Random House, 1970.

Sherman, Howard. *The Business Cycle: Growth and Crisis Under Capitalism*. Princeton: Princeton University Press, 1991.

Sherman, Howard. *Foundations of Radical Political Economy*. Armonk: M. E. Sharpe, 1987.

Sherman, Howard. "Changes in the Character of the U.S. Business Cycle." *Review of Radical Political Economics* 18 (Winter-Spring 1986): 190-204.

Sherman, Howard, and Thomas Stanback. "Cyclical Behavior of Profits, Appropriations, and Expenditures." *Proceedings of the American Statistical Association* 59 (September 1962): 274–286.

Sherman, Howard, and Gary Evans. *Macroeconomics: Keynesian, Monetarist, and Marxist Views.* New York: Harper and Row, 1984.

Sherman, Howard. *Profits in the United States.* Ithaca: Cornell University Press, 1968.

Shleifer, Andrei, and Robert Vishny. "Value Maximization and the Acquisition Process." *Journal of Economic Perspectives* 2 (Winter 1988): 7–20.

Smith, Adam. *The Wealth of Nations.* New York: Modern Library, 1937.

Stanback, Thomas. *Post-War Cycles in Manufacturers' Inventories.* New York: National Bureau of Economic Research, 1963.

Steindel, Charles. "Personal Consumption, Property Income, and Corporate Saving". Ph.D. Dissertation, Massachusetts Institute of Technology, 1977.

Steindl, Joseph. *Maturity and Stagnation in American Capitalism.* New York: Monthly Review Press, 1952.

Stevens, B. H., et al. "A New Technique for the Construction of Non-Survey Regional Input-Output Models." *International Regional Science Review* 8 (1983): 271.

Summers, Laurence. "Good News on the Trade Deficit, But . . . ," *New York Times* May 20, 1988.

Sweezy, Paul. *Theory of Capitalist Development.* New York: Monthly Review Press, 1942. Reprinted 1970.

Szymanski, Albert. "The Decline and Fall of the U.S. Eagle." In David Mermelstein, ed., *The Economic Crisis Reader.* New York: Random House, 1975.

Tamalty, Karen. "Foreigners' Investments in U.S. Rise." *Los Angeles Times,* November 15, 1981.

Tobin, James. "Keynes Policies in Theory and Practice." In Harold Wattel, ed., *The Policy Consequences of John Maynard Keynes.* Armonk: M. E. Sharpe, 1985.

Tobin, James. "A General Equilibrium Approach to Monetary Theory." *Credit and Banking* 1 (February 1969): 421–431.

Torino, M. "History of Kaiser Steel." *Southwest Administrative Review* 2 (Fall 1985).

Turner, Marjorie. *Joan Robinson and the Americans.* Armonk: M. E. Sharpe, 1989.

United Press International. "Tax Cut Seen Having Small Initial Impact." *Honolulu Advertiser,* August 5, 1981.

U.S. Internal Revenue Service. *Statistics of Income, Corporate Income Tax Returns.* Washington, D.C.: GPO, 1935–1990.

U.S. Bureau of the Census. *Money, Income, and Poverty Status of Families and Persons in the United States.* Washington, D.C.: GPO, August 1986.

U.S. Department of Commerce, Bureau of Economic Analysis. "The Input-Output Structure of the U.S. Economy," *Survey of Current Business.* Washington, D.C.: GPO 1991.

Varian, Hal. "Symposium on Takeovers." *Journal of Economic Perspectives* 2 (Winter 1988): 3–5.

Veblen, Thorstein. *The Theory of Business Enterprise*. New York: Augustus Kelly, 1975 reprint.

Wachtel, Howard, and Peter Adelsheim. *The Inflationary Impact of Unemployment: Price Markups During Postwar Recessions, 1947–1970*. Report prepared for U.S. Congress, Joint Economic Committee. Washington, D.C.: GPO, 1976.

Walbank, F. W. *The Decline of the Roman Empire in the West*. London: Cobbett Press, 1956.

Watson, Mark. "Business Cycle Durations and Postwar Stabilization of the U.S. Economy." *American Economic Review* 84 (March 1994): 24–46.

Wattel, Harold, ed. *The Policy Consequences of John Maynard Keynes*. Armonk: M. E. Sharpe, 1985.

Weintraub, Sidney. *An Approach to the Theory of Income Distribution*. Philadelphia: Chilton, 1958.

Weintraub, Sidney. *Keynes, Keynesians, and Monetarists*. Philadelphia: University of Pennsylvania Press, 1978

Weisskopf, Thomas. "Marxian Crisis Theory and the Rate of Profit in the Postwar U.S. Economy." *Cambridge Journal of Economics* 3 (December 1979): 341–378.

Weisskopf, Thomas. "Marxist Perspectives on Cyclical Crisis." In Union for Radical Political Economics, ed., *U.S. Capitalism in Crisis*, pp. 241–260. New York: Monthly Review Press, 1978.

Weisskopf, Thomas, Sammuel Bowles, and David Gordon. "Hearts and Minds—A Social Model of U.S. Productivity Growth." *Brookings Papers on Economic Activity* 2 (1983): 381–441.

White, Laurence. "Anti-Trust and Merger Policy." *Journal of Economic Perspectives* 1 (Fall 1987): 13–22.

Winnick, Andrew. "The Changing Distribution of Income and Wealth in the United States, 1960–1985." In Patricia Voydanoff and Linda Majka, *Families and Economic Distress*, pp. 232–260. Beverly Hills: Sage Publishers, 1988.

Wojnilower, Albert. "The Central Role of Credit Crunches in Recent Financial History." *Brookings Papers on Economic Activity* 2 (1988): 277–326.

Wolfson, Martin. *Financial Crises*. Armonk: M. E. Sharpe, 1986.

Wonnacott, Paul. *Macroeconomics*. Chicago: Irwin, 1974.

Wood, Adrian. *A Theory of Profits*. Cambridge: Cambridge University Press, 1975.

Woodward, Kenneth. "Money, Profits, Credit, and Business Cycles." Ph.D. Dissertation, University of California, Riverside, 1987.

Yaffe, David. "The Crisis of Profitability." *New Left Review* 80 (July-August 1973): 1–21.

Yenkins, J. "Study Outlines Hunger in the U.S." *Press-Enterprise*, June 17, 1993.

Zarnowitz, Victor, and Geoffrey Moore. "Major Changes in Cyclical Behavior." In Robert J. Gordon, ed., *The American Business Cycle*, pp. 519–582. Chicago: University of Chicago Press, 1986.

Zevin, Robert. "Are World Financial Markets More Open?" Paper prepared for Conference on Financial Openness (WIDER), Helsinki, July 1988.

Zimbalist, Andrew, Howard Sherman, and Stuart Brown. *Comparing Economic Systems*. New York: Harcourt, Brace, Jovanovich, 1989.

AUTHOR INDEX

SUBJECT INDEX